Contents

PRINCIPAL SIGHTS

BASLE

ZURICH

Liechtenstein

Lucerne

BERNE

Lake Neuchâtel

SWITZERLAND

Rhine

Inn

Adige

LAUSANNE

St Gotthard

S. Bernardino

Splügen Pass Road

Lake Geneva

Rhône

Simplon

Locarno

Chiavenna

S 38

S 39

Lake Lugano

Lake Como

LAKE DISTRICT

Chamonix

Breuil-Cervinia

Matterhorn

Monte Rosa

Lake Maggiore

Borromean Islands

Camonica Valley

MONT BLANC

Great St-Bernard

Stresa

Como

Bergamo

Lake Iseo

Courmayeur

Aosta

Lake Orta

Monza

Brescia

Lake Garda

Valle d'Aosta

Dora Baltea

Novara

MILAN

A 4

Cremona

Fréjus Tunnel

S 25

PO

Ticino

Pavia Carthusian Monastery

Adda

Sabbionet

TURIN

Pavia

Piacenza

Parm

Sacra di San Michele

Tanaro

Alba

A 7

A 15

GENOA

Portofino Peninsula

FRANCE

WESTERN RIVIERA

Cinque Terre

EASTERN RIVIERA

La Spezia

Carra

Pisa

San Remo

NICE

Leghorn

LIGURIAN SEA

Isle of Elb

Bastia

Worth a journey ★★★

Worth a detour ★★

Interesting ★

The names of towns or sights described in the guide appear in black on the maps. See the index for the page number.

CORSICA

Ajaccio

Conventional signs

● Town described

☩ Ecclesiastical building

⚔ Castle

⁂ Ruins

⌒ Cave

▲ Miscellaneous sights

0   50 Km

Bonifacio

4

5

TOURING PROGRAMMES

Northern Italy : 2200 km - 1370 miles
(15 days including 2 days in Venice)

Central Italy : 1600 km - 995 miles (15 days
including 3 days in Rome and 2 days in Florence)

Lake Neuchâtel

SWITZERLAND

Lake Geneva

Rhône

Locarno

Lugano

★★★ *Lake Maggiore* S 340

Lake Como ★★★

LAKE DISTRICT ★★★

★★★ **Stresa**

★★ *Lake Lugano*

Bergamo ★★

★★ Gardone Riviera

★★★ La Ga

S 525

Brescia ★

S 142

Dora Baltea

★★★ **MILAN**

Pavia Carthusian Monastery ★★★

Ticino

Adda

Oglio

★★★ Sacra di San Michele

A 4

PO

TURIN ★★

Tanaro

★ **Parma** o

A 15

S 589

★★ **GENOA**

★★★ *Portofino Peninsula*

★★★ EASTERN RIVIERA

S 1

La Spezia o

F R A N C E

S 1

WESTERN RIVIERA ★

★★ **Pisa**

N 204

Ventimiglia

San Remo ★★

L I G U R I A N   S E A

C O R S I C A

Overnight stop

THE DOLOMITES ★★★   Region with a local map in the guide

0   100 Km

8

AUSTRIA

YUGOSLAVIA

Bolzano ★   Cortina d'Ampezzo ★★★

THE DOLOMITES ★★★

Trento ★

★ Treviso

★ Padua   VENICE ★★★

Verona ★★★

ADIGE

PO

Ferrara ★★

Modena ★

★★ BOLOGNA

Ravenna ★★★

Rimini ★★

★★★ San Marino   Pesaro ★

★★ Camaldoli

Lucca ★★   ★ Fiesole   Urbino ★★

Arno

FLORENCE ★★★

Sansepolcro ★

★ Arezzo

★★ San Gimignano

★★★ Siena   Perugia ★★   Assisi ★★★

Montepulciano ★   Source of the Clitumnus ★

★ Pienza   Lake Trasimeno

Spoleto ★

★★ Orvieto   Terni   L'Aquila ★

Lake Bolsena

★ Viterbo   Rieti

TIBER

★ Tarquinia   Lake Bracciano

Tivoli ★★★

Cervéteri   ROME ★★★

★★ Ostia   Castelli Romani ★★

★ Anzio

TYRRHENIAN   SEA

ADRIATIC   SEA

Inn
Drava
Adige
S 241
S 48
S 51
A 22
A 27
Tagliamento
S 249
A 13
Brenta
Piave
S 16
Reno
A 14 bis
A 14
A 14
S 16
S 71
S 73 bis
A 11
S 70
S 67
S 429
Potenza
S 71
S 75 bis
S 2
A 1
S 3
S 2
S 1 bis
S 17
A 24
Ombrone
S 5
A 12
S 8
S 207

9

S 150
S 80
Gran Sasso ★★
★ L'Aquila
S. Clemente a Casauria ★★
Termoli
A 14
Sangro
TIBER
★★★ ABRUZZI MASSIF
A 24
A 25
S 17
Scanno ★
★★★ ROME
S 5
Tivoli ★★★
S 83
A 2
Casamari ★★
★★ Ostia
S 8
Volturno
Castelli
Romani ★★
† Monte Cassino ★★
S 207
S 6
★ Anzio

Caserta ★
A 2
VESUVIUS ★★
★★★ NAPLES
△ Pompeii ★★
★★ Herculaneum
Salerno
★★ Sorrento
Amalfi ★

Isle of
Capri ★★★

Maddalena
Archipelago ★★

Emerald
Coast ★★
S 133
Arzachena
S 125
S 127
Sassari
S 127 bis
S 291
Santissima Trinità ★★
Alghero ★
Neptune ★★★
S A R D I N I A
Tirso
Dorgali
S 125
Fonni
Arbatax-Dorgali
Road ★★★
T Y R R H E N I A N
S 389
S 292
★★★ Gennargentu
Mountains
Arbatax
★ Tharros
Oristano
S 198
★ Sta Giusta
★★ Barumini
Lake
Flumendosa
S 197
★★ Nuraghe Su Nuraxi
Mannu
S 131
Muravera
S 125
Muravera
Road ★★★
Cagliari

Mt Pellegrino ★★
★★★ PALERMO
Soluntum ★
★★ Erice
Monreale ★★★
S 113
Cefalù ★★
Trapani
S 113
Segesta ★★★
A 29
S 115
Marsala
S I C I L Y
A 29
★ Enn
★★ Selinus
S 115
S 640
M E D I T E R R A N E A N
★★★ Agrigento
Gela

S E A

0   100 km

10

Gargano Promontory ★★★

Manfredonia

S 159

Trani

Barletta

Bitonto

Bari

★★ Castel del Monte ✕

S 98

S 96

★★★ Castellana

Trulli Region ★★★

Brindisi

A P U L I A

Altamura

★★★ Alberobello

S 379

Lecce ★★

Ofanto

★★ Matera

S 71

★ Taranto

S 611

S 106

Otranto

Bradano

Gallipoli

S 173

Paestum ★★★

★ Rocca Imperiale

Zinzulusa

S 18

Maratea ★★

★ Velia

★★ Gulf
of Policastro

S 18

Crati

Lake
Cecita

S 106

Sila Massif ★★

S 107

Crotone

S 179ª

S E A

Catanzaro

I O N I A N

C A L A B R I A

★ Purple Coast

S 18

S 106

S E A

★ Messina

S 115

★ Tindari

S 114

Reggio di Calabria

Taormina ★★★

★★★ ETNA

Simeto

Catania ★

S 114

Piazza
Armerina ★★

Syracuse ★★★

S 117 bis

S 115

S 115

★ Ragusa

Noto ★

ADRIATIC

SEA

———— Southern Italy : 3500 km - 2175 miles
      (19 days including 3 days in Rome
      and 1 day in Naples)

━━━━ Sicily : 1100 km - 685 miles (7 days)

━━━━ Sardinia : 1100 km - 685 miles (4 days)

11

ITALY TODAY

Political and administrative organisation. — The referendum of June 1946 set up the Republic and the Constitution of 1 January 1948, a Parliamentary Republic headed by a President who holds office for seven years, with two Houses of Parliament—the Chamber of Deputies and the Senate. Members of both houses are elected by universal suffrage.

The Italian state is unusual in that it is neither unitary nor federal. Political power is shared by two autonomous tiers: the state or central government and the regional councils. The latter are also chosen by the people and enjoy some legislative, administrative and financial powers. Their authority must not exceed those prescribed by the laws passed or approved at national level. The 1948 constitution established 20 regions *(map p 3)*, although it was not enacted until 1970. Five of these (Sicily, Sardinia, Trentino-Alto Adige, Friuli-Venezia Giulia and Valle d'Aosta) are special statute regions and enjoy a certain amount of administrative autonomy. The regions are subdivided into 95 provinces, which are themselves composed of districts, each headed by a *Sindaco*.

The socio-political patterns in Italy are dominated by its pronounced regionalism which is part of its heritage from the time when Italy was composed of a multitude of independent states whose capitals were constantly at war with one another. Rome is essentially a residential city with a high percentage of civil servants, while Milan is the acknowledged economic capital and Florence, Bologna and Padua the intellectual centres. The onetime state capitals of Turin, Genoa, Naples and Palermo are now important industrial centres. Venice retains its very own captivating character.

Each of the large Italian towns has its own daily newspaper and only *La Stampa* from Turin, *Corriere della Sera* from Milan and *La Repubblica* from Rome although only recently, have a truly national readership. Numerous illustrated periodicals *(Oggi, Tempo, L'Espresso* and *Gente)* have a wide public.

Economy. — Far from being hampered by its illustrious past, Italy has transformed its essentially agricultural economy into that of an industrial power which is today one of the most active in Europe and ranks seventh in the world.

In addition to the traditional crops and stock raising, Italy has specialised in rice growing (Po Plain) and the production of **silk** (Lombardy and Venetia). Lacking in raw materials such as coal and iron ore the Italian industrial sector has been geared to manufacturing industries where cheap labour is more important than raw materials. Italy has always been an important manufacturer of **motor vehicles** and small machines such as sewing machines, typewriters and other domestic appliances. One of its more unusual industries is the making of **pasta**, the national dish, in all its forms to meet both the home market and export requirements.

The southern part of the peninsula is an exception in that it remains economically underdeveloped. The **Mezzogiorno** (impoverished south) as it is known, extends southwards from a line joining the Gulf of Gaeta to the southern edge of the Abruzzi. The economic backwardness of this area has increased ever since the unification of Italy. In 1950 a special organisation and fund was created to develop both the agricultural (agrarian reform with the subdividing of large estates, soil improvement, land reclamation and reafforestation) and industrial (creation of gigantic complexes often badly integrated, building of dams...) sectors of this area which has a particularly small working population.

Emigration. — As can be expected with such a sizable population there is a high unemployment level. This together with a long tradition of emigration, has been the cause of population movements (south to north) and emigration to other European countries and the Americas. Many of the emigrants return to their homeland in later years.

Urbanism. — The Italian school of town planning is justifiably famous. Throughout the 20C numerous architects have been responsible for some outstanding urban projects. The same is true for interior decoration where many Italians such as Carlo Scarpa and Gae Aulenti have gained a name for themselves.

The genius of the Roman roadmakers has been perpetuated in the road building efforts of today. The Italian motorway network ranks second in Europe and counts numerous audacious projects including great feats of engineering and usually shows a great respect for the landscape and its preservation.

The Italian way of life. — The Italians are a lively, impassioned people who are always ready to render service. These extroverts gesticulate readily and are voluble talkers. Often fanciful they are smart dressers and dare-devil drivers. They are devout Catholics and remain very attached to all kinds of religious events.

In the evening they love to foregather on the cafe terraces to discuss politics or sport. Every evening at the same time the women, children, young men and girls go for the traditional evening stroll *(passeggiata)*.

The Italians are generally eager to speak to foreigners and willing to help them to discover the riches and enchantment of their homeland.

The open-air markets are lively and attractive occasions and a good chance to pick up local products. Shops which are closed for the siesta usually stay open later in the evening. This is especially true in the seaside resorts and the south. Italian fashion ware (shoes, leather goods and clothes) are generally elegant and well displayed and the handicrafts interesting (ceramics, glass ware, objects in wood, gold jewellery, embroidery, materials, etc.).

The various traditional festivals and ceremonies often attract large crowds and numerous participants many dressed in fine local costumes.

Traditional Italy. — For many people Italy, the mother of the Arts, is a museum-country where the masterpieces born of antiquity, Christian and humanist culture are preserved. Here are found the Greek temples of Sicily or Campania; Etruscan burial grounds; the Roman Forum or dead cities now brought to light; basilicas glittering with mosaics; churches splendid with marble and sculpture; and museums housed in palaces with majestic façades where pictures and statues, often celebrated works of art, are brought together.

Introduction
to the tour

The particular attraction of Italy is a happy combination of physical, historical and social factors which make this relatively recently, unified nation one of the richest and most fascinating countries to visit.
The landscapes vary from the Alps in the north to the almost African shores of Sicily. The charms of the country include an exceptional light, an illustrious history peopled by exceptional men and a tolerant and inventive people with a great love of beauty.
Italy with its very own way of life and its inimitable mixture of ancient and modern has contrived to retain a certain realism and elegance for all to appreciate.

(Everts/Rapho)

Lake Orta

Times and charges *for admission to sights described in the guide are listed at the end of the guide.*

The sights are listed alphabetically in this section either under the place–town, village or area–in which they are situated or under their proper name.

Every sight for which there are times and charges is indicated by the symbol ⊙ in the margin in the main part of the guide.

APPEARANCE OF THE COUNTRY

Italy extends for 1 300km–808 miles from north to south and juts like a pier into the Mediterranean between Greece and Spain. The peninsula has an extraordinary variety of climate and topography.

Italy's relief is rugged and contrasting and plains occupy barely one quarter of its total area of 301 262km² – 139 087sq miles. Its almost 7 500km – 4 660 mile long coastline is washed by the waters of four inner seas : the Ligurian, Tyrrhenian, Ionian and Adriatic.

The **Alps,** which arose from the folding of the earth's crust in the Tertiary Era, form a gigantic barrier and a reservoir of electrical power. Several transalpine passes and tunnels link Italy with France and northern Europe. On the southern side of the Alps between the fertile Po Plain and the foothills there are several lakes of glacial origin.

The **Apennines,** a limestone range formed by a more recent Tertiary folding movement, run from Genoa down into Sicily. They are the backbone of the Italian Peninsula and divide the country into two zones of quite different influences, which have for long remained independent of one another. The peaks of this limestone chain are generally lower than those of the Alps. The Corno Grande at 2 914 m–9 560 ft is the main peak of the chain's highest massif the Gran Sasso.

The earth's crust from Naples to Sicily is a zone of instability with much underground activity: volcanoes, changing land and sea levels as well as earthquakes. These processes are all responsible for altering the relief of this southern part of the peninsula.

The distribution of vegetation and crops follows quite closely the subdivision of the peninsula into natural regions *(see map p 3)*.

By the end of 1987 the population of Italy had reached 57 339 108, making it the fifth most densely populated country in Europe after the Benelux countries and West Germany. Towns are more numerous in northern and central Italy and over 54% of the population is urban, residing in towns of 20 000 or more.

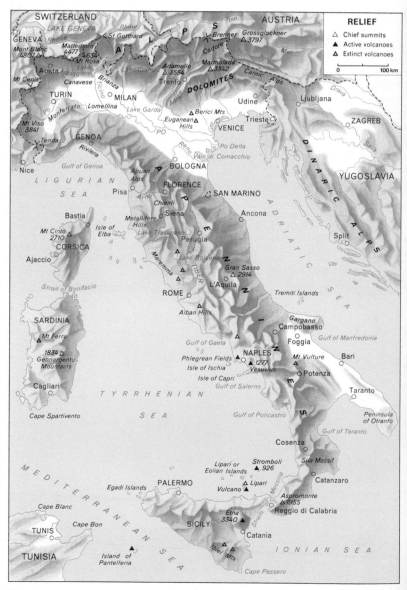

THE REGIONS

The Valle d'Aosta. – This great deep furrow between the highest mountains in Europe, is watered by the Dora Baltea River whose tributaries form picturesque lateral valleys: the Valtournenche, Val di Gressoney, Val d'Ayas, Val Grisenche...
Aosta, well situated in the centre of the valley, is the capital of this region which has enjoyed a certain degree of administrative authority since 1947. In addition to the pastoral activities of the mountain people and the iron mines at Cogne, the valley's economy depends primarily on tourism which has developed as a result of the Great St Bernard and Mont Blanc Tunnels.
From Pont-St-Martin to Courmayeur the local population—essentially mountain people and shepherds—remain attached to their traditions and have retained their French family names. Many still speak French and other varied dialects.

Piedmont. – Piedmont at the foot of the mountain range consists mainly of the extensive Po Plain. Between the Alps and the Apennines this fertile area is intersected with long rows of poplars where grassland alternates with cereals and rice growing. Three-fifths of the Italian rice production is concentrated in the districts of Vercelli and Novara. Southeast of Turin the gently rolling chalk hills of the **Monferrato** bear the well-known Asti vines and produce the Gorgonzola cheese. Numerous hydro-electric power stations supply electricity for the textile factories of Biella and the metal, engineering and chemical works of Turin.
Turin, on the Po, is a dynamic town which attracts followers of fashion and those with a passion for cars.

Lombardy. – This is the busiest region in Italy and it occupies the green Po Plain between the Ticino and the Mincio, which together with the Adda supply Lakes Maggiore, Como and Garda. To the north the great lake valleys give access to the Alpine passes. Lombardy, with the mulberry bushes of the **Brianza** district, takes first place in the production of silk. The permanent grazing and grasslands are used by a modern dairying industry. In the **Lomellina** district, extensive areas are given over to rice growing.
The many towns, scattered over the countryside, were important banking and trading centres in medieval and Renaissance times and spread the name of Lombards all over Europe. Today Como is the centre of the silk industry, Brescia steel, chemical and engineering industries, Bergamo textile and engineering works, Mantua petrochemicals and plastics, Cremona agriculture and Pavia the seat of an important university.
It is Milan, the economic capital of Italy, that has the highest density of population and businesses. This town with its modern architecture and numerous commercial enterprises and cultural institutions has an outer ring of industrial suburbs which are the home base of textile, oil, chemical, steel and food industries.

Venetia (Veneto). – This is essentially comprised of the vast alluvial Po Plain and its tributaries which are overlooked in the north by the Venetian Pre-Alps, and further north again, in the **Cadore** district by the western massifs of the Dolomites. It is an essentially agricultural region growing wheat, maize, mulberry bushes, olive, fruit trees and vines. The industrial sector includes oil refineries, smelting works and chemical plants which are concentrated in the vicinity of Venice at Mestre-Marghera, as well as a large production of hydro-electric energy in the valleys of the Pre-Alps. The latter supplies the textile industry.
The landscape is punctuated by two small volcanic groups, the Berici Mountains south of Vicenza and the **Euganean Hills** near Padua. The slopes of these blackish heights carry vines, peach orchards and are the site of hot springs.
In the **Po delta** (Polesina) and that of the Adige lie improverished, grandiose and desolate areas, subject to river floods. Following reclamation certain areas are farmed on an industrial scale for wheat and sugar beet.
The coastline takes the form of lagoons *(lido)* separated from the sea by spits of sand pierced by gaps *(porti)*. **Venice** whose industrial sector is continually growing, is built on piles in one of these lagoons.

(Aerfoto/Artephot)

Dolomites – Tre Cime di Lavaredo

Trentino-Alto Adige. – This is one of five Italian regions to enjoy a special autonomous statute. The area includes the Adige and Isarco valleys and the surrounding mountains. The Adige Valley, at the southern exit from the Brenner Pass, has always been easy of access and much used for traffic. Though deep, it opens out towards the sunny south and it is fertile. Cereals are grown on the flatter areas of the valley bottom, with vines and fruit trees on the lower slopes and pastures above. Avelengo in the vicinity of Merano is well-known for its breed of horses. **Bolzano** and **Trento** where there is some industrial development, are the regional markets.

The highly eroded, limestone massif of the **Dolomites** extends across Venetia and Trentino-Alto Adige.

Friuli-Venezia Giulia. – This region prolongs Venetia to the east and it forms the Italian boundary with Austria and Yugoslavia. The area enjoys a large degree of autonomy in administrative and cultural affairs. In the north is the schistose massif of the **Carnic Alps** with its forests of conifers and alpine pastures. Friuli-Venezia Giulia is an important silk worm breeding and spinning area. Udine is one of the busiest towns. By way of the **Trieste Riviera** you will reach this town which was once the busy port of Austria and now trades with the Far East. Trieste is still subject to a special statute.

Emilia Romagna. – The plain skirting the Apennines derives its name from the Via Emilia, a straight Roman road that crosses it from Piacenza to Rimini. South and east of Bologna the district is known as **Romagna**. Its soil, which is intensively cultivated, is among the best in Italy for wheat and beet. The monotonous landscape consists of extensive fields intersected at regular intervals by rows of mulberries and vines clinging to tall poles, maples or elms. Other vines grow on the slopes of the Apennines.

The towns are strung out along the Via Emilia : the most important, **Bologna**, famous for its very old university, is today a communications and industrial (steel, engineering and food) centre and a market for wheat and pigs.

The region to the east of Ferrara through which runs the Po river is devoted to rice growing. To the south is an area of great lagoons, **Valli di Comacchio**, where fishermen catch eels. **Ravenna**, which has been somewhat revived by its port and its oil refinery, was once the capital of the Western Roman Empire, and the chief town of Romagna before the creation of Emilia-Romagna, with Bologna as the regional capital.

(Marmounier/CEDRI)

Portofino

Liguria. – Liguria, furrowed with deep, narrow valleys at right angles to the coast, had a maritime civilisation before the Roman era. The steep slopes of the inner valleys are dotted with poor perched villages, watching over groves of chestnut or olive trees and cultivated terraces. The rocky indented coastline has few fish to offer but has enjoyed heavy coastwise traffic since the time of the Ligurians, facilitated by many small deep-water ports. The Roman Empire gave its present appearance to the country, with olive groves and vineyards, to which have been added vegetables, fruit (melons and peaches) and flowers grown on an industrial scale.

The **Riviera di Ponente** (Western Riviera), west of Genoa, is sunnier and more sheltered than the **Riviera di Levante** (Eastern Riviera), but the latter has a more luxuriant vegetation. The chief towns are Imperia, Savona and **Genoa** (shipyards, oil terminal and thermal power station) and La Spezia (naval base, commercial port, thermal power station and the manufacturing of arms).

Tuscany. – Low lying hills with clean, graceful curves under a limpid light, plains, forests and vineyards join with the serenity of cypress and pine to make this country a temple of beauty. By some mysterious influence, sometimes called "the Tuscan miracle", this harmony has gifted the Tuscan people with great artistic sense.

The region has a variety of soils. The Tuscan Archipelago, with the mountainous **Island of Elba** and its rich iron-bearing deposits, faces a shore which is sometimes rocky (south of Leghorn), sometimes flat and sandy as in the area around Viareggio, known as **Versilia**. To the north of the Arno the **Apuan Alps** are quarried for marble.

In the heart of Tuscany the **Arno Basin** lies fertile and beautiful, an ideal setting for **Florence**. Festoons of vines and silvery olives come to meet fields of wheat, tobacco and maize. Peppers, pumpkins and the famous Lucca beans grow among the mulberries. The old farms, with their nobly designed buildings, often stand alone on hill tops.

Southern Tuscany is a land of hills, soft and vine-clad in the **Chianti** district south of Florence, quiet and pastoral near Siena, dry and desolate round Monte Oliveto Maggiore and massive and mysterious in the **Colli Metalliferi** (metal-bearing hills) south of Volterra. On the borders of Latium, **Maremma**, with its melancholy beauty, was formerly a marshy district haunted by bandits and shepherds. Much of the area has now been reclaimed.

Umbria. – The gentle land where St Francis lived is a country of hills, valleys and river basins, where the poplars raise their rustling heads to limpid skies. This is the green Umbria of the **Clitumnus Valley** (Valle del Clitunno), whose pastures were already famous in ancient times.

Umbria has two lakes, **Trasimeno** and Piediluco, and many rivers, including the Tiber. Medieval cities which succeeded Etruscan settlements overlook ravines and valleys: grim Gubbio, haughty **Perugia**, the capital of Umbria, Franciscan Assisi, Spoletto and Spello. Others stand in the centre of a plain, like Foligno and Terni the metallurgical centre.

The Marches. – So-called because they were formerly frontier provinces of the Frankish Empire and the papal domains, the marches form a much sub-divided area between San Marino and Ascoli Piceno, where the parallel spurs of the Apennines run down into the Adriatic, forming a series of deep, narrow valleys. There is, however, a flat and rectangular coastal belt dotted with beaches and canal-ports. The inhabitants of the Marches have a reputation for friendliness, piety and diligence. Apart from the capital, Ancona, a busy port, most of the old towns are built on commanding sites: among them Urbino and Loreto should be noted, one as an art centre and the other for its venerated church.

Latium. – Lying between the Tyrrhenian Sea and the Apennines, from Tuscan Maremma to Gaeta, Latium the cradle of Roman civilisation, borders a sandy coast whose ancient ports, like Ostia at the mouth of the Tiber, have been silted up. Civitavecchia today is the only modern port on the coastline. In the centre of Latium, **Rome** the Italian capital and seat of the Catholic Church, is mainly a residential city attracting civil servants, churchmen and tourists alike.

To the east and north, volcanic hills, with lonely lakes in their craters, overlook the famous **Roman Campagna**, beloved by the writers and painters who have often described its great, desolate expanses, dotted with ancient ruins. Today these waste lands *(latifundia)*, formerly hotbeds of malaria, have regained a certain life: the drainage of the Pontine Marches, near Latina, was the most spectacular achievement of this project. Cassino is the most important industrial centre. A flourishing industrial zone has developed around the atomic centre at Latina.

To the south is the distinctive **Ciociaria**. This area takes its name from the shoes *(ciocie)*, which are part of the traditional costume. They have thick soles and thongs which are wound round the calf of the leg. It is a mainly agricultural area with strong folklore traditions.

The Abruzzi. – Under its harsh climate, this is the part of the Apennines which most suggests a country of high mountains, grand and wild, with its **Gran Sasso** and **Maiella Massifs**. The Upper Sangro Valley is now a nature reserve. In basins sheltered from the wind are vineyards, almond and olive groves, whose products are sent to the market town of Avezzano. Near the latter is the great drained marsh which is now given over to beet growing. The area is slowly acquiring an industrial sector with the development of the Chieti-Pescara zone and implantation of firms in other areas such as Vasto (glass making), Sulmona (car factories) and L'Aquila (steel works).

Molise. – Molise, with its capital, **Campobasso**, extends south of the Abruzzi, with which it has several common features: a mountainous relief, dark valleys and wild forests which are still haunted by wolves. The region is bordered to the west by the Maiella. Agriculture forms the basis of the local economy and the main crops are wheat, oats, maize, potatoes and vines (dried raisins).

Campania. – Campania forms a fertile crescent around the Bay of Naples. Hemp, tobacco and cereals alternate with olive groves and vineyards. **Naples** is the port for a region which is slowly developing its industrial sector (food industries, steel works, oil refineries and engineering works). As for the **Bay of Naples**, its charm and its mystery stirred the imagination of the ancients and it was here that they located the entrance to the Underworld. The characteristic silhouette of **Vesuvius** dominates the landscape at all times. Although the coast has lost much of its charm due to building developments, the **Sorrento Peninsula** and the **Island of Capri** are two notable beauty spots.

Apulia, Basilicata and Calabria. – These three regions cover the foot of the Italian "boot". Apulia, on the east side, facing the Adriatic, is less poor than commonly supposed. Cereal growing flourishes in the plain between Foggia and Manfredonia but also in the plains of Bari, Taranto, Lecce and Brindisi. Vines grow almost everywhere and are associated with olives (the Apulian production of olive oil represents 10% of the world total) and almonds on the coast. The relief of the **Gargano Promontory**, otherwise known as the "boot's spur", is quite high, distinguishing it from the rest of the area. The country to the south of Bari has an almost Oriental aspect, with strange dwellings known as *trulli* and customs.

Bari, the capital of Apulia and a busy port, still enjoys numerous trading links with the Middle East. Along with Taranto and Brindisi it is one of the three main industrial centres in the region.

Basilicata or **Lucania**, and Calabria, comprise very different types of country; the rocky corniche from the Gulf of Policastro to Reggio; the grim, grand mountains of the **Sila Massif** with its extensive mountain pastures and wide horizons; and at the southern extremity of the peninsula between two inner seas, lies the **Aspromonte Massif** clad with pine, beech and chestnut forests.

Sardinia and Sicily. – *Description p 215 and p 222.*

HISTORICAL TABLE AND NOTES

Roman History

From the Origins to the Empire (753-27 BC)

BC	
753	Foundation of Rome by Romulus according to legend. (In fact it was born of the union of Latin and Sabine villages in the 8C).
7-6C	Royal Dynasty of the Tarquins. Power is divided between the king, the senate, representing the great families, and the *comitia*, representing the rich families.
509	Establishment of the Republic: the king's powers are conferred on two consuls, elected for one year.
451-449	Law of the XII Tables, instituting equality between patricians and plebeians.
390	The Gauls invade Italy and take Rome but are expelled by Camillus.
281-272	War against Pyrrhus, King of Epirus; submission of the southern part of the peninsula to Rome.
264-241	First Punic War: Carthage abandons Sicily to the Romans.
218-201	Second Punic War.
	Hannibal crosses the Alps and defeats the Romans at Lake Trasimeno.
	Hannibal routs the Romans at Cannae and halts at Capua *(qv)*.
	In 210, Scipio carries war into Spain and in 204, he lands in Africa. Hannibal is recalled to Carthage.
	Scipio defeats Hannibal at Zama in 202.
146	Macedonia and Greece become Roman provinces. Capture and destruction of Carthage.
133	Occupation of all Spain and end of the Mediterranean campaigns.
133-121	Failure of the policy of the Gracchi, who promoted popular agrarian laws.
118	The Romans in Gaul.
112-105	War against Jugurtha, King of Numidia (now Algeria).
102-101	Marius, vanquisher of Jugurtha, stops invasions of Cimbri and Teutons.
88-79	Sulla, the rival of Marius, triumphs over Mithridates and establishes his dictatorship in Rome.
70	Pompey and Crassus, appointed Consuls, become masters of Rome.
63	Plot of Catiline against the Senate exposed by Cicero.
60	The first Triumvirate: Pompey, Crassus, Julius Caesar. Rivalry of the three rulers.
59	Julius Caesar as Consul.
58-51	The Gallic war (52: Surrender of Vercingetorix at Alesia).
49	Caesar crosses the Rubicon and drives Pompey out of Rome.
49-45	Caesar defeats Pompey and his partisans in Spain, Greece and Egypt. He writes his history of the Gallic War.
early 44	Caesar is appointed Dictator for life.
March 15	Caesar is assassinated by Brutus, his adopted son, among others.
43	The second Triumvirate: Octavius (nephew and heir of Caesar), Anthony, Lepidus.
41-30	Struggle between Octavius and Anthony. Defeat (at Actium) and death of Anthony.

The Early Empire (27 BC to AD 284)

27	Octavius, sole master of the Empire, receives the title of Augustus Caesar and plenary powers.

AD	
14	Death of Augustus.
14-37	Reign of Tiberius.
54-68	Reign of Nero, who causes the death of Britannicus, his mother Agrippina and his wives Octavia and Poppaea, and initiates violent persecution of the Christians.
69-79	Reign of Vespasian.
96-192	The Century of the Antonines, marked by the successful reigns of Nerva, Trajan, Hadrian, Antonius and Marcus Aurelius, who consolidated the Empire.
235-268	Military anarchy; a troubled period. The legions make and break emperors.
270-275	Aurelius re-establishes the unity of the Empire.

The Later Empire (AD 284-476)

284-305	Reign of Diocletian. Institution of Tetrarchy or 4-man government.
303	Persecution of the Christians: reign of Diocletian known as "the age of martyrs".
306-337	Reign of Constantine, who establishes Christianity as the state religion. By the Edict of Milan (313) Constantine decrees religious liberty. Constantinople becomes the new capital.
379-395	Reign of Theodosius the Great, the Christian Emperor. At his death the Empire is divided between his two sons, Arcadius (Eastern Empire) and Honorius (Western Empire) who settled at Ravenna.
5C	The Roman Empire is repeatedly attacked by the Barbarians: in 410, Alaric, King of the Visigoths, captures Rome. Capture and sack of Rome in 455 by the Vandals under Genseric.
476	Deposition by Odoacer of the Emperor Romulus Augustus ends the Western Empire.

From the Roman Empire to the Germanic Holy Roman Empire

493	Odoacer is driven out by the Ostrogoths under Theodoric.
535-553	Reconquest of Italy by the Eastern Roman Emperor Justinian (527-565).
568	Lombard invasion by King Alboin.
752	Threatened by the Lombards, the pope appeals to Pepin the Short, King of the Franks.
774	Pepin's son, Charlemagne (Charles the Great), becomes King of the Lombards.
800	Charlemagne is proclaimed Emperor by Pope Leo III.
9C	The break-up of the Carolingian Empire causes complete anarchy and the formation of many rival states in Italy.
951	Intervention in Italy of Otto I, King of Saxony, who becomes King of the Lombards.
962	Otto I, now crowned Emperor, founds the Holy Roman Empire.

The Quarrel of the Church and the Empire

11C	Progressive establishment of the Normans in Sicily and southern Italy.
1076	Quarrel between Pope Gregory VII and the Emperor Henry IV about Investitures.
1077	Humbling of the Emperor before the Pope at Canossa *(qv)*.
1155	Frederick Barbarossa crowned Emperor. Resumption of the struggle between the Empire and the Papacy, with the **Ghibellines** supporting the emperor and the **Guelphs** supporting the pope.

1167	Creation of the **Lombard League.** An association of Lombard cities with Guelph tendencies to counter the Emperor.
1176	Reconciliation between Frederick Barbarossa and Pope Alexander III.
1216	Triumph of the Papacy on the death of Pope Innocent III.
1227-1250	A new phase in the struggle between the Empire (Frederick II) and the Papacy (Gregory IX). New triumph of the Papacy.

French Influence and Decline of Imperial Power

1265	Charles of Anjou, brother of St Louis, crowned King of Sicily.
1282	Sicilian Vespers: massacre of French settlers in Sicily *(qv)*.
1302	The Anjou Dynasty establishes itself in Naples.
1303	Attack of Anagni, instigated by King Philip of France, on Pope Boniface VIII.
1309-1377	The popes established at Avignon, France. The Avignon popes went from Clement V to Gregory XI who took the papacy back to Rome under the instigation of St Catherine of Siena.
1328	Failure of the intervention in Italy by the Emperor Ludwig of Bavaria.
1378-1418	The Great Schism of the West (anti-popes in Pisa and Avignon) was brought to an end by the Council of Constance (1414-1418).
1402	Last German intervention in Italy (emperor defeated by Lombard militia).
1442	Alfonso V, King of Aragon, becomes King of the Two Sicilies.
1494	Intervention of King Charles VIII of France at the behest of Ludovico il Moro.

From the 16C to the Napoleonic era

16C	France and Spain engage in a struggle for the supremacy of Europe.
1515-1526	François I, victor at Marignano but vanquished at Pavia, is forced to give up the Italian heritage.
1527	Capture and sack of Rome by the troops of the Constable of Bourbon, in the service of Charles V.
1559	Treaty of Cateau-Cambrèsis: Spanish domination over Naples and the district of Milan.
17C	Savoy becomes the most powerful state in northern Italy.
1713	Victor-Amadeus II of Savoy acquires Sicily and the title of King. The Duke of Savoy is compelled to exchange Sicily for Sardinia in 1720.
1796	Napoleon's campaign in Lombardy. Creation of the Cispadan Republic.
1797	Battle of Rivoli. Treaty of Campo-Formio. Creation of the Cisalpine and Ligurian Republics.
1798-1799	Proclamation of the Roman and Parthenopaean (Naples) Republics.
1805	Napoleon transforms the Italian Republic into a Kingdom, assumes the iron crown of the Lombard Kings and confers the vice-royalty on his stepson, Eugène de Beauharnais.
1808	Rome is occupied by French troops. Murat becomes King of Naples.
1809	The Papal States are attached to the French Empire. Pius VII is taken to France as a prisoner (1812).
1814	Collapse of the Napoleonic régime. Pius VII returns to Rome.

Towards Italian Unity (1815–1870)

1815	Congress of Vienna. Hegemony of Austria.
1815-1832	The "Carbonari" patriots oppose the Austrian occupation but their revolts are crushed.
1831	Founding of the Young Italy movement by Mazzini. Growth of national feeling against Austria: the **Risorgimento.**
1834-1837	Revolts at Genoa and in the Kingdom of the Two Sicilies.
1848	General insurrection against Austria, led by the King of Sardinia, ruler of Piedmont. Italian successes followed by a violent Austrian counter-attack.
1849-1852	Accession of Victor Emmanuel II. Cavour's government reorganises the State of Piedmont.
1854	Participation of Piedmont, with Britain and France, in the Crimean War.
1856	Paris Congress. Cavour officially raises the question of Italian unity.
1858	Meeting of Cavour and Napoleon III at Plombières. Alliance between France and Piedmont.
1859	War declared by Austria against Piedmont and France. Franco-Piedmontese victories of Magenta and Solferino and Villafranca Armistice. Piedmont obtains Lombardy and France, Savoy and the County of Nice.
1860	Bologna, Parma, Modena and Tuscany unite with Piedmont. Expedition of Garibaldi and the Thousand to Sicily and Naples. Union of the South.
1861	Proclamation of the Kingdom of Italy with Turin as its capital. Death of Cavour.
1865-1870	Florence becomes the capital of the Kingdom of Italy.
1866	Austria at war with Prussia and Italy. Venetia united to Italy.
1867	Garibaldi, marching on Rome, is defeated at Mentana.
1870	Occupation of Rome by the Piedmontese. Rome becomes the capital of Italy. Italian unity is complete.

From 1870 to the Present Day

1882	Italy, Germany and Austria sign the Triple Alliance.
1885	The Italians gain a footing in Eritrea and on the Somali Coast.
1900	Assassination of King Umberto I by an anarchist. Accession of Victor Emmanuel III.
1904-1906	Rapprochement of Italy with Britain and France.
1915	Italy enters the First World War on the side of the Allies.
1919	Treaty of St. Germain: Istria and the Trentino are attached to Italy.
1921	Social disturbances fomented by Mussolini's Fascist Party.
1922-1926	The March on Rome. Mussolini becomes Prime Minister, then *Duce* (Leader).
1929	Lateran Treaty concluded between the Italian Government and the Papacy *(p 21)*.
1936	Italian occupation of Ethiopia. Rapprochement with Germany. Rome-Berlin Axis formed.
1940	Italy enters the Second World War against Britain and France.
1943	Fall and arrest of Mussolini. Italy goes to war with Germany.
1945	Execution of Mussolini.
May 1946	Abdication of Victor Emmanuel III and accession of Umberto II.
June 1946	Proclamation of the Republic after a referendum.
1947	Treaty of Paris: Italy loses its colonies as well as Albania, Istria, Dalmatia and the Dodecanese. Frontier redefined to the benefit of France.
1954	Trieste is attached to Italy.
March 1957	Treaty of Rome instituting the European Economic Community (Common Market): Italy is one of the six founder member states.

UNIFICATION OF ITALY

Although Machiavelli had already dreamed of a united Italy in the 16C, it was not until after the French Revolution that the question of uniting the various regions under the same political regime was seriously contemplated. The Risorgimento provided the initial impe-

tus which resulted in the uprisings of 1848 against Austrian rule and their defeat at Novara (1849). The problem of Italian unity was brought to the forefront of European affairs with the accession of **Victor Emmanuel II** and the skilful campaigning of his minister **Camillo Cavour**, an ardent advocate of Italian liberty. Napoleon allied himself with the Piedmontese in order to oppose the Austrians. After the combined Franco-Piedmontese victories of 1859 and the disillusionment caused by the Treaty of Villafranca when Savoy was surrendered to France, several regions of central Italy planned a concerted revolt and united with Piedmont. **Garibaldi** liberated Sicily and southern Italy from the domination of the Bourbons. On the 17 March 1861 the inauguration of the Kingdom of Italy was proclaimed with Turin as the capital and Victor Emmanuel as King. Five more years had to pass before the war of independence

UNIFICATION OF ITALY

with the Prussians as allies led to the annexation of Venetia and more than ten before Italian troops captured Rome in 1870, thus achieving the unification of Italy.

THE PAPACY

The Vatican City forms a Free State of which the pope is sovereign. Although the pope in relation to the priesthood has no powers superior to those of a bishop, he is in the hierarchy the head of the whole Roman Catholic Church. As the successor of St Peter and the Vicar of Christ he governs that Church by virtue of powers received from God. In 1870 the Vatican Council declared him infallible in matters of dogma. The pope is elected by the cardinals, forming the Sacred College which meets in conclave in the Sistine Chapel. A majority of two-thirds plus one is required to make an election valid. The spiritual influence of the Roman Catholic Church radiates throughout the world through the person of the Sovereign Pontiff. As the Christian community grew in numbers the pope began to assume an ever growing political role in parallel with his function as Head of the Church. Thus the history of the Papacy is also the history of the relationship between the Church and State.

From the Birth of the Church to that of the Papacy. – Christianity was born in the Levant with the preaching of Jesus and the Passion of Christ but reached the west through the agency of the Apostles and their disciples. By the end of the 1C the early Church was formed of small communities directed by bishops, representing Christ. By the end of the 2C the Bishop of Rome claimed primacy over the other bishops. Gradually the name of Pope (low Latin *Papa*: Father) ceased to be applied to all bishops and was reserved exclusively for the Bishop of Rome.

Growth of the Church. – At first regarded as a harmless cult, Christianity was considered in the reign of Nero to be subversive of public order, and many Christians fell victim to the persecutions instituted by certain emperors such as Domitian, Decius, Valerian and Maximinus. These persecutions failed to check the spread of Christianity and the Church stood out as the only great moral force left in a distracted and divided Empire. In 313, the Emperor Constantine, who himself converted to Christianity the following year, gave complete religious freedom to Christians by the **Edict of Milan**. When it was recognised as the state religion it became the surest support of the imperial power, and when Rome crumbled under the repeated assaults of the Barbarians it formed the last bulwark of civilisation.

Pontifical Authority. – The authority of the pope and the ascendancy of the Church grew all the stronger due to the strong personality of **Gregory the Great** (590-604). In the 8C when faced with the occupation of the imperial territories by the Lombards, the then pope appealed to Pepin the Short, King of the Franks, and initiated an era of alliances with the Carolingian dynasty culminating in two important events. By the **Donation of Quiersy-sur-Oise** (AD 756) the King of the Franks gave an undertaking to return all occupied territories to Pope Stephen II and not to the Byzantine emperor. This donation is the origin of the Papal States and of the pope's temporal power. The second event was the coronation of Charlemagne as Emperor of the West in the year AD 800. The privileged position of the Church vanished with the fall of the Carolingian Empire at the end of the 9C.

The anarchy which then obtained in Europe was for the papacy a period of great laxity. After the foundation of the Germanic Holy Roman Empire, **Gregory VII** (1073-85) stands out as a reformer. His decrees led to the **Quarrel of the Investitures**, a long drawn-out conflict between the pope and the emperor.

The papacy emerged weakened from the Captivity of Avignon (1309-1377) but it had to face a still more serious crisis with the **Great Schism of the West** (1378-1417) and again in 1520, when the Reformation started by Martin Luther began to spread. Every religious crisis tended to be followed in due course by a reaffirmation of papal authority.

The "Roman Question". – As the spiritual head of the Church but also a temporal sovereign, the pope was involved, in the 19C, in the problem of Italian unity. Unity could be complete only if he renounced all temporal power in the peninsula.

(Giraudon)

Pope Paul III (Alessandro Farnese) with his nephews by Titian
(Capodimonte Palace, Naples)

At the occupation of Rome by the troops of Victor Emmanuel II in 1870 Pope Pius IX was forced to consider himself a prisoner in the Vatican Palace.

It was Pius XI who obtained the territorial independence of the Holy See by the **Lateran Treaty** of 1929. From then on the pope enjoyed complete freedom of action within the Papal State which comprises the Vatican City itself, the four major basilicas, the catacombs, the Roman Curia, several colleges and Castel Gandolfo.

The authority of the Church was also recognised in the fields of education and marriage. It was on this basis that in 1947 the Constitution defined the relations between the Church and the State. Another agreement modifying the 1929 Lateran Treaty was signed in 1984.

ANCIENT CIVILISATIONS

Since 2000 BC and throughout antiquity, Italy, the meeting-place of races, has seen the Etruscan, Greek and Latin civilisations flourish on her soil. Two thousand years later, western civilisation is still impregnated with them. Greeks, Etruscans and Romans were preceded by two peoples who came from the north: the Ligurians, who also occupied southern Gaul and the Iberian Peninsula, and the Italics or Italiots, who settled in Umbria and Latium and from whom the Latins sprang. The former transmitted their fair hair and blue eyes to some of the present inhabitants of Liguria. The latter built acropoli of which the gigantic foundations still exist in some places, as for instance at Alatri.

THE GREEKS

Cities and Men. – The shores of Sicily and southern Italy had a sort of fascination for the ancient Greeks, who regarded them as the limits of the inhabited earth. Many scenes of Greek mythology are set there: the Phlegrean Fields, near Naples, hid the entrance to

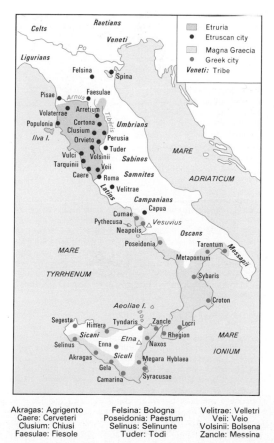

Akragas: Agrigento
Caere: Cerveteri
Clusium: Chiusi
Faesulae: Fiesole

Felsina: Bologna
Poseidonia: Paestum
Selinus: Selinunte
Tuder: Todi

Velitrae: Velletri
Veii: Veio
Volsinii: Bolsena
Zancle: Messina

An ancient temple

the Kingdom of Hades; Zeus routed the Titans, with the help of Hercules, on the site of Etna, where the Cyclops lived and Hephaestus, the God of Fire, had his forges; Kore, the daughter of Demeter, was kidnapped by Hades, who had emerged from the Tartara River near Enna.

In the *Odyssey*, Homer (9C BC) relates the adventures of Ulysses (Odysseus) after the siege of Troy, sailing between Scylla and Charybdis in the Straits of Messina and resisting the temptations of the Sirens in the Gulf of Sorrento. Pindar (5C BC) describes these mysterious shores, to which Virgil (1C BC) also refers in the *Aeneid*.

After the Phoenicians had settled at Carthage and their seamen had set up a few trading posts, the Greeks founded, as early as the 8C BC, a large number of colonies on the coasts of Sicily and southern Italy. The whole settlement took the name of **Magna Graecia**. In it were Ionian, Achaean and Dorian colonies, named after the Greek peoples who had colonised them. The social unit was the "city". One of them, Crotone, was governed by a school of philosophers, the Phytagoreans.

The 6C and 5C BC marked the zenith of Greek civilisation in Italy, corresponding with the period of Pericles in Athens. The Greek cities drew such profit from their seaborne trade that Syracuse soon rivalled Athens. Syracuse and Taranto were the two main centres of this refined civilisation.

Philosophers, scientists and writers settled in Sicily. Aeschylus lived at Gela and Syracuse was where Theocritus defined the rules of bucolic poetry and the geometrician Archimedes was murdered by a Roman soldier.

The number and diversity of these cities led to rivalry and dissension. Warfare between the "tyrants" of neighbouring towns and Carthaginian raids caused a decline which ended in the Roman conquest at the end of the 3C BC.

Today, on the shores of the Ionian and Tyrrhenian Seas, Greek ruins enhance the attractions of the Italian countryside.

Art in Magna Graecia. –

The 6 and 5C BC saw the building of the temples of Paestum, Selinus and Agrigento, magnificent examples of Doric architecture whose vigorous design contrasts with the delicate grace of the Ionic order.

At the end of the 5C BC the Doric style was still used for the beautiful temple at Segesta while in Greece itself the Ionic style was at its height and the Corinthian style was just making its appearance.

Doric Order   Ionic Order   Corinthian Order

Decline began in the 4C BC, after the Peloponnesian War between Sparta and Athens, which impoverished the Greek world. This was the beginning of the so-called **Hellenistic** period, marked by the neglect of architecture in favour of sculpture.

The museums of Naples, Paestum, Reggio di Calabria, Taranto, Palermo and Syracuse illustrate the development of sculpture from the archaic low-reliefs of the metopes of Paestum or Selinus and the monumental telamones (male figures used as pillars) of Agrigento to the delightful statuettes of the decadent period, akin to the Tanagra figures modelled at Taranto in the 3C BC. Between these extremes, innumerable youths, Apollos and Aphrodites issued from the sculptors' studios. They were all more or less copied from Phidias, Praxiteles, Scopas or Lysippus, but their harmony of form and proportion remained admirable.

THE ETRUSCANS

While the Greeks were impregnating the south of the peninsula and Sicily with their civilisation, the Etruscans were building up in central Italy, from the 8C BC onwards, a powerful empire whose growth was checked only by that of Rome (3C BC). They are a little known people whose alphabet along with certain tombstone inscriptions, have now been deciphered. Some authorities think they were natives of these parts; others, following the example of Herodotus, say they came from Lydia in Asia Minor. The Etruscans at first occupied the area between the Arno and the Tiber *(map p 21)* but later spread into Campania and the Po Plain. They reached their zenith in the 6C BC. **Etruria** then comprised a federation of twelve city-states known as *lucumonies*, among which are named Veii, Bolsena, Tarquinia, Volterra, Perugia, etc.

Having grown rich by working iron (Island of Elba), copper and silver mines and by trading in the western Mediterranean, the Etruscans, who were artisans and technicians, had a civilisation derived from a mixture of savagery and refinement.

In religion their gods were the same as those of the Greeks. They believed in life after death and in divination, and they studied the entrails of animals (for haruspices) and the flight of birds (for auspices), a form of superstition which the Romans adopted and developed.

Their towns, built on elevated sites with walls of huge stones, show an advanced sense of town planning. Near them are vast burial grounds with underground chambers or hypogea filled with utensils and adorned with mural paintings. These reveal the customs of the Etruscans, which formed the basis of one branch of Latin civilisation.

Etruscan Art. – Etruscan art is primitive in character, though strongly influenced by the Orient and especially by Greece from the 5C BC onwards. It has a marked individuality sustained by realism and expressive movement.

Etruscan art was discovered in the 18C, but was for long regarded only as an offshoot of Greek art. The discovery in the 19C of masterpieces like the Apollo and Hermes of Veii and the systematic study in the 20C of pottery, bronzes, utensils and ornaments unearthed in excavations made it possible to give this vigorous and refined art the place it deserved.

(Bevilacqua/CEDRI)

Etruscan cist
(Museum of the Villa Giulia, Rome)

Sculpture. – Since architectural specimens are lacking, sculpture appears to us as the artists' favourite medium. The great period is the 6C BC, when large groups of statuary adorned the frontons of the temples: the famous Apollo of Veii (in the museum of the Villa Giulia in Rome) in which Greek influence is obvious, belongs to this period. Some portrait busts are more original in their striking realism, intensity of expression and stylised features: their large prominent eyes and enigmatic smiles are characteristic of the Etruscan style. The same remarks apply to the famous groups of semi-recumbent figures on the sarcophagi, many of which are portraits.

The sense of movement is shown mainly in sculptures of fantastic animals (such as the Chimera from Arezzo in the Archaeological Museum of Florence) and in figurines representing warriors fighting, women at their toilet, etc.

Painting. – The only surviving specimens are in the burial chambers of the cemeteries (Cerveteri, Veii and especially Tarquinia), where they were supposed to remind the dead of the pleasures of life: banquets, games and plays, music and dancing, hunting, etc. The delicate paintings in colour laid on flat show surprising powers of observation. They form an excellent record of Etruscan life.

Pottery and goldsmiths' work. – Even more than artists, the Etruscans were artisans of genius. In pottery they used the **bucchero** technique, about which little is known, producing black earthenware with figures in relief. Initially decorated with motifs in *pointillé*, the vases developed more elaborate shapes with a more complicated ornamentation. In the 5C BC they modelled beautiful burial urns, *canopae*, in animal or human shape adorned with geometric designs. Inca and Aztec pottery bears a striking resemblance to Etruscan work. Greek pottery continued to be popular in Etruria where it was faithfully copied.

In the domain of goldsmiths' work, both men and women wore heavy gold ornaments of remarkable workmanship: often of solid gold they were a good example of the oustanding skill of the Etruscan goldsmiths. They were particularly skilful in the filigrane technique and perfected the granulation technique, splitting the gold into granules only a few tenths of a millimetre in diameter. Engraved mirrors, cists (cylindrical vessels which usually served as marriage coffers), scent-burners and bronze candelabra of great decorative elegance also show the skill of the artisans.

THE ROMANS

For about twelve centuries, from the foundation of Rome in the 8C BC to the end of the Western Empire in AD 476, a civilisation from which Western Europe emerged, reigned in Italy. Royal Rome (753-509 BC) was followed by the Republic (509-27 BC) and then the Empire (27 BC). The Roman eagle then spread its wings from Britain to the Persian Gulf and from Africa to Germany. It was only at the time of the Later Empire (AD 284-476), which was torn by civil wars and harried by Barbarian invasions, that decline set in.

Political and social Life. – At the time of the kings, the political organisation of Rome comprised two bodies, the Senate and the *Comitia*, composed of patricians. These were a privileged class who kept idle but devoted hangers-on. The plebeians had no access to public affairs. At the bottom of the scale the slaves formed the under-privileged section of the population, but they could be freed by their masters.

Under the Republic, power was given to two consuls, elected for one year and assisted by quaestors in charge of public finance and the criminal police, together with censors of public morals, aediles in charge of the municipal police and judicial praetors. The Senate had a consultative role and sanctioned laws. Ten Tribunes of the People watched over the rights of the masses. Consuls or praetors administered the provinces.

Generally speaking, the Empire kept the administrative structure of the Republic, but the powers of the consuls were taken by an emperor *(Imperator)* who was commander-in-chief of the army; he appointed the Senate, and had the right to make peace or war. Under the Later Empire the power of the emperors became absolute.

Outside the State, society was divided into clans *(gentes)*, or groups of people descended from a common ancestor, and families, each under a *pater familias* who wielded absolute authority.

Religion. – Religion played a part in every event of public or private life.

Domestic cults. – A small oratory called the *lararium* enshrined the household gods, Lares and Penates, before whom a sacred flame burned always. The souls of the dead were also venerated.

Public worship. – This took place in buildings copied from the Etruscan or Greek temples *(sketch p 22)*. Sometimes they were circular in form, as in the case of temples dedicated to Vesta.

With the exception of Janus, the chief gods were derived from the twelve (if Pluto god of the Underworld is omitted) Greek gods of Olympus.

A Roman Town *(1)*

Planning. – Roman towns often have a military origin: when the land placed under their control was shared out, the legionaries and veterans who had stayed in the camps were joined by the civil population. Towns which had been surrounded with walls during troubled periods were divided, whenever possible, into four quarters by two main streets, the *decumanus* and the *cardo*, intersecting at right angles and ending in gateways. Other streets parallel to these two gave the town a chess-board plan.

Streets. – The streets were edged with footpaths, sometimes 1ft 6in high, and lined with porticoes to shelter pedestrians. The roadway, paved with large flagstones laid diagonally, was crossed at intervals by stepping-stones laid at the same level as the pavements but between which horses and cart-wheels could pass.

The Roman house. – Excavations at Herculaneum, Pompeii and especially Ostia have uncovered Roman houses of various types: the small bourgeois house, a dwelling of several storeys, shops open to the street and finally large, luxurious patrician mansions.

The latter had a modest external appearance owing to their bare walls and few windows. But the interiors, adorned with mosaics, statues, paintings and marbles and sometimes including private baths and a fish pond, revealed the riches of their owners. The entrance was often surmounted by a mosaic or an inscription warning the visitor to beware of the dog: *Cave canem.* A vestibule overlooked by the porter's lodge led to the *atrium*.

A Roman house

The **atrium (1)** was a large rectangular court open, in the middle, to the sky. A basin called the *impluvium,* under the open section, caught rainwater. The rooms *(cubiculae)* opened off the atrium, which was the only part of the house to which strangers were usually admitted. At the far end was the **tablinum (2)** or study and reception room of the head of the family. Money and books were kept there.

The atrium and the adjoining rooms represent the primitive, simple house of the poorer citizen. High officials, rich colonials and prosperous tradesmen often added a second house, of the more refined Greek type, joining on to the *tablinum.*

The **peristyle (3)** was a court surrounded by a portico (a gallery with a roof supported by columns) in the centre of the part of the house reserved for the family. Here the peristyle was generally made into a garden with basins lined with mosaics, fountains and statues. The living quarters opened on to it all round: bedrooms, dining-rooms, or the **triclinium (4)** and the main saloon or **œcus (5)**.

The bedrooms were simple sleeping chambers. They contained a stone or marble dais built against the wall or a movable bed. There were mattresses, cushions and blankets but no sheets. In the dining-room, the guests reclined on couches placed on three sides of the table, the fourth being left open for service.

The servants' quarters included the kitchen with a sink and drain, a built-in stove and an oven for roasting and pastry; baths, which were like the public baths on a smaller scale, and the slaves' quarters, attics, stables, etc. The latrines with drains were either in a corner of the kitchen or in some other recess.

The forum. – The forum was a large square, often surrounded by a portico. Originally it was a market, usually at the crossing of the two main streets, but it became the centre of the public and commercial life of Roman towns. Men came there to read public notices, listen to political speakers, stroll and talk. The women did their shopping, either in shops round the square or from hawkers and artisans who set up their stalls under the porticos. Slave markets were held on certain days.

Government offices were placed round the forum. These included the *curia* or headquarters of local government; the voting hall for elections; the public tribune from which candidates for office harangued the crowd; the Temple of Money or exchange; the municipal treasury; the public granaries; the Temple of Justice or law courts; the prison, and one or more temples.

---

(1) The personal records of M. Jules Formigé (1879-1960), Inspector-General of Historical Monuments were consulted for this section.

The tombs. – Roman cemeteries were placed along the roads, a little away from the towns. The most famous in Italy is that on the Via Appia Antica, south of Rome. Directly after death the body of the deceased was exposed on a funeral couch surrounded with candlesticks and wreaths of flowers. Then it was buried or burnt by the family. The deceased was provided with funeral furnishings for use in his second life: clothes, arms and tools for the men, toys for the children, as well as jewellery and toilet articles for the women.

Buildings

Great builders. – The art of building was highly developed by the Romans. The speed with which they erected their buildings was due less to the number of workmen employed than to the special training of workers, the methods of work and the use of lifting devices such as levers, winches and tackle to move heavy material into place. The Roman vault is semicircular in shape. At the end of the Empire, brick was used in preference to stone. The Roman architectural orders *(see sketch p 22)* were derived from the Greek orders, from which they are distinguished by certain details. Roman Doric, the simplest and strongest, is found in the ground floors of buildings. The Corinthian order was the most popular one with the Romans.

Temples. – Rome liberally adopted gods from all the mythologies. The emperors, when raised to divine status, were themselves objects of worship. The Roman temple *(see sketch p 22)* consists of a closed chamber, the *cella* (sanctuary), containing the image of the god, and an open vestibule *(pronaos)*. The building is surrounded, partly or completely, by a colonnade or peristyle.

Triumphal arches. – In Rome these commemorated the "triumphs" of generals or conquering emperors. The low-reliefs on the arches recorded their feats of arms. In the provinces, such as Aosta, Benevento and Ancona, are municipal arches commemorating the founding of a city or erected in honour of some member of the imperial family.

The baths. – The Roman baths, which were public and free, were not only baths but centres of physical culture, casinos, clubs, recreation centres, libraries, lecture halls and meeting-places, which explains the amount of time people spent in them. Decoration in these great buildings was lavish: mosaic ornaments, coloured marble facings, columns and statues. The bather followed a medically approved circuit. From the gymnasium *(palestra)* he entered a luke-warm room *(tepidarium)* to prepare him for the high temperature of the hot room *(caldarium)* and the steam-room. Then came the hot cleaning-bath, the tepid transition-bath and the cold plunge *(frigidarium)* to tone up the skin.

To heat air and water a number of underground furnaces *(hypocausts)* were used. The hot air was circulated to heat the rooms from below and from the sides.

(Giraudon)

Roman art: Caracalla

The amphitheatre. – This typically Roman structure, several storeys high encircles the usually oval arena and was destined to seat the spectators. Posts were fixed to the upper part of the wall to carry a huge adjustable awning, the **velum** to shelter the spectators from the sun and rain.

Inside, enclosing the arena, a wall protected the spectators in the front rows from the wild animals, released in the ring.

Three circular galleries forming promenades, various staircases and corridors made it possible for all the spectators to reach their seats quickly without crowding and without any mingling of the classes.

Always very popular, the performances were announced in advance by painted posters, giving the names of the performers and details of the programme which included fighting of three kinds: between animals, between gladiators and animals, and between gladiators. In principle, a duel between gladiators had always to end in the death of one of the opponents. The public could ask for a gladiator's life to be spared and the President of the Games would indicate a reprieve by turning up his thumb. The victorious gladiator received a sum of money if he was a professional or he was freed if he were a slave or a prisoner.

Other performances included chariot races, naval battles *(naumachia)*, Olympic games or impressive boxing contests, when the opponents wore copper gloves.

The theatre. – Theatres had rows of seats, usually ending in colonnades, a central area or **orchestra** occupied by distinguished spectators or used for acting, and a raised **stage**. The actors performed in front of a wall which was the finest part of the building; its decoration included several tiers of columns, niches containing statues, marble facings and mosaics. The perfect acoustics were generally due to an ensemble of subtle architectural features. The scenery was either fixed or mobile and there was an ingenious array of machinery either in the wings or below stage.

The chief function of the theatre was the performance of comedies and tragedies; however Roman theatres were also used for competitions, lottery draws and the distribution of bread or money.

Until 100 BC all actors wore wigs of different shapes and colours according to the nature of the character they represented. After that date they adopted pasteboard masks and again each character had a distinctive mask. Tragic actors, to make themselves more impressive, wore buskins or sandals with thick cork soles.

ITALIAN ART

To appreciate fully Italian art in all its diversity and richness from the 12C to the late 18C it is necessary to keep in mind the illustrious historical backdrop. The rightful heir of the Greek, Etruscan and Roman civilisations, Italian art has adopted from each period some of the most essential principles and characteristics. Italy with its vast geographical extent from the Alps in the north down to Sicily, has always been open to diverse foreign influences. Following the fall of the Western Roman Empire it was Byzantium that held sway and greatly influenced the southern Adriatic shores for several centuries. A succession of invading peoples followed namely the Ostrogoths, Lombards, Franks, Arabs and Normans, and each left their imprint on the conquered territory.

The extraordinary malleable Italian character absorbed the various foreign influences and one after another the cities of Florence, Siena, Verona, Ferrara, Milan, Rome, Venice, Naples and Genoa became the cradle of a flourishing artistic movement. As early as the 12C, in spite of the regional diversities, Italian artists were already beginning to show certain common characteristics. This phenomenon gathered momentum right up until the Renaissance. Initially it was a common taste for harmony, solidity of form as well as an innate sense of space. Both as an idealist and a mystic, the Italian has always worshipped beauty: the Italian landscapes were his source of inspiration where the clearly defined outlines are softened by the effect of the colours and the play of shimmering light.

The Italians rejected the importance accorded to realism which was so popular with northern schools and diminished the excessive emphasis placed on decoration by Oriental artists.

Slowly the Italian artist evolved a representational technique which contained his emotion. A preoccupation with idealisation is particularly evident in the emphasis given to feminity whether it be profane or religious in inspiration.

In spite of this scholarly and well mastered image, Italian art is not all exclusive. Take for example the medieval square, the famous **piazza,** which groups together on the site of the Roman forum the main public buildings: the church, baptistry, communal palace or the princely seat. To these were added at times the law courts, a hospital or a fountain. This was the venue for local markets and meetings. It is this urban decor which gives the best evidence of Italian taste for prestigious illusions and a love of spectacle.

Often designed like stage scenery and embellished with ornamentation the piazza is also the place for business, political decision-making and other important events. History can be interpreted by studying how certain elements were reused, how ornamental motifs were copied and how styles were mingled or superimposed. This is where the artist who also aspires to be architect, sculptor and painter can best accomplish his art where it may be admired by all.

These excellent town planners, however, achieved a harmonious relationship with nature and the Italian countryside. Ever since Roman times they embellished the beautiful countryside with sumptuous **villas,** splendid terraced gardens cooled by refreshing basins, fountains and springs and landscaped with considerable skill to create shade and please the eye. In addition all sorts of follies invited the passer-by to rest, meditate or simply enjoy the intimate or grandiose aspect of nature. Thus the Italian architects and landscape gardeners, often indifferent to the solemn grandeur of French classicism, have created an infinite number of places where man has established a harmonious relationship with nature: from Hadrian's Villa near Rome to the flower decked terraces of the Borromean Islands, passing by the almost Oriental charm of the Villa Rufolo in Ravello, the elegant buildings of the Florentine countryside, the fantastic Mannerist creations of Rome, Tivoli or Bomarzo adorned with grottoes and statues and finally the delightful mansions of the Brenta Riviera, all the work of Palladio.

BYZANTIUM

When Constantine transferred the seat of the Empire to Constantinople in the 4C AD, Rome began to decline and ancient Byzantium became the centre of a brilliant civilisation, while part of Italy was overrun by the Barbarians. After Honorius, who with his sister Galla Placidia fixed the capital of the Empire at Ravenna, and Theodoric, King of the Ostrogoths, who favoured the Greco-Latin civilisation and died there, this town came under Byzantine rule in the reign of Justinian (527-565 AD) and his wife Theodora. The Byzantine Emperors held the region of Ravenna and Venezia Giulia only until the 8C, but they kept a footing in Sicily and part of southern Italy until the 11C.

Byzantine art was born of the Christian art of the catacombs and early Christian basilicas and the Greek Oriental style, with its taste for mass, rich decoration and colour. The capital of Byzantine art in Italy was Ravenna, whose tradition was carried on by Venice, Rome, Sicily and even Lombardy to the beginning of the 13C. The Byzantine artists had a sense of sanctity which appears in their works, with their air of grandeur and mystery.

Architecture and sculpture. – The palaces have vanished but religious buildings remain. They are built in brick, with domes, on the basilical plan inspired by the Roman basilica or on a circular plan for mausolea or baptistries. The sober exteriors of these buildings give no hint of the splendour of the mosaic decorated interiors. The low-reliefs on the sides of sarcophagi, chancel parcloses, ambos and pulpits, assume an essentially decorative character: symbolic and stylised figures, animals facing front to front, etc.

Mosaics. – Byzantine artists showed their full powers in this sumptuous art form. Mosaics were composed of *tesserae*, or fragments of hard stone, glazed and irregularly cut to catch the light. They covered oven-vaults, walls and cupolas, their gold scintillating gently in mysterious semi-darkness. Enigmatic and grandiose figures stood out against midnight blue backgrounds and landscapes enlivened with trees, plants and animals, depicted with surprisingly accurate observation.

The most famous mosaics are those of Ravenna, dating from the 5 and 6C; however, the Byzantine style still prevailed in the 11-12C at St. Mark's in Venice, in Sicily (Cefalù, Palermo Monreale) and as late as the 13C in Rome.

MIDDLE AGES- ROMANESQUE AND GOTHIC (11-14C)

As elsewhere in Europe, cathedrals were built all over Italy, but here the Italian predilection for harmony and the Roman tradition of monumental ensembles meant that architecture did not reach the sublime heights of the great achievements of religious art in France.

Romanesque Period. – Romanesque architecture in Italy received constant contributions from the Orient and, in the 12C especially, was influenced by France, notably by Normandy and Provence.

Lombard Style   Pisan Style   Florentine Style   Sicilian-Norman Style

The most flourishing school was that of Lombardy, whose master masons, the **maestri comacini,** created the **Lombard style** which spread all over north and central Italy. They built great vaulted churches decorated on the outside with bands and arcades, detached campaniles and elaborately carved façades preceded by porches supported by lions (Como, Milan, Pavia, Verona, etc.).

In the **Pisan style,** architecture showed a strong Lombard influence while the decorative work borrowed more from Oriental art. This style included tiers of arcades with a multitude of small columns on the façades, tall blind arcades on the side walls and east end and decorative marble incrustations forming lozenge shapes or other small motifs.

The highly original **Florentine Romanesque style** did not spread beyond the city. It is characterised by simple lines inspired by antique art and by the decoration of façades with white and green marble used alternately.

In Latium and as far as Campania, in the 12-13C, the **Cosmati,** a Roman guild of mosaic and marble workers, held sway. They specialised in assembling fragments of multicoloured marble (pavings, episcopal thrones, ambos or pulpits and candelabra) and the incrustation of columns and friezes in the cloisters with brightly coloured enamel mosaics.

Finally, in southern Italy and Sicily, Lombard, Saracen and Norman influences mingled, the first two exercising their effect chiefly on decoration and the last on the building plan. The combined result was the **Sicilian-Norman style** *(see p 224).*

Sculpture was closely linked with architecture, which was essentially religious and decorative.

Gothic Period. – As far as architecture was concerned it was the Cistercians who systematically introduced Gothic formulae into Italy in the 13C, starting at the Abbey of Fossanova; the Franciscans (at Assisi) and the Dominicans (at Florence) followed their example. In the same period the Angevin architects imported by the Anjou Dynasty, which reigned at Naples, spread arched vaulting and façades flanked by turrets in part of southern Italy.

Arnolfo di Cambio, the architect and sculptor, was influenced by both these traditions. He worked mainly in Florence and Rome.

In the 14C the Cathedral of Genoa and the huge unfinished Duomo at Siena were derived from Burgundian art, but in the 15C the great Church of S. Petronio at Bologna and the gigantic and florid Milan Cathedral marked the end of a style for which the Italians never showed much enthusiasm.

There was more originality in civil architecture of the Gothic period. Numerous prosperous towns chose to concretise their civic pride by embellishing their city centres with municipal palaces and loggias. In Venice *(see over)* the ornate Gothic style relieved bare façades with their numerous window openings and loggias. Venetian Gothic was to persist until the end of the 15C.

(Roy/Explorer)

Siena Cathedral

Romanesque Gothic Renaissance Classical Baroque

Venetian Palaces

The **Pisano** family from Pisa gave a decisive impetus to the art of **sculpture** by combining their continued use of ancient traditions (Nicola) and their vigorously expressive realism (Giovanni). These masters influenced the Sienese **Tino di Camaino** and the Florentines **Andrea Orcagna** and **Arnolfo di Cambio** with their new iconography and ambitious projects for pulpits and funerary monuments, all of which exhibited the new humanism.

The painted Crucifixes in relief which appeared in the 12C were the first specimens of Italian painting. Gradually the hieratic tradition inherited from Byzantine art lost its extreme rigidity. In the 13C a Roman, **Pietro Cavallini,** executed frescoes and mosaics with a greater breadth of style reminiscent of antique art. His Florentine contemporary, **Cimabue** (1240-1302) adorned the Upper Basilica of Assisi with frescoes displaying a new sense of pathos. This new approach influenced **Giotto** (1266-1337) who revolutionised painting by introducing naturalism into his works: movement, depth and atmosphere were indicated or suggested, and emotion came to light in the frescoes at Assisi, Padua and Florence.

In Siena at the same time **Duccio's** (born c1260) work still showed a strong Byzantine influence. He founded the Siena school which continued to employ a graceful linear technique and show a pronounced taste for the decorative use of colour. Some of the most delicate exponents of this school were **Simone Martini** and the brothers, **Pietro** and **Ambrogio Lorenzetti.** A famous school of miniaturists was founded at Rimini.

The leaders of the Florentine Trecento period (14C) were **Andrea Orcagna** and **Andrea di Bonaiuto,** known also as **Andrea da Firenze.** Their mystical and realistic style became known as **International Gothic** which is characterised by harmonies of line and colour as well as a great refinement in the decorative elements. Several artists of the Marches, Umbria, Lombardy and Piedmont, such as **Allegretto Nuzi** and **Gentile da Fabriano,** worked in this style, as also did the Veronese, Stefano da Zevio and **Pisanello** (15C) a portraitist, animal painter and distinguished medallist *(p 209),* as well as the Piedmontese Giacomo Jaquerio.

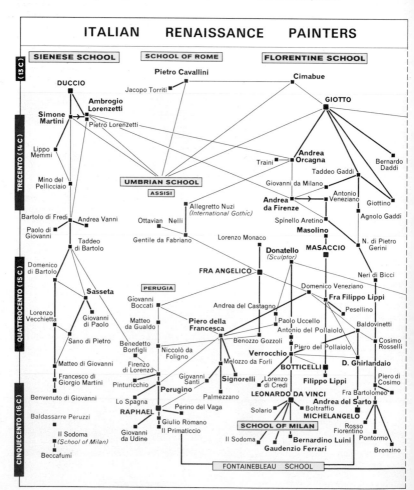

QUATTROCENTO (15C)

The early Renaissance was characterised by an abiding passion for antiquity and distant lands, the well-organised city-states governed by a noble or princely patron, a new vision of man's place at the centre of the universe and a large number of artists, scholars and poets. The Medici city of Florence united all these conditions and it was an appropriate birthplace of this cultural movement, designated much later as the Renaissance.

Architecture. – **Filippo Brunelleschi** (1377-1446) revealed himself as a great innovator in the art of building. Drawing on antique sources he advocated a purity and elegance of line. Among his disciples were **Michelozzo** (1396-1472), **Leon Battista Alberti,** Antonio and Bernardo Rossellino, Giuliano and Benedetto da Maiano, as were Francesco di Giorgio Martini in Siena and Luciano Laurana at Urbino.

Sculpture. – In the design of the doorways of the Baptistry at Florence, **Lorenzo Ghiberti** (1378-1455) shook off the Gothic tradition, still followed by the Sienese, **Jacopo della Quercia,** who like Brunelleschi, was eliminated from the competition.

The most powerful sculptor of the period was undoubtedly **Donatello** (1386-1466) who although a Florentine, worked throughout Italy. His contemporary **Luca della Robbia** (1400-82) specialised in coloured and glazed terracotta works, while Agostino di Duccio, Desiderio da Settignano and Mino da Fiesole continued in the Donatello tradition. At the end of the Quattrocento, **Verrocchio** (1435-88) showed remarkable power in the famous statue of Colleoni at Venice. The most remarkable sculptor outside Florence was the Dalmatian, **Francesco Laurana,** a sculptural portraitist of the greatest sensibility.

(After photo by Hachette)

Florence – Annunciation
by Donatello

Painting. – With **Masaccio** (1401-28), a new era opened for Italian art. He was the first to insist, in the Carmine frescoes, on an illusion of perspective and the notion of space. **Paolo Uccello** (1397-1475) made clever use of foreshortening in his admirable battle scenes. At the same time the Dominican friar, **Fra Angelico** (1387-1435) who remained very attached to Gothic tradition, was attracted to the new theories of the Renaissance.

His successors such as **Domenico Veneziano** and **Fra Filippo Lippi** (1406-69) developed his technique while retaining his delicacy of detail. **Benozzo Gozzoli** (1420-97) also recalls Angelico but adapts his manner to the portrayal of brilliant festivities, always purely secular.

No one has produced better than **Sandro Botticelli** (1444-1510), a pupil of Filippo Lippi, that miraculous purity of line which gives a graceful and almost unreal fragility to the figures and a deep sense of mystery to his allegorical scenes. Baldovinetti (1423-57), adopted Botticelli's manner while **Andrea del Castagno** (1423-57) emphasised modelling and monumental qualities. **Domenico Ghirlandaio** (1449-94) on the other hand had a particularly good gift for narrative painting.

The work of **Piero della Francesca** (c1415-92) from Sansepolcro, is a supreme example of Tuscan Renaissance art displaying faultless harmony and sure draughtsmanship. He influenced other artists such as Melozzo da Forlì.

At the Gonzaga court in Mantua, **Mantegna** (1431-1506) *(p 138)* painted scenes full of grandeur and rigour. In Ferrara **Cosimo Tura** with his realism inherited from northern painters, created his troublingly strange but original compositions.

The first Venetian painters to emerge from the Byzantine manner were the **Vivarini.** It was however the **Bellini** family *(p 201)* which gave Venetian painting its outstanding characteristic of luminosity. **Carpaccio** *(p 200)* and the elegant but somewhat precious artist, **Carlo Crivelli**, with his minutely detailed drawings and refined colours, are both chroniclers.

CINQUECENTO (16C)

The 16C saw the development of human sensibility which had already marked the previous century. Artists were attracted more and more by antiquity, mythology and the discovery of man.

The artistic centre of the Renaissance moved from Florence to Rome where the popes rivalled one and another to embellish palaces and churches. The artist became more independent and acquired a certain prestige.

By the end of the century, the canons of Renaissance art were already being exported and put into practise elsewhere in Europe, notably at Fontainebleau and in the Low Countries.

Architecture. – It was in the course of this century that the style of the Florentine palace was formed. The imposing rustication and elaborate cornices were replaced by a less massive appearance with a strong classical influence.

Bramante (1444-1514) invented the "rhythmic bay" *(p 115)*. He worked at Milan then Urbino before conceiving the original central plan of St Peter's in Rome. **Vignola** (1507-73) also worked in Rome and **Palladio** (1508-80) did much in Vicenza *(qv)*. In his important works on architecture he advocated the Classicism of ancient art and was himself responsible for many churches, palaces and luxury villas in Venetia.

Sculpture. – **Michelangelo** (1475-1564) did most of his life's work in either Florence or Rome and he was the most outstanding character of the century due to his creative, idealist and even troubled genius which found its expression in such works as David, Moses or the groups of slaves for the tomb of Julius II.

His contemporaries paled beside him: neither the elegant and refined **Benvenuto Cellini** (1500-71), a skilled goldsmith and able sculptor known for his Perseus now in Florence nor the powerful sculptor **Giambologna** or **Giovanni Bologna** (1529-1608) of Flemish origin and author of numerous group sculptures, bore comparison with the master Michelangelo.

Painting. – The 16C is an important period for painting with numerous outstanding artists producing works in the new humanist vein in several centres throughout Italy (Rome at first, then Venice, Mantua and finally Parma) and France.

The century began with exceptional but complementary masters. The fascinating **Leonardo da Vinci** (1452-1519) was the archetype of the enquiring mind of the new humanists. He is famous in painting for his *sfumato* (literally mist), a sort of impalpable, luminous veil which created an impression of distance between persons and things. After having worked in Florence and Milan he went to France at the behest of that Renaissance prince, François I.

Raphael (1483-1520) was not only a prodigious portraitist and painter of gently drawn madonnas, but also a highly inventive decorator with an exceptional mastery of composition which was given free rein in the Stanze of the Vatican. **Michelangelo** (1475-1564), the last of the three great men, although he was really a sculptor, took on the formidable task of decorating the ceiling of the Sistine Chapel where his sense of relief and his power are triumphant. His powerful figures are the origins of Roman Mannerism.

(Tetrel/Explorer)

Lady with a Veil by Raphael
(Pitti Palace, Florence)

In addition there was **Andrea del Sarto** and the portraitist **Bronzino** at Florence, **Sodoma** at Siena, **Correggio** at Parma *(qv)*, **Bernardino Luini** at Milan, etc. The 16C Venetian school produced many great colourists. **Giorgione** *(p 70)* had a wonderful sense of landscape and atmosphere. **Titian** (c1490-1576), a disciple of Bellini, was as a youth influenced by Giorgione and imbued with his skill for both mythological and religious compositions. He was also a fine portraitist and was commissioned by numerous Italian princes and European sovereigns. His work represents the high point in Venetian painting. **Tintoretto** (1518-94) added a tormented violence to the luminosity of his predecessors, and ably exploits this in his dramatic religious compositions. He had a strong influence on his amiable pupil, the Cretan, Theotocopoulos, known as **El Greco** who finally took refuge in Toledo. **Veronese** (1528-88) was first and foremost a decorator in love with luxury and sumptuous schemes who delighted in crowd scenes with grandiose architectural backgrounds. As for the very endearing **Jacopo Bassano** (1518-92), he handled rustic and nocturnal scenes with a freedom of touch and composition.

MANNERISM (16-17C)

The art of the Counter-Reformation, with its continued use of Renaissance canon often in an exaggerated or mannered way, marked the transition between Renaissance and baroque. If Mannerism was widely adopted throughout Europe it was countered in Italy by the opposition of the Roman Catholic Church, which following the Council of Trent proposed the purging of religious art. The Counter-Reformation movement was characterised in the domain of architecture by the Church of Gesù in Rome, an austere work by Vignola. The numerous fountains and gardens where the natural and artificial were found side by side are also expressions of the Mannerist taste for festivities and frivolities.

The art of the period shows a certain elongation of the figures, unusual attitudes and rather violent light, factors which would seem to translate a certain anxiety and impatience in the artists of the time. The main exponents include **Beccafumi, Pontormo** (1494-1556), **Rosso Fiorentino** (1494-1540), **Parmigianino** *(p 142),* Giulio Romano, Niccolò dell'Abbate, and the Zuccaro brothers.

BAROQUE (17-18C)

Painting. — In reaction against mannerisms, a group of Bolognese artists founded the Academy of the Eclectic (Incamminati), under the leadership of the **Carraci** family (Annibale, the most original, Lodovico and Agostino). They tried to codify beauty in large, careful but rather cold compositions which paved the way for baroque art. Their Bolognese followers, Guido, Albano and Guercino, continued in this manner with rather more vigour. However it was the work of **Caravaggio** (1573-1610) which revolutionised several centuries of Italian idealism. His intense and often cruel realism drew its inspiration from everyday life in Rome. His unusual use of contrasting light gave a dramatic visual impact to his work. He was widely imitated both in Italy and France and was without doubt the most influential artist in 17C Europe.

The characteristics of baroque art and architecture are effects of movement, inverted perspectives, *trompe-l'œil*, and scrolls. Often painting and architecture were associated giving sumptuous interior decoration schemes as Andrea Pozzo's work in Sant' Ignazio in Rome. Rome was the main centre of this movement but other exponents worked in Florence **(Luca Giordano)**, Venice **(Tiepolo)** and Naples (Giordano again, **Mattia Preti** and **Ribera**). During the 18C Venetian painting became more serene with **Pietro Longhi, Canaletto** and **Francesco Guardi** *(p 202)*.

(Everts/Rapho)

Lecce — Fronton of the Basilica of the Holy Cross

Architecture and sculpture. — Under the sway of the **Jesuits** architecture and sculpture acquired a florid and theatrical quality with architects such as **Carlo Maderno**, author of the façade of St Peter's (1614) in Rome, **Borromini** with his tormented spirit and designer of the elliptical Church of St Charles by the Four Fountains in Rome and especially **Bernini** (1598-1680) the most productive of them all who designed the colonnades of St Peter's, the baldachin and tombs inside the Basilica and numerous other fountains and sculptures. In Piedmont baroque architecture took a new turn with Guarini and **Juvara**. This was also true in Apulia (especially in Lecce) and Sicily where buildings became sumptuously fantastic in a search for decorative effect under the influence of the Spanish Plateresque.

MODERN ART

At the end of the 18C and beginning of the 19C the vogue of all things Classical was current throughout Europe and in Italy. The Italian neo-classical style is exemplified by the sculptor **Antonio Canova** (1757-1822) with his statue of Pauline Borghese now in Rome which displays a purity of line and rather cold elegance. The 19C makes a direct break with the sumptuous richness of the previous centuries.

The architect Alessandro Antonelli was responsible for curious buildings in Milan and his native town, Novara.

The **Macchiaioli** group was formed as a reaction to the strict academic principles then in vogue. The group also known as the "spotters" often worked outside and showed a greater feeling for nature and colour. The main exponents of this movement were **Giovanni Fattori** (1825-1908), Silvestro Lega and Telemaco Signorini (1835-1901) who travelled widely in Britain and was known for his street scenes of Edinburgh and London. Certain artists were in regular contact with the French Impressionists. Of De Nittis, Boldini and Zandomenighi, the latter profited most from his stay in the French capital. At the end of the 19C **Segantini**, leader of the divisionist school assured the transition into the 20C.

The 20C began in an explosive manner with the Futurists who under the leadership of the poet Marinetti proclaimed their belief in the age of machines, high speed and crowds. Members included Boccioni, Balla, Severini and **Carrà**. **Giorgio de Chirico** created metaphysical painting. **Modigliani**, who had belonged to the Paris school, outlined all his figures while Giorgio Morandi united groups of everyday objects on a table while concentrating his thought on the invisible.

20C sculptors include Arturo Martini, Marino Marini and **Giacomo Manzù**. Architecture has produced numerous talented names: Pier Luigi Nervi and Gio Ponti.

LITERATURE

Birth and splendour of Italian literature. – The Italian language acquired a literary form at the same place and time when painting was breaking free from foreign influences and acquiring a character of its own. At Assisi St Francis (1182-1226) wrote his **Canticle of the Creatures** in the vernacular instead of the traditional Latin, so that the people could read the word of God. In Florence and in the other cities where he spent his exile **Dante Alighieri** (1265-1321) established the basis of a national language, the Tuscan or Florentine. As justification of his choice he invoked antiquity and the Christian religion and it was with this new tool that he wrote one of the most powerful masterpieces of Italian literature. The **Divine Comedy** (begun *c*1307) is the account of a lively, enquiring and impassioned visitor to *Inferno, Purgatorio* and *Paradiso*. It is also an epic account of the Christianised western world and the height of spiritual knowledge of the period.

During the 14C **Petrarch**, the precursor of humanism and the greatest Italian lyrical poet *(p 140)* and his friend **Boccaccio** the astonishing story-teller who seems almost modern at times *(p 71)*, continued in the tradition of Dante. Each enriched the Italian language in his own way.

Petrarch in his **Sonnets** brought a fluidity and depth of psychological interrogation, while Boccacio in his **Decameron** added a liveliness of narration and accuracy of description.

Renaissance and the letters. – Florentine humanism reinterpreted the ancient heritage and invented a scholarly poetry in which the tension of the words and images reflected the aspiration of the soul to attain an ideal. Politian, Lorenzo Medici and especially Michelangelo were exponents of the Neo-Platonic notion of ideal poetry. However the Florentine Renaissance also favoured the development of other quite different lines of thought: scientific with Leonardo da Vinci, theorist with Leon Battista Alberti, philosophical with Marsile Fincin and encyclopaedic with the fascinating personality of Pico della Mirandola. Later Giorgio Vasari *(p 85)* became the first ever art historian.

In the 16C writers and poets perfected the Italian language to a height of refinement and elegance rarely attained and all this in the service of princes whom they counselled or entertained. The most famous was **Machiavelli** *(p 85)* the statesman and political theorist whose name now symbolises cunning and duplicity. In his work entitled **The Prince** he defined with clarity and intelligence the processes which control the society of man and the moral and political consequences of these relationships.

In the court at Ferrara it was **Ariosto** (1475-1533) and **Tasso** (1544-95) who provided the element of intellectual brilliance. While the former wrote *Orlando Furioso (Roland the Mad)*, an epic poem in episodes which enjoyed an extraordinary vogue, Tasso, his successor at court in this genre published his *Jerusalem Delivered (Gerusalemme Liberata)*.

In Venice, Aretino (1492-1556) sketched the implacable portrait of his contemporaries. As for Baldassare Castiglione (1478-1529) he was the author of one of the great works of the period *The Courtier (Il cortegiano)* which was read throughout Europe.

From the Renaissance to the Risorgimento. – The 17C and the early 18C was a period of decadence for Italian literature. Exceptions were Galileo (1564-1642) and Giambattista Vico (1668-1744) whose biting yet well thought out vision advanced scientific and philosophical thought.

The 18C was dominated by the Venetian dramatist **Carlo Goldoni** (1707-93) known as the Italian Molière who peopled his plays in an amusing, alert and subtle manner with the stock characters and situations of the *Commedia dell'Arte (p 55)*, an art form which was then highly popular in Venice.

From the end of the 18C writers began to express a new national spirit (consciousness which developed until the upheaval of the Risorgimento), Giuseppe Parini (1729-99) and Vittorio Alfieri (1749-1803) were the precursors of the violent and tormented Ugo Foscolo (1778-1827) whose patriotic pride is given full vent in *Of the Sepulchres*.

It was **Giacomo Leopardi** (1798-1837) who in some of his finest poems of his verse collection *Canzoni* expresses with a certain lucidity and lyrical purity the growing gulf between the old faith and a fear of the unknown future.

The Milanese author, **Alessandro Manzoni** (1785-1873), wrote one of the most important novels of 19C Italian literature, *The Betrothed (I promessi sposi)*.

Modern and contemporary authors. – The Sicilian **Giovanni Verga** (1840-1922) assured the transition between the 19 and 20C with his novels. He was one of the most important members of the Italian Realist *(Verismo)* school of novelists which took its inspiration from the French naturalist movement. In his extravagant fiction series entitled *Vinti* he presents his pessimistic vision of the world and his compassion for the disinherited.

The tortuous and anxious voice of the poet **Giovanni Pascoli** (1855-1912) filled the early years of the century. Then followed the brief interlude known as *Crepuscolari* and after three intense and thoroughly modern lyrical poets: Giuseppe Ungaretti, Eugenio Montale and Umberto Saba.

Early 20C novel writing was dominated by Giovanni Papini while an important school of literary critics developed around the Neapolitan philosopher Benedetto Croce (1866-1953), known for his idealistic theories.

Both the extraordinary character of the novelist, poet and soldier Gabriele D'Annunzio (1863-1938) and Curzio Malaparte (1898-1957) were to the forefront of 20C Italian literature. Another important contemporary, the Sicilian dramatist **Luigi Pirandello** (1867-1936) was the creator of a new stage technique and Nobel Prize Winner in 1934.

The works of Cesare Pavese (1908-1950) have as recurring themes the difficulty of existing described with anguish in his diary which was published posthumously with the title *This Business of Living*.

During recent decades the Italian novel has shown a strong vitality with such diverse personalities as Pratolini *(A Tale of Poor Lovers)*, **Alberto Moravia** *(The Time of Indifference)*, Guido Piovene *(Pietà contro pietà)*, Ignazio Silone *(Fontarama)*, Dino Buzzati *(The Tartar Steppe)*, Mario Soldati *(A cena col commendatore)*, Pasolini *(Ragazzi di vita)*, Carlo Levi *(Christ stopped at Eboli)*, Italo Calvino *(Il Visconte dimezzato)*, Leonardo Sciascia *(Il giorno della civetta)* and Elsa Morante *(Arthur's Island)*.

FOOD AND WINE

Italy is rich in tasty products and its cooking is among the best known in the world. A traditional meal consists of an **antipasto** or hors d'œuvre (raw vegetable salads with a dressing, fine pork-butchers' meats, pickled vegetables); **primo** (*primo piatto:* first course) rice or *pasta* in its numerous forms plain or combined with various sauces and trimmings ; **secundo** (meat or fish course) often accompanied by a **contorno** (vegetable or green salad). After the cheese (**formaggio**) are served fruit (**frutta**) as well as a choice of numerous other desserts: cakes, pastries and sweets (**dolci**), ices (**gelato**) or frozen cakes (**semifreddo**). A young wine is usually served in carafes *(sfuso)* of 1/4 *(quarto)*, half *(mezzo)* or litre *(litro)*. Ask for a wine list if you prefer better quality wines. There is a wide choice of mineral waters available. Traditionally the meal ends with a strong black espresso coffee.

SOME REGIONAL SPECIALITIES

Piedmont. – Cooking here is done with butter. A popular dish is **fonduta**, a melted cheese dip of milk, eggs and white truffles *(tartufi bianchi)*. *Cardi* (chards) are prepared *alla bagna cauda,* i.e. with a hot sauce containing oil or butter, anchovies, garlic and truffles. Monferrato produces the famous **Gorgonzola** cheese and delicious wines: Barolo, Barbaresco, Barbera, Grignolino, red Freisas, white **Asti**, still or sparkling *(spumante),* with a strong flavour of grapes.

Lombardy. – Milan, where cooking is done with butter, gives its name to several dishes: *minestrone alla milanese,* a soup of green vegetables, rice and bacon; *risotto alla milanese,* rice cooked with saffron; **costoletta** alla milanese, a fillet of veal fried in egg and breadcrumbs with cheese; **osso buco**, a knuckle of veal with the marrow-bone; **panettone**, a large fruit cake containing raisins and candied lemon peel. Here the commonest cheese is again the excellent **Gorgonzola**. Few wines are produced, apart from those of Valtellina or the Pavia district.

Venetia. – As in the Po Plain, the people eat **polenta**, a form of semolina made from maize, sometimes accompanied by little birds, *risi e bisi* (rice and peas), and **fegato alla veneziana** (calf's liver fried with onions). The shell-fish, eels and dried cod *(baccalà)* are excellent. The best wines come from the district of Verona; **Valpolicella** and Bardolino, *rosé* or red, perfumed and slightly sparkling, and Soave, which is white and strong.

Liguria. – The chief speciality of Genoa is **lasagne al pesto,** flat leaves of *pasta* baked in the oven and seasoned with *pesto*, a sauce based on olive oil in which basil, pine-kernels, garlic and ewes' cheese have been steeped. Sea-food is famous, including **zuppa di datteri,** a shell-fish soup with which the Ligurians drink Cinqueterre or Coronata, strong, liqueurlike white wines.

Emilia Romagna. – This is an eminently gastronomical region, whose pork-butchers' meat is the most famous in Italy: Bologna **salami** and **mortadella**, Modena *zamponi* (pigs' trotters), Parma **prosciutto** (ham). *Pasta* are varied and tasty when served *alla bolognese* – that is, with meat-gravy and tomato sauce. **Parmesan cheese** *(parmigiano)*, hard and pale yellow, is strong and delicate in flavour. Emilia produces **Lambrusco**, a fruity, sparkling red wine, and white Albano.

Tuscany. – This is where Italian cooking was born, at the court of the Medici. Florence offers its *alla fiorentina* specialities: dried cod *(baccalà)* with oil, garlic and pepper, *costata* grilled steak fillets with oil, salt and pepper, **fagioli** (beans with oil, onions and herbs); Leghorn produces **triglie** red mullet and **cacciucco** (fish soup) and Siena offers the **panforte**, a sugar cake containing almonds, honey and candied melon, orange or lemon. **Chianti** (both red and white) is drunk everywhere.

Umbria, Marches. – The regional dish is the **porchetta**, a whole sucking pig roasted on the spit. One of the Marches specialities is *vincigrassi,* pasta cooked in the oven with meat grary and cream sauce. The wines are white, including the famous **Orvieto** of Umbria, the Verdicchio of the Marches and the delicious Moscato of San Marino.

Latium. – There are many Roman specialities: **fettucine** or strip macaroni, **gnocchi** alla Romana, **saltimbocca**, a fillet of veal rolled in ham, fried in butter and sprinkled with Marsala and flavoured with sage, and **abbacchio al forno** or roast lamb. Vegetables include *carciofi alla Giudia,* or artichokes cooked in oil with garlic and parsley. **Pecorino**, ewes' milk cheese, and the famous white wines of Montefiascone *(see p 213)* and the **Castelli** (Frascati) will satisfy the most discerning gourmet.

Abruzzi, Molise. – Among the *pasta* note **maccheroni alla chitarra**, made by hand and cut into strips. **Latticini** (fresh mountain cheeses) are popular.

Campania. – Naples is the home of **spaghetti**, which is often prepared with shell-fish *(alle vongole).* *Trattorie* and *pizzerie* serve *costata alla pizzaiola*, a fillet steak with tomatoes, garlic and wild marjoram, **mozzarella** *in carrozza* (cheese savoury) and especially the **pizza**, a cheese *(mozzarella)* tart containing tomato and anchovy and flavoured with capers and wild marjoram. Wines from volcanic soil have a delicate, slightly sulphurous taste: red and white Capri, white Ischia, white **Lacryma Christi** and red Gragnano (Vesuvius wines).

Apulia, Basilicata, Calabria. – The oysters *(ostriche)* of Taranto are tasty. The most original dish is **capretto ripieno al forno**, a roast kid stuffed with herbs.

Sicily. – The island is rich in fruit (lemons, oranges, mandarines, olives, almonds), pastries and ices. The real Sicilian **cassata** is a partly iced cream cake containing chocolate cream and candied fruits. Other specialities: **cuscusu** (couscous) and fish – tunny, swordfish, anchovies. The best known wine is **Marsala**, which is dark and strong, but **Malvasia** and the white wines of Etna and Lipari are also delicious.

Sardinia. – *See p 215.*

Key

Sights

★★★ **Worth a journey**
★★ **Worth a detour**
★ **Interesting**

Sightseeing route with departure point indicated
on the road   in town

✕ ❖	Castle – Ruins	🏛 ⸙ Ecclesiastical building
⊥ ◎	Wayside cross or calvary - Fountain	Building with main entrance
⚜ ♈	Panorama – View	Ramparts – Tower
⚓ ✗	Lighthouse – Windmill	Gateway
⌒ ⌂	Cave – Nuraghe	Statue or small building
☆	Fort	Gardens, parks, woods
▲	Miscellaneous sights	B Letter locating a sight

Other symbols

▬▬▬	Motorway (unclassified) (Autostrada)	⌐⌐ Public building
═══	Major through road	⊞ ⊠ Hospital – Covered market
═══	Dual carriageway	✝✝✝ Cemetery
▫▫▫---	Stepped street – Footpath	⚑s Golf course
╫╫╫	Pedestrian street	🏇 Racecourse
⋍⋍⋍	Unsuitable for traffic	⚊ ▦ Outdoor or indoor swimming pool
→1429←	Pass – Altitude	⊤ Viewing table
🚂 🚌	Station – Coach station	⚓ Pleasure boat harbour
⬤	Underground station	Ⓑ Ferry (river and lake crossings)
•—•—•	Tramway	⟨⟩ Stadium
	Ferry services: Passengers and cars Passengers only	⌇ Water tower
✈	Airport	☎ Telephone
₀╫╫╫╫╫	Rack-railway, funicular	✉ Main post office with poste restante (Fermo posta)
₀•••••₀	Cable-car, chairlift	🛈 Tourist information centre
		🅿 Car park

MICHELIN maps and town plans are north orientated.

Main shopping streets are printed in a different colour in the list of streets.

Town plans: roads most used by traffic and those on which guide listed sights stand are fully drawn; the beginning only of lesser roads is indicated.

Local maps: only the primary and sightseeing routes are indicated.

Abbreviations

H Town Hall (Municipio)	**M** Museum (Museo)	**POL.** Police station (in large towns: Questura)
J Law Courts (Pal. di Giustizia)	**P** Préfecture (Prefettura)	**T** Theatre (Teatro)
		U University (Università)

🕐 Times and charges for admission are listed at the end of the guide

SIGHTS

listed alphabetically

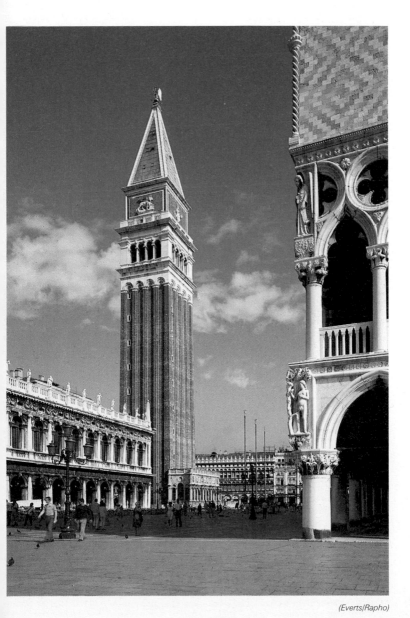

Venice – St Mark's Square

The Abruzzi Massif, the highest of the Apennine range, is a harsh region which due to its isolation and climate has preserved its beautiful landscapes and noble traditions. From the north with the formidable limestone barrier, the Gran Sasso, the massif extends from L'Aquila to Sulmona and beyond to Alfedena and the Abruzzi National Park. The massif has a variety of landscapes composed of gorges, sheer gullies, lakes, forests, desolate high plateaux and green pastures. In recent years there has been a growth in winter sports centres catering for the ski enthusiasts from the capital. Lying as it does not far from Rome, the massif is easily reached by motorway.

Sightseeing. – The adjoining map in addition to locating the towns and sites described in the guide, indicates other beauty spots in small black type.

★★THE GRAN SASSO

From L'Aquila to Castelli *159km – 99 miles – allow half a day*

This is the highest massif in the Abruzzi and its main peak is Corno Grande with an altitude of 2 914m – 9 560ft. On the northern side spines with many gullies slope away gently, while on the southern face, the Gran Sasso drops abruptly to the great glacial plateaux edged by deep valleys. They provide contrasting aspects, on the north it is one of lush pastures and tree covered slopes and on the other one of sheer desolation.

★ **L'Aquila.** – *Description p 47.*
Beyond Paganica the road passes through the gorges and climbs to Fonte Cerreto.

★★ **Campo Imperatore.** – *Take the road from Fonte Cerreto.* It passes through grandiose
ⓥ mountain country grazed by large flocks of sheep or hordes of wild horses. It was from here that Mussolini escaped on 12 September 1943, thanks to a daring raid by German airmen whose plane landed and took off near the hotel, in which the Duce had been interned.

Return to Fonte Cerreto.

The road then skirts the lower slopes of the Gran Sasso, as it follows the long green **Vomano Valley**★★ before entering the magnificent gorges (5km – 3 miles beyond Tintorale) which have amazingly stratified rock walls.

On leaving Montorio, take the S491 to the right, the road to Isola del Gran Sasso.

★ **Castelli.** – This town which stands on a wooded promontory at the foot of Monte Camicia, has been famous since the 13C for its highly colourful and richly decorated faïence (glazed pottery).

THE GREAT PLATEAUX
Round tour leaving from Sulmona
138km — 86 miles — allow 1 day

The Great Plateaux with their wide horizons stretch between Sulmona and Castel di Sangro, at a height of over 1 000m — 3 281ft. Cattle graze these expanses and their herdsmen make soft cheese *(scamorza)* in the form of eggs. These can be purchased at Rivisondoli.

★ **Sulmona.** — *Description p 184.*

Beyond the road runs sometimes along a corniche, or in a tunnel or over a viaduct but leads to the most important of the Great Plateaux, **Piano dei Cinquemiglia**, so-called because it was five Roman miles long (8km — 5 miles).

When you come within sight of the old village of Rivisondoli, take the S84 to the left.

★ **Pescocostanzo.** — This attractive village with its paved streets and old houses is a flourishing craft centre specialising in wrought-iron work, copper, gold and wood work as well as lace-making. The **Collegiate Church of Santa Maria del Colle** although built to a Renaissance plan has several Romanesque features and baroque additions (organ loft, ceiling and grille of the north aisle).

Castel di Sangro. — The town dominates a mountain rimmed basin. The cathedral, built to the plan of a Greek cross, is surrounded by a Renaissance portico.

★ **Alfedena.** — The houses of this small town are grouped about the ruined castle. Paths lead northwards to the ancient city of Alfedena with its cyclopean walls and necropolis.

★ **Scanno.** — From its high mountain site, Scanno overlooks the lovely **Lake Scanno**★ (Lago di Scanno) formed by a landslide which blocked the bed of the river Sagittario. This holiday resort is attractive with steep and narrow streets bordered by houses and churches. Women, still wear the dignified black local dress which is probably of Oriental origin. In the main street note the curious 14C fountain decorated in the Byzantine manner.
Between Lake Scanno and Anversa degli Abruzzi, for a distance of 10km — 6 miles the Sagittario River has hollowed from the grey rock a series of **gorges**★★ (Gole del Sagittario) of impressive depth and wildness, which the road follows with many twists and turns.

Anversa degli Abruzzi. — The village church dating from 1540 has a doorway with a carved tympanum representing the Entombment and other sculptures of masks and Biblical personages.

★★ ABRUZZI NATIONAL PARK (PARCO NAZIONALE D'ABRUZZO)

A nature reserve was founded in 1923, in the very heart of the massif, to protect the fauna, flora and outstanding landscapes of the region. It has an area of approximately 40 000ha — 155sq miles which is mostly forest with beach and maple predominating. The fauna includes the royal eagle, the Apennine wolf, the brown bear, the Abruzzi chamois and the wild cat and more recently roe deer and red deer.

⊙**Access and sightseeing.** — Either start from Gioia Vecchio in the north, Forca d'Acero in the west or Villetta Barrea and Barrea in the east.
Within the park's limits there are four different categories of protection according to the importance of the site to be protected and the type of activity permitted in that zone. The visitor is however free to visit a large part of the park using the well surfaced roads or tracks. Facilities include observation posts, camping and picnic sites as well as visitors' centres. It is only possible to study either the fauna or the flora at close quarters on foot or on horseback in some cases. It is advisable to keep to the signposted footpaths and go along with an official guide if possible.

Pescasseroli. — This is the main centre in the valley and is the home of the park's administrative services. The village lies in a basin whose outer sides are covered with beech and pine forests. Tourism and timber related activities are the village's main industries. Pescasseroli is the birthplace of the philosopher and politician, Benedetto Croce (1866-1952).

ADDITIONAL SIGHTS

★ **Bominaco.** — Two Romanesque churches stand 500m — 1 640ft above the hamlet of Bominaco, and are all that remain of a Benedictine **monastery** which was destroyed in ⊙the 15C. The **Church of San Pellegrino** is a 13C oratory with **frescoes**★ also of the 13C, which portray in a rather maladroit but detailed way the Life of Christ and a giant St Christopher. The **Church of Santa Maria** ★ (11 and 12C) is more characteristic of the local style. This has an elegant chevet and on one of the outer walls an opening flanked by four projecting lions. The bare but well-lit interior has a beautiful 12C cubic **ambo**★ resting on four columns with palm leaf capitals adorned with foliated scrolls and finials.

⊙**Corfinio.** — Away from the village stands the **Basilica of San Pelino** or **Basilica Valvense** in the Romanesque style, with the adjoining 12C Chapel of Sant' Alessandro. Walk round the church to admire the **east end**★. Inside there is a fine 12C pulpit.

Popoli. — The main square, Piazza Grande, of this busy market town, is overlooked by the Church of San Francesco, which has a Gothic façade with a baroque upper part. The **Taverna Ducale**★, near the Piazza Grande is an elegant Gothic edifice formerly used for collecting tithes payable to the prince.

⊙**Alba Fucens.** — These are the ruins of a Roman colony founded in 303BC. Amidst the ruins, mostly cyclopean in nature, are the remains of a basilica, the forum, baths, covered market as well as paved streets, wells and latrines.

Michelin map 988 fold 26

Built in the 6C BC this important city retains a great part of its cyclopean walls (4C BC). The **acropolis**★ can be reached on foot from the grandiose Porta di Città. It is laid out on a trapezoidal plan and is one of the best preserved examples in Italy. It affords a very fine **view**★★ of Alatri and the Frosinone Valley.

The town has a maze of steep flights of stairways, and alleyways lined with Gothic houses. The **Palazzo Gottifredi** *(Largo Luigi di Persiis)* is 13C and the **Church of St Mary Major**★ (Santa Maria Maggiore) in the transitional Romanesque-Gothic style has a façade with three porches. Inside there is interesting 12-15C **carved woodwork**★. On the by-pass is the 13C **Church of St Silvester** (San Silvestro) built in a dry stone technique. Inside are frescoes dating from the 13C to the 16C.

ALBA Piedmont   Pop 30 987

Michelin map 988 fold 12

Alba was the ancient Roman city of Alba Pompeia, which gave Rome the Emperor Pertinax (126-193AD). It is a gourmets' resort made famous by its delicious **tartufi bianchi** or white truffles (annual truffle fair in autumn) and its wines (Barolo, Barbaresco and Barbera). The town boasts several **towers of nobility,** churches and medieval houses. Inside the Gothic Cathedral (**Duomo San Lorenzo**) will be seen Renaissance stalls inlaid with intarsia work of very delicate craftsmanship.

To the south of Alba is the **Langhe** region, an area of limestone hills and clay soils planted with vineyards. Take the Alba-Ceva road, which frequently follows the crests and affords good **views**★ of both slopes. The road passes through some picturesquely situated villages.

★ **ALTILIA SAEPINUM** Molise

Michelin map 988 fold 27 – 25km – 16 miles to the south of Campobasso

The ruins of Roman **Saepinum** spread over 12ha – 30 acres of the fertile plain which lies at the foot of the Matese Mountains. The present day village of Altilia, built with stone quarried from the ruins, stands nearby. This Samnite settlement was occupied by the Romans who made it a municipium and then fortified it in the 1C BC. Saepinum was at the height of its glory at the end of the 5C BC. The Saracens destroyed it in the 9C.

Ⓥ **TOUR** *time: 1 1/2 hours (start in the southwest)*

Terravecchia Gate (Porta di Terravecchia). – This ruined gateway commands the southern end of the north-south Cardo Maximus, one of the city's two main streets.

★ **Basilica, forum and temple** (Basilica, foro e tempio). – These are to be found at the junction of the Cardo Maximus and the Decumanus Maximus, a paved street crossing the city from east to west. To the left are the twenty Ionic columns of the **basilica's** peristyle. To the right is the forum, a vast rectangular paved area and the Decumanus Maximus *(turn right into this street)* which is bordered by the ruined senate house *(curia);* a temple dedicated to Jupiter, Juno and Minerva and a semicircular recess belonging to the "house of the oil presses" with three brick oil containers still visible. Beyond are the remains of a fountain carrying the sculpture of a hippogriff and a Samnite house with an impluvium.

Benevento Gate (Porta di Benevento). – At the eastern end of the Decumanus Maximus the outer face of this arch is decorated with a helmet-clad head. The adjoining Ⓥ **museum** gives an account of the excavations and has displays on the first floor of sculpture, steles and fragments of mosaics.

Mausoleum of Ennius Marsus Volmarso (Mausoleo di Ennius Marsus Volmarso). – This beautiful crenellated semicircular building stands beyond the Benevento Gate. The square plinth is guarded by two very badly damaged lions.

Return to the main crossroads and continue up the Decumanus Maximus.

This is a residential area with the remains of shops on the right.

★ **Boiano Gate** (Porta di Boiano). – This gate with its semicircular main arch is flanked by two round towers. It was dedicated to the future Emperor Tiberius and his brother Drusus. From the top there is a good view of the western part of the fortifications and the ruins of the central part of the city.

Fortified ramparts. – The wall built of finely worked lozenge-shaped stones, with its total length of 1 250m – 1 367yds, describes a rectangle. It has 25 round towers, now reduced to the height of the wall, and four fortified gateways. The western part is the best preserved section.

Mausoleum of Numisius Ligus (Mausoleo di Numisius Ligus). – *Once beyond the wall, turn right.* This tomb has a certain elegant simplicity with its four acroteria.

★ **Theatre** (Teatro). – The theatre standing against the wall has kept its monumental entrance of white stone.

Ⓥ **Museum** (Museo). – *In front of the theatre.* On the ground floor interesting sculpture decorate the sarcophagi and the sepulchral monuments *(cippi).* Upstairs the excavation work is illustrated by photographs and documents.

From the far side of the theatre return to the Cardo Maximus and turn left.

Tammaro Gate (Porta Tammaro). – This simple archway leads to the village of Sepino.

Amalfi, which has given its name to the beautiful Amalfi Coast *(see below)*, is a rather Spanish-looking little town of tall white houses built on slopes facing the sea, which makes a wonderful **site★★★**. Amalfi enjoys a very mild climate, making it a popular holiday resort.

The Maritime Republic of Amalfi. – This is Italy's oldest republic. Founded in 840, by the end of the 9C it was under the rule of a doge. It enjoyed its greatest prosperity in the 11C, when shipping in the Mediterranean was regulated by the *Tavole Amalfitane* (Amalfi Navigation Tables), the oldest maritime code in the world. Amalfi traded regularly with the Orient, in particular Constantinople and the Republic had an arsenal where many large galleys were built. This fleet of galleys played a large part in carrying crusaders to the Levant.

SIGHTS

★ **St Andrew's Cathedral (Duomo Sant' Andrea).** – Founded in the 9C, enlarged in the 10C and 13C and subsequently altered numerous times, the cathedral is a good example of the liking of maritime cities for Oriental splendour. The crypt enshrines those relics of St Andrew which had been removed from Patras to Constantinople, from whence they were transferred in 1206 to Amalfi.

The façade, rebuilt in the 19C on the original model, has a great deal of character: it stands at the top of a stairway and attracts attention with its varied geometrical designs in multicoloured stone. The campanile, on the left, is all that remains of the original church. A beautiful 11C bronze **door★**, cast in Constantinople, opens onto the vast atrium which precedes the church.

The interior of the cathedral is baroque. Admire the two antique columns, two candelabra decorated with mosaics and two 12C ambos.

From the atrium, visit the **Cloisters of Paradise★★** (Chiostro del Paradiso) which date from 1268. Architecturally there is a mixture of Romanesque austerity and Arab fantasy. The arcades shelter some fine sarcophagi.

★ **Via Genova and Via Capuano.** – These two streets starting from the Piazza del Duomo are the main shopping arteries. With a succession of varied shop fronts, balconies and flower bedecked niches they are most attractive. Many alleys, stairways and vaulted passageways lead off the main streets into little squares with fountains.

Piazza Flavio Gioia. – This street takes its name from the native of Amalfi who is said to have perfected the mariner's compass. The workshops of the **arsenal** stood to the left of gateway, Porta della Marina.

★★ AMALFI COAST (COSTIERA AMALFITANA) *79km – 49 miles – allow 1 day*

The corniche road follows the indentations of the rocky coast between Sorrento and Salerno which is Italy's finest coastline, namely the Amalfi Coast. For over 30km – 19 miles its innumerable bends afford constantly changing views of enchanting landscapes, wild, fantastically shaped rocks plunging vertically into a crystal clear sea, deep gorges spanned by dizzy bridges and Saracen towers perched on jagged rock stacks. The Amalfi Coast, with its wild and rugged landscape, is formed by the fringe of the Lattari Mountains, a deeply eroded limestone range. Contrasting with these scenes of sublime awe are the more charming views of fishing villages and the luxuriant vegetation, a mixture of orange trees, citron trees, olives, almonds, vines and all the Mediterranean flora. The region is popular with foreigners and artists and the local cuisine is an important attraction. Seafood is the keyword and fish, crustaceans and shellfish are served regularly. The local cheese *mozzarella (p 33)*

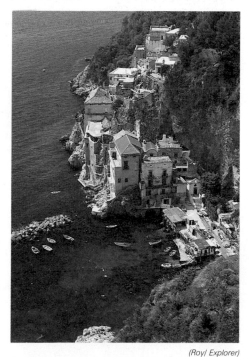

(Roy/ Explorer)

The Amalfi Coast

should be accompanied by the red Gragnano or white Ravello and Positano wines.

Sightseeing. – The map overleaf in addition to locating the towns and sites described in the guide, indicates other beauty spots in small black type.

★★ **Sorrento and the Sorrento Peninsula.** – *Description p 183.*

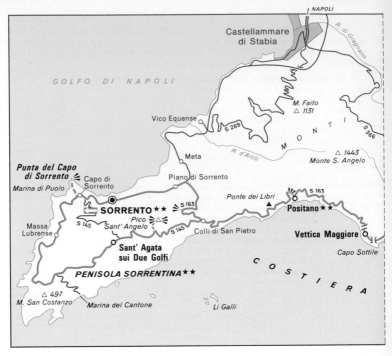

★★ **Positano.** – This fishermen's village is one of the busiest resorts on the coast. The small white cubic houses with a strong Moorish influence are only just visible as they lie scattered on the slopes amid the greenery of their gardens.

Vettica Maggiore. – Its houses are scattered over the slopes. From the esplanade there is a fine **view★★** of the coast and sea.

★★ **Furore Valley** (Vallone di Furore). – The Furore Valley, between two road tunnels, is the most impressive section of the coast owing to the dark depths of its steep, rocky walls and in stormy weather, the thunder of wild, rough seas. A fishermen's village has, nevertheless, been built where a small torrent gushes into the sea. The houses clinging to the slopes and vividly coloured boats drawn up on the shore make a somewhat surprising picture.
For those who wish to discover the spot on foot, take the path that goes along one side of the gorge.

★★ **Emerald Cave** (Grotta dello Smeraldo). – This marine cave at the end of a rocky creek washed by the sea is best visited by boat. The exceptionally clear water is illuminated indirectly by rays of light which give it a beautiful emerald colour. The bottom looks quite near, though the water is 10m – 33ft deep, but it was not always covered by the sea. Fine stalactites add to the interest of the trip. The cave became submerged as a result of variations in ground level under the influence of the volcanoes, which affect the whole region.

★ **Atrani.** – This pleasant fishermen's village at the mouth of the Dragon Valley (Valle del Dragone) has two old churches: Santa Maria Maddalena and San Salvatore. The latter was founded in the 10C and has a fine bronze door which strongly resembles the one in Amalfi Cathedral. An excellent winding road rejoins Ravello.

★★★ **Ravello.** – *Description p 158.*

★ **Cape Orso** (Capo d'Orso). – The cape, consisting of oddly formed rocks, affords an interesting view of Maiori Bay.

Vietri sul Mare. – At the eastern end of this stretch of coastline, the houses of Vietri sul Mare, as elsewhere, climb the slope in tiers. The town is known for its ceramic ware. It affords magnificent **views★★** of the Amalfi Coast.

★ **Salerno.** – *Description p 176.*

*Join us in our never ending task
of keeping up to date.*

*Send us your comments
and suggestions, please.*

**Michelin Tyre Public Limited Company
Tourism Department
Davy House – Lyon Road – HARROW – Middlesex HA1 2DQ**

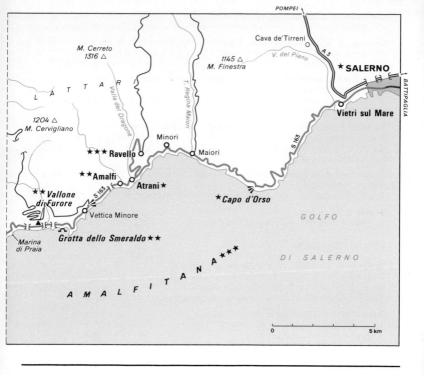

POMPEI
Cava de'Tirreni
A 3
★ SALERNO
M. Cerreto
1316 △
1145 △
M. Finestra
V. del Piano
BATTIPAGLIA
Vietri sul Mare
L A T T A R I
Valle del Dragone
T. Regina Maior
1204 △
M. Cervigliano
Minori
★★★ Ravello
Maiori
★★ Amalfi
Atrani ★
★ Capo d'Orso
★★ Vallone
di Furore
S 163
Vettica Minore
G O L F O
Marina
di Praia
Grotta dello Smeraldo ★★
D I   S A L E R N O
A M A L F I T A N A ★★★
0   5 km

★ ANAGNI Latium

Michelin map 988 fold 26 – 65km – 40 miles southeast of Rome

Anagni is a small medieval town, built on a rocky spur, overlooking the Sacco Valley. This was the birthplace of several popes, including Boniface VIII who excommuni- cated Philip the Fair. Dante confined Boniface to Hell for misusing his authority.

★★ **Cathedral (Cattedrale).** — The town's most important building stands on the site of the former acropolis. This Romanesque edifice was built in the 11 and 12C with Gothic additions. Go round the outside to admire the three Ro- manesque apses with Lombard mouldings and arcades, the 14C statue of Boniface VIII over the loggia on the north side and the detached massive Romanesque campan- ile. The interior contains three aisles of which the 13C **paving**★ was the work of the Cosmati (qv). The high altar is surmounted by a Romanesque ciborium or canopy. The **paschal candelabrum** with a spiral column is adorned with incrustations and rests on two sphinxes. The work like the nearby **episcopal throne** is by Pietro Vassaleto and has strong similarities with the work of the Cosmati. The **crypt**★★★ with its beautiful pavement by the Cosmati also has magnificent 13C **frescoes** depicting the story of the Old Testa- ment, scenes from the lives of the saints and men of science such as Galen and Hip- pocrates. The **treasury** contains some fine liturgical items, notably Boniface VIII's cope of embroidered red silk.

★ **Medieval Quarter.** – This quarter consists almost entirely of 13C buildings and is particularly evocative. The façade of **Boniface VIII's Palace** has two pierced galleries one above the other. One has wide round headed arches while the other consists of attrac- tive twinned windows with small columns. In the Piazza Cavour is the 12-13C **Palazzo Comunale** with a great **arch**★ at ground level. The rear façade is in the Cistercian style.

★ ANCONA Marches

Michelin map 988 fold 16 – Town plan in the current Michelin Red Guide Italia

Ancona, the chief town in the Marches, an Adriatic region of Italy, is built in the form of an amphitheatre on the slopes of a rocky promontory forming an acute angle from which the name of the town is derived (Greek *ankon* – elbow). Ancona was founded in the 4C BC and became an independent maritime republic in the Middle Ages. Ancona is today a busy port and the main point of embarkation for Yugoslavia and Greece. The town specialises in the production of accordions, electric-organs and guitars.

SIGHTS

★ **Cathedral (Duomo San Ciriaco).** – It was placed under the vocation of St Cyriacus, 4C martyr and patron saint of Ancona. The Romanesque building has a mixture of Byzan- tine (the Greek cross plan) and Lombard (mouldings and arcades on the outside walls) architectural features. The façade is preceded by a majestic Gothic **porch** in pink stone, supported by two lions. The interior is articulated by monolithic marble columns with Romanesque-Byzantine **capitals.** Under the dome, note the clever transition from the square base to the 12-sided drum supporting the dome. The tomb (1509) of Cardinal Giannelli in the chancel is the work of the Dalmatian sculptor Giovanni da Traù.

★ **Merchants' Loggia (Loggia dei Mercanti).** – This 15C hall for merchants' meetings has a Venetian Gothic façade which was the work of another Dalmatian, Giorgio Orsini.

★ **Church of Santa Maria della Piazza.** – This small 10C Romanesque church has a
ⓥ charming façade (1210) adorned with amusing popular figures. It was built over the site of two earlier (5 and 6C) churches and their fragments of mosaic pavements.

ⓥ **National Museum of the Marches (Museo Nazionale delle Marche).** – *At the southern end of Piazza del Senato.*
The museum installed in the Palazzo Ferretti, has interesting prehistoric and archaelogical collections on view.

ⓥ **Podesti Public Gallery (Galleria Comunale Francesco Podesti).** – *Via Ciriaco Pizzecolli.*
The museum regroups works by Crivelli, Titian, Lorenzo Lotto, C. Maratta and Guercino. The gallery of modern art has canvases by Luigi Bartolini, Massimo Campigli, Bruno Cassinari and Tamburini.

Church of San Francesco delle Scale. – *Via Ciriaco Pizzecolli, not far from the Podesti Public Gallery.*
This 15C church has a splendid Venetian Gothic doorway bu Giorgio Orsini.

Trajan's Arch (Arco di Traiano). – The arch was erected in AD115 in honour of the Emperor Trajan who built the port at the northern end of Lungomare Vanvitelli.

EXCURSIONS

★ **Portonovo.** – *12km – 8 miles to the southeast.*
Portonovo lies in the picturesque setting formed by the rocky coastline of the **Conero**
ⓥ **Massif.** A private path leads through woodland to the charming 11C **Church of Santa Maria★**, built on an almost square plan inspired by Norman churches.

Jesi. – *32 km – 20 miles to the southwest.*
ⓥ Jesi with all its aspect of a medieval town, has a **picture gallery★** with an important collection of works by Lorenzo Lotto, a Venetian artist of the early 16C, who was influenced by German art. **Palazzo della Signoria★** is an elegant Renaissance building built by Francesco di Giorgio Martini, a pupil of Brunelleschi.

*The **Michelin Guide Italia***

revises annually its selection of establishments offering

– a good but moderately priced meal
– prices with service included or net prices
– a plain menu for a modest price
– free overnight parking

Michelin map 𝟿𝟾𝟾 fold 26

Anzio stands close against a promontory facing out to sea and forms with **Nuttuno** a pleasant modern seaside resort. It has a popular yachting harbour.

Anzio is the Antium of antiquity, a Volscian city where Coriolanus took refuge having abandoned his original intention to engage in a fratricidal struggle with Rome. Antium was also the birthplace of Nero, in whose villa were found the statues of the Apollo Belvedere, the Fanciulla (young girl) of Anzio and the Borghese Gladiator, now respectively in the Vatican, the National Roman Museum in Rome and the Louvre in Paris.

The name of Anzio is also remembered for the Anglo-American landing of 22 January 1944, which, after a long struggle, ended in the taking of Rome on 4 June 1944. Several military cemeteries, monuments, memorials and museums recall those who gave their lives during this operation.

EXCURSION

★ **Island of Ponza.** – *Access: see the current Michelin Red Guide Italia.*
This volcanic island, lying beyond the Gulf of Gaeta, has a verdurous ridge and white or blue-grey cliffs, which are either bordered by narrow beaches or drop abruptly into the sea. At the southeast end of the island, the village of **Ponza**★ aligns its serried ranks of cubic and gaily painted houses in a semicircle around a small harbour. The latter is busy with fishing boats, coasting vessels, pleasure craft and the ferries which ply back and forth to the mainland. The island is popular with underwater fishermen.

★ **AOSTA** Valle d'Aosta   Pop 37 038

Michelin map 𝟿𝟾𝟾 fold 2 or 𝟸𝟷𝟿 fold 2 – Town plans in the current Michelin Red Guide Italia

Aosta stands in the valley of the same name and is capital of the region. It has retained the geometrical plan of a military camp *(castrum)* and some interesting monuments from the Roman period. Aosta, an active religious centre in the Middle Ages, was the birthplace of the theologian St Anselm, who became Archbishop of Canterbury where he died in 1109. Today it is an active industrial town and since the opening of the Mont Blanc Tunnel in 1965, an important tourist centre, at the junction of the transalpine routes to France and Switzerland via the St Bernard Tunnel.

★ **Roman buildings.** – These are grouped in the centre of Aosta and include the **Pretoria Gateway,** the majestic **Arch of Augustus** (Arco di Augusto) both dating from the 1C BC, the **Roman bridge, theatre** and the ruins of the **amphitheatre.**

⊙ **Collegiate Church of St Orso (Collegiata di Sant'Orso).** – The church has some lovely carved 15C **stalls** and a baroque rood screen. Beside the 11C **crypt** a doorway opens onto charming little Romanesque **cloisters**★ with historiated **capitals**★★ illustrating Biblical and secular scenes.

The **Priory of St Orso** (Priorato di Sant' Orso) is a Renaissance style building with elegant **windows**★.

⊙ **Cathedral (Cattedrale).** – Although it was built in the 12C it has been re-modelled several times and now has a neo-classical façade (1848). The chancel has 12C mosaic paving, 15C Gothic stalls and the 14C tomb of Thomas II of Savoy. The sacristy ⊙ contains a rich **treasure.** The cloisters are 15C.

★★VALLE D'AOSTA

The Valle d'Aosta comprising the Dora Baltea and adjacent valleys is surrounded by high peaks of both the French and Swiss Alps : Mont Blanc, the Matterhorn (Cervino), Monte Rosa, Grand Combin, Dent d'Hérens, Gran Paradiso and Grande Sassière. With such a marvellous situation there are some splendid **viewpoints**★★★. Its secluded valleys, numerous castles, villages with balconied and stone slab *(lauze)* roofed houses, a traditional way of life, the numerous possibilities of excursions by cable-car, car or on foot, scenic routes leading up to glaciers all go to make the Valle d'Aosta a captivating place to discover.

The inhabitants of the high valleys are deeply religious and remain strongly attached to their customs and freedom as well as the French language. Since 1948 the Valle d'Aosta has been, for administrative purposes, an autonomous district.

Living in houses roofed with flat stone slabs *(lauzes)*, they raise cattle and prepare a cheese called *fontina* which is often used for a cheese fondue. During the long winter evenings many still carve wood as a pastime.

Sightseeing. – The map on pages 42-43 in addition to locating the towns and sites described in the guide, indicates other beauty spots in small black type.

★★ **Gran Paradiso National Park (Parco Nazionale del Gran Paradiso).** – This park covering an area of almost 70 000 ha – 270sq miles includes an area previously preserved as a royal hunting ground. It can be reached by the Rhêmes, Savarenche, Cogne, Locana valleys or the Nivolet Pass road. The park is rich in wildlife and is important as a reserve for endangered species, such as the Ibex, and some of the rarest specimens of Alpine flora.

FROM COURMAYEUR TO IVREA
162km – 101 miles – allow 1 day

★★ **Courmayeur.** – *Town plans in the current Michelin Red Guide Italia.* This well-known mountaineering and winter sports resort is a good excursion centre. Take a cable-car to the Cresta d'Arp and to cross the Mont Blanc Massif and make a short detour into France *(for the area beyond La Palud see the Michelin Green Guide* Alpes du Nord, *in French only).* By car explore one of the following valleys, Veny, Ferret or Testa d'Arpi and the road to the little St Bernard, one of the most frequented transalpine routes which was used by the Romans in ancient times.
The itinerary follows the Dora Baltea Valley. Once through St-Pierre and having passed the road to the right going up the Cogne valley, there stands on the left **Sarre Castle,** the onetime summer residence of the Counts of Savoy. Further on to the right there is the 14C **Aymavilles Fortress,** impressively quartered with great round crenellated towers.

★ **Aosta.** – *Description p 43.*

★ **Fenis Castle.** – This imposing fortress contains fine carved furniture in the local Valle d'Aosta style. The inner courtyard is remarkable for its frescoes portraying the Golden Legend.

★★ **Breuil-Cervinia.** – This winter sports resort is admirably situated at 2 050m – 6 822ft. Cable-cars will take you up to the Rosa Plateau (Plan Rosa) and the Furggen Pass at 3 491m – 11 453ft.

★ **St-Vincent.** – The Casino de la Vallée in its fine park is very popular.
The road passes Montjovet Castle and then the 14C **Verrès Castle** which curiously enough has no keep or corner towers.

★ **Issogne Castle.** – The castle was built at the end of the 15C by Georges de Challant. It has a remarkable courtyard with a fountain surmounted by the wrought-iron figure of a grenadier. The arcaded gallery is painted with 15C frescoes and inside the furniture is typical of the Valdotain area.

★ **Bard Fortress.** – The colossal fortress, dismantled on the orders of Napoleon in 1800, rebuilt during the 19C, commands the upper Dora Baltea Valley.

Pont St-Martin. – This village is named after the Roman bridge which was guarded by a chapel dedicated to St John Nepomucene.

Ivrea. – This busy industrial town stands at the mouth of the Valle d'Aosta. To the east of Ivrea is the largest moraine in Europe, the Serra d'Ivrea.

★ APULIA

Michelin map 988 folds 28, 29 and 30

This region takes its name from the ancient Roman province of Apulia and extends from the spur to the heel of the boot along the Adriatic coast to the south. With the exception of the Gargano Promontory and the limestone Murge Hills which rise behind Bari, it is a flat plain-like area planted with cereals, olive trees, vines or in pasture.
Away from the main tourist haunts, Apulia offers the visitor the rather severe beauty of its scenery, quiet beaches and some marvellous architectural gems, both religious and military.

HISTORICAL NOTES

As early as the late 8C BC Greeks from Laconia and Sparta founded the towns of Gallipoli, Otranto and especially Taranto on the Apulian coast. In the 5C and 4C BC Taranto was the most prosperous town in Magna Graecia. The local tribe, the Lapyges tenaciously resisted Greek colonisation; in the 3C BC the Greek cities and the Italiots both came under Roman domination.
Taranto declined as Brindisi, a trading post facing the eastern part of the Mediterranean, flourished. The latter was linked to Rome when Trajan prolonged the Appian Way. The Roman colonisation greatly benefited this area with improved communications and political organisation. Christianity was first introduced to the area in the 3C BC and was strengthened in the 5C with the appearances of the Archangel Michael at Monte Sant'Angelo *(qv)*.
The area was occupied successively by the Byzantines, Lombards and Arabs before Apulia sought help in the 11C from the Normans who then dominated the entire area. Apulia greatly increased its trade and its architectural heritage during both the early Crusades, most of which embarked from the Apulian ports, and the reign of Roger II of Sicily (1095-1154).

It was under the Emperor Frederick II of Hohenstaufen, a surprising, authoritarian and cruel person, atheist but cultured and highly intelligent that the region knew a period of splendour in the first half of the 13C. The king was captivated by the country and chose to reside here. This favoured trading, the unification of the country and the establishment of an efficient administration. His son Manfred continued his work but had to submit to Charles of Anjou in 1266. When the French slowly lost interest in the region, it began to lose its vitality and prestige. Apulia then passed to the Aragon dynasty who by isolating the region greatly contributed to its decline.

After a period of Austrian domination, the Bourbons of Naples improved to some small extent the misery and its entrenched opposition to progress to which the country had been reduced by the Spanish. The brief Napoleonic period followed a similar policy. In 1860 Apulia was united with the rest of unified Italy.

During the 20C Apulia progressively emerged from the difficult position of inferiority which was prevalent throughout the rest of the Italian south or Mezzogiorno. The region has achieved a certain independence and vigour and now claims two thriving industrial towns, Taranto and Lecce, a Trade Fair in Bari and several newly founded universities.

TOWNS AND SIGHTS

★★ Castellana Caves (Grotta di Castellana). – *40km – 25 miles to the southeast of Bari, at Castellana-Grotte.*

This system of caves was created by the underground rivers which filter down through the limestones of the Murge Hills. The vast chamber now void of water, was discovered in 1938 and has an infinite variety of magnificent concretions: draperies, richly coloured stalactites and stalagmites. The **White Cave,** 70m – 230ft underground, glistens with calcite crystals.

★★ Gargano Promontory. – *Description p 96.*

(Everts/Rapho)

Apulia – Trulli in Alberobello

★★ Trulli Region and Alberobello. – *Description p 194.*

★★ Castel del Monte. – *29km – 18 miles southeast of Barletta.*

The Emperor Frederick II of Hohenstaufen built this powerful castle *c* 1240. It stands, proud and solitary, on the summit of one of the Murge Hills. With its octagonal plan the Castel del Monte is the unique exception in a series of 200 quadrilateral fortresses built by this sovereign on his return from the Crusades. The octagonal plan of this fortress, built in a pale coloured stone, is quartered at each of its angles by a 24m – 79ft tall octagonal tower. The overall plan combines balance, logic and strict planning with delicate decoration.

The superb Gothic gateway takes the form of an ancient triumphal arch and opens into the inner courtyard. Arranged around this at ground floor level are eight vast trapezoidal chambers with pointed vaulting. Above, the eight identical rooms are lit by delicately ornamented windows. The arrangement of the water conduits is quite ingenious: water runs from the rooftops into the cisterns of the towers and is then piped into the different rooms.

★ Gallipoli. – The old town with its attractive small port is set on an island and linked to the modern town by a bridge. Note the **Hellenistic fountain** *(to the left of the bridge)* with a baroque pediment, the Angevin castle, the cathedral with a baroque façade which recalls Lecce and nearby, the baroque Church of Santa Teresa. The **interior★** of the **church (la Purissima)** is sumptuously decorated like a drawing room.

★★ Lecce. – *Description p 108.*

Locorotondo. – *36km – 22 miles north of Taranto.*
This town takes its name from the layout of its alleyways which wind in concentric circles (*loco rotondo:* round place) around the hill on which it is set. On arriving from Martina Franca there is an astonishing **view**★ of a multitude of white houses with tall pointed gables.
The road from Martina Franca to Locorotondo follows the **Itria Valley**★★, a vast and fertile plain planted with vines and olive trees and dotted with *trulli (qv)*, those peculiar bee-hive shaped houses.

★ **Martina Franca.** – This white city occupies a hilltop in the Murge Hills. The old town, girdled by its ramparts, forms an attractive ensemble of baroque and rococo architecture. The pleasant **Piazza Roma** is bordered by the former ducal palace (1668). The **Collegiate Church of San Martino** with its lovely façade embellished with high reliefs is the principal monument in Piazza Plebiscito. Walk down the **Via Cavour**★ with its numerous baroque palaces.

★ **Monte Sant' Angelo.** – *Description p 123.*

★ **Ostuni.** – *35km – 22 miles west of Brindisi.*
This large market town now spreads over several hillsides. The rampart-encircled old town with its white alleyways centres on the late 15C **cathedral** in the Gothic style. The **façade**★ is crowned by an unusual curved gable which is a precursor of the baroque manner.

★ **Taranto.** – *Description p 185.*

★ **Tremiti Islands.** – *Description p. 189.*

Altamura. – This large market town in the Murge Hills also groups its old quarter on a hilltop. The 13C **cathedral** in the transitional Romanesque-Gothic style forms the focal point at the upper end of the main street. The façade is crowned with two bulbous bell towers, 16C additions, and pierced by a delicately decorated 13C **rose window**★ and a richly sculptured 14-15C **doorway**★.

Bari. – *Description p 52.*

Barletta. – *Description p 54.*

Bitonto. – *17km – 11 miles to the southwest of Bari.*
Set amidst a sea of olive groves this small town has a fine **cathedral**★ which strongly resembles those in Trani and Bari. The three part façade is enlivened by large, richly sculptured openings. On the south side an elegant gallery with small columns surmounts the ground floor arcade. Inside columns with fine capitals support a gallery with triple openings. The remarkable pulpit dates from 1229.

Brindisi. – *Description p 64.*

Canosa di Puglia. – *23km – 14 miles southwest of Barletta.*
The inhabitants of this Greek then Roman city were known for their ceramic vases *(askoi).* The 11C Romanesque **cathedral** which shows a certain Byzantine influence, was remodelled in the 17C following an earthquake. The façade is 19C. Inside note the 11C episcopal throne and the **tomb**★ of Bohemond, Prince of Antioch (d 1111), the son of Robert Guiscard (1015-85), a Norman adventurer who campaigned in southern Italy. This curious mausoleum is in the form of a domed cube. In the Via Cadorna there are three 4C BC **hypogea** (Ipogei Lagrasta) and to the right of the Andria road there are the remains of a paleo-Christian Basilica **(San Leucio)** which was itself built on the site of a Roman temple.

Foggia. – *Town plan in the current Michelin Red Guide Italia.*
Foggia is set in the heart of a vast cereal-growing plain, the Tavoliere. This trading and industrial centre was founded in *c*1050 by the Norman, Robert Guiscard. In 1223 the Emperor Frederick II of Hohenstaufen built a castle which has now disappeared. The present **cathedral** incorporates parts of an earlier building (1172), notably the lower walls with some blind arcading and a sculptured cornice above, and the crypt. This earlier building was destroyed by the 1731 earthquake.

Galatina. – This craft and wine-making centre stands on the flat and stony Salento Peninsula. The Cathedral with its baroque façade recalls the gracious style of Lecce. The 14C **Church of Santa Caterina di Alessandria**★ is decorated with a marvellous cycle of **frescoes**★ by several 15C artists. The frescoes in the cloisters are 18C.

Galatone. – *24km – 15 miles southwest of Lecce.*
The **Church of Crocifisso della Pietà** has a lovely **façade**★ embellished in the baroque style so typical of the Lecce area. The sumptuous interior decoration includes gilding and stucco ornamentation.

Lucera. – Already important in Roman times, Lucera was ceded by the Emperor Frederick II of Hohenstaufen to the Saracens of Sicily, who in turn were expelled by Charles II of Anjou, the grandson of St Louis. Lucera has an imposing 13C **castle**★ built by the Angevins, a **cathedral** (Duomo) dating from 1300 and a **Roman amphitheatre** built during Augustus' reign. The **museum** (Museo Civico) has a marble **Venus**★, a Roman replica of a model by the school of Praxiteles.

Manfredonia. – Manfred, the son of the Emperor Frederick II of Hohenstaufen, founded the port in the 13C. It is guarded by a fine 13C **castle.** The **Church of Santa Maria di Siponto**★ *(3km – 2 miles to the south by the S 89)* is an elegant 11C building in the Romanesque style which shows both an oriental (square plan and terraced roof hiding the dome) and Pisan influence (blind arcades with columns enclosing lozenges). The late 11C **Church of San Leonardo** *(beyond Santa Maria, take the Foggia road to the right)* has a fine delicately sculptured **doorway**★ dating from the early 13C.

Otranto. – *Description p 138.*

Ruvo di Puglia. – *34km – 21 miles to the west of Bari.*
On the edge of the Murge Hills Ruvo has an Apulian style Romanesque **cathedral**★ with a sober façade embellished by a rose window, a twin opening, a sculptured doorway and at the very top a frieze of arches. Inside the lofty nave, tall arches carry a deep cornice supported by sculptured corbels. The **Jatta Archaeological Museum** owns the superb **Crater of Talos**★★, a red-figured vase on a black background.

Trani. – This wine-growing town has an ancient port surrounded by old houses. The 11-13C Romanesque **cathedral**★★ is one of the finest in Apulia and is dedicated to St Nicholas the pilgrim, a humble Greek shepherd who arrived in Trani on the back of a dolphin. Blind arcades encircle the building and there is a lovely **bronze door**★ which was cast in 1180. Beyond the very lofty transept the chancel has a delicately decorated window. Inside one detects a strong Norman influence. The nave and aisles are slightly raised as they are built over two immense crypts, the lower of which is literally a forest of ancient columns. The upper church is well lit but severe with slender twin columns carrying the main arches and an elegant gallery with triple openings.
From the **public gardens**★ to the east of the port there is an attractive view of the old town and its tall cathedral. The **castle** on the seashore was built by Frederick II.

Troia. – *17km – 11 miles to the southwest of Foggia.*
This agricultural market town is well situated on a hilltop overlooking the Tavoliere plain. The Romanesque **cathedral** in the Apulian style was begun in the 11C and completed two centuries later. The façade is embellished with blind arcading and an asymmetrical **rose window**★. A lovely 12C **bronze door**★ in the Byzantine tradition opens into the nave and two aisles separated by columns with finely worked capitals. The north doorway has a sculptured **tympanum** depicting Christ flanked by two angels.

★ L'AQUILA Abruzzi   Pop 66 097

Michelin map 988 fold 26 – Local map p 36 – Town plan in the current Michelin Red Guide Italia

L'Aquila was founded in the 13C on the initiative of the Emperor Frederick II of Hohenstaufen who gave it an imperial eagle for its emblem. Charles I of Anjou took control of the town in 1266 and was responsible for building part of the fortifications. The town has many Romanesque or Renaissance churches and palaces, often marked with the initials IHS (*Iesus Hominum Salvator* – Jesus Saviour of Mankind) after the preaching and motto of St Bernardino of Siena. The saint died here in 1444.

★★ **Basilica of St Bernardino (San Bernardino).** – This superb building, built between 1454 and 1472, was given a remarkable façade by Cola dell' Amatrice in 1527. The interior, in the form of a Latin cross, is spacious and well lit and roofed with a lovely baroque wooden ceiling. The **mausoleum**★ of St Bernardino is adorned with figures by the local sculptor, Silvestro dell' Aquila, as is the elegant **sepulchre**★ of Maria Pereira.

★ **Castle (Castello).** – This square castle quartered with powerful bastions, is a good example of 16C military architecture. The great rooms now house the **National Museum of the Abruzzi**★★ with its archaeological, medieval (mainly interesting examples of local craftsmanship of the period) and modern sections.

★ **Basilica of Santa Maria di Collemaggio.** – This Romanesque building was begun in 1287 at the instance of Pietro da Morone, founder of the Celestine Order and future Pope Celestine V. The wonderful **façade**★★ of white and pink stone is pierced with rose windows and round-headed doorways, all added in the 14C.

★ **Fountain of the 99 Conduits (Fontana delle 99 cannelle).** – This imposing fountain was remodelled in the 15C. 99 masks spout water into its basins. This figure corresponds to the legend which relates that the town sprang up by a miracle with 99 quarters, 99 castles, 99 squares and 99 fountains. Even today a bell in the tower of the Law Courts tolls 99 times every evening.

AQUILEIA Friuli – Venezia Giulia   Pop 3 441

Michelin map 988 fold 6

While the plan of the town was being outlined with the plough, according to Roman custom, an eagle *(aquila)* hovered overhead: hence its name. Aquileia was a flourishing market under the Roman Empire and was used as general headquarters by Augustus during his conquest of the Germanic tribes. The town then became one of Italy's most important patriarchates (554-1751) ruled by bishops.

★★ **Basilica.** – It was built in the 11C on the foundations of a 4C building and restored in the 14C. It is preceded by a porch and flanked by a campanile.
The interior with its nave and two aisles is in the form of a Latin cross. The splendid 4C **paving**★★ is one of the largest and richest in western Christendom. Numerous religious scenes are depicted. The timber ceiling and the arcades are both 14C, the capitals are Romanesque and the decoration of the transept Renaissance. The 9C Carolingian **crypt** is decorated with Romanesque **frescoes**★★.
The **Cripta degli Scavi** is reached from the north aisle. Finds from the excavations are assembled here, notably splendid 4C mosaic **pavings**★★.

★ **Roman Ruins.** – Excavations have uncovered the remains of Roman Aquileia: behind the basilica, the Via Sacra leading to the river port, houses and the forum. The **Archaeological and Paleo-Christian Museums** contain an important collection of finds from local excavations. Note in particular the remarkable series of portraits including ones of Tiberius and Augustus as a youth, in the archaeological museum.

After being first an important Etruscan city and then a rich Roman one, Arezzo was an independent commune before it was annexed by Florence in 1384, following a protracted struggle. The town has many reminders of its past and was the birthplace of several famous men: Guido d'Arezzo (c 990) the inventor of the musical scale, Petrarch the poet (1304-74), Aretino the author (1492-1566), Giorgio Vasari (qv) and probably Maecenas (69-8 BC), the legendary patron of art and letters.

SIGHTS

St Francis' Church (San Francesco) (ABY). – This aisleless church is large, being designed for preaching; it was built for the Franciscans in the 14C, in the Gothic style.

★★★ **Frescoes of Piero della Francesca.** – These frescoes depicting the Legend of the Holy Cross, were executed between 1452 and 1466 on the walls of the apse. This fresco cycle is without doubt one of the greatest masterpieces ever. Scenes include the death and burial of Adam, Solomon and the Queen of Sheba, the dream of Constantine, the victory of Constantine over Maxentius, the making of the Cross, the victorious Heraclius overcoming Chosroes and the announcement of Christ's death to Mary. Piero della Francesa, a pupil of the Florentine school, inherited his subtle handling of light from Domenico Veneziano and was a master of well balanced compositions and colours. The sturdy sculptural forms of his figures appear at times to be held motionless by the perspective. The whole however is treated with a profound realism which is not without humoristic touches, notably in his portrayal of clothes.

★ **Church of Santa Maria della Pieve (BY B).** – This lovely 12C Romanesque church is flanked by a powerful campanile. The Pisan Romanesque style façade★★ is articulated by three tiers of small columns, adorned with various motifs, whose ranks become closer as the height increases. On the high altar is a 14C polyptych by the Sienese, Pietro Lorenzetti.

★ **Piazza Grande (BY).** – This square, behind the above church, is surrounded by medieval houses, Renaissance palaces and the Logge or galleries designed by Vasari (16C). The square is the setting for the **Saracen's Tournament,** when costumed horsemen attack a dummy figure with lances (see the table of Principal Festivals at the end of the guide).

◉ **Archaeological Museum (Museo Archeologico) (AZ M¹)**. – The museum overlooks the 1-2C **Roman amphitheatre (ABZ)**. There is a remarkable collection of 6-5C BC Etruscan statuettes and Aretine vases made in the Roman period.

Cathedral (Duomo) (BY). – This large church was built from the 13C onwards on the town's highest point. Inside are some fine **works of art★**: stained glass by the Frenchman Guillaume de Marcillat (1467-1529), a fresco by Piero della Francesca of Mary Magdalen and the tomb of St Donatus (14C).

St Dominic's Church (San Domenico) (BY). – This 13C church has frescoes by the Duccio school and an admirable painted **crucifix★★** (c1260) attributed to Cimabue.

◉ **Vasari Mansion (Casa del Vasari) (AY A)**. – The house was sumptuously decorated by **Giorgio Vasari** (1511-74), painter, sculptor, architect and early art historian. Also exhibited are works by Tuscan Mannerists.

Church of St Mary of Grace (Santa Maria delle Grazie). – *1km – 1/2 mile to the south via Viale Mecenate* **(AZ)**. In front of the church is a graceful **portico★** by the Florentine, Benedetto da Maiano (15C). Inside is a marble **altarpiece★** by Andrea della Robbia.

◉ **Museum of Medieval and Modern Art (AY M²)**. – The collections are in the Renaissance Bruni-Ciocchi Palace. These include paintings from the 13 to the 19C, sculpture, ceramics, furniture, goldsmith's work, arms, small bronzes and coins.

★★ ASCOLI PICENO Marches Pop 53 399

Michelin map 988 fold 16 – Town plan in the current Michelin Red Guide Italia

Ascoli, an austere but picturesque town lies in a narrow valley at the confluence of the Castellano and the Tronto. This walled town has a medieval quarter which is rich in churches, palaces, houses and picturesque streets.

★★ **Piazza del Popolo**. – The People's Square, elongated and well proportioned and paved with large flagstones, is surrounded by Gothic and Renaissance buildings. It is a popular meeting-place and is the setting for the town's main festivities. The **People's Captains' Palace★** (Palazzo dei Capitani del Popolo) is an austere 13C building with an imposing Renaissance doorway, surmounted by a statue of Pope Paul III which was added in 1549 by Cola dell' Amatrice. At the far end of the square **St Francis' Church★** (San Francesco) was begun in 1262 and consecrated in 1371. The church has several Lombard elements. Abutting the south front is the **Merchants' Loggia★** (Loggia dei Mercanti) a graceful early 16C building, showing Tuscan influence, particularly in the capitals.

★ **Old Quarter (Vecchio Quartiere)**. – The quarter lies between the Tronto River and the **Corso Mazzini★** lined with old mansions, in particular at no 224 the 16C Malaspina Palace. At the beginning of **Via delle Torri** is the Renaissance façade of **St Augustine's** (Sant' Agostino) which has a moving fresco of Christ bearing the Cross by Cola dell' Amatrice. The Via delle Torri ends at the 14C **Church of St Peter the Martyr** (San Pietro Martire). Behind is the Romanesque **Church of Sts Vincent and Anastasius★** (Santi Vincenzo ed Anastasio) with its curious compartmented façade dating from the 14C. The **Ercolani Tower** (Torre Ercolani) in Via Soderini, is the tallest of the feudal towers of Ascoli. Adjoining is the 12C Lombard Romanesque mansion, **Palazzo Longobardo**. Once through the medieval gateway, a single-arched Roman bridge, the **Ponte di Solestà★** spans the Tronto at a height of 25m – 82ft. From the far end there is an attractive view of the old quarters.

Cathedral (Duomo). – The grandiose façade of this 12C building was the work of Cola dell' Amatrice. Inside there is a superb **polyptych★** (1473) by **Carlo Crivelli**. This Venetian artist with a love for meticulous realism settled in Ascoli Piceno in 1470 and he was a motivating force in the development of a local art movement. The **baptistry★**, square at the base and octagonal above, standing to the left of the cathedral, is one of the finest in Italy.

Near the baptistry, in Via Buonaparte, is the **Palazzo Buonaparte**, a lovely example of 16C Renaissance architecture.

◉ **Picture Gallery (Pinacoteca)**. – The collections are displayed in the Communal Palace in Piazza Arringo. The collection regroups works by Crivelli and his pupils, Carlo Maratta, Titian, Van Dyck, Bellotto, Guardi and Callot. Do not miss the precious and delicately worked 13C English relic, the cope of Nicholas IV.

The current Michelin Guide Italia
offers a selection of pleasant, quiet and well situated hotels.

Each entry includes the facilities provided
(gardens, tennis courts, swimming pool and equipped beach)
and annual closure dates.

Also included is a selection of establishments recommended for their cuisine:
– well prepared meals at a moderate price, stars for good cooking.

The city of Assisi is prettily spread across the slopes of Monte Subasio and closely associated with **St Francis** as related in the numerous accounts of his life and work. Under the influence of the Franciscans (Order of Minors) founded by St Francis, a new, essentially religious, artistic movement developed which marked a turning point

in Italian art. Born in 1182 Francis was a rich and brilliant youth who dreamed of military glory, but was converted following an illness in 1201.

Several apparitions of the Virgin and of Christ were seen by Francis, the most famous is that of La Verna *(qv)* during which he received the stigmata. But this mystic also had a deeply poetic soul and was a lover of the beauties of nature which he praised in texts written in the Umbrian language. In addition he befriended a young woman of rare beauty, Clare, who founded the Order of Poor Clares. St Francis himself died in 1226 after having founded, in 1210, the

(Schneiders/ Artephot)

St Francis Preaching to the Birds
by an unknown 13C master, Maestro di San Francesco
(Lower Basilica)

Order of Minors, mendicant monks known thereafter as Franciscans.

The son of the rich Assisi draper preached poverty, obedience and chastity, a credence which gave rise to a new artistic vision which found its expression in the purity and elegance of Gothic art. During the 13C the churches were embellished with a new splendour. At the end of the 14C famous masters came from Rome and Venice to Assisi to work on the Basilica of St Francis. These artists abandoned forever the rigid traditions of Byzantine art in favour of a more dramatic art imbued with a spiritual atmosphere. Cimabue and then Giotto were its most powerful exponents.

★★★ ST FRANCIS' BASILICA (SAN FRANCESCO) (A) *time: 1 1/2 hours*

The basilica consists of two superimposed churches, resting on a series of immense arches. The whole building, built after the death of St Francis to the plans of Brother Elias, was consecrated in 1253. It was this monk who influenced the Franciscans to use more splendour and decoration.

Lower Basilica. – Beyond the long narthex, the walls of the dark and sombre four bay nave are covered with 13 and 14C **frescoes★★★**.

From the narthex pass through the Chapel of St Anthony the Abbot into the 15C **Cloisters of the Dead★★★** with its two storeys so full of gentleness and peace. Return to the nave and the first chapel on the left with **frescoes★★** by Simone Martini illustrating the life of St Martin. These are remarkable for their delicate drawing and colour, graceful composition and beauty of expression. Further along above the pulpit is a fresco of the Coronation of the Virgin attributed to Maso, a pupil of Giotto (14C). The choir **vaulting★★** was painted with scenes symbolising the Triumph of St Francis and the virtues practised by him. They were the work of one of Giotto's pupils. In the south transept admire the majestic work by Cimabue, a **Ma-**

donna with Four Angels and St Francis★★. The north transept is decorated with **frescoes★★** of the Passion. Those on the ceiling, attributed to pupils of Pietro Lorenzetti, are valued for their narrative design and charm of detail; those on the walls, probably by Lorenzetti himself, are striking for their dramatic expression **(Descent from the Cross)**.

From the north transept make for the Renaissance main cloisters and the **treasury★★** with its many valuable pieces and a collection of 14C and 15C paintings.

Upper Basilica. – This accomplished Gothic work with its tall and graceful nave, bathed in light, contrasts with that of the lower church. The apse and transept were decorated with frescoes (many have since been damaged) by Cimabue and his school. In the north transept Cimabue painted a **Crucifixion★★★** with an unforgettable sense of tragedy.

Between 1296 and 1304 **Giotto** and his assistants depicted the life of St Francis in a now famous cycle of **frescoes**★★★. There are twenty-eight clearly distinguished scenes each showing a greater search for realism. They mark a new dawning in the figurative traditions of Italian art, which was to reach its apogee during the Renaissance.

Step out of the basilica onto the esplanade to admire the harmonious façade with its doorway and rose window in Cosmati work *(qv)*.

ADDITIONAL SIGHTS

★★ **Medieval Castle (Rocca Maggiore)** (B). – This is a good example of 14C military architecture. From the top of the keep there is a splendid **view**★★ of Assisi and the surrounding countryside.

★★ **St Clare's Church (Santa Chiara)** (BC). – The church is preceded by a terrace from which there is a pretty view of the Umbrian countryside. It was built between 1257 and 1265 and closely resembles the Gothic Upper Basilica of St Francis'. Inside there are numerous works of art including 14C frescoes depicting the life and history of St Clare. These have been influenced by Giotto.

The Crucifix, which is said to have spoken to St Francis, can be seen in the small Church of St George, which adjoins the south aisle. The crypt enshrines the remains of St Clare.

★ **Cathedral (Duomo San Rufino)** (C). – The cathedral was built in the 12C. The Romanesque **façade**★★ is one of the finest in Umbria, with a harmonious arrangement of its openings and decorative ornamentation.

The interior, on a basilical plan, was rebuilt in 1571. To the right on entering is the baptismal font used for the baptism of St Francis, St Clare and Frederick II.

★ **Piazza del Comune** (B 3). – This square with its attractive fountain occupies the site of the forum: the **Temple of Minerva**★ (B A), converted into a church, with its portico of six Corinthian columns, is one of the best preserved in Italy.

★ **Via San Francesco** (AB). – This picturesque street is lined by medieval and Renaissance houses. At no 13A the **Pilgrims' Oratory** (B B) is decorated inside with 15C frescoes, notably by Matteo da Gualdo.

★ **St Peter's Church (San Pietro)** (A). – A Romanesque church built by the Benedictines. It contains a charming triptych by Matteo da Gualdo.

EXCURSIONS

★★ **Carceri Hermitage (Eremo delle Carceri)**. – *4km – 2 miles to the east.*

The road climbs through olive groves, oaks, cypresses and broom to reach this hermitage, a series of caves where St Francis came to meditate and pray, along with some disciples. The minute church, hollowed out of the rock, already existed when St Francis was wont to retreat to these cells *(carceri)*.

★ **Monastery of St Damian** (Convento di San Damiano). – *2km – 1 mile to the south of the* ⊙ *gateway, Porta Nuova.*
This convent and small adjoining church stand alone amidst olive and cypress trees and are closely associated with St Francis, who received his calling here and also with St Clare who died here in 1253. The humble and austere interior is a moving example of a 13C Franciscan monastery.

★ **St Mary of the Angels Basilica** (Santa Maria degli Angeli). – *5km – 3 miles to the* ⊙ *southwest.*
The basilica was built in the 16C on the site of the chapel, Porziuncola, in which St Francis consecrated St Clare as the Bride of Christ. Inside are two remarkable works of art: above the altar a dazzling **fresco★** dating from 1393 and portraying the Pardon of Assisi and the Annunciation; and in the crypt a charming glazed terracotta **polyptych★** by Andrea della Robbia representing the Coronation of the Virgin. Visit also the Transito chapel where St Francis died on 3 October 1226 and the little courtyard with the rose bush into which St Francis threw himself to overcome temptation. The plant lost its thorns from that moment. The cave to which the saint retired for prayer may also be visited.

★ **Spello.** – *12km – 8 miles to the southeast.*
This picturesque little town preserves some traces of its rich Roman past (fortifications and gateways) and the Church of St Mary Major (Santa Maria Maggiore, the first church on the right when going up Via Consolare). Inside are a series of splendid **frescoes★★** by Pinturicchio which display the realistic verve and freshness of his technique. The life of Christ decorates the walls and the Sibyls the vaulting.

Foligno. – *18km – 11 miles to the southeast.*
Piazza della Repubblica is overlooked by the 14C **Palazzo Trinci,** built by the local overlords and the **cathedral** (Duomo) with its magnificent doorway decorated with Lombard style geometrical decoration.
Foligno is famous for the **Game of the Quintana** when horsemen in 17C costumes representing the ten different quarters of the town, must carry away, with the points of their spears, a ring which is hung from the outstretched hand of the Quintana, an early 17C wooden statue. On the day previous to this tournament there is a procession with over one thousand people also in 17C costumes *(see the table of Principal Festivals at the end of the guide).*

ATRI Abruzzi   Pop 11 522

Michelin map **988** fold 27

The inland town of Atri has a beautiful situation looking out to sea. To the west lies the strange **landscape★★**, known as the **Bolge** of Atri, which has resulted from the fluvial erosion of a Tertiary plateau. The flat topped hills with steep sides and gullies are covered with vegetation.

★ **Cathedral** (Cattedrale). – Built in the 13-14C on the foundations of a Roman edifice, this structure is in the transitional Romanesque-Gothic style. A Romanesque doorway with a rose window above adorns the otherwise sober and compartmented façade. The lower part of the campanile is square but becomes recessed and polygonal in its upper part. Inside there are tall Gothic arches and in the apse **frescoes★** by the Abruzzi artist, Andrea Delitio (1450-73) illustrating in a very realistic way and in detail the Lives of the Virgin and Jesus.

BARI Apulia   Pop 365 630

Michelin map **988** fold 29 – Plan of the built-up area in the current Michelin Red Guide Italia

Bari, the capital of Apulia and an agricultural and industrial centre, is first and foremost a port with shipping connections with both Yugoslavia and Greece. The Levantine Fair *(Fiera del Levante)*, held in September, is an important trade fair which was inaugurated in 1930 to encourage trade with other Mediterranean countries.
Bari comprises the old town, clustered on its promontory and the modern town with wide avenues, laid out on a grid plan in the 19C. Bari was the capital of Byzantium's possessions in Italy and a very prosperous city in the Middle Ages due partly to its role as a pilgrimage centre to St Nicholas' shrine and as a port of embarkation for the Crusades.

★ **OLD TOWN** (CITTÀ VECCHIA) (CDY) *time: 1 1/2 hours*

★★ **St Nicholas' Basilica** (San Nicola) (DY A). – The basilica in the heart of the old town was begun in 1087 and consecrated in 1197 to St Nicholas, Bishop of Myra in Asia Minor, who achieved fame by resurrecting three children, whom a butcher had cut up and put in brine. St Nicholas' relics were brought home by sailors from Bari and it was decided to build a church to him. The building is one of the most remarkable examples of Romanesque architecture and many churches were built locally under its inspiration. The plain but powerful façade, flanked by two towers, is relieved by several twinned openings and a sculptured doorway with bulls supporting the flanking columns.
On the north side there is the richly decorated 12C Lions' Doorway.
Inside, the three naves with a triforium, were reroofed in the 17C with a fine coffered ceiling. A large 12C ciborium (canopy) surmounts the high altar behind which is an unusual 11C **episcopal throne★** in white marble. In the north apse is a painting by the Venetian, Bartolomeo Vivarini. The tomb of St Nicholas lies in the crypt.

★ **Cathedral (Cattedrale) (DY B)**. – This 11-12C Romanesque cathedral was added to and then altered at a later date. Inside the nave and two aisles have oven vaulted terminations and there is a false triforium above the arches. The works of art include a pulpit assembled from 11 and 12C fragments and a baldachin of 13C fragments.
In the sacristy is a precious 11C Byzantine parchment scroll in Beneventan script, typical of medieval southern Italy. The illustrations are upside down so that the congregation could see them as the parchment was unrolled for the choristers.

★ **Castle (Castello) (CY)**. – The Emperor Frederick II of Hohenstaufen built the castle in
⊙ 1233 over the foundations of earlier Byzantine and Norman buildings. The irregular but four-sided courtyard and two of the original towers date from the Swabian period. The castle's defences were strengthened in the 16C.

ADDITIONAL SIGHTS

⊙ **Picture Gallery.** – *On Lungomare Nazario Sauro (**DY**) beyond Piazza A. Diaz.*
The gallery, on the fourth floor (lift) of the Palazzo della Provincia, regroups Byzantine works of art (sculpture and paintings), a 12-13C painted wood statue of **Christ**★, *The Martyrdom of St Peter* by Giovanni Bellini and canvases by the 17-18C Neapolitan school.

⊙ **Archaeological Museum (DZ M¹)**. – *First floor of the university.* Greco-Roman collections from excavations made throughout Apulia.

EXCURSION

The road from Bari to Barletta passes through some small but attractive coastal towns which were fortified against invasion from the Saracens during the Middle Ages and the Turks at the end of the 15C. These include **Giovinazzo** with its small 12C cathedral dominating the fishing harbour; **Molfetta** pinpointed by the square towers of its Apulian Romanesque cathedral in white limestone; and **Bisceglie**, a picturesque fishing village, with its cathedral finished in the 13C. The main doorway is flanked by two lions.

BARLETTA Apulia
Pop 86 205

Michelin map 988 folds 28 and 29 – Town plan in the current Michelin Red Guide Italia

In the 12 and 13C the town of Barletta was an embarkation port for the Crusades and many military or hospitaller Orders chose this as the site for an institution.

Now a commercial and agricultural centre, the town has several medieval religious or secular buildings: the 12-14C **cathedral** (Duomo) in the Apulian style shows a Burgundian influence, especially in the choir; the **Basilica of the Holy Sepulchre** (San Sepolcro), at the junction of Corso Vittorio Emanuele and Corso Garibaldi, dates from the 12-14C and possesses a fine **reliquary★** for a fragment of the True Cross-note the Limoges enamels on the base; and the **castle★** (Castello) which is an imposing fortress built by the Emperor Frederick II of Hohenstaufen and strengthened by Charles of Anjou.

The **Municipal Museum★** (Museo Civico) has in addition to a collection of Apulian ceramics, a particularly fine series of paintings by the local artist, Giuseppe de Nittis (1846-84). This portraitist of Parisian elegance was also a landscape painter influenced by the Macchiaioli *(p 31)*.

The **Colossus★★** (Colosso or Statua di Eraclio) is a gigantic statue over 4.5m – 15ft tall of a Byzantine emperor whose identity is uncertain (Valentinian?). Probably 4C, this work is of interest as it marks the transition from decadent Roman to early Christian art.

★ BASSANO DEL GRAPPA Venetia
Pop 38 754

Michelin map 988 fold 5

Bassano del Grappa, a pottery town which also produces brandy *(grappa)*, is built on the banks of the Brenta River. The town is attractive with narrow streets lined by painted houses and the squares bordered by arcades. In the centre, Piazza Garibaldi is dominated by the 13C square tower, Torre di Ezzelino and overlooked by the **Church of S Francis** (San Francesco). Dating from the 12-14C the church has an elegant porch (1306). Inside the 14C Christ is by Guariento. The **Covered Bridge** (Ponte Coperto) is well known in Italy. Originally built in the 13C it has been rebuilt many times since.

★ Municipal Museum (Museo Civico). – The museum is installed in the monastery next to St Francis . The **picture gallery,** on the first floor, has several works by the local da Ponte family. Jacopo da Ponte, otherwise called **Jacopo Bassano** (1510-92) was the best known member. His works were marked by a picturesque realism and contrasts of light and shade. Look for his masterpiece **St Valentine baptising St Lucia.** Other Venetian painters include Guariento, Vivarini, Giambono (14 and 15C), Pietro Longhi, Tiepolo and Marco Ricci (18C). There are also two lovely canvases by the Genoese painter Magnasco (18C) and a gallery devoted to the sculptor Canova.

EXCURSIONS

★★★ Monte Grappa. – 1 775m – 5 823ft. *32km – 20 miles to the north.*
The road up passes through fine forests and bare mountain pastures, before reaching the summit, from where there is a magnificent **panorama** which reaches as far as Venice and Trieste. The monument is a World War I ossuary.

★ Asolo. – *14km – 9 miles to the east.*
This attractive little town, dominated by its castle, has streets lined with palaces painted with frescoes. The town is closely associated with Robert Browning and Duse, the famous Italian tragic actress who interpreted the works of Gabriele D'Annunzio. Duse is buried in the peaceful cemetery of Sant'Anna.

Marostica. – *7km – 4 miles to the west.*
The **main square★** (Piazza Castello) of this charming small medieval city serves as a giant chessboard for a highly original game of chess **(Partita a Scacchi)** with costumed people as the chessmen *(see the table of Principal Festivals at the end of the guide).*

Cittadella. – *13km – 8 miles to the south.*
This stronghold was built by the Paduans in 1220 by way of a reply to the Trevisans construction of Castelfranco. Cittadella is encircled by lovely brick **walls★**.

Possagno. – *8km – 11 miles to the northwest.*
This was the birthplace of the sculptor **Antonio Canova** (1757-1822) known for his neoclassical works. The **Temple of Canova,** designed by the master himself, crowns an eminence. Inside are the sculptor's tomb and his last sculpture, a **Descent from the Cross★**.

★ BELLUNO Venetia
Pop 36 233

Michelin map 988 fold 5 – Town plan in the current Michelin Red Guide Italia

This pleasant town stands on a spur at the confluence of the Piave and the Ardo rivers and is surrounded by high mountains. To the north are the Dolomites with the Belluno Pre-Alps in the south. An independent commune in the Middle Ages Belluno came under the protection of the Venetian Republic from 1404.

Walk along Via Rialto through the 13C gateway, Porta Dojona (remodelled in the 16C) across the **Piazza del Mercato★**, bordered with arcaded Renaissance houses and adorned with a 1409 fountain, along Via Mezzaterra and Via Santa Croce to the gateway, Porta Rugo. Via del Piave offers a vast **view★** of the Piave Valley and the surrounding mountains. The **Piazza del Duomo★** is surrounded by the late 15C Venetian style **Rectors' Palace★** (Palazzo dei Rettori), the **Episcopal Palace** (Palazzo dei Vescovi) and the cathedral (Duomo), dating from the 16C with its baroque campanile by Juvara. Inside there are several good pictures by the Venetian school, notably by Jacopo Bassano and in the crypt a 15C **polyptych★** by the Rimini school. The Jurists' Palace (Palazzo dei Giuristi) houses the **Municipal Museum** (Museo Civico) with an art gallery (local and Venetian works), a rich coin collection and documents on the Risorgimento *(qv)*.

EXCURSION

Feltre. – *31km – 19 miles to the southwest.*
Feltre, grouped round its castle, has kept part of its ramparts and in **Via Mezzaterra★**, old houses, adorned with frescoes in the Venetian manner. **Piazza Maggiore★** is a beau-
⊙ tiful square with its noble buildings, arcades, stairways and balustrades. The **Municipal Museum** *(Museo Civico, 23 Via Lorenzo Luzzo, near the Porta Oria)* regroups works by Lorenzo Luzzo a local artist, Marescalchi, Bellini, Cima da Conegliano, Ricci and Jan Massys. The museum also includes a historical section on Feltre and an archaeological collection.

BENEVENTO Campania   Pop 65 742

Michelin map 988 fold 27

This was the capital of the Samnites who hindered for some considerable time the Roman expansion. In 321 BC they trapped the Roman army in a defile known as the Caudine Forks (Forche Caudine) between Capua and ancient Beneventum. The Romans occupied the town following the defeat in 275 BC of Pyrrhus and his Samnite allies. During the reign of Trajan the town knew a period of glory and it was designated as starting point for the Trajan Way (Via Traiana) leading to Brindisi. Under Lombard rule it became the seat of a duchy in 571 and later a powerful principality. Following the Battle of Benevento in 1266 when Charles of Anjou defeated Manfred the then king of Naples and Sicily, supported by Pope Urban IV he claimed the kingship.

★★ **Trajan's Arch (Arco di Traiano).** – *At the junction of Via Traiano and Corso Garibaldi.*
Built in AD 114 this is Italy's best preserved triumphal arch. The low-reliefs dedicated to the glory of the emperor are of an exceptionally high standard.

★ **Samnium Museum (Museo del Sannio).** – Go behind the **Church of St Sophia** in Piazza
⊙ Matteotti, an 8C edifice rebuilt in the 17C on a polygonal plan. The columns of the **cloisters★** support Moorish style arches. Adjoining the cloisters, the museum has an important archaeological section and works from the Neapolitan school.

Roman Theatre (Teatro Romano). – *Near Via Port'Arsa.*
This theatre, which is one of the largest still in existence, was built in the 2C during the reign of the Emperor Hadrian.

★★ # BERGAMO Lombardy   Pop 119 427

Michelin map 988 fold 3 – Town plan pp 56 and 57

Situated on the northern edge of the Lombardy plain at the confluence of the Brembana and Seriana valleys, Bergamo is one of the principal towns of Lombardy. As well as being an art centre it is a busy business and industrial centre. The modern **lower town** is pleasant while the old **upper town** is quiet, picturesque and evocative of the past.

From Roman city to Venetian rule. – Around 1200 BC the Ligurians occupied the site of the upper town. The Gauls seized the settlement *c*550 which they called Berghem. It was renamed Bergomum by the Romans when they took over in 196 BC. The city was destroyed by the Barbarians before enjoying a period of peace under the Lombards and in particular in the reign of Queen Theodolinda. An independent commune from the 11 to the 13C she then joined the Lombard League *(qv)* in its struggle against the Emperor Frederick Barbarossa. The town suffered during the struggles between the Guelphs (followers of the pope) and the Ghibellines (followers of the emperor). Under the rule of **Bartolomeo Colleoni** (1400-75) the town fell first to the Visconti family from Milan and then the Republic of Venice. The famous mercenary leader served both successively, before finally ceding Bergamo to the Venetians. Bergamo came under Austrian rule in 1814 and was only liberated by Garibaldi in 1859.

Bergamo and its artists. – In addition to a large group of local artists, namely Previtali, Moroni, Cariani, Baschenis and Fra Galgario numerous others worked in the town, including Lorenzo Lotto, Giovanni da Campione and Amadeo.

Masks and Bergamasques. – The **Commedia dell'Arte** originated at Bergamo in the 16C. The comedy consists of an improvisation *(imbroglio)* based on a pre-arranged theme *(scenario)*, with gags *(lazzi)* uttered by masked actors representing stock characters: the valet (Harlequin), a stubborn but wily peasant from the Brembana Valley, the braggart (Pulcinella), the lady's maid (Columbine), the lover (Pierrot), the knave (Scapino), the old fox (Scaramouch), the clown (Pantaloon) and the musician (Mezzetino). Its element of caricature sometimes springs from triviality. The theatre was popular in France in the 17 and 18C. Bergamo is also the home of the composer Donizetti (1797-1848). The vivacity of the people is displayed in the local folklore such as the Bergamasque, a lively dance, and in the groups of public musicians *(pifferi)*.

Scapino   Pantaloon   Fracasso   Pulcinella   Scaramouch   Mezzetino

★★★ UPPER TOWN (CITTÀ ALTA) (ABY)

No cars allowed in this part of the town – time: 3 hours

When going by car leave it in one of the two car parks *(see town plan below)* or take the funicular *(station in Viale Vittorio Emanuele II)* which ends in **Piazza del Mercato delle Scarpe** (Square of the Shoe Market) **(BY 38)**.

BERGAMO

The Upper Town, with its 16C Venetian perimeter wall, its strategically placed castle, and its winding alleyways lined with old houses, has Bergamo's finest buildings.

★★ **Piazza del Duomo** (AY). – This attractive square is lined by fine buildings. The arcades of the Palazzo Ragione in the north lead to the Piazza Vecchia.

★★ **Colleoni Chapel** (Cappella Colleoni). – The architect of the Carthusian Monastery at Pavia, **Amadeo** designed this gem (1470-76) of Lombard Renaissance architecture, as a mausoleum for Bartolomeo Colleoni. As at Pavia the graceful **façade** is covered with precious multicoloured marble and lavishly decorated with delicate sculptures: figures of children *(putti)*, fluted and spiralling columns, sculptured pilasters, vases and candelabra, medallions and low-reliefs which are typical of one of the tendencies of contemporary art to mix sacred and secular elements (allegories, scenes from the Old Testament, mythological figures including scenes from the life of Hercules with whom Colleoni often used to identify himself).

The interior is sumptuously decorated with low-reliefs of extraordinary delicacy, frescoes by Tiepolo and Renaissance **stalls** with intarsia work. The **Colleoni monument**, also by Amadeo, is surmounted by an equestrian statue of the leader in gilded wood and is delicately carved. The low-reliefs of the sarcophagi represent scenes from the New Testament separated by niches occupied by statues of the Virtues. Between the two sarcophagi are portraits of the leader's children. His favourite daughter, Medea, who died at the age of fifteen, lies near him (to the left) in a tomb by Amadeo which is a marvel of delicacy and purity.

★ **Basilica of St Mary Major** (Santa Maria Maggiore). – This church is 12C but the two lovely north and south **porches** with loggias and supported by lions in the Lombard Romanesque style were added in the 14C by Giovanni da Campione.

The interior, remodelled in the baroque style (late 16C-early 17C) is richly decorated with stucco and gilding. The walls of the aisles and the chancel are hung with nine splendid Florentine **tapestries★★** (1580-86) beautifully designed after cartoons by Alessandro Allori which relate the Life of the Virgin. On the west wall of the nave hangs the sumptuous Flemish tapestry depicting the **Crucifixion★★**. After cartoons by L. Van Schoor it was woven in Antwerp between 1696 and 1698. Note also the curious 18C baroque confessional in the north aisle and the interesting 14C frescoes in the transept. Incorporated in the chancel screen are four superb **panels of intarsia work★★** depicting scenes from the Old Testament. They were made in the 16C after the designs of Lorenzo Lotto.

Once out in Piazza del Duomo again, admire the quatrefoil **Tempietto Santa Croce** which was built *c*1000 in the Romanesque style as well as the 14C south porch and the **chevet★** with its radiating chapels decorated with graceful arcading.

★ **Baptistry** (Battistero) (B). – This charming octagonal work is encircled by a red Verona marble gallery with gracefully slender columns and 14C statues representing the Virtues. It is a reconstruction of Giovanni da Campione's original work dating from 1340. It originally graced the east end of the nave of St Mary Major but was deemed too cumbersome and was demolished in 1660 and rebuilt on its present site in 1898.

Cathedral (Duomo). – It has a richly decorated interior (18C). The very lovely baroque stalls were carved by the Sanzi.

★ **Piazza Vecchia** (AY). – This is the historic centre of the town. The **Palazzo della Ragione (AY C)** the oldest communal palace in Italy dates from 1199 but was rebuilt in the 16C. It has graceful arcades and trefoil windows and a central balcony surmounted by the Lion of St Mark. A 14C covered stairway leads to the majestic 12C **bell tower** with its 15C clock. The **Palazzo Scamozziano (AY D)** opposite is in the Palladian style *(p 211)*. The fountain in the centre was offered to Genoa in 1780 by the Doge of Venice, Alvise Contarini.

⊙ **Via Bartolomeo Colleoni (AY 10).** – This street is lined with old mansions including the Colleoni Mansion, at Nos 9 and 11, which contains frescoes to the glory of the mercenary leader.

Fortress (Rocca) (BY). – Built in the 14C it was remodelled by the Venetians. There are interesting **views★** of the upper and lower towns.

★**LOWER TOWN** *time: 1 1/2 hours.*

The Carrara Academy is in the heart of a district of attractive alleyways while Piazza Matteotti is at the centre of the present day business and shopping district.

★★**Carrara Academy (Accademia Carrara) (CY).** – This collection of 15-18C Italian and foreign
⊙ paintings is housed in a neo-classical palace.
Beyond the early 15C works, which still recall the International Gothic style *(qv)*, note two important portraits of **Giuliano de' Medici** by Botticelli and the elegant and refined one of **Lionello d'Este** by Pisanello. These are followed by works of the Venetian school by the Vivarini family, Carlo Crivelli, Antonello da Messina, Giovanni Bellini (gentle Madonnas with dreamy expressions which are similar to those of his brother-in-law, Mantegna). Gentile Bellini (delicate but penetrating portraits), Carpaccio *(Doge Leonardo Loredan)* and by Lorenzo Lotto. Next come the late 15C and early 16C works represented by Cosimo Tura, master of the Ferrarese school (a very realistic *Virgin and Child* showing the influence of Flemish art), the Lombard, Bergognone (gentle light) and of the Bergamask, Previtali. The 16C covers works by the Venetian Lorenzo Lotto (including a splendid **Holy Family with St Catherine**), the good Bergamask portraitist, Cariani and the Venetian masters Titian and Tintoretto. The colours and delicate draughtsmanship of Raphael greatly influenced Garofalo (Benvenuto Tisi) who was nicknamed the Ferrara Raphael, while the Piedmontese Gaudenzio Ferrari and Bernardino Luini, the main exponents of the Renaissance in Lombardy, were inspired by Leonardo da Vinci. The 16C **portraits** are a particularly rich group with the Ferrarese school which specialised in this art and the Bergamask, Moroni (1523-78). Foreign artists include Clouet (portrait of *Louis de Clève*) and Dürer. The 17-18C Bergamask school is represented by Baschenis (1617-77) and excellent portraits by Fra Galgario (1655-1743). The 17C Flemish and Dutch section (Rubens, Van Dyck, Velvet Brueghel...) is dominated by a delightful Van Goyen seascape. The visit ends with 18C Venetian painting: scenes of domestic interiors by Pietro Longhi, topographical views by Carlevarijs, Bernardo Bellotto, Canaletto and some charming seascapes by Francesco Guardi.

★ **Old quarter.** – The main street of this quarter is **Via Pignolo★ (BC YZ)** which winds among old palaces, mostly 16 and 18C and churches containing numerous works of art. The **Church of San Bernardino (CY)** has in the chancel a Virgin and Saints (1521) by Lorenzo Lotto. **Santo Spirito (CZ)** contains a St John the Baptist surrounded by saints and a polyptych by Previtali, a polyptych portraying the Virgin by Bergognone and a Virgin and Child by Lorenzo Lotto.

★ **Piazza Matteotti (BZ).** – This immense square in the centre of the modern town is overlooked by the **Church of San Bartolomeo** (a superb Virgin and Saints by Lorenzo Lotto), the **Donizetti Theatre (T)** and is bordered by one of the Bergamasks' favourite promenades, the **Sentierone.**

EXCURSION

★ **Brembana Valley (Val Brembana).** – *25km – 16 miles to the north.*
Leave Bergamo by the S 470 which follows an industrial valley. Note the curious two toned limestone strata. The important thermal spa of **San Pellegrino Terme★** has a lovely mountain setting.

★★ **BOLOGNA** Emilia-Romagna   Pop 427 240

Michelin map 𝟿𝟾𝟾 folds 14 and 15 – Plan of the built-up area in the current Michelin Guide Italia

Situated on the southern edge of the Po Plain, on the lower slopes of the Apennine foothills, Bologna the capital of Emilia-Romagna is a city of many facets: its numerous medieval towers, its churches, its long arcaded streets lined by sumptuous 14 to 17C palaces recall the former political and cultural importance of this once independent city.
Bologna was famous for its University, one of the oldest in Europe, which already numbered 10 000 students in the 13C and produced many scholars, including Guglielmo Marconi (1874-1937).
In addition to being an Italian sanctuary of good fare, Bologna is an important industrial and commercial centre well placed on both the national rail and road networks. The city hosts numerous international fairs, shows and exhibitions.

HISTORICAL AND ARTISTIC NOTES

Etruscan Felsina was conquered in the 4C BC by the Boïan Gauls, who were driven out in their turn by the Romans in 190 BC. Roman Bononia fell under the sway of the Barbarians and did not recover until the 12C. From the 13C onwards the city enjoyed independent communal government and developed rapidly. A fortified city wall, palaces and churches were built and the University flourished and acquired an excellent reputation for its teaching of Roman law. In the struggle which confronted the Ghibellines, supporting the emperor, and the Guelphs, partisans of communal independence, it was the latter who prevailed when in 1249 they defeated the Imperial Army of

Frederick II at Fossalta. The emperor's son, Enzo, was taken prisoner and remained at Bologna until his death twenty-three years later. In the 15C, following a period of violent struggles between rival families, the city was ruled by the **Bentivoglio** family. Bologna was greatly influenced by the Tuscan Renaissance during the reign of Giovanni II Bentivoglio. The Bentivoglio family was in its turn vanquished in 1506 by **Pope Julius II** and the city remained under papal control until the arrival of Bonaparte in 1797. In the early 19C several insurrections were severely repressed by the Austrians and in 1860 it was united with Piedmont.

Famous citizens of the city include the Popes, Gregory XIII, who established our present Gregorian calendar (1582), Gregory XV (17C) and Benedict XIV (18C). In 1530 following the defeat of François I at Pavia and the sack of Rome, the Emperor Charles V obliged Pope Clement VII to crown him in the Basilica of St Petronius in Bologna.

The Bologna School of Painting. – This term covers the artistic movement founded by the **Carracci,** a Bolognese family of painters, as a reaction to the excessive formalism of Tuscan Mannerism. Their aim was to create simpler compositions and a greater realism of subject matter. Numerous artists including their Bolognese followers, Albani, Guercino, Domenichino and Guido Reni followed this movement known as the Academy of the Eclectic *(Incamminati)* whose main teaching precept was the study of nature.

The work of Annibale Carracci, the decorator of the Farnese Palace in Rome and the most brilliant of the three cousins, had a decisive influence on this new artistic movement. Annibale was a precursor of baroque art with his purity of tone and the vitality of his decorative schemes.

★★ CITY CENTRE *time: 1 day*

The two adjoining squares, **Piazza Maggiore** and **Piazza del Nettuno**★★★, form with **Piazza di Porta Ravegnana**★★, the heart of Bologna, an ensemble of rare beauty.

★★ **Neptune's Fountain (Fontana del Nettuno) (DT A)**. – This is the work of the Flemish sculptor, known as Giambologna or Giovanni Bologna. The muscular bronze Neptune, nicknamed the Giant, is surrounded by four sirens spouting water from their breasts. The group has a rather rough vigour characteristic of Giovanni Bologna.

★ **Communal Palace (Palazzo Comunale) (DT)**. – The façade is composed of buildings of different periods: 13C to the left, 15C on the right and in the centre the main doorway is 16C (the lower section is by Alessi) and is surmounted by a statue of Pope Gregory XIII. Above and to the left of the doorway is a statue of the Virgin and Child (1478) in terracotta by Niccolò dell'Arca. At the far end of the courtyard, under a gallery on the left is a superb staircase leading to the richly decorated first floor rooms, then up again to the second floor.

Opening off the vast Farnese Gallery with 17C frescoes are the sumptuous rooms containing the **Communal Art Collections** with a sculpture section and an exceedingly good group of Emilian **paintings**★.

To the left of the Communal Palace stands the severe 14-15C Notaries Palace **(DU B)**.

★ **Governors' Palace (Palazzo del Podestà) (ET)**. – The Renaissance façade facing Piazza Maggiore, has arcades separated by Corinthian columns on the ground floor and is surmounted by a balustrade. The upper storey has pilasters and an attic pierced by oculi or round windows.

The 13C **King Enzo's Palace (ET D)** stands next to the Governor's Palace. It has a fine inner courtyard and a magnificent staircase leading up to a gallery, to the left of which is a courtyard overlooked by the Arengo Tower.

★★ **Basilica of St Petronius (San Petronio) (DU)**. – Building began in 1390 to the plans of Antonio di Vincenzo (1340-1402) and was only fully completed in the 17C when the vaulting was finished. The façade, the upper part of which lacks its marble facing, is remarkable chiefly for the main **doorway**★★ on which the Sienese Jacopo della Quercia, worked from 1425 to 1438. The lintel, uprights and embrasures are adorned with small, expressive low-reliefs, rather pagan in spirit. This immense building has many **works of art**★: frescoes by Giovanni da Modena (15C) in the first and fourth chapels off the north aisle; a Martyrdom of St Sebastian by the late 15C Ferrara school in the fifth chapel; a Madonna (1492) by Lorenzo Costa and the tomb of Elisa Baciocchi, Napoleon's sister in the seventh chapel; and at the high altar a canopy (baldachin) by Vignola (16C). The 15C organ on the right is one of the oldest in Italy.

★ **Municipal Archaeological Museum (Museo Civico Archeologico) (EU M[1])**. – Egyptian, Greco-Roman (lovely Roman copy of the head of Athena by Phidias) and Etruscan (bronze historiated water pitcher, *situle)* antiquities.

Near the museum is the 16C **Palazzo dell'Archiginnasio (EU V),** the home of an important library (10 000 manuscripts) and the 17-18C **Anatomy Theatre** (Teatro Anatomico).

(After photo by T.C.I.)

Bologna – Central doorway
of the Basilica of St Petronius

★★ **Leaning towers** (ET R). – There are two strange leaning towers which belonged to noble families in the attractive Piazza di Porta Ravegnana. They are the heritage of continual conflict between rival Guelph and Ghibelline families in the Middle Ages. The taller, **Torre degli Asinelli,** nearly 100m – 328ft high dates from 1109. 486 steps lead to the top from where there is an admirable **panorama★★** of the city. The second, known as **Torre Garisenda** is 50m – 164ft high and has a tilt of over 3m – 10ft. No 1 in the square is the Renaissance **Linen Drapers' Palace** (ET S).

The 14C **Mercanzia★** (EU C) or Merchants' House, in the next square, bears the coats of arms of the various guilds and several small statues.

★ **St Stephen's Basilica** (Santo Stefano) (EU). – This dedication includes a group of three buildings overlooking the square with its Renaissance mansions: the **Church of the Crucifix** (Crocifisso) 11C but remodelled; the 12C **Church of the Holy Sepulchre** (Santo Sepolcro) with its polygonal form and the shrine of Bologna's patron saint, St Petronius. Go through the Church of the Holy Sepulchre to reach the charming 12C Court of Pilate and a Romanesque cloisters transformed into a **museum** (paintings, statues and liturgical objects).

At the far end of the courtyard is the 13C **Church of the Trinity** (Chiesa della Trinità) with a curious 14C multicoloured group representing the Adoration of the Magi.

The 8-11C **Church of Sts Vitalis and Agricola** is plain and massive.

ADDITIONAL SIGHTS

★★ **National Picture Gallery** (Pinacoteca Nazionale). – *Take Via Zamboni* (ET).

The Bologna school is well represented and its characteristics were: in the 14C gold backgrounds, bright colours and Gothic preciosity (affectation), all typical of Byzantine art; under the Renaissance mannerisms, idealism, science and composition; during the baroque period with the Carracci realism, vigour and colour; and with the pupils of the Carracci an academic style.

The first rooms are devoted to the 14C Bolognese painters: Vitale da Bologna (lovely frescoes), Simone dei Crocifissi and Giovanni Bologna.

The following rooms contain works of the early Renaissance: the Venetian school (the Vivarini family and Cima da Conegliano), the Ferrara school with their pronouncedly realistic works (Ercole de' Roberti, Francesco del Cossa and Lorenzo Costa) as well as Bolognese artists such as Francia *(The Adoration of the Child)*.

Beyond *The Ecstasy of St Cecilia,* a famous picture of truly classical beauty by Raphael, there is a series of 16C frescoes by Niccolò dell' Abbate depicting Ariosto's *Orlando Furioso (Roland the Mad)*.

The Bologna school of the 17C follows with the Carracci brothers, to whom an entire room is devoted, Guido Reni, Albani and Domenichino and their disciples, as well as Guercino with his outstanding masterpiece *St William of Aquitaine,* so rich in clever light effects.

★ **Church of St James Major (San Giacomo Maggiore) (ET).** – The church was founded in 1267. On the north side is a lovely Renaissance portico. In the **Bentivoglio Chapel★** (Cappella Bentivoglio) is an altarpiece that is considered to be one of Francia's (late 15C) best pieces and frescoes which are in part attributed to the Ferraran, Lorenzo Costa. Opposite the chapel, in the ambulatory, Jacopo della Quercia made the **tomb★** of the jurist, Antonio Bentivoglio. In St Cecilia's Oratory are remarkable **frescoes★** (1506) by Francia and Lorenzo Costa.

★ **Strada Maggiore (EU).** – The street is lined with crenellated Gothic and classical palaces. No 44, a palace dating from 1658, houses a **Museum of Industrial Art** and the **Davia Bargellini Gallery**: 16-18C Bolognese furniture, 18C puppet theatres, a collection of door handles and locks, and paintings including several on the Madonna and Child theme by the Vivarini family, Garofalo, Francia and Vitale da Bologna.

★ **St Dominic's Church (San Domenico) (EU).** – The church was built at the beginning of the 13C and remodelled in the 18C. The famous and beautiful **tomb★★** (arca) of the saint by Nicola Pisano (1267) was crowned by an arch (1468-73) by the sculptor Niccolò da Bari, who was afterwards known as Niccolò dell' Arca. The two saints and a kneeling angel (1494) were by Michelangelo. The chapel to the south of the choir has a fine painting by Filippino Lippi: **the Mystic Marriage of St Catherine★** (1501).

★ **Bevilacqua Palace (Palazzo Bevilacqua) (DU).** – This, the finest palace in Bologna, is in the Florentine Renaissance rusticated style.

St Francis' Church (San Francesco) (DT). – At the high altar is a magnificent marble **altarpiece★** (1392), a Gothic work by the Venetian sculptor Paolo dalle Masegne.

EXCURSION

Madonna di San Luca. – *5km – 3 miles to the southwest. Leave the city centre by Via Saragozza* (DV).
The 18C church is linked to the city by a **portico★** of 666 arches. In the chancel, is the Madonna of St Luke, a painting in the 12C Byzantine manner. There is a lovely **view★** of Bologna and the Apennines.

BOLSENA Latium   Pop 4 057

Michelin map 988 fold 25

Bolsena, the ancient Etruscan city of Volsinii, stands on the banks of Italy's largest lake of volcanic origin, the level of which is continually changing due to earth tremors. Its shady shores welcome many visitors attracted by a gentle and limpid light. The old part of the town groups its sombre coloured houses upon a small hill; there is a good view from the S2, the Viterbo-Siena road.

The Miracle of Bolsena. – A Bohemian priest had doubts about the Transubstantiation, that is, the incarnation of Christ in the Host. But, it is related, at the moment of Consecration when he was celebrating mass in St Christine's Church, the Host began to bleed profusely. The priest no longer doubted the mystery and the Feast of Corpus Christi was instituted.

★ **St Christine's (Santa Cristina).** – The 3C Saint Christine is said to have belonged to the Bolsena region. She was a victim of the persecutions of Diocletian. Although the building is 11C the façade, articulated by gracefully carved pilasters, is Renaissance. The columns inside are Roman. From the north aisle you enter the **Chapel of the Miracle**, where the pavement stained by the blood of the Host is revered, and then the Grotto of St Christine. In the latter is the Altar of the Miracle and a reclining statue of the saint attributed to the della Robbias.

★ BOLZANO (BOZEN) Trentino – Alto Adige   Pop 102 111

Michelin map 988 fold 4 or 218 fold 20 – Local map p 78 – Town plan in the current Michelin Red Guide Italia

Bolzano, the capital of the Alto Adige, lies on the Brenner transalpine route at the confluence of the Isarco and the Adige. The surrounding slopes are covered with orchards and vineyards. The architecture of the town shows a marked Tyrolean or Austrian influence which was exercised between the 16C and 1918. This industrial and commercial town is now also a busy tourist centre due to its proximity to the Dolomites. The town centre from **Piazza Walther** to **Via dei Portici★** has some lovely houses.

★ **Cathedral (Duomo).** – Built in the Romanesque Gothic style in pinkish sandstone and roofed with multicoloured tiles, the cathedral has several decorative doorways and an open 14-16C campanile. The interior, in the style of a German hall church, has three aisles of equal height. The frescoes (1424) are by Corrado Erlin and the lovely Gothic **pulpit★** is carved with a realism which is wholly northern in spirit.

Dominican Monastery (Convento dei Domenicani). – *Piazza Domenicani.*
The church contains several interesting groups of frescoes: by the followers of Giotto in the Chapel of San Giovanni, by Giovanni Stocinger (14-15C) in the nave and by Friedrich Pacher in the cloisters.

Church of the Franciscans (Chiesa dei Francescani). – *1 Via Francescani.*
The church was begun in the 13C. Inside admire the lovely late 15C **altarpiece★** carved in wood by Hans Klocker. The charming small cloisters have elegant fan vaulting.

Gries Parish Church (Chiesa Parrocchiale di Gries). – *Take Corso Libertà.*
This Gothic church has an **altarpiece★** (1471) carved by Michael Pacher from Brunico.

★★ **BRENTA Riviera** Venetia

Michelin map 988 fold 5 – 35km – 22 miles east of Padua

Standing alongside the Brenta Canal between Strà and Fusina are numerous lovely classical **villas★** by Palladio *(qv)*. These were the summer residences of the Venetian nobility who used to lay on sumptuous night-time festivities to music by Vivaldi Pergolesi or Cimarosa.

⊘ **Sightseeing.** – Boat trips leave from both Venice and Padua. By car take the road which follows the Brenta passing through Strà, Dolo, Mira and Malcontenta.

⊘ **Strà.** – The **Villa Nazionale★** has a majestic garden with a delightful vista and basin. The spacious **apartments★** of this 18C palace were decorated by various artists including Giovanni Battista Tiepolo who painted his masterpiece **The Apotheosis of the Pisani Family★★**.

⊘ **Mira.** – The **Palazzo Foscarini** and **Villa Widmann-Foscari-Rezzonico** are both 18C. The **Ballroom★** of the latter is entirely decorated with frescoes.

⊘ **Malcontenta.** – Palladio built the **Villa Foscari★** in 1574. G.B. Zelotti and B. Franco were responsible for the frescoes. The villa was named after the wife of a Foscari who was ill-pleased *(malcontenta)* at being consigned to the villa.

GREEN TOURIST GUIDES

Picturesque scenery, buildings
Attractive routes
Touring programmes
Plans of towns and buildings.

★ **BRESCIA** Lombardy   Pop 200 790

Michelin map 988 fold 4

The important industrial town of Brescia lies at the foot of the Lombard Pre-Alps. It has retained the regular street plan of the Roman camp *(castrum)* of Brixia. The town is dominated to the north by a medieval castle (Castello) and its centre has numerous fine buildings from all periods: Roman, Romanesque Renaissance and baroque.

HISTORICAL NOTES

Brixia flourished under the Empire and the remains of Roman monuments include the Capitoline Temple and the forum.

In the 8C Brescia became a Lombard duchy and then in the 12 and 13C a free commune and member of the Lombard League *(qv)*. The town was one of the most prosperous in Italy, due to the manufacture of arms and armour. Brescia supplied all Europe until the 18C. From 1426 to 1797 Brescia was part of the Venetian domains and acquired numerous secular and religious buildings. A group of artists formed the Brescia school and the most important members were in the 15C Vincenzo Foppa and in the 16C Romanino and Moretto, Savoldo and Civerchio.

SIGHTS

★ **Piazza della Loggia** (BY 9). – The **Loggia** (BY H), now the town hall, was built from the end of the 15C to the beginning of the 16C to the designs of Bramante for the lower part and Sansovino and Palladio for the upper part. The **Palazzo dell' Orologio,** opposite the Loggia, is surmounted by two Venetian Moorish figures *(Mori)* as jaquemarts. On the south side of the square are the graceful palaces, **Monte Vecchio** (1484) and **Monte Nuovo** (1497) (BY B). To the north of the square is a picturesque popular quarter with arcades and old houses.

Piazza del Duomo (BY 5). – The 17C **New Cathedral** (Duomo Nuovo) seems to crush, with its mass of white marble, the **Old Cathedral** (Duomo Vecchio) a 12C Romanesque building which succeeded an earlier sanctuary known as the rotunda after its shape.

Inside there is a magnificent sarcophagus in rose-coloured marble surmounted by the recumbent figure of a bishop and in the chancel paintings by local artists, Moretto and Romanino. To the left of the Duomo Nuovo the **Broletto (P)** is an austere Romanesque building dominated by a tower. The balcony on the façade was for proclamations.

★ **Tosio Martinengo Picture Gallery (Pinacoteca Tosio - Martinengo) (CZ)**. – Here you will see works of the **Brescia school**, characterised by richness of colour and well balanced composition: religious scenes and portraits by Moretto, more sumptuous religious scenes in the Venetian manner by Romanino and other works, as well as canvases by Vincenzo Foppa and Savoldo. Admire also the works of Clouet, Raphael, the Master of Utrecht, Lorenzo Lotto and Tintoretto.

★ **Via dei Musei (CY)**. – This picturesque street has two interesting museums. The **Roman Museum**★ **(M¹)** in the ruins of the **Capitoline Temple**★ (73 AD) contains a magnificent **Winged Victory** and six bronze Roman **busts**. Beyond the remains of the forum is the **Museum of Christian Art (M²)**, installed in the 16C Church of Santa Giulia. This collection has some priceless works of art such as the 4 and 5C **ivories**★★, the 8C **Cross of Desiderius**★★, a richly encrusted piece, medals by Pisanello and small bronzes by Antonio Riccio (16C).

Churches. – Brescia has a great wealth of Romanesque, Renaissance and baroque churches and nearly all contain paintings of the Brescia school. The 13C **San Francesco**★ **(AY)** has a 14C *Pietà* by Giotto's followers, three saints by Moretto and a Virgin and Child by Romanino. The 15 and 16C **Santa Maria dei Miracoli (AYZ A)** has a lovely marble **façade**★.

San Nazaro - San Celso (AZ N) contains Moretto's masterpiece, the **Coronation of the Virgin**★. **Sant'Alessandro (BZ G)** has a 15C **Annunciation**★ by Jacopo Bellini and a **Descent from the Cross**★ by Civerchio. **Sant'Agata (BY R)** with its rich **interior**★ has a polyptych of the **Virgin of Pity**★ as well as a **Virgin with Coral**★ a charming 16C fresco. **San Giovanni Evangelista (BY E)** is known for its works by Moretto and Romanino, **Madonna delle Grazie (AY C)** for its baroque interior and the **Church of the Carmine (BY D)** for its oriental silhouette.

★ BRESSANONE (BRIXEN) Trentino - Alto Adige   Pop 16 360

Michelin map 988 folds 4 and 5 – Local map p 78 – Town plan in the current Micheli Red Guide Italia

Standing at the confluence of the Rienza and the Isarco, Bressanone is an attractive little town known for its particularly sunny, dry and bracing climate.
The town has remained Tyrolean in character.

Cathedral (Duomo). – The baroque interior is lavish with marble, stucco, gilding and frescoes. To the right of the cathedral are lovely 12C Romanesque **cloisters★** with interesting 14 to 16C frescoes. The **treasury★** has a good collection of liturgical objects and reliquaries and the 11C St John the Baptist's Chapel has both 13C Romanesque and 14C Gothic frescoes.

Palace of the Prince-Bishops (Palazzo Vescovile). – *Entrance is Via Vescovado.*
The lovely **courtyard★** has three storeys of arcades decorated with statues. Inside is the **Diocesan Museum★** with a remarkable collection of painted wood **sculptures★★** typical of Tyrolean art of both the Romanesque and Gothic periods. There is also a series of **carved altarpieces★** dating from the Renaissance and on the ground floor an interesting collection of 18 and 19C **cribs★**.

EXCURSIONS

★★★ **Plose.** – Alt 2 446m – 8 025ft. *To the southeast.*
Firstly the cable-car from Valcroce and then another from Plose take you up to discover a wonderful **panorama★★★** of the Dolomites to the south and the Austrian mountains to the north.

★ **Monastery of Novacella.** – *3km – 2 miles to the north.*
The monastery was founded in 1142 and remodelled in the 15 and 18C. The Church of Our Lady (Nostra Signora) is in the Bavarian baroque style, the cloisters have frescoes by Michael Pacher and the Chapel of St Michael (San Michele) is late 12C.

BRINDISI Apulia   Pop 92 128

Michelin map 988 fold 30 – Town plans in the current Michelin Red Guide Italia

This important naval and trading port, on the Adriatic side of the 'boot's heel', has a daily shipping connection with Greece. Ever since antiquity the town has played the important role of trading post with the rest of the Mediterranean basin. It was Trajan who replaced the old Appian Way beyond Benevento by the new Via Traiana which increased the importance of Brindisi from AD 109 onwards. After the Norman conquest the town, along with Barletta, became a port of embarkation for the crusades to the Holy Land and in particular saw the departure of the Sixth Crusade (1228) led by the Emperor Frederick II of Hohenstaufen. Along with Taranto and Bari, Brindisi makes up the triangle delimiting the Mezzogiorno, an area of industrial redevelopment.

★ **Roman Column (Colonna Romana).** – This marble column near the harbour marked the end of the Appian-Traiana Way. It is crowned by a capital carved with figures.

Archaeological Museum (Museo Archeologico). – *Piazza Duomo.*
The museum regroups the numerous finds from excavations and a precious collection of vases made by early Italic peoples, the Apulians and Messapii.

★ CALABRIA

Michelin map 988 folds 38, 39 and 40

Calabria covers the extreme southwestern 'toe' of the Italian peninsula from the Gulf of Policastro to Reggio di Calabria. This mountainous region lacked a good road network which made it difficult to visit until the prolongation of the motorway to the south as far as the regional capital. For this particular reason the region remained isolated but it was a mistake to consider as a French traveller did at the beginning of the 19C that "Europe ended at Naples". In fact the opposite is true if we consider that the first colonies founded by the Greeks in the 8C BC were located on the Ionian coast of present day Calabria. If it is not always possible – as it is in Sicily at Segesta, Agrigento or Selinunte – to discover the traces of Magna Graecia in the peninsula, the museums of Reggio, Taranto and Naples have collections recalling this period of Greek influence. It lasted until the 3C BC when Rome undertook the conquest of southern Italy, without however gaining a complete and peaceful domination before Sylla reorganised the administration of these provinces in the 1C BC. After the fall of the Roman Empire, Calabria and the neighbouring regions fell under the sway of the Lombards, Saracens and Byzantines before being reunited with the Norman kingdom of the Two Sicilies and finally becoming part of a unified Italy in 1860.
The mountainous massifs which occupy the interior of the peninsula are fringed by narrow coastal plains. Between these physically distinct regions there are considerable vegetational and climatic differences according to the seasons. The Sila Massif is one of rugged mountains and alpine prairies, the Aspromonte is covered with chestnut forests, and has stony and abrupt valleys on the coastline and coastal plains covered with fruit trees bordering the Gulf of Taranto. Recent agrarian reform has been responsible for a slowing down of emigration and the region's emergence from its isolation.

★★ **Sila Massif.** – North of Catanzaro and several miles inland the high granite plateau of the Sila Massif is covered with Italy's most extensive forest of pine, evergreen oak and beech which alternates with pastures and the calm waters of lonely lakes. The recent agrarian reform called for a reappraisal of this once inaccessible region and today it is being redeveloped for its recreational value in both summer and winter.

To the east of the massif the capital, **San Giovanni in Fiore** grew up around the abbey founded by Joachim of Fiore for his new religious order, stricter than that of the Cistercians. La Badia Fiorense has a remarkable pointed doorway and some Cistercian windows in the apse. The small holiday village and ski resort of Lorica has developed on the indented and wooded shores of the immense **Lake Arvo★**.

★ **Aspromonte.** – The Aspromonte Massif composes the southern tip of Calabria and culminates in a peak of 2 000m – 6 561ft. The Tyrrhenian coast descends in terraces to the shore while the Ionian coast slopes more gently down to the sea. The forest cover includes chestnut trees, oaks and beeches. The massif serves as a catchment area from which radiate deep valleys eroded by fast flowing torrents *(fiumare)*. The wide river beds are dry in summer but may fill up rapidly and the waters become destructive. The S183 between the S112 and Melito di Porto Salvo runs through attractive scenery and affords numerous and often quite astonishing **panoramas★★★**.

★ **The Purple Coast (Costa Viola).** – The most southern part of the Tyrrhenian coast from Gioia Tauro to Villa San Giovanni takes its name from the dark purple of its rocky mountain slopes.

Gioia Tauro. – This seaside resort has a hinterland of centuries old olive groves.

Palmi. – This small town perched high above the sea, has a small fishing harbour and a lovely sandy beach. The **Municipal Museum** *(Casa della Cultura, Via San Giorgio)* has an **ethnographic section★** evoking the life and traditions of Calabria: local costumes, handcrafts, ceramics, etc.

★ **Bagnara Calabra.** – In a picturesque site looking out to sea, Bagnara is the main sword-fishing port.

★ **Scilla.** – This small fishing town stands at the foot of a rock which is said to be the female monster Scylla. According to Homer's *Odyssey* it was on this rock that ships often came to grief having successfully avoided the whirlpool of Charybdis near Taormina on the Sicilian coast. Hence the expression "between Scylla and Charybdis".

Villa San Giovanni. – This is the ferry terminal for Sicily.

★ **Rocca Imperiale.** – *25km – 16 miles to the north of Trebisacce.*
This picturesque village has grown up around a castle built by the Emperor Frederick II.

★ **Tropea.** – Built on the clifftop this ancient small town had its hour of glory under Angevin and Aragonese rule. The lovely Norman style **cathedral★** (cattedrale) has three apses encrusted with polychrome stones.

Altomonte. – *30km – 19 miles to the south of Castrovillari.*
The large market town is dominated by an imposing 14C Angevin cathedral dedicated to **Santa Maria della Consolazione.** The façade is embellished with a doorway and an elegant rose window. Inside there are no aisles and the east end is flat. The fine **tomb★** is that of Filippo Sangineto. The small **museum** beside the church has in addition to a statue of **St Ladislas★** attributed to Simono Martini, several other precious works of art.

Catanzaro. – *Town plan in the current Michelin Red Guide Italia.*
Like numerous other Calabrian towns Catanzaro stands perched on a hilltop, at some distance from the sea, away from the danger of invading forces and malaria-infested waters. The town was founded in the 9C by the Byzantines and it prospered until the end of the 15C thanks to its university and its silk industry, for which it was famous throughout Europe. After having successfully resisted the French troops of Marshal de Lautrec in 1528 the town began to decline in the 17C, partly due to the Black Death and partly due to the numerous earthquakes in the 18 and 19C. However the modern town, traversed by Corso Mazzini, has a certain charm.
The **Villa Trieste★** is a terraced public garden with plenty of shade. The **Church of San Domenico** (or of the Rosary) treasures a very fine altarpiece of the **Madonna of the Rosary★** which is probably the work of the 17C Neapolitan school.

Cosenza. – *Town plan in the current Michelin Red Guide Italia.*
The modern town is overlooked by the old town whose streets and palaces recall the prosperity of the Angevin and Aragonese periods. Cosenza was then considered the artistic and religious capital of Calabria. The 12-13C **cathedral** (Duomo) has recently been restored to its original aspect. Inside is the **tomb★** of Isabella of Aragon, the wife of Philip III, King of France and son of St Louis. Isabella was returning from Tunis, where the sainted king had died, when she fell from her horse at Cosenza and being pregnant died as she gave birth to her child (1271).

Crotone. – *Description p 76.*

Gerace. – *Northwest of Locri on the S 111.*
This was the inland refuge of the people from Locri at the time of the Saracen raids. It was abandoned in favour of the coastal area when the latter was rid of malaria. The **cathedral** (Cattedrale) is one of the largest in Calabria and dates back to the time of the Norman Robert Guiscard (11C). Although remodelled several times it has retained its basilical plan with a nave and two aisles separated by lovely antique piers. Quite near stands the **Church of San Francesco** with a lovely doorway and a 17C **altarpiece★** in polychrome marble.

Locri. – *On the east coast of the Aspromonte Massif.*
This modest seaside resort was founded by the Greeks in the 7C BC. The town was ruled by the severe laws edicted by Zaleucos and was one of the rival cities of Crotone which she defeated during the battle of Sagra. Locri repelled all annexation tentatives by the Syracusan 'tyrants'. After having sided with Hannibal, along with the other towns on the Ionian coast during the Second Punic War, it declined in importance and was destroyed by the Saracens in AD 9C. Most of the town's antiquities can be seen in the museum in Reggio di Calabria. There is an interesting excavation site to the south of the town.

Paola. – St Francis of Paola was born here around 1416. A **monastery** visited by numerous pilgrims stands 2km – 1/2 mile away up the hillside. This important group of buildings includes the basilica with a lovely baroque façade which enshrines the relics of the saint, cloisters and a hermitage hewn out of the rock.

★ **Pentedattilo.** – *10km – 6 miles northwest of Melito di Porto Salvo.*
In a bare and sun-scorched valley this little village regroups its houses at the foot of a gigantic and highly eroded rock which resembles a hand pointing upwards to the sky.

Reggio di Calabria. – *Description p 161.*

Rossano. – *96km – 60 miles northwest of Crotone.*
The town spreads over a hillside clad with olive groves. In the Middle Ages it was the capital of Greek monasticism in the west, where expelled or persecuted Basilian monks came for refuge, living in the cells which can still be seen today. The perfect little Byzantine church **San Marco** dates from this period. The flat east end has three projecting semicircular apses with lovely openings. To the right of the cathedral (Cattedrale) the **Diocesan Museum** (Museo Diocesano) or former archiepiscopal residence has a valuable **Purpureus Codex★**, 6C evangelistary with brightly coloured illuminations.
20km – 12 miles to the west of the town is a small church, the **Patirion**, the only remaining building of a large Basilian monastery. The church has three apses ornamented with blind arcading and inside mosaics portraying various animals.

Serra San Bruno. – Between the Sila and Aspromonte Massifs amidst the Calabrian mountains covered with oak and pinewood **forests★**, this small market town grew up around a **hermitage** founded by St Bruno. The 12C charterhouse *(1km – 1/2 mile from the town)* and the cave which served as hermitage *(4km – 2 1/2 miles to the southwest of the latter)* recall the memory of St Bruno who died in 1101.

Sibari. – *15km – 9 miles south of Trebisacce.*
Founded in the 8C BC in a very fertile plain which was the source of the exceptional prosperity of the ancient city of **Sybaris**. The town was razed in 510 BC by the neighbouring city of Crotone. There is a small **Archaeological Museum** (Museo Archeologico) and an **excavation site** (Scavi) to the south of the town.

Stilo. – *15km – 9 miles west of Monsterace Marina.* On the rocky side of this deep valley this town was the bastion of the Basilian monks and is famous for its Byzantine church, **La Cattolica★**. Small in size but of perfect proportions in the form of a Greek cross, it is in the pure Byzantine style and is roofed with five domes. Inside four ancient columns support the arches and vaulting.

(After photo by T.C.I.)

Stilo – La Cattolica

CAMONICA Valley Lombardy

Michelin map 988 fold 4

Camonica Valley stretches from Lovero to Edolo. Industrial in its lower stretches, more picturesque towards the head, its slopes are guarded by a series of ruined castles. Numerous interesting rock engravings have been discovered in the valleys.

★★ **National Park of Rock Engravings (Parco Nazionale delle Incisioni Rupestri di Naquane)** – *Time: 2 hours. This is reached via Capo di Ponte.*
The rock faces, smoothed by glacial erosion, have many very lively engraved scenes depicting day to day life, religious customs, hunting and fighting methods. They date from the Bronze Age (1 800 BC) to the Iron Age (900-200 BC).

Breno. – The main town of the valley has a 10C castle and two interesting churches the 14-15C Sant'Antonio and San Salvatore.

CAPRAROLA Latium   Pop 4 931

Michelin map 988 fold 25 – 19km – 12 miles southeast of Viterbo

★ **Villa Farnese.** – The villa was built, upon a fortified pentagon basement, between 1559 and 1575 for Cardinal Alessandro Farnese to the designs of Vignola and is a good example of the late 16C Mannerist style. The five storey tall ranges surround a delightful circular inner courtyard. To the left of the entrance hall is Vignola's **spiral staircase★★** which rises majestically through tiers of thirty paired Doric columns, and is decorated with grotesques and landscapes by Antonio Tempesta. The many paintings which decorate several of the rooms are by the Zuccaro brothers, Taddeo (1529-66) and Federico (c 1540-1609) as well as Bertoja (1544-74). These are typical of the refined and sophisticated Mannerist style of the late Italian Renaissance period.

Park. – This 18ha – 44 acre park with its many terraces and monumental fountains, is embellished by a charming **palazzina** also designed by Vignola.

Michelin map 988 fold 27 – Local map overleaf – Access: see the current Michelin Red Guide Italia

Capri, the Island of Dreams, has always enchanted with its situation in close proximity to the Sorrento Peninsula *(see local map p 133)*, the incomparable beauty of its rugged landscape, the mildness of its climate and the luxuriance of its vegetation. Capri captivated two Roman emperors: Angustus exchanged Ischia for Capri and Tiberius spent the latter part of his life here. Since the late 19C the island has attracted numerous celebrities: artists, writers, musicians and actors, in all seasons. Capri is one of the high spots of international tourism.

★MARINA GRANDE

This is the disembarkation port for the northern part of the isle. The white and colourful houses nestling round the bay are framed by spectacular cliffs.

A funicular railway goes to Capri (Piazza Umberto I). There is a bus service to Anacapri with a stop off at Capri (Via Roma).

BOAT TRIPS

★★ **Blue Grotto (Grotta Azzurra).** – *Boats leave from Marina Grande. It is also possible to go by road (8km – 5 miles from Capri).*
The Blue Grotto is the most famous among the many marine caves on the island. The light enters, not directly, but by refraction through the water, giving it a beautiful blue colour.

★★ **Tour of the isle.** – *Leave from Marina Grande.*
Visitors will discover a rugged coastline, pierced with caves and small peaceful creeks, fringed with fantastically shaped reefs and lined with sheer cliffs dipping vertically into the sea. The island is quite small: barely 6km – 4 miles long and 3km – 2 miles wide. The particularly mild climate favours the growth of a varied flora: pine, lentisk, juniper, arbutus, asphodel, myrtle and acanthus.
The boats go in a clockwise direction and the first sight is the **Sea Ox Cave** (Grotta del Bove Marino) which derives its name from the roar of the sea rushing into the cave in stormy weather. Beyond is the headland (Punta del Capo) dominated by **Mount Tiberius** (Monte Tiberio). Once past the impressive cliff known as Tiberius' Leap *(see below)* the headland to the south, Punta di Tragara is fringed by the famous **Faraglioni**, rocky islets carved into fantastic shapes by the waves. The **Arsenal Cave** (Grotta dell'Arsenale) **(BZ)** was used as a nymphaeum during the reign of Tiberius. Continue past the small port of Marina Piccola *(p 68)* to reach the generally lower west coast. The last part of the trip covers the north coast and includes the visit to the Blue Grotto *(see above)*.

★CAPRI

Capri is like a stage setting for an operetta with its small squares, little white houses and its quite Moorish-looking alleyways. Another of its charms is that wild and lonely spots can still be found near crowded and lively scenes.

★ **Piazza Umberto I** (BZ). – This famous piazzetta is the centre of town and the spot where fashionable crowds foregather. The busy narrow side streets, like **Via Le Botteghe★** (BZ 10), are lined with souvenir shops and smart boutiques selling luxury goods.

★ **Cannone Belvedere.** – To reach the belvedere take the **Via Madre Serafina★** (BZ 12), which is almost entirely vaulted and presents another aspect of Capri with its quiet and mysterious, covered and winding alleys interrupted by steps.

★ **Tragara Belvedere.** – *Access by Via Camerelle* (BZ) *and Via Tragara.*
There is a magnificent view of the Faraglioni.

★ **Jupiter's Villa (Villa Jovis).** – This was the residence of the Emperor Tiberius. Excavations have uncovered servants' quarters, the cisterns that supplied the baths and the imperial apartments with a loggia overlooking the sea.
From the esplanade overlooked by a church, there is a lovely **panorama★★** of the whole island.
Take the stairway behind the church to have a view of **Tiberius' Leap★** (Salto di Tiberio) the impressive cliff over which he is said to have had his victims thrown.

The main car parks are indicated on the town plans.

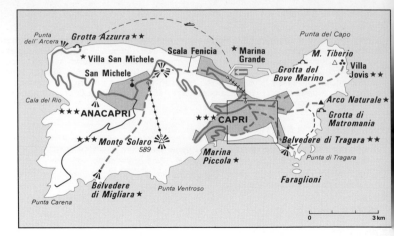

★ **Natural rock arch** (Arco Naturale). – The sea has created this gigantic arch which rises well above sea level. Lower down the **Matromania Cave** is where the Romans venerated the goddess Cybele.

⊘ **Carthusian Monastery of St James** (Certosa di San Giacomo) **(BZ D)** and **Augustus' Gardens** (Giardini Augusto) **(BZ B)**. – This 14C monastery has two cloisters. In the smallest there are Roman statues taken from the nymphaeum of the Blue Grotto.
From Augustus' Gardens there is a beautiful **view★★** of Punta di Tragara and the Faraglioni (p 67). Lower down, **Via Krupp★** **(BZ)**, clinging to the rock face, leads to Marina Piccola.

★ **Marina Piccola.** – There are beautiful small beaches and a haven for fishing boats.

★★★ ANACAPRI

Town plan in the current Michelin Red Guide Italia

Take the Via Roma and a beautiful corniche road to reach Anacapri, a delightful village with shady streets, which is much less crowded than Capri.

★ **Villa San Michele.** – *Access from Piazza della Vittoria.*
⊘ The villa was built at the end of the 19C for the Swedish doctor-writer Axel Munthe (d 1949) who lived there up to 1910 and described the atmosphere of the island in his *Story of San Michele.* The house contains 17 and 18C furniture, copies of antique works and some original Roman sculptures. The pergola at the end of the garden giddily overhangs the sea and provides a splendid **panorama★★★** of Capri, Marina Grande, Mount Tiberius and the Faraglioni.
Just below the villa is a stairway, **Scala Fenicia**, which numbers nearly 800 steps and leads down to the harbour. It was for a long time the only link between the town and its port. This is where Axel Munthe met the old Maria "Porta-Lettere" who delivered the mail although she could not read and who is depicted in his novel.

⊘ **San Michele.** – The fine majolica **pavement★** (1761) represents an earthly paradise after a cartoon by Solimena.

★★★ **Monte Solaro.** – The chairlift swings pleasantly above gardens and terraces brim-
⊘ ming over with a luxuriant vegetation. From the summit there is an unforgettable **panorama★★★** of the whole island and the Bay of Naples as far as the island of Ponza, the Apennines and the mountains of Calabria to the south.

★ **Migliara Belvedere.** – *1 hour on foot Rtn. Go under the chairlift to take Via Caposcuro.* There is a remarkable **view★** of the lighthouse on the headland, Punta Carena and of the dizzily steep cliffs.

CAPUA Campania   Pop 18 904

Michelin map 988 fold 27 – 38km – 24 miles north of Naples

The present town stands quite near to the ancient Roman Capua where Hannibal grew soft in luxury. This small triangular town, enclosed within ramparts, has a certain charm with its narrow alleys, arches, old palaces and churches, many of which are built with material quarried from the numerous Roman ruins.

Cathedral (Duomo). – Although built in the 9C it has been destroyed and rebuilt several times since. The Lombard style campanile incorporates some ancient fragments at its base. The columns of the atrium have lovely **Corinthian capitals,** dating from the 3C. Basilical in plan, the cathedral has numerous works of art.

★ **Campania Museum** (Museo Campano). – *At the corner of Via Duomo and Via Roma.*
⊘ The archaeological section has an astonishing collection of **earth goddesses** dating from the 7C to 1C BC and a charming **mosaic.** The medieval section groups some lovely **sculptures** from the imposing gateway built by the Emperor Frederick II of Hohenstaufen, around 1239 to delimit the boundary of his kingdom.
The lovely **Piazza dei Giudici** is bordered by the baroque church of Sant'Eligio, a loggia surmounted by a Gothic arch and the 16C town hall.

CARRARA Tuscany

Michelin map 988 fold 14

Carrara lies in a smiling basin on the edge of the limestone massif of the Apuan Alps, which is rugged and spectacular and so white it appears to be snow-clad. It is known the world over for its white **marble**, of unequalled texture and purity (except perhaps for that of Paros in Greece). The marble has been quarried since the time of the Romans and Michelangelo used to come in person to choose blocks from which he carved his masterpieces.

Cathedral (Duomo). – The façade, in the Pisan style, is adorned with a delicately carved marble rose-window and flanked by an elegant 13C campanile. Inside there are several interesting 14C statues.

ⓥ **Marble Quarries (Cave di marmo).** – The wild countryside and the gigantic nature of the quarrying operations afford a spectacular sight. The **Fantiscritti Quarries**★★ *(5km – 3 miles to the northeast)* in an impressively wild site and the **Colonnata Quarries**★ *(8.5km – 5 miles to the east)* in a greener setting, are both actively quarried and regularly despatch quantities of marble. **Marina di Carrara** *(7km – 4 miles to the southwest)* is the main port of exportation, where piles of marble blocks are stacked high.

EXCURSION

★ **Sarzana.** – *16km – 10 miles to the north.*
The busy town of Sarzana was once an advanced base of the Republic of Genoa, a rival of Pisa, and its numerous historic buildings bear witness to its past importance. The **cathedral (Cattedrale)** has a marble **altarpiece**★ (1432) delicately carved by Riccomani. In a chapel to the right of the chancel is a phial which is said to have contained the Blood of Christ. In the chapel to the left is a **Crucifixion**★ (1138) the masterpiece of the Roman artist, Guglielmo, probably from Lucca.
ⓥ The **Fortress of Sarzanello**★ (1322) was built on a height to the northeast of the town, by the *condottiere* (leader of mercenary army) from Lucca, Castruccio Castracani. It is a curious example of military architecture with deep moats, massive curtain walls guarded at intervals by round towers. From the top of the keep there is a magnificent **panorama**★★ of the town and the Apennine foothills.

★ CASAMARI Abbey Latium

Michelin map 988 fold 26

ⓥ Casamari Abbey standing in a lonely site was originally Benedictine and was consecrated in 1217 by Pope Honorius III. It was later taken over by the Cistercians who rebuilt the abbey, modelling it on the abbey at Fossanova *(qv)* and in accordance with the rules of austerity and self-sufficiency laid down by St Bernard, the founder of the Cistercian Order.
This is a lovely example of early Italian architecture. Above the entrance porch of the abbey church is a gallery of twinned openings, which served as the abbots' lodging during the Renaissance. The simplicity of the façade is typically Burgundian with a round-headed doorway, the rose window, and rising above all the transept tower.
The interior is spacious, austere and solemn. Built to a Latin cruciform plan, it has a nave and two aisles separated by massive cruciform piers with engaged columns supporting the lofty pointed vaulting. The later canopy seems out of place in the shallow chancel. The apse and arms of the transept are lit by windows with a wheel window above.
On the south side of the church are the cloisters with their twin columns, the well and lovely garden bright with flowers. On the east side, in its traditional position, is the remarkable chapterhouse with delicate ribbed pointed vaulting supported by clustered columns.

★ CASERTA Campania

Michelin map 988 fold 27

Caserta, the Versailles of the Kingdom of Naples, stands in the heart of a fertile plain.

★ **La Reggia.** – This immense palace was begun in 1752 by Vanvitelli for the Bourbon
ⓥ King, Charles III, who dreamed of another Versailles. The palace, one of Italy's most grandiose, was built five floors high on a great rectangular plan 249m – 273yds long and 190m – 208yds wide. The façades, each with a projecting colonnaded centrepiece, are grand but rather monotonous. In all there are some 250 windows. The buildings are arranged around four well proportioned inner courtyards. A magnificent entrance hall leads to the courtyards and the main **staircase**★. The sumptuously decorated apartments are furnished with Empire style pieces.

★ **The park.** – The gardens and park were also designed by Luigi Vanvitelli and his son.
ⓥ The main vista is a succession of fountains and basins, themselves studded with statues. Note in particular the group of Diana and Actaeon by Vanvitelli himself. The focal point is the 78m – 256ft tall monumental **cascade**★★. To the right of the cascade is a picturesque **English garden**★★ created for Maria-Carolina of Austria.

★ **Caserta Vecchia.** – *10km – 6 miles to the north.*
This small town is dominated by the ruins of its 9C castle. The town has a certain charm with its almost entirely abandoned narrow alleyways lined by old buildings with their brown tufa walls.

★ CASTELFRANCO VENETO Venetia Pop 28 793

Michelin map 988 fold 5

Castelfranco is a pleasant citadel surrounded by moats. It has a few prettily arcaded houses and is proud to be the birthplace of the artist Giorgione. In the **cathedral** (Duomo) the visitor can see one of his masterpieces, the **Madonna and Child with Saints★★**.

Born c1477 **Giorgione** died young at the age of 32, no doubt of the Black Death. His twenty or so masterpieces not only influenced Venetian artists (Titian, who was his pupil and doubtless completed several of his master's canvases, Giovanni Bellini in his later works, Sebastiano del Piombo, Palma Vecchio, Savoldo, Dosso Dossi, etc.) but also all of European art with his masterful handling of light.

Giorgione accomplished in his short life-time an admirable synthesis of the human figure and nature, thanks to his flowing draughtsmanship and his knowledge of colour. The cathedral's work is one of his earlier ones and it already shows a preoccupation with achieving this fusion as the figures are disposed on two different planes: the two saints in the shadow of the paved room while the Virgin enthroned on high stands out from the landscape background.

The artist's **birthplace** *(Piazza del Duomo)* is now arranged as a museum.

★ CASTELLAMMARE DI STABIA Campania Pop 68 526

Michelin map 988 fold 27 – Local map p 133

This was the ancient Roman spa town of Stabiae. Occupied successively by the Oscans, the Etruscans, the Samnites and finally the Romans in the 4C, Stabia rebelled against Rome but was crushed by Scylla in the 1C BC. The town was rebuilt in the form of small clusters of houses, while luxury villas for rich patricians spread over the high ground. In the AD 79 eruption of Vesuvius the new town was wiped out along with Herculaneum and Pompeii. The naturalist Pliny the Elder who came by boat to observe the phenomenon at close range perished by asphyxiation.

In the 18C the Bourbons undertook excavations, repaired the port, and built shipyards which are still in use.

★ Antiquarium. – 2 Via Marco Mario.

The finds from the excavations are displayed here and include a magnificent series of **mural paintings** from the villas and some very fine stucco **low-reliefs**.

Roman villas. – *2km – 1 mile to the east by the Gragnano road.*

Ariadne's Villa (Villa di Arianna) was one of the luxurious villas facing the sea with an incomparable view of the bay and of Vesuvius. The architectural refinement of **San Marco's Villa** with its two storeys, was enhanced by gardens and swimming pools. It was in all probability a sumptuous country residence.

★★ CASTELLI ROMANI Latium

Michelin map 988 fold 26

Castelli Romani, or Roman Castles, is the name given to the region of the Alban Hills (Colli Albani), which are of volcanic origin and lie to the southeast of Rome. While anarchy reigned in Rome, the noble families sought refuge in the outlying villages which they fortified. Each of these villages was strategically set on the outer rim of an immense crater, itself pitted with small secondary craters, some of which now contain lakes (Albano and Nemi). Pastures and chestnut groves cover the upper slopes while lower down there are olive groves and vineyards, which produce an excellent wine.

Nowadays the Romans readily leave the capital in summer for the "Castelli" where they find peace, fresh air, good walking country and pleasant country inns.

ROUND TOUR STARTING FROM ROME

122km – 76 miles – allow a whole day

Leave Rome by the Via Appia in the direction of **Castel Gandolfo**, now the Pope's summer residence. It is thought that Castel Gandolfo was built on the site of ancient Alba Longa, the traditional and powerful rival of Rome. Their rivalry led to the famous combat of the Horatios for Rome and the Curiaces for Alba as recounted by the Roman historian Livy (Titus Livius). **Albano Laziale** was built on the site of Domitian's villa. Today the town boasts an attractive church (**Santa Maria della Rotonda★**), large public gardens (**Villa Comunale★**) and not far from Borgo Garibaldi, the so-called tomb of the Horatios and the Curiaces. **Ariccia** has a lovely square designed by Bernini, a palace which belonged to the Chigi banking family and the Church of the Assumption. **Velletri** is a prosperous town lying south of the Alban Hills in the heart of a wine producing region.

Take Via dei Laghi out of Velletri.

This scenic road winds through groves of chestnut and oak trees to reach **Nemi**, a small village in a charming setting on the slopes of the lake of the same name. The road then climbs to **Monte Cavo** (alt 949m – 3 124ft) which was crowned by the Temple of Jupiter. First a monastery and now a hotel occupies the buildings. From the esplanade there is a fine **view★** of the Castelli region with Rome on the horizon. Beyond the attractively set **Rocca di Papa,** facing the Alban lakes, the road passes through **Grottaferrata** with its abbey which was founded in the 11C by Greek monks. **Tusculo** was the fief of the powerful Counts of Tusculum who governed the Castelli region. Next comes **Frascati** pleasantly situated on the slopes facing Rome. It is known for its wines and its 16 and 17C villas, particularly the **Villa Aldobrandini★** set above its terraced gardens.

The road back to Rome passes Cinecittà, the Italian Hollywood.

CERTALDO Tuscany   Pop 15 920

Michelin map 988 fold 14

It was in this village, in the wooded Elsa Valley, that **Giovanni Boccaccio** (1312-75) spent the last years of his life. Along with Dante and Petrarch, he was one of the three great Italian writers. The son of a merchant, he was brought up at the Angevin court in Naples and represented the new urbane bourgeois of the Renaissance with his taste for ironic analysis of different types of character dominated by a variety of ever-changing passions. In his main work **Decameron** (ten days) he describes in a rhythmic, limpid style the accounts of ten young people exiled from Florence because of the plague. He praises intelligence and love and their victory over baseness and routine.

In the upper town visit **Boccaccio's House**, now transformed into a museum, the Church of San Jacopo where the writer is buried and the **Palazzo Pretorio**, which was rebuilt in the 16C.

CERVETERI Latium   Pop 15 767

Michelin map 988 fold 25

The ancient Caere was a powerful Etruscan centre, which stood on an eminence to the east of the present town of Cerveteri. Caere attained great prosperity in the 7 and 6C BC and was renowned as a great cultural and religious centre. In the 4C BC Caere began to decline. It was only at the beginning of the 20C that excavation work began on this site. Most of the finds are now displayed in the Villa Giulia (p 175) in Rome.

The admirable necropolis which is to be found 2km – 1 mile to the north of Cerveteri testifies to the Etruscans belief in an afterlife. The **Banditaccia Necropolis★★** is laid out like a city with numerous tumuli lining a main street. The site is pervaded by a great sense of peace. The tombs generally dating from the 7C BC, add a strange note to the scene. These conical earth mounds, often grass covered, rest on a stone base, which is sometimes decorated with mouldings, with the burial chambers underneath. Other tombs consist of underground burial chambers reached through simply decorated doors. A vestibule leads into the burial chambers which often contain two funeral beds placed side by side: one is adorned with a small column if the deceased was a man (the breadwinner) and the other with a small canopy in the case of a woman (guardian of the home).

One of the tombs without a tumulus, is the **Tomb of the Reliefs★★** with its painted stucco low-reliefs giving a realistic picture of everyday Etruscan life.

CHIAVENNA Lombardy   Pop 7 611

Michelin map 988 fold 3 or 218 fold 14

In this region of wild valleys, Chiavenna, is the key (chiave) to the Splügen and Maloja transalpine passes between Italy and Switzerland.

The Romanesque **Collegiate Church of St Lawrence** (San Lorenzo) was rebuilt in the 16C following a fire. The works of art include a canvas by Pietro Ligari. The **baptistry** contains a Romanesque **baptismal basin★** (1156) with interesting low-reliefs. Outstanding among the items of the **treasure** is a lovely 12C binding for an evangelistary.

The rock, **Il Paradiso**, is a **botanical and archaeological garden** which affords lovely **views★** of the town's setting.

EXCURSION

★★**Splügen Pass Road** (Passo dello Spluga). – *30km – 19 miles from Chiavenna to the pass.*

This road is one of the boldest and most spectacular in the Alps. The **Campodolcino-Pianazzo section★★★** is spectacular as it climbs the sheer mountain side in tight hairpin bends.

CHIETI Abruzzi   Pop 55 733

Michelin map 988 fold 27 – Town plan in the current Michelin Red Guide Italia

Chieti is built on the summit of a hill planted with olive trees and offers varied panoramas. Corso Marrucino is the town's busiest street.

Abruzzi Archaeological Museum (Museo Archeologico degli Abruzzi). – The museum is housed in a building set in lovely **gardens★** (Villa Comunale). There are numerous works which were produced locally from the 6C BC to AD 4C. Note in particular the marble statue of Hercules, discovered at Alba Fucens (qv), a portrait of Sylla, a fine bronze of Hercules and especially the famous **Warrior of Capestrano★** a strange 6C BC limestone statue, and several rare examples of Picenum art. The Picenes occupied the central part of the Italian peninsula prior to the Romans.

Roman remains. – Three adjoining and minute **temples** (Templi Romani) were discovered in 1935 near the post office and Corso Marrucino. A little further to the east are water tanks cut out of the hillside intended to supply the baths which are also fairly well preserved.

The times indicated in this guide
when given with the distance allow one to enjoy the scenery
when given for sightseeing are intended to give an idea
of the possible length or brevity of a visit.

CHIUSI Tuscany   Pop 9 277

Michelin map 988 fold 15

Standing on a hill, covered with olive groves, Chiusi is today a quiet and hospitable little town. It was once one of the twelve sovereign cities of Etruria.

★ **Etruscan Museum (Museo Etrusco).** – *Via Porsenna*. The museum regroups the various objects from the burial grounds in the neighbourhood: sarcophagi, rounded tombstones *(cippi)*, alabaster and stone funerary urns, burial urns *(canopae)* in the shape of heads, clay ex-votos as well as a variety of utensils, vases, lamps and jewellery. The objects all display the Etruscan taste for fantasy and realism.
If you have a car you may be accompanied by the museum custodian to some of the remaining tombs 3km – 2 miles from Chiusi. The most interesting, the **Tomba della Scimmia** (the Monkey Tomb), consists of four decorated chambers and dates from the 5C BC.

★★ CINQUE TERRE Liguria

Michelin map 988 fold 13 – Local map p 164

Lying northwest of the Gulf of La Spezia, the Cinque Terre (Five Lands) even today is an isolated region with no good access road. This rugged coast is wild but hospitable, with its vineyards and fishing villages where the people remain strongly attached to their old customs and traditions.

★★ **Vernazza.** – *Access by train or boat only.*
This is the most attractive village with its tall colourful houses and its church clustered together at the head of a well sheltered cove.

(Aerfoto/Artephot)

The Cinque Terre – Manarola

★ **Manarola.** – This fishing village with its small 14C church is set in a landscape of terraced vineyards. Starting from the station there is a splendid **walk★★** *(1/4 hour on foot)* which offers lovely views of the coast and the other villages.

★ **Riomaggiore.** – *Take the branch road off the La Spezia-Manarola road.*
The old houses of this medieval village lie in a narrow valley. This tiny fishing village stands backed up against the strange black and well stratified rocks which are so typical of the region.

★ CIVIDALE DEL FRIULI Friuli - Venezia Giulia   Pop 11 162

Michelin map 988 fold 6 – 17km – 11 miles to the northeast of Udine

The ancient Forum Julii gave the town its modern name. It is superbly set overlooking the River Natisone. It was for long independent and became the residence of the Patriarchs of Aquileia. From the 15C onward it belonged to Venice. Since the 1976 earthquake, Cividale has been rebuilt.

Cathedral (Duomo). – It was extensively rebuilt in the 16C in the Renaissance style by Piero Lombardo (1435-1515) but retains some Gothic features on the façade and in the interior. The high altar has a 12C Veneto-Byzantine silver-gilt altarpiece. The small **museum** of Lombard art (opens off the south aisle) contains numerous valuable items: the octagonal baptismal font of the Patriarch Callisto, rebuilt using Byzantine fragments and the 8C "altar" of Duke Ratchis in marble with carved sides depicting scenes from the Life of Christ.

★ Archaeological Museum (Museo Archeologico Nazionale). – *To the left of the cathedral.*
⊙ The museum has a collection of silver and gold pieces, representative of 7C Lombard art, including a solid gold cross which belonged to Gisulph, a carved and encrusted ivory plaque which once belonged to Duke Orso (9C). The collection of medieval manuscripts includes a 13C psalter adorned with miniatures which was known as St Elizabeth's.

★★ Tempietto. – *Near the Piazza San Biagio.*
⊙ This elegant 8C Lombard building is a square chamber with quadripartite vaulting and admirable Lombard **decoration** of friezes and stylised stuccos. It is a unique example of the architecture of this period.

CIVITAVECCHIA Latium   Pop 50 610

Michelin map 988 fold 25

Civitavecchia, the Roman Centumcellae, has been the port of Rome since the reign of Trajan and now handles maritime traffic with Sardinia. The port is guarded by the Fort of Michelangelo, a massive Renaissance construction which was begun by Bramante, continued by Sangallo the Younger and Bernini and completed by Michelangelo in 1557. Henri Beyle, alias Stendhal (1783-1842), was appointed Consul at Civitavecchia in 1831. Stendhal took advantage of his moments of leisure to write numerous works, including *The Charterhouse of Parma* (1839).

⊙ **National Archaeological Museum (Museo Nazionale Archeologico).** – *2A, Largo Plebiscito.*
The museum has Etruscan and Roman collections composed of finds from local sites. There is an astonishing collection of Roman anchors.

⊙ **Trajan's Baths (Terme di Traiano** or **Terme Taurine).** – *3km – 2 miles to the northeast.*
There are two groups: the first (to the west) dates from the Republican period and the second, the better conserved, was built by Trajan's successor, the Emperor Hadrian.

COMACCHIO Emilia Romagna   Pop 21 251

Michelin map 988 fold 15

Comacchio is built on sand and water and in many ways it resembles Chioggia. The main activity of the townspeople is eel fishing. Its brightly coloured fishermen's houses, its canals spanned by some curious bridges, including an unusual triple bridge, and the fishing boats all lend it a special charm.

★ Polesina. – This area around the Po delta was once a malaria-infested marshy district. Land reclamation and drainage have since turned it into a fertile agricultural area. The Chioggia to Ravenna road *(90km – 56 miles)* traverses these flat expanses as they reach away to the horizon, interrupted only by large solitary farms. Clumps of poplars and umbrella pines add touches of colour, especially in spring, to the monotony of this countryside where eel fishing is still common on the numerous canals which criss-cross the area. At **Mesola** *(28km – 17 miles to the north of Comacchio)* there is a stout brick castle dating from 1583 which once belonged to the Este family. In the southern part of the area the **Valli di Comacchio,** Italy's most important zone of lagoons, has its own special melancholy beauty.

★ COMO Lombardy   Pop 92 677

Michelin map 988 fold 3 or 219 folds 8 and 9 – Local map p 105 – Town plan in the current Michelin Red Guide Italia

The city was already prosperous under the Romans but reached its zenith in the 11C. Destroyed by the Milanese in 1127 it was rebuilt by the Emperor Frederick Barbarossa and from 1355 onwards followed the fortunes of Milan.
The **maestri comacini** (master masons), known as early as the 7C, were masons, builders and sculptors who spread the Lombard style *(p 27)* throughout Italy and Europe. Their name would appear to mean simply associated masons *(co-macini).*

★★ Cathedral (Duomo). – Begun in the late 14C it was completed during the Renaissance and crowned in the 18C by an elegant dome by the Turin architect, Juvara. It has a remarkable **façade★★** which was richly decorated from 1484 onwards by the **Rodari brothers,** who also worked on the **north door,** known as the Porta della Rana because of the frog *(rana)* carving on one of the pillars. They were also responsible for the exquisitely delicate **south door.**
The **interior★,** full of solemn splendour, displays Gothic architecture and Renaissance decoration. In addition to the curious banners, hung between the pillars, and the magnificent 16-17C **tapestries★** there are numerous works of art including canvases by B. Luini **(Virgin and Child with Saints★),** G. Ferrari as well as a **Descent from the Cross★** (1498) carved by Tommaso Rodari.
Adjoining the façade is the **Broletto★★,** or 13C town hall, with an arcade at street level and a lovely storey of triple arched windows above.

★ Church of San Fedele. – In the heart of the picturesque old quarter, this church in the Romanesque Lombard style, has an unusual doorway at the apse adorned with lovely low-reliefs. The nave and two aisles are terminated by a splendid polygonal Romanesque **chancel★** with radiating chapels. The whole east end is graced by two storeys of arcading.

COMO ★

★ **Basilica of Sant'Abbondio.** – This masterpiece of Romanesque Lombard architecture was consecrated in 1093. The noble but severe **façade**★ has a lovely doorway. The nave and four aisles are separated by elegant columns. The remarkable 14C **frescoes**★ evoke the Life of Christ.

⊙ **Villa Olmo.** – *3km – 2 miles to the north by the S 35 and then the S 340 to the right.* This is a large neo-classical building dating from the late 18C, with a small theatre and gardens, from where there is a lovely **view**★ of Como in its lakeside setting.

CONEGLIANO Venetia   Pop 36 032

Michelin map 𝟵𝟴𝟴 fold 5 – 28km – 17 miles north of Treviso

Conegliano is surrounded by pleasant hills clad with orchards and vineyards, which produce an excellent white wine. This was the birthplace of **Cima da Conegliano** (1459-1518), an admirer of Giovanni Bellini, and superb colourist who introduced idealised
⊙ landscapes bathed in a crystal-clear light to his works. The **cathedral** (Duomo) has a
⊙ lovely **Holy Conversation**★ by this artist. The **castle** houses two small **museums** and provides a lovely **panorama**★ of the town and its setting. Next to the cathedral the walls of the **Scuola dei Battuti** are decorated with 15 and 16C **frescoes**★ in both the Venetian and Lombard styles.

★★★ CORTINA D'AMPEZZO Venetia   Pop 7 815

Michelin map 𝟵𝟴𝟴 fold 5 – Local map p 79 – Town plan in the current Michelin Red Guide Italia

Cortina, the capital of the Dolomites *(qv),* is a winter sports and summer resort with a world wide reputation. Set in the heart of the Dolomites Cortina makes a good excursion centre for discovering the magnificent **mountain scenery**★★★.

★★★ **Tondi di Faloria.** – From the summit there is a grand panorama. There are excellent
⊙ ski slopes.

★★★ **Tofana di Mezzo.** – A cable-car takes you up to 3 244m – 10 743ft, from where
⊙ there is a superb panorama over the surrounding mountains.

★★ **Pocol Belvedere.** – Lying to the southwest, this viewpoint affords a lovely view of
⊙ Cortina which is best at sunset.

★ CORTONA Tuscany   Pop 22 669

Michelin map 𝟵𝟴𝟴 fold 15 – Town plan in the current Michelin Red Guide Italia

The quiet town of Cortona, with its girdle of medieval ramparts, clings to the steep slopes of a hill clad with olive groves. It affords good views as far as Lake Trasimeno. As early as the 14C Cortona attracted artists including the Sienese, Fra Angelico. Cortona was the birthplace of **Luca Signorelli** (1450-1523), who with his dramatic temperament and sculptural modelling, was the precursor of Michelangelo; he died as a result of a fall from scaffolding when he was decorating the Villa Passerini to the east of Cortona. In the 16C Cortona gave France an architect, Domenico Bernabei, known as **Il Boccadoro** (Mouth of Gold) who designed Paris' Hôtel de Ville for François I. **Pietro da Cortona** (1596-1669), painter and architect with a lively imagination was one of the masters of Roman baroque and a talented decorative painter.

SIGHTS

Piazza del Duomo, close up against the ramparts, affords a lovely view over the valley. The Romanesque **cathedral** (Duomo) was remodelled at the Renaissance.

★★ **Diocesan Museum** (Museo Diocesano). – *Opposite the Cathedral.*
⊙ This former church houses a remarkable collection of paintings: a beautiful **Annunciation** and *Madonna and Saints* by Fra Angelico; works from the Sienese school by Duccio, Pietro Lorenzetti and Sassetta; an excellent group of works by **Signorelli**; and a remarkable **Ecstasy of St Margaret** by the Bolognese artist, G.M. Crespi (1665-1747). The lovely 2C Roman sarcophagus has low-reliefs depicting the story of Bacchus.

Praetorian Palace (Palazzo Pretorio). – It was built in the 13C and remodelled later. The façade, on the right, covered with coats of arms, is 13C Gothic, but that which
⊙ faces the Piazza Signorelli, dates from the 17C. Inside the **Museum of the Etruscan Academy**★ regroups, in addition to Etruscan exhibits, Roman, Egyptian, medieval and Renaissance items. Among the Etruscan objects note a curious 5C BC bronze oil lamp, with sixteen burners in the human form.

St Margaret's Church (Santa Margherita). – This enshrines the lovely Gothic **tomb**★ (1362) of the saint.

St Francis' Church (San Francesco). – *At the junction of Via G. Maffei and Via Berrettini.* This church was begun in 1245 to the designs of Brother Elias, St Francis' companion who directed the building operations at Assisi. This Gothic church, remodelled in the 17C, has several works of art including an Annunciation by Pietro da Cortona.

St Dominic's Church (San Domenico). – *Largo Beato Angelico.* In the south apse is a Madonna with angels and saints by Luca Signorelli, a triptych of the Coronation of the Virgin by Lorenzo di Niccolò at the high altar and a fresco attributed to Fra Angelico.

★ Church of Santa Maria del Calcinaio. – *3km – 2 miles to the west.*
Santa Maria, built between 1485 and 1513 by Francesco di Giorgio Martini, strongly resembles the work of Brunelleschi. It is remarkable for the grace and harmony of its design and its well balanced proportions. In the oculus of the façade is a remarkable stained glass window (1516) designed by **Guillaume de Marcillat** (1467-1529). Born at La Châtre in Berry this Dominican monk's skill with stained glass led to his receiving a papal summons from Julius II to work at the Vatican alongside Raphael and Michelangelo. He settled at Arezzo *(qv)*. Vasari said of his work "These are not stained glass windows but marvels fallen from Heaven for the consolation of men".
A short distance westwards is the so-called Tomb of Pythagoras, really a 4C circular Etruscan sepulchre.

★ # CREMONA Lombardy
Pop 77 604

Michelin map 988 folds 13 and 14

Cremona is an important agricultural market town in the heart of a fertile agricultural region. Town life centres on Piazza Roma. The original Gallic settlement became a Latin city before emerging as an independent commune in the Middle Ages. It suffered from the Guelph and Ghibelline troubles of the period. In 1334 the town came under Visconti rule and was united with the Duchy of Milan in the 15C. At the Renaissance the town was the centre of a brilliant artistic movement. In the 18 and 19C the French and Austrians fought for supremacy over Cremona until the Risorgimento *(qv)*.
From the late 16C the stringed-instrument makers of Cremona gained a reputation as violin and cello makers. The Amati and Guarnieri families, and especially **Antonio Stradivarius**, with their knowledge and incomparable skill produced outstanding instruments of unequalled tonal quality. The International School of Violin Making in Piazza Marconi (**BZ 19**) carries on this tradition. The Cremonese composer **Claudio Monteverdi** (1567-1643) created modern opera with his *Orfeo* and *The Return of Ulysses to his Country*.

★★**PIAZZA DEL COMUNE** (**BZ 7**) *time: 1 hour*

This is one of the finest squares in Italy.

★★**Torrazzo** (**BZ**). – The admirable late 13C campanile is linked to the cathedral by a Renaissance gallery. Its massive form is elegantly crowned by an octagonal 14C storey. From the top (112m – 367ft) there is a lovely **view★** over the town.

★★**Cathedral (Duomo)** (**BZ**). – This magnificent Lombard building was begun in the Romanesque and completed in the Gothic style (1107 to 1332). The richly decorated white marble façade is preceded by a porch. Numerous decorative features were later additions, namely the frieze by Antelami and followers, the large 13C rose window and the four statue-columns of the central doorway.

CREMONA

Campi (Corso)	**BZ**	Geromini (Via Felice)	**BY** 9
Cavour (Piazza)	**BZ** 6	Ghinaglia (Via F.)	**AY** 12
Garibaldi (Corso)	**AYZ**	Ghisleri (Via A.)	**BY** 13
Matteotti (Corso)	**BYZ**	Libertà (Piazza della)	**BY** 14
		Mantova (Via)	**BY** 17
Aselli (Via)	**BYZ** 2	Manzoni (Via)	**BY** 18
Boccaccino (Via)	**BZ** 3	Marconi (Piazza)	**BZ** 19
Cadorna (Piazza L.)	**AZ** 4	Marmolada (Via)	**BZ** 22
Comune (Piazza del)	**BZ** 7	Mazzini (Corso)	**BZ** 23
		Melone (Via Altobello)	**BZ** 24
		Monteverdi (Via Claudio)	**BZ** 27
		Novati (Via)	**BZ** 28
		Risorgimento (Piazza)	**AY** 29
		S. Maria in Betlem (Via)	**AY** 32
		S. Rocco (Via)	**BZ** 33
		Spalato (Via)	**AY** 35
		Stradivari (Via)	**BZ** 37
		Tofane (Via)	**BZ** 39
		Ugolani Dati (Via)	**BY** 40
		Vacchelli (Corso)	**BZ** 42
		Verdi (Via)	**BZ** 43
		Vittorio Emanuele II (Corso)	**AZ** 45
		4 Novembre (Piazza)	**BZ** 46
		20 Settembre (Corso)	**BZ** 48

The spacious **interior** is decorated with **frescoes**★ by the Cremona school (B. Boccaccino, the Campi, the Bembo, Romanino da Brescia, Pordenone and Gatti). Note also the lovely 17C Brussels **tapestries**★ and at the entrance to the chancel the **high-reliefs**★★ by Amadeo, the architect-sculptor of the Carthusian Monastery at Pavia.

★ **Baptistry** (BZ L). – This lovely octagonal building, preceded by a Lombard porch and decorated with a gallery, was remodelled during the Renaissance.

⊙ **Town Hall** (Palazzo Comunale) (BZ H). – This 13C palace was remodelled at a later date. Inside, on display, are four famous **violins** by Cremonese instrument-makers (Stradivarius, Guarnieri and the Amati family).
To the left of the palace is the lovely 13C **Loggia dei Militi** (BZ K).

ADDITIONAL SIGHTS

★ **Municipal Museum** (Museo Civico) (ABY M). – Installed in a 16C palace this museum
⊙ has several different sections, notably the **picture gallery** with works of the Cremona school, minor arts (French **ivories**), the **treasure from the cathedral** and a **Stradivarius museum**.

Renaissance Architecture. – The town is embellished with numerous Renaissance palaces including the **Palazzo Fodri**★ (BZ D), the **Palazzo Stanga** (AY E), the **Palazzo Raimondi** (AY F) as well as churches like **Sant'Agostino** (AZ B) rich in works of art: **portraits**★ of Francesco Sforza and his wife by Bonifacio Bembo and an **altarpiece**★ by Perugino.
On the Casalmaggiore road *(2km – 1 mile out of town by no ③ on the town plan)* is the **Church of San Sigismondo** with its lavishly decorated **interior**★. The frescoes are by the 16C Cremona school (Campi, Gatti and Boccaccino).

CROTONE Calabria   Pop 60 798

Michelin map 🔲🔲🔲 fold 40

The ancient Croton was an Achaean colony of Magna Graecia, founded in 710 BC and celebrated in antiquity for its riches, the beauty of its women and the prowess of its athletes, such as Milo of Crotone, so admired by Virgil. Around 532 BC Pythagoras founded several religious communities which devoted themselves to the study of mathematics and which once they had become too powerful were expelled northwards towards Metapontum (present day Metaponto). The rival city of Locari defeated Croton in the mid-6C BC which in turn defeated its other rival Sybaris. The city welcomed Hannibal during the Second Punic War before being conquered by Rome. Crotone is today a prosperous seaport and industrial centre as well as a popular holiday resort.

⊙ **Archaeological Museum** (Museo Archeologico). – *Via Risorgimento*. The archaeological collections regroup local finds from other colonies of Magna Graecia and include displays of ceramics, terracottas, coins and sculpture.

EXCURSIONS

Cape Colonna (Capo Colonna). – *40km – 25 miles to the south*.
At the extremity of this promontory stands a Doric column, the last remaining vestige of an enormous temple dedicated to Hera Lucinia (6 or 5C BC).

★ **Santa Severina.** – *34km – 21 miles to the northwest*.
The 13C cathedral has a remarkable 8C circular **baptistry**★ which shows a strong Byzantine influence. Visit also the Norman Castle.

★ CUMAE (CUMA) Campania

Michelin map 🔲🔲🔲 fold 27 – 7km – 4 miles north of Pozzuoli – Local map p 132

Cumae, one of the oldest Greek colonies, was founded in the 8C BC. The city soon dominated the whole Phlegrean area *(p 131)* including Naples, leaving an important Hellenic heritage. Its splendour was at its height under the tyrant Aristodemus. Captured by the Romans in 334 BC, decline then set in and continued until AD 915 when it was pillaged by the Saracens.
The ancient city of Cumae stands in a serene and solemn setting near the sea. You can visit the ruins of the upper town – the acropolis – where most of the temples stood. In the area of the lower town, excavations have revealed the remains of an amphitheatre, a temple dedicated to the Capitoline Triad (Jupiter, Juno and Minerva) and baths.

★★ **Acropolis.** – The acropolis is built on a hill of volcanic material (lava and tufa) in lovely
⊙ surroundings. It is reached by an alley bordered with laurels. After the vaulted passageway, the path to the left leads to the **Sibyl's Cave**★ (Antro della Sibilla), one of the most venerated spots of antiquity. Here the Sibyl rendered her oracles. The cave was hollowed out of the rock by the Greeks in the 6 or 5C BC and it is rectangular in shape with three small niches.
Take the stairway up to the sacred way (Via Sacra). From the belvedere there is a good **view**★ of the sea. Some finds from the excavations are on display. On the right are the remains of the **Temple of Apollo** (Tempio di Apollo) which was later transformed into a Christian church. Further on is the **Temple of Jupiter** (Tempio di Giove) which was also transformed by the early Christians. Note in the centre a large font and several Christian tombs near the sanctuary.

★ **Arco Felice.** – *Take the minor road in the direction of Naples*.
This triumphal arch was erected on the Domitian Way (Via Domitiana) of which there are still traces of the paved way.

Michelin map 988 folds 4 and 5

This rugged and grandiose limestone massif displays many colours, some harsh, some soft, which change with the light. The massif makes a splendid haunt for mountaineers and skiers. For the ordinary holidaymaker the Dolomites provide excellent roads, good paths, immense panoramas and a large choice of hotels.

GEOGRAPHICAL NOTES

The Dolomites are bounded roughly by the Adige River and its tributary, the Isarco, in the west, the Brenta Massif in the south, the Piave Valley in the east and the Rienza (Val Pusteria) in the north. Most of the range is formed of limestone rocks called "dolomites" after a French geologist, Gratet de Dolomieu, who was the first to study their formation at the end of the 18C. A few nuclei of volcanic rock are to be found in the centre and west and schists in the southwest (Cima d'Asta). The nature of the soil and the effect of erosion have created a distinctive landscape: steep, rugged rocks take the form of towers, belfries or domes with gentler slopes at their feet covered with alpine pastures, conifers or crops. The steepness of the upper slopes prevented the formation of glaciers.

The various massifs. – To the southeast rise Monte Pelmo (3 168m – 10 394ft) and Monte Civetta (3 220m – 10 564ft) while to the south, near the Cima della Vezzana, the Pale di San Martino, which are deeply fissured, are divided into three chains separated by a high plateau. The Massifs of the Latemar (2 842m – 9 324ft) and the Catinaccio (2 981m – 9 780ft), from which rise the well known Towers of Vaiolet (Torri del Vaiolet), enclosing the pass, Passo di Costalunga. To the north of the latter, are the Sasso Lungo and the vast Sella Massif (Gruppo di Sella), which is skirted by a road. To the east, the chief summits in the Cortina Dolomites are the Tofano di Mezzo, the Punta Sorapiss and Monte Cristallo. Finally in the heart of the range stands the formidable **Marmolada Massif** (Gruppo della Marmolada), which rises to the highest point in the Dolomites.

The **Cadore** district prolongs the Dolomites to the east and southeast of Cortina; its axis is the Piave Valley and its capital Pieve di Cadore. Here the highest summits are Antelao (3 262m – 10 705ft) and the triple peak Tre Cime di Lavaredo (2 998m – 9 836ft) *(illustration p 15).*

Fauna and flora. – Birds and animals are those of the Alps: royal eagle, chamois, deer, hawks, and woodcock in the coniferous forests. In spring the prairies are covered with brightly coloured flowers: edelweiss, deep blue gentian, white or mauve crocus, six-petalled anemones, starry white saxifrage or five-petalled rock flowers, fringed mauve soldanellas and purplish pink Turk's Cap lilies. Market gardens and vineyards flourish in valleys dotted with large farmhouses with wooden balconies.

Sightseeing. – The map pp 78-79, in addition to locating the towns and sites described in the guide, indicates other beauty spots in small black type.

★★★ DOLOMITE ROAD

From Bolzano to Cortina *210km – 131 miles – allow 2 days*

The main touring route in the Dolomites is the great Dolomite Road, which is a wonderful and world famous example of road engineering, linking Bolzano and Cortina d'Ampezzo as it follows the central depression of the massif. It runs through a landscape which is always majestic and varied. The road was already used during the Renaissance by merchants travelling from Venice to Germany. It began to be modernised in 1895, was used for military purposes in 1915-18 and was improved after the First World War.

★ **Bolzano.** – *Description p 61.*

★ **Ega Valley Gorge** (Valle d'Ega). – This narrow gorge, with pink sandstone walls, is guarded by **Cornedo Castle.**

★ **Nova Levante.** – Catinaccio Massif rises up behind this attractive village with its bulbous belfry and attractive houses overlooking the Ega. It is now a popular holiday resort.

★★ **Lake Carezza** (Lago di Carezza or Karer See). – This tiny lake is set in a dark expanse of fir trees with the peaks of the Latemar and the Catinaccio Massifs in the background.

★ **Costalunga Pass** (Passo di Costalunga). – From this pass on the Dolomite Road, also called the Passo di Carezza, there is a **view**★ over the Catinaccio on one side and the Latemar on the other.

★ **Vigo di Fassa.** – This resort, very well situated in the famous Val di Farsa, is a mountaineering and excursion centre in the Catinaccio Massif *(cable-car).*

★★ **Canazei.** – Canazei lies deep in the heart of the massif, framed between the Catinaccio, the Towers of Vaiolet (Torri del Vaiolet), the Sella Massif and the Marmolada. This is the usual base for most of the excursions and difficult climbs in the Marmolada range. The church has a shingle roof, a bulbous belfry and a painted façade.

At Canazei turn right into the S 641.

This road affords very fine **views**★ of the Marmolada range and its glacier. On coming out of a long tunnel **Lake Fedaia**★ (Lago di Fedaia) suddenly appears dominated by the Marmolada range.

★★ **Marmolada Massif** (Gruppo della Marmolada). – This is the highest massif in the Dolomites and has its own glacier and very fast ski-runs.

The **cable-car** starting from Malga Ciapela goes up to 3 265m – 10 712ft from where there are admirable **panoramas**★★★ of the Cortina peaks (Tofano and Cristallo), the sugar loaf forms of Sasso Lungo, the enormous tabular mass of the Sella Massif and in the background the summits of the Austrian Alps including the Grossglockner.

Adige/Etsch
Alpe di Siusi/Seiseralm
Badia (Val)/Gadertal
Bolzano/Bozen
Braies (Lago di)/Pragser Wildsee
Bressanone/Brixen
Brunico/Bruneck
Campo Fiscalino/Fischleinboden
Carezza (Lago di)/Karersee
Catinaccio/Rosengarten

Cervina (Punta)/Hirzerspitze
Chiusa/Klausen
Cornedo/Karneid
Corvara in Badia/Kurfar
Costalunga (Passo di)/Karerpass
Croda Rossa/Hohe Geisel
Dobbiaco/Toblach
Ega (Val d')/Eggental
Gadera/Gaderbach
Gardena (Passo di)/Grödnerjoch

Return to Canazei then after 5.5km – 4 miles turn left.

The road follows the **Gardena Valley★★★** (Val Gardena), one of the most famous valleys in the Dolomites for its beauty, its winter sports facilities and its role as an excursion centre in summer. Its slopes are covered with coniferous forests, waterfalls and typical mountain dwellings.

The inhabitants still speak the Ladin dialect and maintain their traditional costumes and customs. They are skilful wood-workers.

★★★ **Sella Pass** (Passo di Sella). – Linking the Val di Fassa and Val Gardena this pass offers one of the most extensive and most characteristic **panoramas★★★** in the Dolomites, including the Sella, Sasso Lungo and Marmolada Massifs.

★ **Selva di Val Gardena.** – This resort is situated at the foot of the impressive vertical mass of the Sella Massif. This is an active craft centre: wooden objects, pewterware and enamels. In the **church** there is a Flamboyant Gothic **altarpiece★**.

★★ **Ortisei.** – Halfway up the valley is the linear settlement of Ortisei, amidst its fir trees. A ⊙ **cable-car** takes you up to **Alpe di Siusi★★**, a winter sports resort and excursion centre in summer. This overlooks the Isarco and Gardena Valleys.

Return to the Dolomite Road.

★★★ **Pordoi Pass** (Passo Pordoi). – This, the highest (2 239m – 7 346ft) pass on the Dolomite Road, passes between huge blocks of rock with vertical sides and shorn-off tops.

Falzarego Pass (Passo di Falzarego). – This wild and desolate pass offers a good view of the Marmolada and its glacier.

★★★ **Cortina d'Ampezzo and excursions.** – *Description p 74.*

Gardena (Val)/Grödnertal
Isarco/Eisack
Lavaredo (Tre Cime di)/Drei Zinnen
le Odle/Geislerspitze
Nova Levante/Welschnofen
Ortisei/St-Ulrich
Plan de Corones/Kronplatz
Plose (Cima d.)/Plose Bühel
Rienza/Rienz
Riscone/Reischach
San Candido/Innichen

San Cassiano (Cima)/Kassianspitze
San Giacomo (Cima)/Jakobspitze
Sta-Cristina/St-Christina
Sarentina (Valle)/Sarntal
Sasso Lungo/Langkofel
Sella (Passo di)/Sellajoch
Selva in Val Gardena/Wolkenstein in Gardena
Sesto (Val di)/Sextental
Talvera/Talfer
Tre Scarperi (Cima)/Dreischusterspitze
Vipiteno/Sterzing

OTHER TOWNS AND SIGHTS

★★ **Lake Braies** (Lago di Braies). – Alt 1 495m – 4 905ft. The lake appears, encircled by grim mountains. Its winding banks fringe the emerald green and crystal clear waters.

★★ **Misurina Lake** (Lago di Misurina). – This popular lake in rolling parkland is overlooked to ⊙ the north by the Tre Cime di Lavaredo. A private toll road leads through larch plantations to Dantesque **scenery★★★** of jumbled, jagged rocks.

★ **Sesto Valley** (Valle di Sesto). – This attractive valley has numerous Tyrolean style villages, the main one being **Sesto★**. A winding road branches southwards following the Fiscalino Valley to end at **Campo Fiscalino★★** set in a grandiose setting, a mountain cirque encircled by jagged mountain peaks.
San Candido★ stands where the Sesto Valley rejoins the main valley, Val Pusteria, not far from the Austrian border. This town has three interesting churches: one in the mountain style with shingle roof and bulbous belfry, another in the Austrian baroque style and the third, a Romanesque one.

★ **Cordevole Valley** (Valle del Cordevole). – The road from Caprile to Bulluno is an extremely picturesque one with its perched villages and impressive gorges. **Alleghe** on the bank of a pale green **lake★** is a good excursion centre.

★ **San Martino di Castrozza**. – In its superb setting, San Martino is an excellent excursion centre with a strong cultural tradition, especially for the wearing of traditional costumes.

★ **Bressanone**. – *Description p 64.*

★ **Chiusa**. – Charming Tyrolean looking village.

★ **Pieve di Cadore.** – This town is pleasantly set at the head of a reservoir. It was the birthplace of the great artist, **Titian**. One of his works is to be found in the church and the
⊙ house where he was born is now a **museum.**

★ **San Vito di Cadore.** – This attractive village with its shingle-roofed churches is oversha-
dowed by the Antelao.

Dobbiaco. – In the centre of this village there is an Austrian-style baroque church.

Vipiteno. – *30km – 19 miles to the northwest of Bressanone.* The picturesque **main street**★
has 15-16C Tyrolean houses with arcades, oriel windows and wrought iron signs.

★ ELBA, Isle of Tuscany   Pop 29 243
Michelin map **988** fold 24

With its beaches, solitary sites, peacefulness and mild dry climate, Elba is a good
island for a stay rather than an excursion. In the distant geological past Elba was a part
of the vanished continent, Tyrrhenia. This, the largest island in the Tuscan Archipel-
ago, like Corsica, Sardinia, the Balearics and the Maures and Estérel Massifs on the
French Riviera coast, has an indented coastline with small creeks, caves and beaches.
The vegetation is typically Mediterranean with palms, eucalyptus, cedars, magnolias
and in great quantity, olives and vines. The wines produced (white Moscato and red
Aleatico) are heady with a strong bouquet.
Elba is closely associated with Napoleon who was exiled here following his abdication.
Between the 3 May 1814 and the 26 February the fallen emperor ruled over his small
court and the island which was garrisoned by about 1 000 soldiers.

Sightseeing. – Start from Portoferraio and follow one of the two itineraries indicated
on the map below: **western Elba** *(66km – 41 miles, about 4 hours)* and **eastern Elba** *(68km
– 42 miles, about 3 hours).*

Portoferraio. – Lying at the head of a beautiful bay, the island's capital is guarded by
⊙ ruined walls and two forts. In the upper part of the town the **Napoleonic Museum** (Museo
Napoleonico dei Mulini) is a simple house, with a terraced garden, which Napoleon
sometimes occupied. His personal library and various mementoes are kept here.
Beyond the great sandy beach at **Biodola**, the road goes towards **Marciana Marina**, a small
port protected by two piers, one of which is dominated by a round tower.

★★ **Monte Capanne.** – 1 018m – 3 339ft. *Cable-cars leave from Marciana.* From the summit
⊙ not far from the terminus there is a splendid **panorama**★★ of Elba, the Tuscan coast to
the east and the coast of Corsica to the west.

Marciana. – From this attractive village there is a lovely **view**★ of Poggio, perched on its
⊙ rocky spur, Marciana Marina and the Bay of Procchio. There is a small **archaeological
museum** with displays of prehistoric items, Greek vases, etc.

Madonna del Monte. – Take the road up to the castle which dominates Marciana and from
there a rocky path leads up to this sanctuary, built on the northern slope of Monte
Giove. Beside the 16C chapel there is a curious semicircular fountain dated 1698.

Marina di Campo. – This small fishing port with its popular beach, lies at the head of a
lovely bay backed by a hinterland plain of olive groves and vineyards.

★ **Napoleon's Villa in San Martino.** – In a setting of silent hills, planted with groves of ever-
⊙ green oaks and vineyards, this modest house was the ex-emperor's summer residence. There is a lovely view of the Bay of Portoferraio.

Capoliveri. – From a spot to the west of this village there is a **panorama**★★ of the Bays of
Portoferraio, Marina di Campo and Porto Azzurro.

Porto Azzurro. – This pretty port is overlooked by a fort which now serves as a prison.

Rio Marina. – Pleasant port and mining village protected by a crenellated tower. Beyond
Cavo, a small port sheltered by the Castello headland, the return **road**★★ to Portoferraio
is a high altitude one *(in bad condition)* affording remarkable views of the ruins of Vol-
terraio, the Bay of Portoferraio and the sea.

FAENZA Emilia-Romagna

Pop 54 769

Michelin map 988 fold 15 – Town plan in the current Michelin Red Guide Italia

Faenza has given its name to the ceramics known as **faïence,** which have been produced locally since the 15C. In Italy faïence is also known as majolica because during
the Renaissance Faenza potters were inspired by ceramics which were imported from
Majorca in the Balearic Isles. The characteristics of Faenza ceramics are fine clay, remarkable glaze, brilliant colours and a great variety of decoration.

★★ **International Ceramics Museum (Museo Internazionale delle Ceramiche).** – These vast
⊙ collections present the development of ceramic making throughout the world. On the
first floor is a very fine collection of Italian Renaissance majolica, examples of the local
work, popular Italian pieces and an oriental section. On the ground floor, as well as the
contemporary Italian collection, there are pieces by Matisse, Picasso, Chagall, Léger,
Lurçat and the Vallauris school.

★ **Municipal Picture Gallery (Pinacoteca Comunale).** – This important collection includes
⊙ works by Giovanni da Rimini, Palmezzano, Dosso Dossi, Rossellino and other canvases from foreign schools (portraits by Pourbus).

Cathedral (Cattedrale). – The cathedral was built in the 15C by the Florentine architect
Guiliano da Maiano, but the façade was left unfinished. Inside is the tomb (1471) of
Bishop St Savinus by Benedetto da Maiano. On the cathedral parvis, Piazza della
Libertà, is a charming 17C baroque fountain.

Piazza del Popolo. – The square is elongated and unusual, with arcades surmounted
by galleries. Lining the square are the 12C governor's residence, Palazzo del Podestà
and the 13-15C Palazzo del Municipio.

★ # FANO Marches

Pop 52 396

Michelin map 988 fold 16 – Town plan in the current Michelin Red Guide Italia

This town, now a favourite seaside resort, was ruled by the Malatesta family from
Rimini in the 13 and 15C. Montaigne passed through Fano in April 1581 and aroused
a controversy concerning the reputed beauty of the local women.

★ **Malatesta Courtyard (Corte Malatestiana).** – This 15C Renaissance ensemble includes a courtyard garden and palace and would make an ideal theatrical set. The palace
⊙ houses the **Municipal Museum** (Museo Civico) with sections on archaeology, coins and
medals and 14-18C sculpture and painting. The latter includes Guercino's well known
work, the **Guardian Angel** (1641).

Church of Santa Maria Nuova. – 16-18C. This contains **works★** by Perugino, which
are admired for their fine draughtsmanship and their delicate colours: an exquisite
Madonna and Child (1497) (third altar on the right) and a graceful Annunciation (1498)
(second altar on the left).

Fountain of Good Fortune (Fontana della Fortuna). – This fountain in Piazza 20 Set-
tembre presents the protecting goddess, perched on a pivoting globe, with her billow-
ing cloak acting as a weathervane.

Arch of Augustus (Arco d'Augusto). – *At the far end of the street of the same name.*
This 1C arch has a main opening and two side ones for pedestrians. A low-relief on
the façade of the Church of St Michael (San Michele) nearby portrays the arch in its
original form. To the left of the arch are the remains of the Roman wall.

★ # FERMO Marches

Pop 35 116

Michelin map 988 fold 16

Fermo is one of the artistic and cultural centres of the Marches. It stands in a good
site★ on the slopes of a hill overlooking the countryside and facing the sea.

★ **Piazza del Duomo.** – From this esplanade in front of the cathedral there are splendid
views★★ of the Ascoli area, the Apennines, the Adriatic and Conero Peninsula.

Cathedral (Duomo). – This Romanesque-Gothic building (1227) has a majestic **façade★**
in white Istrian stone. A delicately carved doorway shows Christ with the Apostles on
the lintel and symbolic scenes or figures on the uprights. In the 18C interior note the
14C sarcophagus of Giovanni Visconti, overlord of the town; a 5C mosaic paving in
front of the chancel, a 13-14C Byzantine icon of the Virgin; and a 4C sarcophagus with
high-reliefs in the crypt.

Piazza del Popolo. – This square in the centre of town, is surrounded with arcades
and elegant porticoes. Numerous palaces including the 15C Palazzo Comunale and the
16C Palazzo degli Studi line the square. Running between these two palaces is the
Corso Cefalonia, a picturesque street lined with towers of nobility, palaces and ancient
churches.

EXCURSION

Montefiore dell' Aso. – *20km – 12 miles to the south.*
Carlo Crivelli (1430-95), a painter of courtesans and fair virgins, on being sentenced at
Venice in 1457, took refuge in the Marches, and Montefiore so gained a masterpiece.
This splendid **polyptych★★**, although incomplete, finely chiselled and highlighted with
gold represents six saints. The most successful panel shows the sinner Mary Magda-
len richly apparelled in gold and silk brocade, holding the symbolic box of ointment.

Michelin map 988 fold 15

In the heart of the fertile Po Plain, Ferrara has kept its urban layout intact from the Renaissance period, when the brilliant court of the Princes of Este rivalled, for splendour and culture, those of Milan, Venice and Mantua. The streets on a gridiron pattern are lined with the red brick houses, severe palaces and great spacious squares which so inspired the 20C metaphysical painter Giorgio de Chirico.

A discerning dynasty of patrons of the arts. – Initially an independent commune Ferrara belonged to the **House of Este** from 1208 to 1598 and despite numerous family dramas, often bloodthirsty, the Estes embellished their native city with fine buildings and patronised both men of letters and artists. **Niccolò III** (1393-1441) murdered his wife and her lover but he begat **Lionello** and **Borso**, generous administators and enlightened patrons. **Ercole I** who assassinated his nephew, encouraged artists, as did his two famous daughters, Beatrice and Isabelle d'Este. **Alfonso I**, the son of Ercole, became the third husband of Lucrezia Borgia and Ercole II married Renée of France. **Ariosto** (1474-1533), spent his lifetime in the service of the Estes, in particular with Alfonso I, and his rare spare time was spent writing his masterpiece **Orlando Furioso** *(Roland the Mad)*. In relating the adventures of the knight, Orlando and Angelica, the poet gives free reign to his imagination. **Tasso** (1544-95), a native of Sorrento, made several visits to Ferrara. During the first he wrote his epic poem **Gerusalemme Liberata** *(Jerusalem Delivered)* recounting the capture of Jerusalem by the Christians, enlivened by the love-story of Rinaldo and Armida.

The Ferrara School of Painting. – The leader of this local school was, **Cosimo Tura** (*c*1430-95) with his strong personality, and its main characteristic was a meticulous realism, borrowed from the Northern schools. It was combined with a rather grim expressionism which derived from Mantegna, whose figures with their sculptural form display a high degree of tension. The main members were **Francesco del Cossa** (1435-77), **Ercole de' Roberti** (1450-96) and **Lorenzo Costa** (*c*1460-1530). In the 16C the colourist **Dosso Dossi** and **Garofalo** abandoned this drawing tradition in favour of a greater harmony of colour, as did the Venetian and Roman schools.

SIGHTS

★★ **Cathedral (Duomo) (BYZ).** – In the Romanesque-Gothic Lombard style, the triple **façade★★**, all in marble, is remarkable for its arrangement and variety of the openings. On the south side is the 15C Merchants' portico and gallery (loggia). The interior was remodelled in the 18C and contains numerous works of art. Above the narthex is the

○ cathedral **museum**★ with amusing 12C **low-reliefs of the Months**★, two statues by Jacopa della Quercia and two outstanding **masterpieces**★★ by **Cosimo Tura**. The four canvases represent an **Annunciation** and a **St George slaying the Dragon.**
The 13C **Palazzo Comunale (BY H)**, facing the cathedral, was once the ducal palace.

★ **Este Castle (Castello Estense) (BY B)**. – This massive castle guarded by moats and four
○ fortified gateways with drawbridges, was the seat of the Estes. Visitors may view the apartments decorated with frescoes by Filippi, and the hanging gardens.

★ **Schifanoia Palace (Palazzo Schifanoia) (BZ E)**. – This 14-15C palace is where the Estes
○ used to come to relax (*schifanoia* means carefree). It now houses the **municipal museum** (Museo Civico). In addition to the interesting archaeological and Renaissance exhibits note the splendid **frescoes**★★ in the Room of the Months (Salone dei Mesi). This complex cycle to the glory of Borso d'Este unfortunately only retains some of the twelve months. The three different levels correspond to three different themes, notably everyday life at court, astrology and mythology. Several artists, including Francesco del Cossa and Ercole de' Roberti, worked under Cosimo Tura to produce these frescoes which demonstrate an extraordinary delicacy when portraying detail and a marvellous vivacity in both the use of colour and draughtsmanship.
The 15-16C **Basilica of Santa Maria in Vado (BZ)**, near the palace is decorated inside with frescoes and paintings.

★ **Palace of Diamonds (Palazzo dei Diamanti) (BY F)**. – The palace takes its name from
○ the distinctive marble façade of 12 500 diamond bosses. This sumptuous 15-16C building now houses the **National Picture Gallery**★: works from the 15 and 16C Emilian and Ferrara schools (Cosimo Tura, Ercole de' Roberti, Garofalo and Dosso Dossi). In the Great Hall there are splendid 13-14C **frescoes**★★ taken from local churches.

★ **Corso Ercole I° d'Este (BY)**. – The main street in the northern part of the town is lined with splendid Renaissance palaces.

★ **Palace of Ludovico the Moor (Palazzo di Ludovico il Moro) (BZ M)**. – This palace, built
○ in the late 15C, for Ludovico Sforza the Moor, husband of Beatrice d'Este is the home of an **archaeological museum** with an important collection of 5-4C BC **Attic vases** ★.

★ **Casa Romei (BZ L)**. – The inner courtyards of this delightful 15C house are bordered
○ by porticoes and loggias.

★ **Palazzina di Marfisa d'Este (BZ N)**. – This elegant single storey residence (1559),
○ set in a shady garden, is where Marfisa d'Este entertained her friends, among whom was the poet Tasso.

○ **Sant' Antonio in Polesine (BZ S)**. – This attractive architectural group includes a convent and church. The latter has three chapels decorated with 14-15C frescoes by the Northern Italian schools.

○ **Ariosto's House (Casa dell' Ariosto) (AY Q)**. – The writer's home is now a cultural centre but it still has the garden where he tended his roses and jasmine.

★ **FIESOLE** Tuscany   Pop 15 146

Michelin map 988 folds 14 and 15 – 8km – 5 miles north of Florence – Town plan in the current Michelin Red Guide Italia

The road from Florence winds uphill to Fiesole through olive-clad slopes, past luxuriant gardens and long lines of cypress trees and affords views of this incomparable **countryside**★★★, so often depicted by the masters of the Italian Renaissance. The Etruscans founded this city in the 7 and 6C BC. Fiesole was the most important city in northern Etruria and it dominated its neighbour and rival Florence, until the 12C.

★★ **View of Florence**. – The small terrace near the convent of St Francis (San Francesco) provides a lovely view of Florence, nestling in a hollow of the Arno Basin.

★ **Convent of St Francis (San Francesco)**. – This humble Franciscan convent, with its
○ charming small cloisters, is admirably set on the hilltop.

Cathedral (Duomo). – Founded in the 11C and enlarged in the 13 and 14C, the building was extensively restored in the late 19C. The austere **interior**★, on a basilical plan with raised chancel has columns supporting antique capitals. There are two handsome **works**★ by the sculptor Mino da Fiesole.

○ **Archaeological Site (Zona Archeologica)**. – This site, in its enchanting **setting**★, regroups a **Roman theatre**★ (c80 BC), which is still used for performances, a small **Etruscan temple** and the remains of baths built in 1C BC by the Romans. The **museum**★ exhibits the finds which date from the Etruscan to the medieval period.

○ **Bandini Museum**. – *Opposite the entrance to the archaeological site.*
This is a collection of 14 and 15C Tuscan works. The sculpture and terracottas are on the ground floor with the paintings on the floor above. Note Petrarch's masterpiece **Triumphs** with illustrations by Jacopo del Sellaio.

San Domenico di Fiesole. – *2.5km – 1 1/2 miles to the southwest. See the plan of the built-up area of Florence in the current Michelin Red Guide Italia.*
It was in this 15C church, remodelled in the 17C, that Fra Angelico made his vows. In the first chapel on the north side is a **Madonna and Saints**★ by the artist. In the second chapel on the south is a **Baptism of Christ** by Lorenzo di Credi.

○ **Badia Fiesolana**. – *3km – 2 miles to the southwest. See the plan of the built-up area of Florence in the current Michelin Red Guide Italia.*
This former Benedictine convent was partially rebuilt in the 15C thanks to the generosity of Cosimo the Elder. The Romanesque **façade** of the original church, with its decorative green and white marble motifs, was incorporated in the new building, left incomplete on the death of Cosimo the Elder.

★★★ **FLORENCE** (FIRENZE) Tuscany   Pop 421 299

Michelin map ⑨⑧⑧ folds 14 and 15 − Town plan pp 88 and 89 − Plans of the built-up area in the current Michelin Red Guide Italia

Florence is without doubt the city where the Italian genius has flourished with the greatest display of brilliance and purity. For three centuries from the 13C to the 16C the city was the the cradle of an exceptional artistic and intellectual activity which evolved the precepts which were to dictate the appearance of Italy of the day and also the aspect of modern civilisation throughout Europe. The main characteristics of this movement, which was later to be known as the **Renaissance,** were partly a receptivity to the outside world, a dynamic open-minded attitude which encouraged inventors and men of science to base their research on the reinterpretation of the achievements of ancient Rome and the expanding of the known horizons. The desire to achieve universality resulted in a multiplication of the fields of interest.

Dante was not only a great poet but also a grammarian and historian who did much research on the origins and versatility of his language. He was one of Florence's most active polemists. Giotto was not only a painter but also an architect. Lorenzo the Magnificent was the prince who best incarnated the spirit of the Renaissance. An able diplomat, a realistic politician, a patron of the arts and poet himself, he regularly attended the Platonic Academy in the Medici villa at Careggi where philosophers such as Marsilio Ficino and Pico della Mirandola and men of letters like Politian and others established the principles of a new humanism. This search to achieve a balance between nature and order had its most brilliant exponent in **Michelangelo,** painter, architect, sculptor and scholar whose work typifies a purely Florentine preoccupation.

Florence is set in the heart of a beautiful **countryside**★★★ which is bathed by a diaphanous, amber light so full of serenity. The low surrounding hills are clad with olive groves, vineyards and cypresses which appear to have been landscaped to please the human eye. Florentine architects and artists have variously striven to recreate this balance of nature in their works, whether it be the campanile of La Badia by Arnolfo di Cambio, or that of the cathedral by Giotto, the façade of Santa Maria Novella by Alberti or the dome of Santa Maria del Fiore by Brunelleschi. The pure and elegant lines of all these works of art would seem to be a response to the beauty of the landscape and the intensity of the light. The Florentine preoccupation with perspective throughout the Quattrocento (15C) is in part the result of this fascination for the countryside and the other great absorption of the period, the desire to faithfully recreate what the eye saw. This communion of great minds, with their varied facets and fields of interest, expressed a common desire to push their knowledge to the limits, and found in the flourishing city of Florence an ideal foyer for their artistic and intellectual development. The city's artists, merchants, able administrators and its princely patrons of the art, all contributed to the creation of just the right conditions for nurturing such an intellectual and artistic community, which for centuries was to influence human creativity.

(Malin/Rapho)

View of Florence

HISTORICAL NOTES

The colony of Florentia was founded in the 1C BC by Julius Caesar on the north bank of the Arno at a spot level with the Ponte Vecchio. The veteran soldiers who garrisoned the colony controlled the Via Flaminia linking Rome to northern Italy and Gaul.

It was only in the early 11C that the city became an important Tuscan centre when Count Ugo, Marquis of Tuscany took up residence here and again towards the end of the same century when the Countess Matilda affirmed its independence. During the 12C Florence prospered under the influence of the new class of merchants who built such fine buildings as the baptistry and San Miniato. This period saw the rise of trades organised in powerful guilds *(arti)*, which soon became the ruling class when Florence became an independent commune. In the 13C one third of Florence's population was engaged in either the wool or silk trades, both of which exported their products to the four corners of Europe and were responsible for a period of extraordinary prosperity. These tradesmen were ably supported by the Florentine moneyhouses which succeeded the Lombard and Jewish institutions, and themselves acquired a great reputation by issuing the first ever bills of exchange and the famous florin, struck with the Florentine coat of arms. The latter was replaced in the late 15C by the Venetian ducat. The main banking families were the Bardi-Peruzzi who advanced huge sums to England at the beginning of the Hundred Years War; they were soon to be joined in the forefront by the Pitti, Strozzi, Pazzi and of course the Medici.

Despite this prosperity, Florence did not escape the internal strife between the Ghibellines, who were partisans of the Holy Roman Emperor and the Guelphs who supported the Pope. The Guelphs at first had the advantage; but the Ghibellines on being driven out of Florence, having allied themselves with other enemies of Florence, notably Siena, recaptured Montaperti in 1260. The Guelphs counter-attacked and retook Florence in 1266. Under their rule the physical aspect of the city changed considerably, notably with the destruction of the fortified tower houses built by the Ghibelline nobility. They created a republic and established government by a single individual or family; lordship *(signoria)* and committees which in Florence were known as *priori*. There then occurred a split between the Black Guelphs and the White Guelphs who opposed the Papacy. During this latter tragedy Dante, who supported the White Guelphs, was exiled for good in 1302. In 1348 the Black Death killed more than half the population and put an end to these periods of internal strife.

Among the numerous wealthy families in Florence, it was the **Medici** who gave the city several leaders who exercised their patronage in both the sphere of fine arts and finance. The founder of this illustrious dynasty was Giovanni di Bicci, a prosperous banker who left his fortune in 1429 to his son **Cosimo the Elder** who in turn transformed his heritage into the city's most flourishing business. He discreetly exercised his personal power through intermediaries, and astutely juggled his own personal interests with those of the city, which assured Florence of a kind of peaceful hegemony. His chief quality was his ability to gather around him both scholars and artists, whom he commissioned for numerous projects. Cosimo the Elder was a passionate builder and Florence owes many of her great monuments to this 'Father of the Land'. His son, Piero Il Gottoso (the gouty) only survived him by five years and he in turn bequeathed all to his son **Lorenzo the Magnificent** (1449-92). Having escaped the Pazzi Conspiracy *(see p 86)* Lorenzo reigned like a true Renaissance prince, although it was always unofficially. He distinguished himself for his skilful politics and managed to retain the prestige of Florence amongst its contemporaries while ruining the Medici financial empire. This humanist and man of great sensitivity was a great patron of the arts, and he gathered around him poets and philosophers, who all contributed to make Florence capital of the early Renaissance.

On Lorenzo's death, which had repercussions throughout Europe, the Dominican monk **Savonarola,** profiting from a period of confusion, provoked the fall of the Medici. This fanatical and ascetic monk, who became the Prior of the Monastery of St Mark, so preached against the pleasures of the senses and of the arts, that the citizens of Florence made a "bonfire of vanities" in 1497 in Piazza della Signoria on which musical instruments, paintings, books of poetry, etc were burnt. A year later Savonarola himself was burnt at the stake on the same spot.

The Medici family returned to power with the help of the Emperor Charles V and they reigned until the mid-18C. **Cosimo I** (1519-74) brought some of the splendour back to Florence which she had lost to Siena and he himself became Grand Duke of Tuscany. He continued the tradition of patron of the arts protecting numerous artists. Francesco I (1541-87), whose daughter Maria was to marry Henri IV King of France, took as his second wife the beautiful Venetian Bianca Cappello. The last prominent Medici was Ferdinand I (1549-1609) who married a French princess, Christine de Lorraine. After the Medici, the Grand Duchy passed to the House of Lorraine, then to Bonaparte until 1814 before it returned to the House of Lorraine until 1859. When it became part of the Italian kingdom, Florence was capital from 1865 to 1870.

FLORENCE, CAPITAL OF THE ARTS

The relatively late emergence of Florence in the 11C as a cultural centre and its insignificant Roman heritage, no doubt contributed to the development of an independent art movement, which developed vigorously for several centuries. One of its principal characteristics was its preoccupation with clarity and harmony which influenced writers as well as architects, painters and sculptors.

Dante Alighieri (1265-1321) established the use of the Italian vernacular in several of his works, thus superseding Latin as the literary language. He made an admirable demonstration with his **New Life** *(Vita Nuova),* recounting his meeting with a young girl Beatrice Portinari who was to be his inspiration for his **Divine Comedy** *(Divina Commedia)* in which Dante, led by Virgil and then by Beatrice visits the Inferno, Purgatory and Paradise. Dante's description of these infernal circles where the damned are chastised, of the mountain of Purgatory where great crowds await redemption and finally the dazzling vision of the divine splendour of Paradise, have inspired for generations, not only Italian writers but men of letters everywhere. In the 14C Dante was responsible for creating an exceptionally versatile literary language to which Petrach *(qv)* added his sense of lyricism and Boccaccio *(qv)* the art of irony.

Machiavelli (1469-1527), born in Florence, was the statesman on whose account Machiavellism became a synonym for cunning, and recounted his experiences as a statesman in a noble and vigorous prose. He was the author of **The Prince** *(Il Principe –* 1513), an essay on political science and government dedicated to Lorenzo Il in which he counselled that in politics the end justified the means. **Francesco Guicciardini** (1483-1540) wrote an important history of Florence and Italy while **Giorgio Vasari** (1511-74), much later, with his work *The Lives of the Most Eminent Italian Architects, Painters and Sculptors* was the first real art historian. He studied and classified local schools of painting, tracing their development from the 13C with the work of Cimabue, whom even Dante had praised in his *Divine Comedy*.

The Florentine school had its origins in the work of **Cimabue** (1240-1302) and slowly it freed itself from the Byzantine tradition with its decorative convolutions, while **Giotto** (1266-1337) in his search for truth gave priority to movement and expression. Later **Masaccio** (1401-28) studied the depth of space and three dimensional world. From then on perspective became the principal preoccupation of Florentine painters, sculptors, architects and theorists who continually tried to perfect this technique.

The Quattrocento (15C) saw the emergence of a group of artists like **Paolo Uccello** (1397-1475), **Andrea del Castagno** (1423-57), **Piero della Francesca** *(qv)* a native of the Marches, who were all ardent exponents in the matters of foreshortening and the strictly geometrical construction of space, while others like **Fra Angelico** (1387-1455), and later **Filippo Lippi** (1406-69) and **Benezzo Gozzoli** (1420-97) were imbued with the traditions of International Gothic *(qv)* and more concerned with the visual effects of arabesques and the appeal of the luminous clarity of the colours. These opposing tendencies were reconciled in the harmonious balance of the work of **Sandro Botticelli** (1444-1510), whom Florence is proud to claim as a son. He took his subjects from antiquity as the humanists in the court of Lorenzo de' Medici recommended, and he invented fables peopled by enigmatic figures with subtle linear movements, which created an impression of inner movement. At times a certain melancholy seems to arrest the movement and pale the luminosity of the colours. Alongside Botticelli the **Pollaiuolo** brothers, **Ghirlandaio** (1449-94) and **Filippino Lippi** (1457-1504) assure the continuity and diversity of Florentine art. The High Renaissance with its main centres in Rome and other northern towns reached Florence in the 16C. **Leonardo da Vinci** *(qv)*, **Michelangelo** *(qv)* and **Raphael** *(qv)*, all made their debut at Florence, and inspired younger Mannerist artists *(p 30)* such as **Pontormo, Rosso Fiorentino, Andrea del Sarto** (1486-1530) or the curious portraitist of the Medici, **Bronzino** (1503-72).

However the emergence of a Florentine school of painting is indissociable with the contemporary movement of the architects who were creating a style, also inspired by antiquity, which united the classical traditions of rhythm, a respect for proportion and geometric decoration. The constant preoccupation was with perspective in the arrangement of interiors and the design of façades. **Leon Battista Alberti** (1404-72) was the theorist and grand master of such a movement. However it was **Filippo Brunelleschi** (1377-1446) who best represented the Florentine spirit, and he gave the city buildings which combined both rigour and grace as manifested in the magnificent dome of Santa Maria del Fiore which has become the symbol of Florence.

Throughout the Quattrocento (15C), buildings were embellished with admirable sculptures which became a harmonious part of the architectural whole. The doors of the baptistry were the object of a competition which confronted the very best. If **Ghiberti** (1378-1455) was finally victorious, **Donatello** (1386-1466) was later to provide ample demonstration of the genius of his art so full of realism and style, as did **Luca della Robbia** (1400-82) and his dynasty, **Verrocchio** (1435-88) and numerous other artists who adorned the ecclesiastical and secular buildings of Florence. In the 16C **Michelangelo** who was part of this tradition, confirmed his origins with his New Sacristy (1520-55) of San Lorenzo which he both designed and decorated with sculpture. Later **Benvenuto Cellini** (1500-71), Giambologna or **Giovanni Bologna** (1529-1608) and **Bartolomeo Ammannati** (1511-92) maintained this polyvalence which was responsible for the exceptional beauty of the city of Florence.

SIGHTSEEING

Florence is such an important art centre that it takes at least four days to see the main sights. These are however situated fairly closely together in the city centre which is not adapted to heavy traffic. It is therefore advisable to do your sightseeing on foot and establish a visiting programme which takes into account the opening times.

★★★ PIAZZA DEL DUOMO (HX) *time: 1/2 day*

In the city centre, the cathedral along with the campanile and baptistry, form an admirable group of white, green or pink marble, which demonstrates the traditions of Florentine art from the Middle Ages to the Renaissance.

★★ **Cathedral (Duomo) (HX A).** — The **Cathedral of Santa Maria del Fiore**, one of the largest cathedrals in the Christian world is a symbol of the city's power and wealth in the 13 and 14C. It was begun in 1296 by Arnolfo di Cambio and was consecrated in 1436. This essentially Gothic cathedral is an outstanding example of the Florentine variant of this style: with its sheer size, predominance of horizontality and taste for polychrome decoration.

Exterior. — Walk round the cathedral starting from the south side to admire the marble mosaic decoration and the sheer size of the **east end ★★★**. The harmonious **dome ★★★** by Brunelleschi took fourteen years to build. To counteract the downward pushing forces he built two concentric domes which were linked by props.

Interior. — The bareness of the interior contrasts sharply with the sumptuous decoration of the exterior. Enormous piers support sturdy arches which themselves uphold the lofty Gothic vaulting. The great octagonal chancel under the dome is surrounded by a delicate 16C marble **balustrade ★**. The dome is painted with a huge **fresco** of the Last Judgment. You can go up to the inner gallery which offers an impressive view of the nave, and then up to the **top of the dome** (464 steps) with its magnificent **panorama ★★** of Florence.

The sacristy doors on either side of the high altar have tympana adorned with pale blue terracottas by Luca della Robbia representing the Resurrection and the Ascension. A dramatic episode of the **Pazzi Conspiracy** took place in the chancel. The Pazzi, who were rivals of the Medici, tried to assassinate Lorenzo the Magnificent on 26 April 1478, during the Elevation of the Host. Lorenzo, though wounded by two monks, managed to take refuge in a sacristy, but his brother Guiliano fell to their daggers.

The axial chapel contains a masterpiece by Ghiberti, the sarcophagus of St Zanobi, the first Bishop of Florence. One of the low-reliefs shows the saint resurrecting a child. Go down the north aisle: in the first bay a fresco of 1465 shows Dante explaining the *Divine Comedy* (Inferno, Purgatory and Paradise) to the city of Florence. Further along on the right two frescoes by Uccello (1436) and Andrea del Castagno (1456) depict portraits of leaders of mercenary armies *(condottiere)*.

A stairway on the other side of the nave, between the first and second pillars, leads to the **Crypt of Santa Reparata**, the only remaining part of a Romanesque basilica which was demolished when the present cathedral was built. The basilica itself was formerly an early Christian church (5-6C). Excavations have revealed traces of mosaic paving belonging to the original building and Brunelleschi's tomb (behind the railing enclosed chamber, at the bottom of the stairs, on the left).

★ **Campanile** (HX B). – The tower is slender and tall (82m – 269ft) and is the perfect complement to Brunelleschi's dome, the straight lines of the former balancing the curves of the latter. Giotto drew the plans for it and began building in 1334, but died in 1336. The Gothic campanile was completed at the end of the 14C; its geometric decoration with its emphasis on horizontal lines is unusual. The admirable low-reliefs at the base of the campanile have been replaced by copies. Those on the lower band were executed by Andrea Pisano and Luca della Robbia and those on the upper band by pupils of Andrea Pisano, but the overall design was by Giotto. The original low-reliefs are in the Cathedral Museum. From the top of the campanile (414 steps) there is a fine **panorama**★★ of the cathedral and town.

★ **Baptistry** (HX C). – The building is encased in white and green marble in a quiet and well balanced Romanesque style. The **bronze doors**★★★ are world famous.
The South Door (entrance) by Andrea Pisano (1330) is Gothic and portrays scenes from the life of St John the Baptist (above), as well as the three Theological Virtues (Faith, Hope, Charity) and the four Cardinal Virtues (below). The door-frames, which show great skill are by Vittorio Ghiberti, son of the designer of the other doors.
The North Door (1403-24) was the first done by Lorenzo Ghiberti. He was the winner of a competition in which Brunelleschi, Donatello and Jacopo della Quercia also took part. Scenes from the Life of Christ are evoked with extraordinary nobility and harmony of composition.
The East Door (1425-52), facing the cathedral, is the one that Michelangelo declared worthy to be the **Gate to Paradise**. In it Ghiberti recalled the Old Testament; prophets and sibyls adorn the riches. The artist portrayed himself, bald and malicious, in one of the medallions.

Interior. – With its 25m – 82ft diameter, its black and white marble and its paving decorated with oriental motifs, the interior is grand and majestic. The dome is covered with magnificent **mosaics**★★★ of the 13C. The Last Judgment is depicted on either side of a large picture of Christ the King; on the five concentric bands that cover the other five panels of the dome, starting from the top towards the base, note the Heavenly Hierarchies, Genesis, the Life of Joseph, scenes from the Life of the Virgin and of Christ, and the Life of St John the Baptist.
On the right of the apse is the tomb of the Antipope John XXIII, friend of Cosimo the Elder, a remarkable work executed in 1427 by Donatello assisted by Michelozzo.
Under the 14C Gothic **Loggia del Bigallo** (HX E) to the south of the baptistry, lost or abandoned children were exhibited.

★ **Cathedral Museum** (Museo dell'Opera del Duomo) (JX M¹). – This contains items from the cathedral, campanile and baptistry. Statues from the former façade of the cathedral (Pope Boniface VIII by Arnolfo di Cambio, the four Evangelists), equipment used by Brunelleschi to build the dome and his death mask as well as gold plate are exhibited on the ground floor.
On the mezzanine is the famous **Pietà**★★ which Michelangelo, at the age of eighty, left unfinished.
In the large room on the first floor are three famous statues by Donatello – an impressive repentant **Magdalen**★ carved in wood, and the prophets Jeremiah and Habakkuk, the latter being nicknamed *Zuccone* (vegetable marrow) because of the shape of his head. In the same room are the famous **Cantorie**★★, choristers' tribunes, from the cathedral: on the left, Luca della Robbia's tribune (the panels on the base are original, the upper section has been remodelled with copies) bears figures of choir boys, dancers and musicians of exquisite charm. Donatello's tribune, opposite, is more elaborate and less natural but its decorative carvings are effective.
In a room on the left are exhibited the admirable **low-reliefs**★★ from the campanile: those by Andrea Pisano and Luca della Robbia which are hexagonal in shape and very picturesque, depict the creation of Adam and Eve and various human activities; the rest are diamond-shaped and represent the planets, the virtues, the liberal arts and the sacraments.
The room to the right of the one with the cantorie, contains the famous silver **altarpiece**★★ depicting the life of St John the Baptist, a masterpiece of 14-15C Florentine craftsmanship.

PIAZZA DELLA SIGNORIA *time: 1 day*

★ **Piazza della Signoria** (HY). – This was, and still is, the political stage of Florence, with a wonderful backcloth formed by the Palazzo Vecchio, the Loggia della Signoria and in the wings the Uffizi Museum. The many statues make it virtually an open-air museum of sculpture: near the centre of the square, the equestrian statue of Cosimo I, after Giovanni Bologna, and at the corner of the Palazzo Vecchio, the Fountain of Neptune (1576) by Ammannati. In front of the Palazzo Vecchio are a copy of the proud Marzocco or Lion of Florence by Donatello and a copy of Michelangelo's David.

★ **Loggia della Signoria** (HY D). – Built at the end of the 14C, the loggia was the assembly hall and later the guardroom of the Lanzi (foot soldiers) of Cosimo I. It contains ancient (Classical) and Renaissance statues: the Rape of a Sabine (1583), Hercules and the centaur Nessus by Giovanni Bologna and the wonderful **Perseus**★★★ holding up the severed head of Medusa, a masterpiece executed by Benvenuto Cellini between 1545 and 1553.

★★★ **Palazzo Vecchio** (HJY). – The Old Palace's powerful mass is dominated by a loft⬛ ⊘ bell-tower, 94m – 308ft high. Built between 1299 and 1314 probably to plans b⬛ Arnolfo di Cambio, it is in a severe Gothic style with a total lack of openings at groun⬛ level, a series of twinned windows above and battlements, parapet walk and crenella⬛ tions on top with the tower.

The refinement and splendour of the Renaissance interior is a complete contras⬛ The **courtyard★** was restored by Michelozzo in the 15C and decorated the following century by Vasari. The 16C fountain is surmounted by a delightful winged goblin, a copy of a work by Verrocchio (the original is in the palace).

Initially the seat of government (Palazzo della Signoria) the palace was then taken over in the 16C by Cosimo I, as his private residence, as it was better suited to accommodating his court. Most of the redecoration work done by Giorgio Vasari dates from this period. When Cosimo I abandoned the palace in favour of the Pitti Palace it was renamed Palazzo Vecchio.

The apartments were lavishly decorated with sculptures by Benedetto and Giuliano da Maiano (15C) and with paintings by Vasari and Bronzino (16C) to the glory of Florence and the Medici. On the first floor the great Sala dei Cinquecento, painted with frescoes by several artists including Vasari, contains a group carved by Michelangelo, *The Genius of Victory*. The walls of the magnificent **studiolo★★** or study of Francesco de' Medici, which was designed by Vasari were painted by several Florentine Mannerist painters including Bronzino who was responsible for the medallion portraits of *Cosimo I* and *Eleanora of Toledo*. Leo X's apartment was decorated by Vasari and his assistants with scenes illustrating episodes of the Medici history.

On the second floor are the Priors' Apartment including the **Sala dei Gigli** which is adorned with a splendid coffered **ceiling★** by Giuliano da Maiano; the **Sala della Guardaroba★** lined with 16C **maps**; the Apartment of Eleonora of Toledo decorated by Vasari with the exception of the chapel which was adorned with frescoes by Bronzino; the Apartment of Cosimo I, known as Quartiere degli Elementi because of the allegorical scenes painted by Vasari and his assistants to decorate the first room (in the Room of Jupiter are three **tapestries★** which were woven in the 16C by the Medici tapestry works).

★★★ **Uffizi Museum** (Galleria degli Uffizi) (HY). – This ⊘ is one of the finest museums in the world. These collections were assembled by several generations of Medici and the visitor can follow the evolution of Italian art from its beginnings to the 17C. The early nucleus was gathered together by Francesco I (1541-87) to which were added the collections of the Grand Dukes Ferdinand I, II and Cosimo III. In 1737 the last member of the Medici dynasty, Anna Maria Ludovica, Electress Palatine bequeathed the Medici collection to her native city of Florence. The Uffizi Museum was then housed in the Renaissance palace, designed by Vasari in 1560, which contained the offices *(uffizi)* of the Medici administration.

The rich collections of drawings and paintings are on the first floor, paintings and sculpture are exhibited in two galleries and adjacent rooms on the second floor.

The galleries. – The walls are hung with an admirable series of 16C **tapestries**: in gallery 1 the Months and the Fêtes given at the court of Catherine de' Medici and Henri II by the Flemish school (look for the Tuileries and the Châteaux of Anet and Fontainebleau). In gallery 2 is the *Passion of Christ* from the Florentine looms. Classical statues, mostly Roman copies and a fine series of busts of the imperial era are also on view.

FIRENZE

East side galleries. – The first room is devoted to archaeology, the next ten contain Florentine and Tuscan paintings from the late 13C to 16C and the remaining rooms are reserved for 15 and 16C Italian and foreign schools.
Late 13-14C Tuscan: note especially the works of Cimabue, Giotto and Duccio (Madonnas: room 2) and the famous **Annunciation** of Simone Martini (room 3), a masterpiece of Gothic art.

15C Florentine: here you can admire in room 7 the famous **Battle of San Romano** (the two other panels are in the Louvre and London) by Paolo Uccello; Fra Angelico *(Coronation of the Virgin)*, Piero della Francesca (Portrait of the *Duke of Urbino)*; in room 8 Filippo Lippi (his famous **Virgin and Child** on an easel between two *Adorations* and a *Coronation of the Virgin*).

(Edimedia)

The Birth of Venus by Botticelli (detail)

The **Botticelli Room★★★** (10-14), which is the most remarkable in the museum, contains the *Madonna of the Magnificat,* the **Birth of Venus** and **Spring** both mature works typical of this artist's lyrical poetry; and the admirable tondo of the *Madonna with a Pomegranate.* In the same room is Van der Goes **Portinari Triptych** which demonstrates the influence that the Flemish primitives had on Italian Renaissance artists. The next room contains the *Baptism of Christ* by Verrochio and two masterpieces by Leonardo da Vinci, the unfinished **Adoration of the Magi** and the famous **Annunciation.**

The Tribune (room 18): this is octagonal in shape and was designed by Buontalenti (1588). It contains the famous **Medici Venus** carved by a Greek sculptor in the 3C BC, and several portraits of the Medici by Pontormo, Bronzino, Vasari...

15 and 16C Italian and foreign schools: note in room 19, Perugino and Signorelli, in room 20, Cranach (**Adam and Eve,** *Luther*) and Dürer (**Adoration of the Magi**); in room 21, Giovanni Bellini (**Sacred Allegory**) and Giorgione; in room 22, portraits by Van Orley, Holbein, Joos van Cleve; in room 23, Correggio *(Rest in Egypt, Adoration)*, Bernardino Luini, Boccacino *(La Zingarella).*

Miniatures Room: *look through railings.* Miniatures from the 15 to the 19C.

West side galleries. – *Parallel to the first series.* Eleven rooms are devoted to the Italian Cinquecento (16C): Michelangelo (room 25: **Holy Family**); Raphael (room 26: **Leo X, Madonna with Goldfinch**); the Florentine Mannerists (rooms 26 and 27: Andrea del Sarto with his famous *Virgin with Harpies,* Pontormo, etc.), Emilian (rooms 29 to 31: Parmigianino, Dosso Dossi) and Venetian.

There are some splendid Titians (room 28: *Flora,* **Urbino Venus,** portraits); Veroneses (room 34: *the Holy Family and St Barbara*) and Tintorettos (room 35: **Leda and the Swan,** portraits).

Next is Italian and foreign painting of the 17 and 18C. The 17C Flemish school is represented (room 41) by Rubens (**Isabella Brandt**) and Van Dyck (portraits). The Niobe Room (42) contains a group of sculpture.

The following room (43) has several **Caravaggio's** *(Bacchus as a Youth)* and works by **Claude;** Dutch works and **Rembrandt** portraits and self-portraits hang in room 44 while room 45 is devoted to the 18C with works by Nattier and Chardin as well as the two Venetian view painters, Canaletto and Guardi.

⊙ **Corridoio Vasariano** (HY). – This corridor by Vasari links the Palazzo Vecchio to the Pitti Palace and is hung with a remarkable collection of portraits. The covered passageway was built by Vasari in 1565 and it is appropriate that the self-portraits should include one of the architect. Other notable sitters include Raphael, Becafumi, Salvator Rosa as well as foreign artists (Rembrandt, Van Dyck, Kneller...).

★★★ **Bargello Palace and Museum** (JY M). – This austere palace was formerly the residence of the governing magistrate *(podestà)* and then became police headquarters *(bargello).* It is a fine example of 13-14C medieval architecture planned round a majestic **courtyard★★** with a portico and loggia.

The palace is now transformed into a museum of sculpture and decorative arts with particularly good sections on Italian and Florentine Renaissance sculpture.

Ground floor. – These rooms are devoted to the works of 16C Florentine sculptors: by Michelangelo there is a **Bacchus Drunk,** a Brutus, an Apollo and the Tondo Pitti (a marble medallion depicting the Virgin and Child with St John); and by Benvenuto Cellini a Narcissus, a **low-relief** from the pedestal of the Perseus bronze in the Loggia della Signoria and a bust of Cosimo I.

First floor. – The great saloon contains an exceptional collection of **sculpture★★★** by **Donatello** and his assistants (Desiderio da Settignano, Agostino di Duccio) as well as works by Luca della Robbia. Donatello's genius made him an important figure in the early Italian Renaissance period. His works include St John the Baptist as a Youth, his **Marzocco** (the Florentine heraldic lion) and his famous mature work the bronze **David.** Note also the low-relief of **St George** from Orsanmichele.

The other rooms in the palace now display the Louis Carrand collection of enamels, jewellery and remarkable ivories bequeathed by this Frenchman from Lyons in the late 19C.

Second floor. – Rooms VII to XI contain colourful enamelled terracottas by Giovanni and Andrea della Robbia, works by **Verrocchio,** including the famous bronze statue of **David,** a series of small Renaissance bronzes and a remarkable collection of arms and armour.

FROM SAN LORENZO TO SANTA MARIA NOVELLA
time: 1/2 day

★★ **San Lorenzo** (HX). – Not far from the Medici Palace, this was the Medici family parish church, and it was here that most of the family was buried. The **church** ★★ was begun by Brunelleschi *c*1420. The interior is a perfect example of the sobriety of style introduced by **Brunelleschi** and typical of his thoughtful, measured, rigorous architectural style and its human dimension. His great achievement is the **Old Sacristy** ★★ *(at the far end of the north transept)*. Donatello was responsible for part of the decoration of the latter and also the two **pulpits** ★★ in the nave with bronze panels which are works of admirable virtuosity and full of a great sense of drama.

★★ **Laurenziana Library.** – Cosimo the Elder's library was added to by Lorenzo the Magnificent. Access is through the charming 15C **cloisters** ★ *(entrance to the left of the church)*. The vestibule was designed as an exterior and is occupied by a magnificent **staircase** ★ supremely elegant as the curved steps of the central flight lead up to the library proper. The staircase was built by Ammannati to Michelangelo's designs. The **library**, also by Michelangelo, displays in rotation some of the 10 000 manuscripts.

★★ **Medici Chapels.** – *Entrance on Piazza Madonna degli Aldobrandini.* This includes the Princes' Chapel and New Sacristy.
The **Princes' Chapel** ★ (17-18C), grandiose but gloomy, is faced with semi-precious stones and marbles and is the funerary chapel for Cosimo I and his descendants.
The **New Sacristy** ★★ was Michelangelo's first architectural work and despite its name was always intended as a funerary chapel. Begun in 1520 it was left unfinished when the artist left Florence in 1534. Michelangelo achieved a great sense of rhythm and solemnity by using contrasting materials, dark grey sandstone *(pietra serena)* and white of the walls and marbles. The famous **Medici tombs** ★★★ were also the work of Michelangelo. Giuliano, Duke of Nemours (d1516) is portrayed as Action, surrounded by allegorical figures of Day and Night, and Lorenzo II, Duke of Urbino (d1519) as a Thinker with Dawn and Dusk at his feet. Of the plans for Lorenzo the Magnificent's tomb only the admirable group of the Madonna and Child flanked by saints was completed. In the plain tomb underneath lie Lorenzo the Magnificent and his brother Giuliano.

★★ **Medici Palace** (Palazzo Medici-Riccardi) (HX). – This noble but austere building, with its ground floor rustication, is typical of the Florentine Renaissance style. It was begun by Michelozzo on the order of his friend, Cosimo the Elder, in 1444. It was a Medici residence from 1459 to 1540 and it was here that Lorenzo the Magnificent held court and welcomed poets, philosophers and artists alike. In the second half of the 17C it passed to the Riccardi who made extensive alterations to the building.

Chapel. – *First floor: entrance by the first stairway on the right.* This tiny chapel was decorated with admirable **frescoes** ★★★ (1459) by **Benozzo Gozzoli.** The Procession of the Kings is a vivid picture of Florentine life with portraits of the Medici and of famous dignitaries from the East who had assembled for the Council of Florence in 1439.

★ **Luca Giordano Gallery.** – *First floor: entrance by the second stairway on the right.* The entire roof of this gallery built by the Riccardi at the end of the 17C and splendidly decorated with gold stucco, carved panels and great painted mirrors, is covered by a brightly coloured baroque fresco of the Apotheosis of the second Medici dynasty masterfully painted by Luca Giordano in 1683.

★ **Santa Maria Novella** (GX).– The Church of Santa Maria Novella and the adjoining monastery were founded in the 13C by the Dominicans. The church overlooks an elongated square which was originally the setting for chariot races.

★ **Church.** – Begun in 1246, the church was completed only in 1360, except for the **façade** with harmonious lines and geometric patterns in white and green marble, designed by Alberti (upper section) in the 15C. It is a large church (100m – 328ft) designed for preaching. On the wall of the third bay in the north aisle is a famous **fresco** ★ of the Trinity with the Virgin, St John and the donors in which Masaccio, adopting the new Renaissance theories, shows great mastery of perspective. In the north chapel, the Strozzi Chapel (raised) is decorated with **frescoes** ★ (1357) by the Florentine Nardo di Cione depicting the Last Judgment on a grand scale. The **polyptych** ★ on the altar is by Nardo's brother, Orcagna di Cione. The sacristy contains a fine **Crucifix** ★ *(above the entrance)* by Giotto and a delicate glazed terracotta **niche** ★ by Giovanni della Robbia. In the Gondi Chapel *(1st on the left of the high altar)* is displayed the famous **Crucifix** ★★ by Brunelleschi, which so struck Donatello that he is said, on first seeing it, to have dropped the basket of eggs he was carrying. The chancel is ornamented with admirable **frescoes** ★★★ by **Domenico Ghirlandaio** who, on the theme of the Lives of the Virgin and of St John the Baptist, painted a dazzling picture of Florentine life in the Renaissance era.
The church is flanked by two cloisters. The finest are the **Green Cloisters** ★, so-called after the dominant colour of the frescoes painted by Paolo Uccello and his school. Opening off these is the **Spaniards' Chapel** with late 14C **frescoes** ★★ by **Andrea di Bonaiuto** (also known as Andrea da Firenze). With an intricate symbolism the frescoes depict the Church Triumphant and the glorification of the action of the Dominicans.

PONTE VECCHIO, PITTI PALACE AND BOBOLI GARDEN
time: 2 hours

★ **Ponte Vecchio** (HY). – This, Florence's oldest bridge, crosses the Arno at its narrowest point and has been rebuilt several times. It has a curious appearance with jewellers' shops lining the roadway and above the Corridoio Vasariano *(p 90)*.

★ **Pitti Palace** (GHZ). – This 15C Renaissance building, of rugged but imposing appearance, with pronounced rustication and many windows, was built to the plans of Brunelleschi for the Pitti family, the rivals of the Medici. It was Cosimo I's wife, Eleanora di Toledo who enlarged the palace by the addition of two wings.

★ ★ ★ **Palatina Gallery.** – *First floor.* The marvellous collection of paintings is hung quite at ran
⏱ dom. There are two wonderful **groups** ★ ★ ★ of works by **Raphael** and **Titian: Portrait of** a
Lady or *La Valata* (Hall of Jupiter; *illustration p 30)*, **Madonna del Granduca** and **Madonna della**
Seggiola (both in the Hall of Saturn); by Titian portraits, **La Bella** and **The Aretino** and **The**
Concert (Hall of Venus) and the **Grey-eyed Nobleman** (Hall of Apollo). Among the many
other paintings which hang in the rooms, splendidly decorated by Pietro da Cortona,
note two seascapes by Salvator Rosa (Hall of Venus), portraits by Van Dyck (Hall of
Apollo), *The Four Philosophers* by Rubens and *Cardinal Bentivoglio* by Van Dyck, a *De*-
scent from the Cross by Fra Bartolomeo, and two large landscapes by Rubens (Hall of
Venus).

Further on are an astonishing **Sleeping Cupid** by Caravaggio (Hall of the Education of
Jupiter), a *Virgin and Child* by Filippo Lippi (Hall of Prometheus), a *St Sebastian* by Sodoma (Castagnoli Room), as well as numerous works from the Italian and foreign
schools by Perugino, Dosso Dossi, Andrea del Sarto, Rosso Fiorentino, Pontormo,
Bronzino, Veronese, Guido Reni, Sustermans, Velasquez, etc.

⏱ **State Apartments.** – *First floor.* These are lavishly decorated with pictures, works of art
and admirable tapestries.

★ ★ **Silver Museum** (Museo degli Argenti). – *Ground floor and mezzanine.* This contains an
⏱ exceptional collection of works in semi-precious stones *(pietre dure)*, ivories, glassware and silver plate largely from the Medici collections.

★ **Modern Art Gallery.** - *Second floor.* Works, mostly Tuscan, illustrating the trends that
⏱ influenced Italian sculpture and painting in the 19C. In the section devoted to Neo-
Classical and Romantic art, note works by the Benvenuti, Canova, Bezzuoli and Hayez,
Bartolini. The **Macchiaioli** movement *(p 31)* is represented by an exceptional **series** ★ ★
by Fattori, Lega, Signorini, Cecioni...

★ **Boboli Garden** (Giardino di Boboli) (GHZ). – This Italian-style terraced garden, behind
⏱ the Pitti Palace, was designed in 1549 by Tribolo and is ornamented with antique and
Renaissance statues. At the end of an avenue to the left of the palace is the grotto by
Buontalenti. Crossing the amphitheatre you reach the highest point of the garden from
which, on the right, the **Viottolone** ★, an avenue of pines and cypresses runs down to
Piazzale dell'Isolotto ★, a circular pool with a small island, bearing citrus trees and a foun-
⏱ tain by Giovanni Bologna. A pavilion houses a **Porcelain Museum** ★ (HZ M²). The **Citadel**
Belvedere, at the top of the hill, affords a splendid **panorama** ★ ★ of Florence and the cele-
brated Florentine countryside. The elegant villa which dominates the bastion was by
Buontalenti.

SAN MARCO QUARTER *time: 2 hours*

★ ★ **Convent and Museum of St Mark** (Convento e Museo di San Marco) (JV). – The
⏱ museum in a former Dominican monastery rebuilt *c*1436 in a very plain style by
Michelozzo is virtually the **Fra Angelico Museum** ★ ★ ★. Fra Angelico took orders in Fiesole
before coming to St Mark's, where he decorated the walls of the monks' cells with
edifying scenes. Humility, gentleness and mysticism were the qualities expressed
by this artistic monk in a technique that was still Gothic. His refined use of colour,
delicate draughtsmanship, timid handling of the subject matter imbued these frescoes with a pacifying power, so appropriate for this oasis of calm and place of
meditation.

Ground floor. – The former guest quarters, opening off the cloisters on the right, contain
many of the Dominican's works on wood, especially the triptych depicting the **Descent**
from the Cross, the famous **Last Judgment** and a series of other religious scenes. The
chapter house has the severe Crucifixion while the refectory contains an admirable **Last**
Supper ★ by Ghirlandaio.

First floor. – The staircase is dominated by his well balanced and sober masterpiece the
Annunciation. The monks' cells open off three corridors, with lovely timber ceilings. Following the corridor to the left of the stairs, note the Apparition of Christ to the Penitent
Magdalen (1st cell on the left), the Transfiguration (6th cell on the left) and the Coronation of the Virgin (9th cell on the left).

At the far end of the next corridor were the cells of Savonarola, who was prior of
St Mark's. Off the corridor on the right is the **library** ★, one of Michelozzo's finest ac-
complishments.

★ ★ **Academy Gallery** (Galleria dell'Accademia) (JV). – The paintings in this collection are
⏱ judiciously hung and give the visitor some idea of the extraordinary personality of
Michelangelo and his conflict between the nature of his raw materials and his idealistic
vision. The **main gallery** ★ ★ ★ contains the powerful figures of **Four Slaves** (1513-20) and
St Matthew (all unfinished) who would seem to be trying to struggle free from the
marble. At the far end of the gallery, in a specially designed apse (1873), is the monumental figure of **David** (1501-4), the symbol of youthful but well mastered force and a
perfect example of the sculptor's humanism. The **picture gallery** ★ has works by 15C
Tuscan masters, including the painted chest by Adimari and two Botticellis.

★ **Piazza della Santissima Annunziata** (JV). – This fine square is adorned with an
equestrian statue of Ferdinand I de' Medici by Giovanni Bologna and two Baroque
fountains.

Church of the Santissima Annunziata (JV S). – This church was rebuilt in the 15C by
Michelozzo. It is preceded by an atrium decorated with **frescoes** ★ (damaged) by
Rosso Fiorentino, Pontormo, Andrea del Sarto, Franciabigio and Baldovinetti. Inside
there is a miraculous image of a Madonna.

Foundlings Hospital (Ospedale degli Innocenti) (JV M⁴) – This is preceded by an elegant 15C **portico** ★ by Brunelleschi, with corners decorated with touching terracotta
⏱ **medallions** ★ of children by Andrea della Robbia. The **art gallery** contains some interesting
works by Florentine artists.

SANTA CROCE AND A TRIP TO THE HILLS *time: 2 hours*

★ **Santa Croce** (JY). — The church and cloisters of Santa Croce give onto one of the town's oldest squares.

★ **Church.** — This is the church of the Franciscans. It was started in 1294 and completed in the second half of the 14C. The façade and the campanile date from the 19C. The **interior** is vast (140m – 460ft by 40m – 130ft) as the church was designed for preaching and consists of a single spacious nave and slender apse with fine 15C stained glass windows. The church is paved with 276 tombstones and along the walls are sumptuous tombs.

South aisle: By the first pillar, a Virgin and Child by A. Rossellino (15C); opposite, the tomb of Michelangelo (d1564) by Vasari; opposite the second pillar, the funerary monument (19C) to Dante (d1321, buried at Ravenna); by the third pillar, a fine **pulpit**★ (1476) by Benedetto da Maiano and facing it the monument to V. Alfieri (d1803) by Canova; opposite the fourth pillar, the 18C monument to Machiaveli (d1527); facing the fifth pillar, an elegant low-relief of the **Annunciation**★★ carved in stone and embellished with gold by Donatello; opposite the sixth pillar, the **tomb of Leonardo Bruni**★★ (humanist and chancellor of the Republic, d1444) by B. Rossellino, and next to it the tomb of Rossini (d1868).

South transept: At the far end, the Baroncelli Chapel with **frescoes**★ (1338) depicting the Life of the Virgin by Taddeo Gaddi and at the altar the **polyptych**★, Coronation of the Virgin from Giotto's studio.

★ **Sacristy** *(access by the corridor on the right of the chancel):* This dates from the 14C and is adorned with **frescoes**★ including a Crucifixion by Taddeo Gaddi and, in the fine Rinuccini Chapel, with scenes from the Life of the Virgin and of Mary Magdalen by Giovanni da Milano (14C). At the far end of the corridor is the harmonious Medici Chapel (1434) built by Michelozzo with a fine **altarpiece**★ in glazed terracotta by Andrea della Robbia.

Chancel: The first chapel to the right of the altar contains moving **frescoes**★★ (*c*1320) by Giotto depicting the life of St Francis; in the third chapel is the tomb of Julie Clary, the wife of Joseph Bonaparte. The chancel proper is covered with **frescoes**★ (1380) by Agnolo Gaddi relating the legend of the Holy Cross.

North transept: At the far end is a famous **Crucifix**★★ by Donatello, which Brunelleschi tried to surpass at Santa Maria Novella.

North aisle *(coming back):* Beyond the second pillar, a fine **monument**★ to Carlo Marsuppini by Desiderio da Settignano (15C); facing the fourth pillar the tombstone of L. Ghiberti (d1455); the last tomb (18C) is that of Galileo (d1642).

Great cloisters. — *Entrance at the far end of the first cloisters, on the right.* These very elegant cloisters were designed by Brunelleschi shortly prior to his death (1446) and were only completed in 1453.

Santa Croce Museum (Museo dell'Opera di Santa Croce). — This is installed in the buildings around the first cloisters and in particular in the former refectory. The museum contains a famous **Crucifix**★ by Cimabue which was seriously damaged by the 1966 floods. Santa Croce was one of the Florentine monuments to suffer most in these floods.

★ **Pazzi Chapel.** — *At the far end of the first cloisters; entrance to the right of the church.* This chapel by Brunelleschi is entered through a domed portico, and is a masterpiece of the Florentine Renaissance remarkable for its original conception, its skilful proportions and the harmony of its decoration (glazed terracotta from the della Robbia workshop).

★ **A Trip to the Hills** (Passeggiata dei Colli). — On the south bank of the Arno *(see the plan of the built-up area in the current Michelin Red Guide Italia)*. This splendid road to the hills was built by Giuseppe Poggi between 1865 and 1870 and offers numerous glimpses of the city, in particular from Piazzale Michelangiolo.

Not far from this square, in a splendid **setting**★★ overlooking the town, the **Church of San Miniato al Monte**★★ built from the 11 to 13C is one of the most remarkable examples of Florentine Romanesque architecture. Its very elegant façade is decorated with geometric designs in green and white marble, not unlike those of the baptistry. The harmonious interior also ornamented with multicoloured marble contains a 13C pavement. The **Chapel of Cardinal James of Portugal**★ opening out of the north aisle is a fine Renaissance structure. In the centre of the nave is a Chapel of the Crucifix by Michelozzo. The pulpit and chancel screen *(transenna)* form a remarkable **ensemble**★★ beautifully inlaid with marble dating from the early 13C. The apse is adorned by a mosaic depicting Christ conferring His Blessing.

The **frescoes**★ (1387) in the **sacristy** are by Spinello Aretino. The 11C **crypt** has fine columns with antique capitals.

ADDITIONAL SIGHTS

★ **Strozzi Palace** (HY F). — Dating from the end of the 15C, this is one of the finest privately owned palaces in Florence with its rusticated stonework, cornice and arcaded courtyard.

★ **Frescoes of Santa Maria del Carmine** (GY). — The outstanding point of interest of this church which was badly damaged by fire in the 18C, is its cycle of frescoes in the **Brancacci Chapel** depicting the life of St Peter. The principal artist was **Masaccio** who at the age of 27 in 1427 was a pioneer of the Renaissance. In all of the scenes, be it **Adam and Eve being banished from the Garden of Eden**, the **Payment of the Tribute, St Peter Baptising** or **St Peter healing the sick** the figures portray an astonishing realism and inner gravity with their solid but simple forms, the dull colours and a new mastery of the play of light. The remaining frescoes are by Masolino (1424) and Filippino Lippi (1481).

★★ **Last Supper of San Salvi** (Cenacolo di San Salvi). – *To the east of Florence (see the pla
of the built-up area in the current Michelin Red Guide Italia,* **FU A**). *Take the Piazza Be
caria, Via V. Gioberti and its continuation beyond the Piazza L.B. Alberti, Via Aretina an
finally Via San Salvi. Entrance at no 16.*
The former refectory of the abbey contains a splendid fresco of the Last Supper (1520
by **Andrea del Sarto** which is a masterpiece of composition and colour and has a dramat
sense of reality.

★ **Orsanmichele** (HY G). – Originally a grain storehouse, Orsanmichele was rebuilt i
the 14C in a transitional Gothic-Renaissance style. The statues in the niches alone ar
a museum of sculpture and portray the patrons of the corporations. There are work
by Donatello, Ghiberti, Verrocchio, etc. Inside, there is a splendid Gothic **tabernacle**★
by Orcagna, decorated with coloured marble.

Holy Trinity Church (Santa Trinità) (HY N). – Despite the sober interior, the **Chapel**
the Annunciation★ has frescoes by Lorenzo Monaco and the **Sassetti Chapel**★★ has other
depicting scenes from the life of St Francis by Ghirlandaio.

★ **Archaeological Museum** (Museo Archeologico) (JVX M³). – *38 Via della Colonna
Important collections of Greek, Egyptian, Etruscan and Roman art. Do not miss th
outstanding Etruscan masterpiece the **Chimera from Arezzo**★★ dating from the 5C BC.

Casa Guidi (GZ). – *8 Piazza S. Felice.*
Florentine home of the Victorian poets Robert and Elizabeth Barrett Browning. Eliza
beth is buried in the English cemetery in the centre of Piazza Donatello.

★ **Church of the Holy Spirit** (Santo Spirito) (GY). – The simple and graceful interior o
this church, built from 1444 onwards to plans by Brunelleschi, resembles Sa
Lorenzo. The numerous **works of art**★ include a Madonna and Saints by Filippino Lipp
(fifth chapel in the south transept).

La Badia (HJ L). – This was originally the church of a former abbey *(badia)* and it ha
one of Florence's most elegant **campaniles**★.
Inside are several works of art including Filippino Lippi's **Virgin appearing to St Bernard**
(to the left on entering), a delicate **relief**★★ sculpture in marble by Mino da Fiesole an
two **tombs**★ also carved by the same artist.

★ **Last Supper of Sant'Apollonia** (Cenacolo di Sant'Apollonia) (HV R). – In this forme
refectory there hangs a remarkable Last Supper (1430) by Andrea del Castagno, wit
the characteristics pure colours of this artist.

★ **Last Supper by Ghirlandaio** (GX A). – Next to **All Saints Church** (Ognissanti) whic
was remodelled in the 17C, is the former monastery refectory *(no 42 to the left of th
church)* containing Ghirlandaio's *Last Supper*.

★ **Florentine House and Museum** (Museo dell'Antica Casa Fiorentina) (HY M⁵). – Thi
tall 14C house contains a museum which evokes the life of a rich Florentine family o
the period.

New Market Loggia (Loggia del Mercato Nuovo) (HY X). – This loggia with its elegan
Renaissance arcades was built in the 16C in the heart of the commercial district. It nov
serves as a market for Florentine crafts.

★ **Science Museum** (Museo di Storia della Scienza) (HY M⁶). – Historical presentation o
a rich collection of scientific instruments and a section on the life and work of th
mathematician and astronomer Galileo.

★ **Semi-precious Stone Workshop** (Opificio delle Pietre dure) (JVX M⁷). – Lorenzo th
Magnificent was responsible for reviving the ancient tradition of decorating with sem
precious stones (quartz, porphyry, onyx, jasper, etc.) in the form of mosaics *(pietr
dure)*. The workshop now specialises in restoration work and there is a small **museu**
with some quite remarkable works on display.

★ **Buonarroti's House** (Casa Buonarroti) (JY). – Michelangelo Buonarroti owned this hous
although he never lived here. There are several of the sculptor's works on displa
inside.

EXCURSIONS

See the plan of the built-up area in the current Michelin Guide Italia.

★★ **Medici Villas** (Ville Medicee). – In the 15 and 16C, the Medici built numerous elegan
villas throughout the Florentine countryside.

Villa della Petraia. – *3km – 2 miles to the north.* In 1576 Cardinal Ferdinand de' Medic
commissioned the architect Buontalenti to convert this former castle into a villa. In th
16C **garden**★, there is a remarkable fountain by N. Tribolo with a bronze statue of Venu
by Giovanni Bologna.

Villa di Castello. – *5km – 3 miles to the north.* This villa was embellished by Lorenzo th
Magnificent and restored in the 18C. It has a very fine garden adorned with statue
and fountains.

★ **Villa di Poggio a Caiano**. – *17km – 11 miles to the northwest by the Pistoia road, the S 66
Sangallo designed this villa for Lorenzo the Magnificent. The loggia is decorated by th
della Robbia. The magnificent drawing-room has a coffered ceiling and **frescoes** b
Pontormo representing Vertumnus and Pomona, goddess of fruit.

Galluzzo Carthusian Monastery (Certosa del Galluzzo). – *6km – 4 miles to the sout
by the Sierra road.*
The monastery was founded in the 14C and remodelled many times. The adjoinin
palace contains frescoes by Pontormo. The monks' cells are grouped around the Ren
aissance **cloisters**★.

FORLÌ Emilia-Romagna

Michelin map 988 fold 15 – Town plan in the current Michelin Red Guide Italia

Forlì is set on the Via Emilia and it was an independent commune ruled by an overlord in the 13 and 14C. The citadel was heroically defended in 1500 by Caterina Sforza against Cesare Borgia.

Basilica of San Mercuriale. – *Piazza Aurelio Saffi.* The basilica is dominated by an imposing Romanesque campanile. The lunette of the doorway is adorned with a 13C low-relief. The numerous works of art, inside, include several paintings by Marco Palmezzano and the tomb of Barbara Manfredi by Francesco di Simone Ferrucci.

⊙ **Picture Gallery (Pinacoteca).** – *72 Corso della Repubblica.* The collection includes works by local 13-15C artists. Note the delicate **portrait of a young girl** by Lorenzo di Credi.

EXCURSIONS

Cesena. – *19km – 12 miles by the Via Emilia.* The town lies at the foot of a hill on
⊙ which stands the great 15C castle of the Malatestas. It contains the Renaissance **Malatestiana Library★** *(Piazza Bufalini).* The interior comprises three long aisles with vaulting supported on fluted columns capped with fine capitals. On display are valuable manuscripts, including some from the famous school of miniaturists at Ferrara, as well as the Missorium, a great silver-gilt dish possibly dating from the 4C.

Bertinoro. – *14km – 9 miles to the southeast.* This small town is famous for its panorama and its yellow wine (Albana). In the middle of the town is a "hospitality column" fitted with rings, each corresponding with a local home. The ring to which the traveller tethered his horse used to decide which family should be his hosts. From the nearby terrace there is a wide **view★** of Romagna.

★★ FOSSANOVA Abbey Latium

Michelin map 988 fold 26

⊙ Standing, as the rule prescribes, in a lonely site, the Cistercian Abbey of Fossanova is the oldest of the Order in Italy. Monks from Cîteaux in France settled here in 1133. In 1163 they began to build their abbey church, which was to serve as a model for many Italian churches (Casamari for instance). Although rather heavily restored, Fossanova has kept its original architecture and arrangements intact. It was designed in accordance with the rules of austerity laid down by St Bernard.

Church. – Consecrated in 1208, it is in the Burgundian style but such decoration as there is, recalls the Lombard tradition with traces of the Moorish style. As regards the exterior, the Latin cross plan with flat east end, the octagonal transept crossing tower, the rose windows and the triple bayed window of the east end are typically Cistercian. The well-lit and lofty interior has a central nave balanced by aisles with groined vaulting.

Cloisters. – These are picturesque with three Romanesque sides and the fourth or south side in the late 13C pre-Gothic style (transitional Romanesque Gothic style). The small columns are Lombard in form and decoration. The fine Gothic chapterhouse opens into the cloisters through wide twin bays. It was in the guest house, which stands apart, that the teacher and scholar St Thomas Aquinas died on 7 March 1274.

★ GAETA Latium

Michelin map 988 fold 27

This former fortress, still partly walled, is admirably sited on the point of a promontory bounding a beautiful **bay★**. The coastal road round the bay affords magnificent views. Gaeta has a pleasant beach of fine sand, Serapo Beach, facing south.

Cathedral (Duomo). – The cathedral is interesting, especially for its 10C and 15C Romanesque Moorish campanile adorned with glazed earthenware and resembling the Sicilian or Amalfi bell towers. Inside the late 13C **paschal candelabrum★** is remarkable for its size and for its forty-eight low-reliefs depicting scenes from the lives of Christ and St Erasmus, the patron saint of sailors.
A picturesque medieval quarter lies near the cathedral.

Castle (Castello). – The castle dating from the 8C, has been altered many times. The lower castle was built by the Angevins while the upper one was the work of the Aragonese.

⊙ **Monte Orlando.** – Standing on the summit is the tomb of the Roman Consul Munatius Plancus, a friend of Caesar's who founded the colonies of Lugdunum (Lyons) and Augusta Raurica (Augst near Basle).

EXCURSION

Sperlonga. – *16km – 10 miles to the northwest.* The village stands on a rocky spur pitted with many caves.
⊙ **Tiberius' Cave and the Archaeological Museum.** – The cave lies below the Gaéta-Terracina road *(to the left after the last tunnel).* It was in this cave that the Emperor Tiberius narrowly escaped death when part of the roof fell in.
In the museum, by the roadside, there are 4-2C BC statues, outstanding heads and busts and some realistic theatrical masks. There is also a reconstitution of a colossal group depicting the punishment meted out to the Cyclops Polyphemus by Ulysses.
At the Gaeta end of the tunnel are the charred ruins of Tiberius' Villa.

★★★ **GARGANO** Promontory Apulia

Michelin map 988 fold 28

The Gargano Promontory, shining white under a blue sky, projects like a spur from the "boot" of Italy. It is one of the most attractive natural regions of Italy with its wide horizons, its deep and mysterious forests and its lonely, rugged coastline.

Physically, Gargano is quite independent from the Apennine Mountains; it is a limestone plateau fissured with crevices into which water runs. Originally an island Gargano was connected to the mainland by an accumulation of deposits brought down by the rivers from the Apennines. Today the massif is riven by high altitude valleys, with fertile valley floors, and is heavily afforested in the east.

The scanty pastures and moors on the plateaux support flocks of sheep and goats and herds of black pigs.

The picturesque **Tremiti Islands** belong to the same geological formation *(access: see the current Michelin Red Guide Italia).*

TOUR

Leave from Monte Sant' Angelo and follow the itinerary indicated on the local map (146km – 91 miles – allow 1 day).

★ **Monte Sant'Angelo.** – *Description p 102.*

★★ **Umbra Forest** (Foresta Umbra). – Forests are rare in Apulia and this vast expanse of venerable beeches covers over 10 000 ha – 24 711 acres of undulating countryside. Visitors are welcome and the forest is well equipped with recreational facilities. Shortly after the road to Vieste there is a forestry lodge (Casa Forestale) which now serves as a **visitor centre.**

★ **Peschici.** – Well situated on a rocky spur jutting out into the sea, this fishing town is now a seaside resort.

★ **Vieste.** – In a similar setting to Peschici, this small but ancient town, crowded on the clifftop, is dominated by its 13C cathedral. To the south is a vast sandy beach with a limestone sea-stack, **Faraglione di Pizzomunno,** standing offshore.

Between Vieste and Mattinata there is a very fine **scenic stretch**★★ of corniche road, overlooking the indented coastline. After 8km – 5 miles the square tower in **Testa del Gargano** marks the easternmost extremity of the massif: fine **view**★ of the inlet, **Cala di San Felice,** which is spanned by a natural arch at the seaward end.

Beyond the popular holiday resort of **Pugnochiuso,** there is another beauty spot the **Bay of Zagare**★ (Baia delle Zagare).

Mattinata. – As you descend towards Mattinata there is a fine **view**★★ of this agricultural market town, a white mass amid a sea of olive groves encircled by a rim of mountains.

★★ **GENOA** (GENOVA) Liguria   Pop 722 026

Michelin map 988 fold 13 – Local maps pp 163 and 164 – Town plan p 98 – Plan of the built-up area in the current Michelin Red Guide Italia

Genoa the superb, the greatest seaport in Italy, spreads over a mountain amphitheatre. It is a city of surprises and contrasts, where the most splendid palaces stand side by side with the humblest alleyways.

HISTORICAL NOTES

Genoese expansion was based on a strong fleet, which already in the 11C ruled supreme over the Tyrrhenian Sea, having vanquished the Saracens. By 1104 the fleet already comprised seventy ships, all built in the famous dockyards, making it a formidable weapon much coveted by foreign powers such as the French Kings, Philip the Fair and Philip of Valois.

The Crusaders offered the Genoese an opportunity of establishing trading posts on the shores of the Eastern Mediterranean. Following the creation of the Republic of St George in 1100, seamen, merchants, bankers and money lenders united their efforts to establish the maritime supremacy of Genoa. Initially Genoa allied itself with Pisa in the struggle against the Saracens (11C) and then became her enemy in the conflict concerning Corsica (13C), and finally the most persistent rival of that other great maritime republic, Venice (14C), disputing with her the trading rights for the Mediterranean. Genoa had colonies as far afield as the Black Sea. In the 14C the Genoese merchant seamen exported the precious cargoes from the Orient, in particular they had the monopoly in the trading of alum used in the dyeing trade to fix colours.

Limited partnership companies flourished. Founded in 1408 the famous Bank of St George regrouping the maritime state's lending houses, administered the finances of the trading posts. The merchants became ingenious money lenders and instituted such modern methods as bills of credit, cheques and insurance to increase their profits.

Following continual struggles between the rival families of Genoa the decision was taken in 1339 to elect a doge for life and to seek, essentially in the 15C, foreign protection.

In 1528 the great admiral **Andrea Doria** (1466-1560) gave Genoa its aristocratic constitution which gave it the status of a mercantile republic. The enterprising and independent Andrea was one of Genoa's most famous sons: admiral, legislator, this intrepid and wise leader distinguished himself against the Turks in 1519 and while serving François I, by covering the French retreat after Pavia. In 1528, indignant at François I's unjust treatment of him, he entered the service of Charles V, who plied him with honours and favours. Following his

(Giraudon)

Andrea Doria by Sebastiano del Piombo

death and the development of ports on the Atlantic coast, Genoa declined as a port and it was Louis XIV who destroyed the harbour in 1684. In 1768 by the Treaty of Versailles Genoa surrendered Corsica to France. Later, after indulging the republican spirit of its own citizen, Giuseppe Mazzini, it became in 1848 one of the cradles of the Risorgimento *(qv)*.

Fine Arts in Genoa. – As in many countries, the decline of commercial prosperity in the 16C and 17C coincided with intense artistic activity, evidenced in the building of innumerable palaces and the arrival at Genoa of well known artists, especially the Flemish. In 1607 Rubens published a work on the *Palazzi di Genova (Palaces of Genoa)* and between 1621 to 1627 Van Dyck painted the Genoese nobility *(grandezza)*. Puget lived at Genoa from 1661 to 1667, working for patricians like the Dorias and the Spinolas.

The art of the Genoese school, characterised by intense drama and the use of muted colours, is represented by Luca Cambiaso (16C), Bernardo Strozzi (1581-1644), the admirable engraver Castiglione, and especially Alessandro Magnasco (1667-1749) whose sharp and colourful brushwork denotes him as a precursor of modern art.

In the domain of architecture, Galeazzo Alessi (1512-72), when at his best, was the equal of Sansovino and Palladio in the nobility and ingenuity of his designs when integrating isolated buildings with the existing urban landscape.

★★ **THE OLD TOWN** *time: allow 1 day*

This quarter extends from the old port up towards Via Garibaldi and Piazza De Ferrari.

★★ **The Port (EXY).** – From the raised road (Strada Sopraelevata – **EXYZ**) which skirts the port, there are good views of Italy's number one port. To the east the old port (Porto Vecchio) includes a pleasure boat harbour, shipyards, and embarkation terminals and quays for ferries leaving for the islands or Africa. To the west the modern port (Porto Nuovo) is fringed by an industrial zone with steel and chemical plants as well as oil refineries. This busy port handles imported raw materials (oil and petrol, coal, minerals, cereals, metal and wood) and exports manufactured goods such as machines, vehicles and textiles. There are organised **boat trips** to visit the port.

★ **Sailors' Quarter (FY).** – At the centre of this district is the 13C Palazzo San Giorgio which was the headquarters of the famous Bank of St George. The building was remodelled in the 16C.

Behind the palace on Piazza Banchi (of the banks) is the Loggia dei Mercanti which is now a fruit and vegetable market.

★ **Piazza San Matteo (FY).** – In the city centre, this small but harmonious square is lined with palaces that belonged to the Doria family. No 17 is a Renaissance building presented by a grateful republic to Andrea Doria.

The **Church of San Mateo** has a Genoese style façade with alternating courses of black and white stone. The tomb and sword of Andrea Doria are in the crypt.

★ **Cathedral of St Lawrence (San Lorenzo) (FY).** – The cathedral built between the 12C and 16C has a splendid Gothic **façade ★★** typical of the Genoese style. French influence appears in the placing of the 13C doorways and the large rose window. Carving on the central doorway represents a Tree of Jesse and scenes from the Life of Christ (on the piers) and a Christ and Martyrdom of St Lawrence between the Symbols of the Evangelists (on the tympanum). The early 13C knifegrinder, at the right corner of the façade, resembles the angel of the sundial at Chartres and performs the same function. The transept crossing is crowned with a dome, designed by Alessi. The severe and majestic **interior★** has marble columns in the nave. The **Chapel of St John the Baptist★** contains the bones of St John.

GENOVA

```
0          200 m
```

NERVI LA SPEZIA   S. Maria di Carignano

⊙ The **treasury★** possesses the famous **Sacro Catino**, a cup given to Solomon by the Queen of Sheba, from which Christ is said to have drunk at the Last Supper.

★ **Via Garibaldi** (FY). – This street of palaces, once known as Via Aurea, was built to designs by Alessi in the 16C. It is one of the loveliest streets in Italy.

At No 1 is Alessi's **Palazzo Cambiaso** (1565); No 3 is the **Palazzo Parodi** (1578); No 4 the
⊙ **Palazzo Cataldi** (1588) again by Alessi has a delightful entrance hall and a dazzling gilded **gallery★**. Both No 6, **Palazzo Doria** and No 7, **Palazzo Podestà** (1565-67) are by the same
⊙ architect G.B. Castello. The **Town Hall** (H), the former Palazzo Doria Tursi, at No 9 has a lovely arcaded courtyard. The collections include the violin of Paganini and manu-
⊙ scripts by Christopher Columbus. No 11, **Palazzo Bianco** contains a very fine **art gallery★** (Flemish and Dutch paintings by Provost, Van der Goes, Gerard David, Van Dyck, Rubens, also French and Spanish works as well as canvases by the Genoese, Strozzi).
⊙ The **Palazzo Rosso** at No 18 also contains a **picture gallery★** with works by the Venetian (Titian, Veronese and Tintoretto) and Genoese schools, a canvas by Dürer and some remarkable **portraits★** by Van Dyck. In addition there are sections on baroque sculpture, Ligurian ceramics and medals.

Via Balbi (EX). – This street is joined to Via Garibaldi by Via Cairoli and is lined
⊙ with palaces. The **Royal Palace** (Palazzo Reale) formerly the Balbi Durazzo, at No 10, dates from 1650 and contains a Van Dyck room. The imposing 17C **University Palace★** at No 5 has a court and majestic staircase. The 17C Palazzo Durazzo Pallavicini is at No 1.

★ **Palazzo Spinola Gallery** (Galleria Nazionale di Palazzo Spinola) (FY). – The beautifully
⊙ decorated apartments of this 16-18C mansion, with their period furnishings make an ideal setting for the works of art. The fine frescoes (17-18C) of the **ceilings★** are by Tavarone, L. Ferrari and S. Galeotti. The **art collection★** regroups works by painters of the Italian and Flemish Renaissance: an **Ecce Homo** by Antonello da Messina, a *Madonna* and especially a sumptuous polyptych, of the **Adoration of the Magi★★** by Joos Van Cleve and finally a *Crucifixion* by Brueghel the Younger. From the 17C there are can-vases by Strozzi, Castiglione Genovese and a ravishing **Portrait of a Child** by Van Dyck.

ADDITIONAL SIGHTS

Piazza De Ferrari (FY). – This square is bordered by the remains of the Opera House, partly destroyed in 1944, and numerous palaces including the Ducal Palace (1778) with its monumental façade overlooking Piazza Matteotti. The **Church of St Ambrose** (Sant'Ambrogio) was built by Tibaldi in 1597 and its sumptuous interior is the setting for an Assumption by Guido Reni and a Circumcision and a St Ignatius Exorcising by Rubens.

Church of St Donatus (San Donato) (FZ). – This 12-13C church has an attractive octagonal **campanile★** in the Romanesque style. The Romanesque interior is also quite charming. Note the 14C Virgin and Child in the chapel to the right of the chancel.

Church of Santissima Annunziata (EFX). – This 17C church is one of the most splendid in Genoa. The sumptuous decoration inside is a happy mixture of gilding, stucco and frescoes and is a good example of the Genoese baroque style.

Church of Santa Maria di Carignano. – *Take Via Ravasco* (**FZ 39**).
This vast church was built in the 16C to plans by Alessi. Inside there is a lovely statue of **St Sebastian★** by Puget.

Villetta Di Negro (GXY). – On higher ground to the northwest of Piazza Corvetto, this is a sort of belvedere-labyrinth with palm trees, cascades and artificial grottoes. From the terrace there is a lovely **view★** over the town and the sea. Standing on the summit is the **Chiossone Museum★ (M)** with sections on Chinese art and Japanese arms and armour, a remarkable collection of prints, ivories and lacquerwork.

Castelletto (FX). – From the terrace *(reached by lift)* there is a fine **view★** of the town.

★ **Staglieno Cemetery (Cimitero di Staglieno)**. – *1.5km – 1 mile to the north. Leave from Piazza Corvetto* (**GY**), *see the town plan in the current Michelin Red Guide Italia.*
This curious cemetery has a mixture of sumptuous tombs and simple clay tumuli.

★ # GRADO Friuli-Venezia Giulia   Pop 9 552

Michelin map 988 fold 6

At the time of the Barbarian invasions the inhabitants of Aquileia founded Grado which was from the 5C to the 9C the residence of the Patriarchs of Aquileia. Today Grado is a busy little fishing port and seaside resort with a growing reputation. The town is surrounded by the waters of the lagoon which have a certain grandeur.

★ **Old Quarter**. – This is a picturesque district with a network of narrow alleys *(calli)* running between the canal-port and the cathedral. The Cathedral (Duomo) of Santa Eufemia, on the basilical plan, dates from the 6C. It has marble columns with Byzantine capitals, a 6C mosaic pavement, a 10C ambo and a valuable silver-gilt **altarpiece★**, a Venetian work of the 14C. Beside the cathedral stands the 6C Basilica of St Mary of Grace (Santa Maria delle Grazie) which has some mosaics and fine capitals.

GROSSETO Tuscany   Pop 70 244

Michelin map 988 folds 24 and 25

This modern looking provincial capital is situated in the fertile Ombrone Plain. The old town is encircled with late 16C ramparts and their powerful bastions built by the Medici.

★ **Maremma Art and Archaeological Museum (Museo Archeologico e d'Arte della Maremma)**. – *Piazza Baccarini.*
The ground floor exhibitions cover Bronze Age jewellery and pottery, and a lovely collection of Etruscan and Roman sculpture. Grouped on the first floor are coins, statuettes, bronzes, Roman objects and a section on Greek and Etruscan ceramics.

Diocesan Museum (Museo Diocesano). – On the second floor this covers 13 to 17C paintings, as well as polychrome sculpture, ivories, bronzes and ecclesiastical plate.

St Francis Church (San Francesco). – *Piazza dell' Indipendenza.*
This 13C abbatial church has some small frescoes by the 14C Sienese school and a lovely painted 13C crucifix.

EXCURSION

Ruins of Roselle. – *12km – 8 miles to the northeast. Leave Grosseto by the Siena road and after 10km – 6 miles turn right into a non-surfaced road.*
Important excavation work has uncovered the Etruscan city of Roselle which was conquered by Rome in the 3C.

Times and charges for admission to sights described in the guide are listed *at the end of the guide.*

The sights are listed alphabetically in this section either under the place – town, village or area – in which they are situated or under their proper name.

Every sight for which there are times and charges is indicated by the symbol ⊘ *in the margin in the main part of the guide.*

The small town of Gubbio, spread out over the steep slopes of Monte Ingino, has preserved almost intact its rich cultural and artistic heritage. Encircling ramparts, the yellow ochre colour of its buildings, the toast-like tint of its Roman tiled roofs, and the outline of its towers and palaces as they stand out against a burnt and austere land scape make it one of the Italian towns in which the harsh atmosphere of the Middle Ages is most easily imagined. In the 11 and 12C the free commune of Gubbio, fiercely Ghibelline *(qv)*, enjoyed a period of expansion before being governed by the Montefel tro family in the 15C and then by the Della Roveres. The town became a papal posse sion from 1624.

Since medieval times the artisans of Gubbio have specialised in ceramics. One of them Maestro Giorgio, produced in the early 16C the famous iridescent red lustre – the secret of which was never discovered by nearby towns.

One of Gubbio's traditional events is the spectacular **Race of the Ceri**. Members of the different guilds *(ceraioli)* wearing ancient costumes and carrying the *ceri,* curious wooden poles over 4m – 13ft tall, race over a distance of 5km – 3 miles to the Basilica o St Ubald *(see the table of Principal Festivals at the end of the guide).*

SIGHTS

★★★ **Old Town (Città Vecchia).** – Wander through the narrow streets of the old town to admire the houses flanked by towers of nobility, palaces, small squares and hermi tages clinging to sheer rocks. A typical house has the shop or workshop on the ground floor with living quarters above and a loggia for storing the wool on the upper floor The façade, often a mixture of dressed stone, brick and rubblework has sometimes two doors, one for everyday use, the other narrower and known as the Door of Death through which coffins were brought out.

★★ **Consuls' Palace (Palazzo dei Consoli).** – Overlooking Piazza della Signoria this imposing Gothic building, supported by great arches rising above Via Baldassini, has a severe façade. Inside are the famous bronze **Tavole eugubine,** a series of tablets pertaining to the political and religious history and language of Umbria. The third floor of the loggia affords a good panorama. The next gallery has works by Signorelli.

★ **Ducal Palace (Palazzo Ducale).** – The palace was built from 1476 onwards to the plans of Francesco di Giorgio Martini, who was inspired by the ducal palace at Urbino. The elegant courtyard is delicately decorated. Of the rooms adorned with frescoes and lovely chimmey pieces, the Salone is particularly interesting.

★ **Roman Theatre (Teatro romano).** – This well preserved theatre dates from the Augus tan period.

Church of St Francis (San Francesco). – The inside walls of the north apse are cov ered with remarkable early 15C **frescoes★** by the local painter, Ottaviano Nelli.

Cathedral (Duomo). – The plain façade is adorned with low-reliefs showing the Sym bols of the Evangelists. The interior consists of a single nave. The **Episcopal Chapel** opens to the right. It is a luxurious sitting room decorated in the 17C, from which the bishop could follow the services.

Church of Santa Maria Nuova. – The church contains a charming **fresco★** by Otta viano Nelli.

EXCURSIONS

Fabriano. – *36km – 22 miles to the east.* The industrial town of Fabriano has manu factured paper since the 13C. This was the birthplace of two delightful artists, **Alle gretto Nuzi** (*c*1320-73) and **Gentile da Fabriano** (*c*1370-1427), who were both exponent of the International Gothic style *(qv)*. **Piazza del Comune★** in the centre of Fabriano, wit its elegant Gothic fountain, is overlooked by the grim 13C Governor's Residence (Palazzo del Podestà). A stairway leads to the quiet and charming **Piazza del Duomo★** bordered by the 15C hospital and the cathedral with frescoes by Allegretto Nuzi.

★★ **Frasassi Caves (Grotte di Frasassi).** – *50km – 31 miles to the northeast by the Sassofer rato road.* A tributary of the River Sentino has formed a vast network of underground caves. The largest, the **Grotta del Vento★★,** is composed of seven chambers where the visitor may admire stalagmites, stalactites and other diverse forms in a variety o colours.

Founded, according to tradition, by Hercules, this Roman town was overwhelmed lik Pompeii during the AD 79 eruption of Vesuvius.

It was a less important and more peaceful town than Pompeii. Its port was frequente by fishing boats, there were numerous craftsmen and many rich and cultured patr cians were drawn to the resort of Herculaneum because of its beautiful setting, ove looking the Bay of Naples. The five quarters of the town were divided by three mai streets *(decumani)*. The town has various examples of different types of dwellings, a of which were overwhelmed by the sea of mud which seeped into every nook. Th particular interest of a visit to Herculaneum is that all timber structures (frameworks beams, doors and partitions) were preserved by a hard shell of solidified mud, wherea at Pompeii they perished, burned. The houses were empty, but death caught up wit the inhabitants as they tried to flee the city.

ⓥ THE RUINS

time: 2 hours

From the access road *(go on foot)* there is a good view of the luxurious villas overlooking the sea.

House of the Inn (Casa dell' Albergo). – This vast patrician villa was about to be converted into apartments for letting, hence its name. It was one of the most badly damaged by the eruption.

★★ **House with the Mosaic Atrium (Casa dell' Atrio a mosaico).** – The atrium is paved with a chequered mosaic. The garden on the right is surrounded by a peristyle. On the left are the bedrooms and at the far end, a pleasant *triclinium* (dining room). The terrace, flanked by two small rest rooms, offers an attractive view of the sea.

★★ **The Wooden Trellis House (Casa a Graticcio).** – The house gets its name from the wooden trellis framework of the walls.

It is a unique example of this type of house from antiquity.

★ **House with the Wooden Partition (Casa del Tramezzo carbonizzato).** – The façade is remarkably well preserved. This is a good example of a patrician dwelling which housed several families. The atrium is separated from the *tablinium* (living room) by a wooden partition *(tramezzo)*. Only the sides of the partition remain standing.
Standing next door is the dyer's shop (**A**) containing an interesting wooden clothes-press.

★★ **Samnite House (Casa Sannitica).** – The house was built on the very simple plan typical of the Samnites. The splendid atrium is surrounded by a gallery with Ionic columns. The rooms are decorated with frescoes.

★★ **Baths (Terme).** – The baths of Herculaneum which are in excellent condition were built at the time of Augustus. They are not sumptuous but they show a remarkable degree of practical planning. In the **men's baths** visit the *palestra*, the cloakroom (**a**), the *frigidarium* (**b**) with frescoes on the ceiling, the *tepidarium* (**c**) and the *caldarium* (**d**). The **women's baths** include the waiting room (**e**), the cloakroom (*apodyterium* - **f**), adorned with a mosaic pavement representing Triton, the *tepidarium* (**g**) with a mosaic representing a labyrinth and the *caldarium* (**k**).

Men's Baths ☐
Women's Baths ■

★ **House with the Charred Furniture (Casa del Mobilio carbonizzato) (B).** – This small but rather elegant house has the remains of a charred bed in one room.

★★ **House with the Neptune and Amphitrite Mosaic (Casa del Mosaico di Nettuno e Anfitrite).** – This house is equipped with a **shop**★ whose counter opened on to the street. Mosaics depicting Neptune and Amphitrite adorn the nympheaum.

★ **House with a Fine Courtyard (Casa del Bel Cortile) (C).** – This is one of the most original houses in Herculaneum with its courtyard, stone staircase and balcony.

★ **The Bicentennial House (Casa del Bicentenario) (D).** – This house was laid bare in 1938, two hundred years after digging officially started. The house has fresco decorations and a small cross incorporated in a stucco panel. This is one of the oldest Christian relics.

★★ **Pistrinum.** – An inscription announces that this bakery belonged to Sextus Patulus Felix. In the shop and back room the visitor can see flour mills, storage jars and a large oven.

★★ **House of the Stags (Casa dei Cervi).** – This rich patrician mansion, probably the most beautiful among those overlooking the bay, is adorned with numerous frescoes and works of art, including an admirable sculptured group of stags being attacked by dogs.

★ **Small Baths (Terme Suburbane) (E).** – These are elegantly decorated.

★ **Theatre (Teatro).** – *Corso Resina.* The theatre could accommodate at least 2 000 spectators.

★★★ ISCHIA, Isle of Campania Pop 44 939

Michelin map 988 fold 27 – Local map p 132 – Access: see the current Michelin Red Guide Italia

Ischia, known as the Emerald Island because of its luxuriant vegetation, is the largest island in the Bay of Naples and one of its major attractions. A clear, sparkling light plays over a varied landscape: a coast covered with pinewoods, indented with bays and creeks sheltering villages with their colourful cubic houses; the slopes covered with olive trees and vineyards (producing the white or red Epomeo wine) and an occasional village with its white houses.

The cottages, sometimes roofed with a dome and with an outside staircase, often have walls covered with vines. The island rose out of the sea during the Tertiary era at the time of a volcanic eruption, and has many hot springs with various medicinal properties. The soil is volcanic in origin.

Sightseeing. – The map above, in addition to locating the towns and sights described in the guide, indicates other beauty spots in small black type. Being fairly small, a tour of the island can be done in a matter of hours *(40km – 25 miles: follow the itinerary on the map)*. The narrow road as it winds between rows of vines, offers numerous fine viewpoints of the coast and the sea.

★ **Ischia.** – *Town plan in the current Michelin Red Guide Italia.* The capital is divided into two settlements, **Ischia Porto** and **Ischia Ponte**. The Corso Vittoria Colona, an avenue lined with cafés and smart shops, links the port, in a former crater, and Ischia Ponte. The latter owes its name to the dyke built by the Aragonese to link the coast with the rocky islet on the summit of which stands the **Castello d'Ischia★★**. This is a group of buildings comprising a castle and several churches. On the outskirts is a large pinewood and a fine sandy beach.

★★★ **Monte Epomeo.** – *Access is by a path which branches off in a bend of the road once level with the public gardens. 1 1/2 hours on foot Rtn or by donkey.* From the summit of this tufa peak there is a vast **panorama** of the entire island and the Bay of Naples.

Serrara Fontana. – Not far from this settlement a belvedere offers a plunging **view★★** of the site of Sant' Angelo with its beach and peninsula.

★ **Sant' Angelo.** – The houses of this peaceful fishing village cluster round the small harbour. Nearby is the vast **Maronti Beach** (Marina dei Maronti) which has been transformed by the presence of many thermal establishments *(access by a footpath)*.

★ **Citara Beach** (Spiaggia di Citara). – This fine beach is sheltered by the majestic headland, Punta Imperatore. Another thermal establishment, Giardini di Poseidone, is laid out with its numerous warm water swimming pools amidst flowers and statues.

Forio. – The town centre is Piazza Municipio, a tropical garden overlooked by old buildings.

Lacco Ameno. – *Town plan in the current Michelin Red Guide Italia.* This was the first Greek colony on the island and was called Pithecusa (meaning lots of monkeys). It is now a holiday resort. The Church of Santa Restituta *(Piazza Santa Restituta)* was built on the remains of a paleochristian basilica and a necropolis. There is a small archaeological museum. The tour of the island ends with the important thermal spa of **Casamicciola Terme.**

★ PROCIDA

Access: see the current Michelin Red Guide Italia.

Procida is formed by craters levelled by erosion and has remained the wildest island in the Bay of Naples. The fishermen, gardeners and winegrowers live in delightful colourful houses with domes, arcades and terraces.

Michelin map 🞮🞮🞮 folds 2, 3 and 4 or 🞮🞮🞮 folds 6 to 10 – Local maps pp 104, 105 and 106

The Lake District extends from Piedmont to Venetia and Switzerland to Trentino in the north. Narrow and long these lakes are all of glacial origin and their banks are covered with a varied and luxuriant vegetation which flourishes with the particularly mild climate.

This fairyland of blue waters, at the foot of shapely mountains has always been a favourite haunt of artists and travellers. The charm and originality of these Pre-Alpine lakes, which are sometimes called the Lombard Lakes, are due to the juxtaposition of Alpine and southern scenery, the numerous villas with attractive gardens on the lakesides, the great variety of flowers throughout the year, the small sailing villages with their flotilla of boats where fresh fish is the speciality. Each lake has its own specific character making it quite different from its neighbour.

ⓥ **Sightseeing.** – The maps overleaf in addition to locating the towns and sites described in the guide, indicate other beauty spots in small black type. *For places in Switzerland see the Michelin Green Guide Switzerland.*

★★ LAKE MAGGIORE (LAGO MAGGIORE)

Maggiore is the most famous of the Italian lakes in part for its legendary beauty at times both majestic and wild, and also for the Borromean Islands. It is fed by the Ticino River, which rises in Switzerland, and its waters change from a jade green in the north to a deep blue in the south. The mountains of the Alps and Pre-Alps shelter the lake which enjoys a constantly mild climate in which a luxuriant and exotic vegetation flourishes.

ⓥ Take one of the **boat trips** on the lake, for the views from the lakeside road with its heavy traffic are often screened.

★★ **Borromean Islands** (Isole Borromee). – *Look under Stresa for a town plan in the current*
ⓥ *Michelin Red Guide Italia.* Since the 12C the islands have belonged to the Borromeos, a princely family who, since the 17C have built a lovely palace with Italian style gardens on **Isola Bella★★★** (Beautiful Island). In the Lombard baroque style the palace is richly decorated with stucco, frescoes, paintings, tapestries and crystal chandeliers. The state apartments include the Medals' Room, the Great Saloon, the Music Room, the Ballroom and the Hall of Mirrors. The basement rooms have been arranged as grottoes with multicoloured pebble mosaics portraying various aquatic scenes. The terraced gardens in the baroque style with statues, fountains and basins are perfumed by numerous aromatic shrubs. The centrepiece is a shell-shaped amphitheatre.

The boat also stops at **Isola dei Pescatori★★** (Fishermen's Island) which remains quite unspoilt, and **Isola Madre★★★** (Mother Island) which is one large garden full of rare and exotic plants and flowers.

★★ **Cannero Riviera.** – The houses of this resort rise in tiers above the lake amidst olive trees, vineyards, orange and lemon groves.

★★ **Pallanza.** – Everywhere flowers deck and scent this wonderful resort. Its **quays★★**, sheltered by magnolias and oleanders, offer lovely views of the lake. On the outskirts of
ⓥ the town on the Intra road is the **Villa Taranto★★** with its gardens. These gardens landscaped in the English manner, regroup several specialised gardens and 20 000 different species of plants and trees.

★★ **Stresa.** – *Town plan in the current Michelin Red Guide France.* This pleasant resort which attracts many artists and writers, enjoys a magnificent situation on the west bank of Lake Maggiore facing the Borromean Islands and is a delightful resort with all the
ⓥ amenities of both a seaside resort and skiing resort. The ski slopes are on **Mottarone★★★** *(take the Armeno road: 29km – 18 miles; the scenic toll road from Alpino: 18km – 11 miles or the cable-car)* which from its summit provides a magnificent **panorama** of the lake, the Alps and the Monte Rossa Massif. Standing on the outskirts of the town,
ⓥ off the Arona road, is the **Villa Pallavicino★** with its wildlife park.

★ **Angera.** – This pleasant resort is dominated by the powerful mass of its **castle** (Rocca).
ⓥ The apartments are decorated with 14C **Lombard frescoes★★** (Hall of Justice) and give a good idea of life in the Middle Ages.

★ **Baveno.** – This quiet holiday resort, once visited by Queen Victoria, has a Romanesque church and an octagonal Renaissance baptistry.

★ **Cannobio.** – Cannobio is a small resort near the Swiss border. In addition to the Renaissance Church of the Madonna della Pietà there are several other fine old houses. 3km – 2 miles out of town *(on the Malesco road)* you can see the **Orrido di Sant' Anna★**, a precipice formed by the torrent.

★ **Cerro.** – This peaceful village on a well shaded part of the lakeside has a tiny fishing
ⓥ port and an interesting **ceramics museum.**

ⓥ **Arona.** – The chief town on Lake Maggiore is overlooked by the gigantic statue, **Colosso di San Carlone★**, of **St Charles Borromeo**, the Cardinal Archbishop of Milan who distinguished himself by the authority he showed in re-establishing discipline and morals in the Church and by his heroic conduct during the plague of 1576.
At the summit of the old town the **Church of St Mary** (Santa Maria) contains a lovely **polyptych★** (1511) by Gaudenzio Ferrari. From the ruined **castle** (Rocca) there is a **view★** of Lake Maggiore, Angera and its mountain setting.

ⓥ **Laveno Mombello.** – From here a cable-car takes you up to the summit of **Sasso del Ferro★★** from where there is a vast **panorama** over the entire Lake District.

Santa Caterina del Sasso. – This hermitage was founded in the 13C by an anchorite, Alberto Besozzo. In a picturesque setting the building clings to a rock overlooking the lake.

★★ **LAKE ORTA** (LAGO D'ORTA)

Orta *(photograph p 13)*, one of the smallest Italian lakes, is separated from Lake Maggiore by the peak, Il Mottarone. It is perhaps the most smiling and the most gracious with its setting of wooded hills and the tiny San Giulio Island. The lakesides have been inhabited since earliest times and in the 4C the people were converted to Christianity by St Julius.

★★ **Madonna del Sasso.** – *5km – 3 miles from Alzo.* From the church terrace there is a magnificent view of the lake in its mountain setting.

★★ **San Giulio Island** (Isola San Giulio). – *Boats leave from Orta.* On this jewel of an island, ⏱300m – 328yds long and 160m – 175yds wide, stands the Basilica of San Giulio which is said to date from the lifetime of St Julius. Inside there is a lovely 12C **ambo★**, frescoes by the school of Gaudenzio Ferrari (16C) and in the crypt, the shrine containing the relics of St Julius.

★★ **Orta San Giulio.** – This small resort has a delightful site on the tip of a peninsula. The alleyways are lined with old houses adorned with elegant wrought iron balconies. The **Palazzotto★** or 16C town hall is decorated with frescoes.

★ **Sacro Monte of Orta.** – *1.5km – 1 mile out of Orta.* This sanctuary dedicated to St Francis of Assisi and set on a hilltop comprises a series of twenty chapels. These are decorated in the baroque manner and the frescoes serve as background to groups of lifelike terracotta statues.

Varallo. – *20km – 12 miles to the west.* This industrial and commercial town in the Val Sesia is famous for its pilgrimage to its **Sacro Monte★★** with its 43 chapels. Again these are decorated with frescoes and groups of lifesize terracotta figures which were the work of several artists including Gaudenzio Ferrari (1480-1546), a local painter who was the pupil of Leonardo da Vinci. Ferrari showed definite originality and picturesque realism in his work.

★★ **LAKE LUGANO** (LAGO DI LUGANO)

Most of Lugano, also known as Lake Ceresio by the Italians, is in Swiss territory. Lugano is wilder than Lakes Maggiore and Como and with its irregular outline it has none of the grandeur nor majesty of the others. Its mild climate and its steep mountain countryside make it an ideal place for a holiday.

⏱There are **boat trips** on the lake.

★★★LAKE District

★ Campione d'Italia. – An Italian enclave in Switzerland, Campione is a colourful, smiling village which is highly popular on account of its casino. St Peter's Oratory (San Pietro) is a graceful building dating from 1326. It was the work of the famous **maestri campionesi,** who vied with the *maestri comacini (qv)* in spreading the Lombard style throughout Italy.

★ Lanzo d'Intelvi. – Set in the heart of a pine and larch forest this resort (alt 907m – 2 976ft) is also a ski centre in winter. 6km – 4 miles away is the **Sighignola Belvedere★★★** also known as the "balcony of Italy", because of its extensive view of Lugano, the Alps as far as Monte Rosa and on a clear day Mont Blanc.

Varese. – *13km – 8 miles to the southwest of Porto Ceresio. Town plan in the current Michelin Red Guide Italia.* This busy but pleasant modern town stands not far from the lake of the same name. It benefits from a mild and sunny climate due to its proximity to the Italian lakes.

8km – 5 miles to the northwest rises the hilltop, **Sacro Monte★★** with its important pilgrimage church dedicated to the Virgin. The road up to the basilica is lined with fourteen chapels decorated with frescoes in *trompe-l'œil* and groups of lifesize terracotta figures. From the summit there is a magnificent **view★★** of the lakes and surrounding mountains.

10km – 6 miles to the northwest is the long mountainous ridge, **Campo dei Fiori★★,** which raises its forest-clad slopes above the plain. There is a vast **panorama★★** of the Lake District.

★★LAKE COMO (LAGO DI COMO)

Set entirely within Lombardy, Lake Como of all the Italian lakes, has the most variety. Smiling villages, tiny ports, villas in shady exotic gardens succeed one another along the banks of this Pre-Alpine lake. Bellagio stands on a promontory at the confluence of its three arms. This lake may also be visited by **boat.**

★★ Bellagio. – Bellagio occupies a magnificent site on a promontory dividing Lake Lecco from the southern arm of Lake Como. It has a world-wide reputation for the warmth of its welcome and its excellent amenities. The splendid lakeside **gardens★★** of **Villa Serbelloni** and **Villa Melzi** with their fragrant and luxuriant vegetation are the main sights in Bellagio.

★★ Tremezzo. – A mild climate and a beautiful site combine to make Tremezzo a favourite place for a stay. The terraced **public gardens★** are a haven of peace.

105

LAKE District ★★★

⊘ The 18C **Villa Carlotta**★★★ *(entrance beside the Grand Hotel Tremezzo)* occupies an admirable site facing the Grigne Massif. The numerous statues include a copy by Tadolini of the famous group of Love and Psyche by Canova. The main attraction is however the beautiful terraced **gardens.**

★★ **Cadenabbia.** – This delightful resort occupies an admirable site opposite Bellagio. A splendid avenue of plane trees, Via del Paradiso, links the resort with the Villa Carlotta and Tremezzo. From the **Chapel of St Martin** *(1 1/2 hours Rtn on foot)* there is a good **view**★★ of Bellagio on its promontory, Lakes Como and Lecco and of the Grigne.

★★ **Cernobbio.** – The monumental 16C **Villa d'Este** was once the residence of the Cardinal of Como and a British Queen. Now a luxury hotel it has splendid terraced **gardens**★★ in the Italian manner.

★★ **Menaggio.** – Favoured by a cool summer breeze, this is one of the lake's smart resorts.

★ **Piona Abbey** (Abbazia di Piona). – *2km – 1 mile from Olgiasca.* This graceful little Cluniac ⊘ monastery has an 11C church and remarkable Lombard Romanesque **cloisters**★ (1252).

★ **Como.** – *Description p 73.*

★ **Varenna.** – This delightful town with its many gardens and cypresses stands on a small ⊘ promontory. The 16C **Villa Monastero** has beautiful **gardens**★★.

Bellano. – This small industrial town stands on the Pioverna River at the mouth of the valley (Valsassina) with the great mass of the Grigne towering behind. The attractive 14C **church** with a façade by Giovanni da Campione is in the Lombard Gothic style.

Dongo. – It was in this village that Mussolini and his mistress, Clara Petacci, were captured on 27 April 1945.

Gavedona. – This fishing village has an attractive Romanesque Church, **Santa Maria del Tiglio**★. The 5C baptistry was remodelled in the Lombard style in the 12C.

Torno. – On the outskirts of this attractive port, the 14C Church of **San Giovanni** has a fine Lombard Renaissance **doorway**★.

★ **LAKE ISEO** (LAGO D'ISEO)

Though Lake Iseo is not very well-known its wild scenery, its high mountain fringe, its banks sometimes steep and often indented and its peaceful villages, all lend a certain charm to this small lake. From the midst of the deep blue waters emerges the island of Monte Isola (alt 600m – 1 969ft).
⊘ There are **boat trips** on the lake.

★ **Iseo.** – The Pieve di Sant'Andrea has a 13C campanile.

★★ **Monte Isola.** – From the Church of the Madonna della Ceriola, crowning the summit of ⊘ this green island, there is a vast **panorama**★★ of the lake and the Bergamaschian Alps.

⊘ **Lovere.** – In this small industrial town the **Tadini Museum** has a collection of arms, paintings (Bellini and Parmigianino), porcelain and sculpture by Canova.

★ **Pisogna.** – This small port has an attractive lakeside setting. The **Church of Santa Maria della Neve** contains 16C **frescoes**★ by Romanino da Brescia.

★★★ **LAKE GARDA**
(LAGO DI GARDA)

This, the largest lake, is also considered one of the most beautiful. Its many assets include low lying banks which are alluvial in the south, steep slopes on the west bank, and the mountain chain of Monte Baldo on the east.

The Dolomites in the north, shelter the lake from the cold north winds, creating a very mild climate which already earned it the name of "beneficient" lake in ancient times. It had both a strategic and commercial importance and throughout history it has been coveted by neighbouring powers.

Artistically, the region was greatly influenced by the Venetian Republic which ruled the region from the 15 to the 18C.

Even in Roman times the banks of the lake were appreciated as a place to stay and today's travellers have a large number of resorts from which to choose.

⊘ There are **boat trips** on the lake.

★★ **Gardone Riviera.** – This small resort enjoys many hours of sunshine and offers the tourist
ⓥ a wide choice of hotels. One km – 1/2 mile from the town is the **Vittoriale**★ estate
which belonged to the poet **Gabriele D'Annunzio** (1863-1938) who is buried here. The
neo-classical villa, La Priora, is full of the solemn atmosphere which this writer-
aesthete so cultivated. The museum and park regroup numerous souvenirs of his
turbulent life.

★★ **Punta di San Vigilio.** – This headland is in a romantic setting. The 16C **Villa Guarienti** was
ⓥ built to the plans of Sanmicheli for the Veronese humanist, Agostino Brenzoni.

(Everts/Rapho)

Sirmione – Scaligers' Castle

★★ **Sirmione.** – This important resort clusters around the 13C **Scaligers' Castle**★ (Rocca
ⓥ Scaligera) at the tip of the narrow Sirmione peninsula, as it stretches out into the lake.
The small 15C Church of Santa Maria has interesting 15 and 16C frescoes. On the
rocky tip of the peninsula are the remains of a Roman villa which belonged to the poet
ⓥ Catullus. The excavation site is known as the **Grottoes of Catullus** and it is possible to
distinguish the remains of buildings in this attractive **site**★★.

★ **Garda.** – This resort which gave its name to the lake shows a strong Venetian influence.
Both the Captains' Palace and the Palazzo Fregoso are 15C.

★ **Limone sul Garda.** – This is one of the lake's most attractive villages. Terraced lemon
groves often under glass stretch along the lake shores. Starting from Limone there is a
panoramic route★★ which climbs up to the Tremosine plateau before redescending to
Tignale. It offers superb **views**★★★ of the lake and its mountainous setting.

★ **Malcesine.** – This attractive town stands on a promontory at the foot of Monte Baldo,
and is dominated by the crenellated outline of another Scaliger **Castle**★ (Castello Scaligero). This 13-14C castle belonged to the Scaligers of Verona. The 15C Captains'
ⓥ Palace in the Venetian style stands on the edge of the lake. From the summit of **Monte
Baldo** *(cable-car)* there is a splendid **panorama**★★★ of the lake and in the north the Massifs of Brenta and Adamello.

★ **Riva del Garda.** – This small resort is dominated to the west by a rocky escarpment.
Already in ancient times it was an important trading and communication centre set on
the route between Verona and the Alps. Today the picturesque **old town**★ is a maze of
ⓥ narrow shopping streets. The **castle** (Rocca) has a municipal **museum** with archaeological and historical sections.

★ **Salò.** – This was the seat of the Venetian Captain under the Venetian Empire and
from this period of splendour it has retained its 15C **cathedral** (Duomo). Inside is a
large gilt **polyptych**★ (1510) in wood and several works by Moretto da Brescia and
Romanino.

Bardolino. – This village famous for its red wine has an elegant Romanesque **church**★
dating from the 11C, which is dedicated to St Severinus.

Campione del Garda. – The Bishops of Trento, Brescia and Verona met here to bless the
lake.

Gargnano. – This charming resort is surrounded by great expanses of glasshouses for
the growing of lemon and citron trees.
The **Church of San Francesco** has lovely 15C cloisters with curious Moorish style galleries
with capitals carved with oranges and lemons recalling the fact that it was supposedly
the Franciscan monks who introduced citrus fruits to the area.
ⓥ The lakeside promenade leads to the neo-classical **Villa Feltrinelli** which served as
Mussolini's headquarters during the Facist Republic (end of 1943 to April 1945).

Torbole. – This was the venue for a most unusual event in 1439. Venice in an attempt to rescue the town of Brescia, under seige by the Visconti of Milan, armed a fleet which sailed up the Adige and crossed the mountains towards Torbole on Lake Garda. From there the fleet set sail to occupy Maderno on the west bank. The following year Venice was able to capture Riva and finally achieve suzerainty over the lake.

Desenzano del Garda. – The old port, picturesque Piazza Malvezzi and the neighbouring old quarter are all good places to stroll through. The 16C **parish church** (Parrocchiale) has a very intense **Last Supper★** by Tiepolo. To the north of the town in Via Scavi Romani, the ⊘ **Villa Romana** has a remarkable series of multicoloured **mosaics★** dating from the Roman period.

★★ LECCE Apulia   Pop 99 643

Michelin map ⑨⑧⑧ fold 30 – Town plan in the current Michelin Red Guide Italia

Set in the very heart of the Salento region, Lecce was in Roman times the prosperous town of Lupiae. The Normans greatly favoured the town and made it the capital of the region known as Terra d'Otranto.

From the 16C to the 18C, Lecce knew a period of great splendour during which it was embellished with Renaissance, rococo and baroque monuments. The local finely grained limestone was particularly easy to work and the town's numerous baroque buildings are remarkable for the abundance of decorative work which has earned the city the nickname of "the baroque Florence". When seen at night with the illuminations the whole ressembles some sumptuous theatrical set.

The most inventive artists came from the Zimbalo family: their work is to be found in both churches and palaces and is widespread throughout the Salentina Peninsula.

★★ BAROQUE LECCE   *time: 1 hour*

★★ **Basilica of the Holy Cross** (Santa Croce). – Although several architects worked on this basilica in the 16 and 17C, it is the best example of Lecce's baroque style. The façade *(photograph p 31)* is sumptuously decorated without being overbearing. The interior is light and airy and the plainer architectural style is reminiscent of Brunelleschi. There is also an abundant baroque decoration of great delicacy. The side chapel contains a fine **high altar** with sculptured low reliefs by Francesco Antonio Zimbalo.

Governor's Residence (Palazzo del Governo). – Adjoining the basilica this former Celestine monastery has a rusticated façade with a frieze above and intricately decorated window surrounds, especially at first floor level.

★★ **Piazza del Duomo.** – The unity of the buildings bordering this square make it one of the finest in southern Italy. The **campanile** and the **cathedral** (Duomo) are by Giuseppe Zimbalo (1661-82), the 17C **Episcopal Palace** (Palazzo Vescovile) and the **Seminary** (Seminario) dating from 1709 by Giuseppe Cino. In the courtyard of the latter there is a sumptuously decorated **well★** by the same sculptor.

ADDITIONAL SIGHTS

★ **Provincial Museum** (Museo Provinciale). – Housed in a modern building the museum ⊘ has a rich archaeological section *(ground floor)* and a very important **ceramics collection★★** *(first floor)*. Of particular interest are the proto-Italiot and Italiot vases decorated with painted figures. The art gallery is on the third floor.

★ **San Mateo.** – This church with its harmonious façade by Achille Carducci shows the distinct influence of Barromini and his Roman work, the Church of St Charles by the Four Fountains.

★ **Rosario** or **San Giovanni Battista.** – This was Giuseppe Zimbalo's last work and the façade is an abundance of decoration which is both intricately detailed and yet gracious. The **interior★** has several altarpieces which are incomparably sumptuous.

Santi Nicolò e Cataldo. – *To the north of the town near the cemetery.*
The church was built in 1180 by the Norman Tancred and rebuilt in 1716, undoubtedly by Giuseppe Cino who retained intact, the central part of the Romanesque façade with its small rose window and Norman doorway. There is an attractive baroque niche in the 16C cloisters.

Sant' Irene (or **Chiesa dei Teatini**). – The church was built by Francesco Grimaldi for the monks of the Theatine Order and it contains several sumptuous **altarpieces★** which are attributed to Francesco A Zimbalo.

Gesù (or **Chiesa del Buon Consiglio**). – *Via Francesco Rubichi.*
Built by the Jesuits between 1575 and 1579 the austere style of this church makes a sharp contrast with the other churches of the town.

Sant' Angelo. – *Via Manfredi.*
Although incomplete this façade is typical of Francesco Giuseppe Zimbalo (1663) and is decorated with garlands, cherubs, angels...

Piazza Sant' Oronzo. – This busy square is the town centre and is dominated from on high by the statue of the town's patron saint St Oronzo who crowns one of the two columns which used to mark the end of the Appian Way in Brindisi *(qv)*.
On the south side of the square parts of the Roman amphitheatre have been uncovered.

LEGHORN (LIVORNO) Tuscany

Michelin map 988 fold 14 – Town plan in the current Michelin Red Guide Italia

This important seaport deals mainly in timber, marble, alabaster, cars and craft work from Florence. Cosimo I de' Medici started rebuilding the harbour to replace the silted up Porto Pisano, and it was finished in 1620 under Cosimo II. The main streets are Via Grande lined with arcaded buildings, Via Cairoli and Via Ricasoli. In the Piazza Micheli, from which the Fortezza Vecchia (Old Fortress) can be seen, stands the **monument**★ to the last prominent Medici, the Grand Duke Ferdinand. The four bronze Moors (1624) were the work of Pietro Tacca.

EXCURSION

Montenero. – *9km – 6 miles to the south.*
The 18C pilgrimage church dedicated to Our Lady of Grace consists of a richly deco-rated baroque church, a monastery and behind railings the *famedio,* a series of chapels reserved for the burial of distinguished citizens of Leghorn.

★ # LORETO Marches

Michelin map 988 fold 16 – Town plan in the current Michelin Red Guide Italia

The small city of Loreto is grouped around its well-known church which is the scene of a famous pilgrimage to the "House of Mary". The old quarter is partially encircled by massive brick ramparts dating from the 16C. It is said that the Santa Casa (Holy House) or House of Mary was miraculously carried from Nazareth in several stages by angels and set down in a wood of laurels (*lauretum* in Latin), which gave its name to Loreto. The most popular pilgrimages take place on the Feast of the Virgin, the Nativity (8 September) and the Translation of the Santa Casa (10 December) *(see the table of Principal Festivals at the end of the guide).* The Venetian painter **Lorenzo Lotto** (1486-1556), who imbued his portraits with a new psychological meaning, lived at Loreto from 1535 to his death. Towards the end of his life he became an Oblate in the Santa Casa.

★★SANCTUARY OF THE HOLY HOUSE
⊘ **(SANTUARIO DELLA SANTA CASA)** *time: 1 hour*

Numerous famous architects, painters and sculptors contributed to the building and decoration of this church started in 1468 and only completely finished in the 18C. These included Giuliano da Sangallo firstly, then Bramante who built the side chapels and finally Vanvitelli who designed the bulbous campanile. Go round the outside of the church to admire the lovely triple **apse**★★ and Sangallo's elegant dome. The façade is typical of the late Renaissance, sober and harmonious, with its double buttresses sur-mounted by clocks at the corners.

The three **bronze doors**★★ are adorned with lovely late 16 and early 17C statues. The interior has a nave and two aisles. At the end of the south aisle the **Sacristy of St Mark**★ (San Marco) has a dome painted with frescoes (1477) by Melozzo da Forli with an exceptional sense of foreshortening showing angels carrying the Instruments of the Passion. In the **Sacristy of St John**★ (San Giovanni) is a lavabo designed by Benedetto da Maiano under a vault painted with frescoes by Luca Signorelli. Standing at the transept crossing is the **Santa Casa**★★ which was sumptuously faced with marble carved in the 16C by Antonio Sansovino and other sculptors. From the north transept you enter a room decorated by Pomarancio (1605-10).

Piazza della Madonna★, in front of the basilica, is lined by the unfinished portico of the ⊘ Apostolic Palace, which now houses a **picture gallery.** This contains a remarkable series of **works**★ by Lorenzo Lotto, paintings by Simon Vouet and Pomarancio. The Flemish tapestries were woven to designs by Raphael and there is a superb collection of Urbino faience vessels.

EXCURSION

Recanati. – *7km – 4 miles to the southwest.*
This little town, perched on a hill, was the birthplace of the poet **Giacomo Leopardi,** the ⊘most perceptive but melancholy of men whose work was melodious. The **Palazzo** ⊘**Leopardi** contains mementoes of the writer. The **picture gallery** has several important works by Lorenzo Lotto, including an Annunciation.

Michelin Guides

The Red Guides (hotels and restaurants)

  Benelux – Deutschland – España/Portugal – main cities Europe – France – Great Britain and Ireland – Italia

The Green Guides (beautiful scenery, buildings and scenic routes)

  Austria – Canada – England: The West Country – Germany – Greece – Italy – London – New England – New York City – Portugal – Rome – Scotland – Spain – Switzerland and 7 guides on France

Michelin Main Road Maps

  Greece 980*, Great Britain/Ireland* 986*, Germany* 987*, Italy/Switzerland* 988*, France* 989*, Spain/Portugal* 990*, Yugoslavia* 991*.*

Situated in the centre of a fertile plain, Lucca has conserved within its girdle of ramparts often tree-topped, a rich heritage of churches, palaces, squares and streets which gives the town a charming air, unscathed by contemporary developments.

HISTORICAL NOTES

Lucca was colonised by the Romans in the 2C BC and it has retained the plan of a Roman military camp, with the two principal streets perpendicular to one another.

During the Middle Ages a complicated system of narrow alleys and oddly shaped squares was added to the original network. The town became an independent commune at the beginning of the 12C and flourished until the mid-14C with the silk trade as its main activity. In the early 14C the town enjoyed a great period of prosperity and prestige under the control of the mercenary leader Castruccio Castracani (d 1328). Lucca's finest religious and secular buildings date from this period. Luccan architects adopted the Pisan style to which they added their own characteristics of refinement and fantasy.

From 1550 onwards the town became an important agricultural centre and with this new prosperity came a renewed interest in building. The countryside was dotted with villas, the town encircled by ramparts and most of the houses were either rebuilt or remodelled.

In the early 19C, Elisa Bonaparte ruled the city for a brief period from 1805 to 1813. Following Napoleon's Italian campaigns he bestowed the titles of Princess of Lucca and Piombino on his sister. She showed a remarkable aptitude for public affairs and ruled her fief with wisdom and intelligence encouraging the development of the town and the arts.

The Legend of the Holy Cross. – The **Volto Santo** (Holy Visage) is a miraculous Crucifix kept in the cathedral. It is said that Nicodemus, after Calvary, depicted the features of Christ on it. The Italian Bishop Gualfredo, when a pilgrim in the Holy Land, obtained possession of the Volto Santo and embarked in a boat without a crew or sails which drifted ashore on the beach at Luni, near La Spezia. As the worshippers at Luni and Lucca disputed possession of the Holy Image, the Bishop of Lucca had it placed on a cart drawn by two oxen; they immediately set off towards Lucca.

The fame of the Volto Santo, spread by merchants from Lucca, became great throughout Euroupe. A most unusual commemorative procession **Luminara di Santa Croce** passes through the illuminated town after dark *(see the table of Principal Festivals at the end of the guide)*.

THE IMPORTANT CHURCHES *time: 3 hours*

From the great **Piazza Napoleone** *(car park)* you will reach the Piazza San Giovanni, overlooked by the church of the same name, and then the Piazza San Martino, bordered on the left side by the 16C Palazzo Micheletti designed by Ammannati with pretty terraced gardens.

★★ **Cathedral (Duomo).** – Dedicated to St Martin, the cathedral was built in the 11C and the exterior was almost entirely remodelled in the 13C and the interior in the 14 and 15C.

The imposing green and white marble **façade**★★ by the architect Guidetto da Como gives a great feeling of strength and balance despite its asymmetry. It is typical of the Lucca-Pisan style with its three great arches and above three superimposed galleries, their columns carved with marvellously delicate and inventive ornamentation by local architects.

The slim and powerful campanile harmoniously combines the use of brick and marble and the number of openings increases with the height.

The sculptural decoration of the porch is extremely rich: pillars with naïvely carved columns, arcading, friezes and a variety of scenes (barking dogs, Roland sounding his horn, a man wrestling with a bear and another stroking his beard).

The Gothic interior has elevations where the round-headed main arches with their robust piers contrast with the delicacy of the elegant triforium. On the west wall is an astonishing Romanesque sculpture of St Martin dividing his cloak. The classical and sober traits of this sculpture herald the style of Nicola Pisano. In the north aisle is the lovely shrine *(tempietto)* buit by the local artisan Matteo Civitali (1436-1501) to shelter the Volto Santo. The great 12C figure of **Christ**★ in wood blackened through time shows a distinctly Oriental influence because of its hieratic aspect. It is said to be a copy of the legendary one.

In the north transept is one of the masterpieces of Italian funerary sculpture by Jacopo della Quercia: the **tomb**★★ of Ilaria del Carretto, wife of Paolo Guinigi, lord of Lucca in the early 15C. The recumbent figure wears a long robe with flowing folds and there is a small dog at her feet, a symbol of fidelity. Other works of art include the large scale **Last Supper**★ by Tintoretto with its fantastic lighting.

★ **St Michael's Church (San Michele in Foro).** – The 12-14C church on the site of the Roman forum dominates with its white mass the adjoining square which is lined by old mansions and the Palazzo Pretorio.

The exceptionally tall **façade**★★ (the nave itself was to have been taller) is a good example of the Lucca-Pisan style, despite the fact that the lower part was remodelled last century. The four superimposed galleries surmount blind arcading and are decorated with varied ornamentation. At the top two instrument-playing angels flank a statue of the Archangel Michael slaying the dragon.

The simplicity of the Romanesque **interior** is a direct contrast. The triumphal arch is very lofty. On the first altar of the south aisle is a **Madonna**★ by Andrea della Robbia. The north transept has a Madonna (1480) carved by Matteo Civitali and a lovely **painting**★ with brilliant colours by Filippino Lippi.

★ St Frigidian's Church (San Frediano). — This 12C Romanesque church, one of the largest in the town, has a façade which differs greatly from those of San Martino and San Michele. The bare façade is faced with white marble from the Roman amphitheatre. The tall central part is dominated by an immense mosaic representing the Ascension which was executed by local artists in the 13C after the Byzantine fashion. The Romanesque interior, on the basilical plan, is equally sober. Ancient columns with fine capitals flank the tall nave. To the right on entering is a surprising Romanesque **font★** (12C) with low-reliefs depicting the story of Moses. In the north aisle the Gothic marble **polyptych★** by Jacopo della Quercia represents the Virgin and Child surrounded by saints. The chapel of Sant' Agostino is decorated with frescoes by the Ferarran painter Amico Aspertini: one of these evokes the transportation of the Volto Santo from Luni to Lucca.

ADDITIONAL SIGHTS

★ Old Town (Città Vecchia). — The streets and square of old Lucca are full of atmosphere with their Renaissance and Gothic palaces, their towers of nobility, old shops, sculptured doorways and coats of arms, elegant wrought iron railings and balconies. Starting from Piazza San Michele, follow Via Roma and Villa Fillungo to Piazza del Anfiteatro situated inside the Roman amphitheatre. From this go towards Piazza San Pietro (12-13C church) and then take Via Guinigi where you will see at no 29, **Casa Guinigi**, a tower (**view★** of town from the top) crowned with trees which rises above the great façade with Gothic multiple opening windows some of which are blind. The houses opposite at Nos 2 and 22 also belonged to the Guinigi family.
Continue to the Romanesque Church of **Santa Maria Forisportam**, so-called because it stood outside the Roman walls.
Via Santa Croce, the delightful Piazza dei Servi and the Piazza dei Bernardini, where the 16C palace of the same name stands, lead you back to Piazza San Michele.

★ Walk round the ramparts (Passeggiata delle Mura). — The 4km – 3 mile long ramparts encircling Lucca give the town a special charm. They were built in the 16 and 17C and include eleven well-projecting bastions, linked to one another by curtain walls, and four gateways.

National Museum in the Palazzo Mansi. — The **apartments** of this 17C palace have a remarkable interior **decoration★** (17-18C). The **art gallery** includes works by 17C Italian artists (Salimbeni, Guido Reni and Barocci) and foreign paintings (portrait of *Princess Elisa* by Marie Benoist).

National Museum in the Villa Guinigi. — *Via della Quarquonia.*
The villa which once belonged to Paolo Guinigi now contains archaeological, sculpture (Romanesque, Gothic and Renaissance) and painting (Lucca and Tuscan) sections. There are some remarkable panels of intarsia work.

EXCURSIONS

Villa Reale, Marlia. — *8km – 5 miles to the north.*
The Villa Reale is surrounded by magnificent 17C **gardens★★** modified by Elisa Bonaparte. Unusual features include a lemon grove, a 17C nympheaum and an open-air theatre.

Villa Mansi. — *11 km – 7 miles to the north.*
This very fine 16C villa, transformed in the 18C, has a façade covered with statues and a vast shady **park★** where statue-lined alleys lead to a lovely pool.

★ Villa Torrigiani (or Camigliano). — *12km – 8 miles to the northeast.*
This 16C villa, was converted in the 17C into an elegant summer residence by Marques Nicolao Santini, ambassador of the Lucca republic to the Papal Court and to the Court of Louis XIV. The gardens designed by Le Nôtre, are adorned with fountains, grottoes and nymphea. The villa which has a delightful rococo façade, contains rooms adorned with frescoes and a picture gallery. There are some extremely fine Venetian and French pieces of furniture (18C) as well as mementoes of the many illustrious guests who have stayed at the villa.

★ MANTUA (MANTOVA) Lombardy   Pop 57 718

Michelin map 988 fold 14 – Town plan in the current Michelin Red Guide Italia

Mantua is set in the heart of a flat fertile plain which was formerly marshland on the southeastern border of Lombardy. It is encircled to the north by three lakes formed by the slow flowing Mincio. This active and prosperous town has numerous important industries including plastics which is one of the most important in Italy.

HISTORICAL NOTES

Although according to a legend quoted by Virgil, Mantua was founded by Monto, daughter of the divine Tiresias, its origins would seem to be Etruscan dating back to the 6 or 5C BC. It passed to the Gauls before becoming Roman in the 3C BC. In 70BC **Virgil** (Publius Virgilius Maro) that gentle poet, was born in the Mantua area. Author of the *Aeneid* in which he recounts the wanderings of Aeneas the exiled Trojan prince and the foundation of the earliest settlement, from which Rome was to spring, Virgil describes his beloved Mantuan countryside, with its soft misty light, and the pleasures of rural life in his own harmonious but melancholy style in the *Eclogues* or *Bucolica* and the *Georgics*.

In the Middle Ages Mantua was the theatre for numerous struggles between rival factions which successively sacked the town, before it became an independent commune in the 13C and finally the domain of Luigi Gonzaga nominated Captain General of the People. Under the **Gonzaga** family, who were enlightened rulers and patrons of the arts and letters, Mantua became an important intellectual and artistic centre in northern Italy of the 15 and 16C. Thus Gian Francesco Gonzaga (1407-44) confided his children to the famous humanist Vittorio da Feltre (1379-1446) and commissioned the Veronese **Pisanello** to decorate his ducal palace. His son Lodovico II (1448-78), a mercenary army leader by profession, was a typical Renaissance patron. The Sienese humanist Politian (1454-94), the Florentine architect Leon Battista Alberti (1404-72) and the Paduan painter **Mantegna** (1431-1506) all belonged to his court. Francesco II (1484-1519) married Isabella d'Este, a beautiful and wise woman who contributed to the fame of Mantua. Their son Federico II was made duke by the Emperor Charles V in 1530 and he commissioned the architect and artist **Giulio Romano** (1499-1546), Raphael's pupil, to embellish his native town, rearrange his ducal palace and build another, the Palazzo del Te.

★★★ DUCAL PALACE (PALAZZO DUCALE) *time: 1 1/2 hours*

⊘ This comprises the largely 16C palace proper, facing Piazza Sordello, the Castello di San Giorgio, a 14C fortress and the Renaissance ducal chapel.

★ Piazza Sordello. – In the past this square was the political and artistic centre of town and has retained its medieval aspect. To the west is the 13C Palazzo Bonacolsi, then the Episcopal Palace (Palazzo Vescovile) where telamones adorn the 18C façade and finally the Cathedral (Duomo) with its campanile and the Chapel of the Incoronata, attributed to Alberti. On the eastern side is the entrance to the Ducal Palace.

★★★ The Apartments. – This luxurious ensemble was sumptuously decorated in the 16 and 18C and has some outstanding ceilings and numerous works of art. The three Pisanello rooms on the first floor have fragments of frescoes and remarkable **sinopie★★** (rough sketches using a red earth pigment) which have recently been discovered and are a good example of the refined and penetrating work of this 15C artist from Verona versed in the Gothic tradition. These lyrical scenes portray the fantastic world of courtly novels and medieval chivalry. The **Tapestry Room,** formerly known as the Green Apartment, in the neo-classical style is hung with nine splendid Brussels tapestries after Raphael. You can also see the **Room of the Rivers** with 18C frescoes, the **Moors Room** in the Venetian manner, the **Corridor of the Months** which leads to the famous 17 and 18C **Hall of Mirrors** and the elegant **Archers Saloon** with works by Rubens, Tintoretto and Fetti. The Duke's suite has a late 16C decoration by Antonio Viani: the **Paradise Apartment** is so-called because of its marvellous views of the lakes and it leads to the tiny **Dwarfs' Apartment.** On the ground floor are the **Isabella Rooms,** with delicately carved ceilings. The **Summer Apartment** *(first floor)* with its early 16C decoration by Giulio Romano is the setting for Greco-Roman sculptures acquired by Isabella d'Este.

Inside the **Castello** may be seen the famous **Spouses' Room** (Camera degli Sposi) with **frescoes★★★** (1465-74) by **Mantegna**. The walls of this single cube room are covered with a cycle of frescoes to the glory of the superb and refined world of the Gonzaga court. Mantegna creates an illusion of space by his knowledge of foreshortening and perspective. Note in particular his treatment of the ceiling oculus with its rich painted *trompe l'œil* or carved stucco decoration.

On the north wall fresco look for Lodovico II with his secretary and his wife Barbara seated opposite them. The children cluster round their parents, as do other members of the court including a dwarf. On the west wall the fresco presents Ludovico with his son, Cardinal Francesco, against the background of a town with splendid monuments which could well be Rome where Mantegna had sojourned not long before. Mantegna has portrayed himself as the figure in purple which we glimpse on the right. To the left servants hold the dogs on leases. Looking down from the ceiling oculus are cupids and the servants. This invention of Mantegna's was highly successful and introduces a certain note of wry humour and even strangeness to this otherwise rather solemn ensemble.

(Nimatallah/Artephot)

Ducal Palace in Mantua – detail of ceiling

ADDITIONAL SIGHTS

Piazza Broletto. – In this square stands the Palazzo Broletta, a 12-15C communal palace. On its façade it has a seated statue of Virgil (1225). The tall Torre della Gabbia (Tower of the Cage) still bears on its façade the cage *(gabbia)* in which wrongdoers were exhibited.

★ **Piazza delle Erbe.** – The Square of Herbs has retained a medieval appearance with the 13C Palazzo della Ragione, flanked by the 15C Clock Tower and the Romanesque church, **Rotonda di San Lorenzo**★. Sober and elegant, this circular building has a colonnaded ambulatory with a loggia above, and a dome over all.

★ **Basilica of St Andrew (Sant' Andrea).** – This church, built in the 15C to the plans of Alberti, has a very wide nave. The vaulting of the nave, chancel and transepts are painted with *trompe l'œil*. The first chapel on the left contains the tomb of Mantegna and one of his works.

★ **Palazzo del Te.** – This palace was built between 1525 and 1535 by Giulio Romano for Federico II in the typical Mannerist style with its rustication and monumental columns. The interior was decorated by Giulio Romano and his pupils. The room decorated with the **Story of Psyche** and the **Giants' Room** are perfect examples of Romano's decorative art which is so full of movement.

Law Courts (Palazzo di Guistizia). – *Via Roma.* The monumental façade with caryatids is early 17C. At No 18 in the same street is Romano's house built in 1544 to his own designs.

Mantegna's House (Casa del Mantegna). – *47 Via Acerbi.* This rather severe looking brick building was undoubtedly built to designs by the artist himself in 1476. It has a delightful courtyard.

Teatro Accademico (or **Teatro Scientifico).** – *47 Via Accademia.* This tiny but graceful 18C theatre by Bibiena has a curious decoration of imitation marble and pasteboard.

Palazzo d'Arco. – *Piazza d'Arco.* This neo-classical palace in the Palladian *(p 211)* tradition contains interesting collections of 18C furniture, paintings and ceramics.

★ MASSA MARITTIMA Tuscany   Pop 9 880

Michelin map 988 fold 14

Massa Marittima stands on the lower foothills of the Colli Metalliferi (metal-bearing hills). It has a rich historic past particularly for the Romanesque and Gothic periods.

★ **Piazza Garibaldi.** – This lovely square, paved with broad flagstones, is lined by the town's main buildings: two Romanesque palaces, Palazzo Pretorio and Palazzo Comunale, as well as the cathedral (Duomo) which also dates from the Romanesque period.

★ **Cathedral (Duomo).** – This majestic building in the Pisan Romanesque style, is adorned with blind arcades and dominated by a fine **campanile**★ pierced with windows which increase in number with the height. The façade is richly decorated. Inside there is an unusual baptismal font and in the undercroft below the chancel is the monumental sarcophagus *(arca)* (1324) of St Cerbone.

★ **Candeliere Tower, Sienese Fortress and Arch.** – In the upper part of the town an arch with pure lines links a massive tower to the remains of a 14C Sienese fortress.

Municipal Museums. – These are housed in the Palazzo Pretorio and include a Museum of the Risorgimento *(ground floor)*, an Archaeological and Local Ceramics Museum *(basement)* and a picture gallery *(first floor)* which has a **Virgin in Majesty** by Ambrogio Lorenzetti (14C).

Church of St Augustine (Sant' Agostino). – *Corso Diaz.* Dating from the early 14C, the church has a Romanesque façade, a lovely Gothic apse and a 17C crenellated campanile added in the 17C.

Mining Museum (Museo di Mineralogia). – *Entrance in Via E. Corridoni.* The museum evokes the mining activities in the surrounding area.

EXCURSION

★ **San Galgano Abbey (Abbazia di San Galgano).** – *32km – 20 miles to the northeast.* This ruined Gothic Cistercian Abbey was built by monks between 1224-88, and dedicated to St Galgan, a dissipated youth from Siena who later took holy orders. Siena Cathedral was modelled on this church.

Michelin main road maps

    980 *Greece*
    986 *Great Britain, Ireland*
    987 *Germany, Austria, Benelux*
    988 *Italy*
    989 *France*
    990 *Spain, Portugal*
    991 *Yugoslavia*

Michelin map 📖 fold 29

Matera overlooks a ravine separating it from the Murge Hills in Apulia. The town stands in the heart of a region dissected by deeply eroded gorges, in all a desolate landscape with wide horizons. The modern part of Matera, provincial capital and centre of all activity, is laid out on a platform which overlooks the lower town with its many rock and semi-rock dwellings (*sassi*), now often abandoned.

In the town and its surrounding area there are some 130 churches hewn out of the living rock. These date back to the 8C BC and the arrival of oriental (non-Latin) monastic communities who settled locally and in Apulia. They were adept in this form of underground architecture which shows a Byzantine influence.

★★ **The Sassi.** – The two main troglodyte quarters are on either side of the rock crowned by the cathedral. Many streets run close to the roofs on some houses while the lower storeys are hewn out of the rock. Little white-washed houses and stairways overlap and overhang one another in a labyrinth which is difficult to unravel.

★★ **Strada dei Sassi.** – This panoramic street skirts the wild gorge and runs round the cathedral rock. The natural rock walls are riddled with natural and man-made caves.

★ **Cathedral (Duomo).** – In the 13C Apulian Romanesque style the façade is divided into three sections and has above the single doorway a lovely rose window and a projecting gallery. The walls are embellished with blind arcades. On the south side are two richly sculpted doorways. The interior was remodelled in the 17 and 18C. The Byzantine fresco portraying the Madonna is 12 to 13C, the Neapolitan crib 16C and the lovely carved stalls of the choir are 15C. The **Chapel of the Annunciation**★ *(the last one on the south side)* has a beautiful Renaissance decoration.

ⓥ **San Pietro Caveoso.** – This baroque church stands at the foot of Monte Errone, which has several churches hewn out of the rock and decorated with frescoes, namely Santa Lucia alle Malve, Santa Maria de Idris and San Giovanni in Monterrone.

ⓥ **Ridola National Museum.** – This museum in a former monastery has an interesting collection of archaeological finds discovered locally.

★★ **Views of Matera.** – *4km – 2 1/2 miles by the Altamura road and then the one to Taranto and finally a right turn to follow the signpost rock churches (chiese rupestri).*
The road leads to two belvederes from which there are astonishing views of Matera. On the left below the parking are several churches hollowed out of the rock face.

Michelin map 📖 fold 4 or 📖 fold 10 – Town plan in the current Michelin Red Guide Italia

Merano, lying at the start of the wider upper valley of the Adige, known as the Val Venosta, is an important tourist centre and spa. It is appreciated for its mild climate. There are numerous cable-cars and chairlifts to take you up to **Merano 2000**, a good winter sports centre and popular in summer for excursions into the mountains.

★★ **Winter and Summer Promenades (Passeggiate d'Inverno e d'Estate).** – These promenades follow the Passirio River. The winter one, facing south, is shady and flower-decked and attractively lined with shops, cafés and terraces and is by far the busiest. It is prolonged by the Passeggiata Gilf which ends near a powerful waterfall. The summer promenade, on the opposite bank, meanders through a lovely park.

★★ **Passeggiata Tappeiner.** – This magnificent promenade 4km – 2 1/2 miles long winds high above Merano affording remarkable viewpoints.

Cathedral (Duomo). – This Gothic building, dedicated to St Nicholas, is dominated by a massive bell-tower and a façade with a crenellated gable. It is adorned on the outside with frescoes. Inside there is lovely ribbed **Gothic vaulting**★ and two carved 15C **polyptychs**★.

★ **Via Portici (Laubengasse).** – This arcade-lined street is overlooked by houses with painted façades and oriel windows. The shops beneath the arcades have curiously sculpted façades.

★ **Princes Castle (Castello Principesco).** – This castle with its crenellated gables and pep-
ⓥ perpot roofs was built in 1480 by the Hapsburgs. The apartments are richly furnished.

EXCURSIONS

★ **Avelengo (Hafling).** – *10km – 6 miles to the southeast.*
A scenic road leads to the plateau of Avelengo which dominates Merano in its valley.

★ **Merano 2000.** – *Access by cable-car from Val di Nova, 3km – 9 miles to the east.*
ⓥ This conifer-covered plateau is a growing winter sports centre. It also makes a good centre for excursions into the mountains in summer.

★ **Tirolo.** – *4km – 2 1/2 miles to the north.*
This charming Tyrolean village is surrounded by vineyards and orchards. The village itself is dominated by a 12C castle which was the family seat of the Counts of Tyrol.

★ **Passiria Valley (Val Passiria).** – *50km – 31 miles to the Rombo Pass; 40km – 25 miles to the Monte Giovo Pass.*
The road follows the Passiria Valley as far as the attractive Tyrolean village of **San Leonardo**, which clusters round its church. The **Rombo Pass Road**★ (Timmelsjoch), steep and often cut out of the living rock, offers impressive views of the mountain peaks on the frontier. The **Monte Giovo Pass Road**★ (Jaufenpass) climbs amidst conifers. On the way down admire the **views**★★ of the snow-capped summits of Austria.

Michelin map 🔢 fold 3 or 🔢 fold 19 – Town plan in the current Michelin Red Guide Italia

Milan, the lively capital of Lombardy, is the second city in Italy in population, politics and cultural affairs and first in the field of commerce, industry and banking. Set in the heart of northern Italy at the foot of the Alps, the enterprising spirit of its people has combined with certain historic circumstances to make this the country's most dynamic town which is even today in full expansion.

The town is bounded by two concentric boulevards: the shorter enclosing the medieval centre, has taken the place of the 14C ramparts, of which traces remain, among them the Porta Ticinese *(p 120)* and the Porto Nuovo **(CV)**. The outer wall corresponds with the town's expansion during the Renaissance. After 1870 Milan expanded rapidly beyond its fortifications particularly along the main communication axes.

HISTORICAL NOTES

Milan is probably Gallic (Celtic) in origin, but it was the Romans, who subdued the city of Mediolanum in 222 BC and ensured a certain prosperity. At the end of the 3C Diocletian made Milan the seat of the Emperors of the West and in 313 Constantine published the **Edict of Milan** making Christianity the official religion of the Empire. In 375 **St Ambrose** (340-396), a Doctor of the Church known for his eloquence, became bishop of the town thus adding to its prestige. The Barbarian invasions of the 5 and 6C were followed by the creation of a Lombard Kingdom with Pavia as capital. In 756 Pepin, King of the Franks, conquered the area and his son Charlemagne was to wear the Iron Crown of the Kings of Lombardy from 774. In 962 Milan once again became capital of Italy.

In the 12C Milan grouped with other cities to form the Lombard League (1167) to thwart the attempts of the Emperor Frederick Barbarossa to conquer the region. With the decisive victory at **Legnano** the cities of the league achieved their independence. In the 13C the **Visconti**, Ghibellines and leaders of the local aristocracy, seized power. The most famous member was **Gian Galeazzo** (1347-1402), an able war leader, man of letters, assassin and pious builder of Milan's Cathedral and the Carthusian Monastery of Pavia. His daughter, Valentine, married Louis, Duke of Orleans, the grandfather of Louis XII. This family connection was the reason for the later French expeditions into Italy.

After the death of the last Visconti, Filippo-Maria (d1447), and three years of the Ambrosian Republic, the Sforza took over the rule of Milan, thanks to Francesco, the son of a simple peasant and son-in-law of Filippo-Maria Visconti. The most famous figure in the **Sforza** family, **Ludovico il Moro** (1452-1508) made Milan a new Athens by attracting to his court the genuises of the time, Leonardo da Vinci and Bramante. Louis XII of France proclaimed himself the legitimate heir to the Duchy of Milan and set out to conquer the territory in 1500. His successor François I renewed the offensive but was thwarted at Pavia by the troops of the Emperor Charles V. Between 1535 and 1713 Milan was under Spanish rule. During the plague which ravaged the town from 1576 to 1630 members of the Borromeo family, St Charles (1538-84) and Cardinal Frederico (1564-1631) distinguished themselves for their humanitarian work.

Under Napoleon, Milan became the capital of the Cisalpine Republic (1797) and later of the Kingdom of Italy (1805). In 1815 Milan assumed the role of capital of the Venetian-Lombard Kingdom.

LIFE IN MILAN

The most frequented parts of Milan are around Piazza del Duomo **(CY)**, Via Dante **(BX)** and Via Manzoni **(CDX)**. At the **Galleria Vittorio Emanuele★** **(CY)** which was laid out in 1877 to the plans of Guiseppe Mengoni, the Milanese come to talk, read their *Corriere della Sera* or drink a coffee. Shops and in particular those specialising in antiques are to be found in Corso Vittorio Emanuele **(CDY)**, Corso Venezia **(DVX)** and Via Monte Napoleone **(CDX)**. The night life is centred on Piazza San Babila **(DY)**. The most remarkable gardens are the Parco Sempione and the Giardini Pubblici.

The **Scala Opera House** with its prestigious programme is always a great attraction as is the **Piccolo Teatro (BCY T)** with its international reputation. In addition there are numerous sports facilities allowing the visitor to Milan to enjoy a sport or go along to a match or competition.

Milanese cooking is known for its fillets of veal in breadcrumbs *(scaloppina alla milanese)*, a marrow bone (shin of veal) with its meat *(osso buco)*, saffron-tinted *risotto* and vegetable and pork soup *(minestrone)*. Taste these with the Valtellina wines or those from the Pavia region.

FINE ARTS

In architecture the Cathedral (Duomo) marks the climax of the Flamboyant Gothic period. Prominent architects under the Renaissance were the Florentine, Michelozzo (1396-1472) and especially **Donato Bramante** (1444-1514), favourite master mason of Ludovic il Moro before he left for Rome. An admirer of Classical art, he was both a classicist and a man of great imagination who invented the **rythmic bay** (a façade which combined an alternance of bays, pilasters and niches) which imported much of their harmony to so many Renaissance façades.

In painting, the Lombard school sought beauty and grace above all else. Its principal exponents were Vincenzo Foppa (1427-1515), Bergognone (1450-1523) and Bramantino (between 1450 and 1465-1536). The works of Andrea Solario (1473-c1520), Boltraffio (1467-1516) and especially the delicate canvases of **Bernardino Luini** (c1480-1532) attest to the influence of **Leonardo da Vinci** who stayed in Milan for some time.

Today Milan is the capital of Italy's printing industry and is an important centre with its numerous art galleries, for contemporary art.

MILANO

★★★THE CATHEDRAL (DUOMO) (CY) AND ITS PRECINCTS

time: 1 1/2 hours

Parking is difficult in the centre of town. There are however paying car parks in Piazza Diaz (CYZ), Via San Marco (CV) and Via Santa Radegonda (CY 84). Cars may also be parked in the outer boulevards or in the car parks built beside certain peripheral underground stations.

★★★ Exterior.

This marvel of white marble, both colossal and ethereal, bristling with belfries, gables, pinnacles and statues, stands at one end of a great paved esplanade. It should be seen late in the afternoon in the light of the setting sun.

Building began with the chevet in 1386 on the orders of Gian Galeazzo Visconti, and continued in the 15 and 16C under the direction of Italian, French and German master masons. The façade was only finished between 1805 and 1809, on the orders of Napoleon.

You should walk round the cathedral to see the **east end** with three huge bays of curved and counter-curved tracery and wonderful rose windows. The overall design is the work of a French architect, Nicolas de Bonaventure, and of a Modenese architect,

(Giraudon)

Milan Cathedral

ⓒ Filippino degli Organi. The ruins of a 4C **baptistry** have been found under the parvis.

★★★ Interior.

In contrast with the exterior this is bare, severe and imposing. The nave and four ailes are separated by fifty-two pillars of tremendous height (148m – 486ft). The width across the transepts is 91m – 299ft. The windows of the nave and transept have some lovely stained glass, some of which dates back to the 15 and 16C.

The mausoleum of Gian Giacomo Medici in the south transept is a fine work by Leoni (16C). On the left is the curious statue of St Bartholomew (who was flayed alive), a work of the sculptor Marco d'Agrate. Pass under the dome and in front of the monumental chancel (1570-90) with the high altar, by the architect Pellegrino Tibaldi. The magnificent bronze candelabrum in the north transept is French work of the 13C. In the crypt, the silver urn containing the relics of St Charles Borromeo, Archbishop ⓒ of Milan who died in 1584, was the gift of Philip II of Spain.

In the **treasury** is a fine collection of gold plate and ivories dating from the 4C to the present day.

★★★ Walk on the roofs.

The building is adorned with 135 pinnacles and numerous ⓒ white marble statues (2 245 in all!), full of grace and elegance. They can be admired in detail by going up on to the roof and thence to the top of the Tiburia or central tower (108m – 354ft), surmounted by a small gilt statue, the Madonnina (1774).

★★ Cathedral Museum (CY M¹).

This is installed in the 18C Royal Palace by Pier ⓒ marini and includes sculptures, stained glass, tapestries and religious vestments from the 14 to the 20C. The 11C **Aribert Crucifix★★** in embossed gilt copper is outstanding. Models and documents describe the different stages in the building of this great cathedral.

★ Via and Piazza Mercanti (CY).

In Via Mercanti stands the Palace of Jurisconsults (C), built in 1564 with a statue of St Ambrose teaching on the façade.

The Piazza Mercanti is quiet and picturesque. The charming Loggia degli Osii (1316) is decorated with blasons, statues of saints and the balcony from which penal sentences were proclaimed. To the right of the loggia is the baroque palace of the Palatine school with statues of the poet Ausonius and St Augustine, in the niches. Opposite is the town hall or Broletto Nuovo (D) which was built in the 13C and extended in the 18C. The equestrian statue on the façade is of the governing magistrate *(podestà)* Oldrado da Tresseno. It is a Romanesque work by Antelami.

★ La Scala (Teatro alla Scala) (CX).

The most famous opera house in the world was built from 1776 to 1778 and can accommodate an audience of over 2 000. The acoustics are perfect. The four statues in the foyer are of Italian composers (Rossini, Bellini, Donizetti and Verdi).

ⓒ The **Scala Museum★** is rich in documents and mementoes covering its past. It is possible to visit the auditorium from the museum.

★★ THE MUSEUMS

Milan has numerous museums with rich and varied collections.

★★ **Brera Picture Gallery** (Pinacoteca di Brera) (CX). – The gallery is in a 17C palace. You are greeted in the court by a statue of Napoleon I, whom Canova depicted in 1809 as a victorious Caesar. This is one of Italy's best collections and it is particularly rich in Lombard and Venetian works.

Venetian school: a *Last Supper* and a *Baptism of Christ* by Veronese; a *Pietà* by Lorenzo Lotto; a *Miracle of St Mark* and a *St Helena* by Tintoretto; **St Mark Preaching in Alexandria★★★** by Gentile and Giovanni Bellini; the *Madonna with a Candle* by Crivelli; the museum's masterpiece is Mantegna's **Dead Christ★★★**, admirable in its realism and knowledge of foreshortening. In addition there are works by Carpaccio, Michele da Verona, Cima da Conegliano, Giovanni Bellini, Tiepolo, Longhi, Canaletto, Guardi, etc.

Lombard school: the **Madonna of the Rose Tree★★★** by Bernardino Luini is a perfect example of the gentleness and grace of the Lombard artists, influenced by Leonardo da Vinci; *Christ* by Bramante; and works by Boccaccino, Bergognone, Foppa, Moroni, etc.

Italian schools: one of Piero della Francesca's masterpieces is the balanced composition so full of grace **Madonna with Saints★★★** and kneeling Duke of Montefeltro (1474); **Betrothal of the Virgin★★★** (1504) by the 20 year old Raphael. The perspective focuses on a small circular building in the manner of Bramante; in addition there are works by Signorelli, the Carrachi family, Guido Reni, Caravaggio and Barocci.
There are also sections on 19 and 20C Italian art.

Foreign schools: this groups canvases by Ribera, El Greco, Goya, Velvet Brueghel, Van Dyck, Rembrandt and Rubens.

★★ **Castle of the Sforza** (Castello Sforzesco) (BX). – This huge brick quadrilateral building was the seat of the Dukes of Milan. The **municipal art collections★★★** are now on display in the castle.

Sculpture department. – *Ground floor.* The Romanesque, Gothic and Renaissance works are mainly by Lombard sculptors. Interesting works include the **tomb of Bernabò Visconti★★** surmounted by his equestrian statue from the Romanesque period and the **reclining figure of Gaston de Foix★★★** (1523) by Bambaia in his usual classical and well balanced style, as well as the unfinished **Rondanini Pietà★★★** by Michelangelo both from the Renaissance.

Picture Gallery. – *1st floor.* The gallery regroups works by Mantegna, Giovanni Bellini, Crivelli, Bergognone, Luini, Moretto, Moroni, Magnasco, Tiepolo, Guardi, etc.
In addition there is a decorative arts section and a remarkable collection of **musical instruments★★**.

★ **Sempione Park** (Parco Sempione) (ABVX). – Beyond the castle lies this vast park which is the setting for an exhibition centre (Palazzo dell' Arte), a stadium (Arena), the 1838 Arch of Peace (Arco della Pace) and a 109m – 358ft tall tower (Torre).

★★ **Ambrosian Library** (Biblioteca Ambrosiana) (CY). – The library is in a palace built in 1609 for Cardinal Frederico Borromeo. In addition to the many manuscripts there is a **picture gallery** on the first floor. Of interest are Italian Renaissance works (Ghirlandaio, Bartolomeo Vivarini and Bergognone), **low-reliefs★★** from the tomb of Gaston de Foix *(see above)* by Bambaia, allegorical paintings and the delightful **Mouse with a Rose★** by Velvet Brueghel (1568-1625), several canvases by Luini and a portrait by Giorgione. Note two remarkable **portraits★★★**, one of the musician Gaffurio by Leonardo da Vinci, the other presumed to be of Beatrice d'Este by Ambrogio da Predis. Both are outstanding works. The lovely **Basket of Fruit★** is by Caravaggio and the **Nativity★** by the Mannerist artist Barocci.
Room 10 has Raphael's splendid **cartoons★★★** for the frescoes of the School of Athens in the Vatican. Another room has the collection of reproductions from the drawings in the great *Codex Atlanticus*, where the universal genius of Leonardo is powerfully displayed.

★★ **Poldi Pezzoli Museum** (Museo Poldi Pezzoli) (CX M^2). – The valuable and varied exhibits are well presented in a mansion furnished and decorated with taste. There are collections of paintings, arms and armour, fabrics, **clocks★★** and small 16 to 18C **bronzes★**. Grouped on the first floor the paintings include Lombard works (Bergognone, Luini, Foppa and Solario), two lovely **portraits★★** of Luther and his wife by Cranach and in the Gold Saloon with its splendid **Persian carpet★** a delicate **profile portrait of a woman★★★** by Antonio del Pollaiolo, St Nicholas of Tolentino by Piero della Francesca, an astonishing composition, *Descent from the Cross* and a **Virgin and Child★★** by Botticelli, a rather pathetic **Dead Christ★★** by Giovanni Bellini and a remarkable **View of the Lagoon** by Francesco Guardi. Other rooms have works by Lorenzetti, Tiepolo, Lotto, Boltraffio, Canaletto, Palma Vecchio, etc.

Modern Art Gallery (Galleria d'Arte Moderna) (DVX M^3). – This, the former Villa Belgioioso built in 1790, was once the residence of Napoleon and Eugène de Beauharnais. It now contains one of the most important Italian collections especially in the domain of 19C Lombard painting. Note Canova's neo-classical paintings, others from the Romantic Period and the sculptures of the Milanese Medardo Rosso (1858-1928). On the second floor, the Grassi Collection regroups works by the French Impressionists. To the right of the courtyard there is a group of works by the famous contemporary Italian sculptor, Marino Marini (1901-80).

★ **Leonardo da Vinci Museum of Science and Technology** (Museo della Scienza e della Tecnica Leonardo da Vinci) (AY M^4). – This vast museum has exhibits on various scientific and technological projects. The **Leonardo da Vinci Gallery★★** has reproductions of the scientific drawings by the Tuscan genius. Other sections cover the railways, aeronautics and the sea.

ADDITIONAL SIGHTS

Church of St Mary of Grace (Santa Maria delle Grazie) **(AY)**. – This Renaissance build-ing erected by the Dominicans between 1465 and 1490 was finished by Bramante. Inside (restored) you will see frescoes by Gaudenzio Ferrari in the fourth chapel on the right, and the impressive **dome★**, gallery and cloisters all by Bramante. The best view of the **east end★** is to be had from Via Caradosso **(AXY 15)**.

⊙ **Refectory** (Cenacolo). – In what used to be the former monastery refectory is the world famous **Last Supper★★★** painted by **Leonardo da Vinci** from 1495-97 at the request of Ludovico il Moro. The fresco depicts with dramatic expressiveness the moment when Jesus says: "One of you will betray me". Opposite is a lovely **Crucifixion★** (1495) by Montorfano.

★ **Basilica of St Ambrose** (Sant' Ambrogio) **(AY)**. – The basilica was founded at the end of the 4C by St Ambrose and it is a magnificent example of the 11-12C Lombard Romanesque style with its pure lines and fine **atrium★**. The façade pierced by arcading is flanked to the right by a 9C campanile and a 12C one to the left. The doorway was renewed in the 18C and has 9C bronze panels. In the crypt, behind the chancel, lie the remains of St Ambrose, St Gervase and St Protase. Inside the basilica there is a mag-nificent Byzantine-Romanesque **ambo★**, to the left of the nave, and at the high altar a precious gold-plated **altar front★★** which is a masterpiece of the Carolingian period (9C). From the far end of the north transept one can visit Bramante's portico.

★ **Church of St Eustorgius** (Sant' Eustorgio) **(BZ)**. – This Romanesque basilica was founded in the 9C and belonged to the Dominicans. The side chapels were added in the 15C. Behind the choir is the **Portinari Chapel★★**, a jewel of the Renaissance of really Classical purity by the Florentine, Michelozzo. The architecture, frescoes illustrating the life and martyrdom of St Peter by Vincenzo Foppa and sculpture (richly sculptured marble tomb, 1339) by Giovanni di Balduccio are all in complete harmony.

Church of San Satiro (CY). – The square campanile dates from the 9C, the façade from 1871. The rest of the church and baptistry are by Bramante. The artist has re-solved the problem of lack of space by a skilful use of *trompe l'œil* decoration. The **dome★** is particularly remarkable.

★ **General Hospital** (Ospedale Maggiore) **(CDZ)**. – This hospital, founded by Francesco Sforza in 1456, was completed in the 17C and is at present occupied by the Faculty of Medicine. It is composed of three different ranges and the loggias of the façades are decorated with the busts of famous men.

★ **Church of St Maurice** (San Maurizio or Monastero Maggiore) **(BY)**. – This is a monastery church in the Lombard Renaissance style (early 16C), adorned with **frescoes★** by Bernardino Luini and, in the gallery, with figures of saints most probably by Boltraffio. An ⊙ **Archaeological Museum (BY M⁵)** has been installed inside the former conventual build-ings: Greek, Etruscan and Roman art. The outstanding piece is a 4C **silver plate★**. Opposite is the **Palazzo Litta (BY)** with its 18C façade.

★ **Church of St Lawrence** (San Lorenzo Maggiore) **(BZ)**. – The basilica was founded in the 4C and rebuilt in the 12 and 16C. It has kept its original octagonal plan. In front of the façade is a majestic **portico★** of sixteen Roman columns, all that remains of the Roman town of Mediolanum. The majestic interior is in the Byzantine-Romanesque style and has galleries, exclusively reserved for women, a vast dome and spacious ambulatory. From the south side of the chancel pass through the atrium and then a 1C ⊙ Roman doorway to the **Chapel of Sant' Aquilino★** dating from the 4C. It has retained its original plan and the paleo-christian mosaics. Farther on, the **Porta Ticinese (BZ)**, a vestige of the 14C ramparts, leads to the attractive quarter (Naviglio Grande), where the artists used to foregather.

EXCURSION

★ **Chiaravalle Abbey** (Abbazia di Chiaravalle). – *7km – 4 miles to the southeast. Leave by* ⊙ *Porta Romana* **(DZ)** *then consult the plan of the built-up area in the current Michelin Red Guide Italia.* The abbey, founded by St Bernard of Clairvaux (hence Chiaravalle) in 1135, is domi-nated by an elegant polygonal **bell tower★**. Brick and white stone are combined in the typical Cistercian style. The porch was a 17C addition. Inside there is a nave and two aisles and 14C frescoes on the dome. Another fresco in the south transept represents the Tree of the Benedictine Saints. The small cloisters are delightful.

★ **MODENA** Emilia-Romagna   Pop 178 051

Michelin map **988** fold 14 – Town plan in the current Michelin Red Guide Italia

Modena, situated between the Secchia and Panaro Rivers, at the junction of the Via Emilia and the Brenner Autostrada, is an active commercial and industrial (manufacture of shoes and cars and railway engineering) centre and one of the most important towns in Emilia-Romagna. However, Modena with its archbishopric and university, remains a quiet town whose old quarter in the vicinity of the cathedral is adorned by several spacious squares lined with arcades. It is in this part of the town that one finds such gastronomic specialities as *zamponi* (stuffed pigs' trotters) and Lambrusco, a spar-kling red wine which is produced locally. The original Roman colony of Mutina then became independent before becoming part of the Lombard League *(qv)*, falling under the domination of the Estes from Ferrara to avoid being ruled by Bologna. In 1453 the duchy of Modena was created for Borso d'Este. In 1598 they were expelled from Ferrara by the pope and they took refuge at Modena which reached the peak of its prosperity during the 17C.

SIGHTS

★★ **Cathedral (Duomo).** – The cathedral is dedicated to St Geminian and is one of the best examples of Romanesque architecture in Italy. In it the Lombard architect, Lanfranco, gave vent to his sense of rhythm and proportion. The *maestri campionesi (qv)* put the finishing touches to his work. Most of the sculptural decoration is due to Wiligelmo, a 12C Lombard sculptor. The central porch is supported by marble lions and surmounted by a loggia and a large marble rose window. The doorways are framed by low-reliefs by Wiligelmo; from left to right, they represent the Creation, the Life of Adam and Eve, and Cain and Abel. The south side is remarkable for its architectural rhythm. From left to right may be seen: the Princes' Doorway, crowned by low-reliefs carved by pupils of Wiligelmo; the 13C main doorway, known as the Royal Door; and an outside pulpit (1501) ornamented with the Symbols of the Evangelists.

The Fish Market Doorway on the north side was also carved by the pupils of Wiligelmo, showing fantastic animals and people, the Work of the Months on the inner faces of the pilasters, and an attack on the town on the outer curve of the arches. The massive Romanesque campanile built of white marble, 88m – 289ft high, is nicknamed Ghirlandina because of the bronze garland on its weather-vane: it was completed in 1310.

The sober and solemn interior of the cathedral is of brick and roofed with pointed vaulting. The great arches rest on massive brick and slender marble piers, placed alternately. The graceful **rood screen★★** supported by Lombard lions was carved from 1170 to 1220 by the *maestri campionesi* with Scenes from the Passion.

The crypt, supported on many slender columns, contains a terracotta Holy Family (1480) by the Modena artist Guido Mazzoni, and the tomb of St Geminian.

The chancel is encircled by 15C carved stalls ornamented with realistic intarsia work. In the north apse there is a 15C statue of St Geminian and a 1384 polyptych of the Coronation of the Virgin.

The **Cathedral Museum** contains the famous 12C **metopes★★**, low-reliefs which used to surmount the flying buttresses. They represent buffoons or symbols incomprehensible today, but whose modelling, balance and style have an almost Classical air.

Museums Palace (Palazzo dei Musei). – This 18C palace contains the two most important art collections gathered by the Este family.

★ **Este Library** (Biblioteca Estense). – *1st floor, staircase on the right.* This is one of the richest libraries in Italy, containing 600 000 books and 15 000 manuscripts, the most interesting of which are on display. The prize piece is the **Bible of Borso d'Este.** It has 1 020 pages illuminated by a team of 15C Ferrara artists including Taddeo Crivelli.

★★ **Este Gallery** (Galleria Estense). – This excellent collection regroups 14C Emilian, 15C Venetian (Cima da Conegliano), Ferrarese (notably the astonishing **St Anthony** by Cosima Tura) and Florentine (Lorenzo di Credi) works. The 16C is represented by Veronese, Tintoretto, Bassano, El Greco, Correggio, Il Parmigianino, Dosso Dossi, as well as by works of the local artist, Nicolò dell' Abbate. The 17C is illustrated by the Emilian painters, the Carrachi and the "Caravaggists", while the 18C includes Venetian landscape painters. The foreign schools are also well represented. Among the sculptures, note a powerful bust of Francesco I d'Este by Bernini.

The glass cabinets display around 100 **coins and medals,** several of which were executed by the Verona artist Pisanello. These form only a fraction of the remarkable collection (35 000 exhibits) belonging to the Gallery.

★ **Ducal Palace (Palazzo Ducale).** – This noble and majestic building was begun in 1634 for Francesco I d'Este and has an elaborately elegant design. Today it is occupied by the Infantry and Cavalry schools.

EXCURSIONS

Abbey of Nonantola (Abbazia di Nonantola). – *11km – 7 miles to the north.*
The abbey was founded in the 8C and flourished during the Middle Ages. The 12C abbey church has some remarkable **Romanesque sculpture★** carved by Wiligelmo's assistants in 1121.

Carpi. – *18km – 11 miles to the north.*
This attractive small town has a 16C Renaissance cathedral by Peruzzi, overlooking **Piazza dei Martiri★.** The **Castello dei Pio★,** an impressive building bristling with towers, has a courtyard by Bramante and contains a small museum. The 12-16C Church of Sagra has a tall Romanesque campanile, **Torre della Sagra.**

★ MONTE CASSINO Abbey

(ABBAZIA DI MONTECASSINO) Latium

Michelin map 988 fold 27

The access road to one of the holy places of Roman Catholicism climbs in hairpin bends, affording remarkable views of the valley. The monastery of Monte Cassino, the mother house of the Benedictines, was founded by St Benedict in 529. It was here that the saint drew up a remarkably complete and precise set of rules. Intellectual study and manual labour were combined with the virtues of chastity, obedience and poverty. In the 11C under Abbot Didier the abbey's influence was at its height. The monks were skilled in the arts of miniatures, frescoes and mosaics and their work greatly influenced Cluniac art. The abbey was destroyed on several occasions including 1944 during the allied assault against this German key stronghold in the system of defences guarding the approaches to Rome. It was rebuilt to the original plan and today stands four square on its powerful foundations on the summit of Monte Cassino.

MONTE CASSINO Abbey ★★

★★ **The abbey.** – It is preceded by a suitably solemn suite of four communicating clois-
⊙ ters. The bare façade of the basilica quite belies the sumptuousness of the **interior**★★
where marble, stucco, mosaics and gilding create a dazzling if somewhat austere ensemble in the 17-18C style. The chancel has lovely 17C walnut stalls and the marble
tomb enshrining the remains of St Benedict.

★★ **Museum.** – This regroups documents on the abbey's history and works of art
⊙ which survived the 1944 bombing.
⊙ On the way down to Cassino you pass a **National Archaeological Museum** and the neighbouring excavation site (amphitheatre, theatre and tomb of Umidia Quadratilla).

★★ **MONTECATINI TERME** Tuscani   Pop 21 086

Michelin map 988 fold 14 – Town plan in the current Michelin Red Guide Italia

Montecatini is Italy's most frequented and most fashionable thermal spa and speci-
⊙ alises in treating stomach, intestinal and liver ailments. There is an interesting **Museum
of Modern Art** (Museo dell' Accademia d'Arte) which has works by Italian (Fattori,
Guttaso, Primo Conti) and French artists (Fernand Léger, Dufy).

EXCURSION

Collodi. – 15km – 9 miles to the west. Collodi was the pen-name adopted by Carlo
Lorenzini, the author of Pinocchio, whose mother was born in the village. A **Pinocchio
Park** in the form of a maze is laid out on the banks of the Pescia River.
⊙ The **Villa Garzoni** built in the 18C by the Marquess Garzoni has fine terraced **gardens**★
dating from the 17C. Vistas, pools, clipped trees, grottoes, sculpture and mazes are
all part of this exuberant baroque creation.

★ **MONTEFALCO** Umbria   Pop 5 488

Michelin map 988 fold 16

14C ramparts still girdle this charming little town, which lies among vineyards and
olive groves. It is perched – as its name suggests – like a falcon on its nest and has
been called the Balcony of Umbria. Owing to its strategic position it was destroyed by
the Emperor Frederick II and then coveted for two centuries by the popes. Montefalco, won over to Christianity in 390 by St Fortunatus, has its own saint, Clara not to
be confused with the companion of St Francis of Assisi.
The ring road (Circonvallazione) affords remarkable views of the Clitumnus Basin.

⊙ **Communal Tower** (Torre Comunale). – From the top (110 steps) there is a beautiful
panorama★★★ of nearly all Umbria.

⊙ **St Francis' Church** (San Francesco). – This Franciscan church has been converted into
a museum. The mid-15C **frescoes**★★ by the Florentine Benozzo Gozzoli are full of freshness and colourful realism. In addition there are frescoes by Perugino and Francesco
Melanzio (15-16C), a native of Montefalco.

Santa Illuminata. – The church is Renaissance in style. The tympanum of the main
doorway and several niches in the nave were painted by Francesco Melanzio.

St Augustine's Church (Sant' Agostino). – Corso G. Mameli.
The church is Gothic with frescoes by Umbrian painters of the 14, 15 and 16C.

St Fortunatus' Church (San Fortunato). – 1km – 1/2 mile to the south.
The church is preceded by a small 14C colonnaded courtyard. On the tympanum of
the doorway Benozzo Gozzoli painted a **fresco**★ showing the Madonna between
St Francis and St Bernard. Inside, the south altar is adorned with another fresco by
Gozzoli of St Fortunatus.

★ **MONTE OLIVETO MAGGIORE Abbey** Tuscany

Michelin map 988 fold 15 – 36km – 22 miles southeast of Siena

⊙ The extensive pink brick buildings of this famous abbey lie hidden among cypresses,
in a countryside of eroded hillsides. Monte Oliveto is the Mother House of the Olive-
tans, a congregation of the Benedictine Order which was founded in 1319 by Blessed
Bernard Tolomei of Siena.

Great Cloisters. – The cloisters are decorated with a superb cycle of thirty-six
frescoes★★ depicting the life of St Benedict by **Luca Signorelli** from 1498 and by
Il Sodoma between 1505 and 1508. The frescoes begin near the entrance to the church,
at the great arch with two of Sodoma's masterpieces the Christ of the Column and the
Christ bearing His Cross. The majority of the frescoes are by Sodoma who shows a
greater preoccupation with the attractive evocation of different human types, landscapes and picturesque details while Signorelli, who did eight frescoes, is more concerned with the powerful, sculptural portrayal of his figures and the dramatic effect of
the compositions. Note especially the third fresco in which Sodoma has included himself, turning towards the spectator, with his hair falling to his shoulders; the nineteenth
fresco, also by Signorelli, shows courtesans who have been sent to seduce the monks,
the twenty-seventh one, by Signorelli, shows St Benedict discovering the ruse of the
Barbarian Totila, who had changed clothes with his standard-bearer.

Abbey Church. – The interior was remodelled in the baroque style in the 18C. The
nave is encircled by **stalls**★★ (1505) with intarsia work by Fra Giovanni da Verona.

Michelin map 988 fold 15

Montepulciano, perched on the crest of a hill of volcanic rock between valleys, has numerous religious and secular buildings influenced by the Florentine Renaissance. Inhabitants of Chiusi, fleeing from the Barbarian invasion, founded the town in the 6C. This was the birthplace of **Politian** (1454-94) one of the most exquisite Renaissance poets. The poet was a great friend of Lorenzo de' Medici, whom he called Lauro (Laurel) and whom he saved from assassination during the Pazzi Conspiracy *(qv)*. The *Stanzas* Politian's masterpiece, describe a sort of Garden of Delight haunted by attractive women. Politian's verse matches the painting of his friend Botticelli.

Old city (Città antica). – Having passed through the fortified gateway, Porta al Prato, one enters the street that crosses Montepulciano from end to end. It is lined with many interesting **palaces**★ and churches.

★ **Piazza Grande.** – Forming the centre of the city, this square with its irregular plan and varying styles avoids architectural monotony while blending into a harmonious whole. ⊘ The **Town Hall**★ (Palazzo Comunale) is a Gothic building which was remodelled in the 15C by Michelozzo. From the top of the square tower you will see an immense **panorama**★★★ of the town and its environs. The majestic Renaissance **Palazzo Nobili-Tarugi**★ facing the cathedral is attributed to Antonio da Sangallo the Elder, a member of that famous family of artists and sculptors. Sangallo was responsible for several of the city's most famous buildings. The palace has a portico and great doorway with semi-circular arches; six Ionic columns, standing on a lofty base, support the pilasters of the upper storey. The square also has an attractive **well**★ adorned with an admirable sculpture of lion supporters holding aloft the Medici coat of arms. Inside the 16-17C **cathedral** (Duomo), to the left of the entrance is the recumbent figure of Bartolomeo Aragazzi, secretary to Pope Martin V, a work by Michelozzo. On the high altar is the monumental **altarpiece**★ (1401) by the Sienese Taddeo di Bartolo.

EXCURSIONS

★★ **Madonna di San Biagio.** – *1km – 1/2 mile. Leave by the Porta al Prato and then take* ⊘ *the Chianciano road before turning right.*
This pale coloured stone church stands in a grassy setting, high above the valley.
The church, which was consecrated in 1529 by the Medici Pope Clement VII, is the masterpiece of **Sangallo the Elder**. The variety and harmony of its architectural lines and the reliefs which create a play of light and shade will please the tourist in search of beauty. The building is planned in the shape of a Greek cross and is surmounted by a dome. The south transept is prolonged by a semicircular sacristy. Two campaniles flank the main façade. One is unfinished; the other includes the three orders: Doric, Ionic and Corinthian. The interior gives the same impression of majesty and nobility. To the left of the entrance is a 14C Annunciation.
Opposite the church stands the Canonica (chanonry) an elegant porticoed building.

★★ **Chianciano Terme.** – *10km – 6 miles to the southeast.*
This fashionable thermal spa is pleasantly situated. The curative properties of its waters were known to the Etruscans and the Romans. There are some fine shady parks.

Michelin map 988 fold 28 – Local map p 96

Monte Sant'Angelo stands on a **curious site**★★. The town is built on a spur (803m – 2 634ft) dominated by the massive form of its castle and overlooks both the Gargano Promontory and the sea. It was in a nearby cave between 490 and 493 that the Archangel Michael, chief of the Heavenly Host, appeared three times to the bishop of Siponto. After a further apparition in the 8C it was decided to found an abbey. During the Middle Ages all the Crusaders came to pray to the Archangel Michael, the saintly warrior, before embarking at Manfredonia.
On the 29 September the annual feast day includes the procession of the Archangel's Sword.

★ **Church of St Michael (Santuario di San Michele).** – The building, designed in the transitional Romanesque-Gothic style, is flanked by a detached octagonal campanile dating from the late 13C. The very beautiful and richly worked **bronze door**★ is of Byzantine origin and dates from 1076. It gives access to both the nave with pointed vaulting and the cave in which St Michael is said to have made his apparition. Note the marble statue of the saint by Andrea Sansovino (16C) and the 11C episcopal pulpit in a style characteristic of Apulia.

★ **Tomb of Rotharis (Tomba di Rotari).** – *Go down the stairs opposite the campanile.*
⊘ The tomb is to the left of the apse of the ruined Church of St Peter's. Above the entrance are scenes from the life of Christ. Inside the tower rises in stages through a square, an octagon and finally a triangle to the dome. The tomb was supposed to contain the remains of Rotharis, a 7C King of the Lombards, but is really a 12C baptistry.

ROME
A Michelin Green Guide
29 walks in the Eternal City :
*   the most famous sites,*
*   30 centuries of history*
*   the art treasures in the museums.*

Monza is quite an attractive industrial town specialising mainly in textiles. It stands on the edge of the Brianza, a lovely green hilly area dotted with lakes, attractive towns and villas set in lovely gardens.

★ **Cathedral (Duomo).** − This cathedral was built in the 13-14C and has an attractive Lombard façade★★ (1390-96) in alternating white, green and black marble, which is remarkable for its harmonious proportions and variety of openings. It was the work of Matteo di Campione architect and sculptor and one of the famous *maestri campionesi (qv)*, who spread the Lombard style throughout Italy.

The **interior**★ was remodelled in the 17C. The splendid silver gilt **altar front**★ dates from the 14C. To the left of the chancel is the Chapel of the Queen of the Longobards, Theodolinda (6-7C) adorned with fascinating 15C **frescoes**★ depicting scenes in the life of this pious sovereign.

⊙ The **treasury**★ has the famous 5-9C **Iron Crown**★★ of the Kings of Lombardy, which was offered by Pope Gregory I the Great to the queen. In addition there are fine pieces of 6 to 9C plate, 17C reliquaries and 16C tapestries.

★★ **Park of the Royal Villa (Parco di Villa Reale).** − This majestic neo-classical building
⊙ was the residence of Eugène de Beauharnais and Humbert I of Italy, who was assassinated at Monza by an anarchist in 1900. This vast park is landscaped in the English manner.

In the northern part of the park there are several sporting facilities and the Monza racing circuit which is the venue for the annual Grand Prix Formula One race.

★★★ **NAPLES** (NAPOLI) Campania   Pop 1 200 958

Michelin map 988 fold 27 − Local map p 133 − Town plan pp 126 and 127 − Plan of built-up area in the current Michelin Red Guide Italia

The beauties of Naples have been praised by innumerable travellers. A lovely bay, a horizon bounded by Posillipo, the islands, the Sorrento Peninsula and lofty Vesuvius, all contribute to the fame of this favoured spot. As for Naples itself, its attractive climate, the mingling of gaiety and sadness, vivacity and fatalism of the people make this town "the permanent playhouse of Italy", and add to its celebrity.

However, the industrial quarters to the east, the alleys littered with rubbish, the dilapidation of buildings damaged by the serious earthquake of 1980, the heavy traffic, which throttles the city at certain times of the day and the light haze that clouds the horizon may at first disappoint tourists who dream of a picturesque Naples basking under an ever blue sky in a harmonious setting.

Visiting Naples. − Although the discovery of this city is not easy it is always a rewarding experience. When visiting the older areas like Spacca Napoli, visitors are advised to avoid attracting undue attention to themselves either by their behaviour or their way of dress, to refrain from night-time strolls, to leave nothing in the car and to be on the alert at all times.

HISTORICAL NOTES

According to legend, the siren Parthenope gave her name to a town which had sprung up round her tomb, that is why Naples is called the Parthenopaean City. In fact, Naples originated as a Greek colony named Neapolis, which was conquered by the Romans in the 4C BC. Rich inhabitants of Rome like Virgil, Augustus, Tiberius, Nero, etc used to spend the winter there, but the Neapolitans themselves retained the Greek language and customs until the decline of the Empire.

Since the 12C seven princely families have reigned over Naples: the Normans, Hohenstaufens, Angevins, Aragonese, Spanish and Bourbons. The French Revolution of 1789 brought in French troops, and in 1799 a **Parthenopaean Republic** was set up, followed by a French kingdom (1806-15), under Joseph Bonaparte (Napoleon's brother) and afterwards Joachim Murat (Napoleon's brother-in-law), both of whom promoted excellent reforms. From 1815 to 1860 the restored Bourbons remained in spite of the 1820 and 1848 revolts.

ART IN NAPLES

A royal patron of the arts. − Under the princes of the House of Anjou, Naples was endowed with many ecclesiastical buildings, which were greatly influenced by the French Gothic style. **"Good King Robert" of Anjou** (1309-43) attracted poets, scholars and artists from various regions of Italy, to his court in Naples. Boccaccio spent part of his youth in Naples where he fell in love with Fiammetta, whom some believe to be the king's own daughter. His friend Petrarch also spent some time in this city. In 1324 Robert the Wise brought the Sienese sculptor, Tino da Camaino to adorn many of the churches with his monumental tombs. Other churches were embellished with frescoes by the Roman artist, Pietro Cavallini, and slightly later Giotto whose works have unfortunately disappeared, and Simone Martini.

The Neapolitan School of Painting (17C − early 18C). − With the arrival in Naples in 1606 of the great innovator in Italian painting, **Michelangelo Merisi Caravaggio** (1573-1610), a new local school of painting flourished, whose members were inspired by the master's bold and dramatic style. The principal followers were Artemisia Gentileschi, the Spaniard José Ribera alias Spagnoletto, the Calabrian Mattia Preti and Salvator Rosa. One pupil who differed greatly from the others was **Luca Giordano** (1632-1705) who specialised in decorating ceilings with spirited compositions full of light. His decorative work was a step towards Roman baroque art. Francesco Solimena perpetuated the former's style.

(Lauros/Giraudon)

Ferdinand of Aragon's fleet in Naples harbour (15C)

Original works. – Numerous were the architects who built fine baroque buildings in Naples and the surrounding area. **Ferdinando Sanfelice** (1675-1748) had a highly inventive and theatrical approach to staircases which he placed at the far end of the courtyard where they became the palace's most important decorative feature. It was however **Luigi Vanvitelli** (1700-73) who was the great Neapolitan architect of the 18C. The Bourbon King, Charles III entrusted Vanvitelli with the project to build another Versailles at Caserta *(qv)*.

It was in the 17C that Naples began to specialise in the marvellous **cribs** *(presepi)* which were to become so famous.

Music and the theatre. – Neapolitans have always shown a great love of music, be it for **opera** where great importance is placed on the virtuosity of the singer, or for more **popular music**, sometimes joyful, sometimes melancholy, practised to the accompaniment of a guitar or a mandolin. Naples gave the character Scaramouch (old fox) to the *Commedia dell' Arte (qv)*.

Religious festivals. – In Naples these are sumptuous and the best known are the Madonna di Piedigrotta, Santa Maria del Carmine and especially the Feast of the Miracle of St Januarius *(p 130)*. Between Christmas and Epiphany (Twelfth Night) the local churches are adorned with splendid cribs. *See the table of Principal Festivals at the end of the guide.*

IN THE STREETS OF NAPLES

The Neapolitans are small and dark, with almost Graecian profiles. They speak a very expressive dialect in a sing-song way. They have lively imaginations, they readily give vent to their emotions and they fear the Evil Eye *(jettatura)*. Religious festivals are numerous and very popular and even sporting events, in particular football matches, become a pretext for outrageous behaviour.

There are numerous novels and films which have captured the peculiarities of the Neapolitans and their way of life. Popular scenes which used to charm the tourists are now a thing of the past. Traffic is hectic. The town with its narrow streets is ill-suited to heavy traffic but cars weave in and out frenetically and only the genius for improvisation, the daring and virtuosity of Neapolitan drivers compensate for their lack of discipline.

The quarters. – The busy port handles more passengers than any other in Italy but is second to Genoa in goods traffic. The city centre extends around **Piazza del Plebiscito** *(p 126)* and the **Galleria Umberto I (JKZ)**. The working class quarters, with their streets drawn close together and hung with washing, are to be found in the Spacca Napoli *(p 128)* and in the area to the west of the Via Toledo **(KY)**. To the west of the town lie the residential areas spread over the hillsides of **Vomero** and **Posillipo** *(p 131)*.

Neapolitan cuisine. – One can usually have a meal at any time of the day and late into the night at any one of the many restaurants and *trattorias* .

The numerous pizzerias are only usually open in the evening. Try the cow-buffalo's-milk cheese *(mozzarella)* served with ham or tomatoes as a starter or as a sort of toasted sandwich *(in carrozza)*, the various forms of spaghetti served lightly cooked *(al dente)* seasoned with fresh tomatoes or mussels or other shellfish *(alle vongole)*. The local vines grown in volcanic soil give a slightly sulphur tasting wine: red and white from Capri, white from Ischia, the red Gragnano wine and the liquorous wine of Vesuvius known as *Lacryma Christi*.

★★CITY CENTRE *time: 2 1/2 hours*

★★ **New Castle (Castel Nuovo) (KZ)**. – This imposing castle, surrounded by deep moats, was built in 1282 by Pierre de Chaulnes and Pierre d'Agincourt, the architects of Charles I of Anjou. It was modelled on the castle at Angers. A remarkable **triumphal arch**★★ embellishes the entrance on the town side. This masterpiece bearing sculptures to the glory of the House of Aragon, was built to designs by Francesco Laurana in 1467. At the far end of the inner courtyard stands an elegant Renaissance doorway surmounted by a Virgin by Laurana (1474).

★ **St Charles Theatre (Teatro San Carlo) (KZ T)**. – The theatre was built under Charles of Bourbon in 1737 and rebuilt in 1816 in the neo-classical style. The opera house is an important institution in the Italian world of music.
The sumptuous auditorium, with boxes on six levels, is built entirely of wood and stucco to achieve perfect acoustics.

★ **Piazza del Plebiscito (JKZ)**. – This noble semicircular "square" was laid out in the reign of Murat. It is enclosed on one side by the royal palace, on the other by the neo-classical façade of the **Church of St Francis of Paola** (San Francesco di Paola) built on the model of the Pantheon in Rome and prolonged by a curving colonnade. The equestrian statues of Ferdinand I and Charles III of Bourbon in the centre are by Canova.

126

★ **Royal Palace (Palazzo Reale) (KZ)**. – The palace was built at the beginning of the 17C
by the architect Domenico Fontana and was remodelled several times. The façade
retains more or less its original appearance. Since the late 19C the niches on the façade contain eight statues of the most famous Kings of Naples.

A huge staircase with twin ramps and crowned by a coffered dome, leads to the apartments and the sumptuously decorated **royal chapel**. It was only after 1734 that royalty
lived in the apartments. The richly decorated rooms have retained their numerous works
of art, tapestries, paintings, period furniture and fine porcelain.

★ **Port of Santa Lucia.** – *Town plan in the current Michelin Red Guide Italia.* Santa Lucia
is the name of the small suburb that juts out toward the sea. It is best known as the
name of a tiny port, immortalised by a famous Neapolitan song, nestling between a
rocky islet and the jetty linking it to the shore. **Egg Castle** (Castel dell' Ovo) is a severe
edifice built by the Normans and remodelled by the Angevins in 1274. Legend has it
that Virgil hid a magic egg within its walls and the destruction of the egg would result
in a similar fate for the castle.

From the jetty there is a splendid **view**★★ of Vesuvius on one hand and of the western
side of the bay on the other. In the evening, go further along to Piazza Vittoria which
offers a **view**★★★ of the residential suburbs on the Vomero and Posillipo hillsides brightly
lit up by a myriad of twinkling lights.

NAPLES ★★★

★★ OLD NAPLES (SPACCA NAPOLI) (KLY) *time: 2 1/2 hours on foot*

This is the heart of old Naples. With its numerous churches, dilapidated palaces, small crafts and businesses, its ancient streets where swarms a lively populace, it is undoubtedly the most engaging part of the town. Its main axis, formed by the Via Benedetto Croce and S. Biagio dei Librai, follows the course of the Roman *Decumanus Maximus* and is nicknamed Spacca Napoli, meaning the street which cuts Naples in two.

★ **St Clare's (Santa Chiara) (KY C).** – Sancia of Majorca, the wife of Robert the Wise of Anjou had this Church of the Poor Clares built in the Provencal Gothic style. The interior is sober and lofty. In the chancel are several memorials to the Anjou dynasty: behind the high altar is the **tomb★★** of Robert the Wise, the work of Florentine sculptors in 1345; the **tomb★** of Marie de Valois, near the wall on the right, is by Tino di Camaino and his pupils.

Behind the church are **cloisters★** which Vaccaro transformed in the 18C into an original garden and embellished with Capodimonte faience *(see opposite)*.

St Dominic Major (San Domenico Maggiore) (KY L). – Its apse gives on to a square ornamented with a small baroque votive monument *(guglia)*. The interior has both Gothic (**caryatids★** by Tino di Camaino support a hugh paschal candelabrum) and baroque (high altar) features. The 18C sacristy with its panelling contains numerous coffins of members of the court of Aragon.

Chapel of San Severo (KY V). – This 16C church has an amazingly exuberant baroque interior which dates from the 18C. There are some astonishing marble **sculptures★**: on either side of the choir are Chastity and Despair (the latter being symbolised by a man struggling with a net); the central one depicts the recumbent figure of Christ covered by a thin shroud and is the work of Giuseppe Sammartino.

Not far from the Church of St Dominic is the charming Piazzetta Nilo, adorned with a statue of the Nile from which it derives its name.

A little further along the Via S. Biagio dei Librai opens onto the picturesque Via S. Gregorio.

St Lawrence Major (San Lorenzo Maggiore) (LY K). – The spacious and well-lit church, on the plan of a Latin cross, has a fine Gothic nave (early 14C) lined with chapels. Following renovation, the interior has assumed its original bare appearance except for the west wall which has kept its baroque additions. An elegant **arch★** spans the transept crossing. To the south of the choir is the remarkable mosaic-covered **tomb★** of Catherine of Austria, the daughter-in-law of Robert the Wise. The late 13C **polygonal apse★** by Thibaud de Saumur is an interesting specimen of French architecture in southern Italy; the chancel opens onto the ambulatory through elegant arches crowned by twin bays.

In the Via Tribunali (KY) at no 362 is the **Palazzo Spinelli di Laurino (A)** with a curious elliptical courtyard embellished by one of Sanfelice's staircases. The Via Tribunali ends at the **Piazza Dante (KY)** overlooked by a semicircular range of buildings by Vanvitelli.

★★★ NATIONAL ARCHAEOLOGICAL MUSEUM
(MUSEO ARCHEOLOGICO NAZIONALE) (KY) *time: 2 hours*

The museum occupies a 16C building which was originally intended to house the royal cavalry, and then became the seat of the university from 1610 to 1777. The collections are essentially composed of works or art belonging to the Farnese family and treasures discovered at Pompeii and Herculaneum. It is one of the richest museums in the world for Greco-Roman antiquities.

★★★ **Greco-Roman sculpture.** – This department is on the ground floor.

Tyrant-Slayers' Gallery. – *Turn right on entering.* This gallery is devoted to Archaic art. The **Aphrodite Sosandra** with a fine, proud face and elegantly draped robe is a splendid copy of a Greek bronze (5C BC) while the powerful marble group of the **Tyrant-Slayers,** a copy of a Greek bronze, represents Harmodios and Aristogiton who delivered Athens from the tyrant, Hipparchus, in the 6C BC.

Great Masters' Gallery. – *Parallel to the above gallery on the entrance side.* Room II contains the majestic statue of the Farnese Pallas (Athena) and Orpheus and Eurydice bidding each other farewell, a low-relief of touching simplicity copied from the Phidias original (5C BC). In Room III is the **Doryphorus,** the spear-bearer, a copy of the famous bronze by Polykleitos.

Farnese Bull Gallery. – The gallery derives its name from the colossal group, the **Farnese Bull** (Room VI), depicting the death of Dirce. Carved from a single block of marble it was restored by Michelangelo. The famous **Callipygian Venus,** a Roman copy of the Greek original, stands in the centre of Room X. Room XII contains the **Aphrodite of Sinuessa,** a Greek original of admirable delicacy as well as the **Farnese Hercules,** a Greek copy of an original by Lysippus who was greatly admired by Renaissance artists. In Room XIV is the **Psyche of Capua,** with a beautifully spiritual face.

Works in coloured marble. – The most famous work is the statue of **Artemis of Ephesus** (2C) in alabaster and bronze, representing the deity venerated at the famous temple by the Aegean Sea. She is sometimes considered as a nature goddess in the oriental tradition and is represented with numerous breasts symbolising her motherly nature.

Great Hall. – Note against the second pillar on the right the statue of the priestess Eumachia, discovered at Pompeii. The robe is beautifully draped and the face expressive.

Greek Portrait Gallery *(on the left at the far end of the hall)* **and the Emperors' Gallery** *(at right angles to the former gallery).* – In these galleries admire the portrait busts of Socrates, the blind Homer, Euripides and other excellent portraits of Roman emperors.

★★ **Mosaics.** – *To the left on the mezzanine.*
Although most of these come from Pompeii they offer a wide variety of styles and subject matter. Note two small works by Dioscurides of Samos (Room LIX): Roving Musicians and Visit to a Magician as well as the famous mosaic of the **Battle of Alexander** (Room LXI) which paved the floor of the House of the Faun at Pompeii. It depicts with a remarkable sense of movement the victory of the King of Macedon over Darius, King of Persia.

★★ **Works from Villa Pison.** – *First floor, on the right.*
The villa which was discovered at Herculaneum in the 18C but was later reburied, is thought to have belonged to L. Calpurnius Pison who was Julius Caesar's father-in-law. The owner had turned the house into a museum. The documents and splendid works of art from his collections are priceless. The Papyri Room (CXIV) contains photographs of some of the 800 papyri from the library. In Room CXVI are exhibited **bronze statues** that adorned the peristyle of the villa: the **Drunken Faun** lost in euphoria, a **Sleeping Satyr** with a beautiful face in repose; the two lifelike **Wrestlers** are inspired from Lysippus (4C BC); the famous **Dancers from Herculaneum** are probably in fact water carriers; the famous **Hermes at Rest** with a tall strong figure, reflects Lysippus' ideal. In Room CXVII, in addition to the **portrait** mistakenly identified as that of **Seneca** and one of the most remarkably expressive works from antiquity, are exhibited an Ideal Head identified as Artemis, and the majestic statue of Athena Promachos (1C BC).

★★ **Small bronzes, paintings and minor arts.** – *First floor, on the left.*
Rooms XC to XCV display works of art from Pompeii and Herculaneum, notably a remarkable collection of **small bronzes,** vases, plates, lamps, musical and surgical instruments, heating apparatus and kitchen utensils. Rooms LXVIII to LXXV have a collection of **mural paintings** from the various villas. The great diversity of style, variety of colours and themes are all ample proof of the richness of decorative traditions in Rome *(see Pompeiian Painting).*

★★CARTHUSIAN MONASTERY OF ST MARTIN
(CERTOSA DI SAN MARTINO) (JZ) *time: 1 hour*

This immense Carthusian monastery is beautifully situated on a spur of the Volmero hill. The **Castel Sant' Elmo** a massive structure with bastions overlooks the monastery to the west; it was rebuilt by the Spaniards in the 16C and was for a long time used as a prison. The monastery was founded by the Anjou dynasty and was almost completely remodelled in the 16 and 17C. The monastic buildings can be visited as well as the museum with its historical collections which are arranged in the buildings overlooking the Procurators' Cloisters.

Church. – The **interior**★★ is lavishly baroque. The choir has a superb marble communion table by Sammartino and several paintings by Guido Reni and Caracciolo. The sacristy has marquetry panelling. In the treasury chapel there are paintings by Ribera and Luca Giordano.

Great Cloisters. – This harmonious ensemble is the work of the architect-sculptor Cosimo Fanzago.

★ **Museum.** – The section devoted to festivals and costumes contains an exceptional collection of figurines and Neapolitan **cribs**★★ *(presepi).* The historical section retraces the history of Naples from the Bourbon reign (1734) to the arrival of Garibaldi in 1860. From Room 25 there is an outstanding **view**★★★ of Naples and its bay. The **art gallery** regroups works from the 15 to the 19C. There is also a rich section of **sculptures** including works by Tino di Camaino.

★★CAPODIMONTE PALACE AND NATIONAL GALLERY
(PALAZZO E GALLERIA NAZIONALE DI CAPODIMONTE) *time: 1 1/2 hours*

On the northern outskirts of Naples: take the Via S. Teresa degli Scalzi (JKY).

This former **royal estate**★ extends over high ground to the north of the city. The whole includes a massive and austere palace which was built between 1738 and 1838, an extensive park, and the remains of the famous 18C porcelain factory. The palace itself has an art gallery in addition to the royal apartments.

★★ **National Gallery.** – *2nd floor.* Pleasantly presented this important Italian collection regroups both Italian and foreign works. The Primitives include the remarkable **St Louis of Toulouse** by Simone Martini, a masterpiece from the Sienese school (Room 4), several works including a *Madonna* by Taddeo Gaddi, others by Masolino (Room 5) as well as the dramatic **Crucifixion** by Masaccio (Room 6).
The Renaissance period is illustrated by canvases by Botticelli, Filippino Lippi and Raphael (Room 7), Lorenzo Lotto, Vivarini, Mantegna and in particular the admirable **Transfiguration** by Giovanni Bellini whose subtle combination of balanced landscape, harmony of colours and vivid light enhances the religious theme.
The Neapolitan school is represented by a picture of a *Lion being cared for by St Jerome* (Room 10) executed in the detailed Flemish style by Colantonio (15C). In the rooms containing works from the Mannerist movement note the elegant *Portrait of a Youth* by Rosso Fiorentino (Room 15), works by Correggio (Room 17) – notably the tender and delicate **Zingarella Madonna** *(Gipsy woman)* – and portraits by Il Parmigianino including that of the sumptuously dressed **Antea.** Room 18 regroups some fine canvases by El Greco while Room 19 has an exceptional **group of Titians.** The outstanding ones are the portrait of *Danae* with its superb colour effects and the admirable family portrait of *Pope Paul III (Alessandro Farnese) with his nephews (photograph p 21)* which is wonderfully expressive. Room 20 regroups northern European painters: Joos Van Cleve and especially Breughel the Elder with his celebrated **Parable of the Blind** (1568).

Further on are several Carracci (Room 25) who with their reaction against Mannerism paved the way for baroque art as well as works by Guido Reni (Room 27). Outstanding however is the remarkable **Flagellation** by Caravaggio (Room 29) who inspired such followers as Andrea Vaccaro, Ribera, Artemisia Gentileschi and Stanzione who are all represented in the following galleries.

The last rooms are devoted to the Neapolitan school with paintings by Salvator Rosa, Bernardo Cavallino, Mattia Preti, Luca Giordano, Giuseppe Recco, Paulo Porpora...

Royal apartments. – *1st floor.* These have some lovely pieces of furniture. Rooms 67 to 71 house the porcelain museum. The Chinese style **porcelain room★★** executed in the 18C at Capodimonte for the royal summer residence at Portici, has been reassembled in Room 94.

ADDITIONAL SIGHTS

★ **Mergellina.** – *Plan of the built-up area in the current Michelin Red Guide Italia.*
Mergellina, at the foot of the Posillipo hillside with the small port of Sannazzaro, is one of the few places in Naples ideal for a stroll. It affords a splendid **view★★** of the bay: the Vomero hillside, crowned by Castel Sant' Elmo, slopes down gently towards the Santa Lucia headland and Egg Castle beyond, with Vesuvius in the distance.

★ **Villa Floridiana.** – *To the west of Naples. Town plan in the current Michelin Red Guide Italia.*
This graceful small white palace *(palazzina)* in the neo-classical style stands at the foot of the Vomero hillside. The palace houses the **Duca di Martina National Ceramics Museum★** with sections devoted to enamels, ivories, faïence and especially porcelain. Its fine gardens afford an attractive **view★** from the terrace.

★ **Catacombs of St Januarius (Catacombe di San Gennaro).** – *To the north of Naples. Plan of the built-up area in the current Michelin Red Guide Italia.*
The catacombs have been associated with the name of St Januarius since the 5C when the remains of the martyred saint were transferred here from Pozzuoli. They extend over two floors and consist of vast galleries, some of which have interesting paleo Christian paintings.

★ **Santa Maria Donnaregina (LY B).** – Cross the cloisters adorned with 18C faïence. A baroque church of the same name precedes the small 14C Gothic church which shows a decidedly French influence. Inside is the **tomb★** of the founder, Mary of Hungary, widow of Charles II of Anjou by Tino di Camaino. The walls of the monks chancel are decorated with 14C **frescoes★**.

★ **St John's (San Giovanni a Carbonara) (LY G).** – An 18C stairway leads to the elegant Gothic doorway of this 14C church. Inside note the tomb of Ladislas of Anjou (15C) and the many works of art in two chapels, the Carracciolo del Sole behind the choir and the Carracciolo del Vico, to the left of the previous one.

★ **Capua Gate (Porta Capuana) (LMY D).** – This is one of the fortified gateways in the walls built in 1484 to the plans of Giuliano da Maiano. The **Capuan Castle** (Castel Capuano) **(LY)** nearby was the former residence of the Norman princes and the Hohenstaufens.

Cathedral (Duomo) (LY). – Built in the 14C the cathedral was considerably altered at a later date. Held in great veneration by the people, the **Chapel of St Januarius** (San Gennaro), in a rich baroque style, is preceded by a remarkable 17C bronze grille: behind the high altar are two glass phials containing the saint's blood which is supposed to liquefy, failing which disaster will befall the town. The Feast of the **Miracle of St Januarius** is held twice annually on the first Sunday in May and on the 19 September. The dome is decorated by a Lanfranco fresco with an admirable sense of movement. A door in the middle of the north aisle gives access to the 4C **Basilica of Santa Restituta**, which was transformed in the Gothic period and again in the 17C. At the far end of the nave, the 5C baptistry contains remains of mosaics of the same period.

★ **Cuomo Palace (Palazzo Cuomo) (LY Q).** – This majestic late 15C palace, with its rusticated stonework, is a reminder of the Florentine Renaissance. It contains the **Filangieri Municipal Museum**. There are collections of arms and armour, ceramics and porcelain, furniture and paintings by Ribera, Carracciolo, Mattia Preti, etc.

St Anne of the Lombards (Sant' Anna dei Lombardi) (KYZ R). – This Renaissance church is rich in contemporary Florentine **sculptures★**. Inside is the tomb of Mary of Aragon (1st chapel on the left) by Antonio Rossellino and an Annunciation (1st chapel on the right) by Benedetto da Maiano. In the oratory to the right of the choir is a Descent from the Cross, a late 15C terracotta by Guido Mazzoni who introduced this style of rather theatrical realism to Naples and was to become very popular in southern Italy. The former sacristy has lovely stalls which are attributed to Fra Giovanni da Verona (1457-1525).

Public Gardens (Villa Comunale). – *Town plan in the current Michelin Red Guide Italia.*
Vanvitelli laid out these gardens along the waterfront in 1780. It is very popular with the Neapolitans for the evening walk. The aquarium stands within the gardens.

Aquarium (Acquario). – Discover the large variety of sea creatures to be found in the Bay of Naples.

If you are puzzled by an abbreviation or a symbol in the text or on the maps, look at the key on p 34.

The Bay of Naples, extending from Cumae to Sorrento, has a rich history and is one of the most beautiful Italian gulfs. It is an area of striking contrasts where one may find in close proximity, places of solitude conducive to meditation such as the archaeological sites, the bare slopes of Vesuvius, the Cave or Lake Averno and others bustling with activity, noisy, dense with traffic, enlivened by a population which lives with the ever present fear of earthquakes and a new volcanic eruption. Its legendary beauty is somewhat marred by the uncontrolled sprawl of industrial development which has reached the outskirts of Naples. However its islands, capes, and mountains offer unforgettable excursions.

Sightseeing. – Follow the itineraries indicated on the local map pp 132 and 133.

★ 1 FROM NAPLES TO CUMAE

The Phlegrean Fields (CAMPI FLEGREI)
45km – 28 miles – about 6 hours

This volcanic area, which received its name from the ancients ("phlegrean" is derived from a Greek word meaning "to blaze"), extends in an arc along the Gulf of Pozzuoli. Hot springs, steam-jets and sulphurous gases rise from the ground and from the sea, and are proof of an intense underground activity. Lakes have formed in the craters of extinct volcanoes. This stretch of coastline is subjected to variations in ground level due to volcanic activity.

★ **Naples.** – *Description p 124.*

★ **Posillipo.** – This famous hill forms a promontory and separates the Bay of Naples from Pozzuoli Bay. Posillipo, dotted with villas and their lovely gardens and modern buildings is Naples' main residential area. It affords splendid views of the bay.

★ **Marechiaro.** – This small fishermen's village built high above the sea, was made famous by a Neapolitan song *Marechiare*.

Garden of Remembrance (Parco Virgiliano or Parco della Rimembranza). – From the point there are splendid **views**★★ over the Bay of Naples, from Cape Miseno to Sorrento Peninsula, as well as the islands of Procida, Ischia and Capri.

★ **Pozzuoli.** – *Description p 157.*

★ **Solfatara.** – *Description p 157.*

Lake Lucrino (Lago Lucrino). – In antiquity, oyster farming was practised here and the banks were lined with elegant villas. One of these belonged to Cicero and another was the scene of Agrippina's murder, on the orders of her son Nero.

★ **Baia: the Baths.** – This Greek colony was in Roman times a fashionable bathing-beach as well as a thermal spa with the most complete equipment in the world for hydrotherapy. The Roman emperors and patricians had immense villas, all of which disappeared under the sea after a change in ground level. However ruins of the famous baths subsist, sitting on the hilltop overlooking the sea. When facing the hill these include from left to right the baths of Venus, the baths of Sosandra and the baths of Mercury.

Bacoli. – On the high ground in the old town, you can visit the **Cento Camerelle**★ *(Via Cento Camerelle, to the right of the church)*. This huge reservoir, which belonged to a private villa, is built on two levels: the grandiose upper level built in the 1C has four sections and immense arches. The lower part, built much earlier, has a network of narrow galleries forming a cross, that emerge high above sea level. The famous **Piscina Mirabile**★ *(at the church take the road to the left, Via Ambrogio Greco, and then Via Piscina Mirabile to the right)* was an immense cistern designed to supply water to the Roman fleet in the port of Miseno. It is 70m long, 25m wide and nearly 15m high (230ft×82ft×49ft) and is divided into five sections with 48 pillars supporting the roof. There are remarkable light effects.

Miseno. – This name is given to a lake, a port, a promontory, a cape and a village. Lake Miseno, a former volcanic crater, was believed by the ancients to be the Styx, across which Charon ferried the souls of the dead. Under the Emperor Augustus it was linked by a canal to the port of Miseno, which was the base of the Roman fleet. The village of Miseno is dominated by Monte Miseno, on which Misenus, the companion of Aeneas, is said to have been buried. The slopes of the promontory were studded with luxurious villas, including the one where in AD 37 the Emperor Tiberius choked to death.

Lake Fusaro (Lago di Fusaro). – A lagoon containing a small island on which Vanvitelli built a hunting lodge for King Ferdinand IV of Bourbon in 1782.

★ **Cumae.** – *Description p 76.*

★ **Lake Avernus (Lago d'Averno).** – *The lake lies below the Cumae-Naples road: belvedere on the right approximately 1km – 1/2 mile beyond Arco Felice.*
This lake within a crater is sad, still and silent and wrapped in an atmosphere of mystery which was all the more intense in antiquity as birds flying overhead were hit by the fumes and dropped into the lake to be swallowed up. Homer and Virgil regarded it as the entrance to the Underworld. Under the Roman Empire, Agrippa, a captain in the service of the Emperor Augustus, developed it as a naval base and linked it by canal with Lake Lucrino *(see above)*, which in turn was linked to the open sea. An underground gallery 1km – 1/2 mile long known as **Cocceio's Cave** (Grotta di Cocceio), connected Avernus with Cumae, and was used by chariots.

★★★ 2 FROM NAPLES TO TORRE ANNUNZIATA

Vesuvius

*44km – 27 miles by the west face or 39km – 24 miles by the south face -
allow 1 day*

The coast road relieves the Salerno motorway but crosses a densely populated zon
of industrial sprawl. Here were however the favourite resorts of the Neapolitan aris
tocracy in the 18 and 19C.

Portici. – The road crosses the courtyard of the **royal palace** built in 1738 for the Bour
bon King Charles III. Today the palace buildings are the home of the Naples Faculty c
Agronomy. In his opera *The Mute Girl of Portici (Muette de Portici)* the French com
poser, Auber features the 17C revolt against the Spaniards, instigated by Masaniello
young fisherman from Portici.

★★ **Herculaneum.** – *Description p 100.*

★★★ **Vesuvius.** – The outline of Vesuvius, one of the few still active volcanoes in Europe
is inseparable from the Neapolitan landscape. It has in fact two summits: to the nort
Monte Somma (alt 1 132m – 3 714ft) and to the south Mount Vesuvius prope
(alt 1 277mp – 4 190ft). With time the volcanic materials on the lower slopes hav
become fertile soil which supports vines producing the famous *Lacryma Christi* wine

The eruptions of Vesuvius. – Until the earthquake of AD 62 and the eruption of AD 7
which buried Herculaneum and Pompeii, Vesuvius seemed extinct; its slopes wer
clothed with famous vines and woods. By 1139, seven eruptions had been recorded
Then came a period of calm during which the slopes of the mountains were cultivated
On 16 December 1631 Vesuvius had a terrible awakening, destroying all the settle
ments at its foot: 3 000 people perished. The eruption of 1794 devastated Torre de

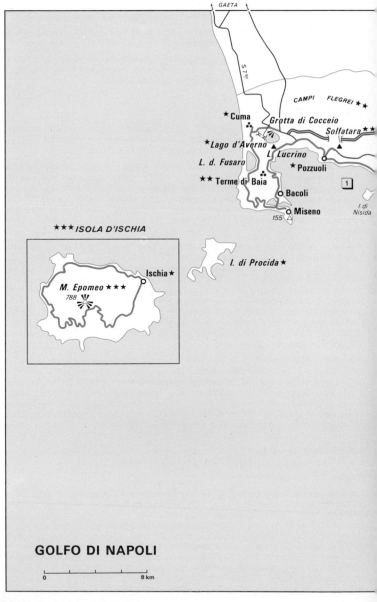

Greco. The volcano had minor eruptions in 1858, 1871, 1872, from 1895 to 1899, 1900, 1903, 1904 and a major eruption in 1906. Following the eruption of 1929 that of 1944 altered the shape of the crater. Since then, apart from a short period of activity linked with the 1980 earthquake, Vesuvius has emitted only a plume of smoke.

Ascent by the west face. – *Start from Herculaneum and return by Torre del Greco: 27km – 17 miles plus 3/4 hour on foot Rtn. Wear stout walking shoes.* This is the easiest route. This good road leads to a junction in the midst of lava flows. Take the left fork *(the car park is several kilometres further on)*. The path offers an easy but most impressive climb up the side of the volcano, scattered with cinders and lapilli.

From the summit there is an immense **panorama**★★★ over the Bay of Naples enclosed by the Sorrento Peninsula in the south and Cape Miseno in the north. Beyond is the Gulf of Gaeta. The crater affords an unforgettable sight for its sheer size and the desolation of the slopes of its jagged walls, for the great yawning crater, which takes on a pink colour in the sun, and the spouting steam jets.

Ascent by the south face. – *Start from Torre Annunziata (see overleaf) and take the toll-road from Boscotrecase (to be taken only in dry weather): 19km – 12 miles Rtn, plus 3/4 hour on foot Rtn. Wear stout walking shoes.* The first part of the route is surfaced but after it becomes a track through the ash and lapilli from the last eruption (1944) and is quite difficult towards the end. It does however afford splendid **views**★★ of the Sarno plain and the coast as far as Sorrento.

Torre del Greco. – This town which has been repeatedly destroyed by the eruptions of Vesuvius, is well known for its coral ornaments and cameos.

Torre Annunziata. – This town is the centre of the famous Neapolitan spaghetti and macaroni industry. It has been buried under the lava of Vesuvius seven times. The sumptuous **Roman Villa Oplontis**★★ is decorated with 2nd style Pompeiian paintings *(p 153)*.

NAPLES, Bay of ★★★

★★★ ③ FROM TORRE ANNUNZIATA TO SORRENTO
69km – 43 miles – allow 1 day

Torre Annunziata. – *Description p 133.*

★★★ **Pompeii.** – *Description p 152.*

★ **Castellammare di Stabia.** – *Description p 70.*

★★ **Monte Faito.** – *Access by a toll-road.* Monte Faito is part of the **Lattari range**, a headland which separates the Bay of Naples and the Gulf of Salerno and forms the Sorrento
Peninsula. Its name is derived from the beech trees (*fagus* in Latin) which are a source
of pleasantly cool shade in summer. The steeply winding road leads to a roundabout
(Belvedere dei Capi) which provides a splendid **panorama**★★★ of the Bay of Naples. The
road continues upwards to the **San Michele Chapel** from where there is another **panorama**★★★; the wild landscape of the Lattari mountains contrasts strongly with the
smiling scenery of the Bay of Naples and the Sarno plain. There is a fine run down
towards Vico Equense.

★ **Vico Equense.** – This small health and seaside resort occupies a picturesque site on
a rocky headland.

★★ **Sorrento and Sorrento Peninsula.** – *Description p 183.*

★★★ THE ISLANDS

★★★ **Capri.** – *Description p 67.*

★★★ **Ischia.** – *Description p 102.*

★ **Procida.** – *Description p 102.*

NOVARA Piedmont   Pop 102 619

Michelin map **988** folds 2 and 3 or **219** fold 17 – Town plan in the current Michelin Red
Guide Italia

Novara is situated on the borders of Piedmont and Lombardy to the north of the
Lomellina, a vast rice growing area. It is a busy commercial and industrial town as well
as being an important road junction in the road network of northern Italy.

★ **Basilica of San Gaudenzio.** – Built between 1577 and 1659 to the designs of the
Lombard architect, Pellegrino Tibaldi, it was crowned with a lovely tall slender **dome**★★
(1844-78), an audacious addition by a local architect A. Antonelli. Inside there are
several interesting works of art including paintings by Morazzone (17C) and Gaudenzio
Ferrari (16C) as well as the silver **sarcophagus**★ of the city's patron saint (St Gaudentius).

Cortile del Broletto. – This lovely courtyard is bordered by several interesting buildings including the 15C Palazzo Podestà, the 13C Broletto (Town Hall) and the Palazzo
degli Paratici which now houses the **Municipal Museum** with an art gallery and archaeological section.

Cathedral (Duomo). – This neo-classical monumental building by Antonelli has a 6-7C
paleo-Christian baptistry. The chancel has a Byzantine style **pavement**★ in black and
white mosaic.

EXCURSION

The Lomellina. – This region lying between the Ticino and the Po is the great rice
growing area of Italy and has a landscape of vast stretches of flooded land divided by
long lines of willows and poplars. The chief towns are **Vigevano** with its outstanding
elliptical shaped **Piazza Ducale**★★ at the foot of the Sforza Castle. **Mortara** has a 14C
Church of San Lorenzo with interesting paintings by G. Ferrari. **Lomello**, after which the
region is named, has the attractive 11C Church of Santa Maria with its 8C baptistry.

★ ORBETELLO Peninsula Tuscany

Michelin map **988** folds 24 and 25

This small limestone outcrop, culminating in Monte Argentario (635m – 2 083ft), is
now linked to the mainland by a build-up of sand. Three causeways lead to the peninsula which has a good coastal road ideal for discovering its charms.

Orbetello. – This town stands on the causeway set in the middle of the lagoon. The
rampart-girdled town has retained the Gothic façade of its cathedral which was remodelled in the Spanish style in the 16 and 17C.

Porto Santo Stefano. – The peninsula's main town, and port, spreads up the hillside on either side of the 17C Aragonese fort. There is a lovely **view**★ from the latter.

Port' Ercole. – This seaside resort has a tiny ancient quarter to which access is gained
through a medieval gateway complete with hoarding and machicolations. From Piazza
Santa Barbara, lined by the arcades of the former 16C governors' palace there is a
view of the port, bay and the two old Spanish forts perched on Monte Filippo.

Ansedonia. – The ruins of the **ancient city of Cosa**★ crown a height at the neck of Orbetello Peninsula. They are within sight of the lagoon, the former island of Orbetello and
Monte Argentario. This former Roman town, girt with cyclopean walls, flourished from
3C BC to AD 4C.
A tower where Puccini is said to have composed part of *Tosca,* stands by the sea.

★ ORVIETO Umbria Pop 22 400

Michelin map 988 fold 25 – Town plan in the current Michelin Red Guide Italia

This important Etruscan centre later became a papal stronghold and it was here that Clement VII took refuge in 1527 when Rome was put to sack by the troops of the French King, Charles V.

Orvieto is a pleasant city with its wealth of historic buildings and it enjoys a particularly remarkable **site★★★** on the top of a plug of volcanic rock. Those arriving by the Bolsena or Montefiascone roads have particularly good views of this site. The region produces a pleasant, white wine, Orvieto cool and fragrant.

★CATHEDRAL (DUOMO) *time: 1 hour*

In the heart of the town the quiet Piazza del Duomo, of majestic proportions, regroups several interesting buildings. Apart from the cathedral there is the austere **Palace of the Popes★** which now houses the Cathedral Museum. The cathedral, a perfect example of the transitional Romanesque-Gothic style was begun in 1290 to enshrine the relics of the Miracle of Bolsena *(qv)*. Over one hundred architects, sculptors, painters and mosaicists took part in the building of the cathedral which was only completed in 1600.

★ **The façade.** – This is the boldest and richest in colour among Italian Gothic buildings. The vertical lines are accentuated by the slender gables and especially by the soaring buttresses, which are clad with small panels of coloured marble, elongated in shape and further prolonged by pinnacles. The sumptuous decorative effect is obtained by the use of sculptures lower down with multicoloured marbles and mosaics above. The façade was designed by the Sienese, Lorenzo Maitani (1310-30) and continued by Andrea Pisano, Orcagna and Sanmicheli.

Maitani was also the author of the astonishing **low-reliefs★★** adorning the pillars. The second shaft to the right of the main doorway has a very realistic **Last Judgment.** Orcagna was the designer of the rose window, fitted into a square frame, further adorned with niches containing the Apostles and the Prophets.

(Ciganovic/Explorer)

Orvieto Cathedral – detail of façade

Interior.– A nave and two aisles built in alternating courses of black and white stone rest on semicircular arches supported by lovely bracketed capitals. A moulding projects above the arches. The nave and aisles are roofed with a timber ceiling, while Gothic vaulting covers the transepts and the chancel. The paving slopes up towards the chancel, reducing the perspective. Alabaster window-panes let in plenty of light. At the entrance note the 15C stoup and the Gothic font. A fresco of the Virgin and Child (1425) in the north aisle is by Gentile da Fabriano.

In the north transept under the 16C monumental organ is the entrance to the **Corporal Chapel,** which enshrines the relics of the Miracle of Bolsena and notably the linen cloth (corporal) in which the bleeding Host was wrapped. A tabernacle encloses the **Reliquary★★** of the Corporal, a masterpiece of medieval goldsmiths' work (1338) encrusted with enamels and precious stones. In the chapel on the right is a Madonna of Pity (1320) by the Sienese painter, Lippo Memmi.

A fine Gothic stained glass **window★** in the chancel illustrates the Gospel with recognisable figures of theologians and prophets.

From the south transept, beyond a wrought iron grille (1516), you reach the famous chapel **(Cappella della Madonna di San Brizio),** painted with admirable **frescoes of the Apocalypse★★.** These were begun in 1447 by Fra Angelico with the help of Benozzo Gozzoli and were entrusted, from 1499 to 1504, to Luca Signorelli and they are considered to be his masterpiece. With his careful portrayal of human anatomy, his dramatic compositions, his appealing faces and his vigorous draughtsmanship, he was a precursor of Michelangelo. On the ceiling, Fra Angelico painted Christ among angels and prophets; the apostles, doctors, virgins, martyrs and patriarchs are by Signorelli. The latter was responsible for the wall frescoes of extraordinary power: the Preaching of the Antichrist (first lunette on the left) containing portraits of Signorelli and Fra Angelico; the End of the World (on the west wall) and the Resurrection of the Body (first lunette on the right). The end wall of the chapel is devoted to the Last Judgment. There is a *Pietà* of astonishing power in a niche in the right hand wall.

ADDITIONAL SIGHTS

★★ **St Patrick's Well** (Pozzo di San Patrizio). – The well was dug in the volcanic rock by
⊘ order of Pope Clement VII de' Medici to supply the town with water in case of siege.
Sangallo the Younger was entrusted with the work. Two spiral staircases, lit by seventy-two windows, wind up and down without meeting. The well is over 62m – 203ft
deep and its water cold and pure.

★ **People's Palace** (Palazzo del Popolo). – The palace is built of weather-worn volcanic
rock in the Romanesque-Gothic style. The façade has a majestic balcony, elegant windows and curious fluted merlons.

★ **Old Quarter** (Quartiere Vecchio). – This quiet, unfrequented quarter has retained its old
houses, medieval towers and churches. At the western extremity the Church of San
Giovenale is decorated inside with 13-15C frescoes.

⊘ **Faina Archaeological Museum.** – This important **Etruscan Collection** ★ includes some
splendid painted vases, sculpted terracotta funerary urns and a rare 4C sarcophagus.

St Bernard's Church (San Bernardino). – A charming baroque church with the refined
decoration of a theatre. The oval interior is delightfully decorated and has an organ
carved with figures.

Piazza della Repubblica. – On the site of the ancient forum it is dominated by the
Church of St Andrew (Sant' Andrea) with its lovely twelve-sided Romanesque tower.

*The annual **Michelin Guide Italia**
gives the addresses and telephone numbers
of the main car dealers, tyre specialists,
and general repair garages.*

OSTIA (EXCAVATIONS)

Michelin map 988 fold 26 – 24km – 15 miles southwest of Rome

Ostia, at the mouth of the Tiber, takes its name from the Latin word *ostium* meaning mouth. According to Virgil, Aeneas disembarked here but its foundation dates in reality back to the 4C BC when Rome embarked on her conquest of the Mediterranean. From that time on Ostia's development has reflected that of Rome: a military port during the period of expansion, a commercial port once Rome had established an organised system of trade. At first there was simply a castle to protect the port from pirates but by 1BC Ostia had become a real town around which Sulla built ramparts in 79BC. Like Rome, Ostia began to decline in the 4C. Slowly the harbour silted up and malaria decimated the population. Ostia was soon covered by alluvium deposited by the Tiber. It was 1909 before Ostia was discovered and regular excavations began.

On this extensive site the visitor can discover a variety of interesting remains: warehouses *(horrea);* baths; sanctuaries; the more substantial dwelling house, the *domus* built around its atrium or courtyard ; and the more usual block of flats, several storeys high *(insula)*. They were nearly all built of brick and unrendered. Some had elegant entrances framed by a triangular pediment resting on two pillars. Here and there a porch or a balcony added interest to the street front.

In addition there are the numerous meeting-places for both business and pleasure and the forum which was the hub of both political and social life. During the empire Ostia was a town with a population of 100 000 which included numerous foreigners.

⏱ EXCAVATION SITE *time: 3 hours*

Follow the itinerary indicated on the accompanying plan, which in addition to locating sights described below, indicates other ruins of particular interest. A tour of this extensive ruined site usually means a pleasant tree-lined walk.

Decumanus Maximus. – The Rome Gate (Porta Roma), the main entrance to the town, led into this street, the main east-west axis of all Roman towns. In Ostia it was paved with large slabs and lined with porticoed houses and shops.

— — Non-extant parts

Neptune Baths (Terme di Nettuno). – This 2C building has a terrace with a view of the fine **mosaics**★★ which depict the marriage of Neptune and Amphitrite.

★ **Hortensius' Warehouses (Horrea di Hortensius).** – These grand 1C warehouses are built round a pillared courtyard which is lined with shops.

Theatro (Teatro). – It has been much restored but is nevertheless very evocative of life in a Roman city. The three fine masks come from the stage.

★★★ **Piazzale delle Corporazioni.** – Under the portico in the square were the offices of the 70 trading corporations which represented the trading links with the known world. The mosaic pavement portrays their emblems which in turn indicate the commodity they traded in and the country of origin. The temple in the centre of the square is sometimes attributed to Ceres, goddess of corn and the harvest.

★ **Thermopolium.** – This bar with a marble counter served hot drinks.

★ **Diana's House (Casa di Diana).** – This is a striking example of an *insula* (block of flats) with rooms and passages arranged around an inner courtyard.

★ **Museum.** – The museum displays the finds of Ostia in a clear well-lit presentation: ⏱ crafts, oriental religious cults, numerous in Ostia, sculptures, **portraits**★ and examples of the rich interior decoration (mosaics, paintings and frescoes) found in Ostia.

★ **Capitol and Forum.** – The Capitol was the largest temple in Ostia, built in the 2C and dedicated to the Capitoline triad: Jupiter, Juno and Minerva. The forum was enlarged in the 2C and the few pillars still standing belonged to the surrounding portico. At the far end stands the 1C Temple of Rome and Augustus, a grandiose building once faced with marble.

★ **House of Cupid and Psyche (Domus d'Amore e Psiche).** – This 4C building, facing the seashore, has interesting remains of mosaic and marble floors and a lovely nymphaeum.

★ **Seven Sages Baths (Terme dei Sette Sapienti).** – The baths are part of a complex. There is a handsome mosaic floor in the large circular room.

★ **Schola di Traiano.** – This impressive 2 to 3C building was the headquarters of a guild of merchants. Inside there is a statue of Trajan, several porticoed courtyards and a rectangular basin.

Christian Basilica. – In this 4C Christian building, a row of columns separates the aisles which end in apses. An inscription on the architrave of a colonnade marks the entrance to what has been identified as the baptistry.

★ **Forum Baths.** – These are the largest baths in Ostia. The heating ducts are still visible in the walls.
Along one side is a good example of a **public lavatory.**
On the left of the Cardo Maximus are several millstones beneath a pergola.

Precinct of the Great Mother. – This sacred enclosure contains the remains of a temple dedicated to Cybele the Great Mother *(Magna Mater)*. The Sanctuary of Attis has a statue of the goddess in the apse and two fauns flanking the entrance.
The Cardo Maximus ends at the Laurentina Gate in Sulla's wall.

OTRANTO Apulia   Pop 5 061

Michelin map 988 fold 30

Otranto lies on the Adriatic coast of the "heel". This fishing port was once capital of 'Terra d'Otranto' the last remaining Byzantine stronghold and resisted the Lombards and then the Normans for some considerable time. In the 15C when the town was besieged by the troops of Mohammed II the townspeople took refuge in the cathedral where they were massacred. Eventual survivors were killed on the summit of Colle della Minerva where a sanctuary was built to the memory of the martyrs of Otranto.

Old town. – There is a good view of this from the northeast pier; to the left is the 15C **Aragonese castle** flanked by its massive cylindrical towers. To reach this stronghold perched on the clifftop pass through the gateways Porta di Terra and the 15C Porta Alfonsina.

★ **Cathedral (Cattedrale).** – This 12C building was altered in the late 15C. Inside, antique columns separate the nave and the two aisles and there is a remarkable mosaic **pavement**★★★ dating from 1165. It was the work of a local craftsman Pantaleone. The stylisation of the figures, the vivacity of their poses and attitudes, the freshness of the colours and variety of the symbols make this a fascinating illustrated story.

EXCURSION

★ **The coast to the south.** – Between Otranto and Santa di Leuca *(51km – 32 miles)* ⊙ the road offers fine views of this wild and indented coastline. At the head of an inlet is the cave, **Grotta Zinzulusa,** with concretions and two lakes, one salt water and one fresh water, which are inhabited by rare marine species.

★ # PADUA (PADOVA) Venetia   Pop 227 528

Michelin map 988 fold 5

A busy town and art centre, Padua's historic centre is **Piazza Cavour (BY4)**, with the neo-classical Café Pedrocchi, which was a meeting-place of the liberal élite including Musset, in the Romantic period.

HISTORICAL NOTES

There are few traces of ancient Patavium which was one of the most prosperous Roman cities in Venetia during the 1CBC due to its fluvial trade, its agriculture and the sale of horses. In the 7C it was destroyed by the Lombards, and from the 11 to 13C Padua became an independent city-state and knew its greatest period of economic and cultural prosperity under the enlightened rule of the lords of Carrara (1337-1405). The university was founded in 1222 and soon developed. Dante and Petrarch both came to Padua as did Giotto in 1304 to decorate the Scrovegni Chapel. This was the period when numerous churches and palaces were built. In 1405 Padua came under Venetian rule and remained thus until 1797. Padua is also a pilgrimage centre where St Anthony the Hermit, a Franciscan is venerated. He was born in Lisbon in 1195 and died in the environs of Padua aged 36. An elegant preacher his help was invoked by the shipwrecked and those in prison. He is generally represented holding a book and a lily.

PADUAN ART

Art in Padua flourished in the 15C under the guiding influence of the Paduan artist **Andrea Mantegna (1431-1506).** He was a painter of powerful originality, fascinated by anatomy and archaeology and a technical innovator in the representation of perspective. Previously the Renaissance in Padua had been represented by the Florentine Donatello who stayed in the city from 1444 to 1453. In the 13C the university attracted numerous scholars: Galileo was a professor and students included the Renaissance scholar Pico della Mirandola, Copernicus and Tasso.

⊙ SIGHTS

★★★ **Frescoes by Giotto (BY).** – The frescoes decorate the walls of the **Scrovegni Chapel** ⊙ (Cappella degli Scrovegni) which was built as part of a palace in 1303. They illustrate the lives of the Virgin and Christ; on the entrance wall is a Last Judgment; the Virtues and Vices are represented in grisaille below on the lower parts of the wall. This cycle of thirty-eight frescoes shows an exceptional unity and constitutes Giotto's masterpiece displaying his usual powerful drama and harmony of composition and intense spirituality. The **Virgin**★ on the altar is by the Tuscan sculptor Giovanni Pisano.

PADOVA

★ **The Saint's Basilica** (Basilica del Santo) (BZ). – This important pilgrimage church is dedicated to St Anthony and overlooks the square in which Donatello erected an **equestrian statue**★★ of the Venetian mercenary leader **Gattamelata** (nickname of Erasmo da Nardi who died in Padua in 1443). This bronze was the first of this size to be cast in Italy.

Built from 1232 to 1300 in the transitional Romanesque-Gothic style, the basilica with its eight tiered domes brings to mind St Mark's in Venice. The imposing **interior**★★ contains numerous works of art: off the north aisle is the **Saints Chapel**★★, a Renaissance masterpiece, which contains the tomb of St Anthony (Arca di Sant' Antonio) and the tomb cum altar of Tiziano Aspetti (1594); around the walls are magnificent 16C **low-reliefs**★★ by several artists. In the chancel the **high altar**★★ is adorned with bronze panels (1450) by Donatello. The third chapel, off the south aisle, has 14C **frescoes**★ by Altichiero.

From the cloisters to the right of the basilica there is a fine **general view**★ of the basilica.

★ **St George's Oratory** (Oratorio di San Giorgio) (BZ B). – St George's Oratory was built as a funerary chapel and is decorated with twenty-one **frescoes**★ (1377) by Altichiero and his pupils evoking various religious scenes.

★ **Scuola di Sant' Antonio** (BZ B). – Standing alongside, this building has, on the first
⊘ floor, a chamber with eighteen 16C **frescoes**★ relating the life of St Anthony. Four are
by Titian.

★ **Law Courts** (Palazzo della Ragione) (BZ J). – This building, standing between two at-
⊘ tractive **squares**★ the Piazza della Frutta (BZ 13) and the Piazza delle Erbe (BZ 8), is
remarkable for its loggias and its roof in the form of an upturned ship's keel. The first
floor **Salone**★★ (Great Hall) has a 15C cycle of frescoes depicting the Work of the
Months, Liberal Arts, Trades and the Signs of the Zodiac.

Piazza dei Signori (AYZ). – Along one side of this square is the 14-16C Palazzo
del Capitanio, onetime residence of the Venetian Governors, the **Clock Tower**★ (Torre
dell'Orologio) with its arcade and the graceful Renaissance Loggia del Consiglio.

★ **Municipal Museum** (Museo Civico) (BZ M). – Installed in the former Monastery of St
⊘ Anthony, this museum has a rich collection of Venetian paintings. Alongside works by
Giotto, Guariento **(Madonna and Heavenly Host**★★**)**, Giovanni Bellini, Veronese, Bassano,
Piazzetta and Longhi, note the very lovely **Crucifixion**★★ by Tintoretto. There is also a
splendid 15C tapestry entitled **Uri's Expedition**★★.

★ **Church of the Hermits** (Chiesa degli Eremitani) (BY). – This 13C church was badly
damaged in 1944 but has been restored to its original Romanesque style. In the
Ovetari Chapel at the far end of the south transept, are fragments of **frescoes**★
by Mantegna. The various scenes (the Martyrdom of St James on the north wall,
Assumption in the apse and Martyrdom of St Christopher on the South wall) display
his powerful visionary talent and his careful attention to perspective and architectural
detail. The chancel chapel has splendid **frescoes**★★ attributed to Guariento, Giotto's
Venetian pupil.

⊘ **University** (BZ U). – The university is in a palace known as the "Bo" from the name
of an inn with an ox as its sign which once stood on the site. It has retained a lovely
16C courtyard and an anatomy theatre, **Teatro Anatomico** (1594).

⊘ **Botanical Gardens** (Orto Botanico) (BZ). – This garden is one of the oldest of its
kind in Europe; it was laid out in 1545. You may admire many exotic species and
the palm tree which inspired Goethe in his reflections on the metamorphosis of
plants.

Prato della Valle (BZ). – This 17C oval garden is planted with plane trees and encircled by the still waters of a canal, lined with statues of famous men.

Church of St Justina (Santa Giustina) (BZ). – This 16C classical building with its domes
reminds us of the Saint's Basilica. At the far end of the chancel is an **altarpiece**★ by
Veronese.

Baptistry (Battistero) (AZ D). – Adjoining the cathedral (Duomo), the baptistry has
interesting frescoes and a polyptych by Menabuoi (14C).

EXCURSIONS

★ **Montagnana.** – *47 km – 29 miles to the southwest.*
This small town is girt with impressive 14C **ramparts**★★ with at intervals twenty-four
polygonal towers and four gateways. The **cathedral** (Duomo), attributed to Sansovino
contains a Transfiguration by Veronese at the high altar, 16C frescoes and stalls.
The Church of San Francesco with its lovely Gothic belfry stands against the town
wall.

★ **Euganean Hills** (Colli Euganei). – These hills to the south of Padua, also known as
Monti Euganei, are of volcanic origin. This pleasant hilly area has many orchards and
vineyards and was already appreciated in Roman times for its numerous hot springs
and its wines.

★ **Abano Terme.** – *Town plan in the current Michelin Red Guide Italia.* This modern
and elegant thermal spa well shaded by pines is one of Italy's most famous spa
towns.

Montegrotto Terme. – Although less important than Abano it is rapidly growing in importance. This was the ancient Mons Aegrotorum or mountain of the sick.

★ **Monselice.** – This town has retained an important section of its walls and is dominated
by the ruins of a castle. From Piazza Mazzini, go up the picturesque Via del Santuario
to reach the 13-14C castle, the Romanesque cathedral (Duomo), the early 17C Sanctuary of the Seven Churches and the Villa Balbi with its Italian garden. The upper terrace affords a lovely **view**★ of the region.

★ **Arquà Petrarca.** – *6.5km – 4 miles to the northwest of Monselice.* **Petrarch** (Francesco Petrarca) the leading humanist of the Renaissance, died in this medieval-looking town in
1374. Born in 1304 Italy's most important lyric poet skilfully manipulated his sensitive
and flowing language to suit the strict form of the sonnet. A diplomat and great traveller, he spent nearly all his youth, at the Papal Court in Avignon, and it was in a church
there that he met Laure de Sade to whom he dedicated all the poems of the *Canzoniere*.
His house stands on the top of a hill and his tomb, a plain pink marble sarcophagus
was set up in the church square in 1380.

Este. – Cradle of the Este family, rulers of Ferrara, the town still has an attractive sec-
⊘ tion of **town wall**★ to the north. The **Atestino National Museum**★ (Museo Nazionale Atestino) has an interesting collection of local archaeological finds. The cathedral (Duomo
on an elliptical plan, contains a large canvas (1759) by Tiepolo.

★ **Brenta Riviera.** – *Description p 190.*

One of Italy's most important archaeological sites, Paestum was discovered by chance around 1750, when the Bourbons started work on the building of the road which crosses the area today.

The initial settlement was an ancient Greek colony founded around 600 BC under the name of Poseidonia by colonists from Sybaris *(qv)*. Around the year 400 BC the city fell to a local tribe, the Lucanians. It became Roman in the year 273 BC but began to decline towards the end of the Empire because of the malaria which finally drove out its inhabitants.

Paestum is also a seaside resort and its long beach is sheltered by a fine pinewood.

TOUR *time: 2 hours*

★★ **Museum (Museo).** – The masterpieces on display include the famous **metopes★★**, low-reliefs in the Doric style of the 6C BC which adorned a small temple alongside the temple of Hera *(10km – 6 miles to the north near the mouth of the Sele River)* as well as the **metopes★★** from the latter. Also admire the **Tomb of the Diver★★** (Tomba del Tuffatore) with its paintings which are unique examples of Greek funerary art.

★★ **Ruins.** – *Follow the itinerary indicated on the accompanying plan.*

The temples, built of a fine yellow limestone, stand amidst the ruins of dwellings interrupted by the occasional cypress or oleander. Take the Justice Gate to pass through the 5km – 3 miles long **city wall★** and follow the **Sacred Way** (Via Sacra) which leads to the Temple of Hera.

★★ **Basilica.** – The rear of the 'Basilica', so-called by 18C archaeologists, stands to the right of the Sacred Way. This mid-6C BC temple was dedicated to Hera (Juno). The peristyle comprises 50 archaic columns all fluted and with a slight swell. The porch *(pronaos)* leads into the central chamber divided into two naves.

★★ **Temple of Neptune** (Tempio di Nettuno). – When Paestum was first discovered this well preserved temple was thought to have been dedicated to Neptune (or Poseidon in Greek, hence the town's name Poseidonia). It has since been proved that it was dedicated to Hera. Dating from the mid-5C BC it is in an admirably pure Doric style. The entablature and the two triangular frontons are almost intact. Inside the central chamber is divided into three naves.

The **forum** surrounded by a portico and shops, is in the centre of the city. The Roman **amphitheatre,** built at the end of the Republic, is today divided by the main road. The small **Underground Temple** contained superb bronze vases.

★★ **Temple of Ceres** (Tempio di Cerere). – Originally erected in the late 6C BC in honour of Athena, the temple is surrounded by 34 columns and retains parts of its frontons. A sacrificial altar stands nearby.

Parma, at the junction of the Via Emilia and the Mantua-La Spezia road, is an important market town and industrial centre which has a rich heritage from its past. Parma has a certain refined charm and is often bathed in a diaphanous light. Piazza Garibaldi (**BZ 9**) is a popular meeting place for the townspeople. The famous 20C conductor Arturo Toscanini was born in Parma.

HISTORICAL NOTES

A settlement was founded on this site by the Etruscans in 525 BC and it became a Roman station on the Via Emilia in 183 BC. It declined but revived in the 6C under the Ostrogoth King, Theodoric. From being an independent commune from the 11-13C, it then became a member of the Lombard League *(qv)* and was finally annexed by the papacy in 1513. In 1545 Pope Paul III Farnese gave two papal territories, Parma and Piacenza, having made them a duchy, which he passed to his son Pier Luigi Farnese, who was assassinated in 1547. However the Farnese dynasty continued to reign until 1731 and numerous members of the house were patrons of the arts and letters, collectors and great builders.

When Don Philip, the son of Philip V of Spain and Elizabeth Farnese, married Louise Elizabeth the favourite daughter of Louis XV, the town knew a period (1748-1801) of great French influence in several domains (customs, administration and the arts).

Numerous Frenchmen came to work in Parma while others like Stendhal chose to live here; he made Parma the setting of his well-known novel, *The Charterhouse of Parma*. The Bourbon-Parma had their Versailles, now in ruins, at Colorno, north of the town.

The Parma School. – The school is represented by two main artists, Correggio and Il Parmigianino whose works formed the transition between the Renaissance and baroque. Antonio Allegri (1489-1534) known as **Correggio,** was a master of light, chiaroscuro sensuality, and a gracefully optimistic vision which seemed to herald 18C French art. Francesco Mazzola (1503-40) or **Il Parmigianino** (The Parmesan) as he was commonly known was a more troubling and melancholy personality. His elongated forms, new rather cold colours were characteristic of Mannerism *(qv)*. His canon of feminine beauty influenced the Fontainebleau school and all the other European Mannerists of the 16C, through the intermediary of Niccolò dell' Abbate and Il Primaticcio.

★★★CITY CENTRE *time: 1/2 day*

This historic core of the city comprises the Romanesque **episcopal centre**★★★ (**CYZ**) including the cathedral and baptistry a most harmonious group of faded rose brick, the baroque Church of St John and the surrounding palaces as well as the Palazzo della Pilotta (16-17C) and Correggio's Room.

★★ **Cathedral (Duomo) (CY).** – This is in the Lombard Romanesque style and is flanked by an elegant Gothic campanile. The façade includes a Lombard porch supported by lions and surmounted by a loggia and three tiers of galleries with little columns. Inside, the dome is decorated with the famous **frescoes**★★ of Correggio painted between 1522 and 1530. They represent the Assumption of the Virgin amidst a swirling group of cherubim. In the south transept is a **Descent from the Cross**★ (1178) by the Parmesan sculptor Benedetto Antelami.

★★★ **Baptistry (Battistero) (CY A).** – This baptistry is one of the most remarkable in Italy for the harmony of its architecture and decoration, both carved and painted. It is a Romanesque building in Veronese rose coloured marble, on an octagonal plan and is almost certainly the work of the great local sculptor Antelami. The doorways are decorated with a rich array of figures. Inside, the remarkable 13C **frescoes**★★ depict scenes from the Life of Christ and the Golden Legend. The statues in the niches were by Antelami.

St John the Evangelist's Church (San Giovanni Evangelista) (CYZ D). – This Renaissance church has a baroque façade. Inside, the dome has very fine **frescoes**★★ by Correggio portraying The Vision of St John.

ⓥ In the couvent next door you can visit the Renaissance **cloisters.**

ⓥ **Pharmacy (Farmacia di San Giovanni Evangelista).** – *1 Borgo Pipa.* This 13C pharmacy was started by the Benedictine monks.

Palazzo della Pilotta (BY). – The palace was so-called because the game of fives *(pilotta)* was played in its courtyards. This rather austere building, erected by order of the Farnese between 1583 and 1622, now houses three museums, the Palatine Library and the Farnese Theatre.

★ **National Museum of Antiquities (M).** – The pre-Roman and Roman exhibits include the ⓥ finds made in the excavation of Velleia to the west of Parma.

★★ **National Gallery** (Pinacoteca) **(M).** – Emilian, Tuscan and Venitian paintings of the 14, 15 ⓥ and 16C. Leonardo da Vinci *(Head of an Adolescent),* Fra Angelico, Dosso Dossi, El Greco, Canaletto, Bellotto, Piazzetta and Tiepolo. Il Parmigianino is represented by his astonishing portrait **Turkish Slave,** of considerable elegance and Correggio by one of his masterpieces **The Virgin with St Jerome** (1528) as well as other works. The last rooms are devoted to French painters who had a connection with Parma: Nattier, Largillière, Hubert Robert, Vigée-Lebrun, etc.

★★ **Farnese Theatre.** – This delightful theatre in wood was built in 1619 by G.B. Aleotti ⓥ following the model of Palladio's Olympic Theatre in Vicenza *(qv).*

★ **Correggio's Room (Camera del Correggio) (CY).** – Also known as St Paul's Room ⓥ **(Camera di San Paolo)** this was the former dining-room of the Abbess of the Convent of St Paul. Correggio decorated the ceiling with a mythological theme: the Triumph of Diana, Adonis, the Three Graces, etc.

PARMA

		Repubblica (Strada della)	CZ	Pilotta (Piazza)	BY 17
				Ponte Caprazucca	BZ 19
Cavour (Strada)	BY 3	Basetti (Viale)	BZ 2	Ponte di Mezzo	BZ 21
Farini (Strada)	BZ	Duomo (Strada al)	CY 8	Ponte Verdi	BY 22
Garibaldi (Strada)	BCY	Garibaldi (Piazza)	BZ 9	Regale (Borgo)	CZ 23
Mazzini (Strada)	BZ 13	Pace (Pza della)	BY 15	Studi (Borgo degli)	CY 24
				Toscanini (Viale)	BZ 25

ADDITIONAL SIGHTS

★ **Glauco–Lombardi Museum** (Museo Glauco–Lombardi) (BY M¹). – The museum is chiefly devoted to life in the Duchy of Parma in the 18 and 19C. It contains paintings and mementoes of the former Empress Marie-Louise who governed the duchy with wisdom until 1847. There are numerous works by French artists: Nattier, Mignard, Chardin, Watteau, Fragonard, Greuze, La Tour, Hubert Robert, Vigée-Lebrun, David and Millet.

Madonna della Steccata (BZ E). – This 16C church, designed by the architects Bernardino and Zaccagni, contains fine **frescoes★** by Il Parmigianino representing the Foolish and the Wise Virgins, Adam and Eve, and Moses and Aaron. The mausoleum of Neipperg, Marie-Louise's husband, is on the left, and the tombs of the Farnese family and the Bourbon-Parma are in the crypt.

Garden Palace (Palazzo del Giardino) (BY B). – The **ducal garden★** (Parco Ducale) was landscaped by the French architect Petitot and adorned by statues by another Frenchman, Boudard.

EXCURSIONS

★ **Torrechiara.** – *17km – 11 miles to the south by the Langhirano road.*
Built on a hilltop, this 15C fortress is powerfully fortified by double ramparts, massive corner towers, a keep and machicolated curtain walls. The upper rooms (the Gaming and Gold Rooms) have remarkable **frescoes★**. From the terrace there is a superb **view★** which reaches as far as the Apennines.

Fidenza. – *23km – 14 miles to the west. Leave Parma by Via Massimo D'Azeglio* (AY). This attractive agricultural town has a remarkable 11C **cathedral★** (Duomo) which was completed in the Gothic style in the 13C. The lovely sculptured decoration of the **central porch★★** is most likely the work of the Parmesan sculptor, Antelami.

Fontanellato. – *19km – 12 miles to the northwest by the Fidenza road and then the road to Soragna, to the right.*
The vast moat-encircled castle, **Rocca San Vitale,** stands in the centre of town. One of the bathrooms has a **fresco★** decorated ceiling by Il Parmigianino depicting Diana and Actaeon.

143

This proud city on the banks of the Ticino River, is rich in buildings from the Romanesque and Renaissance periods.

This important military camp under the Romans then became successively, the capital of the Lombard Kings, rival of Milan in the 11C, famous intellectual and artistic centre during the 14C under the Visconti, a fortified town in the 16C and one of the most active centres of the 19C independence movements. The university, one of the oldest and most famous in Europe, was founded in the 11C and its students included Petrarch, Leonardo da Vinci and the poet Ugo Foscolo *(Letters to Jacopo Ortiz)*.

SIGHTS

★ **Castle of the Visconti** (**Castello Visconteo**). – This impressive brick building was built by the Visconti. It now houses the **Municipal Collections**★ (Musei Civici) which are rich in archaeological finds, medieval and Renaissance sculpture and particularly paintings. The **picture gallery**★, on the first floor, has numerous masterpieces including a lovely altarpiece by the Brescian artist Vincenzo Foppa, a *Virgin and Child* by Giovanni Bellini and a very expressive *Christ bearing the Cross* by the Lombard artist, Bergognone. The last room contains a 16C model of the cathedral by Fugazza after the plans by Bramante.

★ **Cathedral** (**Duomo**). – This vast building, surmounted by one of Italy's largest domes, was begun in 1488: both Bramante and Leonardo da Vinci are said to have worked on the plan. The façade is 19C. To the left of the façade stood an 11C municipal tower, which fell down in March 1989, while opposite is the 16C Bishop's Palace. The adjoining Piazza Vittoria is overlooked by the 12C **Broletto** or town hall. The square affords an interesting view of the cathedral's chevet.

★ **Church of St Michel** (**San Michele**). – This lovely Romanesque church has a pale-coloured sandstone **façade**★ which is quite remarkable for the balance and variety of its sculptural ornamentation. A remarkable Romanesque doorway on the south side has a lintel on which Christ is seen giving a papyrus volume to St Paul and the Keys of the Church to St Peter. Inside there are some interesting architectural features (dome on squinches, the friezes and modillions beneath the galleries, the elevated chancel, mosaics, capitals, etc). The apse is decorated with a lovely 15C **fresco**★ portraying the Coronation of the Virgin.

Church of St Peter (**San Pietro in Ciel d'Oro**). – This Lombard Romanesque Church was consecrated in 1132. It is preceded by a richly decorated **doorway**★. In the chancel is the **tomb**★ of St Augustine (Arca di Sant' Agostino), the work of the *maestri campionesi (qv)*.

Church of St Lanfranc (**San Lanfranco**). – *2km – 1 mile to the west.*
A graceful **tomb**★ by Amadeo in the late 15C, holds the remains of Lanfranc, who died when Bishop of Pavia in 1198.

★★★ PAVIA Carthusian Monastery

(CERTOSA DI PAVIA) Lombardy

Michelin map 988 fold 13 – 9km – 6 miles to the north of Pavia

The "Gra Car", Gratiarum Cartusia (Charterhouse of the Graces) is one of the most remarkable and characteristic examples of Lombard art. It was founded as a family mausoleum in 1396 by Gian Galeazzo Visconti of Milan. Most of the monastery was built in the 15 and 16C to the plans of successive architects. The former palace of the Dukes of Milan (1625), is on the right of the courtyard, and on the left are the studios of the sculptors in charge of the decoration.

★★★ **Façade.** – Even unfinished the façade is nevertheless famous for the care and richness of its decoration. The more ornate lower part (1473-99) was the work of the Mantegazza brothers, the famous architect and sculptor Amadeo, who worked also in Bergamo, and his pupil, Briosco. The upper part was completed in 1560 by another architect and sculptor, Cristoforo Lombardo.

The façade is adorned with multicoloured sculptures in marble, with medallions, copied from antiquities, at the base, statues of saints in the niches and an endless variety of foliage, garlands and ornaments. Round Amadeo's famous windows are scenes from the Bible, the Life of Christ and the life of Gian Galeazzo Visconti. The low-reliefs round the central doorway by Briosco depict events in the history of the Carthusians. Before entering the church walk round to the left for a general view of the late Lombard Gothic style, with its galleries of superimposed arcades.

★★★ **Interior.** – The interior has a certain solemn grandeur and although it is essentially Gothic, the beginnings of the Renaissance can be detected in the transept and the chancel.

There are numerous works of art. The chapels of the south aisle are decorated with late 15C frescoes by Bergognone who was also responsible for a **Crucifixion,** an altarpiece and a polyptych. The second chapel on the north side contains an **altarpiece** by Perugino. The north transept has an **Ecce Homo** by Bergognone, superb candelabra (1580) by Fontana and the famous **reclining figures** (1497) of Ludovico il Moro and Beatrice d'Este by Cristoforo Solari. The doorway to the former sacristy was the work of Amadeo. In the lavatorium there is a splendid Renaissance marble **lavabo** and a **fresco** by Luini. The south transept has the magnificent **tomb of Gian Galeazzo Visconti** by Cristoforo Romano dated 1497.

There are two **cloisters.** The smaller one is decorated with charming terracottas and a baroque fountain. The larger one with 122 richly decorated arcades is bordered by twenty-four cells.

Michelin map 988 fold 15

Perugia was one of the twelve Etruscan city-states known as *lucumonies* which comprised the federation of Etruria in the 7 and 6C BC. The massive Etruscan wall with its gateways gives some idea of the splendour of that age. The town also has numerous ecclesiastical and secular buildings from the Middle Ages. Today the capital of Umbria, in addition to being an industrial and commercial centre, is a university town.

Umbrian Painting. – Like their peaceful countryside, the Umbrian painters had gentle, mystic souls. They loved landscapes with pure lines, punctuated with trees and stylised their compositions giving the women a tender gracefulness, sometimes too mannered. Extremely delicate draughtsmanship and soft colours characterise their technique. The masters were Giovanni Boccati (1410-85), Fiorenzo di Lorenzo (d1520) and especially Pietro Vannucci alias **Perugino** (1445-1523), the teacher of Raphael. His favourite subjects were religious; in them he showed his sense of space, atmosphere and landscape, marred only by a touch of mannerism. The historical artist **Pinturicchio** (1454-1518) was influenced by Perugino but his charmingly realistic scenes were painted more naïvely than those of his predecessor.

PERUGIA

Matteotti (Piazza)	**BY**	34
Mazzini (Via)	**BY**	35
Vannucci (Corso)	**BYZ**	51
Alessi (Via)	**BY**	2
Asilo (Via dell')	**BY**	3
Baglioni (Via)	**BZ**	4
Bartolo (Via)	**BY**	7

Bonazzi (Via L.)	**AZ**	8
Bontempi (Via)	**BY**	9
Cupa (Via della)	**AY**	12
Danti (Piazza)	**BY**	13
Fabretti (Via)	**BY**	14
Fortebraccio (Piazza)	**BY**	17
Forze (Via delle)	**AZ**	18
Imbriani (Via M.)	**BY**	23
Indipendenza (Viale)	**ABZ**	24
Innamorati (Via F.)	**AY**	25
Italia (Piazza)	**BZ**	26
Maestà delle Volte (V.)	**BY**	29
Mariotti (Piazza A.)	**AZ**	30
Marzia (Via)	**BZ**	32
Morlacchi (Piazza)	**AY**	38
Oberdan (Via)	**BZ**	39
Partigiani (Piazza dei)	**AZ**	40
Piccinino (Piazza)	**BY**	43
Repubblica (Pza della)	**BY**	45
Roma (Viale)	**BZ**	46
Roscetto (Via del)	**BY**	47
S. Elisabetta (Via)	**BY**	50
Viola (Via della)	**BY**	52
Volte delle Pace (Via)	**BY**	55

145

★★PIAZZA 4 NOVEMBRE (BY) *time: 2 hours*

This square in the heart of Perugia is one of the grandest in Italy. Here are grouped the chief buildings of the glorious 'communal' period: the Priors' Palace, the Great Fountain and the Cathedral. Leading off from the far end of the square is the picturesque **Via Maestà delle Volte★** (ABY 29) with its medieval houses and vaulted passageways.

★★ **Great Fountain** (Fontana Maggiore). – The fountain was built to the designs of Fra Bevignate and is admirably proportioned. The sculpted panels are the work of Nicola Pisano (lower basin) and his son Giovanni (upper basin). Copies replace some of the originals which are on display in the National Gallery of Umbria.

★★ **Priors' Palace** (Palazzo dei Priori) (BY D). – The palace was begun in the 13C and enlarged in the following centuries. It forms an ensemble of impressive grandeur. The façade overlooking the square has a majestic outside staircase leading up to a marble pulpit from which the priors harangued the people. The Corso Vannucci (BY 51) façade has a fine 14C doorway. Inside, the palace rooms are either decorated with 14C frescoes or beautifully carved 15C panelling.

★★ **National Gallery of Umbria** (Galleria Nazionale dell' Umbria). – This collection, housed ⊘ on the top floor of the Priors' Palace, has an extremely good selection of Umbrian art showing its development from the 13C to the late 18C. Here is a **Madonna** by Duccio, a **Crucifix** by the unknown master, Maestro di San Francesco, a **polyptych of St Anthony** by Piero della Francesca and works by Fra Angelico, Boccati and Fiorenzo di Lorenzo. The most interesting room is that containing the masterpieces of Pinturicchio and Perugino, including a **Dead Christ** with its black background and an admirable **Madonna of Consolation.** Another room is devoted to the marble statuettes by Nicola and Giovanni Pisano from the Great Fountain and other works by Arnolfo di Cambio. The 17C is represented by Federico Barocci, Pietro da Cortona, Orazio Gentileschi, etc.

The 15C Priors' Chapel is dedicated to the city's patron saints: St Herculanus and St Louis of Toulouse, whose story is told by Benedetto Bonfigli (d1496) in a remarkable cycle of **frescoes.** The museum also has some lovely 13 and 14C French enamels and ivories.

★ **Cathedral** (Cattedrale) (BY F). – The cathedral is Gothic, but the Piazza Danti façade was completed with a baroque doorway. The right hand chapel contains an interesting **Descent from the Cross,** by Barocci which inspired Rubens in his *Antwerp Descent.* In the chapel on the left are lovely 16C **stalls** with intarsia-work and a ring said to be the Virgin's wedding ring.

ADDITIONAL SIGHTS

★★ **St Peter's Church** (San Pietro) (BZ L). – To reach the church, go through the **Porta San Pietro★** (BZ N), a majestic but unfinished work of the Florentine Agostino di Duccio. The church was built at the end of the 10C and remodelled at the Renaissance. Inside are eleven excellent canvases by Vassilacchi, alias Aliense, a Greek contemporary of El Greco. Note also the **carved tabernacle** by Mino da Fiesole and the marvellous 16C **stalls★★.**

★ **St Dominic's Church** (San Domenico) (BZ). – An impressive Gothic church. The interior was altered in the 17C. To the right of the chancel is the 14C **funerary monument** of Benedict XI.

★★ **National Archaeological Museum of Umbria** (Museo Archaeologio Nazionale dell' ⊘ Umbria) (BZ M). – The museum unites prehistoric, Etruscan and Umbrian sections. The remarkable collections include funerary urns, sarcophagi and Etruscan bronzes.

★ **Exchange Building** (Collegio del Cambio) (BY E). – This was built in the 15C for the ⊘ money changers. In the courtroom (council chamber) are the famous **frescoes★★** of Perugino and his pupils. These frescoes display the humanist spirit of the age, which sought to combine ancient culture and Christian feeling. Admire the statue of Justice by Benedetto da Maiano (15C).

★★ **Oratory of St Bernardine** (San Bernardino) (AY). – To reach the church walk along the picturesque **Via dei Priori★.** This Renaissance jewel (1461) by Agostino di Duccio is exquisite in its harmonious lines, the delicacy of its multicoloured marbles and its sculptures. The low-reliefs on the façade display, on the tympanum, St Bernardine in glory, the life of the saint on the lintel and delightful angel musicians on the shafts.

★ **Via delle Volte della Pace** (BY 55). – This picturesque medieval street is formed by a long 14C Gothic portico as it follows the Etruscan town wall.

★ **St Angelo's Church** (Sant Angelo) (AY R). – This small church is circular in shape and dates from the 5-6C. The interior includes sixteen ancient columns.

★ **Porta Marzia and Via Bagliona Sotterranea** (BZ Q). – This Etruscan gateway of ⊘ the 2C BC gives access to this curious street, which runs underground and is lined with 15 and 16C houses.

★ **Etruscan Arch** (Arco Etrusco) (BY K). – This imposing structure is built of huge blocks of stone. A 16C loggia surmounts the tower on the left.

Alongside, the majestic 18C **Palazzo Gallenga** (U) serves as a summer school for foreign students.

Carducci Gardens (Giardini Carducci) (AZ). – There is a superb **view★★** from these gardens, dominating the San Pietro quarter, over the Tiber Valley.

EXCURSIONS

★ Hypogeum (Ipogeo dei Volumni). – *6km – 4 miles to the southeast. Leave by ② on the* ⊙ *town plan.*
This Etruscan cemetery hewn out of the rock, comprises an atrium and nine burial chambers. The Volumnian tomb is the largest; it contains six rounded tombstones *(cippi),* the biggest being that of the head of the family (2C BC).

Torgiano. – *16km – 10 miles to the southeast. Leave by ② on the town plan.*
⊙ This village dominating the Tiber Valley, has an interesting **wine museum★** presenting exhibits with the help of documents and photographs.

★ **PESARO** Marches	Pop 90 491

Michelin map 988 fold 16 – Town plan in the current Michelin Red Guide Italia

Pesaro is on the Adriatic coast at the mouth of the smiling Foglia Valley, which is terraced with vineyards, orchards and Italian poplars. The town was the birthplace of
⊙ the composer **Gioacchino Rossini** (1792-1868) whose **house** (No 34 Via Rossini) is now a museum.

★ Municipal Museum (Musei Civici). – The **picture gallery** contains several works by the
⊙ Venetian Giovanni Bellini *(qv).* The famous **Pala di Pesaro** (1475) is an immense altar-piece representing the Virgin being crowned on the central panel and numerous other scenes on the predella.
In the **ceramics section★★** the Umbrian potteries are well represented but there are also examples of work from the Marches region.

Ducal Palace (Palazzo Ducale). – The great mass of this palace, built for a Sforza in the 15C, overlooks the Piazza del Popolo with its fountain adorned with tritons and sea horses. The crenellated façade has an arcaded portico with above windows adorned with festoons and cherubs.

⊙ **Oliveriano Museum (Museo Oliveriano).** – *97 Via Mazza.*
Interesting collection of archaeological items of varied origins: Italic, Greek, Etruscan and Roman.

Former Church of St Dominic (San Domenico). – *In Via Branca behind the post office.*
All that remains is the 14C façade with a lovely pointed doorway flanked by twisted columns and sculpture.

EXCURSION

Gradara. – *15km – 9 miles to the northwest.*
Gradara is a medieval town, almost intact, surrounded by walls and battlemented
⊙ gateways. The **Rocca★** built on a square plan with corner towers, is a well preserved example of military architecture in the 13 and 14C. It is here that Gianni Malatesta is said to have surprised and then murdered his wife, Francesca da Rimini, and her lover, Paola Malatesta. Dante portrayed the inseparable couple in his *Divine Comedy.*

★ **PIACENZA** Emilia-Romagna	Pop 106 365

Michelin map 988 fold 13 – Town plan in the current Michelin Red Guide Italia

Piacenza was originally built by the Romans on the south bank of the Po at the end of the Via Emilia. It flourished in the Middle Ages and became a member of the Lombard League *(qv).* In 1545 Pope Paul III Farnese gave Piacenza and its neighbour Parma to his son along with the title of duke. After this its destiny was linked with that of Parma.

SIGHTS

★★ Palazzo del Comune. – Also called 'Il Gotico', this building is a masterpiece of Lombard Gothic architecture and has a severe but harmonious appearance. There is a curious contrast between the marble lower part and the brick upper storeys, the great openings and the elegantly decorated windows. Standing in the square in front are two remarkable 17C **equestrian statues★★** of Alessandro Farnese and Ranuccio I Farnese.

★ Cathedral (Duomo). – This remarkable Lombard Romanesque building dates from the 12-13C. The façade is pierced with three doorways and a rose window. The interior on the plan of a Latin cross is simple and forceful. Some of the dome frescoes are by Guercino.

Church of St Savin (San Savino). – *Near the junction of Via G. Alberoni with Via Roma.*
The crypt of this 12C church with very pure architectural lines, has a magnificent mosaic pavement.

Church of St Sixtus (San Sisto). – *At the northern end of Via San Sisto.*
This is a rather curious 16C building. The façade is preceded by an atrium and a doorway with rustication and grotesque masks. The interior has an interesting Renaissance decoration.

Madonna di Campagna. – *Via Campagna.*
This 16C church, in the form of a Greek cross, contains interesting frescoes, notably by the 16C Venetian Pordenone.

PIACENZA ★

ⓥ **Farnese Palace (Palazzo Farnese).** – This imposing late Renaissance building was never completed, but it now houses the **Municipal Museum** (Museo Civico). On the lower floor are paintings including a *Virgin* by the school of Botticelli, Murano glassware, 17-19C ceramics, sculpture, and mainly 16-17C arms. The upper floor is devoted to the Risorgimento *(qv)*.

ⓥ **Alberoni Gallery (Galleria Alberoni).** – *No 77 Via Emilia.*
On view are 16 and 17C Italian and Flemish tapestries and numerous paintings by Antonello da Messina, Raphael, Signorelli, Correggio, Caravaggio and Veronese, amongst others.

★ **PIENZA** Tuscany   Pop 2 429

Michelin map 🔢🔢🔢 fold 15 – 52km – 32 miles to the southeast of Siena

This little city in southern Tuscany, is an interesting example of Renaissance town planning by the Florentine architect **Bernardo Rossellino** (1409-64). It was the humanist pope, Æneas Silvius Piccolomini (1405-64) who asked the architect to transform his native village, which took the name of Pienza in memory of its son who became Pope Pius II.

★ **Cathedral (Cattedrale).** – The cathedral, which was completed in 1462, has a Renaissance façade. The interior (restored) shows Gothic influences and contains several paintings by the Sienese school, including an **Assumption★★**, the masterpiece of Vecchietta.

ⓥ **Cathedral Museum.** – The museum contains pictures of the 14 and 15C Sienese school and a remarkable 14C historiated cope made in England.

★ **Palazzo Piccolomini.** – Inspired by the Florentine palaces, this is the master-
ⓥ piece of Rossellino. The inner courtyard is extremely elegant with its slim Corinthian columns.

★ **Pieve di Corsignano.** – *1km – 1/2 mile to the east.*
This solitary and sober Romanesque building has a façade adorned with a sculptured doorway and a window with a statue-column.

*The **Michelin Map of Greece** no 🔢🔢🔢 at a scale of 1: 700 000 has all the practical information needed to make driving a pleasure.*

★★ **PISA** Tuscany   Pop 104 244

Michelin map 🔢🔢🔢 fold 14

This calm and pleasant town, near the sea, has splendid buildings recalling the past grandeur of the Pisan Republic.

HISTORICAL NOTES

Sheltered from raiding pirates, Pisa was a Roman naval base and commercial port until the end of the Empire. It became an independent maritime republic at the end of the 9C and continued to benefit from its geographical location. Pisa became the rival of Genoa and Venice and the Pisans waged war against the Saracens in the Mediterranean basin. It was in the 12C and the beginning of the 13C that Pisan power and prosperity reached its zenith. This period was marked by the construction of some fine buildings and the foundation of the university.
During the 13C struggles between the Emperor and the Pope, Pisa supported the Ghi-bellines *(qv)* and thus opposed Genoa on the seas and Lucca and Florence on land. In 1284 the Pisan fleet was defeated at the **naval battle of Meloria**. Ruined and wracked by internal strife Pisa's maritime empire foundered, Corsica and Sardinia which she had ruled since the 11C were ceded to Genoa. Pisa herself passed under Florentine rule and the Medici were particularly attentive to this city, especially in the world of sci-ence. The most famous son was the astronomer and physicist **Galileo** (1564-1642). His patron was Cosimo II Grand Duke of Tuscany. Nevertheless Galileo, aged seventy, had to defend his theory of the rotation of the universe before the Inquisition and ren-ounced his theory.

PISAN ART

The economic prosperity of the powerful maritime Pisan Republic from the 11C to the 13C fostered the development of a new art style which is particularly evident in the domains of architecture and sculpture. The **Pisan Romanesque style**, with the cathedral as the most rigorous example, is characterised by external decoration: the alternate use of different coloured marbles to create geometric patterns, a play of light and shade due to the storeys of loggias with small columns on the upper parts of the façade and intarsia decoration showing a strong oriental influence. Alongside architects such as Buscheto, Rainaldo and Diotisalvi there were numerous sculptors to embellish the ex-teriors. Pisa became an important centre for Gothic sculpture in Italy thanks to the work of **Nicola Pisano** (1220-c1280), originally from Apulia, and his son **Giovanni Pisano** (1250-c1315). Their work included carved pulpits with two good examples in the Baptistry and the Cathedral, which greatly influenced the early Tuscan Renaissance.

★★ PIAZZA DEL DUOMO (AY) *time: 3 hours*

Regrouped on and around this famous square are four buildings which form one of the finest architectural ensembles in the world. Enter on foot from the west through the Porta Santa Maria to have the best view of the leaning tower.

★★ Cathedral (Duomo). – This sumptuous church was built with the fantastic spoils captured during the expeditions against the Mussulmans. Building operations started in 1063 under Buscheto and were continued by Rainaldo, who designed the façade. The **west front★★★** is light and graceful with three tiers of small marble columns and a decorative facing of alternating light and dark marble. The church itself is built on the plan of a Latin cross. The original doors were replaced by bronze **doors★** cast in 1602 to designs by Giovanni Bologna. The south transept door has very fine Romanesque bronze **panels★★** (late 12C) by Bonanno Pisano, depicting the Life of Christ in a naive but prodigiously free and creative style.

The **interior★★**, with its nave and four aisles, is impressive for its length (100m – 328ft), its deep apse, its three bay transept and the forest of piers which offer an astonishing variety of perspectives. Note in particular the beautiful **pulpit★★★** of **Giovanni Pisano** on which he worked from 1302 to 1311. It is supported by six porphyry columns and five pillars decorated with religious and allegorical statues. The eight panels of the basin evoke the Life of Christ and regroup a multitude of personages with dramatic expressions. Near the pulpit is the lamp of Galileo which gave the scholar his original idea for his theory concerning the movement of the pendulum.

★★ Leaning Tower (Torre Pendente or Campanile) (V). – This tower in a very pure Romanesque style serves as a campanile or belfry. Built in white marble it was begun in 1173 by Bonanno Pisano and completed in 1350. Its leaning (4m – 13ft at the top) is caused by the settling of the alluvium subsoil, which lacks the resistance to withstand the weight of the tower. Architects have tried in vain to rectify this weakness.

The tower is cylindrical, like most Byzantine ones, and comprises six open galleries, which give an illusion of spiralling upwards due to the inclination. Lower down the blind arcades are adorned with lozenges in the true Pisan style. From the top there is a fine **view**★ of the square and the town.

★★★ **Baptistery (Battistero)** (R). – Begun in 1153, the two lower storeys are in the Romanesque Pisan style, while the frontons and pinnacles above the first floor arcades are Gothic. The building is roofed with an unusual dome and has four doorways with lovely carving. The majestic interior is full of light and has a diameter of 35m – 115ft. The sober decoration consists of light and dark coloured marble and in the centre is a lovely octagonal **font**★ (1246) by an artist from Como, Guido Bigarelli. The masterpiece of the baptistry is the admirable **pulpit**★★ (1260) by Nicola Pisano. Less ornate than the one done by his son for the cathedral, it stands on simple columns. The basin composes five panels depicting the Life of Christ: its sculptures are no doubt inspired by Roman art and the sarcophagi to be found in the neighbouring Composanto.

★★ **Cemetery (Camposanto)** (S). – This burial ground was begun in 1277 by Giovanni di Simone, one of the architects of the leaning tower. Work was interrupted by the naval Battle of Meloria, and only completed in the 15C. The burial ground takes the form of cloisters with lovely graceful quatrefoil windows. In the centre, the Camposanto (sacred field) proper consists of earth taken from the Hill of Calvary by the Crusaders. The galleries paved with 600 tombstones shelter numerous Greco-Roman sarcophagi. The admirable frescoes which adorned the walls were destroyed by bomb damage in 1944. One of the most famous **The Triumph of Death**★★★ was miraculously saved and is now on display in a room off the north cloister. This fresco, like that of the **Last Judgment**★★ and **Hell**★ which accompany it, was the work of a 14C artist. The brevity and vanity of worldly pleasures are portrayed with much realism.

★ **Sinopia Museum (Museo delle Sinopie)** (M¹). – This contains the sketches or *sinopias* (sketches in a reddish brown pigment, sinopia, which came from Sinope on the Black Sea) which were under the frescoes and were brought to light by the fire following the 1944 bombing. They have been well restored and they give a good idea of the vitality and free draughtsmanship of these 13-15C painters.

ADDITIONAL SIGHTS

★★ **National Museum (Museo Nazionale)** (BZ M²). – This museum regroups the works of medieval sculptors such as Giovanni Pisano and his school. Of particular note is the **Annunciation** by Andrea Pisano and a delightful **Nursing Madonna** by Nino Pisano. The numerous paintings include **St Paul** by Masaccio and a polyptych by Simone Martini.

★ **Piazza dei Cavalieri** (AY). – This the historic centre of Pisa, gets its name from the Cavalieri di Santo Stefano (Knights of Stephen), a military order which specialised in the struggle against the infidels. Around the square are: the **Palazzo dei Cavalieri** (ABY F) with a **façade**★ decorated by Vasari; the **Church of St Stephen** (Santo Stefano) (BY) built in 1569 with its white, green and pink marble façade; and the **Palazzo Gherardesca** (AY K) designed in 1607 by Vasari to stand on the site of a former prison, Torre della Fame, where Count Ugolino della Gherardesca and his children were condemned to die by starvation, having been accused of treason after the naval defeat at Meloria.

★★ **Church of St Mary of the Thorn (Santa Maria della Spina)** (AZ). – This early 14C church resembles a finely worked reliquary shrine with all its gables, pinnacles, statues and statuettes by the two Pisano, their assistants and followers. Some of the originals have been replaced by replicas.

Church of St Paul (San Paolo a Ripa d'Arno) (AZ D). – This church like the previous one stands on the banks of the Arno. It has a lovely Pisan Romanesque **façade**★.

Church of the Holy Sepulchre (San Sepolcro) (BZ Q). – This original 12C building in the form of a pyramid was built by Diotisalvi. Inside the nobly proportioned **chancel**★ is roofed with a tall dome. The tomb belongs to Maria Mancini, Louis XIV's mistress and Mazarin's niece who came to Pisa to die in 1715.

Church of St Catherine (Santa Caterina) (BY E). – The Church has a graceful Pisan Gothic **façade**★. Inside are statues by Nino Pisano, in particular an Annunciation (on either side of the chancel).

Church of St Michael (San Michele in Borgo) (BY L).– The **façade**★ of this church is an excellent example of the transitional Pisan Romanesque-Gothic style.

The quays. – Prestigious palaces line the quays such as **Lungarno Pacinotti** (ABY) and **Lungarno Mediceo** (BZ), notably **Palazzo Upezzinghi** (AY Y) a 17C building now occupied by the university; **Palazzo Agostini**★ (ABY Z) a 15C mansion with a highly decorated entrance front (the Caffè dell' Ussero was the haunt of the Risorgimento poets) and opposite on the other bank is Palazzo Gambacorti (BZ H), a late 14C building; Palazzo Toscanelli (BZ W) where Byron wrote *Don Juan*; and the Palazzo Medici (BZ P) a 13-14C palace.

EXCURSIONS

★ **San Piero a Grado.** – *6km – 4 miles to the southwest. Leave by ⑤, the Via Conte Fazio.* The Romanesque **basilica**★ stands on the spot on which St Peter is said to have landed when he came from Antioch. The apse with its three apsidal chapels is remarkable.

Viareggio. – *20km – 12 miles to the northwest. Leave by ① on the town plan.* This fashionable seaside resort, on the Tyrrhenian Coast, has some lovely beaches and plenty of amenities for the holidaymakers. At **Torre del Lago Puccini** *(5km – 3 miles to the southeast)* the composer, Puccini wrote *La Bohème, Tosca* and *Madame Butterfly.* The **Villa Puccini** has the tomb and other mementoes of Puccini.

★ PISTOIA Tuscany

Michelin map 988 fold 14 – Town plan in the current Michelin Red Guide Italia

This industrial town has a rich historic centre which is the heritage of its importance in the 12-14C. Both Lucca and Florence coveted Pistoia, but it was Florence and the Medici who annexed it for good in 1530.

★★ PIAZZA DEL DUOMO *time: 1 hour*

This is a most attractive and well-proportioned square lined with a harmonious ensemble of secular and religious buildings.

★ **Cathedral (Duomo).** – Rebuilt in the 12 and 13C, the cathedral's **façade** ★ is a harmonious blend of the Pisan Romanesque style (tiers of colonnaded galleries) and the Florentine Renaissance style (porch with slender columns added in the 14C). The lower part of the campanile is quite massive becoming more graceful towards the top with three tiers of colonnaded galleries. The interior was remodelled in the 17C. Inside is the famous **altar of St James** ★★★, a masterpiece of silversmith work dating from the 13C, which was modified and extended in the following centuries. The saints surround the apostle seated in a niche, with Christ in Glory above. Scenes from the Old and New Testaments complete the composition. In the chapel to the left of the chancel is a lovely **Madonna in Majesty** ★ (*c* 1480) by Lorenzo di Credi.

★ **Baptistry (Battistero).** – This Gothic octagonal baptistry with polychrome marble facing dates from the 14C. The tympanum of the central doorway bears a statue of the **Virgin and Child** between St Peter and St John the Baptist attributed to Nino and Tommaso Pisano.

Palazzo Pretorio. – This palace was built in the 14C as the residence of the governing magistrate *(podestà)* and remodelled in the 19C.

Town Hall (Palazzo del Comune). – Built between 1294 and 1385 it has a graceful façade over arcades with elegant paired windows or triple bays. The palace houses a **documentation centre** on the 20C sculptor **Marino Marini** (1901-80) and the **Municipal Museum** (Museo Civico) with a collection of paintings from the 13-16C Tuscan school.

ADDITIONAL SIGHTS

Hospital (Ospedale del Ceppo). – The portico on the façade has a magnificent **frieze** ★★ in terracotta (1530) by Giovanni della Robbia, brightly coloured and expressive, showing the Seven Works of Mercy.

★ **Church of St Andrew (Sant'Andrea).** – This church in the pure Pisan Romanesque style has the famous **pulpit** ★★ executed (1298-1308) by Giovanni Pisano in his dramatic but intensely lively manner: the panels represent five scenes from the Life of Christ. Also admire the lovely **crucifix** ★ in gilded wood by Giovanni Pisano *(in a niche beyond the first altar on the right).*

Church of St John outside the City (San Giovanni Fuorcivitas). – This church, built from the 12C to the 14C has a long and spectacular **north façade** ★ in the Pisan Romanesque style. Inside there is a **pulpit** ★ (1270) by Fra Guglielmo from Pisa, a polyptych by Taddeo Gaddi *(to the left of the altar)* and an admirable glazed terracotta of the **Visitation** ★★ by Luca della Robbia.

Church of St Bartholomew (San Bartolomeo in Pantano). – This church in the Pisan Romanesque style has a lovely sculptured doorway, and a beautiful **pulpit** ★ (1250) by Guido da Como.

EXCURSION

★ **Vinci.** – *24km – 15 miles to the south.* The great Leonardo da Vinci was born not far from this town. The castle has a **museum** (Museo Vinciano) and **library** (Biblioteca Leonardiana) in honour of its famous son.

The **birthplace** of the artist lies 2km – 1 mile to the north amidst olive trees, bathed in a pellucid light.

POLICASTRO, Gulf of Campania - Basilicata - Calabria

Michelin map 988 fold 38

This magnificent gulf extending from the tip of Infreschi to Praia a Mare, is backed by high mountains whose sharp needle-like peaks soar skywards.
The lower slopes carry cereals and olive groves with clumps of chestnut trees above. Between Sapri and Praia a Mare the corniche road overlooks the green coloured waters which lap the numerous charming creeks. A series of small villages succeed one another along this enchanting coast.

★★ **Maratea.** – This seaside resort has numerous beaches and creeks and its hotels and villas are hidden behind a screen of luxuriant vegetation. The village itself is spread over the slopes of Monte Biagio, on the summit of which stands the Basilica of San Biagio and the great white figure of the 22m – 72ft tall Statue of the Redeemer the work of Innocenti (1965). Nearby there is a superb **panorama** ★★ of the Gulf of Policastro and the Calabrian coast.

Respect the life of the countryside
Go carefully on country roads
Protect wild life, wild plants and trees.

Michelin map 🔢🔢🔢 fold 27 – Local map p 133

Pompeii, the sumptuous town which was buried in AD 79 in one of the most disastrous volcanic eruptions, provides first-class evidence of the ancient way of life. The extensive and varied ruins of this dead city, in its attractive setting, movingly evoke on a grand scale a Roman city at the time of the Empire.

HISTORICAL NOTES

Pompeii was founded in the 8C BC by the Oscans but by the 6C BC a Greek influence was already prevalent in the city from its neighbour Cumae, which was then a powerful Greek colony. From the end of the 5C BC when it became Samnite, to the beginning of the AD 1C the city knew great prosperity, when town planning and art flourished. In the year 80 BC, the town fell under Roman domination and then it became a favourite resort of rich Romans. Roman families settled there. Pompeii adopted Roman organisation, language, life style, building methods and decoration. When the eruption of Vesuvius struck, Pompeii was a booming town with a population of about 25 000. As it was situated in a fertile region, trade flourished and even some industrial activity and the town had an active port. There were numerous shops and workshops.

The people had a lively interest in spectacles, games and active politics. In the year AD 62, an earthquake extensively damaged the town but before all this could be put to right, Vesuvius erupted (August AD 79) and also destroyed Herculaneum and Stabiae. In the space of two days Pompeii was buried by a layer of cinder 6 to 7m – 20 to 23ft deep. Bulwer-Lytton describes these events in *The Last Days of Pompeii*.

It was only in the 18C, under the reign of Charles of Bourbon, that systematic excavations began. The finds had a tremendous effect in Europe, creating a revival of antique art and the development of a so-called Pompeiian style.

ARCHITECTURE AND DECORATION

Building methods. – Pompeii was destroyed before a degree of uniformity in building methods had been achieved and it presents diversity in both the methods and materials used: **opus quadratum** (large blocks of freestone piled on top of one another, without mortar of any kind); **opus incertum** (irregularly shaped blocks of tufa or lava bonded with mortar); **opus reticulatum** (small square blocks of limestone or tufa arranged diagonally to form a decorative pattern); **opus testaceum** (walls are faced with triangular bricks laid flat with the pointed end turned inwards). Sometimes the walls were faced with a layer of plaster or marble. There are several types of dwellings in Pompeii: the sober and severe house of the Samnites, which became larger and more richly decorated through Greek influence. With the arrival of the Romans and the problems arising from a growing population, a new kind of house evolved in which limited space is compensated for by richness of decoration.

POMPEII
(EXCAVATIONS)

0   200 m

--- Non-extant parts

Pompeiian painting. – A large number of paintings which adorned the walls of the dwellings have been transferred to the Archaeological Museum in Naples. However, a visit to the dead city gives a good idea of the pictorial decoration of the period. There are four different **styles.** The 1st style by means of relief and light touches of colour imitates marble. The 2nd style, by far the most attractive of them all, adopts a decoration where walls are divided into large panels by fake pillars surmounted by pediments or crowned by a small shrine, with false doors all designed to create an illusion of perspective. The artists show a partiality for the famous Pompeiian red, cinnabar obtained from mercury sulphide, and a dazzling black, both of which make for a quite striking style. The 3rd style abandoned false relief in favour of scenes and landscapes altogether more ethereal and painted in pastel colours. Most of the frescoes uncovered at Pompeii belong to the 4th style. It combines elements from the 2nd style with others from the 3rd style to produce opulent compositions.

⊙ THE DEAD CITY *time: allow 1 day*

Sea Gate (Porta Marina). – This was the gateway through which the road passed to go down to the sea. There are separate gates for animals and pedestrians.

★★ **Antiquarium.** – This contains historical records, objects in daily use and reconstructions of mills. There are mouldings of human beings and animals in the attitudes in which they died.

The streets. – The streets are straight and intersect at right angles. They are sunk between raised pavements and are interrupted at intervals by blocks of stone to enable pedestrians to cross without getting down from the pavement. This was particularly useful on rainy days when the roadway turned into a stream; these stepping stones were positioned so as to leave enough space for chariots. Fountains, of simple design, adorned square basins all similar.

★★ **Forum (Foro).** – This was the centre of the town and the setting for most of the large buildings. In this area, religious ceremonies were held, trade was carried out and justice was dispensed. The immense square was paved with broad marble flagstones and adorned with statues of past emperors. A portico surmounted by a terrace enclosed it on three sides.

The **Basilica★★**, the largest building in Pompeii, measures 67m by 25m – 220 by 82ft. Judicial affairs and business were conducted there.

The **Temple of Apollo★★** (Tempio di Apollo), built before the Roman occupation, stood against the majestic background of Vesuvius. The altar was placed in front of the steps leading to the shrine *(cella)*. Facing each other are copies of the statues of Apollo and Diana found on the spot (the originals are in the Naples Museum). The **Horreum**, a warehouse probably used for storing cereals, has a display of archaeological artifacts.

The **Temple of Jupiter**★★ (Tempio di Giove), in the place of honour, is flanked by two triumphal arches, formerly faced with marble.

The **Macellum** was a large covered market lined by shops. In the centre, a kiosk surrounded by pillars and crowned by a dome contained a basin.

The **Temple of Vespasian** (Templio di Vespasiano) contained a marble altar adorned with a sacrificial scene.

A fine doorway with a marble frame decorated with carvings of plants gave access to the **Building of Eumachia** (Edificio di Eumachia) built by the priestess for the powerful guild of the *fullones (see below)* of which she was the patron.

★ **Triangular Forum (Foro Triangolare).** – A majestic propylaeum, of which several Ionic columns remain, preceded the forum. A few vestiges of its small **Doric temple** provide rare evidence of the town's existence in the 6C BC.

★ **Great Theatre (Teatro Grande).** – The theatre was built in the 5C BC, remodelled in the Hellenistic period (200-150 BC) and again by the Romans in the AD 1C. It was an open theatre which could be covered by a canopy and could accommodate 5 000 spectators.

Gladiators' Barracks (Caserma dei Gladiatori). – This has a large esplanade bounded by a gateway, originally used as a foyer for the theatres.

★★ **Odeon.** – Odeons, or covered theatres, were used for concerts, oratorical displays and ballets. This held only 800 spectators. It had a wooden roof and it dates from the early days of the Roman colonisation.

★ **Temple of Isis (Tempio di Iside).** – This small temple is dedicated to the Egyptian goddess Isis, adopted by the Romans, who were very liberal in their choice of gods.

House of Lucius Ceius Secundus (Casa di L.C. Secundus). – This is an interesting house with its façade faced with stucco in imitation of marble as in the 1st style, and with its pretty little *atrium*.

★★ **House of Menander (Casa di Menandro).** – This large patrician villa richly decorated with paintings (4th style) and mosaics, had its own baths. Part of the building was reserved for the servants' quarters. There is a Tuscan *atrium (p 24)* with a *lararium* arranged as a small shrine in one corner. It has a remarkable peristyle with Doric columns faced with stucco between which stands a low wall adorned with plants and animals.

The house opens on to **Via dell' Abbondanza**★★, a commercial street which is now most evocative with its shops and houses.

House of the Criptoportico (Casa del Criptoportico). – *No 2, Via dell' Abbondanza.*
After passing through the peristyle (note the painting in the *lararium*: Mercury with a peacock, snakes and foliage), go down to the Criptoportico, a wide underground passage surmounted by a fine barrel vault lit by small windows. This type of corridor, which was very popular in Roman villas during the Empire, was used as a passage and for exercise as it was sheltered from the sun and from bad weather.

★★ **Fullonica Stephani.** – *No 7, Via dell' Abbondanza.*
This was an example of a dwelling-house converted into workshops. The clothing industry flourished in Roman times as the full, draped costume required a lot of material. In the *fullonicae*, new fabrics were finished and used clothing was laundered. Several of these workshops have been uncovered in Pompeii. The **fullones** (fullers) cleaned the cloths by trampling them underfoot in vats filled with a mixture of water and soda or urine.

★ **Thermopolium of Asellina (Termopolio di Asellina).** – This was a bar which also sold pre-cooked dishes. A stone counter giving directly on to the street formed the shop front; jars embedded in the counter contained the food for sale.

Great Thermopolium (Termopolio Grande). – Similar to the previous one, this bar has a painted *lararium*.

House of Trebius Valens (Casa di Trebius Valens). – The inscriptions on the wall are electoral slogans. At the far end of the peristyle the polychrome fresco is in imitation of a stone wall.

★ **House of Loreius Tiburtinus (Casa di Loreius Tiburtinus).** – This was a rich dwelling judging from the fine marble *impluvium*, the *triclinium* adorned with frescoes and the **decoration**★ against a white background of one of the rooms, which is among the best examples of the 4th Pompeiian style. But its most luxurious feature was the splendid **garden**★ which was laid out for water displays.

★ **Villa di Giulia Felice.** – Built just within the town boundary, it has three main parts: the dwelling, the baths which the owner opened to the public, and a section for letting including an inn and shops. The large garden is bounded by a fine **portico**★ and embellished by a fine series of basins.

★ **Amphitheatre (Anfiteatro).** – This is the oldest Roman amphitheatre known (80 BC). Alongside is the great **palestra** used a training ground by athletes.

★ **Necropolis at the Nocera Gate.** – According to custom, tombs line one of the roads leading out of town.

Take the Via Porta Nocera to return to the Via dell' Abbondanza, then turn left.

★★★ **Stabian Baths (Terme Stabiane).** – *See plan p 153 and details of Roman baths p 25.*
These baths, the best preserved and most complete in Pompeii, are divided into sections for men and women. You enter through the *palestra* (A) for athletic games, to the left of which is a swimming pool, *piscina* (B) with adjacent changing-rooms, *spogliatoio* (C). The **women's baths** begin at the far end, on the right with changing-rooms (e) fitted with lockers, a *tepidarium* (lukewarm, f) and a *caldarium* (hot, g). The central heating

apparatus (**D**) is between the men's and women's baths. The **men's baths** have large, well preserved changing-rooms (**h**), a *frigidarium* (cold, **k**), a *tepidarium* (**l**) and a *caldarium* (**m**). There is a fine stucco decoration on the coffered ceiling.

Lupanare. – The decorations are licentious.

★ **Pistrinum.** – Baker's oven and flourmills.

★★ **House of the Faun (Casa del Fauno).** – This vast, luxurious house had two atriums, two peristyles and dining-rooms for all seasons.The bronze original of the famous statuette of the faun that adorned one of the impluviums is in the Naples Museum. The rooms contained admirable mosaics including the famous Battle of Alexander (Naples Museum) which floored the area between the two peristyles.

House of the Labyrinth (Casa del Labirinto). – One of the rooms opening onto the peristyle has a mosaic of the labyrinth with Theseus killing the Minotaur.

★★ **House of the Vettii (Casa dei Vettii).** – The Vettii brothers were rich merchants. Their dwelling, the most lavishly decorated in the town, is the finest example of a house and garden that have been faithfully restored. The reroofed *atrium* opens directly on to the peristyle surrounding a delightful garden with statues, basins and fountains.
The **frescoes** in the *triclinium*, on the right of the peristyle, depicting mythological scenes and friezes of cupids are among the finest of antiquity.

★ **House of the Golden Cherubs (Casa degli Amorini Dorati).** – This house shows the refinement of the owner who probably lived during the reign of Nero, and his taste for the theatre. The glass and gilt medallions depicting cupids have deteriorated. But the building as a whole, with its remarkable peristyle with one wing raised like a stage, is well preserved. Note the obsidian mirror set in the wall near the passage between the peristyle and *atrium*.

Casa dell' Ara Massima. – Well preserved **paintings★** (one in *trompe-l'œil*).

★ **Tower of the God Mercury (Torre di Mercurio).** – A tower on the town wall now affords an interesting **view★★** of the excavations.

House of the Great Fountain (Casa della Fontana Grande). – Its main feature is the large **fountain★** shaped as a niche decorated with mosaics and fragments of coloured glass in the Egyptian style.

★ **House of the Tragic Poet (Casa del Poeta Tragico).** – This house takes its name from a mosaic now in a Naples Museum. A watchdog in mosaic at the threshold bears the inscription *Cave Canem.*

Casa di Pansa. – A very spacious house partly converted for letting.

★★ **Herculaneum Gate (Porta Ercolano).** – This was the main gateway of Pompeii, having two gates for pedestrians and one for vehicles.

★★ **Via dei Sepolcri.** – A great melancholy feeling pervades this street lined with monumental tombs and cypresses. There are examples of all forms of Greco-Roman funerary architecture: tombs with niches, small round or square temples, altars resting on a plinth, drum-shaped mausoleums, simple semicircular seats or exedrae...

Villa of Diomedes (Villa di Diomede). – This important dwelling has a loggia overlooking the garden and the swimming pool.

★★ **Villa of the Mysteries (Villa dei Misteri).** – Standing outside the city walls this patrician villa although it has lost much of its ornamentation still comprises numerous rooms. Near the present entrance were the out-buildings *(partly excavated)*. These were reserved for all domestic work, agricultural use and as the servants quarters.
In the main dwelling, the room on the right contains the splendid **fresco** for which the villa is famous. This vast composition which fills the whole room, depicts against a Pompeiian red background, the initiation of a young bride to the mysteries of the cult of Dionysius (Child reading the rites; scenes of offerings and sacrifices; flagellation; nuptials of Ariadne and Dionysius; dancing Bacchante; dressing of the bride). The mistress of this house was no doubt a priestess of the cult of Dionysius, which was then very popular in southern Italy. There is a fine peristyle and an underground passage *(cryptoportico).*

★★ POMPOSA Abbey Emilia-Romagna

Michelin map 𝟿𝟾𝟾 fold 15 – 49km – 30 miles east of Ferrara

⊙ Pomposa is the name of a Benedictine Abbey, founded in the 6C. It enjoyed great fame in the Middle Ages, especially from the 10 to the 12C, when it was distinguished by its Abbot, St Guy (Guido) of Ravenna, and by another monk Guido d'Arezzo, the inventor of the musical scale.
The fine Pre-Romanesque **church★★** in the style of Ravenna is preceded by a narthex whose decoration exemplifies the Byzantine style. To the left, an admirable Romanesque campanile (1063) rises heavenwards: note on the one hand the progression in the number and size of its windows, on the other the elegant simplicity of the Lombard bands and arches adorning its nine storeys; and finally, the variety of geometrical decoration obtained by the use of bricks.
The nave has some magnificent mosaic **paving**, a Romanesque stoup and a second in the Byzantine style. The walls bear an exceptional cycle of 14C **frescoes** based on the illuminator's art. From right to left the upper band is devoted to the Old Testament while the lower band has scenes from the Life of Christ; the corner pieces of the arches depict the Apocalypse. On the west wall are a Last Judgment and in the apsidal chapel, Christ in Majesty.
Opposite, stands the Palazzo della Ragione, where the abbot dispensed justice.

Michelin map 988 fold 13

This rocky, rugged promontory forms one of the most attractive landscapes on the Italian Riviera. The coastline is dotted with small villages in sheltered bays. Part of the peninsula has been designated as a **Nature Reserve** (Parco Naturale) to protect the fauna and flora. By taking one of the few corniche roads and one of the numerous footpaths the visitor can discover the secret charms of this region.

★★★PORTOFINO

To reach the port which gave the peninsula its name take the road that passes via **Santa Margherita Ligure**★ *(5km – 3 miles)* a fashionable seaside resort and then the **corniche road**★★ (Strada Panoramica) which affords lovely views of the rocky coast. This small fishing village with its gaily coloured houses lies at the head of a sheltered creek *(photograph p 16)*. The **walk to the lighthouse**★★★ *(1 hour on foot Rtn)* is beautiful, especially in the evening, when the setting sun shines on the Gulf of Rapallo. Wonderful views unfold between the olive trees, yews and sea pines.

⊘ From the **castle** – formerly Castello San Giorgio *(take the stairway which starts near the harbour and the Church of San Giorgo)* – there are splendid **views**★★★ of Portofino and the Gulf of Rapallo. Continue along the pathway to the lighthouse, from where the view extends right round the coast as far as La Spezia.

EXCURSIONS

San Lorenzo della Costa. – *10km – 6 miles*.
At Santa Maria Ligure take the **scenic road**★★ which offers a succession of lovely views over the Gulf of Rapallo. The **Church of San Lorenzo** contains a **triptych**★ (1499) by an artist from Bruges. It may have been the work of Gerard David (Gheeraert Davit) who spent some time in Genoa.

★★ **Portofino Vetta.** – *14km – 9 miles by a toll road*.
⊘ From this elevated site (450m – 1 476ft) there is a lovely view of the peninsula and the Ligurian coast.

★★ **San Fruttuoso.** – *No car worthy road leads to this village*.

On foot: *take the signposted footpath starting in Portofino (4 1/2 hours Rtn) or another from Portofino Vetta, but the final stages are difficult (3 hours Rtn)*.

By boat: *services operate from Rapallo, Santa Margherita Ligure, Portofino and Camogli*.
This delightful fishing village stands at the head of a narrow cove in the shadow of Monte Portofino.

★★ **San Rocco's Belvedere.** – *13km – 8 miles*.
From the terrace beside the church there is a view of Camogli and the western coast from the headland, Punta Chiappa right round to Genoa. A path leads to **Punta Chiappa**★★★ *(2 1/2 hours on foot Rtn by a stepped footpath which starts to the right of the church)*. There are unforgettable views of the peninsula, a chapel and the Genoa Coast.

★★ **Camogli.** – *15km – 9 miles*.
Tall houses crowd round a small harbour.

POTENZA Basilicata   Pop 66 519

Michelin map 988 fold 28 – Town plan in the current Michelin Red Guide Italia

Potenza overlooks the upper Basento Valley with wide mountain views. The ancient town founded by the Romans, flourished during the Empire. Today it is an active town, the growth of which was favoured by the development of the road and rail networks in the region. Its tall, modern buildings, curiously terraced, make an unusual sight which is quite dazzling by night. The old town suffered extensive damage in the 1980 earthquake. The 13C **Church of San Francesco** with its lovely Renaissance **doorway**★ carved in wood, has inside, a marble Renaissance tomb and a 13C Madonna.
Potenza is situated in the district of **Lucania**, an indescribably wild region which is ravaged by erosion.

Michelin map 988 fold 27 – 16km – 10 miles west of Naples – Local map p 132

Of Greek origin Pozzuoli became an active trading port under the Romans. The town is at the centre of the volcanic area known as the Phlegrean Fields *(qv)* and has suffered on several occasions from the changes in the level of the land, which affected this region. The town has given its name to *pozzolana*, a volcanic ash with a high silica content, which is used in the production of certain kinds of cement.

★★ **Amphitheatre (Anfiteatro Flavio).** – *Corso Terracciano.*
⊙ This amphitheatre is one of the largest in Italy and dates from the reign of Vespasian the founder of the Flavian dynasty. It could accommodate 40 000 spectators. Built of brick and stone it is relatively well preserved: note the outer walls, entrances and the particularly well preserved **basements★★**.

★ **Temple of Serapis (Tempio di Serapide).** – *Standing back from Via Roma.*
Situated near the sea, this was really the ancient market place and was lined with shops. There is a sort of apse in the end wall which contained the statue of Serapis, the protecting god of traders. The central edifice shows the effects of variations in ground level: the columns show signs of marine erosion.

★ **Temple of Augustus (Tempio di Augusto).** – The temple dated from the early days of the Empire and was converted into a Christian church in the 11C. A recent fire has revealed a grandiose marble colonnade with its entablature.

★★ **Solfatara.** – *2km – 1 mile to the northeast by the Naples road.*
⊙ Although extinct this crater still has some of the phenomena of an active volcano such as jets of steam charged with sulphurous fumes, strong smelling and with traces of yellow, miniature volcanoes spitting hot mud and bubbling jets of sand. The soil resounds hollowly and is hot to touch. The sulphurous vapours have been used for medicinal purposes since Roman times.

Michelin map 988 fold 14

In spite of the peaceful and provincial air of its old quarter, Prato is a bustling and important town which has developed in the textile industry since its early beginnings in the 13C. For a long time Prato was in conflict with Florence but in 1351 she fell under the sway of her illustrious neighbour and remained thus until the 18C. In the 14C a fortified wall in the form of a hexagon was erected around the old town.

SIGHTS

★ **Cathedral (Duomo) (B).** – This church built in the 12 and 13C and extended in later centuries, mingles harmoniously the Romanesque and Gothic styles. The façade, with its partial facing of white stone and green marble, owes its elegance to its lofty central part, its finely carved decoration and the graceful circular pulpit with its canopy (15C) by Michelozzo. The south side has blind arcading in the true Pisan tradition. The campanile has a Gothic upper storey.
The interior of the church, sober in style, has massive columns of green marble and numerous works of art: the **Chapel of the Holy Girdle** (Capella del Sacro Cingolo) contains the precious relic which the Virgin had given to Thomas as proof of her Assumption. The girdle was brought from Jerusalem by a citizen of Prato in the 12C. The chapel is enclosed by two delicately worked bronze **screens★** and decorated by frescoes (1392-5) by Agnolo Gaddi and his pupils. **The Virgin and Child★** (1317) is by the sculptor Giovanni Pisano. The **frescoes★★** by **Filippo Lippi** in the axial chapel form a striking picture of the lives of St Stephen and St John the Baptist. Between 1452 and 1465 this artistic monk, renowned for his libertine ways, painted this masterpiece with its pleasantly fresh colours and spontaneous attitudes: the graceful melancholy of the feminine figures in two scenes, the **Banquet of Herod★★★** and Salome's Dance, are more typical of the work of one of his pupils', Botticelli. On the walls of the chapel to the right are **frescoes★** started by Paolo Uccello and completed by Andrea di Giusto. Note also the marble **pulpit★** with the original shape of a chalice and in a niche a moving **Virgin with an Olive★**, a terracotta statue (1480) by Benedetto da Maiano.

⊙ **Cathedral Museum (Museo dell' Opera del Duomo) (B M).** – This is housed in several rooms overlooking a delightful courtyard. Amongst the exhibits are the seven **panels★** carved between 1428 and 1438 by Donatello for the pulpit from which the Holy Girdle used to be displayed. The pulpit was set at the corner of the cathedral's west front. Also on display are pieces of ecclesiastical plate and paintings by Filippino Lippi, the son of Filippo, who was born in Prato around 1457.

★ **Palazzo Pretorio (A A).** – This austere and massive building, a curious mixture of the Romanesque and Gothic styles, overlooks a charming small square. **Piazza del Comune** with a gracious bronze fountain (1659) by Tacca. Three floors of the building are occupied by the **Municipal Gallery** (Galleria Comunale) which regroups works by the 14 and 15C Tuscan school and notably an important collection of **polyptychs★** by Bernardo Daddi, Lorenzo Monaco, Filippo Lippi, etc. There are also works by the Neapolitan Caracciolo (17C) and the Dutchman Van Wittel the Elder.

★ **Imperial Castle (Castello dell' Imperatore) (B).** – This is one of the rare existing examples in northern and central Italy of a castle built by the Emperor Frederick II of Hohenstaufen. This imposing and balanced structure on a square plan around a central courtyard, has massive walls of cyclopean blocks with very few openings and enormous projecting towers. The castle is modelled on Castel del Monte *(qv)* in the south. With its cleft Ghibelline crenellations, this fortified stronghold guarded the route between the emperor's northern empire and his Kingdom of Sicily in the south.

Garibaldi (Via)	**B**	Dante (Via)	**B** 12	S. Domenico (Piazza)	**A** 34
Guasti (Via Cesare)	**A** 13	Guizzelmi (Via)	**A** 15	S. Francesco (Piazza)	**A** 35
Mazzoni (Via G.)	**B** 20	Lippi (Via)	**B** 16	S. Jacopo (Via)	**AB** 37
Ricasoli (Via)	**A** 32	Martini Arcivesco (V.A.)	**B** 18	S. Marco (Piazza)	**B** 38
		Mazzini (Via G.)	**B** 19	S. Silvestro (Via)	**B** 40
Abbaco (Via P. dell')	**A** 2	Misericordia (V. della)	**A** 22	S. Maria d. Carceri (Pza)	**B** 42
Bettino (Via)	**B** 3	Monte Grappa (Viale)	**B** 24	Savonarola (Corso)	**A** 43
Bologna (Via)	**AB** 4	Muzzi (Via L.)	**A** 25	Serraglio (Via del)	**B** 45
Cairoli (Via)	**B** 5	Pellegrino (Via)	**A** 27	Simintendi (Via A.)	**B** 46
Cambioni (Via)	**A** 6	Ponte Mercatale	**B** 28	Stufa (V. della)	**A** 48
Carducci (Largo)	**A** 9	Porta Serraglio (V. di)	**A** 30	Tintori (Via de')	**B** 50

Santa Maria delle Carceri (B K). – This attractive late 15C building was designed by Giuliano da Sangallo. The **interior★** displays both a severity and nobility which was typical of Florentine architecture as influenced by Brunelleschi.

Church of St Francis (San Francesco) (AB D). – This church was built from the 13C to the 15C. The chapterhouse has **frescoes★** by Nicolo di Pietro Gerini, a Florentine artist who was influenced by Giotto.

★★★ RAVELLO Campania   Pop 2 369

Michelin map 988 south of fold 27 – Local map 41

Ravello with its alleys, stairways and roofed passages clings to the steep slopes of the Dragon Hill. The **site★★★**, suspended between sea and sky, is unforgettable. The road from Amalfi climbs in hairpin bends up the narrow Dragon Valley, planted with vines.

★★★ Villa Rufolo. – *Like the cathedral it overlooks Piazza Vescovado.*
The villa was built in the 13C by the rich Rufoli family of Ravello and was the residence of several popes, of Charles of Anjou and more recently in 1880, of the German composer Wagner. A well shaded avenue leads to a Gothic entrance tower. Beyond is a Moorish style courtyard with typical sharply pointed arches in the Sicilian-Norman style and interlacing above. This was originally cloisters in the 11C. A massive 11C tower overlooks the well tended gardens and the elegant villa.
From the terraces there is a splendid **panorama★★★** of the jagged peaks as far as Cape Orso, the Bay of Maiori and the Gulf of Salerno.

★★★ Villa Cimbrone. – A charming **alley★** leads from Piazza Vescovado to the villa, passing through on the way the Gothic porch of the convent of St Francis, founded by the saint of the same name in 1222 (cloisters). On entering the grounds visit first the charming cloisters and a lovely hall with pointed vaulting and some curious grilles. A wide alley leads through the garden to the belvedere, adorned with a series of marble busts. There is an immense **panorama★★★** over the terraced hillsides, Maiori, Cape Orso and the Gulf of Salerno.

Cathedral (Duomo). – Founded in 1086, the church was transformed in the 18C. The campanile is 13C. The fine **bronze door★** with panels of reliefs was cast in 1179 by Barisana da Trani. In the nave the antique columns have been uncovered and there is a magnificent mosaic-covered **pulpit★★** with a remarkable variety of motifs and fantastic animals (1272). On the left is an elegant 12C **ambo** with green mosaics representing Jonah and the Whale. The small **museum** in the crypt has sculptural fragments, mosaics, a silver **head-reliquary** with the relics of St Barbara.

★ St John's (San Giovanni del Toro) – This small 11C church was restored in the 18C. Inside antique columns support the arches. There is a richly decorated 11C **pulpit★**, a Roman sarcophagus (north aisle) and 14C frescoes in the crypt.

Michelin map **988** fold 15

In the peaceful provincial-looking town of Ravenna, the sober exteriors of its buildings belie the wealth of riches accumulated when Ravenna was an imperial city, the Byzantium of the West and an Exarchate of Byzantium. Indeed the many wonderful mosaics which adorn the city's ecclesiastical buildings are the finest in Europe. Their bright colours, richness of decoration and powerful symbolism are evocative of a great spirituality.

Since the division of the Empire in 395 by Theodosius, Rome already in decline was abandoned in AD404 by Honorius who made Ravenna the capital of the Roman Empire. Honorius' sister **Galla Placidia** lavishly governed the Western Empire before the Barbarian invasions brought the Ostrogoth Kings Odoacer (476-493) and **Theodoric** (493-526) to Ravenna, who also embellished Ravenna in their turn.

The strategic location of Ravenna's port, Classis, facing the Greek world, inevitably led to trading with Byzantium which had become capital in 476. Ravenno came under Byzantine rule in 540 in the reign of the Emperor Justinian, and was administered by Exarchs. From then on Ravenna exercised considerable influence over the whole of northern Italy and beyond.

★★ **THE MOSAICS** *time: one day*

The oldest mosaics are in the Orthodox Baptistry and the Galla Placidia Tomb. Next in chronological order are those adorning the Arians' Baptistry, St Apollinaris the New, St Vitalis, and finally, St Apollinaris in Classe.

★★ **Tomb of Galla Placidia (Mausoleo di Galla Placidia) (Y).** – This mid-5C mausoleum in the form of a Latin cross has a great architectural harmony and is embellished by wonderful mosaics. The vaulting shines with stellar and floral motifs and the dome is painted a deep blue. On the tympanum and pendentives the scenes exude a serenity of symbolism, in particular the Good Shepherd, on the west wall. The sarcophagi at either end of the projecting arms are the tombs of Galla Placidia and her family.

★★ **Church of St Vitalis (San Vitale) (Y).** – This church consecrated in 547 by Archbishop Maximian is a masterpiece of architecture, expressing a taste for splendour, originality and the play of light, features which are typical of the later period of ancient art. The church has an octagonal plan, two storeys of concave exedrae encircled by an ambulatory and a deep apse. The interior is of a dazzling richness: precious marbles, Byzantine capitals splendidly carved, frescoes and especially the **mosaics** of the apse with their brilliant colours. On the sides and end wall of the chancel are scenes from the Old Testament; on the side walls inside the chancel are wonderful groups representing the **Empress Theodora** with her suite and the **Emperor Justinian** attended by his court. These works display splendour, a hieratic power and a strong Byzantine influence. On the ceiling **Christ the King** is enthroned between St Vitalis and Bishop Ecclesio, the founder of the church.

To the left of St Vitalis is the **National Museum** (Museo Nazionale) (**Y M**) with its Roman, Oriental, Byzantine, Romanesque and Renaissance collections.

★ **Orthodox Baptistry (Battistero degli Ortodossi) (Z).** – Known generally as the Neoni Baptistry because it was built in the 6C by a bishop of this name. It contains superb **mosaics** in brilliant and contrasting colours. The main arches over the bays are adorned with decorative motifs while the dome portrays the **Baptism of Christ** and the Twelve Apostles. The Byzantine low-reliefs over the arches of the rotunda represent the prophets.

The 18C **cathedral (Z E)** adjacent to the baptistry, is dominated by a round 10-11C campanile. It contains a 6C marble ambo adorned with symbolic animals.

(Lauros/Giraudon)

Basilica of St Apollinaris in Classe – Mosaics

★ **Basilica of St Apollinaris the New (Sant' Apollinare Nuovo) (Z).** – Built in 519 by Theodoric, this lovely church with three naves separated by Corinthian columns is adorned with brilliant **mosaics** with a gold background. On the upper walls are scenes from the Life of Christ, then pictures of saints and prophets. Below is the famous **procession of saints** depicting holy virgins leaving the town and port of Classis, behind the Magi, bearing offerings to the Virgin. Opposite is a procession of twenty-six martyrs leaving the palace of Theodoric, moving solemnly towards Christ the King, who is surrounded by angels.

Arians' Baptistry (Battistero degli Ariani) (Y D). – The baptistry is thought to have been built by Theodoric in the 6C. The dome is decorated with fine **mosaics** portraying the Baptism of Christ and in the surrounding band, the twelve Apostles and a throne adorned with a cross.

★★ Basilica of St Apollinaris in Classe (Sant' Apollinare in Classe). – *5km – 3 miles to the south. Leave Ravenna by ④ on the plan, the S 67.*
The basilica stands in open country not far from the sea. Begun in 534 and consecrated in 549 the basilica was completed in the 11C with the construction of a cylindrical campanile.
The majestic interior has a nave and two aisles separated by twenty-six arches supported by marble columns. In the side aisles lie superb early Christian sarcophagi carved with symbols (5-8C). The triumphal arch and the chancel are adorned with magnificent 6-7C mosaics with a marked freedom and simplicity of composition and a lovely harmony of colour. The mosaics full of symbolism portray Christ the Saviour and the Transfiguration.

ADDITIONAL SIGHTS

★ Theodoric's Tomb (Mausolea di Teodorico) (Y B). – This curious monument, erected by Theodoric around 520 is built of huge blocks of free stone assembled without mortar. The two storey building is covered by a remarkable monolithic dome 11m – 36ft in diameter in Istrian stone. Inside, the decoration is sober and austere. A Romanesque porphyry basin has been transformed into a scarcophagus.

Episcopal Palace Museum (Museo dell' Arcivescovado) (Z M¹). – Part of this collection is the pulpit★★ of Archbishop Maximian (6C), a masterpiece of carved ivory. The Archiepiscopal Chapel★★ contains remarkable mosaics.

Municipal Picture Gallery (Pinacoteca Comunale) (Z M²). – This collection includes works from most of the Italian schools from the 14C to the 20C. Note in particular the recumbent figure★ (1526) of a young knight, Guidarello Guidarelli, which is the masterpiece of Tullio Lombardo.

Dante's Tomb (Sepolcro di Dante) (Z A). – Dante was exiled from Florence and took refuge first at Verona and then at Ravenna where he died in 1321. The classical building in which the tomb now stands was erected in 1780.

Church of St Francis (San Francesco) (Z). – This 10C Romanesque church is flanked by a campanile of the same period. Remodelled after the Second World War it still retains some lovely Greek marble columns, a 5C high altar and a 9-10C crypt.

REGGIO DI CALABRIA Calabria

Reggio, which stands close against the Aspromonte Massif, is a pleasant town of modern appearance, rebuilt after the earthquake of 1908 along the Straits of Messina. Reggio is surrounded with rich groves of olives,vines, orange and lemon trees and flowers used for making perfume. Half the world production of bergamot (a citrus fruit) comes from Reggio. There are daily boat and car ferry services to Sicily *(see the current Michelin Red Guide Italia)*.

★ **Lungomare.** – This long and elegant marine promenade lined with palm trees and magnolias, affords views of the Sicilian coastline and Etna.

★★ **National Museum (Museo Nazionale).** – This modern museum, in the centre of town, ⊘ regroups an important **archaeological collection** covering the history of Magna Graecia. There is also an interesting art gallery. The museum was selected to house *(ground floor)* the **Riace Warriors** ★★★ dating in all probability from the 5C BC which were discovered in 1972 off the coast of the small Calabrian harbour of Riace. The two warrior figures are exceptionally well conserved and are striking for their imposing appearance, their harmonious proportions and the refinement of their details. The sculptor remains an enigma. The ground floor also has displays on local prehistory, finds dating from Magna Graecia (especially the excavations at Locri which have uncovered Greek and locally produced pottery, terracotta votive tablets, a marble group, etc). On the first floor are the Hellenistic works and the coin collection. The second floor **art gallery** has two remarkable works by **Antonello da Messina**: a *St Jerome* and *Three Angels appearing before Abraham*.

EXCURSION

★ **Aspromonte.** – *From its junction (burio Brandano) with the S 112, the S 183 crosses the Aspromonte Massif from north to south, allowing the visitor to discover its many varied aspects. Description p 65.*

The practical information chapter,
at the end of the guide, regroups
– a list of the local or national organizations supplying additional information
– a section on times and charges.

REGGIO NELL'EMILIA Emilia-Romagna

This rich industrial and commercial centre, set on the Via Emilia, was the birthplace of Ariosto *(qv)*. Like Modena and Ferrara, it belonged to the Este family from 1409 to 1776.

★ **Parmeggiani Gallery (Galleria Parmeggiani).** – *2 Corso Cairoli.*
⊘ The collections comprise gold plate, fabrics, costumes, arms, furniture and paintings: works by El Greco and Ribera as well as Flemish and Italian Mannerist paintings.

Madonna della Ghiara. – *Corso Garibaldi.*
Lovely 17C church with a dome. The interior was richly decorated by the Bolognese school.

EXCURSION

Castle of Canossa (Castello di Canossa). – *32km – 20 miles to the southwest. Follow the San Polo d'Enza road and then turn left to Canossa.*
Only the romantic runs, perched on a rock, remain of the imposing stronghold which belonged to the great Countess of Tuscany, Matilda (1046-1115), who supported the pope against the emperor for thirty years during the quarrel over the investiture of bishops and abbots *(qv)*. The Emperor Heinrich IV of Germany came barefoot and in his shirt sleeves through the snow, to make amends to Pope Gregory VII in 1077. He had to wait three days for his absolution. This is the origin of the expression "to go to Canossa", that is, to humble oneself after a quarrel.

RIETI Latium

Rieta lies at the junction of several valleys in the heart of a fertile plain and is the geographical centre of Italy. It is also a good excursion centre from which to follow in the footsteps of St Francis of Assisi who preached locally.

Piazza Cesare Battisti. – This is the centre of the town, where the most important buildings are to be found. Take the gateway to the right of the 16-17C Palazzo del Governo with its elegant loggia to reach the pleasant **public garden** ★, from where there is a lovely view of the town and its surroundings.

Cathedral (Duomo). – This has a 15C porch and a lovely Romanesque campanile dating from 1252. Inside, the fresco of the Madonna dates from 1494 while the **crypt** is 12C.

Episcopal Palace (Palazzo Vescovile). – *Behind the cathedral.*
This 13C building has heavily ribbed **vaulting** ★ over the two vast naves which are now used as a garage.

EXCURSIONS

🕙 **Fonte Colombo Monastery (Convento di Fonte Colombo).** – *5km – 3 miles to the south-west. Take the Contigliano road and after 3km – 2 miles turn left.*
It was in the old monastery that St Francis underwent an eye operation. He dictated the Franciscan Rule in the grotto having fasted for forty days. You will see the 12C Chapel of St Mary Magdalen adorned with frescoes with the "T" the emblem of the Cross designed by St Francis; the St Michael Chapel and the grotto where he fasted; the tree-trunk in which Jesus appeared to him; the old monastery and the 15C church.

★ **Greccio Monastery (Convento di Greccio).** – *15km – 9 miles to the northwest. Take the*
🕙 *Contigliano road and after this town continue for 2km – 1 mile. Leave the car on the esplanade at the foot of the monastery.*
This 13C monastery clings to a rocky overhang at an altitude of 638m – 2 093ft. It was here that St Francis celebrated Christmas in 1223 and said mass at a manger *(presepio)* between an ox and an ass, thus starting the custom of making cribs at Christmas.
You will see the Chapel of the Crib (frescoes by the school of Giotto) and where St Francis and his companions lived. On the upper floor is the church of 1228 with its original furnishings.

🕙 **Poggio Bustone Monastery (Convento di Poggio Bustone).** – *10km – 6 miles to the north by the Terni road.*
Perched at an altitude of 818m – 2 684ft in a lovely green setting, the monastery consists of a 14C church, very altered, with its 15 to 17C frescoes, charming 15-16C cloisters, a 14C refectory and two caves in which St Francis is said to have lived.

🕙 **La Foresta Monastery (Convento La Foresta).** – *5km – 3 miles to the north.*
It was in this mountain retreat that St Francis wrote his *Canticle of the Creatures* and performed the miracle of the vine. Visit the wine cellar which was filled by the miraculous grape and the cave where St Francis stayed.

★★ **RIMINI** Emilia-Romagna   Pop 130 344

Michelin map 988 fold 15 – Town plan in the current Michelin Red Guide Italia

Like Janus, Rimini has two faces: that of an ancient city rich in history and that of an international ultra-modern seaside resort with its marina, airport and in particular, a great beach of fine sand. This Umbrian and Gallic colony with its strategic situation at the junction of the Via Emilia and the Via Flaminia, flourished during the Empire. In the 13C the town grew to fame with the notoriety of its ruling house, the **Malatesta**. They combined extreme refinement with savagery. Dante immortalised the fate of the tragic lovers, Paolo Malatesta and Francesca da Rimini, who were murdered by Gianni Malatesta, the brother of Paolo and the husband of Francesca. Later Sigismondo Malatesta, cultured patron of the arts and protector of the humanists, repudiated, poisoned and strangled his first three wives, before making an irregular marriage with his mistress, Isotta. After the fall of the Malatesta, Rimini became a papal town.

SIGHTS

★ **Malatesta Temple (Tempio Malatestiano).** – The building was erected to shelter the tomb of Isotta, the last wife of Sigismondo Malatesta. The Florentine architect Alberti designed this Renaissance building, which was left unfinished. The remarkable façade in some respects recalls the nearby Arch of Augustus with its fluted columns with Corinthian capitals and medallions. The frieze running round the base of the columns bears the rose of the Malatesta and the intertwined initials of Sigismondo and Isotta.
The spacious and imposing interior includes an allegorical decoration of exquisite grace and subtlety, due in large part to Agostino di Duccio. The same motifs are also found in the side chapels. In the reliquary chapel, to the right, Piero della Francesca painted the **portrait of Sigismondo Malatesta★**. In the adjacent chapel, the tomb of Isotta faces an admirable **painted 14C crucifix★** of the Rimini school. The first chapel on the left contains the cenotaph of Sigismondo's ancestors, adorned with low-reliefs.

Arch of Augustus (Arco d' Augusto). – *Piazzale Giulio Cesare.*
The arch was built in 27BC and has a majestic appearance, with fine fluted columns and Corinthian capitals.

Bridge of Tiberius (Ponte di Tiberio). – The bridge was begun under Augustus and completed under Tiberius in AD21. The building material is massive blocks of Istrian limestone.

Times and charges for admission to sights described in the guide are listed at the end of the guide.

The sights are listed alphabetically in this section either under the place – town, village or area – in which they are situated or under their proper name.

Every sight for which there are times and charges is indicated by the symbol 🕙 in the margin in the main part of the guide.

Michelin map 🔢 folds 12 and 13 or 🔢 folds 19, 20 and 29

From Ventimiglia to the Gulf of La Spezia the coast describes an arc backed by the slopes of the Alps and the Ligurian Apennines, with Genoa in the middle.
The enchanting Italian or Ligurian Riviera is like the French Riviera, a tourist's paradise. The mild climate makes it particularly popular in winter. The coast is dotted with popular resorts with good amenities and a wide choice of hotels. The hinterland provides a large choice of walks for those who prefer solitude.

Sightseeing. – The map below in addition to locating the towns and sites described in the guide, indicates other beauty spots in small black type.

★ 1 RIVIERA DI PONENTE (WESTERN RIVIERA)

From Ventimiglia to Genoa 175km – 109 miles – allow a day

The main road artery of the Riviera is the Via Aurelia, of Roman origin – difficult, for it is winding and narrow, and carries heavy traffic. Nevertheless it offers remarkable viewpoints when it is a corniche road or when it runs close to the blue waters of the Ligurian Sea. Slightly inland the A10 motorway with its many tunnels and viaducts runs parallel. The road passes through a succession of resorts and villas, often screened by luxuriant and varied vegetation, or crosses a stretch of coastal plain traversed by mountains torrents. With its exceptionally good exposition the Riviera specialises in the growing of flowers often in glass houses, throughout the year.
The hinterland provides a sharp contrast with the peacefulness of its wild forested landscapes.

Ventimiglia. – *Town plan in the current Michelin Red Guide Italia.* Not far from the French border, Ventimiglia has an old quarter (Città Vecchia) criss-crossed by narrow alleyways, an 11-12C cathedral (Duomo), an 11C octagonal baptistry, an 11-12C Church of San Michele and the 17C Neri Oratory. The **Hanbury Gardens★★** in **Mortola Inferiore** *(6km – 4 miles ot the west, in the direction of the French border)* with their varied and exotic vegetation, are laid out in terraces, overlooking the sea.

★ **Bordighera.** – The villas and hotels of this famous resort are scattered among flower gardens shaded by splendid palm trees. The old town, with its winding alleys, still has several fortified gateways.

★ **San Remo.** – *Description p 179.*

★ **Taggia.** – Taggia, set amidst the vineyards, orchards and olive groves, commands the Argentina Valley. In the 15 and 16C Taggia was an important art centre frequented by Louis Bréa from Nice, the Piedmontese Canavese and the Genoese Perino del Vaga and Luca Cambiaso.
The **Church of St Dominic** (San Domenico) has a fine collection of **works**★ by Louis Bréa (Virgin of Pity and the Baptism of Christ).

Diano Marina. – From here it is possible to visit the fortified village of **Diano Castello** and its 12C Chapel of the Knights of Malta with its multicoloured wooden roof.

Albenga. – Albenga lies a short distance inland, in an alluvial plain with rich market gardens. The medieval **old town★** is clustered round the **cathedral** (Cattedrale) with its imposing late 14C campanile. The vaulting of the nave is covered with *trompe l'œil* frescoes. The octagonal 5C baptistry has a baptismal font and a charming paleo-Christian mosaic in the style typical of Ravenna.

Finale Ligure. – **Finale Marina** has a basilica with a fanciful baroque façade. In **Finale Pia** the abbey church is graced with an elegant late 13C campanile. The old town of **Finale Borgo★**, 2km – 1 mile inland, still has its town walls and its Collegiate Church of San Biagio with its elegant 13C polygonal campanile. Inside is a polyptych of St Catherine (1533) and a 16C painting of St Blaise surrounded by saints.

From **San Giovanni Castle** *(1 hour on foot Rtn, start from Vial del Municipio)* there is a **view**★ of Finale Ligure, the sea and inland. Higher up, **Gavone Castle** conserves a 15C round tower with diamond shaped rustication.

★ **Noli.** – This fishing village still has ancient houses, 13C towers and a Romanesque church with a huge wooden statue of Christ also of the Romanesque period.

Savona. – *Town plan in the current Michelin Red Guide France.* Italy's seventh port, Savona handles crude oil, coal, cellulose and Italian cars for export to Britain and the United States. The old town has several Renaissance palaces, a 16C cathedral (Duomo and on the sea front the 16C **Priamar Fortress** where the Italian patriot Mazzini was imprisoned in 1830.

★ **Albisola Marina.** – This town is known for its production of ceramics which carries on a 13C tradition. At the end of the 16C a Duke of Nevers, a member of the Italian Gonzaga family, summoned the Conrade brothers from Albisola to Nevers to found a faïence factory. The 18C **Villa Faraggiana** with its exotic **park**★ now houses the Ligurian Ceramics Centre. Note in particular the rich Empire decoration, ceramic pavements and flooring and the superb **ballroom**★ with its stucco and fresco decoration.

★★**Genoa.** – *Description p 96.*

★★★② **RIVIERA DI LEVANTE**

(EASTERN RIVIERA)

From Genoa to La Spezia *173km – 108 miles – allow 1 day*

This stretch of coast has more character and is wilder than the Riviera di Ponente. Sharp promontories, little sheltered coves, tiny fishing villages, wide sandy bays, cliffs, the pinewoods and olive groves of the hinterland, all lend it charm. The road is often winding and hilly but less often a corniche and often much further from the coast.

★★ **Genoa.** – *Description p 96.*

★★★ **Portofino.** – *Description p 156.*

★ **Rapallo.** – *Town plan in the current Michelin Red Guide Italia.* This sophisticated seaside resort is admirably situated at the head of a bay to the east of the Portofino peninsula. The Lungomare Vittorio Veneto is a lovely palm-shaded **promenade**★ along the sea front.

Chiavari. – This seaside resort has a vast beach and a pleasure boat harbour. In San Salvatore 2km – 1 mile to the northeast, is the small 13C **Basilica dei Fieschi**★ with its alternating courses of black and white marble. The vaulting is pointed. Opposite stands the Palazzo Fieschi, a graceful 13C Genoese Gothic building.

★★ **Cinque Terre.** – *Description p 72.*

La Spezia. – *Town plan in the current Michelin Red Guide Italia.* This naval base and important port has Italy's largest naval dockyard and specialises in the manufacture of arms. The **naval museum** comprises souvenirs, arms and models.

★★ **Portovenere.** – This small, severe-looking town is dominated by a 12-16C citadel. Some of the houses date as far back as the 12C and were in fact once fortified by the Genoese.
The Church of San Lorenzo dates from the 12C while the Church of San Pietro incorporates parts dating from the 6C. From the terrace there is a very fine view of the Gulf of La Spezia and the Cinque Terre region.

★ **Lerici.** – Lerici at the head of a well sheltered cove has an important 13C castle (castello) which was rebuilt in the 16C by the Genoese.
It was near this village that the Shelleys rented a small house in 1822. Percy Bysshe drowned on the return trip from Leghorn to greet Leigh Hunt, who was to edit a new journal with Shelley and Byron. He was cremated on the beach, Il Gombo north of the mouth of the Arno and his ashes are buried in the Protestant Cemetery in Rome.

Women in trousers and men and women wearing shorts or with bare shoulders are not allowed into churches and monasteries.

Michelin map 988 fold 26 – Town plan pp 168-169 – Plan of the built-up area in the current Michelin Green Guide Italia

Since 1870 when it became the capital of Italy, Rome has undergone extensive urban development. Then it was a city of barely 200 000 while today there are almost 3 million inhabitants. The treasures of Rome are not always easy to visit, as the city centre is a dedale of narrow streets, traffic snarls up easily and Roman drivers are notoriously undisciplined.

We strongly recommend you when you visit the Eternal City to use the **Michelin Green Guide Rome** with its suggested itineraries, descriptions of selected sights, plans of certain quarters and buildings, and notes on the city's history and its artistic traditions. Discover Rome's charms and don't waste precious time.

HISTORICAL NOTES

The lengendary origins of Rome were perpetuated by both Roman historians and poets like Livy in his *Roman History* and Virgil in the *Aeneid*. Both claimed that Aeneas, son of the goddess Venus, fled from Troy when it was captured and landed at the mouth of the Tiber. Having defeated the local tribes he founded Lavinium. His son Ascanius (or Iulus) founded Alba Longa. It was here that Rhea Silvia the Vestal, following her union with the god Mars, gave birth to the twins Romulus and Remus, who were abandoned on the Tiber. The twins came to rest at the foot of the Palatine where they were nursed by a wolf. Later Romulus marked a furrow round the sacred area on which the new city was to be built. Jesting, Remus stepped over the line; Romulus killed him for violating the sacred precinct. Romulus populated his village with outlaws who settled on the Capitol and he provided them with Sabine wives. An alliance grew up between the two peoples who were ruled by a succession of kings, alternately Sabine and Latin, until the Etruscans arrived.

Modern historians emphasize the strategic location of Rome's seven hills especially that of the Palatine, which was a staging post on the salt road (Via Salaria). These favourable features no doubt led to the development of settlements around the Palatine in the 8C BC.

Two centuries later the Etruscans had transformed these villages of shacks into a well organised town, with a citadel on the Capitol. The last Etruscan king, Tarquin the Superb, was thrown out in 509 BC and the Consulate was instituted.

The Republican era was an ambitious one of territorial expansion. During the 2C and 1C BC the Republican regime tore itself to pieces in a civil war. To restore order disrupted by the rival political factions and rule the newly conquered territories it required a clever man of very determined character. **Julius Caesar** (101-44 BC) emerged from amidst the contenders in part due to his audacious strategies (he conquered the whole of Gaul in 51), his grasp of political affairs, his talents as an orator and his unbounded ambition; appointed consul and dictator for life he was assassinated on the Ides of March, 15 March 44 BC. He was succeeded by his nephew, **Octavian**, a young man who had delicate health and had won no military glory. Octavian was to demonstrate tenacity of purpose and political genius and ably rid his path of possible rivals. In 27 BC the Senate granted Octavian the title **Augustus** which invested him with an aura of holiness. He soon became the first Roman emperor. His achievements were considerable: he extended Roman government and restored peace to the whole of the Mediterranean basin.

Among Augustus' successors there were those who were motivated by madness and cruelty (Caligula, Nero and Domitian) and others who continued the good work of Roman civilisation; the good administrator, Vespasian; Titus who was known as the love and delight of the human race; Trajan, the "best of Emperors" and great builder; and Hadrian, an indefatigable traveller and passionate Hellenist.

Christian Rome. – As the old order passed away, undermined from within by economic misery, the concentration of authority in the hands of one man and from without by Barbarian attacks, a new force – Christianity – emerged. It had first reached Rome in the reign of Augustus. The religion of Jesus originated in Palestine and Syria, and was spread throughout the pagan world by his disciples. As the world fell into disarray, Christianity preached a new doctrine of brotherly love and the hope of happiness after death. During the last years of the 1C and the early years of the 2C the Christian Church became organised but transgressed the law from the beginning because the Emperor embodied religious power. It was not until the **Edict of Milan** (313), which allowed Christians to practise their religion openly, and the conversion of **Constantine** (314) that the Church could come out into the open.

From the first days of Christianity, the bishop was Christ's representative on earth. The bishop of Rome, traditional capital of the Empire, claimed primacy. Gradually the name **"Pope"**, derived from the vulgar Latin *papa* meaning father, which had been used for all bishops, was reserved for the Bishop of Rome alone. For nineteen centuries the popes at the head of the Roman church have influenced the history of Christianity and given the Eternal City its particular character. In the 11C **Gregory VII** restored order to the Christian church which had by then an appalling reputation. He dealt with two scourges, the buying and selling of church property and the marriage of the clergy. In so doing he started the Investiture Controversy which opposed the Sovereign Pontiff and the emperor.

During the Renaissance numerous popes were scholarly, ambitious and great patrons of the art and greatly contributed to the embellishment of the capital by bringing to their court such artists as Raphael and Michelangelo. They included Pius II, Sixtus IV (builder of the Sistine Chapel, Santa Maria della Pace and Santa Maria del Popolo), Julius II (who commissioned Michelangelo to decorate the ceiling of the Sistine Chapel), Leo X (who had a great personal fortune and nominated Raphael as intendant of the arts), Clement VII, Sixtus V (who was a great builder) and Paul III who built the Farnese Palace.

ROME TODAY

No other city in the world has managed to combine so successfully such a diverse heritage of Classical antiquities, medieval buildings, Renaissance palaces and baroque churches. Far from being discordant they constitute a logical continuity where revivals, influences and contrasts are the results of the subtleties of genius of Roman architects and builders. Of course the ruins no longer enjoy their former splendour when they were faced with marble under the Empire and only a few of the palaces have retained the painted decoration of their façades. The Rome so loved by Goethe and Stendhal has changed due to the depredations of heavy traffic and the developments resulting from the modernisation of a capital city.

However today's visitor cannot fail to be impressed by the immensity of this great town planning project, which is Rome. The best overall views of this urban complex sprawling over the seven hills are from the belvederes on the Janiculum (Gianicolo - AY), the Aventine (CZ) and the Pincio (BV). At dusk the visitor will discover a city bathed in a golden light, the green masses of the gardens, the silhouettes of umbrella pines shading the areas of ruins, as well as the numerous domes and bell towers rising above the pink tiled roofscape. Rome with some 300 churches is the city of churches, where it is not uncommon to find two side by side. It is often impossible to stand back and admire their façades but the richness of the decoration and the ingenious use of *trompe-l'œil* tend to compensate. Often the interiors are astonishing for their silence and light and the inventiveness and audacity of the ultimate design. In the older districts of Rome (Vecchia Roma) around the Pantheon (BX), the Piazza Navona (BX) and the Campo dei Fiori (BY), there is a wealth of palaces. For those who wander through these districts it is often possible to get a glimpse between a pair of ochre coloured façades of a small square with all the bustle of a market, or several flights of stairways descending to a fountain. These areas are lit by tall street lights which diffuse an unreal light giving them a certain charm, a pleasant change from the bustle of the main arteries.

Luxury shops are to be found around the Piazza del Popolo (BV), Via del Corso (BCX), Piazza di Spagna (CX) and the streets which open off them. Via Veneto (CX) lined with cafés and luxurious hotels is a fashionable tourist centre. Piazza Navona is another fashionable meeting place while the **Trastevere** (BY), which has never lost its popular character, has a variety of restaurants. Antique and second-hand shops line Via dei Coronari (BX 25).

SIGHTSEEING

On the following pages the reader will find a very brief description of some of the sights, which will enable him to see in three days some of the masterpieces which make Rome famous. In the section Additional Sights, a thematic classification includes other important monuments, sites or museums which are further proof of the exceptional riches of this city.

FIRST DAY *(morning)*

★ PIAZZA VENEZIA (CXY)

The Piazza in the centre of Rome is lined with palaces: Palazzo Venezia, Palazzo Bonaparte, where Napoleon's mother died in 1836, and the early 20C Palazzo delle Assicurazioni Generali di Venezia.

★ Palazzo Venezia (CY A). – This palace, built by Pope Paul II (1464-71), is one of the first Renaissance buildings. The **museum,** on the first floor, contains ceramics, a collection of 13-15C statues, tapestries (15-17C) and arms (15-18C) arranged in the three rooms of Paul II's apartment. The **Basilica of St Mark** (San Marco), incorporated within the palace in the 15C, has a fine Renaissance **façade★** overlooking Piazza di San Marco (CY 60).

Monument to Victor Emmanuel II (Vittoriano) (CY B). – This huge memorial by Giuseppe Sacconi begun in 1885 in honour of the first king of a united Italy, overshadows the other monuments of Rome by its sheer size and dazzling white colour. It affords a **view★★** of the Eternal City.

★★★ CAPITOL (CAMPIDOGLIO – CY)

On the hill which symbolized the power of ancient Rome, there now stand the city's administrative offices, also the Church of Santa Maria d'Aracoeli, Piazza del Campidoglio and its palaces, and pleasant gardens.

★★ Church of Santa Maria d'Aracoeli (CY C). – The church has a beautiful staircase built as an ex-voto after the plague of 1346, and a flat, austere façade. It was built in 1250 on the spot where the Sibyl of Tibur (Tivoli) announced the coming of Christ to Augustus. In the first chapel on the right are **frescoes★** painted by Pinturicchio in about 1485.

★★★ Piazza del Campidoglio (CY 17). – Capitol Square was designed and partly laid out by Michelangelo from 1536 onwards. It is framed by three palaces and a balustrade with statues of the Heavenly Twins or Dioscuri. The **equestrian statue of Marcus Aurelius★★** (late 2C) in the centre was installed and restored by Michelangelo.
The **Palazzo dei Conservatori★★★ (CY M¹)**, built in the 15C and remodelled in 1568 by Giacomo della Porta, houses a **museum★★★** of antique art which includes the **She-Wolf★★★** (6-5C BC), the **Boy Extracting a Thorn★★★**, a Greek original or a very good copy dating back to the 1C BC and a **Bust of Junius Brutus★★**, a remarkable head dating from the 3C BC placed on a bust in the Renaissance period. The **picture gallery★** *(2nd floor)* contains mainly 17C paintings.

The **Palazzo Nuovo** (New Palace) **(CY M²)**, built in 1655 by Girolamo Rainaldi, houses the **Capitoline Museum**★★ where you will see the **Dying Gaul**★★★, a Roman sculpture based on a bronze of the Pergamum school (3-2 BC): the **Emperors' Room**★★ with portraits of all the emperors; the **Capitoline Venus**★★, a Roman work inspired by the Venus of Cnidus by Praxiteles; and the **Mosaic of the Doves**★★ from Hadrian's Villa at Tivoli.

The **Palazzo Senatorio**★★★ (the Senate) **(CY H)** is a 12C building, remodelled between 1582 and 1602 by Giacomo della Porta and Girolamo Rainaldi.

FIRST DAY (afternoon)

★ ROMAN FORUM (FORO ROMANO - CY)

From Via del Campidoglio **(CY 19)** there is a beautiful **view**★★★ of the ruins. The remains of the Roman Forum, the religious, political and commercial centre of ancient Rome, reflect the twelve centuries of history which created Roman civilisation. The forum was excavated in the 19 and 20C.

At the foot of the Capitol is the **Portico of the Di Consentes**★, a colonnade of pillars with Corinthian capitals dating back to restoration work of AD 367; the portico was dedicated to the twelve principal Roman deities. The three elegant Corinthian columns nearby belonged to the **Temple of Vespasian**★★ (late 1C).

Further on stands the **Mamertine Prison**★, state prison in antiquity in which Jugurtha (105 BC) and Vercingetorix (52 BC) both died. According to legend, the apostles St Peter and St Paul caused a spring to gush forth in order to baptise their gaolers.

Opposite is the **Church of St Luca and St Martina (CY V)**, built in the 17C by Pietro da Cortona.

Take Via della Salara Vecchia to reach the entrance to the Forum.

Take the **Via Sacra**★★★ (Sacred Way) along which victorious generals marched in triumph to the **Curia**★★, rebuilt in the 3C by Diocletian. Senate meetings were held here; nowadays it houses **Trajan's low-reliefs**★★★, sculpted panels depicting scenes from the life of the Emperor, and sacrificial animals.

Nearby, the imposing **Triumphal Arch of Septimus Severus**★★ was built in AD 203 to commemorate this Emperor's victories over the Parthians. Only eight 4C columns of the **Temple of Saturn**★★★ (Tempio di Saturno) remain. The **Column of Phocas**★ (Colonna di Foca) was erected in AD 608 in honour of the Byzantine Emperor Phocas who presented the Pantheon to Boniface IV. The **Basilica Julia**★★ which has five aisles, was built by Julius Caesar and completed by Augustus. It served as a law court and exchange.

Three beautiful columns remain of the **Temple of Castor and Pollux**★★★ (Tempio di Castore e Polluce). The circular **Temple of Vesta**★★★ (Tempio di Vesta) stands near the **House of the Vestal Virgins**★★★ (Casa delle Vestali). The **Temple of Antoninus and Faustina**★★ (Tempio di Antonino e Faustina) was dedicated to the Emperor Antoninus the Pius and his wife. The grandiose **Basilica of Maxentius**★★★ (Basilica di Massenzio) was completed by the Emperor Constantine. The **Triumphal Arch of Titus**★★ (Arco di Tito), erected in 81 commemorates the capture of Jerusalem by this emperor, who only reigned for two years.

★ PALATINE (PALATINO - CY)

The Palatine Hill, where Romulus and Remus were discovered, was chosen by Domitian as the site for the Imperial Palace. The building included three main areas: the **Domus Flavia**★ or official state apartments, the **Domus Augustana**★★ or private imperial apartments and the **Stadium**★. The **House of Livia**★★ (Casa di Livia) probably belonged to Augustus (fine vestiges of paintings). The **Farnese Gardens** (Orti Farnesiani), laid out in the 16C on the site of Tiberius' palace, afford **views**★★ of the Forum and town.

Leave the Palatine by an exit alongside the Arch of Titus.

★ Temple of Venus and Rome (CY R).

The temple built between 121 and 136 by Hadrian was the largest in the city (110m – 361ft by 53m – 174ft). It was unique in that it comprised two *cellae* with apses back to back. One was dedicated to the goddess of Rome and faced the Forum; the other was dedicated to Venus and faced the Coliseum.

★ COLISEUM (COLOSSEO - CY)

This amphitheatre, inaugurated in AD 80, is also known as the Flavian Amphitheatre after its initiator, Vespasian, first of the Flavian emperors. With its three superimposed classical orders (Doric, Ionic and Corinthian), it is a masterpiece of classical architecture. Fights between men and beasts, gladiatorial contests, races and simulated naval battles took place in the arena.

★ ARCH OF CONSTANTINE (ARCO DI CONSTANTINO - CY)

The arch was erected to commemorate Constantine's victory over Maxentius in AD 315. Some of the low-reliefs were removed from other 2C monuments.

★ IMPERIAL FORUMS (FORI IMPERIALI - CY)

These were built by Caesar, Augustus, Trajan, Nerva and Vespasian. There are hardly any remains of the latter two. The Via dei Fori Imperiali, laid out in 1932 by Mussolini, divides the imperial forums.

Of **Caesar's Forum**★★ (Foro di Cesare - *view from Via del Tulliano*) **(CY 77)** there remains three lovely columns from the Temple of Venus Genitrix. Of the **Augustan Forum**★★ (Foro di Augusto - *view from Via Alessandrina*) **(CY 2)** there remain a few columns of the Temple of Mars the Avenger, vestiges of the stairway and of the wall enclosing the forum (behind the temple).

ROMA

169

The forum is dominated by the House of the Knights of Rhodes, built in the Middle Ages and rebuilt in the 15C amidst the ancient ruins.

All that remains of the largest and finest, **Trajan's Forum★★★** (Foro di Traiano), is **Trajan's column★★★** (Colonna Traiana) which depicts in over 100 scenes, episodes of the war waged by Trajan against the Dacians. It is an unrivalled masterpiece.

⊙ The **markets★★★** (entrance in Via 4 Novembre - **CXY 87**) have kept their semicircular façade. The **Tower of the Militia★** (Torre delle Milizie) is part of a 13C fortress.

SECOND DAY (morning)

★★★ CASTEL SANT' ANGELO (ABX)

⊙ This imposing fortress was built in AD 135 as a mausoleum for the Emperor Hadrian and his family. In the 6C, Gregory the Great erected a chapel on top of the mausoleum to commemorate the apparition of an angel who by putting his sword back into its sheath, announced the end of a plague. In the 15C Nicholas V crowned the ancient building with a brick structure and the fortress with corner towers. Alexander VI (1492-1503) added octagonal bastions. In 1527, during the sack of Rome, Clement VII took refuge in the castle and installed an apartment which was later embellished by Paul III; the **Popes' Apartment★** stands isolated at the summit of the fortress and testifies to the graciousness of the popes' life style. A long passageway links the fortress to the Vatican palaces. A fine spiral ramp dating from antiquity leads to the castle. From the terrace at the summit there is a splendid **panorama★★★** of the whole town.

The Castel Sant' Angelo is linked to the left bank of the Tiber by the graceful **Ponte Sant' Angelo★** (**BX 57**) which is adorned with baroque angels carved by Bernini and with statues of Sts Peter and Paul (16C).

⊙ THE VATICAN CITY (CITTÀ DEL VATICANO - AV)

The Vatican City is bounded by a wall, overlooking Viale Vaticano and to the east by the colonnade of St Peter's Square. This makes up the greater part of the Vatican state as laid down in 1929 in the Lateran Treaty. The Vatican City, now only 44 hectares – 109 acres and with less than one thousand inhabitants, stems from the Papal States, a donation made in the 8C by Pepin the Short to Pope Stephen II and lost in 1870 when Italy was united into one Kingdom with Rome as its capital. The Vatican State, with the pope as ruler, has its own flag and anthem; it prints stamps and mints its own coinage which is legal tender throughout Italy. In 1970, Pope Paul VI dissolved the armed forces retaining only the Swiss Guard who wear a colourful uniform.

The Pope, who is the Head of State, is also the supreme head of the Universal Church and from this very small state, the spiritual influence of the church radiates throughout the world through the person of the sovereign pontiff. When the pope is in residence ⊙ in Rome, he grants **public audiences.**

★★★ VATICAN MUSEUMS (AV M⁶)

⊙ Entrance: Viale Vaticano.

The museums of the Vatican occupy part of the palaces built by the popes from the 13C onwards which have been extended and embellished to the present day.

These include on the first floor the **Pio-Clementino Museum★★★** (Greek and Roman antiquities) with its masterpieces: the **Belvedere Torso★★★** (1C BC), greatly admired by Michelangelo; **the Venus of Cnidus★★**, a Roman copy of Praxiteles' Venus; the **Laocoön Group★★★**, a 1C BC Hellenistic work; the **Apollo Belvedere★★★**, a 2C Roman copy; **Perseus★★**, a neo-classical work by Canova, which was purchased from the artist to make up for the loss of certain works removed under the terms of the Treaty of Tolentino (1797); **Hermes★★★**, a 2C Roman work inspired by the work of Praxiteles; and the **Athlete★★★**, scraping his skin with a strigil after taking exercise, is a 1C Roman copy of the Greek original by Lysippus.

The **Etruscan Museum★**, on the second floor, has a remarkable 7C BC gold **fibula★** adorned with lions and ducklings in high relief (Room II) and the **Mars★★** found at Todi, a rare example of a large bronze statue from the 5C BC (Room III).

The **Room of the Biga** derives its name from the **two horse chariot** (biga), a 1C Roman work reassembled in the 18C. The four **Raphael Rooms★★★** (Stanze di Rafaello), the private apartments of Julius II, were decorated by Raphael and his pupils between 1508 and 1517. The result is a pure Renaissance masterpiece. Admire the frescoes: the Borgo Fire, the School of Athens, the Parnassus, the Expulsion of Heliodorus from the Temple, the Miracle of the Bolsena Mass and St Peter delivered from prison. The **Collection of Modern Religious Art★★**, assembled by Pope Paul VI, is displayed in the apartment of Pope Alexander VI.

On the first floor the **Sistine Chapel★★★** (Cappella Sistina) is once again open to the public, with its splendid vault painted by Michelangelo between 1508 and 1512, illustrating the Bible, the Creation, the Flood and above the altar the Last Judgment which was added by the same artist in 1534. The lowest sections of the side walls were decorated by Perugino, Pinturicchio and Botticelli. The **Picture Gallery★★★** (Pinacoteca) also contains some first-class works: three **compositions★★★** by **Raphael** (The Coronation of the Virgin, The Madonna of Foligno and The Transfiguration - Room VIII); **St Jerome★★** by Leonardo da Vinci (Room IX) and a **Descent from the Cross★★** by Caravaggio (Room XII).

★★★ ST PETER'S SQUARE (PIAZZA SAN PIETRO - AV)

This architectural masterpiece was begun in 1656 by Bernini, master of the baroque. The two semicircles of the colonnade which adorn the square and frame the façade of the basilica, form an ensemble of remarkable sobriety and majesty. At the centre of the square stands a 1C BC obelisk brought from Heliopolis in Egypt to Rome in 37 by order of Caligula. It was erected here in 1585 on the initiative of Sixtus V by Domenico Fontana. At the top is a relic of the Holy Cross.

(Gould/Scope)

Rome – St Peter's Square

★ ST PETER'S BASILICA (BASILICA DI SAN PIETRO - AV)

Constantine, the first Christian Emperor, decided in AD 324 to build a basilica on the site where St Peter was buried after he had been martyred in Nero's circus. In the 15C it proved necessary to rebuild. For two centuries, the plan of the new basilica was constantly revised. The plan of a Greek cross surmounted by a dome designed by Bramante and adopted by Michelangelo, was altered to a Latin cross at the behest of Paul V in 1606 when he instructed Carlo Maderna to add two bays and a façade to Michelangelo's square plan.

From 1629 onwards, the basilica was decorated in a sumptuous baroque style by Bernini.

The **façade** which was completed in 1614 by Carlo Maderna is 115m – 377ft long and 45m – 151ft high; it is surmounted by colossal figures and masks the dome. In the centre is the balcony from which the Sovereign Pontiff gives his benediction *Urbi and Orbi* (to the City and the World).

Under the **porch**, note the first door on the left which has bronze panels carved by Giacomo Manzù (1964); the bronze central door which dates from the Renaissance (1455); and the door on the right or Holy Door which is opened and closed by the Pope to mark the beginning and end of a Jubilee Year.

Inside, it is customary to approach the stoups in the central nave which at first glance, appear of normal size but are in fact huge. Such size emphasises the gigantic dimensions of the basilica otherwise not apparent because of the harmony of its proportions. The length of St Peter's can be compared to that of other great basilicas throughout the world by means of markers inlaid in the pavement of the nave.

The first chapel on the right contains the **Pietà ★ ★ ★**, the masterpiece carved by Michelangelo in 1499-1500, which shows his creative genius.

In the right aisle, adjoining the Chapel of the Blessed Sacrament, **Gregory XIII's Monument★** is adorned with low-reliefs illustrating the institution of the Gregorian calendar devised by that pope. Immediately beyond the right transept, **Clement XIII's Monument★ ★ ★** is a fine neo-classical design by Canova dating from 1792. The apse is dominated by **St Peter's Throne ★ ★ ★** by Bernini (1666), a great carved throne in bronze encasing a 4C episcopal chair but symbolically attributed to St Peter, and surmounted by a glory in gilded stucco. In the chancel on the right is **Urban VIII's Monument★ ★ ★**, again by Bernini (1647) a masterpiece of funerary art. On the left stands **Paul III's Monument★ ★ ★** by Guglielmo della Porta (16C) a disciple of Michelangelo.

St Leo the Great's Altar *(chapel to the left of the chancel)* has a fine baroque **altarpiece★** carved in high-relief by Algardi. Nearby, **Alexander VII's Monument★**, characterised by extreme exuberance, is a late work by Bernini (1678) assisted by his pupils. The **baldachin★ ★ ★** which crowns the pontifical altar, which is 29m – 95ft tall (the height of the Farnese Palace), was strongly criticised. Partly because the bronze had been taken from the Pantheon and partly because it was thought to be too theatrical and in bad taste. It does however fit in well with the overall architectural plan.

The **dome★ ★ ★** designed by Michelangelo, which he himself built as far as the lantern, was completed in 1593 by Giacomo della Porta and Domenico Fontana. From the **summit** *(access from the left aisle opposite the pillar between the first and second bays)* there is a **view★ ★ ★** of St Peter's Square, the Vatican City and Rome from the Janiculum to Monte Mario.

The 13C bronze **Statue of St Peter★ ★** overlooking the nave is attributed to Arnolfo di Cambio and is greatly venerated by pilgrims, who come to kiss its feet.

Innocent VIII's Monument★ ★ ★ *(between the second and third bays in the left aisle)* is a Renaissance work (1498) by Antonio del Pollaiuolo. The **Stuart Monument** *(between the first and second bays in the left aisle)* carved by Canova is adorned with beautiful **angels★** in low-relief.

The **Treasury and Historical Museum★ ★** *(entrance in the left aisle, opposite the Stuart Monument)* has many treasured items.

SECOND DAY *(afternoon)*

★★★ FARNESE PALACE (PALAZZO FARNESE - BY)

🕐 The most beautiful of Roman palaces, now the French Embassy, was built from 1515 by Cardinal Alessandro Farnese, who reigned as pope under the name of Paul III (1534-49). He employed several architects: Antonio da Sangallo the Younger, Michelangelo (who designed the upper cornice of the façade, the Farnese coat of arms above the central balcony and the second floor of the inner court), Vignola who collaborated on the inner court and built the palace's rear façade, and Giacoma della Porta who designed the loggia of the same façade.

★★★ GESÙ CHURCH (BY)

The mother-church of the Jesuits in Rome, built by Vignola in 1568, is a typical building of the Counter-Reformation. On the outside, the engaged pillars replace the flat pilasters of the Renaissance, with light and shade effects and recesses. The interior, spacious and ideal for preaching, was lavishly decorated in the baroque style: on the dome, the Baciccia frescoes★★ illustrate the Triumph of the Name of Jesus (1679); the St Ignatius Loyola Chapel★★★ *(north transept)*, where the remains of St Ignatius Loyola rest, is the work (1696-1700) of the Jesuit Brother Andrea Pozzo and is sumptuously decorated.

★★★ PANTHEON (BX)

🕐 The Pantheon, an ancient building perfectly preserved, founded by Agrippa in 27 BC and rebuilt by Hadrian (117-125), was a temple which was converted into a church in the 7C. Access is through a porch supported by sixteen single granite columns, all ancient except for three on the left. The doors are the original ones.
The interior★★★, a masterpiece of harmony and majesty, is dominated by the dome, the diameter of which is equal to its height. The side chapels, adorned with alternately curved and triangular pediments, contain the tombs of the kings of Italy and that of Raphael *(on the left)*.

★★ SAN LUIGI DEI FRANCESI (BX L)

🕐 This is the French church in Rome. Its façade, probably designed by Giacomo della Porta, heralds baroque art with its projecting columns. Many Frenchmen have been laid to rest within this church.
In the second chapel on the right are frescoes★ by Domenichino illustrating the legend of St Cecilia. In the fifth chapel on the left, note the three paintings★★★ by Caravaggio depicting scenes from the life of St Matthew: his Calling, Martyrdom and the angel dictating the Gospel. The artist's violent yet refined realism captures through his personal and unusual use of chiaroscuro, the religious drama of the moment.

★★ PIAZZA NAVONA (BX)

The square built on the site of Domitian's stadium, retains its shape. A pleasant and lively pedestrian precinct, it is adorned at the centre with the baroque masterpiece Bernini's Fountain of the Four Rivers★★★ completed in 1651. The statues represent the four rivers symbolising the four corners of the earth.
Among the churches and palaces lining the square, note Sant' Agnese in Agone (BX N) with a baroque façade by Borromini (attractive interior★ on the plan of a Greek cross) and the adjoining 17C Palazzo Pamphili.

THIRD DAY *(morning)*

★★★ BASILICA OF ST JOHN LATERAN (SAN GIOVANNI IN LATERANO - DY)

St John Lateran, the cathedral of Rome, is among the four major basilicas in Rome. The first basilica was founded by Constantine prior to St Peter in the Vatican. It was rebuilt in the baroque era by Borromini and again in the 18C.
The main façade by Alessandro Galilei dates from the 18C and the central door has bronze panels that originally belonged to the Curia of the Roman Forum (modified in the 17C). The vast and grandiose interior has a 16C ceiling★★ which was restored in the 18C. In the nave the Statues of the Apostles★ by pupils of Bernini stand in niches built by Borromini. The elegant Corsini Chapel★ *(first in the north aisle)* was designed by Alessandro Galilei. The transept ceiling★★ dates from the end of the 16C. The Chapel of the Blessed Sacrament *(north transept)* has fine ancient columns★ in gilded bronze. The pretty cloisters★ are the work of the Vassalletto (13C), marble-masons who were associates of the Cosmati *(qv)*. The baptistry★ (DY R) built in the 4C, is decorated with beautiful 5 and 7C mosaics.
In Piazza di San Giovanni in Laterano rises a 15C BC Egyptian obelisk, the tallest in Rome. The Lateran Palace (DY A) rebuilt in 1586 was the papal palace until the papal court returned from Avignon. The staircase, Scala Sancta, (DY B) is a precious vestige from the medieval papal palace and is traditionally identified as the one Christ used in the palace of Pontuis Pilate. Worshippers climb the stairs on their knees. At the top is the papal chapel (Sancta Sanctorum) with its many precious relics.

★★ CARACALLA'S BATHS (TERME DI CARACALLA - CZ)

🕐 These baths built by Caracalla in AD 212 extend over more than 11 hectares – 27 acres and could take 1 600 bathers at a time.
The ruined caldarium for the very hot bath, a circular room with a 34m – 112ft diameter, is the setting for operatic performances in summer.

★★ THE CATACOMBS

Leave Rome by Via di Porta S. Sebastiano (DZ). Plan of the built-up area in the current Michelin Red Guide Italia.

There are numerous underground Christian cemeteries alongside the Via Appia Antica. In use from the 2C they were rediscovered in the 16 and 19C. They consist of long galleries radiating from an underground burial chamber *(hypogeum)* which belonged to a noble Roman family of the Christian faith. They permitted fellow Christians to use the galleries.
The decorations of the catacombs (carvings or paintings of symbolic motifs) are precious examples of early Christian art.
The visitor with little time to spare should visit the following ones:
⊙ **St Callistus' Catacombs**★★★ near the Appian Way famous for its exceptional collection of paintings.
⊙ **St Sebastian's Catacombs**★★★ near the Appian Way.
⊙ **Domitilla's Catacombs**★★★ *entrance at no 282 Via delle Sette Chiese.*
⊙ The **Via Appia Antica**★★★ (Old Appian Way) was laid out in 312 BC to link Rome with Brindisi and was also lined with tombs. The **Tomb of Cecilia Metella**★ is an example of a 1C BC patrician tomb.

★★ BASILICA OF ST PAUL WITHOUT THE WALLS (SAN PAOLO FUORI LE MURA)

Leave by Via Ostiense (BZ). Plan of the built-up area in the current Michelin Red Guide Italia.

One of the four major basilicas. It was built by Constantine in the 4C on the site of St Paul's tomb. It was rebuilt in the 19C, after it had been wholly destroyed by fire in 1823, on the original basilical plan of early Christian churches.
The impressive **interior**★★★ contains: an 11C bronze door cast in Constantinople *(at the entrance of the first south aisle);* and a Gothic **ciborium**★★ (1285) by Arnolfo di Cambio placed on the high altar which stands above a marble plaque inscribed with the name Paul and dated 4C. In the **Chapel of the Blessed Sacrament**★ *(on the left of the chancel)*, note a 14C wooden figure of Christ attributed to Pietro Cavallini, a statue of St Brigitta kneeling by Stefano Maderno (17C), a 14 or 15C statue of St Paul; and the **paschal candelabrum**★★, a 12C Romanesque work of art by the Vassalletto.
The **cloisters**★ are also attributed, at least in part, to this same family of artists.

THIRD DAY *(afternoon)*

★★ BASILICA OF ST MARY MAJOR (SANTA MARIA MAGGIORE - DX)

One of the four major basilicas in Rome built by Sixtus III (AD 432-440) it has an 18C façade and a 14C campanile.
The impressive **interior**★★★ contains remarkable **mosaics**★★★: in the nave, those above the entablature are among the most ancient Christian mosaics in Rome (5C) and depict scenes from the Old Testament; on the 5C triumphal arch are scenes from the New Testament; in the apse, the mosaics are composed of 5C elements but were completely redone in the 13C.
The coffered **ceiling**★ is said to have been gilded with the first gold brought from Peru.

Leave the church by the door at the far end of the south aisle.

From **Piazza dell' Esquilino**, with its Egyptian obelisk, there is a **view**★★ of the imposing 17C chevet.

★★ TREVI FOUNTAIN (FONTANA DI TREVI - CX)

This late baroque creation was commissioned by Clement XIII from Nicola Salvi in 1762. The fountain fills the whole width of the palace façade which acts as backdrop and gives the impression of a triumphal arch. The central figure, the Ocean, rides in a chariot drawn by two sea horses and two tritons.
Tourists continue to play their traditional role by throwing two coins over their shoulders into the fountain — one coin to return to Rome and the other for the fulfilment of a wish.

★★ PIAZZA DI SPAGNA (CX)

This square, a popular tourist attraction, was so named in the 17C after the Spanish Embassy occupied the Palazzo di Spagna. It is dominated by the majestic **Spanish Steps**★★ (Scalla della Trinità dei Monti) built in the 18C by the architects de Sanctis and Specchi who adopted the baroque style of perspective and *trompe-l'œil.* At the foot of the stairway is the Boat Fountain (Fontana della Barcaccia) by Bernini's father, Pietro (17C) and Keats' House where the poet died in 1821. At the top of the stairs, **Holy Trinity on the Hill**★ (Trinità dei Monti) (CX X) is the French church built in the 16C and restored in the 19C. It contains a **Deposition from the Cross**★ *(2nd chapel on the left)* dating from 1541 by Daniele da Volterra, a great admirer of Michelangelo.
Leading off from this square is **Via dei Condotti** (BCX 23) lined with elegant shops. It was also renowned for the Caffè Greco, a famous establishment which was opened in 1760 and frequented by the famous (Goethe, Berlioz, Wagner, Stendhal, etc.).

★ PIAZZA DEL POPOLO (BV)

This square was designed by Giuseppe Valadier (1762-1839). The central obelisk was brought from Egypt in the reign of Augustus and set up here in the 16C on the orders of Sixtus V. The **Porta del Popolo**★ was pierced in the Aurelian wall in the 3C, and adorned with an external façade in the 16C and an inner façade designed by Bernini in the 17C.

The Renaissance **Church of Santa Maria del Popolo**★★ (N) was remodelled in the baroque period. It contains 15C **frescoes**★ by Pinturicchio *(first chapel on the right)*; two **tombs**★ by Andrea Sansovino *(in the chancel)*; two **paintings**★★★ by Caravaggio: the Crucifixion of St Peter and the Conversion of St Paul *(first chapel to the left of the chancel)*; and the **Chigi Chapel**★ *(2nd on the left)* designed by Raphael.

Leading off the Piazza del Popolo is the main street of central Rome, **Via del Corso**★★ (BCX) lined by handsome Renaissance palaces and fashionable shops.

THE PINCIO (BV)

This fine public park was laid out in the 19C by Giuseppe Valadier. It affords a magnificent **view**★★★ particularly at dusk when the golden glow so typical of Rome is at its mellow best.

Viale della Trinità dei Monti (BCVX) leads southwards and is overlooked by the Villa Medici (CX) now the home of the French Academy.

ADDITIONAL SIGHTS

Churches

★ **Chiesa Nuova** (BX Q). – This church dates from the Counter-Reformation. Alongside is the building originally built to house the assemblies of the Congregation of the Oratory, with an elegant **façade**★ by Borromini.

★★ **Sant'Andrea al Quirinale** (CX L). – This masterpiece **by Bernini** with its elliptical **interior**★★ demonstrates his sure taste in the use of coloured marbles, gilding and stucco figures to create a rich and beautiful decor.

★ **St Augustine's Church** (BX E)). – The church contains Jacopo Sansovino's **Madonna del Parto**★, Raphael's fresco of the **Prophet Isaiah**★ and Caravaggio's **Madonna of the Pilgrims**★★★.

★★ **San Carlo alle Quattro Fontane** (CX K). – **Borromini's** masterpiece with a façade which reveals the torment of the architect and an **interior**★★ on an elliptical plan.

★★ **San Clemente** (DY). – There are in fact two basilicas. Upper one: 12C **mosaics**★★★ in the apse and **frescoes**★ by Masolino.

★ **Sant'Ignazio** (BX G). – The façade and central ceiling **frescoes**★★ are by the Jesuit Andrea Pozzo.

★ **Basilica of St Lawrence without the Walls** (San Lorenzo Fuori Le Mura). – *Take Via dei Ramni* (DX 53). *Town plan in the current Michelin Red Guide Italia.*
Basically 13C: 5-6C **harvest sarcophagus**, 13C **ambos**★ and a 13C **papal throne**★.

★ **St Peter in Chains** (San Pietro in Vincoli) (CY G). – Julius II's mausoleum and **Moses**★★★ by Michelangelo.

★ **St Agnes without the Walls** (Sant'Agnese fuori le Mura). – *Take Via Nomentana* (DV). *Town plan in the current Michelin Red Guide Italia.*
Mosaic★ in the apse. **The Church of St Constance**★ originally a 4C mausoleum has a fine **mosaic**★.

★ **St Cecilia in Trastevere** (Santa Cecilia in Trastevere) (BY). – Much altered 9C building ○ St Cecilia's Statue★ (1599) by Stefano Maderno and a **Last Judgment**★★★ *(c*1293) by Pietro Cavallini.

★★ **Santa Maria degli Angeli** (DX E). – This prestigious church was built amidst the ruins of Diocletian's baths. The **transept**★ gives a good idea of the solemn magnitude of the ancient building.

★★ **Santa Maria della Vittoria** (CX E). – This is Carlo Maderna's masterpiece. The sumptuous **interior**★★★ provides the setting for Bernini's **Estasy of St Theresa of Avila**★★★ (1652).

★★ **Santa Sabina** (BY F). – This 5C building is one of Rome's oldest basilicas. Beautiful cypress wood **door**★★. The **interior**★★ is well proportioned and full of light.

★★ **Santa Suzanna** (CX F). – 9-16C church with a beautiful **façade**★★★ by **Carlo Maderna**.

Sts Cosmas and Damian (SS Cosma e Damiano) (CY E). – 5C church with a beautiful 16C coffered **ceiling**★ and 6 and 7C **mosaics**★.

★ **San Pietro in Montorio** (BY D) – This 15C church has Sebastiano del Piombo's **Flagellation**★ and Bramante's **Tempietto**★ in the courtyard. **View**★★★ of Rome from the esplanade.

★ **Sant' Andrea della Valle** (BY C). – This early 17C church has a **façade**★★ by Rainaldo (17C) and a lovely **dome**★★ by Carlo Maderna, painted by Lanfranco. Domenichino decorated the **apse**★.

Santa Maria dell' Anima (BX Y). – One of Rome's rare Gothic interiors.

★ **Santa Maria della Pace** (BX X). – The four **Sybils**★ by Raphael were inspired by ○ Michelangelo's angels in the Sistine Chapel.

★ **Santa Maria in Cosmedin** (CY W). – Elegant 12C **campanile**★. In the porch is the **Bocca della Verità** (Mouth of Truth).

★ **Santa Maria in Trastevere** (BY Z). – 12C basilica with 12-13C **mosaics**★★ in the chancel.

★ **Santa Maria Sopra Minerva** (BX A). – The church has numerous works of art: **frescoes**★ by Filippino Lippi and both Gothic and baroque **tombs**★.

Monuments from antiquity

Arch of Janus (Arco di Giano) **(CY S)**. – Through this public gateway passed some of Rome's busiest roads.

★★ **Area Sacra del Largo Argentina (BY)**. – These ruins of four temples date from the days of the ancient Roman Republic.

★★ **Augustus' Altar of Peace** (Ara Pacis Augustae) **(BX V)**. – The altar is the major work ⊙ of the Augustan 'golden age' and is decorated with magnificent **low-relief** carvings.

Circus Maximus (Circo Massimo) **(CY)**. – This was the largest circus in Rome and was used exclusively for chariot races.

Augustus' Mausoleum (BX B). – The mausoleum takes the form of an Etruscan tumulus tomb.

★ **Caius Cestius' Pyramid (CZ A)**. – Rome's most original mausoleum was erected in the 12C BC by a simple citizen.

★★ **Temple of Apollo (BY V)**. – The temple was dedicated to Apollo medicus and retains three elegant fluted **columns**★★.

★ **Temple of Fortuna Virilis (CY Y)**. – This rectangular and austere temple dates from the late 2C BC.

★ **Temple of Vesta (CY X)**. – Elegant circular construction dating from the Augustan period.

★★ **Theatre of Marcellus (BY T¹)**. – One of Rome's largest theatres it was inaugurated by Augustus in the 11C BC.

Museums and palaces

★ **National Gallery of Modern Art (CV M¹²)**. – Italian painting and sculpture from ⊙ the 19C to the present day.

★★★ **Borghese Gallery** (Museo Borghese) **(CV M⁹)**. – Sculptures by Canova and Bernini and ⊙ paintings by Raphael, Correggio, Titian and Caravaggio.

★★★ **National Roman Museum (DX M⁷)**. – Greek and Roman antiquities: paintings from ⊙ various Roman villas.

★★★ **Villa Giulia National Museum (BV M¹⁰)**. – Exceptional collection of antiquities ⊙ bearing light on the Etruscan Civilisation. The setting is Julius III's elegant country villa.

★★ **Palazzo della Cancelleria (BXY S)**. – Elegant palace built between 1483 and 1513 with a harmonious inner courtyard.

★★ **Quirinal Palace** (Palazzo del Quirinale) **(BXY S)**. – This handsome 16C palace was de- ⊙ signed as a summer residence for the popes and is now the official residence of the President of the Republic.

★★ **Barberini Palace (CX M⁸)**. – This baroque palace now houses a remarkable **Picture** ⊙ **Gallery**★★ (Fra Angelico, Raphael, Titian, Holbein, Pietra da Cortona, etc.).

★ **Palazzo Braschi (BX M⁴)**. – Late 18C papal family palace now housing the **Rome** ⊙ **Museum**★ covering Rome from the Middle Ages.

Palazzo Chigi (BX C). – This 16C palace now belongs to the Presidency of the Council of Ministers.

Palazzo della Consulta (CX Q). – This palace with its **façade**★ by Ferdinando Fuga (18C) is now the seat of the Constitutional Court.

★ **Palazzo Doria Pamphili (CX M³)**. – Handsome 16C palace with a **collection**★ of ⊙ paintings by Caravaggio, Velasquez, the Carrachi, etc.

Palazzo Madama (BX R). – 16C palace now the seat of the Senate.

Palazzo di Montecitorio (BX). – This 17C palace houses the Chamber of Deputies.

⊙ **Palazzo della Sapienza (BX K)**. – 16C palace with Borromini's masterpiece, **St Ivo's Church**★ in the inner courtyard with its bell tower.

★ **Palazzo Spada (BY M⁵)**. – The **Spada Gallery**★ presents in its original setting the pri- ⊙ vate collection of the 17C churchman, Cardinal Spada.

★★ **Villa Farnesina (ABY)**. – This villa was built from 1508 to 1511 for Agostino Chigi ⊙ who commissioned Raphael and his pupils to decorate the interior.

Squares, streets, sites, parks and gardens

★ **Piazza Bocca della Verità (CY 15)**. – A combination of ancient (Arch of Janus, Temple of Fortuna Virilis and Temple of Vesta, *p 167*), medieval (Santa Maria in Cosmedin, *p 174*) and baroque buildings, makes a typical Roman scene.

★ **Piazza Campo dei Fiori (BY)**. – This well-known square and one of the most popular in Rome is the site of a picturesque food market every morning.

★ **Piazza Colonna (BX)**. – At the centre of this busy square stands the 2C **column**★ in honour of Marcus Aurelius.

★★ **Quirinal Square** (Piazza del Quirinale) (**CX**). – This elegant and gently sloping square is adorned with a fountain, an obelisk, statues of the Dioscuri and overlooked by the Quirinal Palace and Palazzo della Consulta *(p 175)*.

★ **Piazza Sant' Ignazio** (**BX 58**). – This charming square was designed in imitation of a theatre set.

★ **St Paul's Gate** (Porta San Paolo) (**CZ**). – This gate opens onto Via Ostiense which led to St Paul's Basilica, from which the gate took its present name.

★ **St Sebastian's Gate** (Porta San Sebastiano) (**DZ**). – This is without doubt Rome's most spectacular gate (3C).

★ **Via dei Coronari** (**BX 25**). – This attractive street known for its second-hand and antique shops is lined with palaces glowing in ochre and stone.

★★ **EUR.** – *Take Via Cristoforo Colombo* (**DZ**). *Town plan in the current Michelin Red Guide Italia.*
Ⓥ This new district to the south of Rome with its colossal modern architecture is the site of the **Museum of Roman Civilisation** ★★.

★ **Tiber Island** (Isola Tiberina) (**BY**). – This peaceful spot is linked to the bank by the **Fabrician Bridge** (Ponte Fabricius) (**BY 31**), the only Roman bridge to survive intact.

Janiculum (Gianicolo) (**AY**). – This attractive promenade affords extensive **views** ★★★ over the city.

★★★ **Vatican Gardens** (**AV**). – The gardens provide a good view of the dome of St Peter's which rises majestically above the gardens.

★★ **Villa Borghese** (**CV**). – This is Rome's largest public park.

*To find a hotel, restaurant,
garage or car dealer
look in the current Michelin Guide Italia.*

★ **SABBIONETA** Lombardy   Pop 4 666

Michelin map 988 fold 14 – 33km – 21 miles to the southwest of Mantua

Ⓥ This little town, clustering within its walls, was built on a regular plan and is a curious example of 16C **town planning** ★. Vespasiano (1531-91), the youngest of the Gonzaga family, held a refined court which earned Sabbioneta the nickname of Little Athens.
The **Ducal Palace,** which contains interesting equestrian statues of the Gonzaga family, has finely carved wooden and coffered ceilings.
The **Olympic Theatre** ★ was the masterpiece of Vicentino Scamozzi (1552-1616) and is one of the oldest in Europe. It has a ducal box adorned with colonnades, statues of the gods and frescoes by the school of Veronese.
The **Palazzo del Giardino** (Garden Palace) was designed for festivities. The great **Gallery of Antiquities** ★ was entirely painted with frescoes by Bernardino Campi and his school. Vespasiano Gonzaga is buried in the **Church of the Incoronata** ★ with its octagonal plan and surprising *trompe-l'œil* decoration. Vespasiano's remarkable **mausoleum** ★ was by Leone Leoni.

★★★ **SACRA DI SAN MICHELE** Piedmont

Michelin map 988 fold 12 – 37km – 23 miles to the west of Turin

Ⓥ Perched on a rocky site (alt 962m – 3 156ft), this **Benedictine Abbey** was a powerful establishment in the 13C with over 100 monks and 140 sister houses. It was built at the end of the 10C by Hugues de Montboissier from Auvergne and its layout has a strong resemblance with that of the Mont St Michel in Normandy. After passing through the iron doors of the entrance gatehouse you climb the great staircase leading to the **Zodiac Door,** whose pilasters and capitals were decorated by the famous Master Nicolò (1135). The Romanesque-Gothic **church** built on top of the rocky eminence, has 16C frescoes. The early 16C triptych on the high altar is by Defendente Ferrari. The carved capitals are outstanding. From the esplanade there is a lovely **view** ★★★ of the Alps, the Dora Valley, the Po and Turin plains.

★ **SALERNO** Campania   Pop 155 755

Michelin map 988 fold 28 – Local map p 41 – Plan of the built-up area in the current Michelin Red Guide Italia

Lying along the graceful curve of its gulf, Salerno has retained a medieval quarter on the slopes of a hill crowned by a castle. The town is now an active port and industrial centre while market gardening is the main activity of the surrounding area.
Salerno was at first Etruscan, then Roman and became a principality under the Lombards. The Norman Robert Guiscard made it his capital in 1077. A rich trading city, Salerno became famous for its university which attracted some of the greatest scholars of the time and in particular its school of medicine which flourished from the 11 to 13C. The town acquired the nickname of City of Socrates. With the arrival of the Kings of Anjou Salerno declined and witnessed the rise of its neighbour and rival, Naples. It was just south of Salerno that the 5th US Army landed on 9 September 1943.

SALERNO

★★ **Cathedral (Duomo)** (B). – The cathedral is dedicated to St Matthew the Evangelist, who is buried in the crypt. It was built on the orders of Robert Guiscard and consecrated by Pope Gregory VII in 1085. In the Norman style it was remodelled in the 18C and suffered considerable damage in the 1980 earthquake. The church is preceded by a delightful arcaded **atruim** built of multicoloured stone with ancient columns. The square tower to the right is 12C. The central doorway has 11C bronze doors cast in Constantinople.

The interior is of impressive dimensions. The two **ambos**★★ encrusted with decorative mosaics and resting on slender columns with marvellously carved capitals, along with the **paschal candelabrum,** form an outstanding 12-13C group. The Crusaders' Chapel at the far end of the south aisle is where the Crusaders had their arms blessed. Under the altar is the tomb of Pope Gregory VII who died in exile at Salerno (1085).

In the north aisle is the tomb of Margaret of Durazzo, the wife of Charles III of Anjou.

★ **Via Mercanti** (AB). – This street is one of the most picturesque with its shops, old houses and oratories. At its west end stands the **Arechi Arch (A A)** built by the Lombards in the 8C.

★ **Lungomare Trieste** (AB). – From this promenade, planted with palm trees and tamarisks, there is a wide view of the Gulf of Salerno.

★★ # SAN CLEMENTE A CASAURIA Abbey Abruzzi

Michelin map 🗺 fold 27 – 40km – 25 miles southwest of Pescara – Access: by the A25 motorway and the Torre de' Passeri exit road

The San Clemente Abbey was founded in 871 and rebuilt in the 12C by the Cistercians in the transitional Romanesque-Gothic style. The secularized church is all that remains today.

Church. – The façade is quite remarkable: a deep portico has three arches resting on lovely capitals; the main doorway is decorated with exceptional sculpture, notably on the uprights, tympanum and lintel (the bronze door was cast in 1191). The interior comprises a nave and two aisles and a semicircular apse and is typical of the architectural simplicity dear to St Bernard. Both the monumental pulpit and the paschal candelabrum are 13C. The high altar is surmounted by a finely carved Romanesque **ciborium**★★★. The 9C crypt has survived from the original structure and has vaulting supported by ancient columns.

Make up your own itineraries

– The map on pages 4 to 11 gives a general view of tourist regions, the main towns, individual sights and recommended routes in the guide.

– The above are described under their own name in alphabetical order or are incorporated in the excursions radiating from a nearby town or tourist centre.

– In addition the **Michelin Map** *no 🗺 shows scenic routes, places of interest, viewpoints, rivers, forests...*

Michelin map 988 fold 14 – Town plan in the current Michelin Red Guide Italia

San Gimignano with its many medieval towers stands on a hilltop in the rolling Tuscan countryside where vineyards and olive groves predominate. Its numerous towers of nobility have earned it the nickname of San Gimignano of the Fine Towers.

In the 12C the town was an independent commune and it prospered for the following two centuries although it did not escape the internecine fighting between the Ghibellines and Guelphs. The towers of nobility built by local noble families date from this troubled period. A network of gangways (the holes used to fix these can still be seen in the walls) was used when various families wanted to meet in times of danger.

★★ **Piazza della Cisterna.** – The square is paved with bricks laid on their edges in a herring-bone pattern and it derives its name from a 13C cistern or well *(cisterna)*. It is one of the most evocative squares in Italy with its tall towers and austere 13-14C mansions all around.

★★ **Piazza del Duomo.** – The Collegiate Church, palaces and seven towers of nobility line this majestic square.

★ **Collegiate Church** (Collegiata). – This 12C Romanesque Church was extended in the 15C by Giuliano da Maiano. The façade was restored in the 19C. Inside is a **Martyrdom of St Sebastian** (1465) by Benozzo Gozzoli and an Annunciation in wood by Jacopo della Quercia *(on the west wall)*. The walls of the north aisle are adorned by **frescoes**★ evoking scenes from the Old Testament by Bartolo di Fredi (14C) while the **frescoes**★★ (c1350) of the south aisle are by Barna da Siena and depict scenes from the Life of Christ (start at the top). They display an elegant draughtsmanship and delicate colours. In the **Chapel of Santa Fina**, designed by Giuliano da Maiano, the harmonious **altar**★ is by his nephew Benedetto da Maiano and the **frescoes**★ (1475) by Domenico Ghirlandaio.

★ **People's Palace** (Palazzo del Popolo). – The 13-14C palace is dominated by a tall **tower** from the top of which you can enjoy an unusual **view**★★ over the brown roofs and towers of the town. The Council Chamber has a remarkable **Maesta**★ (Madonna and Child enthroned in Majesty) (1317) by Lippo Memmi which was restored c1467 by Benozzo Gozzoli. The **Municipal Museum**★ (Museo Civico) on the second floor regroups paintings from the 12 to 15C Florentine and Sienese schools.

Governor's Palace (Palazzo del Podestà). – This 13C palace has a vast porch on the ground floor. It also comprises the impressive Rognosa Tower. Close by stands the 13C Palazzo Chigi.

Church of St Augustine (Sant' Agostino). – This 13C church has in its chancel a cycle of seventeen **frescoes**★★ painted between 1463 and 1467 by Benozzo Gozzoli. The life of the famous theologian St Augustine is depicted with the fresh colour, sense of perspective and love of detail so typical of this artist.

★★★ **SAN MARINO, Republic of**　　　　　　　　　Pop 22 418

Michelin map 988 fold 15 – Town plan in the current Michelin Red Guide Italia

One of the smallest states in the world (61km² – 23sq miles) stands in an admirable **site**★★★ on the slopes of the jagged sandstone ridge of Monte Titano. This ancient republic strikes its own coinage, issues its own postal stamps, has its own army and police force.

San Marino is believed to have been founded in the 4C by a pious mason, Marinus, who was fleeing from the persecutions of the Emperor Diocletian. The system of government has changed little in nine centuries, and the leading figures are still the two Captains Regent, who are chosen from among the sixty members of the Grand Council and installed every six months, during a colourful ceremony *(see the table of Principal Festivals at the end of the guide)*. The economy is based on tourism, trade, the sale of postage stamps, craft industries and agriculture. When in San Marino taste the very pleasant wine Moscato.

SIGHTS

Government House (Palazzo del Governo). – *Piazza della Libertà.*
This was rebuilt in the Gothic style in the late 19C. Visit the Great Council Chamber.

Basilica of St Marinus (Basilica di San Marino). – *Piazzale Domus Plebis.*
The basilica contains the relics of the saint.
In the nearby Church of St Peter (San Pietro) there are two niches hewn in the rock which are said to have been used as beds by St Marinus and his companion St Leo.

Rocca Guaita; Rocca della Fratta; Rocca Montale. – These three peaks are crowned with three towers *(torri)* which are linked by a watchpath. From the towers there are splendid **views**★★★ of the Apennines, the plain, Rimini and the sea as far as the Dalmatian coast. In one of the towers there is an **arms museum** with a mainly medieval collection. It also features gunpowder firearms, as well as guns and rifles dating from the 16, 17 and 18C.

Museum-Picture Gallery (Museo-Pinacoteca). – This includes paintings (Strozzi, Ribera, Guerchino and Domenichino), Egyptian and Etruscan items and Roman coins and statuettes, etc.

St Francis' Museum (Museo di San Francesco). – 12 to 17C and modern paintings and Etruscan potteries and funerary objects.

Coin and Stamp Museum (Museo Filatelico et Numismatico). – *Same location as above.*
Collection of stamps and coins issued by the Republic since the mid-19C.

EXCURSION

★★ **San Leo.** – *16km – 10 miles to the southwest. Leave to the north then take the road to the left leading down to the Marecchia Valley. Just before Pietracuta and the S 258 bear left.*

A steep winding road climbs to the summit of the huge limestone rock (alt 639m – 2 096ft) in an impressive **setting**★★ made famous by Dante in his *Divine Comedy,* with the historic village of San Leo and its 15C **fortress**★ (Forte) perched on the edge of the cliff where the charlatan Count Cagliostro (18C) was imprisoned and died. It now houses a **museum and picture gallery** (arms, furniture and 15 to 18C paintings).

From the fortress there is an immense **panorama**★★★ of the Marecchia Valley, Montefeltro and San Marino.

The cathedral which is in the Lombard-Romanesque style (1173) and the pre-Romanesque parish church (restored) are noteworthy.

★★ SAN REMO Liguria   Pop 61 265

Michelin map 988 fold 12 or 195 fold 20 – Local map p 163 – Town plan in the current Michelin Red Guide Italia

San Remo curves round its wide bay protected by two headlands, and is backed by a rim of mountains. The luxurious capital of the Riviera di Ponente, enjoys a pleasantly warm temperature all the year round and the highest number of sunshine hours on the Ligurian coast. In addition to these advantages San Remo boasts a wide choice of hotels, thermal establishments, a pleasure boat harbour, casino, racecourse, lively festivals and other cultural and sporting events.

San Remo is the principal Italian flower market and millions of roses, carnations and mimosa are exported worldwide. The flower market takes place from October to June between 6am and 8am.

Corso Imperatrice. – It is Liguria's most elegant seafront promenade and it is particularly known for its Canary palms.

★ **La Pigna.** – This is the name given to the old town, because of its pointed shape (*pigna* meaning beak). It has a medieval aspect with its winding alleys lined by tall and narrow houses. From Piazza Castello climb up to the baroque Church of Madonna della Costa, from where there is an attractive **view**★ of the town and bay.

★ **Monte Bignone.** – Alt 1 299m – 4 262ft. *13km – 8 miles to the north.*
From the summit of this pine-covered peak there is a splendid **panorama**★★ which extends as far as Cannes in France.

★ SANSEPOLCRO Tuscany   Pop 15 727

Michelin map 988 fold 15

The small industrial town (manufacture of macaroni) has retained its ramparts and some old houses. It was in this town that the most important artist of the Italian Quattrocento (15C), **Piero della Francesca** (*qv*) was born.

See the table of Principal Festivals at the end of the guide.

Municipal Museum (Museo Civico). – *65 Via Aggiunti.*
This museum occupies twelve rooms of the former town hall. It contains several leading **works**★★ by Piero della Francesca: an impressive Ressurrection showing his mature genius, a very lovely polyptych of the Virgin of Pity, a St Julian and a St Ludovic. You will also see works by his pupil Luca Signorelli, by Pontormo, Bassano, Palma the Younger, Andrea and Giovanni della Robbia and other artists, all native of Sansepolcro (Raffaelino dal Colle, Santi di Tito, Giovanni Alberti...). In addition there are 14C fragments of frescoes, sinopie (*qv*), engravings, reliquaries, etc.

EXCURSIONS

★ **Camaldoli.** – *76km – 47 miles to the northwest.*
Camaldoli, in the heart of the mountains and a great forest, was the cradle of the Camaldulian Order, founded in the 11C by St Romuald. The monastery, standing at the head of a dismal valley, was rebuilt in the 13C. Higher up in a grim, isolated site is the **Hermitage**★ (Eremo), a cluster of buildings encircled by ramparts. These include St Romuald's cell and a lovely 18C church.

★ **La Verna Monastery (Convento della Verna).** – *36km – 22 miles to the northwest.*
The monastery was founded in 1214 by St Francis of Assisi, who received the stigmata there. The visitor can see the Chapel of Santa Maria degli Angeli, the Chapel of the Stigmata, St Francis' sleeping place and the enormous projecting rock under which he used to pray. The basilica has terracottas by Andrea della Robbia.

★ **Poppi.** – *61km – 38 miles to the northwest.*
This proud and attractive city, formely the capital of the Casentino, overlooks the Arno Valley. The city itself is crowned by its proud looking **castle,** former seat of the Counts of Guidi. This Gothic palace has a curious **courtyard**★ decorated with coats of arms.

Monterchi. – *17km – 11 miles to the south.*
The cemetery chapel has a strange but compelling work by Piero della Francesca, the **Madonna with Child**★ (Madonna del Parto), which has been detached and placed above the altar. This is a rare example of the pregnant Virgin in Italian art.

Siena "the Beloved" is a mystical, gentle, passionate and generous art centre. Siena invites the visitor to stroll through its narrow Gothic streets, lined with palaces and patrician mansions, which converge on the famous Piazzo del Campo. It is encircled by ramparts which seem too big for it.

More than anywhere else Siena brings to life the reality of a medieval city. Its plan extends over three converging red clay hills (from which the colour burnt sienna is named) at the very heart of the high Tuscan plateau.

HISTORICAL NOTES

Its greatest period of prosperity was the 13 and 14C when it was an independent republic with a well organised administration of its own. Siena flourished essentially on trade and banking.

During the period of strife between Guelphs and Ghibellines (qv) Siena was opposed to its powerful neighbour Florence. One of the most memorable episodes of this long struggle was the Battle of Montaperti (1260) when the Sienese Ghibellines resoundingly defeated the Florentine Guelphs. It was during this troubled time that Siena acquired her most prestigious buildings and that a local school of painting evolved which played a notable part in the development of Italian art.

In 1348 the plague decimated Siena's population and the city began to decline as dissension continued to reign among the rival factions. By the early 15C Siena's golden era was over.

The mystical city of Siena was the birthplace in 1347 of **St Catherine**. By the age of 7 she had decided on her mystic marriage with Christ. She entered the Dominican Order aged sixteen and had many visions and trances and received the Stigmata at Pisa. In 1377 she helped to bring the popes back from Avignon to Rome, which they had left in 1309. **St Bernardine** (1380-1444) is also greatly venerated in Siena. He gave up his studies in order to help the victims of the plague in Siena. Aged 22 he entered the Franciscan order and was a leader of the Observants who favoured a stricter observance of the rule of St Francis. A great preacher he spent much of his time travelling throughout Italy.

SIENESE ART

It was not only in political matters that Siena opposed Florence. In the city of Dante, Cimabue and Giotto innovated, but were greatly influenced by the Roman traditions of balance and realism which led to the development of Renaissance art in all its glory. Siena, on the other hand, remained attached to the Greek or Byzantine traditions, in which the graceful line and the refinement of colour gave a certain dazzling elegance to the composition, which was one of the chief attractions of Gothic painting.

Duccio di Buoninsegna (c1260-1318) was the first to experiment with this new combination of inner spirituality and increased attention to space and composition as well as the splendour of the coulours.

Simone Martini (c1285-d 1344 in Avignon) followed in Duccio's footsteps but imitated nature more closely with his exquisite harmonies of colour and taste for detail. He had a considerable reputation in Europe and worked at the Papal Court in Avignon.

His contemporaries **Pietro** and **Ambrogio Lorenzetti** introduced an even greater realism with minute delicate details, while at the same time remaining true to the sense of line of their predecessors. One of the favourite themes of the Sienese school was the Virgin and Child.

The Sienese artists of the Quattrocento (15C) continued in the spirit of the Gothic masters. While Florence concentrated on rediscovering antiquity and its myths, minor masters such as **Lorenzo Monaco, Giovanni di Paolo** and **Sassetta** continued to emphasise affectation in figure design, flexibility of line and subtlety of colour which made Siena an ideal refuge for Gothic sensibilities.

In the domain of secular architecture, the Gothic style gave Siena its own special character with the use of elements which made for a more graceful aspect. Brick and stone were often associated on the lower storeys while windows became more numerous especially the Sienese one with a depressed three centred arch supporting a pointed one.

Building activity concentrated on the cathedral where construction work and transformations lasted over two centuries. There again the façade is in a unique Gothic style where one can detect the transition from the Romanesque to the Flamboyant Gothic in an interpretation full of affectation.

Sculpture, also influenced by the building of the cathedral, was enriched by the presence of two Pisans, Nicola and Giovanni Pisano (qv). The latter decorated the cathedral façade with a series of highly expressive figures and his work influenced **Tino di Camaino**, born in Siena in 1280 but who spent the last years of his life at the Angevin Court in Naples. However the important name in Sienese sculpture is **Jacopo della Quercia** (1371-1438) who successfully combined Gothic traditions with the Florentine Renaissance manner.

★★★ PIAZZA DEL CAMPO (BZ) time: 1 1/4 hours

This "square" forms a monumental ensemble of almost matchless harmony. It is shaped like a scallop or a fan and is paved with brick and encircled by a ring of stone slabs. The "square" slopes down to the long brick and stone façade of the Palazzo Pubblico. Eight white lines radiate outwards dividing the area into nine segments, symbolising one of the forms of government which ruled Siena. This consisted of nine members representing trade and banking who ruled the city during its greatest period of prosperity from the late 13C to the mid-14C.

At the upper end is the **Fonte Gaia** (Fountain of Joy) so-called because of the festivities which followed its inauguration in 1348. Fountains were at that time a symbol of the city's power. It was embellished with panels sculpted by Jacopo della Quercia, but these now badly deteriorated have been replaced by replicas.

The Piazzo del Campo is the venue twice annually *(see the table of Principal Festivals at the end of the guide)* of the popular festival **Palio delle Contrade.** The whole town participates in the preparation of this event for weeks beforehand and it recalls the medieval administrative organisation of Siena with its three main quarters, themselves subdivided into parishes *(contrade)*.

The festivities begin with a procession of the *contrade* in costume, who then compete in the dangerous horse race round the square. There is much betting on the outcome. The *palio,* a standard bearing the effigy of the Virgin, the city's protectress, is awarded to the winner.

★★★ **Town Hall (Palazzo Pubblico).** – Built between the late 13C and mid-14C in the Gothic
ⓔ style this building is of a rare elegance with its many triple bays under supporting arches
which give the impression of a curving movement to the façade. High up on the central
part is a circular bronze panel inscribed with the monogram IHS (*Iesus Hominum Salvator* Jesus Men's Saviour) used as a badge by St Bernardine. From one end of the façade rises the slim form of the **Torre del Mangia**, a 88m – 289ft high tower designed by
Lippo Memmi. At the foot of the tower, **Cappella di Piazza** is a chapel in the form of a
loggia dating from 1352, built to mark the end of the plague. It was remodelled in the
Renaissance style a century later.

This palace was the seat of Siena's successive governments and most of the great
artists of the Sienese school contributed to its decoration.

Priors' Room: frescoes (1407) by Spinello Aretino recount the struggles between Pope
Alexander III and the Emperor Frederick Barbarossa.

★ **Chapel:** this contains frescoes by Taddeo di Bartolo portraying the Life of the Virgin, a
very lovely **railing**★ and its magnificent early 15C **stalls**★★ with intarsia work illustrating
the Creed and, on the high altar a Holy Family by Sodoma.

Globe Room: the admirable **Maestà**★★ (1315) is Simone Martini's earliest known work
and opposite is the famous **equestrian portrait**★ of the Sienese general, Guidoriccio da
Fogliano by the same artist. Note the curious contrast between the realism with which
the figure is portrayed and the unreality of the background landscape.

Peace Room: here are the famous frescoes, although badly damaged (1335-40) of
Ambrogio Lorenzetti entitled **Effects of Good and Bad Government**★★ where the artist has
achieved a happy combination of a scholarly and noble allegorical approach with that
of meticulous narrative detail.

ⓔ **Tower:** from the top there is a superb **panorama**★★ of Siena's chaotic rooftops and of
the gently rolling Sienese countryside beyond.

★★★ THE CATHEDRAL AND ITS PRECINCTS *time: 1 1/2 hours*

★★★ **Cathedral (Duomo) (AZ).** – The richly decorated façade *(photograph p 27)* was begun
in the 13C by Giovanni Pisano who added some remarkably expressive statues. The
upper part was modelled on Orvieto Cathedral. The sober Romanesque campanile dates
from 1313.

The walls of the **interior** are faced with alternating bands of black and white marble.
The profusion of pillars provide a multitude of perspectives as one moves
ⓔ about. The 15-16C **paving**★★★ is unique. About forty artists including **Beccafumi** worked
on the 56 marble panels which portray, either in graffiti or intarsia work, mythological
figures such as Sibyls, Virtues and Allegories and scenes from the Old Testament in a
lively and delicate manner.

In the chancel is a 15C bronze tabernacle by Vecchietta and richly decorated 14-16C
stalls★★ At the entrance to the north transept in the famous **pulpit**★★★ carved between 1266 and 1268 by **Nicola Pisano** who relates the Life of Christ in seven panels in
a grandiose and exceptionally dramatic style.

From the north aisle a charming doorway leads to the famous **Piccolomini Library** (Libreria
Piccolomini) built in 1495 by Cardinal Francesco Piccolomini, the future Pius III, to house
his uncle's books. The Umbrian painter **Pinturicchio** adorned it with **frescoes**★★ (1502-9)
depicting episodes in the life of Aeneas Silvius Piccolomini (Pius II). The delicate
draughtsmanship is typical of miniatures while the brilliant colours are more typical of
illuminations. In the centre stands the famous marble statue of the Three Graces,
Roman sculpture (3C) showing Hellenistic influence.

★★ **Cathedral Museum (Museo dell'Opera del Duomo) (ABZ M).** – The museum is in the
ⓔ remains of a huge cathedral, the building of which began in 1339. The present cathedral was to have been its transept. The museum regroups Giovanni Pisano's statues
which originally adorned the cathedral façade, a low-relief by Jacopo della Quercia and
the famous **Maestà** (Virgin in Majesty) by **Duccio**. This altarpiece was originally painted
on both sides (now separated). The panels of the reverse side depict scenes from the
Passion of Christ, with a wealth of intimate details.

★ **Baptistry of St John (Battistero San Giovanni) (AZ V).** – This lies below the cathedral
ⓔ under a prolongation of the chancel, and dates from the 14C. The façade started in the
Gothic style was never completed. The interior is adorned with 15C frescoes. The
font★★ is adorned with panels designed by Jacopo della Quercia. The bronze panels
were by several Tuscan masters such as Lorenzo Ghiberti and Donatello. Admire in
particular the latter's Feast of Herod.

ADDITIONAL SIGHTS

★★ **Picture Gallery (Pinacoteca) (BZ).** – The extensive collection of 13-16C Sienese paint-
ⓔ ings is displayed in the 15C **Palazzo Buonsignori**★.

On the second floor is the rich section of **Primitives**. Beyond the late 12C to early 13C
Crucifixes are the works of a local artist, Guido da Siena and then the better known
Sienese artists, such as Duccio with a youthful work, the **Virgin of the Franciscans** (Room 4).
The flowing line and grace so characteristic of the Sienese school are already visible.
The **Virgin and Child** (Room 6) by Simone Martini is a rare work so full of gentleness and
purity. Room 7 is important for the numerous works by the Lorenzetti brothers including the **Pala del Carmine**, a large altarpiece by the elder, Pietro, in which he displays his
aptitude for portraying narrative details (see the scenes on the predella). The long sin-
uous silhouette of the small **Virgin of Humility** (Room 13) with rose bushes screening of
the meticulously portrayed landscape-background, is an exquisite work by Giovanni di
Paolo.

On the first floor note Pinturicchio's works and a **Birth of the Virgin** by Beccafumi
(Room 31) with its audacious colour tones and **Christ of the Column** by Sodoma.

★ **Via di Città** (BZ), **Via Banchi di Sopra** (BYZ). – These narrow, flagstoned streets bordered with remarkable **palaces**★ bustle with life.

Coming from Via San Pietro you will see in the Via di Città, on the left the 15C **Palazzo Piccolomini** or Palazzo dell Papesse (**A**) with the lower part of its façade rusticated in the Florentine manner. Practically opposite stands the long curving Gothic façade of the **Palazzo Chigi-Saracini** (**B**), now the home of the Academy of Music. Farther along, on the right, the **Loggia dei Mercanti** (**C**) or Merchants Loggia, in the transitional Gothic-Renaissance style with a 17C top storey, is the seat of the Commercial Courts.

Shortly afterwards on the left is the 13C **Palazzo Tolomei** (**D**) an austere but elegant building. Robert of Anjou, King of Naples stayed here in 1310. The **Piazza Salimbeni**★ (**BY**) is enclosed on three sides by buildings with different architectural styles: at the far end the 14C **Palazzo Salimbeni** (**E**) is Gothic; on the left the 15C **Palazzo Spannocchi** (**F**) is Renaissance while the 16C **Palazzo Tantucci** (**G**) on the left is baroque.

Basilica of St Dominic (**San Domenico**) (AYZ). – St Catherine had her trances in this 13-15C Gothic conventual church. Inside there is an authentic portrait of the saint by her contemporary Andrea Vanni.

In the Chapel of St Catherine, half-way down the south aisle, is a lovely Renaissance **tabernacle**★ carved in marble by Giovanni de Stefano which contains the head of the saint. The **frescoes**★ on the walls by Sodoma depict scenes from the life of the saint.

⊘ **Birthplace of St Catherine** (**Casa di Santa Caterina**) (AZ). – *Entrance in Via Santa Caterina.*

The saint's house has been transformed into a series of superimposed oratories. In the basement is the cell where St Catherine lived. Above is the 13C painted crucifix in front of which the saint is said to have received the Stigmata.

Church of St Augustine (**Sant' Agostino**) (BZ). – This 13C church has a baroque interior. There is a remarkable **Adoration of the Crucifix**★ by Perugino and in the Sacramento Chapel **works**★ by Ambrogio Lorenzetti, Matteo di Giovanni and Sodoma.

★★ SORRENTO Campania   Pop 17 648

Michelin map **988** fold 27 – Local map p 40

This important southern Italian resort known for its many beautiful gardens, overlooks the gulf of the same name. Orange and lemon groves are to be found in the surrounding countryside and even encroaching on the town. Local craftsmen produce various marquetry objects. The poet **Torquato Tasso** *(qv)* was born in Sorrento in 1544.

Church of St Francis' (**San Francesco**). – This baroque church with its bulbous belfry masks delightful 13C **cloisters**★. The capitals are carved with water leaf motifs while the interlaced arcades are typical of the Sicilian-Arab style *(p 224)*.

The public gardens, **Villa Comunale,** next door offer a good **viewpoint**★★ for admiring the Bay of Naples.

★ **Correale di Terranova Museum** (**Museo Correale di Terranova**). – Housed in an 18C ⊘ palace the museum has mementoes of the poet Tasso, a small archaeological section and above all a fine collection of 17 and 18C furniture. From the terrace, beyond the orange grove, there is a very fine **view**★★ over the Gulf of Sorrento.

EXCURSION

★★ **Sorrento Peninsula** (**Penisola Sorrentina**). – *Round tour of 33km – 21 miles. See the local map p 40. Leave Sorrento to the west by the S 145 and at the junction take the road to the right to Massa Lubrense.*

This winding road goes round the peninsula and affords fine views of the hillsides covered with olive groves, orange and lemon trees and vines. The latter cling to the trelliswork which supports rush matting in winter to protect the citrus from the cold. From the point of Cape Sorrento (**Capo di Sorrento**) *(footpath: from the church in the village of Capo di Sorrento take the road to the right and after the college the paved path, 1 hour Rtn)* there is a superb **view**★★ of Sorrento.

Beyond **Sant' Agata sui Due Golfi**, perched on a crest overlooking both the Gulf of Salerno and the Bay of Naples, the road descends steeply to Colli di San Pietro. The return to Sorrento by the S 163 offers on the way down some superb **views**★★ over the Bay of Naples.

★ SPOLETO Umbria   Pop 37 871

Michelin map **988** fold 26 – Town plan in the current Michelin Red Guide Italia

This former Roman municipium then became the capital of an important Lombard duchy from the 6 to the 8C. The town covers the slopes of a hill crowned by the Rocca dei Papi. The city was dear to St Francis, who loved its austere character, tempered by the grace of the narrow winding alleys, the palaces and numerous medieval buildings.

Each summer the town hosts an international arts festival, **Festival dei Due Mondi** *(see the table of Principal Festivals at the end of the guide).*

★★ **Cathedral** (**Duomo**). – Flanked by a baptistry it provides the focal point of **Piazza del Duomo**★. The façade is fronted by a fine Renaissance porch and adorned above by a rose window and 13C mosaic. Inside are frescoes *(first chapel on the south side)* by Pinturicchio, a tomb *(south transept)* by Fra Filippo Lippi and in the apse **frescoes** depicting the life of the Virgin, also by Fra Filippo Lippi and his assistants.

★★ **Bridge of Towers** (**Ponte delle Torri**). – The bridge was built in the 13C over a Roman aqueduct which was used as a foundation. The bridge with its ten Gothic arches is guarded by a small fortified gatehouse at one end.

★ **St Saviour's Basilica (San Salvatore).** – This, one of the first Christian churches in Italy, was built by Oriental monks in the 4C and modified in the 9C. Many Roman materials were re-used in the building of the later edifice.

★ **St Gregory Major's Church (San Gregorio Maggiore).** – This 12C Romanesque church was modified in the 14C. The 14C baptistry to the left of the entrance porch has walls covered with frescoes (Massacre of the Innocents). The campanile is built of blocks from ancient buildings. The dark, bare nave and aisles rest on massive columns with roughly hewn capitals. In the chancel is a 15C fresco and a carved stone cupboard of the same period.

Drusus' Arch (Arco di Druso). – This arch was built in AD 23 in honour of Tiberius' son.

St Dominic's Church (San Domenico). – This lovely 13 and 14C church is built of alternating courses of white and pink stone. The nave is decorated with 14 and 15C frescoes and the south transept contains a canvas by Lanfranco.

EXCURSIONS

★ **Monteluco.** – *8km – 5 miles to the east.*
An attractively winding road leads up to Monteluco. On the way up the **Church of St Peter's** (San Pietro) has a lovely 13C Romanesque **façade**★ with relief sculptures. On the summit, **Monteluco**★ was once the seat of an ancient cult, but is now a health resort. The monastery founded by St Francis still exists.

★ **Source of the River Clitumnus (Fonti del Clitunno).** – *13km – 8 miles to the north.*
These crystal clear waters which rise amid aquatic plants were sacred to the Romans. They plunged animals into these waters for purification prior to sacrifice. 1km – 3 mile
⊘ below stands the **temple**★ of Clitumnus, a minuscule early Christian building dating from the 5C. It boasts columns and a carved pediment.

SUBIACO   Latium   Pop 9 084
Michelin map ▨▨▨ fold 26

St Benedict, founder of the Benedictine Order, and his twin sister Scolastica retired to this spot at the end of the 5C and built twelve little monasteries.
To reach the monasteries of Santa Scolastica and San Benedetto (3km – 2 miles) take the Frosinone road and shortly before the Aniene Bridge, turn left.

⊘ **Monastery of St Scolastica (Santa Scolastica).** – Standing in a fine site overlooking the Aniene Gorges the monastery has conserved a majestic 11C campanile, its church which was remodelled in the 18C, and three cloisters. The third, the work of the Cosmati is admirable in its simplicity.

★ **Monastery of St Benedict (San Benedetto).** – This monastery stands above the latter
⊘ in a wild site above the flank of a rock, overhanging the gorge. The buildings date from the 13 and 14C.
The church has two storeys. The **upper church** has walls painted with frescoes of the 14C Sienese school and the 15C Umbrian school. The **lower church**, itself with two storeys, is covered with frescoes by Magister Consolus, an artist of the 13C Roman school.
You then enter the **Sacred Cave** (Sacro Speco) where St Benedict lived a hermit's existence for three years. A spiral staircase then leads up to a chapel which contains the earliest portrait of St Francis (without stigmata or halo), painted to commemorate the saint's visit to the sanctuary. The **Scala Santa** (Holy Staircase) leads down to the Chapel of the Virgin (frescoes by the Sienese school) and the Shepherd's Cave. From there pass to the rose garden where St Benedict threw himself into brambles to resist temptation.

★ SULMONA   Abruzzi   Pop 24 356
Michelin map ▨▨▨ fold 27 – Local map p 36

Lying at the head of a fertile basin framed by majestic mountains, Sulmona was the birthplace of the Roman poet **Ovid** best known for his long poem *Metamorphoses*. The town has retained its medieval character.

★★ **Palazzo dell' Annunziata.** – The palace was built by a Brotherhood of Penitents and has an original façade which displays varying styles: on the left the Gothic doorway has statues of the Virgin and St Michael while the triple-arched opening with four statues of Doctors of the Church, dates from 1415; the central and right hand parts are both later (1483 and 1522). Halfway up the façade is an astonishingly carved frieze. The sober façade of the adjacent church was built in 1710 by Pietro Fontana.

★ **Porta Napoli.** – *Southern town gateway.* This Gothic gate has historiated capitals (14C). The exterior has an unusual decoration of an opening, bosses and rosettes.

Piazza Garibaldi. – This square is the scene on Wednesdays and Saturdays of a large and highly colourful market. The square is bordered on two sides by a medieval aqueduct and overlooked by the Gothic doorway of the Church of St Martin (San Martino) and the Renaissance fountain, **Fontana del Vecchio.**
On Easter Sunday, the **feast of the "Madonna che scappa in piazza"** is celebrated in Piazza Garibaldi: the statue of the Virgin is borne to a meeting with the Risen Christ; as she comes within sight of Him, she sheds her mourning clothes and appears in resplendent green.

Michelin map 🔢 fold 29 – Town plan in the current Michelin Red Guide Italia

Taranto is a well protected naval base at the end of a great roadstead, closed at the seaward end by two fortified islands. Taranto was founded in the 7C BC and became one of the most important colonies of Magna Graecia. The old quarter lies on an island and is linked to the modern town by a swing brige.

During Holy Week many impressive ceremonies take place in the town, including several processions between Thursday and Saturday, one lasting twelve hours and another 14 hours, which go from church to church at a very slow pace *(see the table of Principal Festivals at the end of the guide)*.

★★ **National Museum** (Museo Nazionale). – The museum has a good collection of local ⊙ archaeological finds which illustrate the history of Magna Graecia. On the first floor in addition to sculpture, architectural fragments and grave artifacts, is an exceptional **collection of pottery**★★★ with vases in the Corinthian, Attic, proto-Italiot and Apulian styles. A large collection of Hellenistic jewellery (4-3C BC) found in tombs locally, is displayed in the **Gold Room**★★★ (Sala degli Ori).

★★ **Lungomare Vittorio Emanuele.** – Long promenade planted with palm trees.

★ **Public Gardens** (Giardini Comunali). – From this haven of exotic and luxuriant vegetation there is a magnificent view over the harbour's inner basin, the Mare Piccolo.

Cathedral (Duomo). – The 11-12C cathedral with a baroque façade has been greatly remodelled. The nave and two aisles are separated by ancient columns with Roman or Byzantine capitals. The ceiling is 17C while the **Chapel of San Cataldo**★ was faced with the polychrome marble and embellished with statues in the 18C.

Michelin map 🔢 fold 25 – 21km – 13 miles to the northwest of Civitavecchia

The town of Tarquinia crowns a rocky platform, facing the sea, in a barley and corn growing region interspersed with olive groves. Tarquinia is famous for the Etruscan burial ground which lies quite near. According to legend, the town was founded in the 12 or 13C BC. Archaeologists have found 9C BC vestiges of the Villanovian civilisation which derived its name from the village of Villanova near Bologna, and developed around the year 1000 BC in the Po Plain, in Tuscany and in the northern part of Latium, where the Etruscans later settled. Standing on the banks of the Marta River, Tarquinia was a busy port and in the 6C BC ruled the coast of Etruria. Under Roman rule, Tarquinia was decimated by malaria in the 4C BC and was sacked by the Lombards in the 7C. The inhabitants then moved to the present site about a mile to the northeast of the original position.

★★ **Etruscan Necropolis** (Necropoli Etrusca). – *4km – 2.5 miles.*
⊙ The burial ground is on a bare, windswept ridge parallel with that on which the former Etruscan city stood. The necropolis extends over an area 5km – 3 miles long and 1km 0.5 mile wide and contains around six hundred tombs dating from the 6-1C BC. As at Cerveteri there are no visible remains at ground level but there are remarkable **paintings**★★★ on the walls of the underground burial chambers. Colourful and lively these are of the utmost importance for the light they shed on the Etruscan civilisation.

The most important tombs include: the **tomb of the Baron**, dating from the 6C BC; the 5C BC **tomb of the Leopards,** one of the finest tombs, has as well as the leopards, scenes of a banquet and dancing; the 6C BC **tomb of the Bulls** with its erotic paintings; the **tomb of the Lionesses** dating from around 530-520 BC; the 4C BC **tomb of Giglioli** decorated with *trompe-l'œil* paintings of costumes and arms; and the late 6C BC **tomb with Hunting and Fishing Scenes**, which consists of two chambers displaying the return from the hunt, a banquet and the art of fishing.

★ **National Museum** (Museo Nazionale Tarquiniese). – The museum is housed in the **Palazzo** ⊙ **Vitelleschi**★ built in 1439 and has a most remarkable collection of Etruscan antiquities originating from the excavations in the necropolis. Items include sarcophagi, pottery, ivories, ex-votos and 6C BC Attic kraters and amphorae. Note the two admirable **winged horses**★★★ in terracotta and on the second floor several reconstructed tombs, notably the **tomb with the Funeral Bed** (460 BC) and the **tomb of the Triclinium** (480-470 BC) one of the finest in the necropolis.

★ **Church of St Mary** (Santa Maria ⊙ **in Castello**). – *Take the Via Mazzini, then the Via di Porta Castello beyond the wall.* This Romanesque church (1121-1208) stands near a tall tower built in the Middle Ages and was part of the fortified citadel guarding the town. It has an elegant doorway decorated with Cosmati work *(qv)* and an imposing interior.

(Ross/Rapho)

Tarquinia – The Winged Horses

TERNI Umbria Pop 111 302

Michelin map 988 fold 26 — Town plan in the current Michelin Red Guide Italia

Terni, an important industrial centre, has an old town with several fine palaces, the Church of St Francis with its 15C bell tower and St Saviour's Church, which has early Christian (5C) origins. The main streets are Piazza della Repubblica and Via Roma.

EXCURSIONS

★★ Marmore Cascade (Cascata delle Marmore). — *Take the Macerata road the S 209 (7km — 4 miles east of Terni) or the Rieti road, the S 79 (9km — 6 miles to the east plus 1/2 hour Rtn on foot).*
This artificial cascade created by the Romans falls in three successive drops down sheer walls of marble *(marmore)* to disappear at the bottom of a wooded ravine.

Carsulae: Roman Ruins. — *16km — 10 miles to the northwest. Go via S. Gemini and S. Gemini Fonte.*
These are the remains of a Roman town destroyed in the 9C.

Ferentillo. — *18km — 11 miles to the northeast.*
This picturesque village is dominated by two ruined castles. From here *(5km — 3 miles to the north, then 2km — 1/2 mile more by a poor road)* you may reach the solitary **Abbey of San Pietro in Valle**, which was founded in the 7C and rebuilt in the 12C. It has cloisters with 12C frescoes and there are Roman sarcophagi.

★ TERRACINA Latium Pop 38 352

Michelin map 988 fold 26

Terracina stands in an attractive setting at the head of a bay and is backed by a limestone cliff. Already in the Roman era it was a fashionable country resort. Terracina has retained part of its medieval wall and some Roman remains.

Cathedral (Duomo). — This overlooks the attractive **Piazza del Municipio** which still has the paving of the Roman forum. It was consecrated in 1075 and is fronted by a portico on ancient columns which support a 12C mosaic freize. The campanile with its small columns is in the transitional Romanesque-Gothic style.
Inside note in particular the **pulpit** and **paschal candelabrum★**, a lovely 13C work by the Cosmati *(qv)*.

★ Temple of Jupiter (Tempio di Giove Anxur). — *4km — 2.5 miles plus 1/4 hour on foot Rtn by the Via San Francesco Nuovo.*
Although there are few remains other than the foundations, a vaulted gallery and a cryptoporticus, it is worth visiting the site for its beauty alone and for the extensive **panorama★★** of the town, the canals and port, Monte Circeo and the Pontine marshes, the plain of Fondi with its lakes and the coast as far as Gaeta.

EXCURSION

★ Circeo National Park (Parco nazionale del Circeo). — Designated in 1934 this park covers a narrow coastal strip between Anzio and Terracina and includes part of the former Pontine marshes. Some of the most attractive beauty spots are: **Monte Circeo,** the refuge of the wicked witch Circe who transformed Ulysses and his companions into a herd of pigs; **Lake Sabaudia** (Lago di Sabaudia) which can be reached by a bridge leading to the town of Sabaudia, a pleasant country resort; the **scenic route** *(5km — 3 miles from the San Felice — Torre Cervia road)* is lined by luxury villas and brightened by a succession of typically Mediterranean plants and flowers.

★★★ TIVOLI Latium Pop 53 299

Michelin map 988 fold 26 — 31km — 19 miles east of Rome — Town plan in the current Michelin Red Guide Italia

Tivoli is a small town on the lower slopes of the Apennines where the river Aniene plunges in cascades into the Roman plain.
The villas testify to Tivoli's importance as a holiday resort from the Roman period through to the Renaissance. Tivoli or Tibur in antiquity came under Roman control in the 4C BC and it was there that a Sybil prophesied the coming of Jesus Christ to the Emperor Augustus.

★★★ VILLA D'ESTE *time: 2 hours*

See the plan in the Michelin Green Guide Rome.

In 1550 Cardinal Ippolito II d'Este, who had been raised to great honours by François I of France but had fallen into disgrace when the king's son Henri II succeeded to the throne, decided to retire to Tivoli, where he immediately began to convert the former Benedictine convent into a pleasant country seat. The Neapolitan architect, Pirro Ligorio, was invited to prepare plans. The simple architecture of the villa contrasts with the elaborate gardens which descend in a series of terraces. The statues, pools and fountains enhance the natural beauty with all the grace of the Mannerist style.
To the left of the main entrance stands the old abbey church of **St Mary Major** (Santa Maria Maggiore) with its attractive Gothic façade and a 17C bell tower. Inside, in the chancel, are two 15C triptychs: above the one on the left is a painting of the Virgin by Jacopo Torriti, who also worked in mosaic at the end of the 13C.

★★★ Palace and gardens. – From the former convent cloisters you go down through the ⊙ elaborately decorated Old Apartments. From the ground floor level there is a pleasant **view★** of the gardens and Tivoli itself. A double flight of stairs leads to the upper garden walk. The **Bicchierone Fountain** with its shell-shaped basin is attributed to Bernini. To the left the **Rometta Fountain** or "Mini Rome" reproduces some of the well known monuments of Classical Rome. From here the splendid **Avenue of a Hundred Fountains★★★** (Viale delle Cento Fontane) leads to the **Oval Fountain★★★** (Fontana dell' Ovato) dominated by a statue of the Sybil.

At a lower level the **Fishpond Esplanade** (le Peschiere) is overlooked at one end by the **Organ Fountain★★★** (Fontana dell' Organo) which used to play music on a water-powered organ concealed in the upper part of the fountain. Right at the very bottom of the garden is the **Nature Fountain** (Fontana della Natura) with a statue of Diana of Ephesus. Return by the central avenue to admire the **Dragon Fountain** (Fontana dei Draghi), built in 1572 in honour of Pope Gregory XIII, then turn right to pass the **Bird Fountain** (Fontana della Civetta) which used to produce bird song and finally the modernised **Fountain of Proserpina.**

★★★ HADRIAN'S VILLA (VILLA ADRIANA) *time: 2 1/2 hours*

⊙ *6km – 4 miles southwest by the Rome road the S 5 and then a local road to the left, 4.5km – 3 miles from Tivoli.*

This was probably the richest building project in antiquity and was designed entirely by Hadrian, who had visited every part of the Roman empire. With a passion for both art and architecture, he wished to recreate the works and sites he had visited during his travels. In 134 the villa was almost finished, but the 58 year old Hadrian, ill and griefstricken by the death of his young favourite Antinoüs was to die four years later. Although the succeeding emperors probably continued to visit Tivoli, the villa was soon forgotten and fell into ruin. The site was explored from the 15 to the 19C and the recovered works were dispersed to various museums and private collections. It was only in 1870 that the Italian government organised the excavation of Tivoli, thus revealing this magnificent ensemble.

Before exploring the site it is advisable to study a model of the villa which is displayed in a room next to the bar. *Follow the itinerary shown on the accompanying plan.*

★★ Poikile. – The water-filled Poikile takes its name from a portico in Athens. It was built in the shape of a large rectangle with slightly curved ends and is lined with a portico; it was oriented so that one side was always in the shade.

The apsidal chamber called the **philosophers' room** (**1**) was perhaps a reading room.

★★ Maritime Theatre. – The circular construction consists of a portico and a central building surrounded by a canal. It provided an ideal retreat for the misanthropic Hadrian. Bear south to pass the remains of a **nymphaeum** and the great columns which belonged to a building comprising three semicircular rooms round a courtyard (**2**).

★★ Baths. – The arrangement of the baths shows the high architectural standards attained in the villa. First come the Small Baths and then the Great Baths with its apse and remains of some superb vaulting.

The tall building, called the **Praetorium**, was probably a storehouse.

HADRIAN'S VILLA

0   100 m

CANOPUS ★★★

Praetorium

Museum

Great Baths ★★

★★ Piazza d'Oro

Small Baths ★★

4

5

6   7

3

Imperial   9   8

Palace

Nymphaeum

2

Library Court

1

★★ Poikile

10

MARITIME THEATRE ★★★

13   12   11

Bar

P

Terrace

of Tempe

14

Theatre

N

TIVOLI / ROMA

TIVOLI ★★★

★★★ **Canopus.** – Having passed the **museum** which contains the finds from the most recent
excavations, you come to the canopus which evokes the Egyptian town of Canope
with its famous Temple of Serapis. The route to Canope from Alexandria consisted of
a canal lined with temples and gardens. At the southern end of this site is a copy of the
Temple of Serapis.
Having reached the ruins, overlooking the nymphaeum turn right before skirting the
large **fishpond** (3) surrounded by a portico.

Imperial Palace. – The complex extended from Piazza d'Oro to the Libraries.

★★ **Piazza d'Oro.** – The rectangular piazza was surrounded by a double portico and was an
aesthetic caprice serving no useful purpose. On the far side are traces of an octagonal
chamber (4) and opposite is a domed chamber (5).

★★ **Doric Pillared Hall** (6). – It takes its name from the surrounding portico which was composed of pilasters with Doric bases and capitals.

Also visible are the **firemen's barracks** (7), remains of a summer dining room (8) and a
nymphaeum (9). These buildings overlook a courtyard which is separated from the
library court by a cryptoporticus, part of a network of underground passages which ran
from one villa to another without coming above ground.
The series of ten rooms along one side of the library court was an infirmary (10). Note
the fine mosaic **paving★**. According to custom the **library** was divided in two for a Greek
section (11) and a Latin section (12).
Going towards the **Terrace of Tempe** one passes a group of rooms paved with mosaic
which belonged to a dining room (13).
The path runs through the trees on the slope above the valley past a **circular temple** (14)
attributed to the goddess Venus, and skirts the site of a **theatre**, on the left, before
ending at the entrance.

ADDITIONAL SIGHT

★ **Villa Gregoriana.** – This wooded park has a tangle of paths which wind down the
steeply wooded slopes to the river Aniene where it cascades through the ravine. The
waters of the Aniene plunge down at the **Great Cascade★★**, disappear out of sight at the
Siren's Cave and burst from the rock face in **Neptune's Cave**. Climb the slope overlooking
the ravine to leave the Villa Gregoriana and visit **Sibyl's Temple**, also known as the Temple of Vesta. This elegant Corinthian structure dates from the end of the Republic. An
Ionic temple stands alongside.

★★ **TODI** Umbria   Pop 16 999
Michelin map 988 folds 25 and 26

Todi, a charming old town perched on an attractive **site,** has preserved three sets of
walls: the Etruscan (Marzia Gateway), the Roman and the medieval.

★★ **Piazza del Popolo.** – This square in the centre of Todi is surrounded by buildings
which are evidence of the town's flourishing commercial life in the Middle Ages. The
13C Gothic **Palazzo dei Priori★** was formerly the seat of the governor (podestà). Its windows were remodelled at the Renaissance and it is dominated by a curious 14C tower
on a trapezoidal plan.
The 13C **Palazzo del Capitano★** has attractive windows in groups of three flanked by
small columns. Both this and the neighbouring building have arcades with round headed
arches at ground level. Adjoining is the **Palazzo del Popolo★**, one of the oldest communal
palaces in Italy dating from 1213. It houses a lapidary museum, a picture gallery as
well as a museum of Etruscan and Roman antiquities.

★★ **Church of St Fortunatus** (San Fortunato). – Piazza della Repubblica.
Building lasted from 1292 to 1460, so that Gothic features mingle with those of the
Renaissance. The **central doorway★★** catches the eye by the richness and delicacy of its
decoration.
The well-lit and lofty interior has in the fourth chapel on the south **frescoes** (1432) by
Masolino and the tomb of Jacopone da Todi (1230-1307), a Franciscan monk, a poet
and author of the Stabat Mater.

★ **Cathedral** (Duomo). – This great Romanesque building dating from the early 12C is
preceded by a majestic staircase leading up to its harmonious façade, all in pink and
white marble, with a great rose window pierced and fretted in the Umbrian manner.
Inside note the Gothic capitals, the Renaissance font and the lovely stalls with intarsia
work dating from 1530.

Piazza Garibaldi. – This square adjoining the Piazza del Popolo is graced with a monument to Garibaldi. From the terrace there is a pretty **view★★** of the valley and distant
rounded hills.

Castle (Rocca). – Passing to the right of St Fortunatus, walk up to the ruins of the 14C
castle. Well shaded and pleasant public garden.

★ **Church of Santa Maria della Consolazione.** – 1km – 1/2 mile to the west on the
Orvieto road.
This Renaissance church was built of pale stone between 1508 and 1609 by several
architects who drew inspiration from the designs of Bramante. The plan is that of a
Greek cross; four polygonal apses are reinforced by pilasters with composite capitals.
The dome, whose drum is designed in accordance with Bramante's rhythmic princi-
ples (see p 115), rises roundly from the flat terrace roof. The dome was decorated in
the 16C and the twelve statues of the Apostles are by Scalza (16C).

TOLENTINO Marches Pop 18 338

Michelin map **988** fold 16

This small town in the Marches region was where Bonaparte and Pope Puis VI signed the Treaty of Tolentino ratifying the surrendering of Avignon to France. Tolentino with the Basilica of St Nicholas is known as a pilgrimage centre. Numerous miracles are attributed to this Augustinian hermit who died in Tolentino in 1305.

★★ BASILICA OF ST NICHOLAS (SAN NICOLA DA TOLENTINO)

time: 1 hour

The building of this basilica lasted from 1305 to the 18C and the exterior reflects the different construction periods. The façade, although remodelled in the 17C in the baroque manner has however retained an elegant late Gothic doorway attributed to Nino di Bartolo (15C).

Ⓥ **Interior.** – The vast rectangular nave is striking for the rigour of its ordonnance, the splendour of its marble, gold and stucco decoration and the magnificent coffered ceiling (1628). The side chapels contain numerous works of art: in the first chapel on the south side an admirable canvas by Guercino (1640) and in the fourth on the same side a 14C polychrome recumbent Madonna in wood and an effigy of St Lorenzina.
The **Chapel of the Holy Arms★** *(south side of chancel)* has a remarkably rich decoration. Note the high altar with its chased silver steps. The **Chapel of the Cappellone★★** (Cappella Cappellone) serves as south transept and is the most famous part of this pilgrimage church due to its cycle of 14C **frescoes** by an unknown master of the Rimini school on its vaulting and walls. The lower frescoes recount episodes from the life of St Nicholas of Tolentino while those on the vaulting evoke the Life of Christ.

Great Cloisters. – These are 13 and 14C. The galleries and the adjoining oratory are decorated with baroque frescoes (17C) illustrating the life of the saint.

Crypt. – *Go back through the Capella Cappellone.*
Only completed in 1932 the crypt enshrines the remains of St Nicholas of Tolentino in a reliquary-coffin.

Museums. – These include a gallery of ex-votos, a ceramics and archaeological section, pottery and Roman objects (municipal museum).

★ TREMITI Islands Apulia Pop 336

Michelin map **988** fold 28 – Access: see the current Michelin Red Guide Italia

This tiny archipelago, the only one on the Adriatic coast, lies offshore from the Gargano Promontory *(qv)* and belongs to the same geological formation. There are two main islands, San Nicola and San Domino as well as two uninhabited isles Capraia and Pianosa which is much further out in the Adriatic. The boat trip out from Manfredonia offers unforgottable **views★★★** of the Gargano coastline with its dazzling white limestone cliffs. As the boat rounds the promontory there are also good views of the coastal towns of Vieste, Peschici and Rodi Garganico set on their precipitous sites. Note also on the points of the rocky headlands platform areas *(trabocco)* equipped with fishing nets.

★ **San Nicola.** – High on the clifftop stands the **Abbey of Santa Maria al Mare,** originally
Ⓥ founded by the Benedictines in the 9C. A fortified ramp leads up to the abbey. Of particular interest are the remains of an 11C mosaic pavement, a 15C Gothic polyptych and a 13C Byzantine crucifix. From the cloisters there are good glimpses of the second island, San Domino.

★ **San Domino.** – Take the boat trip to circumnavigate this island and discover the
Ⓥ wild beauty of the very indented and rugged coasts of this forest (pines) covered island.

★ TRENTO Trentino-Alto Adige Pop 99 983

Michelin map **988** fold 4 – Town plan in the current Michelin Red Guide Italia

Trent, capital of Trentino, stands on the Adige not far from the Brenta Massif and is encircled by rocky peaks and valleys. Austrian and Italian influences meet here. This agricultural and industrial centre stands at an important crossroads with the converging of routes from the Brenner Pass, Brescia and Venice.

HISTORICAL NOTES

This Roman colony under the Empire, became an episcopal see in the 4C, was occupied successively by the Ostrogoths under Theodoric, the Lombards in the 6C before being united to the Holy Roman Empire in the late 10C. From 1004 to 1801 the town was governed by a succession of Prince-Bishops. The **Council of Trent** (1545-63) called by Pope Paul III to study methods of combating Protestantism met in the town. These deliberations marked the beginning of the Counter-Reformation and the findings were to change the character of the church. The main decisions concerned the re-establishment of ecclesiastical credibility and authority, compulsory residence for bishops and the abolition of the sale of indulgences.
After a period of Napoleonic rule in the 19C, Trento was ceded to the Austrians in 1814. It was only after a long hard struggle that the town was liberated in 1918 by Italian troops.

★CITY OF THE PRINCE—BISHOPS *time: 2 hours*

★ **Piazza del Duomo.** – This cobbled square is the centre of town. Round it stand the cathedral, the Palazzo Pretoria (13C restored), the belfry and the Rella houses painted with 16C frescoes.

Cathedral (Duomo). – This 12 to 13C majestic façade is in the Lombard Romanesque style. The façade of the north transept is pierced with a window forming a Wheel of Fortune: Christ stands at the summit, the Symbols of the Evangelists rise towards him. Inside, note the unusual sweep of the stairway leading to the towers. To the right, in the 17C Chapel of the Crucifix, is a large wood Christ in front of which the decrees of the Council of Trent were proclaimed. In the south transept is the tomb of the Venetian mercenary leader Sanseverino who was killed in 1486.

⊙ The remains of a 5C **paleo-Christian basilica** have been uncovered beneath the chancel.

★ **Diocesan Museum (Museo Diocesano).** – The museum installed in the Palazzo Pretorio
⊙ regroups the most important items from the cathedral's treasure, paintings, carved **wooden panels★, altarpiece★** and eight early 16C **tapestries★** which were woven in Brussels by Peter Van Aelst.

Via Belenzani. – This street is lined with palaces in the Venetian style. Opposite the 16C town hall (Palazzo Comunale) are houses with walls painted with frescoes.

Via Manci. – The Venetian (loggias and frescoes) and mountain (overhanging roofs) styles are intermingled all along the street. At No 63 the Palazzo Galazzo with its embossed stonework and huge pilasters is 17C.

★ **Castle of Good Counsel (Castello del Buon Consiglio).** – This castle was formerly the
⊙ residence of the prince-bishops and now houses the Trentino National Museum. On the left are the 13C Castelvecchio (Old Castle) and the Torre Grande known as the Tower of Augustus; in the centre is the 16C Renaissance Palazzo Magno, the bishop's residence; and on the extreme right the square Torre dell' Aquila (Eagle Tower).
The interior of the castle gives the impression of being made up of a maze of courts, staircases, passages and sundry buildings. The Castelvecchio has a beautiful court in the Venetian Gothic style with four tiers of galleries adorned with frescoes, including the portraits of the prince-bishops. The Palazzo Magno leads to the Romanino Loggia with its 16C frescoes.
The loggia overlooks the charming Renaissance Lions Courtyard. The apartments of the prince-bishops with coffered ceilings decorated with stucco and frescoes are the setting for rich collections of 16-18C paintings, furniture and ceramics.

ADDITIONAL SIGHTS

★ **Palazzo Tabarelli.** – A remarkable building in the Venetian Renaissance style with pilasters, pink marble columns and medallions.

St Mary Major's Church (Santa Maria Maggiore). – Numerous meetings of the Council of Trent were held in this Renaissance church with a Romanesque campanile. The elegant marble organ loft (1534) in the chancel is by Vincenzo and Girolamo Grandi. At the second altar on the right, in the nave, is a 16C altarpiece of the Madonna and saints by Moroni.

Church of St Apollinaris (Sant' Apollinare). – This small Romanesque church on the west bank of the Adige has a curious pointed roof covering two Gothic domical vaults.

★★★BRENTA MASSIF (GRUPPO DEL BRENTA)
Round tour starting from Trento
233km – 145 miles – allow two days

This wild limestone Brenta Massif prolongs the Dolomites beyond the Adige Valley. Its characteristic features are deep valleys, solitary lakes and erosion worn rocks.

Sightseeing. – The map opposite, in addition to locating the towns and sites described in the guide indicates other beauty spots in small black type.

Take the S 45ᵇ in the direction of Vezzano.

★ **Lake Toblino** (Lago di Toblino). – This charming lake fringed with tall rushes, stands against a background of rocky walls. An attractive little castle, once the summer residence of the Bishops of Trent, stands on a small peninsula.

★ **Rendena Valley** (Valle Rendena). – This wide valley clad with firs and larches has charming villages with churches covered with frescoes, protected by overhanging roofs.
The **Church of San Vigilio** near Pinzolo has a remarkable Dance of Death (1539) by Simone Baschenis.

★★★ **Genova Valley** (Val di Genova). – This valley crosses the granite Adamello Massif and is known for its wild grandeur. The road follows a fast flowing river as it tumbles and foams along the rock-strewn bed to reach the **Nardis Waterfall★★** (Cascata di Nardis) where the waters drop over 100m – 328ft.

★★ **Madonna di Campiglio.** – This pleasant resort and winter sports centre has many hotels and numerous possibilities for excursions.

★★ **Campo Carlo Magno.** – A supposed visit by Charlemagne gave this place its name. It has
⊙ become a winter sports centre.
From **Grosté Pass** (Passo del Grostè) *(cable-car and then on foot)* there is a fine **panorama★★** of the Brenta Massif.

Continue to Dimaro and Malè and at Cles turn right towards Tuenno.

★★★ **Lake Tovel** (Lago di Tovel). – Pass through wild gorges to reach this lovely lake fringed by wooded slopes. In hot weather the waters of the lake take on a reddish tinge due to the presence of microscopic algae.

★ **Andalo.** – This small holiday resort is set in majestic scenery, amidst a great pine forest and overlooked by the crests of the Brenta Massif.

⊙ From the summit of **Monte Paganella** *(cable car)* at 2 125m – 6 9/2ft there is a splendid **panorama**★★ of the whole region, and in clear weather, as far as Lake Garda.

★ **Molveno.** – This choice resort is situated among gently sloping meadows at the north end of a **lake**★★ which lies on the floor of a cirque.

★ **TREVISO** Venetia   Pop 85 677

Michelin map 988 fold 5 – Town plan in the current Michelin Red Guide Italia

Standing on the rich Venetian plain, Treviso is an important agricultural and industrial centre but has retained its old walled town. Ever since the 14C its fortunes have been linked with those of Venice.

★ **Piazzo dei Signori.** – This forms the historic centre of Treviso and is bordered by numerous impressive monuments: the Palazzo del Podestà with its tall municipal bell tower, the **Palazzo dei Trecento**★ (1207) and the Renaissance Palazzo Pretorio. Lower down
⊙ in Piazza del Monte di Pietà is the former pawn shop **(Monte di Pietà)** with the Chapel of the Rectors (Cappella dei Reggitori).
In Piazza San Vito there are two churches side by side: **San Vito** and **Santa Lucia** which is adorned with remarkable **frescoes**★ by Tommaso da Modena, one of the finest 14C artists after Giotto.

★ **Church of St Nicholas (San Nicolò).** – This large Romanesque-Gothic church contains interesting frescoes, especially those on the columns which are by Tommaso da Modena. In the Onigo Chapel there are portraits of Trevisans by Lorenzo Lotto (16C). The Christ in Majesty at the far end of the chancel was by Savoldo (16C).
⊙ In the adjoining **monastery** the chapterhouse has portraits of famous Dominicans by Tommaso da Modena.

★ **Bailo Municipal Museum (Museo Civico).** – *22 Borgo Cavour.*
⊙ There are works by Tommaso da Modena, Girolamo da Treviso (15C) and others of the Venetian school such as Cima da Conegliano, Giovanni Bellini, Titian, Paris Bordone, Jacopo Bassano and Lorenzo Lotto.

Cathedral (Duomo). – The 15 and 16 church has seven domes, a neo-classical façade and a Romanesque crypt. Left of the cathedral is an 11-12C baptistry. In the Chapel of the Annunciation, to the right of the chancel, are mannered frescoes by Pordenone and on the altarpiece an Annunciation by Titian.

Church of St Francis (San Francesco). – *Viale Sant' Antonio da Padova.*
This church in the transitional Romanesque-Gothic style has a fine wooden ceiling, the tombstone of Petrach's daughter, the tomb of one of Dante's sons as well as frescoes by Tomasso da Modena in the first chapel to the left of the chancel.

EXCURSIONS

Maser. – *29km – 18 miles to the northwest by the S 348.*

ⓒ This small agricultural town is known for its famous **villa**★★★ built in 1560 by Palladio for the brothers, Barbaro Daniele, patriarch of Aquileia and Marcantonio, ambassador of the Venetian Republic. The interior was decorated between 1566 and 1568 with an amazing ensemble of **frescoes**★★★ by Veronese. One of his best decorative schemes he used all his amazing knowledge of perspective, *trompe-l'œil*, foreshortening and his sense of movement and colour. Not far from the villa is a **Tempietto,** a graceful circular chapel with a dome which was also the work of Palladio.

Vittorio Veneto. – *41km – 26 miles to the north.*

The name of this town recalls the great victory of the Italians over the Austrians in

ⓒ 1918. In Ceneda to the south of the town, the **Battle Museum** regrouping documents on this victory, is installed in a 16C loggia (Loggia Cenedese) with a frescoed portico by Sansovino. The suburb of Serravalle in the north has retained a certain charm. The **Church of San Giovanni** *(take Via Roma and then Via Mazzini)* has interesting **frescoes**★ attributed to Jacobello del Fiore and Gentile da Fabriano (15C).

★ **TRIESTE** Fruili-Venezia Giulia   Pop 241 386

Michelin map 𝟵𝟴𝟴 fold 6 – Plan of the built-up area in the current Michelin Red Guide Italia

Trieste is a modern town which stands at the head of a bay of the same name and at the foot of the Carso Plateau. The edge of the latter forms a steep coast with magnificent white cliffs as far as Duino in the north. Trieste is the largest seaport on the Adriatic. Its extensive port (12km – 8 miles of quays stretch as far as the Yugoslavian border) handles more Austrian and Yugoslavian goods than Italian. An oil pipeline links Trieste with refineries in Austria and Bavaria. The important shipyards, specialising in the building of large vessels, are important to the local economy.

HISTORICAL NOTES

The origins of the town are very ancient, the Celts and Illyrians disputed it before the Romans made it their important trading centre of Tergeste, which had the important role of defending the eastern frontiers of the Empire. It came under the sway of the Patriarch of Aquileia and then, in 1202, under Venice. In 1382 Trieste rebelled and placed itself under the protection of Austria and it played the role of mediator between the two opponents until the 15C. In 1719 Charles VI declared it a free port and established the headquarters of the French Trading Company (Compagnie d'Orient et du Levant) in the city. Trieste then enjoyed a second period of prosperity and was embellished by numerous fine buildings. Many political exiles sought refuge in Trieste. It was only in 1919 after fierce fighting that Trieste was united with the Kingdom of Italy.

At the beginning of the 20C Trieste had an active literary group under the leading influence of the novelist Italo Svevo and the poet Umberto Saba. James Joyce lived in the town for some years until 1914.

★★ THE HILL OF ST JUSTUS (COLLE DI SAN GIUSTO) *time: 1 hour*

This hilltop was the site of the ancient city and today the **Piazza della Cattedrale**★ (BY) is bordered by the ruins of a Roman basilica, a 15-16C castle, a 1560 Venetian column, the altar of the Third Army (1929) and the Basilica of St Justus.

Basilica of St Justus (San Giusto) (BY). – It was founded in the 5C on the site of a Roman building, but the present buildings date in large part from the 14C. The façade is pierced with a fine Gothic rose window and decorated with a low-relief and bronze busts. The powerful looking campanile has fragments of Roman columns built into its lowest storey and bears a 14C statue of St Justus. From the top there is an attractive **view**★ of Trieste.

The **interior**★ comprises a nave and four aisles. The side aisles belonged to two separate basilicas which were joined together in the 14C by the building of the central nave. In the south aisle there is a lovely 13C mosaic and 11C frescoes depicting the life of St Justus. A magnificent 12C **mosaic**★★ in the north apse shows the Virgin in Majesty between the Archangels Michael and Gabriel, and the Apostles.

ⓒ **Castle (Castello di San Giusto)** (BY). – This houses a **museum (M¹)** of furniture and a remarkable collection of **arms**★.

ⓒ **History and Art Museum (Museo di Storia e d'Arte)** (BY M²). – This regroups a remarkable collection of red-figured **Greek vases**★ and charming **small bronzes**★ dating from the Roman Archaic period.

Roman Theatre (Teatro romano) (BY). – The remains of an early 2C Roman theatre lie at the foot of the Hill of St Justus.

THE LOWER TOWN *time: 1 hour*

★ **Piazza dell'Unità d'Italia** (AY). – Three palaces with typically 1900 architecture line this square, namely the Palazzo del Governo (Government Palace), Palazzo del Comune (Town Hall) and the offices of Lloyd Trieste.

★ **Maritime Museum (Museo del Mare).** – *Via A. Ottaviano. Take Riva Nazario Sauro* (AY).

ⓒ The history of seafaring is traced from its beginnings in the 18C. The **fishing section**★ is quite remarkable.

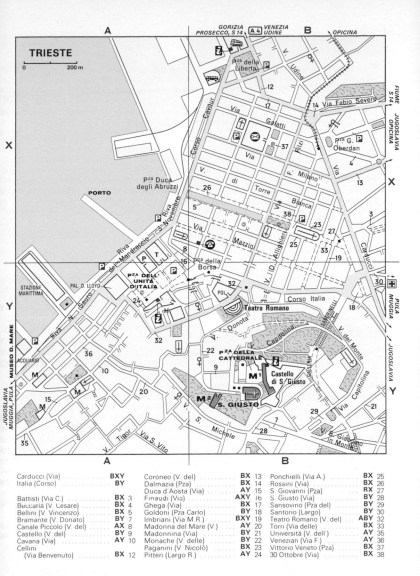

TRIESTE

0   200 m

EXCURSIONS

Sanctuary of Monte Grisa. – *10km – 6 miles to the north. Leave by Piazza della Libertà (**BX**) in the direction of Prosecco and then Villa Opicina and follow the signposts to "Monte Grisa".*
This modern sanctuary is dedicated to the Virgin. From the terrace there is a splendid **panorama**★★ of Trieste and its bay.

Villa Opicina. – *9km – 6 miles to the north. Leave by Via Fabio Severo (**BX**). After 4.5km – 3 miles turn left off the S 14 to take the S 58. It is also possible to take the funicular which leaves from Piazza Oberdan.*
Villa Opicina stands on the edge of the Carso Plateau (alt 348m – 1 142ft). From the belvedere with an obelisk there is a magnificent wide-reaching **view**★★ over Trieste and its bay.

★ **Miramare Castle (Castello di Miramare).** – *8km – 5 miles to the northwest by the coast road.*
Standing on the point of a headland, this castle with its lovely terraced **gardens**★ was built in 1860 for the Archduke Maximilian of Austria, who was executed by shooting in Mexico in 1867 and his wife, Princess Charlotte, who died insane.

★ **Grotta Gigante.** – *13km – 8 miles to the north. Follow the above directions to Villa Opicina and then turn left in the direction of Borgo Grotta Gigante.*
An impressive stairway leads down to this chamber of astonishing size where one can walk among the splendid concretions. There is a **speleological museum** at the entrance to the cave.

Muggia. – *14km – 9 miles to the south. Leave by Riva Nazario Sauro (**AY**).*
Facing Trieste, this small very Venetian-looking town has a 15C Gothic cathedral (Duomo) with an attractive pointed campanile and an elegant façade in Istrian limestone.

*When looking for a pleasant, quiet and well situated hotel consult the current **Michelin Red Guide**.*

Michelin map **988** fold 29

This region extending between Fassano, Ostuni, Martina Franca and Alberobello takes its name from the very curious buildings, the *trulli (photograph p 45)*, which are to be found almost everywhere. These strange white, dry-stone structures have conical roofs covered with grey stone slabs. Each dome corresponds to a room. The *trulli* usually stand in groups of three or four. The external staircase leads to the attic. The doorway stands in the recessed arch of a stepped gable. Inside the rooms are domed.

★★★ **Alberobello.** – This small town has an entire district of *trulli* which often abut one another. They spread over the hillside to the south of the town (Zona Monumentale). On the hilltop stands the **Church of Sant' Antonio** also in the form of a *trullo (take Via Monte Sant' Angelo)*. Inside the transept crossing is covered with a dome, similar to those in the *trulli*. It is possible to visit some of these strange dwellings: from the rooftops there is often a good view of the town. The **Trullo Sovrano★**, a two-storeyed *trulli,* the largest in Alberobello stands near the principal church on Piazza Sacramento.

★★ **TURIN** (TORINO) Piedmont   Pop 1 025 390

Michelin map **988** fold 12 – Plan pp 196-197 – Plan of the built-up area in the current Michelin Red Guide Italia

Turin stands at the confluence of the Dora Riparia and the Po and is the meeting-place of important transalpine routes from France and Switzerland. The capital of Piedmont is an elegant, lively and prosperous town. Most of the town was built on a regular plan in the 17 and 18C and it has wide avenues, spacious squares and numerous parks.

HISTORICAL NOTES

During the 1C the capital of the Celtic tribe the Taurini was transformed by the Romans into a military colony and given the name of Augusta Taurinorum. Converted to Christianity it became the seat of a bishopric in the early 5C and then a century later a Lombard duchy before passing under Frankish rule. From the 11C onwards and for nearly nine centuries the destiny of Turin was linked to that of the **House of Savoy**. This dynasty descended from Umberto the Whitehanded, who died in 1056, reigned over Savoy and Piedmont and then Sardinia and all of Italy. It was Italy's reigning royal family from 1861 to 1946. They were skilful rulers often siding with the pope rather than the emperor, and playing France off against the Dukes of Milan. They slowly extended their rule over the area. It was in the early 18C that Charles Emmanuel II and Victor Emmanuel II embellished their adopted city with splendid buildings by Guarini and Juvara. Charles Emmanuel II increased the importance of Turin during his reign by reorganising the kingdom's administration and by establishing in his capital a court with very formal etiquette, similar to the one at Versailles. In 1798 Charles Emmanuel IV was expelled from Turin by French troops full of the new revolutionary spirit. On the fall of Bonaparte, Victor-Emmanuel I was restored to his kingdom. Turin then became the centre of the struggle against the Austrians and for the unification of Italy.

Following the reorganisation of the Piedmont by the statesman Camillo Cavour, the Franco-Piedmontese alliance against Austria, the victories at Solferino and Magenta (1859), Victor Emmanuel II was proclaimed king of Italy and Turin became the seat of the Italian goverment. The House of Savoy reigned over Italy until the proclamation of an Italian Republic in 1946.

ECONOMY

Thanks to the intense activity of its suburban industries, Turin is the capital of Italian engineering. The people of Turin are born mechanics and most of the motor engineers come from the Politecnico of Turin University. It is here that the Italian motor industry, represented by FIAT and Lancia was born. Turin is responsible for about 77 per cent of Italy's car production. Many of the modern FIAT works are established in the southern suburb of Mirafiori.

Important tyre manufacturers and well known coachbuilders (one of the most famous having been Pinin Farina) contribute to the prosperity of the motor industry of Turin, whose products are displayed at the Turin Motor Show every even year.

The textile and clothing industries are also highly developed.

LIFE IN TURIN

The life of the town is concentrated in Via Roma (**BXY**), Piazza San Carlo *(see p 195)*, and Via Po (**CXY**), which leads to the huge Piazza Vittorio Veneto (**CY**), built in the classical style. The modern-looking Via Roma is lined with arcades beneath which are the luxury shops with attractive window displays of refined and reputed articles from Turin such as silk and leather goods and of course fashion wear.

The Piazza San Carlo, halfway along the Via Roma, is the meeting-place of fashionable women, while connoisseurs linger in the antiquaries' and book-sellers' shops. The large cafés built in the neo-classical style which open onto the Via Po played a part in the politics of the 19C. The courteous and refined atmosphere of Turin is that of a cultural centre distinguished by many publishing houses, well-known newspapers *(Stampa)*, a Music Conservatory and a large university.

But the cult of the spirit does not compel neglect of the flesh, and the people of Turin with appetites whetted by their famous Vermouths (Martini, Cinzano or Carpano) do not disdain good cooking. *Cardi in bagna cauda* (cardoons in piquant sauce) and *tartufi bianchi* (white truffles) are specialities eaten with crisp rolls and accompanied by the delectable wines of the region. Sweetmeats, nougat *(torrone piemontese),* chocolates and chocolate creams, are also excellent.

CITY CENTRE

★ **Piazza San Carlo** (BXY). – This is a graceful piece of town planning. The **Churches of San Carlo** and **Santa Cristina**, symmetrically placed on the south side, frame the Via Roma. The curious façade of Santa Cristina, surmounted by candelabra, was designed by the famous Sicilio-Turinese architect Juvara, who was responsible for many of Turin's lovely buildings. On the east side is the 17C palace which was the French Ambassador's residence from 1771 to 1789. In the centre of the square stands the statue (1838) of Emanuele Filiberto of Savoy.

Academy of Science (Palazzo dell' Accademia delle Scienze) (BX M). – This 17C palace by Guarini now houses two exceptional museums.

★ **Egyptian Museum.** – *Ground and first floors.* This is one of the richest collections of Egyptian antiquities. On the ground floor is the section on **statuary art** with twenty seated or standing figures, of the lion-headed goddess Sekhmet from Karnak, and an important **series of pharaohs** of the New Kingdom (1580-1100 BC), Egypt's Golden Age. The **Rock Temple of Thutmose III** (*c*1450 BC), a present from the United Arab Republic, originated from Ellessya 200km – 124 miles to the south of Aswan.

The collections on the first floor evoke all aspects of Egyptian civilisation. Note in particular the **sarcophagi** dating from the Middle Kingdom (2100-1580 BC) and sculpted during the New Kingdom; a collection of **canopic urns**; and an important number of mummies and copies of funerary papyri rolls known as the **Book of the Dead.** In addition to the recreated **funeral chambers** *(mastabas)* (Giza 2500 BC) there is an exceptional collection of **funerary steles** dating from the Middle and New Kingdoms. Jewellery and pottery from the pre-dynastic civilisations, known as Nagadian date from the 4000-3000 BC. The influence of the Greek world made itself felt following the conquest of Alexander the Great (masks and statuettes) followed by the Romans from 30BC (bronze vases). Another room is devoted to **inscriptions**; the hieroglyphs deciphered by Champollion in 1824 and texts in hieratic script using cursive on papyrus, limestone flakes and fragments of pottery.

★ **Galleria Sabauda.** – *Second floor.*
This art museum comprises five different sections.

First section: this is a very comprehensive collection of 15 to 17C **Piedmontese painting**.

Second section: other Italian schools. There is a remarkable collection of **15C Tuscan painting**: a *Madonna* by Fra Angelico, *Tobias and the Archangel* (Il Toblino) by Antonio and Piero Pollaiuolo, *Eleanor of Toledo* by Bronzino and a dazzling portrait of a *Young Man with a Red Scarf* by Lorenzo di Credi. *The Assumption* (1623) by Orazio Gentileschi is outstanding among the works by the followers of Caravaggio who specialised in violent realism and contrasted light effects. The 15-16C **Lombard school** is well represented. The paintings include a polyptych (1462), the only signed work by Paolo da Brescia, and the *Adorations of the Infant Jesus (presepi)* by Savoldo da Brescia, and a charming little picture of a *Madonna with a Carthusian Monk* by Bergognone. Francesco del Cairo and Tanzio da Varallo illustrate the development of Mannerism in Lombardy and Piedmont. The **Ferrara school** of the 15 and 16C is represented by Ercole de' Roberti *(Virgin and Child),* Garofalo, the Raphael of Ferrara and Mazzolino. Albani and Guercino, both pupils of the Carracci, represent the 17C **Bolognese school** and Crespi the 18C.
The 15-16C **Venetian school** covers a *Virgin and Child* and lovely portrait of a *Lady with a small dog* by Palma Vecchio, altarpieces by Lorenzo Veneziano, *The Feast in the House of Simon* by Veronese, *Leda* and the *Portrait of a Senator* by Titian, the *Portrait of Doge Sebastiano Venier* by Tintoretto, the large canvases by the Bassano family which are precursors of Caravaggio with the contrasting light and shade, scenes of Turin by Bernardo Bellotto, *The Triumph of Aurelian* by Tiepolo and Venetian townscapes by Francesco Guardi. Note also the lovely *Madonna* with a thoughtful expression so characteristic of the Paduan artist, Mantegna who so influenced Venetian Renaissance art.

Third section: the **Dutch and Flemish collections** are probably the richest in Italy. Among the most outstanding works are small religious paintings by Rogier Van der Weyden *St Francis receiving the Stigmata* by Van Eyck, *The Passion* by Memling, an impressive group of official portraits including the famous *Children of Charles I of England* by Van Dyck in his masterly style and the celebrated *Old Man Asleep* by Rembrandt.

Fourth section: the section devoted to **French,** German and Spanish artists displays portraits by François Clonet *(Marguerite de Valois),* a *St Jerome* by Valentin de Boulogne. *Louis, Duke of Burgundy* by Rigaud, *The Knife-Grinder (Arrotino)* by Casper Netscher and the *Portrait of a Man* by Velasquez.

Gualino Collection. – On the upper floor, this is a fine selection of paintings, sculpture, furnishings and gold and silver plate. Note in particular the Oriental and Greco-Roman sculpture, a set of small paintings on a gilded background, several Renaissance masterpieces and 18C pastels by Rosalba Carriera.

★ **Palazzo Madama** (BX A). – The palace stands in the centre of Piazza Castello. It was so-called because the mother of Charles Emmanuel II, "Madama Reale", Marie-Christine of France, lived there. The Porta Decumana, part of the old Augustinian ramparts, forms the original nucleus of the building. The eastern section, in brick, is late medieval (15C), but the west façade, in stone, was designed in the 18C by Juvara.
There is a **Museum of Ancient Art★** (Museo d'Arte Antica) on the ground floor. The exhibits include Gothic carvings, 15C stalls, canvases of the 15-16C Piedmontese school (Gian Martino Spanzotti, Macrino d'Alba, Defendente and Gaudenzio Ferrari), a *Portrait of a Man* (1475) by Antonello da Messina and a 14C *Madonna* by Barnaba da Modena. The decorative arts section regroups Greek, Roman and Barbarian gold work, enamels, ivories, wooden caskets, ceramic ware and 15C furniture.
Standing slightly back from the Piazza Castello is the **Church of San Lorenzo (BX)** which was adorned with a dome and a bold crown by Guarini. Next door, the Palazzo Chiablese is the home of a **National Film Museum (BX M¹)** *(entrance: 2 Piazza San Giovanni).*

★ **Royal Palace (Palazzo Reale)** (BCVX). – The princes of the House of Savoy lived in
⊘ this plain building until 1865. The **apartments** *(first floor)* are sumptuously decorated in
the baroque style.

⊘ The **Royal Armoury** ★ (Armeria Reale) contains a splendid collection of arms and armour
and interesting military memorabilia.

Palazzo Carignano (BX M²). – This palace dating from 1680 has an impressive baroque façade by Guarini. Italy's first king, Victor Emmanuel II, was born in this palace in
⊘ 1820. There is an interesting **Museum of the Risorgimento** ★ with a collection of a documents illustrating the out-
standing people and
events in the history of
19C Italy.

★ **Cathedral of St John
(Duomo San Giovanni)** (BX).
– This Renaissance ca-
thedral was built at the
end of the 15C for Cardi-
nal Della Rovere. The fa-
çade has three delicately
carved doorways while
the crown of the brick
campanile was designed
by Juvara in 1720.
Inside, on the floor above
the apse *(staircase to the
right of the chancel)* the
Chapel of the Holy Shroud
(Cappella della Santa Sin-
done) was the work of
Guarini (17C). An urn on
the high altar contains the
precious but much con-
tested **Holy Shroud** ★★★
(never on view to the
public: there is a series of
photographs alongside
the altar) in which Christ
is said to have been
wrapped after the De-
scent from the Cross.

★ **Mole Antonelliana**
⊘ (CX). – Built between
1863 and 1890 this unu-
sual building towering
167m – 548ft up into the
air, is the symbol of Turin.
The summit affords a vast
panorama ★★ of Turin.

ADDITIONAL
SIGHTS

★ **Motor Museum** (Museo
⊘ dell' Automobile Carlo Biscaretti di Ruffia). – *South of the
town. Take Corso Mas-
simo d'Azeglio* (BZ) *and
then follow the plan of the
built-up area in the current
Michelin Red Guide Italia.
The address is No 40
Corso Unità d'Italia.*
A vast modern building
houses this exhibition of
cars, chassis and engines
as well as a large library
and historic archives.

**Valentino Park (Parco del
Valentino)** (BCZ). – The
park extends along the Po
and contains the **Castello
del Valentino** built in 1688
for the Duchess Marie-
Christine of France, the
Exhibition Hall, the New
Theatre (Teatro Nuovo **T**)
⊘ and the **Borgo Medioevale** ★
a curious and faithful
reconstruction of a me-
dieval town with its
castle.

EXCURSIONS

Plan of the built-up area in the current Michelin Red Guide Italia.

★ **Basilica of Superga.** – *10km – 6 miles to the east.*

This masterpiece was built by Juvara between 1717 and 1731 on a summit of 670m – 2 198ft. Circular in plan and roofed with a dome its most remarkable feature is its monumental façade with its imposing columns and pilasters. The chapel dedicated to the Virgin, in the chancel, is a pilgrimage centre. The basilica is the Pantheon of the Kings of Sardinia.

TORINO

Carlo Felice (Piazza)	**BY** 16
Roma (Via)	**BXY**
San Carlo (Piazza)	**BXY**
Consolata (Via della)	**BV** 25
Diaz (Lungo Po A.)	**CY** 29
Ponte Isabella	**BZ** 45
Ponte Umberto I	**CZ** 47
Repubblica (Piazza della)	**BV** 53
Vitt. Emanuele II (Largo)	**ABY** 75
20 Settembre (Via)	**BY** 78

★ Royal tombs: the crypt is the resting-place of Victor Amadeus II who built the basilica to
⏱ fulfil a vow made when his capital was being besieged by a French and Spanish army
in 1706. Alongside are the tombs of Charles-Albert and other princes of the House of
Savoy. From the esplanade there is a fine **view★★★** of Turin, the Po Plain and the Alps.

★ Colle della Maddalena. – *32km -- 20 miles to the east.*
From Superga take the scenic route via Pino Torinese which affords good **views★★** of
Turin. From Pino Torinese continue to the hilltop, **Colle della Maddalena** and the **Parco della
Rimembranza,** a very popular large public park which commemorates those who died in
the First World War. On the way down there are more lovely **views★** of Turin. The
Europa Park at Cavoretto overlooks the southern part of the town.

★ Stupinigi Palace (Palazzina Mauriziana). – *11km – 7 miles to the southwest.*
⏱ This huge building was a hunting lodge built by Juvara for Victor Amadeus II of Savoy.
Napoleon stayed here before assuming the crown of Italy. The palace now houses a
Fine Arts and Furniture Museum. The apartments are richly decorated in the rococo style of
the 18C. A magnificent park surrounds the palazzina.

★ MONFERRATO

The itinerary described below *(150km – 93 miles – allow 1 day)* takes you through this
attractive region of limestone hills with its numerous castles and vineyards producing
most of the Piedmontese wines, the best known of which is Asti.

Leave Turin to the east by the S 10.

Chieri. – This town is known for its gastronomy. Note the Triumphal Arch (1580), the
15C Gothic cathedral and the 13-15C Church of San Domenico with its fine campanile.

Asti. – *Town plan in the current Michelin Red Guide Italia.* The home town of the tragic
poet, Vittorio Alfieri (1749-1803) is the scene of an annual horse race *(palio)* which is
preceded by a procession with over one thousand participants in 14 and 15C costume
(see the table of Principal Festivals at the end of the guide). The 12C **St Peter's Baptistry★**
the 15C Church of St Peter and the Gothic cloisters form an attractive group. In the
heart of the old town the 14C Gothic **cathedral** (Cattedrale) is decorated with baroque
paintings.

Take the S 231 and then the S 456 to reach Ovada.

★ Tour of the castles of the Monferrato. – Between Ovada and Serravalle Scrivia this scenic
route also known as the wine route, follows the crest of these hillsides covered with
vineyards. You pass on the way a series of perched villages each one guarded by a
castle.

★ TUSCANIA Latium   Pop 7 594

Michelin map 988 fold 25 – 24km – 15 miles west of Viterbo

Tuscania was a powerful Etruscan town, a Roman municipium and an important medieval centre. The town retains fragments of its walls and two superb churches, a little
way out of town. Tuscania's artistic heritage was considerably damaged by the earthquake of February 1971.

★★ St Peter's Church (San Pietro). – The golden-hued façade of St Peter's stands at the
far end of an empty square on the site of the Etruscan acropolis. To the left are two
medieval towers and to the right the former bishop's palace. The well balanced façade
dates from the early 13C. The symbols of the Evangelists surround a rose window
probably of the Umbrian school. Lower down an atlante (or a dancer?) and a man
(Laocöon?) being crushed by a snake came no doubt from Etruscan buildings.
The interior was built by Lombard masons in the 11C. Massive columns with beautiful
capitals support curious denticulated arches. The nave has its original and highly dec-
⏱ orative paving. The fescoes in the apse are 12C. The **crypt★★** is a forest of small columns, all different and of various periods – Roman, Pre-Romanesque and Romar-
esque – supporting groined vaulting.

★ St Mary Major's Church (Santa Maria Maggiore). – This late 12C church is modelled
on St Peter's. Note the 13C Romanesque **doorways★★** with their masterly sculptures.
Inside is an ambo rebuilt with 8C, 9C and 12C fragments. Above the triumphal arc
there is a realistic 14C fresco of the Last Judgment.

★ UDINE Friuli-Venezia Giulia   Pop 100 469

Michelin map 988 fold 6 – Town plan in the current Michelin Red Guide Italia

This charming town was the seat of the Patriarchs of Aquilea from 1238 to 1420
when it passed under Venetian rule. Udine nestles round a hill encircled by the picturesque alley, the Vicolo Sottomonte, with a castle on its summit. The charm of Udine
lies in its Gothic and Renaissance monuments, its secluded squares and narrow streets
often lined with arcades. The town was badly damaged, like most of Friuli, by the
1976 earthquake.

★★ Piazza della Libertà. – This very harmonious square has kept its Renaissance air
and is bordered by several public buildings. The former town hall, also known as the
Loggia del Lionello (1457) from the name of its architect. Its Venetian Gothic style is
characterised by the lightness and grace of its balconies and its white and rose stonework. Opposite on a slightly higher level is the 16C **Loggia di San Giovanni,** a Renaissance
portico surmounted by a 16C clock tower, with Moorish jacks *(Mori)* similar to the
ones in Venice. A 16C fountain plays in the centre of the square, not far from statues
of Hercules and Cacus and the columns of Justice and St Mark.

⊙ **Castle (Castello).** – This imposing early 16C building is preceded by an esplanade from which there is a good view of Udine and the surrounding Friuli countryside. This was the seat of the representatives of the Most Serene Republic (Venice).

Alongside is the 13C **Church of Santa Maria del Castello** with a 16C façade and campanile which bears a statue of the Archangel Gabriel at its summit. Inside there is a 13C fresco of the Descent from the Cross.

Cathedral (Duomo). – This 14C Gothic building remodelled in the 18C, has a lovely Flamboyant Gothic doorway. The massive campanile has, on one of its faces, a fine Annunciation and an Archangel Gabriel dating from the 14C. Inside there is attractive **baroque decoration★**: organ loft, pulpit, tombs, altarpieces and historiated stalls. Tiepolo painted the *trompe-l'œil* frescoes in the Chapel of the Holy Sacrament which are a remarkable piece of illusionism.

⊙ The **Oratory of Purity** (Oratorio della Purità), to the right of the cathedral, has a ceiling decorated with a remarkable Assumption (1757) by Tiepolo.

⊙ **Archbishop's Palace (Palazzo Arcivescovile).** – The 16-18C palace boasts **frescoes★** by Tiepolo. The ceiling of its grand staircase has a Fall of the Rebel Angels while the apartments are decorated with scenes from the Old Testament.

Piazza Matteotti. – This lovely square bordered by arcaded houses is the site of a lively open-air market. Note also the elegant 16C baroque Church of San Giacomo, a 16C fountain and a 15C column of the Virgin. It is pleasant to stroll in Via Mercato Vecchio and Via Vittorio Veneto with their shops beneath the arcades.

★ URBINO Marches   Pop 15 740

Michelin map 988 folds 15 and 16 – Town plan in the current Michelin Red Guide Italia

Urbino is built on two hills overlooking the undulating countryside bathed in a glorious golden light. Urbino was ruled by the Montefeltro family from the 12C onwards and reached its zenith in the reign (1444-82) of **Duke Federico da Montefeltro,** a wise leader, man of letters, collector and patron of the arts. Urbino was the birthplace of **Raphael** (Raffaello Sanzio) (1483-1520).

★ DUCAL PALACE **(PALAZZO DUCALE)** *time: 1 1/2 hours*

This masterpiece of balance and taste was begun in 1444 on the orders of Federico who until 1472 entrusted the work to the Dalmatian architect Luciano Laurana. The palace was completed by Francesco di Giorgio Martini. Overlooking the valley, to the west, the tall façade consists of superimposed loggias between two towers. To the east, a wing pierced with elegant paired windows borders the square overlooked by the cathedral. The inner court of honour is a classic example of Renaissance harmony.

★ **National Gallery of the Marches (Galleria Nazionale delle Marche).** – The palace rooms
⊙ with their original decoration are the setting for some tremendous masterpieces: the predella of the *Profanation of the Host* (1465-9) by Paolo Uccello, the *Madonna* of Senigallia, the astonishing *Flagellation* by Piero della Francesca and the famous portrait of a woman, known as **The Mute,** by Raphael. The astonishing **studiolo★★★** (study) of Duke Federico is panelled with magnificent intarsia work probably after Botticelli.

ADDITIONAL SIGHTS

★ **Raphael's House (Casa di Raffaello).** – *57 Via Raffaello.*
⊙ Raphael lived here up to the age of fourteen. This typical 15C house belonged to the boy's father, Giovanni Sanzio or Santi and contains mementoes of the artist.

⊙ **Oratory Churches of St John** (San Giovanni Battista) **and St Joseph** (San Giuseppe). – *Via Barocci.*
Of these two neighbouring churches the first is 14C and has curious **frescoes★★** by the Salimbene brothers depicting the life of St John the Baptist. The second, dating from the 16C, has in the nave a colossal statue of St Joseph (18C) painted in grisaille and a very lovely stucco **crib★**, a life-size work by Federico Brandani (1522-75).

★ **Strada Panoramica.** – Starting from Piazza Roma, this road skirts a hillside and affords admirable **views★★** of the town walls, the lower town, Ducal Palace and cathedral: a wonderful scene in various hues of pink brick.

★ VELIA Campania

Michelin map 988 fold 38 – 14km - 9 miles northwest of Pisciotta

⊙ The extensive ruins of the ancient city of **Elea** are situated in the vicinity of Castellammare di Velia in the region of Cilento. Excavations have only uncovered part of the site. This colony was founded in 535 BC by Phocean Greek refugees who had been expelled by the Persians. Before settling in Massilia (Marseilles) they lived in the Corsican settlement of Alalia (Aleria) where they were victorious in a naval battle (c538) against the combined Carthaginian and Etruscan fleet. The busy and prosperous port of Velia – known for a long times as Elea – is famous for its school of the Eleatic philosophers (5C). Two of the better known philosphers were Parmenides and his pupil Zeno.

Lower town. – *Go under the railway line to reach this quarter.* From the entrance there is an interesting general view of the ruins which include the former lighthouse, 4C BC town wall, the south sea gateway and the 4C BC **Pink Gateway★**.

Acropolis. – A medieval castle stands up against the remains of a 5C Greek temple. Laid out below are the ruins of the amphitheatre. A small **museum** houses statues of Parmenides, Zeno and Aesculapius which were found amidst the ruins.

A fascinating city between sea and sky, like Venus rising from the waves, Venice welcomes tourists from the five continents drawn to her by the charm of her water pellucid light and coolness of the sea breezes. She also offers the intellectual pleasures to be derived from her masterpieces which mark the meeting of East and West.

The vanished greatness of Venice accounts for the myth of an artificial, voluptuous and tragic city, the scene of intrigues plotted in an atmosphere of corruption where dreams became nightmares. The Romantics especially have described this atmosphere of a city capable of both disturbing and fascinating. Many have described this Venice including Barrès, Thomas Mann in his novel *Death in Venice* which the Italian film-maker Luchino Visconti made into a film.

Today the exceptional position of Venice constitutes a threat to its very existence The nature of the terrain on which it is built induces a sinking while the level of the surrounding waters is constantly rising. Various measures have already been taken and a plan to safeguard and remedy the position has been elaborated.

Access. – The classic approach, ① on the town plan, is through Mestre and the road and railway bridge 4km – 2 1/2 miles long. The trip across the lagoon is somewhat spoilt by the sight of smoke from the port of Marghera and its factories. The bridge leads to the Piazzale Roma (AT), where you must leave the car in one of the paying garages *(autorimesse)* in the square, or in the specially provided car parks on the nearby man-made island of Tronchetto *(July to mid-October, allow at least an hour's delay)*.

Transport. – The best way to make contact with Venice from the Piazzale Roma is to take the little steamer *(vaporetto* – line No 1 *accelerato:* omnibus service) that runs to St Mark's in 1/2 hour, via the Grand Canal. The motor-boats *(motoscafi)* are quicker (line No 2; direct service; 1/4 hour), taking a short-cut through the Rio Nuovo (ATU) The gondolas (1 hour) are delightful, but it is wise to agree in advance on the charge as one would with a porter *(facchino)*. In Venice itself, the canals can be crossed in the gondolas and ferries *(traghetti)*.

Seasons. – The best are spring and autumn. The Venice 'Season' is in summer, time of the sumptuous festivals: Feast of the Redeemer on the Island of Giudecca, the historical Regatta on the Grand Canal; an International Film Festival at the Lido towards the end of summer; concerts in the various churches; the Arts Biennale brings together the works of the world's leading artists. *See the table of Principal Festivals at the end of the guide.*

VARIOUS ASPECTS OF VENICE

Venice is built on 117 islands; it has 150 canals and 400 bridges. A canal is called *rio*, a square a *campo*, a street a *calle* or *salizzada*, a quay a *riva* or *fondamenta*, a filled in canal *rio Terrà*, a passageway under a house *sotto-portego*, a courtyard a *corte* and a small square a *campiello*. The narrow streets, with their historic names, are paved with flagstones but have no footpaths. They are lined with flower-decked balconies, madonnas, shop signs and lanterns. Artisans' stalls and palaces stand side by side. The squares are charming with their well curbs often sculpted *(vera da pozzo)*.

The hub of public life is the Piazza San Marco *(p 203)* where tourists and citizens sit on the terraces of the famous Florian and Quadri cafés to listen to the music, dream and see the mosaics of St Mark's glow under the rays of the setting sun. The Quadri is more popular but the Florian is the best-known café: founded in 1720 it has received Byron, Goethe, George Sand, Musset and Wagner within its mirrored and allegory painted walls.

The shops in St Mark's have sumptuous window displays of lace, jewellery, looking glasses and the famous Murano glassware. The **Marzarie (CTU)**, shopping streets, lead to the Rialto Bridge *(p 205)*.

(Visue

Venice – Gondolas

On the far side of this are the displays of greengrocers *(erberie)* and fishmongers' shops *(pescherie)*. In addition to these well-known and busy areas there are the **Frari Quarter** (ABT) and that of **Santa Maria Formosa** (CT), which have a certain peaceful charm with their brick façades and silent canals.

Meals in the restaurants *(trattorie)* are among the attractions of Venice. The fare consists chiefly of sea-food, squid *(calamaretti)*, cuttlefish, eels and mussels in the Venetian way but also calf's liver also cooked in the Venetian way, with onions. These dishes should be accompanied by the pleasant local wines: Valpolicella, Bardolino and Amarone for red wines and Soave and Prosecco for the whites.

Gondolas and Gondoliers. – Gondolas are inseparable from a mental picture of Venice: gondolas dancing over the ripples or moored to the tall posts called *pali* near the **Paglia Bridge** (CU), where the gondoliers' Madonna stands; gondolas for serenades lit with lanterns, gliding on the small canals at night, police gondolas, refuse-collecting gondolas, fire service gondolas, goods delivery gondolas and even funeral gondolas with black pompoms.

As for the gondoliers, wearing sailors' jumpers and straw hats with coloured ribbons, they murmur gondola, gondola as they propel their craft with a single oar, humming their songs.

The Venetians. – Venetians have pale complexions and lisp slightly. Venetian is an Italian dialect. Their sense of intrigue and their subtlety were displayed equally in love and in politics: Venetian procuresses, spies and ambassadors used to be equally famous for their skill. The black velvet mask and domino, so often worn in Venice, added to the secrecy.

Venetians love pomp and are fond of the Carnival, other festivals *(see previous page)* and gorgeous processions with Venice as the perfect setting.

The Marriage of Venice and the Sea. – Every year, from 1173 to 1797, a gorgeous ceremony perfectly expressed what used to be the greatness of Venice and is still its beauty. After the Venetian Republic supported Pope Alexander III in his struggle against the Emperor Frederick Barbarossa, the Pontiff gave the Doge a ring as a symbol of his 'rule of the sea'. In memory of this, every year on Ascension Day, the Doge, dressed in cloth of gold, boarded *Bucentaur*, his gilded state galley, and sailed out to throw a ring into the sea with the words: "We wed thee, Sea, in token of our perpetual rule".

HISTORICAL NOTES

Venice was founded in AD 811 by the inhabitants of Malamocco, near the Lido, fleeing from the Franks. They settled on the Rivo Alto, known today as the Rialto. In 828 the bones of St Mark the Evangelist were brought from Alexandria; he became the protector of the town. The Republic was developed under the rule of a doge, a name derived from the Latin *dux* (leader).

The Venetian Empire. – From the 9 to the 13C Venice grew steadily richer as It exploited its position between East and West. With such maritime and commercial power it conquered Istria and Dalmatia. The Crusaders, led by Doge Dandolo, captured Constantinople in 1204. The products of its sack flowed to Venice, while trade in spices, fabrics and precious stones from markets established in the East grew apace. **Marco Polo** (1254-1324) returned from China with fabulous riches and related his adventures in French in his *Book of Marvels*. The 14C war with its rival Genoa ended in victory for the Venetians in 1381.

Zenith. – The first half of the 15C saw Venetian power at its zenith: the Turks were defeated at Gallipoli in 1416 and the Venetians held the kingdoms of Morea, Cyprus and Candia (Crete) in the Levant.

In mainland Italy, between 1414 and 1428, they captured Verona, Vicenza, Padua, Udine, and then Brescia and Bergamo. The Adriatic became the Venetian Sea from Corfu to the Po.

Decline. – The capture of Constantinople by the Turks in 1453 started the decadence. The discovery of America caused a shift in the patterns of trade and Venice had to keep up an exhausting struggle with the Turks, who seized Cyprus in 1500 but were defeated in 1571 in the naval battle of **Lepanto,** in which the Venetians played an important part. Their decline, however, was confirmed in the 17C when the Turks captured Candia (Crete) after a twenty-five year siege. The "Most Serene Republic" came to an end in 1797. Bonaparte entered Venice and abolished a ten century old constitution.

The long-lasting oligarchy. – The government of the Republic was from its earliest days organised to avoid the rise to power of a single man. The role of doge was supervised by several councils: the Grand Council elaborated the laws; the Senate was responsible for foreign affairs, military and economic matters; the Council of Ten, responsible for security, kept a network of secret police and informers which created an atmosphere of mistrust.

VENETIAN PAINTING

The Venetian school of painting with its affirmed sensuality is characterised by the predominance of colour over draughtsmanship and by an innate sense of light in landscapes whose outlines are veiled by a general haze. Art historians have often noted the contrast between the scholarly and idealistic art of the Florentines and the freer more spontaneous work of the Venetians, whose example has been perpetuated up until the Impressionists. The real beginnings of Venetian painting are exemplified by the **Bellini** family; Jacopo, the father and Gentile (1429-1507) and **Giovanni** or **Giambellino** (1430-1516), his sons. The latter and younger was a profoundly spiritual artist and one of the first Renaissance artists who integrated his figures harmoniously with landscape backgrounds. Their pupil **Carpaccio** (1455-1525) recorded Venetian life with his usual imagination and care for detail while **Giorgione** *(qv)* continued to exercise his influence. His pupil, **Lorenzo Lotto**, assimilated the lesson of realism as practised by Northern artists.

The Renaissance ended in splendour with three great artists: **Titian** (*c*1490-1576) who introduced movement into his dramatic scenes and was also a skilled colourist; **Veronese** (1528-88) sumptuous decorator who described the luxurious lives of the patricians of the Most Serene Republic; and finally **Tintoretto** (1518-94), a visionary whose dramatic technique reflects an inner anxiety.

The artists of the 18C recalled Venice and its peculiar light, grey-blue, iridescent and slightly misty: **Canaletto** (1697-1768) whose works were so popular with English Grand Tourists and his pupil Bellotto (1720-80) were both inspired by townscapes, **Francesco Guardi** (1712-93) who painted in luminous touches, **Pietro Longhi** (1702-58), the author of intimate scenes, **Giovanni Battista Tiepolo** (1696-1770), a master decorator and creator of graceful transparent and illusionist frescoes and his son, Gian Domenico (1727-1804).

Spontaneity and colour are also found in the musicians of Venice, of whom the best known is **Antonio Vivaldi** (1678-1743).

★★ ST MARK'S SQUARE (PIAZZA SAN MARCO) (CU) *time: 1/2 day*

St Mark's Square is famous all over the world; it forms a great marble saloon. All around covered galleries shelter famous cafés and luxury shops. In front of the basilica are three flag-poles symbolising the Venetian Kingdoms of Cyprus, Candia (Crete) and Morea.

The square opens on the Grand Canal through the delightful **Piazzetta (CU 46)**. The two granite columns surmounted by a statue adapted to look like the Winged Lion of St Mark and the statue of St Theodore, the first patron saint of Venice, were brought from Constantinople.

★★ St Mark's Basilica (Basilica San Marco) (CU).

St Mark's is a structure of mingled Byzantine and Western style, built from 1063 to 1073 to shelter the tomb of the Evangelist Mark. Changes were made at the time of the Renaissance and in the 17C. Despite the great variety of styles (Byzantine, Romanesque, Gothic and Renaissance) the outcome is a unified and harmonious ensemble. The rich decoration of marbles and mosaics on gilded backgrounds is magnificent and has earned the basilica the name of the golden church (Chiesa d'Oro).

Built on the plan of a Greek cross, it is surmounted by a bulbous dome flanked by four smaller domes of unequal height placed on the arms of the cross.

Façade. – This is pierced with five large doorways adorned with variegated marbles and sculptures. The central doorway has lovely 13-14C sculptures on the archivolt and recessed arches and above are copies of the four famous **Bronze Horses** *(the originals are in the Museum of the Basilica: see below)*. The doors have lovely Byzantine bronze panels.

At the lateral doorways, mosaics depict the Translation of the body of St Mark. There is a picture of the basilica in its original form on the last door on the left. The porphyry group, known as the **Tetrarchs** (4C), stands to the right of the façade, near the Doge's Palace. At the corner is the proclamation stone (pietra del bando), where laws were proclaimed. The pretty Piazzetta dei Leoncini (**CU 41**) lies to the left of the façade.

Narthex. – The narthex is faced with multicoloured marbles and mosaics and roofed with six little domes. The 13C **mosaics★★** depict with plenty of detail scenes from the Old Testament.

Interior. – The dazzling decoration, composed of rare marbles, porphyry and outstanding **mosaics★★★** of Byzantine (12-13C) and Renaissance (16C) inspiration on a gilded background harmonises perfectly with the architecture. The 12C paving is highly decorative. In the nave, on the west wall, a 13C mosaic portrays Christ, the Virgin and St Mark. The Arch of Paradise over the narthex is adorned with 16C mosaics illustrating the Last Judgment based on cartoons by Tintoretto. The early 12C mosaic on the first dome above the nave, symbolises Pentecost. Christ and the Virgin, surrounded by Prophets, are seen in the Byzantine mosaics on the walls. On the arch dividing the dome above the nave from the central dome is a fine Crucifixion in the Byzantine style, also in mosaic (13C).

From the south aisle, you enter the **baptistry**, adorned with mosaics (14C) depicting the Life of Christ and that of St John the Baptist. The baptistry contains the Sansovino Font (1545) and doges' tombs. The adjoining Chapel of St Zeno, with interesting 13C mosaics of the life of St Mark, occupies part of the narthex.

In the north aisle stands the *capitello*, a small marble shrine topped by a large oriental agate. The north transept contains interesting mosaics (episodes in the life of St John the Evangelist, Last Supper and Miracles of Jesus) after Veronese and Tintoretto. An Ascension, in mosaic, on the dome over the transept crossing, is 13C. The iconostasis in front of the chapel was made in 1394 and carries fine sculptures of Christ on the Cross, the Virgin and the Apostles.

The **chancel** is roofed with a dome whose Byzantine mosaics represent Christ and the Virgin among the Prophets. On the roof to the right another mosaic shows the Translation of the Relics of St Mark. The Evangelist is entombed under the high altar, above which rises a green marble canopy supported by splendid alabaster columns carved with scenes from the Gospels.

The famous **Pala d'Oro★★★**, gold altarpiece, displays a wonderful assemblage of gold, silver, enamel and jewels. It was made at Constantinople in 976 and restored at Venice in 1105 and 1345.

Through the south transept you reach the rich **treasury★★★** partly formed in the 13C from booty from the pillage of Constantinople by the Crusaders in 1204. At the far end of the chancel are translucent **alabaster columns★★** and to the left a bronze door by Sansovino (16C) leading to the sacristy.

Go up, through the narthex, to the **galleries** which now house the **Museum of the Basilica** where one can now admire the **Bronze Horses★★★** which once adorned the façade. These masterpieces of the Greco-Roman period were brought from Constantinople by Doge Dandolo in 1204. Bonaparte had them removed to the Carrousel Arch in Paris, where they remained until the fall of the French Empire.

There is an attractive view of St Mark's Square from the Bronze Horses' platform.

★★ **Campanile** (CU F). – From the top of this 99m – 325ft high bell-tower there is a fine **panorama★★** of Venice. The campanile collapsed in 1902 but was rebuilt stone by stone. The **loggetta★★** (small loggia) at its base has very pure lines. Note the fine 18C bronze doors and in the niches the statues (Minerva, Apollo, Mercury and Peace) by Sansovino. A delightful Madonna, also by Sansovino, will be found inside.

★★★ **Doges' Palace** (Palazzo Ducale) (CU). – The palace is a symbol of Venetian power and glory and was the residence of the doges and the seat of government and the law courts as well as being a prison. Built in the 12C it was completely transformed between the end of the 13C and the 16C.

A pretty geometrical pattern in white and pink marble lends great charm to the two **façades**. The ground floor gallery is supported by thirty-six columns with exquisite 14-15C historiated capitals. The groups at the corners of the palace represent, from left to right, the **Judgment of Solomon** (attributed to Jacopo della Quercia), Adam and Eve, and **Noah's Drunkenness** (14-15C Gothic sculptures). The open upper gallery has seventy-one columns surmounted by quatrefoil oculi.

The main entrance is the **Porta della Carta,** so-called because decrees were posted on it. It is in the Flamboyant Gothic style (1442) and has on its tympanum a Lion of St Mark before which Doge Foscari (19C copy) is kneeling. In the niches on the uprights are figures representing Strength and Prudence (right) and Temperance and Charity (left).

Courtyard. – The main façade is a splendid example of Renaissance style, richly adorned with sculptures. The wells with bronze curbs date from the 16C.

Standing against the Foscari Portico is the small clock façade, dating from 1615 by B. Monopola while alongside and rising above the portico is a curious 15C building crowned with pinnacles and allegorical statues of the Arts. Beyond the portico is the famous **Giants' Staircase★★★** (Scala dei Giganti) so-called after the massive figures of Mars and Neptune by Sansovino.

Interior. – By way of Sansovino's **Golden Staircase★★★** (Scala d'Oro), which starts from the gallery on the first floor, one reaches the **doges' apartments**: a picture gallery regroups the works of Giovanni Bellini, Carpaccio and Hieronymus Bosch.

Follow the stairway up to the second floor.

The square vestibule has a gilded ceiling with paintings by Tintoretto.

The elegant **Four Doors Room** is adorned with paintings by Tintoretto, who decorated the ceiling.

The **Anticollegio** is a former waiting-room. It contains a fine chimney-piece with atlantes. The **Rape of Europa**, on the wall to the right, is a famous work by Veronese. On the other walls, Tintoretto painted an exceptional series of mythological subjects (the Marriage of Ariadne and Bacchus, Minerva repelling Mars, the Forge of Vulcan as well as Mercury and the Graces).

The **College Hall** used to be where the Doge and his councillors met and ratified treaties and agreements. The ceiling is decorated with eleven paintings by Veronese and his pupils (1577). Above the ducal throne Veronese painted the Doge, Sebastiano Venier, giving thanks to Christ for the naval victory of Lepanto over the Turks. On the walls are allegories by Tintoretto with portraits of the doges.

The ceiling of the **Senate Chamber** is decorated with a remarkable **Triumph of Venice**★★★ by **Tintoretto**, who also painted the Descent from the Cross.

The **Meeting Chamber of the Council of Ten** has a remarkable coffered ceiling painted with two scenes (Old Oriental with a Young Woman and Juno offering the Doges' Headdress to Venice) by a youthful Veronese.

Go down the Censors' Stairway (Scala dei Censori) to reach the **Grand Council Chamber**★★★ which is the finest room in the palace and measures 52m – 171ft by 23m – 75ft. The walls are adorned with paintings illustrating Venetian history. Over the doge's throne **Tintoretto** painted **Paradise**★★★, one of the largest compositions in the world (22m – 72ft by 7m – 23ft). On the ceiling (near the throne) **Veronese** painted the **Apotheosis of Venice**★★★ while the cornice bears the portraits of the seventy-six first Doges: the missing one is Faliero the traitor. His portrait has been replaced by a black veil and his condemnation. Henri II, on his way back from Poland, is said to have attended a banquet in this chamber and pronounced "If I was not King of France, I would like to be a citizen of Venice".

The **Ballot Room**★★★ is ornamented with paintings depicting Venetian naval victories. The visit ends with the Censors' Room and the Avogaria.

★ **Bridge of Sighs (Ponte dei Sospiri)** (CU). – The Bridge of Sighs connects the Doges Palace with the **prisons (CU X)**, in which Casanova was incarcerated but from which he made a fantastic escape. It dates from the 17C and owes its name to the lamentations of prisoners who were conducted across it to their place of execution.

★★ **Law Courts (Procuratie)**. – With their galleries and columns these buildings make a graceful background for the square. The **Clock Tower**★ (Torre dell' Orologio) (CU K) dates from the end of the 15C. The dial bears the signs of the zodiac. On its summit are the famous Moors *(Mori)*, a pair of giant bronze jacks which have been striking the hours for 500 years.

To the left of the Clock Tower, the **Procuratie Vecchie** (Old Law Courts) (CU B) built at the beginning of the 16C, served as a residence for the procurators attached to the building committee of the basilica, who were responsible for its upkeep. The **Procuratie Nuove** (New Law Courts) (CU L), opposite, date from the 17C.

The **Ala Napoleonica** which completes the square, was built by order of Napoleon in 1810. Under the arches is the entrance to the **Correr Museum**★ (CU M) which contains the historical and artistic collections of the city. In the picture gallery, on the second floor, note a Virgin and Child by Thierry Bouts; a Crucifixion by Van des Goes; a *Pietà* by Antonello da Messina; the portrait of Doge Mocenigo by Gentile Bellini; a *Pietà* by Cosimo Tura; a **Pietà, Madonna** and **Transfiguration** by Giovanni Bellini; and the famous **Courtesans** by Carpaccio.

★ **Old Library (Libreria Vecchia)** (CU N). – This noble and harmonious building was designed by Sansovino in 1553 and now contains at No 17 the **Archaeological Museum** and at No 7 the **Marciana Library** with its illuminated manuscripts and the famous Grimani Breviary (15-16C Flemish school).

★★ GRAND CANAL (CANAL GRANDE) *time: half a day including sightseeing*

The French writer and ambassador, Philippe de Commines wrote of the Grand Canal in the 15C: "I think it is the finest street in all the world and has the finest houses". Venice's widest canal winds in a large double bend from the station to St Mark's basin and is lined with sumptuous palaces in various styles. These were the residences of the patricians whose names were in the Golden Book. Tour the Grand Canal in a steamer starting from St Mark's Square.

★ Rialto Bridge (Ponte di Rialto) (CT)

The graceful Rialto Bridge, halfway along the canal, was built from 1588 to 1592 by Antonio da Ponte, and was designed to allow an armed galley to pass under it. It is a hump-backed bridge with a central street lined with shops and gangways on either side affording views of the Grand Canal.

The nearby **Fondaco dei Tedeschi** (CT), now a Post Office, was used in the 12-14C as a warehouse by German merchants.

Right bank (East)

★★ **Palazzo Corner-Spinelli (BTU D)**. – A late 15C-early 16C Renaissance palace with splendid basket-handled arched windows.

★★ **Palazzo Grimani (BT Q)**. – This majestic white palace is a masterpiece of the High Renaissance by Sammicheli (late 16C).

★ **Ca' Loredan (BT H)**. – This former warehouse *(casa fondaro)* in the Veneto-Byzantine style has 16C additions.

★★★ **Ca' d' Oro** (BT). – The "golden house" used to be gilded all over. This the most
ⓥ elegant palace in Venice, is in the ornate Gothic style (1440). It houses the **Franchetti
Gallery★★** (tapestries, sculpture and a fine collection of paintings: Mantegna, Carpaccio, Titian, Van Dyck and Guardi).

★★ **Palazzo Vendramin-Calergi** (BT R). – It was in this rich Renaissance palace (1509)
with its admirable twinned openings, that Wagner died in 1883.

Left bank (West)

★★ **Church of Santa Maria della Salute.** – *Description below*.

★★ **Palazzo Dario** (BV S). – Charming Early Renaissance palace (1487) where Henri de
Régnier lived.

★★ **Palazzo Rezzonico** (AU). – This imposing and well balanced baroque edifice was
built in the 17C by Longhena, but only completed a century later. Inside there is a
museum on 18C Venice *(p 207)*.

★★ **Palazzo Giustiniano** (AU X). – This comprises two identical 15C buildings which
are good examples of the ornate Gothic style.

★★ **Ca'Foscari** (AU Y). – This 15C palace was the residence of Doge Foscari when he
was deposed by the Council of Ten in 1457. He died here the very next day.

★★ **Palazzo Bernardo** (BT Z). – One of the best examples of the ornate Gothic (1442)
style.

★★ **Palazzo dei Camerlenghi** (CT A). – Elegant white building of the Renaissance
period.

★★ **Palazzo Pesaro** (BT M¹). – Longhena's baroque masterpiece now houses a Gallery
of Modern Art *(p 207)*.

★★★ ACADEMY OF FINE ARTS (GALLERIE DELL'ACCADEMIA) (BV)
time: 2 hours

ⓥ The Academy is housed in the School and Church of St Mary of Charity (Santa Maria
della Carità) and in the Lateran Canons' Monastery. It is one of the finest art collections
in Italy and reviews Venetian painting from the 14 to the 18C.
The first room contains works by the few Venetian Primitives, notably Paolo and
Lorenzo Veneziano. The Renaissance is well represented in the following rooms with
works by Giovanni Bellini (the majestic composition of the **San Giobbe altarpiece**, scholarly allegories, numerous madonnas with landscape backgrounds including the *Madonna of the Orange Tree*), Carpaccio, Cima da Conegliano, Mantegna *(St George)*, Piera
della Francesca, Cosimo Tura, and Hans Memling (a fine **Portrait of a Young Man**). One of
the jewels of the collection, is Giorgione's **Tempest** in which nature has become the
main subject and seems to be subjugating the personages with its mysterious power.
Further on pause before Tintoretto's famous *Virgin of the Treasurers of the Republic* and
Lorezzo Lotto's lovely **Portrait of a Gentleman**.
In the **Meal in the House of Levi**, Veronese used all the magic of his decorative technique.
There are also several fine works by Tintoretto, including his *Miracles of St Mark*, and
Titian's moving but unfinished **Pietà** (1576).
In the following rooms, the 17 and 18C are represented by Tiepolo, Piazzetta, Rosalba
Carriera, Canaletto, Pietro Longhi and Guardi.
Room XX contains the **Miracles of the Holy Cross**, a cycle of paintings of which three are
by Gentile Bellini and one by Carpaccio. Note especially a Gentile Bellini, *The Procession
of Relics in St Mark's Square* which is a faithful record of Venetian life in 1500, and
Carpaccio's *The Healing of Someone Possessed, beside the Rialto Bridge*. The **Legend of
St Ursula** in the next room is a series of nine pictures (1480-*c*1500) by Carpaccio in
which the painter shows an eye for picturesque detail and a remarkable clarity of composition.
Finally in Room XXIV the **Presentation of the Virgin at the Temple** is one of Titian's masterpieces.

PRINCIPAL CHURCHES

★★ **Church of St Mary of Salvation** (Santa Maria della Salute) (BV). – The Salute was
ⓥ built at the entrance to the Grand Canal in the 17C by Longhena after an epidemic of
plague, to fulfil a vow. This baroque church stands on an admirable site at the water's
edge. The monumental interior is built on an octagonal plan and is surmounted by a
central dome. The sacristy contains **Tintoretto's Marriage at Cana★★★** (1561) with its
warm luminous colours. Note also the **ceiling** painted by Titian, the **St Mark's altarpiece**
on the left altar and the eight **medallions of the Evangelists.**
Near Santa Maria are the charming square, **Campo San Gregorio** (BV) and a Gothic church
with a fine 15C doorway. At the end of the Punta della Salute is the **Dogana di Mare** (CV
(1677), or Maritime Customs House, with a revolving statue of Fortune aloft.

★★ **Church of St George Major** (San Giorgio Maggiore) (CV). – This church on the Island
of San Giorgio, facing St Mark's Square, was begun by Palladio in 1566 and completed in 1610 by Scamazzio, the designer of its noble façade. The tall brick **campanile★★** was built in 1791 using St Mark's one as a model.
The interior is severe but of majestic proportions. Two **paintings★★★** by **Tintoretto** face
one another on the walls of the chancel: the Harvest of Manna and the Last Supper
which is remarkable for its chiaroscuro. There are also splendidly carved 16C
ⓥ **stalls★★**. From the **terrace of the campanile** *(lift in the north transept)* there is a **panorama★★★** of Venice and its lagoon.

★★ **Church of St John and St Paul** (Ss Giovanni e Paolo or San Zanipolo) (**CT**). – This Gothic church (1234-1430) built by the Dominicans, stands in a spacious square. Also in the square is a 16C well curb and an admirable **equestrian statue**★★ (1480), full of power and energy, of the mercenary leader Bartolomeo Colleoni by Verrocchio.

This vast church is the pantheon of Venice; it contains many **tombs**★★ of doges and patricians. Among the paintings is a beautiful **altarpiece figuring St Vincent Ferrier**★★★ by Giovanni Bellini (second altar in the south aisle) and an Annunciation, Adoration of the Shepherds and an Assumption of the Virgin by **Veronese** on the **ceiling**★★★ of the Rosary Chapel *(entrance in the north transept)*.

To the left of the church, in the square, is the **Scuola di San Marco** (St Mark's School) with a Renaissance **façade**★ richly decorated with sculptures by Pietro and Tullio Lombardo. The **Rio dei Mendicanti**★ (Beggars' Canal) (**CT**) which runs beside the Sculo di San Marco, frequently figured in the works of Canaletto and Guardi.

★★ **Church of St Mary** (Santa Maria Gloriosa dei Frari) (**AT**). – This Franciscan Gothic ⓒ church is the largest in Venice. Inside there are numerous **tombs**★★ including Canova's monument and Titian's mausoleum. Examine the magnificent painted altarpieces and particularly two **works by Titian**★★★: the famous Assumption on the high altar and the admirable Virgin of the Pesaro Family on the second altar in the north aisle. A **triptych** of a **Madonna and Saints**★★ by Giovanni Bellini is shown in the sacristy.

★ **Church of St Zachary** (San Zaccaria) (**CU**). – San Zaccaria, which dates from the Renaissance, stands in a pleasant square. It has a 13C campanile. In the north aisle (at the second altar) is an **altarpiece of the Madonna with Four Saints**★★★ by Giovanni Bellini. In the San Tarasio Chapel there is a fresco by Andrea del Castagno, and three splendid **altarpieces**★★ by Antonio Vivarini and Ludovico da Forli.

SCHOOLS (SCUOLE)

The *Scuole*, typically Venetian institutions were confraternities which often assumed charitable roles. A *Scuola* usually included an assembly room, a chapel and sometimes an almshouse.

★★ **Scuola di San Rocco** (**AT**). – The Renaissance building has a graceful façade of ⓒ basket-handled arches, fluted columns and marble incrustations. There is an outstanding series of fifty-six **paintings**★★★ by **Tintoretto** on which he worked for eighteen years. The best are: on the ground floor, an *Annunciation* and a *Massacre of the Innocents*; on the first floor, in the Great Hall, *Moses drawing Water from the Rock,* the *Miracle of the Brazen Serpent, Manna raining down from Heaven, the Last Supper, the Nativity, the Ascension* and in the small Albergo Room an immense *Crucifixion* so full of drama that Tintoretto regarded it as his best work. Note also Titian's *Dead Christ* and Giorgione's admirable *Christ carrying the Cross.*

★ **Scuola di San Giorgio degli Schiavoni** (**DT**). – This institution received natives of ⓒ Dalmatia, nicknamed Esclavonians by the Venetians, who were citizens of the Venetian Republic, and in particular old seamen. The Renaissance oratory is adorned with exquisite **paintings by Carpaccio**★★ relating the *Legend of St George,* the *Miracle of St Tryphonius* and the *Story of St Jerome.* There is a remarkable portrait of *St Augustine* in his cell.

★ **Scuola dei Carmini** (**AU**). – Inside the ceiling (first floor) is decorated with a masterly ⓒ **cycle of paintings**★★ by Giovanni Battista Tiepolo including a fresco depicting the Virgin in glory appearing to the Blessed Simon Stock.

ADDITIONAL SIGHTS

★★ **Peggy Guggenheim Collection** (BV M²). – The 18C **Palazzo Venierdei Leoni**, al-ⓒ though never completed, is the setting for an exceptional collection of paintings and sculpture by the best 20C artists. The collector Peggy Guggenheim was the muse of the Surrealists.

★ **Venice in the 18C** (Museo del Settecento Veneziano) (AU M³). – This is housed in the ⓒ Palazzo Rezzonico *(p 206).* The collection includes (on the first floor) Venetian baroque furniture, black, gold and heavily carved; genre pictures by Pietro Longhi as well as two **masterpieces**★★ by Guardi: *The Ridotto* (a famous Venetian gambling club) and the *Nuns' Parlour*; and **frescoes**★★ by Gian Domenico Tiepolo portraying the frivolity of Venetian society.

★ **Palazzo Querini-Stampalia** (**CT**). – Picture gallery containing a series of works by ⓒ Donato and Caterino Veneziano, the Florentine Lorenzo di Credi, Giovanni Bellini *(Presentation of Jesus in the Temple)*, Palma Vecchio, V. Catena and Pietro Longhi.

★ **Museum of Modern Art** (BT M¹). – The Palazzo Pesaro *(p 206)* houses this collecⓒ tion which is essentially devoted to 19C Italian painting.

Churches. – There are approximately two hundred churches in Venice, nearly all interesting. Among them are:

West of the Grand Canal: 16C **San Sebastiano (AU)** with remarkable **interior decoration**★★ including paintings (Story of Queen Esther on the ceiling) by Veronese and a curious organ dating from the late 16C; nearby the Church of **Angelo Raffaele (AU)** contains an organ loft decorated with seven delightful 18C **paintings**★, attributed to Guardi; and also not far away from the Scuola di San Rocco, the **Church of San Pantaleone (AT)** with its magnificent 18C **ceiling**★ painted in *trompe-l'œil.*

East of the Grand Canal: **Santa Maria dei Miracoli**★ (**CT**) built in 1489 by P. Lombardo, is a jewel of the Renaissance adorned with multicoloured marbles; and **San Francesco della Vigna (DT)** designed by Sansovino (16C), with a façade by Palladio, classical cloisters and two remarkable paintings of the **Virgin and Child**★, one of which is by Giovanni Bellini.

ⓥ **Palazzo Labia** (AT). – This 18C palace contains a room magnificently covered in **frescoes★** by Tiepolo depicting the story of Antony and Cleopatra. Several other ceilings in the palace are also by the artist.

Arsenal (DU V). – The Arsenal was founded in 1104 and rebuilt in the 15 and 16C. The entrance to the basin is guarded by two towers dating from 1574. The monumental gateway (1460) to their left is preceded by baroque statues and lions of Greek origin. The Arsenal was famous throughout Europe and in its heyday it could build and equip a small galley in a single day.

ⓥ **Naval Museum** (DU M⁴). – The museum near the Riva San Biagio, contains several models of 16-18C Venetian ships (galleys, barges, galleons...) and a small model of one of the doges' famous state barges (Bucentaur). In addition there is a section on modern firearms.

Giudecca Island (Isola della Guidecca) (AV-CV). – The **Church of the Redeemer** (Redentore) *(Fondamenta S. Giacomo)*, built after the 1576 plague, is at the heart of a quiet quarter embellished with many small gardens. There is a **Madonna and Child** with Angel Musicians by Alvise Vivarini in the sacristy.

Ghetto (AT). – In the 16C the Jews were relegated to the area around Campo del Ghetto Nuovo. This square is impressive for its calm and austerity.

ⓥ **San Michele** (DT). – This is Venice's burial ground and the resting place of Stravinsky and Diaghilev. The pretty 15C Renaissance church has 14C cloisters.

THE LAGOON

See the plan of the Venetian suburbs in the current Michelin Red Guide Italia.

The Lagoon, separated from the sea by a coastal strip known as the Lido is tidal and ⓥ very pleasant to explore by boat. *There are also regular sailings (see Michelin Red Guide Italia) and excursions to the islands of the lagoon.*

★★ **The Lido.** – This is one of the most fashionable resorts on the Adriatic. The harmoniously modern casino is one of the few in Italy in which gambling is allowed.

★★ **Murano.** – This town on an island in the Lagoon, whose main street consists of a Y-shaped canal lined with Renaissance houses, has been a great glass-making centre since 1292. In the 15C it was also the headquarters of a school of painting founded by Antonio Vivarini. Continuing up the left branch of the canal, is the 17C Palazzo ⓥ Giustiniani which now houses the **Museum of Glass★★★** (Museo Vetrario) with its unique collection of glassware from ancient to modern times. The jewel of the collection is the 15C Barovier Marriage Cup.
A little further on the right, the early 12C **Church of Santi Maria e Donato★★** which is in the Veneto-Byzantine style has a lovely **chevet** with two superimposed blind arcades, the upper of which is emphasised by a white marble balustrade. Inside there is a splendid 12C mosaic **paving**.

★★ **Burano.** – This fishing village is known for its lace-making and its brightly painted houses. Inside the **Church of San Martino** there is a dramatic **Crucifixion** by Tiepolo.

★★ **Torcello.** – The village was from the 7C onwards an important lagoon community and bishopric. Decline set in the early 14C. The chief buildings are grouped around the **main square★** which is now grass-grown.
The 9-11C **Cathedral of Santa Maria Assunta★★** in the Veneto-Byzantine style has a nave and two aisles which rest on Greek marble columns with lovely 11C Corinthian capitals. The nave is closed by a magnificent **iconostasis** adorned with 11-12C Byzantine low-reliefs (peacocks face to face, lions and foliage). To the left of the iconostasis is a remarkable 10-11C ambo sculpted in marble. The cathedral contains several fine Byzantine **mosaics★★★**: the most spectacular, on the west wall are 12-13C and depict the **Last Judgment**; others in the apse, date from the 13C and picture with admirable purity and nobility the Mother of God, with the apostles above; yet another decorates the vaulting of the south chapel and portrays the Mystic Lamb with a luxuriant background of floral decoration.
The 10C Veneto-Byzantine **Church of Santa Fosca★**, built on a central plan, is surrounded by a **peristyle★★** with raised arches. Inside the lovely Greek marble **columns★★** have carved capitals.

★ **Chioggia.** – Chioggia has been a port since ancient times and has an active fishing industry. Follow the two main canals lined with colourful fishing boats and spanned by hump-backed bridges. The 17C bridge, Ponte Vigo, offers a picturesque view of the **Vena Canal**, overlooked by the fish market.
The main street, **Corso del Popolo**, is lined with some lovely 16 to 18C houses. At one end stands the **cathedral★** (Duomo) which was rebuilt in the 17C in the Palladian style and has a lovely 14C campanile. Alongside is the attractive **Piazza Vescovile** so popular with artists.

★ **Brenta Riviera.** – *Description p 62.*

For travelling in Italy

the **Green Guide Italy,**
the **Michelin Map** no 🄹🄹🄹, scale 1:1 000 000,
the **Red Guide Italia** *(hotels and restaurants)*

are complementary.

Verona stands on the banks of the Adige in a hilly setting and is, after Venice, the finest art centre in Venetia. The fashionable **Piazza Bra (ABVX)** is linked by the Via Mazzini **(BV)** to the heart of the old town. The opera and theatrical summer seasons *(see the table of Principal Festivals at the end of the guide)* both draw large crowds.

This Roman colony under the Empire was coveted by the Ostrogoths, Lombards and Franks. The town reached its zenith under the **Scaliger**, Princes of the Scala, who governed for the emperor from 1260 to 1387. Then it passed to the Visconti of Milan before submitting to Venetian rule from 1405. Verona was occupied by the Austrians in 1814 and united as part of Venetia with Italy in 1866.

Romeo and Juliet. – These two young people immortalised by Shakespeare, belonged to rival families: Romeo to the Montecchi (Montagues), who were Guelphs and supported the Pope, and Juliet to the Capuleti (Capulets), who were Ghibellines and supported the Emperor. Verona was the setting for this drama which took place in 1302.

Pisanello and the Veronese School. – Artists of this school were influenced by northern art from the Rhine Valley and they developed a Gothic art which combined a flowing line and a meticulous attention to detail.

Pisanello (*c*1395-*c*1450) a great traveller, active painter, prodigious medal-maker and untiring draughtsman was the greatest exponent of this school. His painting with the unreality of his colours, the meticulously observed details and the flowing line was both reminiscent of the rapidly disappearing medieval world and a precursor of the realism so typical of the Renaissance.

SIGHTS

★★ **Piazza delle Erbe** (BV). – The Square of Herbs was the former Roman forum and it is today attractive and lively, especially on market day.

In line, down the middle of the square, stands the market column; the *capitello* (a rostrum from which decrees and sentences were proclaimed) of the 16C governors *(podesti)*; the fountain known as the Madonna of Verona, with a Roman statue; and a Venetian column surmounted by the winged Lion of St Mark (1523).

Palaces and old houses, some with pink marble columns and frescoes, make an attractive framework round the square: on the north side is the baroque **Palazzo Maffei (B)**.

⊙ In the Via Cappello (No 23) is **Juliet's House** (Casa di Giulietta) **(K)**; in fact it is a Gothic palace with the famous balcony which belonged to the Capulet family.

★★ **Piazza dei Signori** (BV). – Take Via della Costa to reach this square which resembles
⊙ an open-air drawing room with all its sober elegance. On the right is the 12C **Palazzo del Comune** (Town Hall) **(D)**, also known as the Palazzo della Ragione dominated by the **Lamberti Tower** built of brick and stone, with an octagonal upper storey. This building is connected by an arch with the Palazzo dei Tribunali (Law Courts) **(J)** formerly the Palazzo del Capitano (Governor's Residence) which also has a massive brick tower, Torrione Scaligero. The **Loggia del Consiglio (E)** on the opposite side is an elegant edifice in the Venetian Renaissance style.

At the far end of the square the late 13C Palazzo del Governo **(P)** with its machicollations and fine classical doorway (1533) by Sammicheli was initially a Scaliger residence before it became that of the Venetian Governors.

★★ **Scaliger Tombs** (Arche Scaligere) (BV). – The Scaliger built their tombs between
⊙ their palace and their church. The sarcophagi bear the arms of the family, with the symbolical ladder *(scala)*.

They are elegant Gothic mausolea surrounded by marble balustrades and wrought iron grilles. They are decorated with sculptured religious scenes and statues of saints in niches.

Over the door of the Romanesque **Church of Santa Maria Antica** is the tomb of the popular Cangrande I (d1329) with his equestrian statue above.

★★ **Roman Arena** (Arena) (BVX). – This amphitheatre, among the largest in the Roman
⊙ world, could accommodate 25 000 spectators with its 44 tiers of seats. Its particular building material, agglomerated blocks of pink marble, flint and brick, would seem to date its construction as being in the late 1C. This is the venue each summer for a prestigious opera season. From the topmost row there is a good **panorama**★★ of the town in its hilly setting, which on a clear day reaches as far as the Alps.

★★ **Old Castle and Bridge of the Scaliger** (Castelvecchio e Ponte Scaligero) (AV). – This splendid fortified group was built in 1354 by Cangrande II Scaliger. The castle itself is divided into two parts separated by a passageway guarded by a keep.
⊙ The castle contains a **Museum of Art**★★ **(M)** well presented by the architect Carlo Scarpa. The **collection** shows the development of Veronese art from the 12 to 16C and its links with Venice and the International Gothic *(qv)*. There are frescoes by local artists and' canvases by Stefano da Verona, Pisanello, Giambono, Carlo Crivelli (splendid *Madonna of the Passion*), Mantegna, Carpaccio as well as Bellini.

The rooms on the upper floor contain Veronese works from the Renaissance period: Morone, Liberale da Verona *(Virgin with a Goldfinch)*, Girolamo dai Libri and Veronese. There are also some Venetian works by Tintoretto, Guardi, Tiepolo and Longhi. In addition there are arms, jewellery and sculpture sections.

★★ **Church of St Zeno Major** (San Zeno Maggiore). – Take the Rigaste San Zeno (AV 44).
Town plan of the built-up area in the current Michelin Red Guide Italia.
St Zeno is one of the finest Romanesque churches in northern Italy. It was built on the basilical plan in the Lombard style.

VERONA ★★★

Its most remarkable and sober features are the campanile and the façade. The entrance porch supported by two lions, shelters admirable 11-12C bronze **doors★★★** with scenes from the Old and New Testaments. On either side are 12C low-reliefs by the master sculptors Nicolò and Guglielmo. On the tympanum of the doorway is a statue of St Zeno, patron saint of Verona. The imposing interior has a keel-shaped roof. At the high altar is a splendid **triptych★★** (1459) a good example of Mantegna's work displaying both a wealth of ornamentation and a rigorous vision. Note on the chancel parclose the 14C statues and in the north apse a curious polychrome statue of St Zeno laughing. To the north of the church are small Romanesque cloisters.

★ **Church of St Anastasia** (Sant'Anastasia) **(BV N)**. – This church was begun at the end of the 13C and completed in the 15C. The campanile is remarkable and the façade is pierced with a 14C double doorway adorned with frescoes and sculpture. The spacious and lofty interior contains several masterpieces: four **figures of the apostles** painted by Michele da Verona and seventeen **terracottas**★ by Michele da Firenze in the Pellegrini Chapel, on the right of the chancel; the famous fresco showing **Knights of the Cavalli family being presented to the Virgin**★ (1380) by the Veronese Altichero (first chapel in the south transept); and the **Giusti Chapel** *(opening off the north transept)* has Pisanello's famous fresco depicting **St George delivering the Princess of Trebizond**★★ (1436), a strangely unreal scene which is a combination of meticulously observed details and Gothic fantasy.

★ **Cathedral** (Duomo) **(BV)**. – The cathedral has a 12C Romanesque chancel, Gothic nave and classical tower. The remarkable main doorway in the Lombard Romanesque style is adorned with sculptures and low-reliefs by Nicolò. The interior has fine pink marble pillars. The altarpiece on the first altar on the left has an Assumption by Titian. The marble chancel parclose is by Sammicheli (16C).
The canons' quarters are pleasant to walk through.

★ **Roman Theatre** (Teatro romano) **(BV)**. – The theatre dates from the time of Augustus but has been heavily restored. Theatrical performances are still given here.
Do not fail to go up *(lift)* to the former **Monastery of San Girolamo** which now has a small **Archaeological Museum (M²)** and from where there is a lovely **view** over the town.

Castle of St Peter (Castel San Pietro) **(BV)**. – *Take the stairway which leads off Regaste Redentore* (BV 42).
The castle dates back to the Visconti and the period of Venetian rule. The terraces afford splendid **views**★★ of Verona.

★ **Church of St Firmanus Major** (San Fermo Maggiore) **(BVX)**. – The church was built in the 11 and 12C and remodelled later. The Romanesque and Gothic styles are mingled in the façade. Inside there is a fresco of the **Annunciation**★ by Pisanello, surrounding the Brenzoni mausoleum (1430).

Juliet's Tomb (Tomba di Giulietta) **(BX)**. – *Via del Pontiere.*
The tomb is in the cloisters of the Church of San Francesco al Corso, in which Romeo and Juliet were married.

*Each year the **Michelin Guide France***
presents a multitude of up-to-date facts in a compact form.
Whether on a business trip, a weekend away from it all
or on holiday take the guide with you.

★★ **VICENZA** Venetia   Pop 111 119

Michelin map 988 folds 4 and 5 – Town plan in the current Michelin Red Guide Italia

The proud and noble city of Vicenza lies in a pretty setting at the foot of the Berici Mountains. This busy commercial and industrial centre in addition to its traditional textile industry now has mechanical and chemical industries and a reputation as a gold working centre. Vicenza is strategically set at the crossroads of routes between Venetia and Trentino.
The gastronomic speciality of Vicenza is *baccalà alla Vicentina,* cod with a sauce and slices of maize semolina *(polenta)* which is best with wine from the Berici Mountains (Barbarano, Gambellara and Breganze).

HISTORICAL AND ARTISTIC NOTES

The ancient Roman town of Vicetia became an independent city state in the 12C. After several conflicts with the neighbouring cities of Padua and Verona, Vicenza sought Venetian protection at the beginning of the 15C. This was a period of great prosperity when Vicenza counted many rich and generous art patrons among its citizens and it was embellished with an amazing number of palaces.

Palladio. – Vicenza was given the nickname of Venice on *terra firma* due to the tremendous amount of building activity which was largely the work of one man, Andrea di Pietro, known as Palladio. The last great architect of the Renaissance, Palladio was born at Padua in 1508 and died at Vicenza in 1580. He succeeded in combining, in a supremely well balanced manner, the precepts of ancient art with the contemporary preoccupations. Encouraged by the humanist Trissino he made several visits to Rome to study her monuments and the work of Vitruvius, a Roman architect of the time of Augustus. He perfected the Palladian style and in 1570 he published his **Treatise on Architecture,** in four volumes, which made his work famous throughout Europe.
The **Palladian style** is characterised by rigorous plans where simple and symmetrical forms predominate and by harmonious façades which combine pediments and porticoes as at San Giorgio Maggiore in Venice. Palladio was often commissioned by wealthy Venetians to build residences in the countryside around Venice. Architectural rhythm, noble design and in the case of the country mansions a great sense of situation and decoration with the utmost attention being paid to the base so that the villas seemed to rise like a series of new temples on the banks of the Brenta *(qv)* or the slopes of the Berici Mountains. His pupil, Vincenzo Scamozzi (1552-1616) completed several of his master's works and carried on his style.

★★THE PALLADIAN CITY *time: 1/2 day*

★★ **Piazza dei Signori.** – Like St Mark's Square in Venice, it is an open-air meeting-place recalling the forum of antiquity. As in the Piazzetta in Venice, there are two columns bearing effigies of the Lion of St Mark and the Redeemer.

With the lofty **Torre Bissara★**, a 12C belfry, the **Basilica★★** (1549-1617) occupies one whole side of the square. The elevation is one of Palladio's masterpieces, with two superimposed galleries in the Doric and Ionic orders, admirable for their power, their proportion and their purity. The great keel-shaped roof destroyed by bombing, has been rebuilt. The building was not a church but a meeting-place for the Vicenzan notables. The 15C **Monte di Pietà** (pawn shop) opposite, with buildings framing the baroque façade of the Church of St Vincent, is adorned with frescoes. The **Loggia del Capitanio★**, formerly the residence of the Venetian Governor, to the left, at the corner of the Contrà del Monte, was begun to the plans of Palladio in 1571 and left unfinished. It is characterised by its colossal orders with composite capitals and its statues and stuccoes commemorating the naval victory of Lepanto *(qv)*.

★★ **Olympic Theatre (Teatro Olimpico).** – This splendid building in wood and stucco is ⊙ designed by Palladio in 1580 on the model of the theatres of antiquity. The hemicycle of tiers of seats is surmounted by a lovely **colonnade** with a balustrade carrying statues. The **stage★★★** is one of the finest in existence with its superimposed niches, columns and statues and its amazing perspectives painted in *trompe-l'œil* by Scamozzi who completed the work.

★ **Corso Andrea Palladio.** – This, the main street of Vicenza and several neighbouring streets are embellished by many palaces designed by Palladio and his pupils. At the beginning is the **Palazzo Chiericati** *(see below)*, an imposing work by Palladio; at No 147 the 15C **Palazzo Da Schio** in the Venetian Gothic style was formerly known as the Ca d'Oro (Golden House) because it was covered with frescoes with gilded backgrounds. The west front of **Palazzo Thiene** overlooking Contrà S. Gaetano Thiene was by Palladio, while the entrance front at No 12 Corso Palladio is Renaissance dating from the late 15C. The **Palazzo Porto-Barbaran** opposite is also by Palladio. At No 98 the **Palazzo Comunale** (1592) is one of Scamozzi's most successful works. Next you reach the Corso Fogazzaro, where the **Palazzo Valmarana** (1566) at No 16 is another work by Palladio.

★ **Municipal Museum (Museo Civico).** – This occupies one of Palladio's palaces, Pallazzo ⊙ Chiericati. The collection of paintings is on the first floor and includes Venetian Primitives (*The Dormition of the Virgin* by Paolo Veneziano); a **Crucifixion★★** by Hans Memling; canvases by Bartolomeo Montagna (pupil of Giovanni Bellini), Mantegna and Carpaccio, one of the most active artists in Vicenza. There are Venetian works by Lorenzo Lotto, Veronese, Bassano, Piazzetta, Tiepolo and Tintoretto as well as Flemish works by Velvet Bruegel and Van Dyck.

ADDITIONAL SIGHTS

Church of the Holy Crown (Santa Corona). – *Contrà Santa Corona.* The church was built in the 13C in honour of a Holy Thorn presented by St Louis, King of France to the Bishop of Vicenza. The nave and aisles have pointed vaulting while the chancel is Renaissance. Works of art include: a **Baptism of Christ★★** by Giovanni Bellini (fifth altar on the left) and an **Adoration of the Magi★★** (1573) by Veronese (third chapel on the right). The fourth chapel on the right has a lovely coffered **ceiling★** richly painted and adorned with gilded stucco and Mary Magdalen and the Saints by Bartolomeo Montagna.

Cathedral (Duomo). – Built between the 14 and 16C it has an attractively colourful Gothic façade and a Renaissance east end. Inside the lovely **polyptych★** (1356) is by Lorenzo Veneziano (fifth chapel on the right).

Salvi Garden (Giardino Salvi). – This garden is attractively adorned with statues and fountains. A canal runs along two sides of the garden and two lovely Palladian 16 and 17C loggias are reflected in its waters.

EXCURSIONS

★★ **Villa Valmarana "ai Nani".** – *2 km – 1 mile to the south by the Este road and then the* ⊙ *first road to the right.* The villa dates from the 17C and was adorned in 1757 with splendid **frescoes★★★** by **Gian Domenico Tiepolo**, the son. He portrays with plenty of verve and vigour the different aspects of daily life in the province and in particular carnival scenes.

★ **Rotonda.** – *2km – 1 mile to the southeast by the Este road and then the second road to* ⊙ *the right.* The Rotonda is one of Palladio's most famous creations and the plan of Chiswick House in London was inspired by it. The gracefully proportioned square building is roofed with a dome and fronted on each side by a pedimented portico making it look like an ancient temple.

★ **Monte Berico Basilica and the Berici Mountains.** – *2km – 1 mile to the south by Viale Venezia and then Viale X Giugno.* As the Viale X Guigno climbs uphill it is lined with an 18C portico and chapels. On the summit is the baroque basilica roofed with a dome. From the esplanade there is a wide **panorama★★** of Vicenza, the Venetian plain and the Alps. Inside there is a *Pietà* (1500) by Bartolomeo Montagna.

From here the road runs southwards to Arcugnano and Barbarano where from time to time one can catch glimpses of former patrician villas now used as farmhouses in this attractive countryside of volcanic hills.

Montecchio Maggiore. – *13km – 8 miles to the southwest by the S 11.* The ruins of these two castles remind one of Romeo and Juliet. There are good **views★** of the Po Plain and Vicenza. On the outskirts of Montecchio on the Tavernelle road the ⊙ **Villa Cordellina-Lombardi** has one room entirely covered with **frescoes★** by Tiepolo.

Michelin map 988 fold 25 – Town plan in the current Michelin Red Guide Italia

Viterbo, still girdled by its walls, has kept its medieval aspect notably in the **San Pellegrino quarter**★★, a working-class area with many craftsmen. Here there are many vaulted passageways, towers and external staircases.

★★ **Piazza San Lorenzo.** – This square, which occupies the site of the former Etruscan acropolis, transports you back to the Middle Ages with a 13C house on Etruscan foundations (now a chemist's) with its cathedral dating from 1192 and adorned with a fine Gothic campanile and its 13C **Papal Palace**★★ (Palazzo dei Papi) – one of the most interesting examples of medieval secular architecture in Latium. From the Piazza Martiri d'Ungheria there is a lovely view of the ensemble.

ⓥ **Municipal Museum (Museo Civico).** – *Piazza F. Crispi.*
The museum is housed in the former Monastery of Santa Maria della Verità and contains collections of Etruscan and Roman objects discovered in the area: sarcophagi and grave artifacts from the tombs. The picture gallery, on the first floor has a terracotta by the della Robbias as well as works by Salvator Rosa, Sebastiano del Piombo and a local painter, Pastura (15-16C).

EXCURSIONS

Church of the Madonna of the Oak (Madonna della Quercia). – *3km – 2 miles to the northeast.*
The church is in the Renaissance style with a rusticated façade and tympana by Andrea della Robbia. The cloisters are half Gothic, half Renaissance.

★★ **Villa Lante in Bagnaia.** – *5km – 3 miles to the northeast.*
ⓥ This elegant 16C villa was built to the designs of Vignola and became the residence of several popes. A lovely Italian terraced garden with geometric motifs and numerous fountains makes an ideal setting for the villa.

★ **Roman Theatre in Ferento.** – *9km – 6 miles to the north.*
ⓥ The 1C BC theatre is quite well conserved and is the most important vestige of the ancient Ferentium, the ruins of which lie scattered over a melancholy plateau. The theatre ruins stand between the road and the Decumanus and consist of a brick back wall as well as a portico of well dressed blocks without any mortar and thirteen tiers of seats.

Bomarzo. – *21km – 13 miles to the northeast by the S 204.*
ⓥ Extending below the town is the **park** of the 16C **Villa Orsini** (Parco dei Mostri) which is a Mannerist creation with a series of fantastically shaped **sculptures**★.

Montefiascone. – *17km – 11 miles to the northwest.*
Montefiascone stands in the vineyard country which produces the delicious white wine *Est, Est, Est.*
The imposing **cathedral** (Duomo) has a dome designed by Sammicheli, while the curious **Church of St Flavian**★ (San Flaviano) in the Romanesque Lombard style is in reality two churches superimposed. In the lower church frescoes illustrate the story of the Three Dead and the Three Living Men symbolising the brevity and vanity of human life; opposite stands the tombstone of Johann Fugger, the German prelate who had to visit Rome. As he was fond of good food and wine, he sent one of his servants ahead of him with orders to mark the inns where the wine was the best with the word *est* ("is" in Latin). When he arrived at Montefiascone the faithful servant found the wine so good that he wrote, in his enthusiasm, *"Est, Est, Est".* And his master becoming enthusiastic in his turn, drank so much, much, much of it that he died.

★ **Lake Vico (Lago di Vico).** – *18km – 11 miles to the southeast by the Via Santa Maria di Gradi.*
This solitary but charming lake occupies a crater with forested slopes (beech, chestnut, oak and on the lake shores hazel trees).

Civita Castellana. – *36km – 22 miles to the southeast.*
Civita Castellana occupies the site of the Etruscan city Falerii Veteres which was destroyed by the Romans in 241, but rebuilt in the 8C or 9C. The **cathedral** (Duomo) is fronted by an elegant **portico**★ built in 1210 by the Cosmati *(qv).*
The late 15C **castle** (Rocca) was built by Sangallo the Elder and became the residence of Cesare Borgia.

★ **VOLTERRA** Tuscany   Pop 13 645

Michelin map 988 fold 14 – Town plan in the current Michelin Red Guide Italia

The Tuscan hills, so different from those around Florence, a commanding position and well preserved walls make a harmonious setting for the Etruscan, Roman and medieval town of Volterra. The town has numerous alabaster workshops. Large salt pans to the west are used in the manufacture of fine salt and soda. To the northwest of the town there is a view of the **Balze**★, impressive precipices, which are part of a highly eroded landscape furrowed by gully erosion.

★★ **MEDIEVAL TOWN** *time: 1 hour*

★★ **Piazza dei Priori.** – The piazza is surrounded by grim palaces. The 13C Palazzo Pretorio, on the right, is pierced with twin windows and linked with the Torre del Porcellino, so-called because of the wild boar sculpted on the upper part of the tower. The 13C Palazzo dei Priori, opposite, is adorned with emblems of the Florentine Governors.

★ **Cathedral and Baptistry** (Duomo e Battistero). – The cathedral in the Pisan Roman-esque style, although it has been remodelled several times, stands in the picturesque Piazza San Giovanni. The interior comprises a nave and two aisles with monolithic columns and 16C capitals. In the second chapel on the left is a lovely late 13C Annun-ciation. The transept which is lit by alabaster windows, contains, in the second chapel of the north arm, a Virgin of the 15C Sienese school, and in the second chapel in the north arm, a 13C painted wooden sculpture, Descent from the Cross. The nave has a superb 17C pulpit with 13C low-reliefs. The octagonal baptistry dates from 1283.

Take the Via Roma and then pass through the Arco Buonparenti.

Via dei Sarti. – This street is lined with palaces: note No 1, Palazzo Solaini attributed to Antonio da Sangallo which now houses the picture gallery *(see below)* and No 37 the Palazzo Incontri with its superb Renaissance façade designed by Ammanati.

ⓥ **Picture Gallery.** – *1 Via dei Sarti*. This regroups numerous works of art by 14 to 17C Tuscan artists, notably a lovely Annunciation by Luca Signorelli and a Descent from the Cross, a masterpiece of Florentine Mannerism by Rosso Fiorentino.

Piazza San Michele. – Overlooking this square is the church of the same name with its Romanesque façade and a curious tower-house.

Take the narrow but picturesque Via Matteotti, then turn right into the Via Marchesi which leads back to the Piazza dei Priori.

ADDITIONAL SIGHTS

★ **Etruscan Museum** (Museo Etrusco Guarnacci). – Ceramics and more than 600 funerary
ⓥ urns, some of which are cleverly carved with reclining figures and domestic scenes, make up the exhibition.

★ **Porta all'Arco.** – This Etruscan gateway is built of colossal blocks of stone.

Roman ruins. – The ruins of a 1C Roman theatre lie to the west of the Porta Fioren-tina.

Porta Docciola. – 13C fortified gate near which there is a curious medieval washtub.

Viale dei Ponti. – The Viale is a favourite walk with Volterrans. It affords splendid views★★ of the Colli Metalliferi *(see below)*. Above stands the Fortezza, now used as a prison, an impressive mass of military architecture formed by the 14C Rocca Vecchia and the Rocca Nuova, built in 1742 with a keep and four corner towers.

EXCURSION

Larderello. – *33km – 21 miles to the south.*
Larderello is situated in the heart of the **Colli Metalliferi** or metal-bearing hills as the name suggests. In the past they were mined for iron ore, copper and pyrites. Larderello is one of Tuscany's more unusual places with its desolate landscapes, the hissing of its volcanic steam jets, belching smoke from the blast furnaces and the rumble of machinery.

(Pasquier/Rapho)

Procession in Naples

SARDINIA

With an area of 24 089km² – 9 300sq miles, Sardinia (Sardegna) is the largest island in the Mediterranean, after Sicily. It has a population of over 1 630 000. The Punta la Marmora in the Gennargentu Mountains is its highest peak with an altitude of 1 834m – 6 017ft. Sardinia lies 200km – 124 miles off mainland Italy from which it is separated by the Tyrrhenian Sea and 12km – 8 miles south of Corsica which it resembles in many ways. Both islands were part of the Primary Era Tyrrhenian shield which was later submerged during the Quaternary. The Island is quite mountainous and its scrub vegetation consists mainly of holm oaks and aromatic plants and shrubs, all typical of the Mediterranean basin.

Since prehistoric times the island has had a mainly pastoral economy and more than half of Sardinia is suitable for grazing. Ewes milk is used to make the famous Sardinian cheese *(pecorino)* with its pronounced flavour. The Sardinians often cook their meat over hot embers, under a layer of earth and the pecorino cheese is used to flavour numerous dishes. Specialities include the roussette *(burrida),* smoked ham of wild boar *(proscuitto di cinghiale)* and a strong meat stock with semolina balls *(succutundu).* Taste one of the local wines, red or white: Nuragus and Vernaccia (dry white wine from the Oristano region, which is taken as an aperitif) are the best known.

Historical notes. – Sardinia has traces of human settlement going back to prehistoric times. The **nuraghi** or fortified tower-houses date from the 2nd millennium BC and are the island's earliest monuments. These strange structures in the form of a truncated cone were built of huge blocks of stone without any mortar. The only opening was a low door with a massive lintel stone. Inside each storey was roofed by a corbelled dome. The basic design evolved and towers were added and linked by stout walls, which reinforced the primitive structure. The *nuraghi* have a family resemblance to the brochs of Scotland. It is assumed that these fortified tower-houses served as refuges in times of danger. The island has over 7 000 nuraghi with a large concentration between Porto Torres and Barumini.

Other native monuments from this period are the **Giants' Tombs** (Tomba dei Giganti) or collective graves, no doubt intended for the ruling families. Five hundred of these remain today and they are usually to be found at some distance from the nuraghic settlements.

The funeral chambers lined and roofed with megalithic slabs (like a dolmen) were preceded by an arc of standing stones. In form they resemble a horned gallery grave. The dressed central stone had a small entrance at ground level.

The first settlers were the Phoenicians, followed by the Carthaginians, but these seafaring traders only colonised the coasts. The Romans however completely colonised the island for its agricultural land. From the 6 to the 8C BC the Byzantines ruled over Sardinia. Following a period of comparative independence, the country was ruled by the Pisans and Genoese before falling to the Spanish and the Austrian Empire in 1713. It was not long before the Emperor exchanged Sardinia for Sicily with the dukes of Savoy. The latter took the title of Kings of Sardinia. The various settlers left few artistic traces with the exception of the Pisans, whose influence can be detected in the Romanesque and Gothic Churches.

Sardinia today. – The economy of Sardinia was for a long time based on agriculture and was essentially pastoral. More recently tourism and industry have been developed. The intense industrialisation programme has accentuated the differences between the modern urban way of life and that of the many Sardinian shepherds, clinging to their traditional ways. The Sardinians have retained their keen sense of honour and hospitality. They still speak their own language and wear their magnificent costumes on feast days. Many cottage industries are still popular with the women (baskets, carpets, tapestry and fabrics).

Access. – **By air:** see the current Michelin Red Guide Italia.

By sea: see the Michelin map ▨▨▨ as well as the current Michelin Red Guide Italia.

Sightseeing. – A quick tour of the island can be made in 5 days (petrol pumps are few and far between on the east coast). The map opposite in addition to locating the towns and sites described in the guide, indicates other beauty spots in small black type.

Times and charges for admission to sights described in the guide are listed at the end of the guide.

The sights are listed alphabetically in this section either under the place – town, village or area – in which they are situated or under their proper name.

Every sight for which there are times and charges is indicated by the symbol ⊙ in the margin in the main part of the guide.

CORSE

0   40 km

Bonifacio

*Arcipelago
della Maddalena* ★★

Sta-Teresa Gallura
Capo Testa
Porto
Rafael
Palau
Arzachena
Baia Sardinia
Porto Cervo
Costa Smeralda ★★
Cala di Volpe
Porto Rotondo

Li Muri
S 133
Liscia
S 125

Isola Asinara

Golfo dell' Asinara

I. Tavolara

Olbia

*Capo del
Falcone*
*Spiaggia
della Pelosa*
l'Elefante
Castelsardo

Porto Torres
S 200
S. Pietro di Simbranos
S 127

△ 1362
M. Limbara

971 △
M. Nieddu

S 199

S 131dir

SASSARI
Anghelu Ruiu
**Santissima
Trinità di Saccargia** ★★
S 131
S 127b
Lago del Coghinas
S 133

Porto Ferro

Porto Conte
Palmavera ★
S 597
M. Albo
1127 △

**Grotta di
Nettuno** ★★★
Alghero ★
San Pietro
di Sorres
Torralba

Dorgali

Santu Antine
Nuoro
Golfo di Orosei

S 129bis
S 129

S 128

Macomer
Santa Sabina
S 131dir

Fonni

★★★ *Strada
Arbatax-Dorgali*

Losa
Lago Omodeo
S 125

**Monti
del**
P. la Marmora
1834

△
M. Ferru
1050
Abbasanta
Sorgono
Tonara

Santa Cristina
Tirso
Aritzo

S 131
S 292

Stagno di Cabras

Oristano
Sta-Giusta ★

Gennargentu ★
S 198
Arbatax

★ **Tharros**
*Golfo di
Oristano*
Isili
*Lago di
Flumendosa*

S 128

Arborea
★★ **Barumini**
Santa Vittoria di Serri ★
S 125

★★ **Nuraghe Su Nuraxi**
L. Mulargia
Menhirs
Goni
Flumendosa

S 197
S 131
S 128

△ 1236
M. Linas
Dolianova
S'Oro
Muravera

S 126
△ 1069
M. Serpeddi

Iglesias
S 130
★★★ *Strada
di Muravera*

S 125
Costa Rei

I. di San Pietro
CAGLIARI
Villasimius

S 126
S 195
1116 △
M. is Caravius
Golfo di Cagliari
Capo Carbonara

Sud
del

★ *I. di S. Antioco*
Sta-Margherita
Nora

S 195
Costa
C. Teulada
Capo Spartivento
Capo Malfatano

S 389
T. Sologo
F. Cedrino

▲ **Tomba dei Giganti**
S 125

S 131dir
Serra Orrios ★

↯↯ **M. Ortobene** ★
955
○ **Ispinigoli** ★
Golfo

NUORO
R. d'Oliena
★ *Su Gologone*
▲ **Dolmen Motorra** ★
di

M. Bardia
△ 882
Cala Gonone

DORGALI
Orosei

Oliena
Fluminéddu

P. Corrasi
△ 1463
⌒ **Grotta del Bue Marino**

Sopramonte
★★★ *Strada
Arbatax-Dorgali*

*Barbagia
Ollolai*
Orgosolo
S 125

0   10

★ ALGHERO

Pop 39 466

Michelin map 988 fold 33

The early history of this pleasant little port set amid olive trees, eucalyptus and parasol pines is unknown. Coral divers operate from the port which has become popular as a seaside resort. In 1354 Alghero was occupied by the Catalans and its Spanish air has earned it the nickname of the Barcelonetta of Sardinia. The people still wear Catalan costumes and speak Catalan.

The beach extends 5km – 3 miles to the north of the village.

★ **Old town (Città Vecchia).** – The fortifications encircle a network of narrow streets. The **cathedral** *(Via Roma)* has a remarkable doorway and a campanile in the Catalan Gothic style. The 14-15C **Church of San Francesco** has a Gothic interior and lovely **cloisters** in golden-coloured tufa. The fishing harbour stands close against the fortifications in the northern part of the town. The harbour is the embarkation point for the boat trips to **Neptune's Cave**★★★ *(p 220)*.

ARBATAX

Michelin map 988 fold 34

The name of this small port is Arab in origin. Arbatax is isolated in a beautiful mountain setting overlooking the Tyrrhenian Sea and is used by cargo ships carrying the island's exports of wood and cork. Not far from the harbour there is a small cliff face of porphyry rock. This outcrop has been exploited for some time now.

A large, gently sloping beach lies at the head of the bay.

The magnificent stretch of **road**★★★ between Arbatax and Dorgali *(71km – 44 miles)* skirts impressive gorges.

ARZACHENA

Pop 8 591

Michelin map 988 southeast of fold 23

Arzachena is an agricultural market town situated in the fine basin of Gallura at the foot of a mountain range. The town is dominated by the curious mushroom-shaped eroded rock (le Fungo).

2km – 1 mile outside the town on the Olbia road is a *nuraghe* (round tower) perched on a rock.

10km – 6 miles to the southwest *(by the Luogosanto road and after 7km – 4 miles a path to the right which you follow for 3km – 2 miles)* is the **Li Muri Giants' Tomb**★ *(p 215)* a particular type of collective grave. On the hilltop 15 stone slabs laid out in an arc of a circle.

★★ BARUMINI

Pop 1 509

Michelin map 988 fold 33

The town of Barumini is surrounded by numerous traces of the earliest period of Sardinian history.

★★ **Nuraghe Su Nuraxi.** – *2km – 1 mile to the west, on the lefthand side of the Tuili road.*

This is an excellent example of a massive nuraghic fortress formed by several towers interconnected by galleries. To the east is a large nuraghic settlement.

★ **Santa Vittoria di Serri.** – *38km – 24 miles to the east by the Nuoro road and a road to the right in Nurallao.*

There are remains of a prehistoric religious centre. On the way out pass through the village of **Isili** with two thriving craft industries (furniture-making and weaving).

CAGLIARI

Pop 223 487

Michelin map 988 fold 33

Cagliari is the capital of the island. It is a modern-looking town with a busy harbour and an old nucleus surrounded by fortifications, built by the Pisans in the 13C. Before becoming Roman it was a flourishing Carthaginian city called Karalis.

The **Feast of St Efisio** (an officer in Diocletian's army who converted to Christianity and became the patron saint of Sardinia) is one of the most fabulous in the whole of Italy *(see the table of Principal Festivals at the end of the guide)*.

The **Terrazza Umberto 1°** (Z) affords a remarkable **view**★★ of the town, harbour and bay.

Cathedral (Cattedrale) (Y). – Built in the 13C style of Pisa, the cathedral was remodelled in the 17C. Inside are magnificent **pulpits**★★ (1162) by Guglielmo of Pisa with carved panels illustrating the Life of Christ. Once through a little door on the right of the choir go down to the **Santuario**, a crypt with 17C decoration, which enshrines numerous relics. A door opens on the right into a chapel containing the tomb of Marie-Louise of Savoy, the wife of the future King Louis XVIII of France and sister of the King of Sardinia.

★ **National Archaeological Museum (Museo Nazionale Archeologico)** (Y). – The museum has a large collection of arms, pottery and small **bronzes**★★★, grave artifacts from the earliest period of Sardinian history. Phoenician, Punic and Roman art are represented in the other rooms.

CAGLIARI

Elephant (Y A) and St Pancras Towers (Y B). – These early 14C towers were part of the Pisan fortifications.

Roman Amphitheatre (Anfiteatro Romano) (Y). – This is the most important Roman monument in Sardinia.

Botanical Gardens (Orto Botanico) (Y). – The displays are of both Mediterranean and tropical vegetation.

EXCURSION

★★★ **Muravera Road (Strada di Muravera).** – *Leave by* ① *on the town plan.*
Thirty kilometres – 19 miles from Cagliari, the road enters wild gorges with reddish coloured walls of porphyritic granite.

Churches and monasteries are often closed between 12 noon and 4 pm.

DORGALI   Pop 7 807

Michelin map 988 fold 34

Monte Bardia stands between this important agricultural town and the sea. Dorgali makes an ideal excursion centre especially for visiting the nearby megalithic sites.

Cala Gonone. – *10km – 6 miles to the east.*
A winding **road**★★ leads to this resort with its small harbour. Boats leave from the port to visit the **Sea Ox Cave** (Grotta del Bue Marino). The cave was occupied by the last monk seals, survivors from the Ice Age. The galleried cave has some lovely concretions.

★ **Motorra Dolmen and Ispinigoli Cave.** – *8km – 5 miles to the north by the Nuoro road and then the S125 or Orosei road to the right.*
The **Motorra Dolmen**★ (Dolmen Motorra) consists of an almost circular slab of schist supported by eight uprights. The **Ispinigoli Cave**★ (Grotta di Ispinigoli) *(continue along the Orosei road, then turn right and continue for a further 3km – 2 miles)* is an immense cavity at an altitude of 400m – 1 312ft. The roof is supported by an extraordinary **column**★★ 38m – 125ft tall.

★ Serra Orrios and Sa Ena e Tomes Tomb (Tomba dei Giganti). – *19km – 12 miles by the Nuoro road.*
The important nuraghic village of **Serra Orrios★** *(signposted to the right is 10km – 6 miles from Dorgali)* stands on a plateau strewn with asphodels.
Two temples remain. One immediately to the west of the village and the other, in the same direction but further out, is surrounded by a circular wall.

> *At the next crossroads go straight ahead towards Lula and almost 6km – 4 miles later, after a small pass, turn right at the signpost, "Tomba dei Giganti" 700m – 766yds.*

Although overrun by vegetation one can still make out the **Sa Ena e Tomes Tomb★** which has the traditional layout of a Giants' Tomb. The funerary chamber in the form of a passage roofed with large slabs, like a dolmen, is preceded by a series of stones forming an arc of a circle. The larger central stone is carved with a moulding and pierced with a small passageway at ground level.

★★ Dorgali to Arbatax Road. – *Description p 217.*

★★ EMERALD COAST (COSTA SMERALDA)

Michelin map 988 folds 23 and 24

In the northeastern part of the island the wild and undulating region of **Gallura** has one of the most indented coastlines. It is a succession of pink granite headlands, forest covered mountain ridges, sandy creeks and deeply indented bays and has become a favourite area with holidaymakers.
The development of the **Emerald Coast**, started in 1961, was promoted by a consortium originally presided by the Aga Khan. The coast was endowed with luxury facilities (palatial hotels, marinas and golf courses) to attract the an upmarket clientele. The main resorts are **Porto Cervo,** Cala di Volpe and Baia Sardinia.

★★ GENNARGENTU Mountains (MONTI DEL GENNARGENTU)

Michelin map 988 folds 33 and 34

The immense Gennargentu Massif in the centre of the island, culminates in Punta La Marmora (1 834m– 6 017ft). These bare, deserted and rounded peaks are to be found in the region of **Barbagia,** which was never completely conquered by the Romans. The relative isolation of the area has contributed to the shy and almost inhospitable manner of the people and to the preservation of local costumes and traditions.
During a run through the area you will see many *nuraghi* and scenes of unforgettable wildness on a lonely massif whose slopes are covered with groves of cork-oaks and chestnut trees.
The water which runs off the green slopes of the Gennargentu Mountains, supplies the man-made reservoir of **Lago di Flumendosa** (good **view★★** of the lake from the road that climbs to Villanovatulo) which in turn is used to irrigate the plain of Campidano. **Aritzo** is the main holiday resort of the area. The town of **Tonara** standing at an altitude of 930m – 3 051ft in a green pass is known for its nougat made with honey, almonds and hazel nuts. To the north **Fonni** is the island's highest village at an altitude of 1 000m – 3 281ft.

★★ MADDALENA Archipelago   Pop 11 766
(ARCIPELAGO DELLA MADDALENA)

Michelin map 988 fold 23 or 90 fold 10

Access. – See the maps given above as well as the current Michelin Red Guide Italia.

The Maddalena Archipelago (Arcipelago della Maddalena) consists of fourteen rocky islands and islets, greatly appreciated by the tourists for their wild state. The two busiest islands, Maddalena and Caprera, are linked by a causeway.

★★ Maddalena (Isola Maddalena). – Under 20km² – 8sq miles this, the largest island of the archipelago, has a magnificent coastline. A lovely scenic route *(20km – 12 miles)* follows the coast.

★ Caprera (Isola di Caprera). – This sparsely inhabited island attracts many visitors to the ⊙ onetime home, now a **museum★**, and tomb of Garibaldi, who died here in 1882.

NUORO   Pop 37 264

Michelin map 988 fold 33

Nuoro lies at the foot of Monte Ortobene, on the borders of the Barbagia region to the north of the Gennargentu Mountains. In this large town of central Sardinia the customs, traditions and folklore have remained unchanged since ancient times. The **Sagra del Redentore** (Feast of the Redeemer) includes a procession through the town in local costumes and a folk festival *(see the table of Principal Festivals at the end of the guide).*

★ Museum of Popular Traditions (Museo della Vita e delle Tradizioni Popolari Sarde). – ⊙ *55 Via A Mereu.*
The museum has a fine collection of Sardinian costumes. The author Grazia Deledda, a native of Nuoro, won the Nobel Prize for Literature in 1926 for her description of Sardinian life.

EXCURSIONS

★ **Monte Ortobene.** – *9km – 6 miles to the east.*
This is a popular excursion with local people. The summit affords several good view-points.

★ **Su Gologone.** – *20km – 12 miles to the southeast by the Oliena-Dorgali road.*
The large town of **Oliena** stands at the foot of a particularly steep slope of the Sopra-monte. Locally the women still wear the traditional costume.

Just beyond Oliena take a local road to the left for about 6km – 4 miles.

The lovely spring at Su Gologone gushes from a rocky face in a green setting.

Orgosolo. – *20km – 12 miles to the south.*
This large market town with its calm appearance is reputed for being the stronghold of bandits and outlaws. The Italian film producer Vittorio de Seta popularised them in his film *Banditi a Orgosolo* (1961).

ORISTANO   Pop 31 673

Michelin map 〖988〗 fold 33

Oristano is the main town on the west coast. Founded in 1070 by the inhabitants of nearby Tharros *(qv),* Oristano put up a strong fight against the Aragonese in the 14C.

★★ **Piazza Roma.** – The crenellated tower, Torre di San Cristoforo, overlooking this vast esplanade, was originally part of the town wall built in 1291. Opening off Piazza Roma is **Corso Umberto,** the town's main shopping street.

San Francesco. – Rebuilt in the 19C the church has some interesting **works of art**★ including a wooden statue of Christ by the 14C Rhenish school, a fragment of a polyp-tych (St Francis receiving the Stigmata) by Pietro Cavaro, a 16C Sardinian artist, and a statue of St Basil by Nino Pisano (14C).

EXCURSIONS

★ **Basilica of Santa Giusta.** – *3km – 2 miles to the south.*
This 12C edifice stands in the town of the same name, on the banks of a lake.
The sober elegance of Santa Giusta is characteristic of all Sardinian churches where Pisan and Lombard influences mingle. The façade divided into three sections in the Lombard manner has an attractively carved doorway typical of the Pisan style. Inside the piers are either of marble or granite. There is a crypt under the slightly raised choir.

Arborea. – *18km – 11 miles to the south.*
This charming little town was planned and laid out in 1928 by the Fascist govern-ment following the draining of the marshes and the extermination of the malaria mosquito.

PORTO CONTE

Michelin map 〖988〗 fold 33

This, the ancient Portus Nympharum or Port of Nymphs, lies on the shores of a beauti-ful bay.

★★★ **Neptune's Cave (Grotta di Nettuno).** – *9km – 6 miles to the southwest leaving from the* ⊙ *head of the bay. Boats leave from Alghero.*
The road out to the headland, **Capo Caccia,** offers splendid **views**★★ of the rocky coast. This large cave is on the point. A stairway (654 steps) leads down the cliff face. Ad-mire the small inner lakes, the forest of columns and the concretions in the form of organ pipes.

★ **Nuraghe Palmavera.** – *2km – 1 mile from the bay on the lefthand side of the Alghero road.*
This nuraghi is surrounded by the remains of a prehistoric village. The individual dwell-ings were crowded closely together. This nuraghi is a particularly fine building in white limestone with two vaulted towers and two separate entrances.

PORTO TORRES   Pop 21 523

Michelin map 〖988〗 folds 23 and 33

Situated at the head of a large bay, Porto Torres is the port for Sassari. Founded by Caesar it enjoyed considerable importance in the Roman period as can be testified by the remains in the vicinity of the station.

★ **San Gavino.** – It was built at the end of the 11C by the Pisans (the long series of blind arcades on the north side are characteristic of the Pisan style) and enlarged shortly afterwards by the Lombard master builders. It is a fine example of medieval Sardinian art. A 15C doorway in the Catalan Gothic style interrupts the arcades.
Inside, piers alternate with groups of four clustered columns giving a harmonious re-sult. A large **crypt** enshrines the relics of St Gavin and a very fine Roman **sarcophagus**★, decorated with sculptures portraying the muses.

★ SANT'ANTIOCO Island   Pop 12 595

Michelin map 988 fold 33

This volcanic island is the largest of the Sulcis Archipelago, lying off the southwest coast of Sardinia. It has a hilly terrain with high cliffs on the west coast.
The chief town, also Sant'Antioco, is linked to the mainland by railway.

★ **The remains of Sulcis.** – The ancient town of Sulcis, founded by the Phoenicians, gave its name to this group of islands.
Before entering the necropolis, visit the **museum** which regroups all the finds from the excavations and includes a fine collection of **steles** ★.
The **tophet** ★ *(500m – 1 640ft from the museum)* is where the Phoenicians gathered the remains of their first-born child, who was always sacrificed according to Phoenician custom. The **necropolis** was apart and has sixty tombs cut in the rock.
The **catacombs**, under the parish church, were originally a Phoenician necropolis transformed by the Christians during the Roman period.

SASSARI   Pop 119 871

Michelin map 988 fold 33 – Town plan in the current Michelin Red Guide Italia

Sassari is the second largest town in Sardinia. It offers the tourist a contrast between its spacious, airy modern quarters and its medieval nucleus, nestling round the cathedral. The busiest arteries are the Piazza d'Italia and the Corso Vittorio Emanuele II.
Sassari is known for its festivals. The famous **Cavalcata Sarda** is a colourful procession of people from nearly all the provinces of Sardinia in their local costumes. This is a particularly good chance to admire the great variety and beauty of Sardinian costumes. The procession ends with a frenetic horse race. The **Festa dei Candelieri** (Feast of Candles), dating from the late 16C, was the result of a vow to the Virgin, made during an epidemic of the Black Death. The procession comprises the different trade guilds with each carrying huge beribboned wooden candles, gilded or painted silver *(see the table of Principal Festivals at the end of the guide)*.

★ **Sanna National Museum (Museo Nazionale Sanna).** – The museum contains rich archaeological collections including an interesting section devoted to Sardinian ethnography and a small picture gallery.

Cathedral (Duomo). – The cathedral is built in many styles and has a 13C campanile with a 17C crown, a late 17C Spanish baroque **façade** ★ and a Gothic interior.

EXCURSION

★★ **Holy Trinity Church (Santissima Trinità di Saccargia).** – *17km – 11 miles to the southeast by the Cagliari road, the S131 and then the road to Olbia, the S 597.*
This former Camaldulian abbey church was built in the 12C in decorative courses of black and white stone, typical of the Pisan style. The elegant façade includes a porch, added in the 13C and is flanked by a slender campanile. Inside, the apse is adorned with fine 13C frescoes showing a strong Byzantine influence.

★ THARROS

Michelin map 988 fold 33 – 1.5km – 1 mile to the south of San Giovanni di Sinis

The Phoenicians founded Tharros on the Sinis Peninsula to the north of the Gulf of Oristano. It was an important depot on the trading route between Marseilles and Carthage, before it was conquered by the Romans in the 3C BC. The inhabitants abandoned the site in 1070, before it was overwhelmed by wind-blown sand. They settled in Oristano.

Excavation site. – The site lies near the hill which is crowned by a Spanish tower (Torre di San Giovanni). In the lower part of the settlement there were zones of housing, baths and a paleochristian baptistry dating from the 5C. To the right of the road leading to the hill are the remains of a Punic temple and a Semitic temple. On the hilltop are the ruins of a Roman temple with further on a tophet *(see above)*. Beyond all this are the impressive basalt remains of the town's fortifications.

Necropolis. – Climb to the summit of the headland crowned by a lighthouse to see the Punic necropolis (6-4C BC). Some of the rectangular tombs are cut in the rock while others are hypogea (underground chambers).

SICLIY

Sicily (Sicilia), the largest of the Mediterranean islands has an area of 25 709km² – 9 927sq miles. It is triangular in shape and was named Trinacria by the ancients. Nearly 5 million people live on the island which is generally mountainous and reaches at its highest point, Mount Etna (an active volcano), an altitude of 3 340m – 10 958ft. Throughout its history Sicily has suffered numerous earthquakes: the 1908 one almost entirely destroyed Messina and the 1968 one affected the western part of the island.

Access. – **By air**: consult the current Michelin Red Guide Italia. **By sea**: see the Michelin map 988 as well as the current Michelin Red Guide Italia.

Sightseeing. – The island can be visited in a quick tour of 6 to 7 days. The map below in addition to locating the towns and sites described in the guide, indicates other beauty spots in small black type.

Look in the introduction at the Map of Touring Programmes for the suggested itinerary for Sicily.

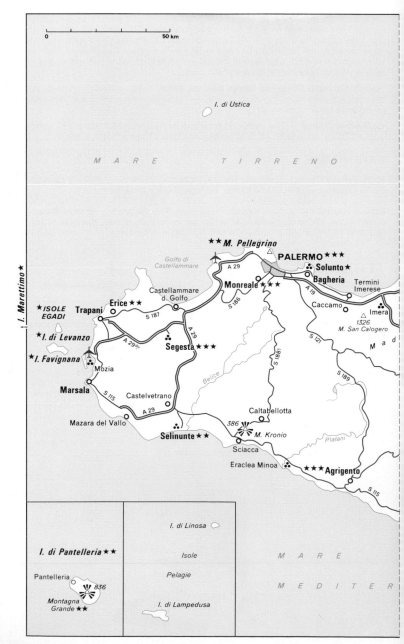

Sicily has been a constant pawn for marauding forces in the Mediterranean due to its strategic location, lying near the peninsula and controlling the Mediterranean. Firstly there were the Greeks in the 8C who discovered an island divided between two ethnic groups, the oldest inhabitants, the **Sicani** and the **Siculi** (Sicels) who came from the peninsula.

The Carthaginians were for several centuries the main rivals of the Greeks. They had colonised the coastal areas but were finally pushed back to the western part of the island where they remained until the siege of Mozia by Denys the Elder in 397BC.

The 5C BC, excluding the rules of the tyrants of Gela and Syracuse *(p 236)*, was the apogee of Greek rule in Sicily (Magna Graecia). They built some magnificent buildings, they neutralised their enemies and Syracuse grew to become the rival of Athens.

This fragile peace was broken by the arrival of the Romans who coveted the island for the richness of its soil. By 241BC, at the end of the First Punic War, the whole of Sicily had been conquered and it became a Roman province, governed by a praetor. The island was also victim of the numerous Barbarian invasions which unfurled on southern Italy.

In 535 the island passed to the Byzantines before experiencing a period of great prosperity under the Aghlabid dynasty (Tunisia), in the 9C. The Saracens were in turn expelled by the Normans (11C). The son of the Great Count Roger I of Sicily, **Roger II** (1095-1154) created the Norman Kingdom of Sicily. He established his court at Palermo and during his reign the island was to enjoy a period of considerable political power and cultural influence.

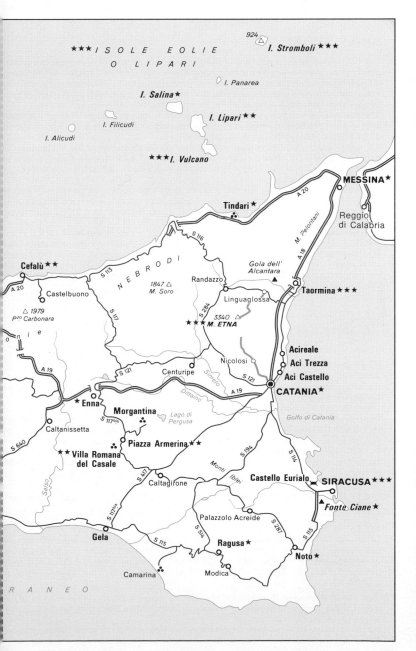

The name of the Hohenstaufen Emperor, **Frederick II,** dominated the reign of this Swabian dynasty. The house of Anjou followed in 1266, however Charles of Anjou was expelled following the Palermo revolt of 1282 known as the **Sicilian Vespers.** Power passed to the Aragon dynasty and it was Alfonso V the Magnanimous who reunited Naples and Sicily and took the title of King of the Two Sicilies (1442).

The island passed to the Bourbons of Naples by marriage until they were overthrown by the Expedition of Garibaldi and the Thousand.

Each period has left its mark on the island's heritage be it in the field of art or customs and daily life. The Greeks built admirable Doric temples with the mellow local limestone and sumptuous theatres. During the brief period when the Normans dominated the island, Sicily knew an era of economic prosperity and artistic development. This style was unique for its blending of a variety of different influences. The architectural style was still essentially Norman but the decoration (horseshoe-shaped arches, bulbous bell-towers and intricately decorated ceilings) showed a strong Moorish influence while the decoration of the walls with dazzling mosaics on golden backgrounds was Byzantine.

Known variously as the **Sicilian-Norman** or **Sicilian-Arab,** this style can be seen at Palermo, Monreale, Cefalu and Messina.

If the Renaissance has left few traces in the island – with some outstanding exceptions by **Antonello da Messina** (qv) who usually worked on the mainland – the Sicilians adopted the baroque style with great fervour in the late 18C. The main exponents were the architects, **Rosario Gagliardi** in Noto and Ragusa, **Vaccarini** in Catania and **Giacomo Serpotta** who embellished numerous oratories in Palermo with his sculpted fantasies.

Sicilian literature is particularly rich, especially in the 19C, with **Giovanni Verga** (qv) who created a new form of Italian novel and **Luigi Pirandello** (qv). Noteworthy among the 20C writers to describe contemporary life are **Elio Vittorini** (1908-66) and **Leonardo Sciascia** (born 1921).

SICILY TODAY

Due to the mountainous nature of the land citrus fruit, vines and olive trees are grown mainly along the coast or on the rare plains which exist such as Catania and the Conca d'Oro inland from Palermo. In the interior which has a rather desolate but grandiose landscape, the main crops are cereals. Isolated dwellings are rare, as the Sicilian prefers to live in fairly large villages where the houses huddle closely together.

The industries which have been implanted on the outskirts of large towns have done little to stem the flow of emigration. Sicily has particularly suffered from the isolation which affected the whole of the Mezzogiorno.

The island's difficulties have been exacerbated by the existence of the Mafia, a formidable secret society whose abiding rule is to defend its members to the extent of braving the law if need be, and to impose a reign of silence (omerta) which creates an atmosphere of fear and mistrust.

The Mafia first appeared in the 19C – although its true foundation goes much further back – and flourished initially in the countryside where it tyrannized the peasant folk for the profit of the large landowners. Today it has become an urban phenomenon using definitely more violent methods.

The folk traditions and customs which once animated the streets have almost completely disappeared. It is only on feast days and in the museums that the visitor can now see the famous **Sicilian carts** which were so gaily decorated. These carts were masterpieces of craftsmanship and decorative ingenuity. However one can still see the popular puppet (pupi) theatres which are mentioned in the 12C Song of Roland or Ariosto's (p 82) Orlando Furioso (Roland the Mad).

★★★ AGRIGENTO   Pop 54 018

Michelin map 🔢 fold 36 – Town plan in the current Michelin Red Guide Italia

Agrigento, the Greek Akragas, is attractively set on a hillside facing out to sea.

The Greek poet Pindar referred to Agrigento as "man's finest town". It includes a medieval quarter on the upper slopes, above the modern town, and below the impressive ancient ruins are strung out along a ridge, which is miscalled the Valley of the Temples. The town was founded in 580BC by people from Gela who themselves originated from Rhodes. Of the governing "tyrants", the cruellest in the 6C was **Phalaris,** while **Tero** (7C) was renowned as a great builder. The 5C philosopher **Empedocles** was a native of Agrigento as was **Luigi Pirandello** (1867-1936), winner of the Nobel Prize for Literature in 1934. He was an innovator in modern Italian drama (Six Characters in Search of an Author) and his plays were woven around the themes of incomprehension and absurdity.

★★★ VALLEY OF THE TEMPLES (VALLE DEI TEMPLI) time: allow half a day

Access from the west by the S 115 and then a left turn in the direction of Piazzale dei Templi (car park). Walk along the Sacred Way which is lined by the principal temples.

Of the ten temples built between the late 6C and the late 5C BC parts of nine are still visible. The destruction of the temples was for long thought to be the work of earthquakes but is now also attributed to the anti-pagan activities of the early Christians. Only the Temple of Concord was spared when it became a church in 579 BC.

★★ **Temple of Hercules** (Tempio di Ercole). – Dating from 520BC this is believed to be the oldest of the Agrigento temples. Eight of its columns have been raised and the others lie amid a jumble of ruins.

Further on to the left amid mimosa, pine and olive trees can be seen the deeply grooved traces of the wheeled vehicles used to transport the building stone for the temples.

★★ **Temple of Concord** (Tempio della Concordia). – This temple was built between 450 and 440BC; it is the most massive, majestic and best preserved of the Doric temples in Sicily. It has a peristyle of thirty-four tufa limestone columns, the original stucco facing having since disappeared.

It is not known to what deity it was dedicated and its present name is taken from a Roman inscription found nearby. The internal arrangement dates from the Christian period.

★★ **Temple of Juno** (Tempio di Giunone). – Set on the edge of the ridge, this temple was built in 470BC and conserves part of its colonnade and its architrave. On the east side you will see a sacrificial altar and behind the temple an ancient cistern.

Return to Piazzale dei Templi.

★★ **Temple of Jupiter** (Tempio di Giove). – Had this now ruined temple been completed, its size (113m – 371ft long by 56m – 184ft wide) would have made it one of the largest in the ancient world.

Its entablature was supported by 20m – 66ft tall columns, between which stood **telemones** (columns in the form of male figures), colossal statues, one of which the Gigante, a giant 7.5m – 25ft tall has been reconstructed and is now on view in the Archaeological Museum. A reproduction, lying on the ground, gives some idea of the immense size of the building.

Temple of Castor and Pollux (Tempio dei Dioscuri). – This lies lower down the slope than the previous temple. This temple was also dedicated to Persephone, goddess of the harvest and protectress of Sicily. Only four of the columns supporting part of the entablature remain. The small rose at the corner of the entablature is the symbol of Rhodes.

Alongside is a **sacred area** dedicated to the Chthonic or underground gods: with two sacrificial altars, one of which is circular and the second square.

ADDITIONAL SIGHTS

★ **Regional Archaeological Museum** (Museo Archeologico Regionale). – *Enter via the* ⊙ *cloisters of the Church of St Nicholas (see below).* The museum contains a collection of Greek vases (including the original **Krater of Perseus and Andromeda** on a white ground). One room is devoted to the telamones from the Temple of Jupiter. There are also mosaics and the 5C BC marble statue of **Ephebus.**

★ **Phalaris' Oratory** (Oratorio di Falaride). – *Access via a passageway leading off the* ⊙ *cloisters of the Church of St Nicholas.* Legend has it that the palace of Phalaris, the first tyrant of Agrigento, was in the vicinity. The building is in fact a small Hellenistic temple which was transformed during the Christian period.

St Nicholas (San Nicola). – This sober church in the transitional Romano-Gothic style contains a magnificent **Roman sarcophagus**★ on which the death of Phaedra is portrayed. From the terrace there is a fine **view**★ of the temples.

★ **Greco-Roman Quarter** (Quartiere Ellenistico-Romano). – The layout of the main streets ⊙ lined by the houses is a good example of 4C BC town planning.

★ **Tero's Tomb** (Tomba di Terone). – *Visible from the Caltagirone road.* The tomb, said to be that of Tero, Tyrant of Agrigento, is 3m – 10ft high and really dates from the Roman era.

★ **The town today.** – The shady **Piazzale Aldo Moro,** often thronged with birds at certain times of the day, is the centre of the town. The **Via Atenea** is a busy shopping street. Crowning the old town with its stepped streets, is the **cathedral** (Duomo), a Norman building which was greatly altered in the following centuries. On the way back down to Piazzale A Moro visit the small **Abbey Church of the Holy Spirit** (Abbaziale di Santo Spirito) which has four charming **low-reliefs**★ in stucco by Giacomo Serpotta.

⊙ **Pirandello's House** (Casa di Pirandello). – *6km – 4 miles to the west by the Porto Empedocle road, the S 115.* Shortly after the Morandi viaduct turn left. This small house surrounded by vineyards was the birthplace of the famous dramatist Luigi Pirandello (1867-1936), who is buried under the nearby pine tree.

★ **CATANIA**   Pop 376 312

Michelin map 988 fold 37 – Plan of the built-up area in the current Michelin Red Guide Italia

Catania is a busy seaport and industrial town which has developed quite considerably in recent years, despite the fact that it was destroyed several times by the eruptions of Mount Etna. It is a fine city with wide, regular streets overlooked by numerous baroque buildings by the architect **Vaccarini,** who rebuilt Catania following the 1693 earthquake.

Natives of the town include the musician **Vincenzo Bellini** (1801-35), composer of the opera *Norma,* and the novelist, **Giovanni Verga** *(qv).*

Catania holds the heat record for the whole of Italy over 40°C (104°F) and the less enviable one of the highest crime rate, which has earned it the nickname of "Sicilian Chicago".

★ **Via Etnea** (DXY). – The town's main shopping artery is over 3km – 2 miles long. All the way along it affords a view of Etna. It is bordered by numerous palaces, churches and the **Bellini Gardens**★ (Villa Bellini).

★ **Piazza del Duomo** (DZ). – This square is the centre of town and is surrounded by a baroque ensemble designed by Vaccarini and includes the **Elephant Fountain** (A) dating from 1735, the **Palazzo del Municipio** (H) with its well-balanced façade and the **cathedral** (Duomo) (EZ) dedicated to St Agatha, the town's patron saint. Built at the end of the 11C by the Norman, Roger I, the cathedral was remodelled after the 1693 earthquake.

★ **Ursino Castle** (Castello Ursino) (DZ). – This bare, grim castle was built in the 13C by the ⊘ Emperor Frederick II of Hohenstaufen. It houses an interesting **Municipal Museum** (M).

EXCURSION

Acireale. – *17km – 11 miles to the north.*
The itinerary passes through two fishing villages, both small resorts, **Aci Castello** and **Aci Trezza**. Offshore the **Cyclops' Reefs** (Isole dei Ciclopi) emerge from the sea. These are supposed to be the rocks hurled by the Cyclops Polyphemus after Ulysses had blinded him by thrusting a blazing stake into his single eye.
The road leads to **Acireale**, a modern town with numerous baroque buildings which include those of the **Piazzo del Duomo** with the Basilica of Sts Peter and Paul and the Town Hall as well as the **Church of San Sebastiano** with its harmonious **façade★** embellished with columns, niches and friezes.

Michelin map 988 fold 36

Cefalu is a small fishing town in a fine **setting**★★, hemmed in between the sea and a rocky promontory. It boasts a splendid Romanesque cathedral.

★ **Cathedral (Cattedrale).** – Built of a golden tinted stone which blends in with the cliff behind, this cathedral was erected to fulfil a vow made by the Norman King, Roger II (12C), when in danger of shipwreck. The church, built between 1131 and 1240, has well marked Norman features in its tall main apse flanked by two slightly projecting smaller ones and especially its façade, abutted by the two square towers. The portico was rebuilt in the 15C by a Lombard master and is emblasoned with the arms of a former bishop, Gatto.

The timber ceiling of the two aisles and the transept galleries are also Norman. Columns with splendid **capitals**★★ in the Sicilian-Norman style *(qv)* support the typically Moorish horseshoe arch. The oven vault of the central apse is covered with beautiful **mosaics**★★ on a gilded background displaying a surprising variety of colour and forming an admirable expression of Byzantine art in its decline (12C). Above is Christ Pantocrator (Ruler of All) with underneath on three different levels, the Virgin with four archangels and the twelve apostles. In the choir the angels on the vaulting and the prophets on the side walls date from the 13C. The two marble and mosaic thrones are the episcopal one (south side) and the royal one (north side).

⏚ **Mandralisca Museum (Museo Mandralisca).** – The museum, facing the cathedral in the picturesque Via Mandralisca, has a fine **Portrait of a Man** by Antonello da Messina.

Michelin map 988 folds 34 and 35. **Access:** see the Michelin map 988 and the current Michelin Red Guide Italia

⏚ The three islands – Favignana, Levanzo and Marettimo – which go to make up this small archipelago lie offshore from Trapani. The islands are popular for their wild aspect, transparent blue sea and the beauty of their coastlines. It was here in 241BC that the treaty ending the First Punic War was concluded in which Carthage surrendered Sicily to Rome.

★ **Favignana.** – In the form of a butterfly this island covers an area of 20km² – 8sq miles. The **Montagna Grossa** with a highest point of 310m – 1017ft runs right across the island and ends as an indented coastline. The islanders are masters in the art of tunny fishing which they do for about fifty days between May and June. Having captured the tunny in a series of nets, the fish are pulled in towards the shore where they are harpooned.

The main town of the group of islands, **Favignana,** is guarded by the fort of Santa Caterina a former Saracen lookout tower, which was rebuilt by the Norman King, Roger II and served as a prison under the Bourbons. To the east of the harbour are the former **tufa quarries**★ now drowned by the sea. Boat trips take visitors to the various caves, including the **Grotta Azzurra**★ which is situated on the west coast.

★ **Levanzo.** – This tiny island (6km² – 2sq miles) has no surfaced roads nor springs. Few people therefore stay overnight. In 1950 traces of life in prehistoric times were found in the **Grotta del Genovese,** which is reached by boat from Cala Dogana.

★ **Marettimo.** – Off the beaten tourist track, Marettimo with its attractive **harbour**★ *(no landing stage, rowing boats take you to the quay)* has several restaurants but no hotels. Take a **trip** around the island in a boat to discover the numerous caves which riddle the cliff faces.

Michelin map 988 fold 38

Enna lies in an isolated, sun-scorched landscape at the centre of the island. Its panoramic **site**★★ at an altitude of 942m – 3 091ft has earned it the nickname of the Belvedere of Sicily.

According to legend it was on the shores of **Lake Pergusa** *(10km – 6 miles to the south)* that Pluto carried off the youthful Proserpine, future Queen of the Underworld.

★ **Castle (Castello).** – This medieval castle has six of its original twenty towers. From the top of the tallest there is an exceptional **panorama**★★★ of the perched village of Calascibetta, Etna and most of the Sicilian mountain peaks.

Belvedere. – *Beyond the castle.* From the far side of the hillock, which was the site of a temple to Demeter, there is a fine **view**★ of Calascibetta and of Enna itself.

Cathedral (Duomo). – This was rebuilt in the baroque style in the 16 and 17C but still has its 14C Gothic apses. The lovely classical façade is 16C.

*Walkers, campers, smokers
please take care*

Fire is the scourge of forests everywhere

★★ ERICE — Pop 28 047

Michelin map 988 fold 35 – 14km – 9 miles northeast of Trapani

This ancient Phoenician and Greek city occupies an unforgettably beautiful **setting**★★★ almost vertically (750m – 2 461ft) above the sea. Erice is clustered within its tow walls and is criss-crossed by a labyrinth of quiet alleyways where numerous craftsme offer their wares for sale. In antiquity Erice was a religious centre famous for its templ consecrated to Astarte, then Aphrodite and finally Venus who was venerated by an cient mariners.

Castle of Venus (Castello di Venere). – This castle built by the Normans in the 12-13C crowns an isolated rock on Monte Eryx, on the site of the Temple of Venus. From her and the nearby gardens (Giardino del Balio) there are admirable **views**★★: in clear weathe the Tunisian coast can be seen.

Chiesa Madre. – This church was built in the 14C using stones quarried from th ancient temples. The porch was added in the 15C and flanked by the square battle mented campanile with its elegant openings.

★★★ ETNA, Mount

Michelin map 988 fold 37 – Alt approx. 3 340m – 10 958ft

Etna is the highest point in the island and is snow-capped for most of the year. It is st active and is the largest and one of the most famous volcanoes in Europe.
Etna was born of undersea eruptions which also formed the Plain of Catania, formerl covered by the sea. Its eruptions were frequent in ancient times: we know of 135. Bu the greatest disaster occurred in 1669, when the flow of lava reached the sea, largel devastating Catania as it passed.
The outstanding eruptions in our time were those of 1910, when twenty-three ne craters appeared, of 1917, when a jet of lava squirted up to 800m – 2 500ft above it base, and of 1923, when the lava ejected remained hot eighteen months after th eruption. The last stirrings of Etna took place in 1928, 1954, 1964, 1971, 197 1978, 1979, March 1981, March 1983 and 1985; the volcano still smokes and ma erupt at any time.
The mountain has the appearance of a huge, black, distorted cone which can be see from a distance of 250km – 155 miles. On its lower slopes, which are extremely fe tile, orange, mandarin, lemon and olive trees flourish as well as vines which produc the delicious Etna wine. Chestnut trees grow above the 500m – 1 500ft level and giv way higher up to oak, beech, birch and pine. Above 2 100m – 6 500ft is the barre zone, where only a few clumps of *Astralagus Aetnensis* (a kind of vetch) will be see scattered on the slopes of secondary craters, among the clinker and volcanic rock.

★★★ Ascent of Etna. – The ascent of Etna can be made by the south face from Catan via Nicolosi or by the northeast face from Taormina via Linguaglossa. *Wear war clothing and strong shoes.*

By the south face. – From a point almost 3 000m – 9 843ft up on the central crater in th area of Torre del Filosofo (the refuge was destroyed in the 1971 eruption), the thre craters can be distinguished: the one to the southeast which appeared in 1978, th immense **central crater** and the highest one to the **northeast**, which has been dormar since 1971. On the way up go over towards the eastern face to see the grandios valley **Valle del Bove** which is hemmed in by 1 200m – 3 937ft high walls of lava pierce with pot-holes and crevasses belching smoke.
Night-time excursions are possible on request: you will see a Dantesque spectacle of mo ten lava at the bottom of the crater and an impressive sunrise with a view of the Lipa Islands and the Bove Valley.

By the northeast face. – The road goes through Linguaglossa, a lovely pinewood of th Laricio species and the winter sports resort of Villaggio Mareneve. The surfaced roa ends at Piano Provenzana (1 800m – 5 906ft).
The area around the new observatory affords a magnificent view of the central ar northeast craters. The climb ends amidst an extraordinary landscape of lava, whic still smokes at times.
Night-time excursions are also organised on this slope. The intrepid are able to enjo from the edge of the crater, the grandiose sight of the sun setting and rising.

GELA — Pop 79 188

Michelin map 988 fold 36

Gela was founded in 688 BC by islanders from Rhodes and Crete. The town was d stroyed and restored several times and it was completely rebuilt in 1230 by the Em peror Frederick II of Hohenstaufen. It was in the plain of Gela, one of the island's mo fertile areas, that the U.S. troops landed in 1943. The town prospered with the di covery of oil in the vicinity. Gela is however also a resort and an interesting archae logical centre.

Ancient remains. – For those interested in archaeology there are the ancient Gre **fortifications**★★ *(at Caposoprano to the west of the town)* dating from the 4C BC with the regular stonework of skilfully dressed blocks below and brickwork above. The mo interesting section is the part facing the sea. This type of construction is particula fragile and is now protected by plexiglass. These walls owe their preservation to th fact that they were encroached upon by sand. The **regional archaeological museum**★ *(Cors Vittorio Emanuele, at the far eastern end of the town)* has a particularily attractive pre entation of pottery and medals.

Michelin map 988 folds 36 and 37 — **Access**: see the Michelin map 988 and the current Michelin Red Guide Italia

The Lipari Islands are also called the **Æolian Islands** because the ancients thought Æolus, the God of the Winds, lived there. The archipelago comprises seven main islands, Lipari, Vulcano, Stromboli, Salina, Filicudi, Alicudi and Panarea all of exceptional interest for their volcanic nature, their beauty, their light and their climate.

A deep blue, warm, clear sea, ideal for underwater fishing, peculiar marine creatures including flying-fish, sword-fish, turtles, sea-horses and hammer-fish, make the Lipari Islands a refuge for those who like to live close to nature. The inhabitants fish, grow vines and quarry pumice-stone.

★★ **Lipari.** – This, the largest island in the archipelago, is formed of volcanic rock dipping vertically into the sea. In ancient times Lipari was a source of obsidian, a glazed black volcanic rock. Today the islanders grow cereals and capers, fish and quarry pumice stone on the east coast.

Two bays (Marina Lunga with its beach and Marina Corta) frame the town of **Lipari★**, which is dominated by its old quarter encircled by 13-14C walls. Inside is the castle rebuilt by the Spaniards in the 16C on the site of a Norman building. The castle houses
Ⓞ the **museum★**: recreation of a Bronze Age necropolis, lovely collection of painted **kraters** (two-handled vases) imported from Greece and terracotta **theatrical masks**.
Ⓞ There are **boat trips★★** leaving from Marina Corta which take the visitor round the very rugged southwest coast of the island. When making a **tour of the island by car★★**, stop at Canneto and Campo Bianco to visit the pumice stone **quarries**. The view from the headland overlooking the **Puntazze** islands includes five of the islands: Alicudi, Filicudi, Salina, Panarea and Stromboli. However it is the belvedere in **Quattrocchi** which affords one of the finest **panoramas★★★** of the whole archipelago.

★ **Vulcano.** – This 21km² – 8sq mile island is in reality four volcanoes and according to mythology it is here that Vulcan, the God of Fire had his forges. This is also the derivation of the term volcanism. Although there has been no eruption on the island since 1890 there are still important signs of activity: fumaroles (smoke-holes), spouting steam jets often underwater, hot sulphurous mud flows greatly appreciated for their therapeutic nature. This island has a wild but foreboding beauty, with its rugged rocky shores, its desolate areas and its strangely coloured soils due to the presence of sulphur, iron oxides and alum.

The island's main centre, **Porto Levante,** stands below the great crater. The beach is known for its particularly warm water due to the spouting steam jets underwater.

Excursions to the **Great Crater★★★** *(2 1/2 to 3 hours on foot Rtn)* are interesting for the impressive views they afford of the crater and of the archipelago. From **Cape Grillo** there is a view of several islands.
Ⓞ On the other hand, **a tour of the island by boat** *(starting from Porto Ponente)* gives the visitor a chance to see the many curious views, especially along the northwestern coast, which is fringed with impressive basalt reefs.

★ **Stromboli.** – The volcano of Stromboli, with its plume of smoke, has a sombre beauty, forming a wild island with steep slopes. There are very few roads and such soil as can be cultivated is covered with vines yielding a delicious golden-coloured Malvasia wine. The little square white houses are markedly Moorish in style.

The **crater**, in the form of a 924m – 3 032ft cone, has frequent minor eruptions with
Ⓞ noisy explosions and accompanying ejections of lava. You can see the spectacle by climbing to the crater *(7 hours on foot Rtn, difficult climb)* or watch from a boat the famous flow of smoking and incandescent lava along the crevasse named Sciara del Fuoco towards the sea. At night the scene becomes both beautiful and awesome.

Strombolicchio, near Stromboli, is a picturesque rocky islet with a steep stairway leading to its summit which affords a splendid view of Stromboli, the Lipari Archipelago and the coasts of Calabria and Sicily.

★ **Salina.** – The island is formed by six extinct volcanoes of which two have retained
Ⓞ their characteristic outline. The highest crater, **Monte Fossa delle Felci** (962m – 3 156ft) dominates the archipelago. There is a pleasant panoramic road round the island. Caper bushes and vines grow on the lower terraced slopes. The latter yield the delicious golden Malvasia wine.

MARSALA   Pop 80 486

Michelin map 988 fold 35

Marsala, the ancient Libybaeum, on Cape Lilibeo, the westernmost point of the island is an African-looking town in all its whiteness. The Saracens first destroyed and then rebuilt it and called it Marsah el Allah (Port of God). It is known for its wines which a certain English merchant, John Woodhouse, rediscovered in the 18C.

It was at Marsala in 1860 that Garibaldi landed at the start of the **Expedition of the Thousand**, which freed southern Italy from the sway of the Bourbons.

The **Piazza della Vittoria**, near the public gardens (Villa Cavalotti) on the northern outskirts of the town, is a favourite meeting-place of the townsfolk.
Ⓞ A former wine cellar, near the sea, now houses the **archaeological museum** *(Via Boeo)*: note in particular the wreck of a **war ship★** which fought in the Punic War and was found off Capo San Teodoro. Only the prow has been rebuilt.

A gourmet ....?

If you are, look in the current Michelin Guide Italia
for the establishments with stars.

★ MESSINA

Michelin map 988 fold 37 – Town plan in the current Michelin Red Guide Italia

Despite having been destroyed numerous times throughout the centuries, Messina or the ancient Zancle of the Greeks, is today an active market town. Messina has suffered repeated earthquakes (especially the 1908 one which destroyed 90% of the town and killed 80 000 in the region), epidemics and bombings.

Antonello da Messina. – Born in 1430 he studied in Naples where he was influenced by the then popular Flemish art. Later he was to be attracted by the innovations of Tuscan painting which with its increasing use of perspective emphasised volume and architectural details. His works show a complete mastery of his art: forms and colours, skilfully balanced, enhance the portrayal of interiors, an aspect which greatly influenced the Venetian painters of the Renaissance, notably Carpaccio and Giovanni Bellini. Antonello died on his native island around 1479.

SIGHTS

★ **Museum (Museo Regionale).** – *To the north of the town at the end of the Viale della Libertà* There is an art gallery and a sculpture and decorative arts section. In the painting section note the polyptych by Antonello da Messina, **Virgin and Child with Saints** (1473) a remarkable composition which combines certain Tuscan traits with the earliest Flemish influences, a remarkable **Descent from the Cross** by the Flemish artist, Colin van Coter two works by Polidoro da Caravaggio, one of Raphael's pupils and two Caravaggios **Adoration of the Magi** and a **Resurrection of Lazarus**, both painted towards the end of his life between 1608 and 1610. In the sculpture section there is a late 14C Crucifixion in wood and two sculptures representing **Neptune** and **Scylla** attributed to the Tuscan sculptor Montorsoli (16C) who was perhaps one of Michelangelo's assistants.

Cathedral (Duomo). – The cathedral, almost entirely rebuilt after the 1908 earthquake and the bombings of 1943, still displays the main features of its original Norman style (12C). The finely carved narrow central **doorway**★ dates from the 15C. To the left stands the 60m – 196ft tall campanile with its **astronomical clock**★ which was made in Strasbourg in 1933 and is believed to be the world's largest.

Church of the Annunciation (Annunziata dei Catalani). – *Take the Via Cesare Battisti from the south side of the cathedral.*
Built in 1100 during the Norman reign and altered in the 13C this church takes its name from the Catalan merchants who owned it. The apse is characteristic of the composite Norman style which blends Romanesque (small columns supporting blind arcades) Moorish (geometric motifs and polychrome stonework) and Byzantine (dome on a drum influences.

★★★ MONREALE

Michelin map 988 fold 35 – 8km – 5 miles to the southwest of Palermo

The town, dominating the green plain Conca d'Oro (Golden Conch Shell) of Palermo *(p 231)*, grew up around the famous Benedictine **abbey** founded in the 12C by the Norman King, William II.

★★★ **Cathedral (Duomo).** – The finely carved central doorway has beautiful **bronze doors** (1186) embellished with stylised figures, which were the work of Bonanno Pisano The more Byzantine north door is the work of Barisano da Trani (12C). The decoration of the **chevet** is remarkable for the blending of Moorish and Norman styles.

The cathedral has a basilical plan. The interior is dazzling with multicoloured marbles, paintings, and especially, the 12 and 13C **mosaics**★★★ covering the oven vaults and the walls. They represent the complete cycle of the Old and New Testaments.
A gigantic **Christ conferring His Blessing** is enthroned in the central apse. Above the episcopal throne, in the choir, a mosaic represents King William II offering the cathedral to the Virgin. Another mosaic opposite, over the royal throne, shows the same King William receiving his crown from the hands of Christ.

★★★ **Cloisters (Chiostro).** – The cloisters to the right of the church are as famous as the mosaics. They offer views of the abbey church. On the south side there is a curious fountain that was used as a lavabo by the monks. The galleries, with their sharply pointed arches, are supported by twin columns with remarkably carved capitals.

Terraces. – These offer magnificent **views**★★ of the cloisters and over the fertile plain known as the Conca d'Oro.

(Loirat/Explorer)

Monreale – detail of the cloisters

Michelin map 988 fold 37 – 32km – 20 miles to the southwest of Syracuse

Dating from the time of the Siculi, Noto was completely destroyed by the terrible earthquake of 1693. It was rebuilt on a new site 10km – 6 miles distant from the original town. Bordering the streets, laid out on a grid plan, are handsome palaces, churches and other baroque monuments in the local white limestone which has mellowed with time to give a golden colour. Several Sicilian architect worked together on this project. The most inventive was probably **Rosario Gagliardi**.

** **Corso Vittorio Emanuele.** – This rectilinear artery is the town's most popular street. The street widens in three places which are overlooked by the monumental façades of churches designed in an imposing but flexible baroque style. From east to west these are San Francesco all'Immacolata, the cathedral and San Domenico.

* **Via Corrado Nicolaci.** – This gently downward sloping street is lined with palaces sporting exuberantly fanciful balconies. The focal point of this perspective is provided by the church of Montevergine.

** **PALERMO** Pop 728 843

Michelin map 988 folds 35 and 36 – Plan of built-up area in the current Michelin Red Guide Italia

This, the capital and the chief seaport of Sicily, is built at the head of a wide bay enclosed on the north by Monte Pellegrino and on the south by Cape Zafferano. It lies on the edge of a wonderfully fertile plain bounded by hills and nicknamed the **Conca d'Oro** (Golden Conch Shell), on which lemon and orange groves flourish.

HISTORICAL NOTES

Palermo was founded by the Phoenicians, conquered by the Romans and then became Byzantine. From 831 to 1072 it was under the sway of the Saracens, who gave it the peculiar atmosphere suggested today by the luxuriance of its gardens, the shape of the domes on some buildings and the physical type and mentality of the people.
Conquered by the Normans in 1072, Palermo became the capital under **Roger II** who took the title of King of Sicily. This great builder succeeded in blending Norman architectural styles with the decorative traditions of the Saracens and Byzantines: his reign was the golden age of art in Palermo. Later the Hohenstaufen and Angevin kings introduced the Gothic style (13C). After more than three centuries of Spanish rule, the Bourbons of Naples gave Palermo its sumptuous baroque finery.

The Sicilian Vespers. – Since 1266 the brother of St Louis, Charles I of Anjou, supported by the pope, had held the town. But his rule was unpopular. The Sicilians had nicknamed the French, who spoke Italian badly, the *tartaglioni* or stammerers. On the Monday after Easter 1282, as the bells were ringing for vespers, some Frenchmen insulted a young woman of Palermo in the Church of Santo Spirito. Insurrection broke out, and all Frenchmen who could not pronounce the word *cicero* (chick-pea) correctly were massacred. The governor, Jean de St-Rémy was besieged in his palace.

FROM QUATTRO CANTI
TO THE PALACE OF THE NORMANS *time: 3 hours*

Three pretty squares form the busy centre of Palermo. Their charm is enhanced by floodlighting in the evening.

* **Quattro Canti** (BY). – Two main streets, Corso Vittorio Emanuele and the Via Maqueda intersect to form this busy crossroads with four corners *(Quattro Conti)* with their canted walls. The crossroads forms a fine early 17C ensemble in the Spanish baroque style.
The Church of San Giuseppe has an astonishingly decorative interior.

* **Piazza Pretoria** (BY). – The square has a spectacular **fountain**** (B) surmounted by numerous marble statues, the work of a 16C Florentine artist. The **town hall** (H) occupied one side of this square.

** **Piazza Bellini** (BY). – This delightful square combines both Moorish and Norman features and has two buildings typical of Palermo: the Martorana and San Cataldo.

** **La Martorana** (BYZ). – This church is also called Santa Maria dell' Ammiraglio (St Mary of the Admiral) because it was founded in 1143 by the Admiral of the Fleet to King Roger II. In the 16 and 17C it was altered by the addition of a baroque façade on the north side. Pass under the elegant 12C belfry-porch to enter the original church which is decorated with beautiful Byzantine **mosaics****: two panels depict Roger I crowned by Christ and Admiral George of Antioch kneeling before the Virgin.

** **San Cataldo** (BZ). – Founded in the 12C this marvellous church recalls Moorish architecture with its severe rectangular plan, its domes, its decorative crenellations and the traceried openings of the façade.

* **Cathedral (Cattedrale)** (AYZ). – Founded at the end of the 12C, the cathedral is built in the Sicilian-Norman style *(qv)* but has often been modified and added to (15C south porch and the 18C dome). The **apses*** of the east end have retained their typically Sicilian-Norman decoration. In the interior, which was modified in the 18C, see on the right the tombs of the Emperor Frederick II and other members of the Hohenstaufen dynasty as well as other Angevin and Aragonese rulers.
The **treasury** has the sumptuous **imperial crown*** which belonged to Constance of Aragon.

PALERMO ★★★

★★ **Palace of the Normans** (Palazzo dei Normanni) (AZ). — Of the immense royal palace
Ⓥ built by the Normans on the site of an earlier Moorish fortress, only the central part
and the massive Pisan Tower are of the Norman period. The **Palatine Chapel**★★★ on the
first floor was built in the reign of Roger II between 1130 and 1140. It is a wonderful
specimen of Arab-Norman decoration. Ten ancient columns support horseshoe-shaped
arches which separate the nave and two aisles. The upper walls, the dome and the
apses are covered with dazzling **mosaics**★★★ which along with those of Constantinople and Ravenna are the finest in Europe. This prestigious ensemble is completed by
the carved stalactite ceiling, richly decorated marble paving, pulpit and paschal candelabrum. On the second floor the 12C **King Roger's Room**★★ is adorned with mosaics of
the chase.
The attractive gardens, **Villa Bonanno**★ (AZ), boast superb palm trees.

ADDITIONAL SIGHTS

★★ **Church of St John of the Hermits** (San Giovanni degli Eremiti) (AZ). — The church,
Ⓥ which Arab architects helped to construct, was built in 1132 at the request of King
Roger II and is picturesquely crowned with pink domes. Beside it is a garden of tropical
plants with pleasant 13C **cloisters** of small twin columns.

★★ **Capuchin Catacombs** (Catacombe dei Cappuccini). – *Access by Via dei Cappuccini*
⊘ **(AZ 14)**. These catacombs are an impressive sight. About 8 000 mummies were
placed here between the 17C and 19C and have been preserved by the very dry air.

★ **Zisa Palace** (Palazzo della Zisa). – *Access by Corso Finocchiaro Aprile* **(AY 31)**.
⊘ This magnificent pleasure palace in the Arab-Norman style was built in the 12C. Austere on the outside it has a very refined decoration inside.

★★ **Regional Gallery of Sicily** (Galleria Regionale della Sicilia) **(CY M¹)**. – This museum is
⊘ installed in the attractive 15C **Palazzo Abbatellis**★ which is built in the Catalan Gothic
style. It includes a medieval art and painting sections. The works include a very fine
bust of Eleonora of Aragon by Francesco Laurana (15C), a dramatic 15C fresco of **Death
Triumphant**★★★ and the **Madonna of the Annunciation**★★ by Antonello da Messina.

★ **Archaeological Museum** (Museo Archeologico) **(BY M)**. – The museum, which is hou-
⊘ sed in a 16C convent, contains the finds from excavations of the numerous ancient
sites in Sicily. On the ground floor note the Phoenician sarcophagi, an Egyptian inscription known as the Palermo Stone and especially the remarkable **metopes**★★ from temples at Selinus (6 and 5C BC). On the first floor are bronzes including the famous **ram**★★,
a Hellenistic work which originated from Syracuse.

PALERMO

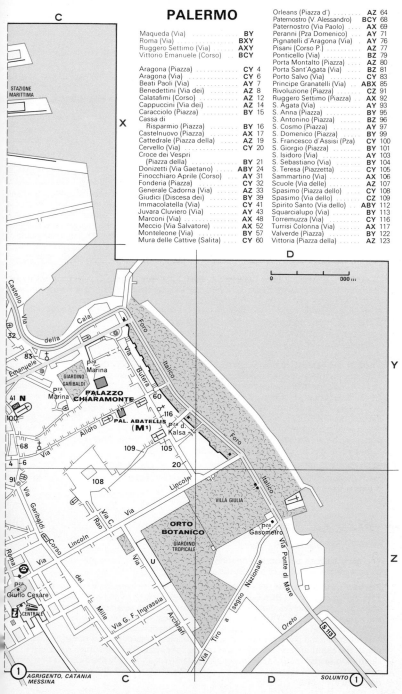

PALERMO ★★★

★ **St Lawrence Oratory (Oratorio di San Lorenzo)** (CY N). – The interior is decorated with curious baroque plaster mouldings by Serpotta and has a Nativity by Caravaggio at the altar. The carved wood supports of the marble benches are remarkable.

★ **Chiaramonte Palace (Palazzo Chiaramonte)** (CY). – A fine Gothic palace (1307) which ⊘ served as a model for many buildings in Sicily and southern Italy.
The Garibaldi Gardens opposite have two spectacular **magnolia-fig trees**★★ (ficus).

★ **Botanical Garden (Orto Botanico)** (CDZ). – A quiet and secluded garden with a vari-⊘ ety of exotic plants and trees.

Park of the Favourite (Parco della Favorita). – *3km – 2 miles to the north. Leave by* ③ *on the town plan.*
This park was laid out for the Bourbons in the 18C. Beside the Chinese pavilion (Palaz-⊘ zina Cinese) is the **Pitrè Ethnographic Museum** which displays some fine **Sicilian carts**★ *(p 242).*

EXCURSIONS

★★★ **Monreale**. – *8km – 5 miles to the southwest. Leave by* ② *on the town plan, the S 186 p 230.*

★★ **Monte Pellegrino**. – *14km – 9 miles to the north. Leave by* ③ *on the town plan, Via Crispi* (BX).
The road out affords some splendid glimpses of Palermo and the Conca d'Oro. On the way up you may visit the 17C sanctuary of Santa Rosalia.

★ **Ruins of Soluntum (Solunto)**. – *19km – 12 miles to the east. Leave by* ① *on the town plan, the S 113* (DZ). *Description p 235.*

Bagheria. – *16km – 10 miles to the east by the A 19 motorway and then 4km – 2 miles southwest of Soluntum.*
⊘ Bagheria is known for its baroque villas and especially for the **Villa Palagonia**, which is decorated with **sculptures**★ of grotesques and monsters.

★★ PANTELLERIA, Island of   Pop 7 717

Michelin map **988** fold 35

Situated in the Sicilian Channel, the Island of Pantelleria is only 84km – 52miles away from Cape Bon in Tunisia. It it the most westerly island of the Sicilian group and lies on the same latitude as Tunis. With an area of 83km² – 32sq miles it is also the largest island in the group. Nicknamed the "Black Pearl of the Mediterranean" the island is full of character with its indented coastline, steep slopes covered with terraces, cultivated for crop growing, its cubic Moorish-looking houses *(dammusi)*. The highest point of this volcanic island is **Montagna Grande** (836m – 2 743ft). The vineyards produce some pleasant wines like the sparkling Solimano and the muscat Tanit. Capers are also grown on Pantelleria.
Pantelleria suffered the same invasions as Sicily, the Phoenicians, Carthaginians, Greeks, Romans, Vandals, Byzantines, Moors and Normans who in 1123 united the island with Sicily.
Access. – By air: see the current Michelin Red Guide Italia. **By sea:** see the Michelin map **988** as well as the current Michelin Red Guide Italia.

TOUR *time: 3 hours*

★★ **Tour of the island by car**. – *40km – 25 miles.*
The very picturesque road following the coast gives the visitor a good chance to discover the beauty of the indented coastline, cliffs, inlets, caves, thermal springs and lakes. On the west coast, 11.5km – 7 miles to the south of the town of Pantelleria, the village of **Scauri** has a lovely site. On the south coast towards **Dietro Isola** the corniche road affords beautiful plunging **views**★★ of this coastal area. The cape, **Punta dell' Arco**, is terminated by a splendid natural rock arch in grey volcanic stone known as the Elephant Arch. On the northeast coast the inlet **Cala dei Cinque Denti** and the rest of the coastline further north make a lovely volcanic landscape.

★★ **Montagna Grande**. – *13km – 8 miles to the southeast of Pantelleria.*
From the summit of this peak there is a splendid **panorama** of the island. In clear weather the view extends as far as Sicily and Tunisia.

★★ PIAZZA ARMERINA   Pop 22 207

Michelin map **988** fold 36

The grey houses of Piazza Armerina huddle round their baroque cathedral on the pleasantly green slopes of a valley side.

★★ **Roman Villa of Casale (Villa Romana del Casale)**. – *6km – 4 miles to the southwest.*
⊘ This immense 3 or 4C BC villa (3 500m² – 37 670sq ft) in all probability belonged to some important dignitary and is important for its **mosaic pavements** which cover almost the entire floor space. These picturesque mosaics, in a wide range of colours, are at times rather primitive and often show a certain North African influence.
The most famous pavements are those showing the **cupids** fishing or playing with dolphins, the capturing and selling of **wild animals** for circus use (in the main corridor); those illustrating **sports** practised by young bikini-clad girls and finally the mosaics of the **triclinium** portraying the **Labours of Hercules**, notably his struggle with the giants. Other scenes decorate the baths.

EXCURSION

Morgantina. – *16km – 10 miles to the northeast by the the Enna road the S 117, then the S 228 to the right. Continue for 6km – 4 miles beyond Aidone.*
Not far from the village of Aidone excavations have uncovered an ancient site in an attractive setting. It has been identified as the early Siculi settlement of Morgantina which was later colonised by the Greeks. The city declined slowly from the 1C onwards.
Amidst the extensive **area of ruins,** note on the valley floor the remains of an agora and a small, rebuilt, theatre. The buildings on the hillside to the north house a number of mosaics which once adorned the 3C BC villas. The village of Aidone features a small **museum** displaying the results of the nearby excavations.

★ RAGUSA   Pop 67 467

Michelin map 🔢🔢🔢 fold 37

Ragusa, partly rebuilt following the 1693 earthquake, lies in a typical **setting**★ on a plateau between deep ravines. The modern town lies to the west while the old town, Ragusa Ibla, clusters on an outlier of the hills, Monti Iblei to the east. The Syracuse road offers magnificent **views**★★ of the old town.
Asphalt and oil are produced or refined locally in large industrial complexes.

★ **Ragusa Ibla.** – The medieval area is a maze of streets, but much of the old town was rebuilt in the baroque style. The lovely 18C **Church of San Giorgio**★ on Piazza del Duomo was designed by the architect Rosario Gagliardi who also worked in Noto. The pink stone façade has a slightly convex central section which is flanked by projecting columns.

Ibleo Archaeological Museum. – *Palazzo Mediterraneo, Via Natalelli.*
In the modern town, below the viaduct, Ponte Nuovo, which spans the Via Roma, this museum contains the finds from excavations undertaken locally, notably from the ancient Greek city of Camarina.

★★ SEGESTA

Michelin map 🔢🔢🔢 fold 35 – 35km – 22 miles southeast of Trapani

The ruins are all that remain of Segesta, the great rival of Selinus in the 5C BC, and it was in all probability destroyed by the Saracens about 1000 AD.

★★ **Temple (Tempio).** – The temple of Segesta stands alone, on an eminence encircled by a deep ravine, in a landscape of receding horizons. The temple is a Doric building (430 BC), pure and graceful, with a peristyle of thirty-six columns in a golden-coloured limestone. The road leading up to the theatre *(2km – 1 mile)* affords a magnificent **view**★★ of the temple.

★ **Theatre (Teatro).** – This Hellenistic theatre with a diameter of 63m – 207ft is built into the rocky hillside. The tiers of seats are slightly orientated towards the Gulf of Castellammare, which is visible beyond the hilltops.

★★ SELINUS (SELINUNTE)

Michelin map 🔢🔢🔢 fold 35

Selinus was founded in the mid-7C by people from the east coast city of Megara Hyblaea and was destroyed twice, in 409 and 250 BC, by the Carthaginians. The huge ruins of its temples with their enormous platforms, wrecked by earthquakes, will impress the visitor. The admirable metopes which adorned these temples are in the National Museum at Palermo.

Archaeological site. – You first reach an esplanade around which are grouped the remains of three **temples** of uncertain attribution. To the right of the road **temple G**, probably dedicated to Apollo, was one of the largest in the ancient world. Over 100m – 328ft long, its columns were built of blocks each weighing several tonnes. The rubble of the fallen stonework gives some indication of its great size. To the left of the road, behind temple F, stands the **temple E** (5C BC) which was rebuilt in 1958.
Cross the depression, Gorgo Cottone to reach the **acropolis** with its perimeter wall. The site is dominated by the rebuilt (1926) columns of temple E (6C BC) the oldest. There are four more ruined temples in the immediate vicinity.
Westwards, on the opposite bank of the Modione stand the remains of a sanctuary to Demeter Malophoros (the dispenser of fruits).

★ SOLUNTUM (SOLUNTO)

Michelin map 🔢🔢🔢 fold 36 – 20km – 12 miles to the east of Palermo

Soluntum stands in an admirable **site**★★ on a rocky ledge on the promontory which overlooks Cape Zafferano. It was a Phoenician city before it fell under the sway of Rome in the 3C BC.
The **archaeological site** *(access by a narrow road which branches off from the S 113 in Porticello, in the direction of a small hill)* includes ruins of a forum, theatre, streets, houses, drainage system and numerous cisterns. Take the Via Ippodamo da Mileto to reach the summit. There is a splendid **view**★★ of the bay of Palermo and Monte Pellegrino.

Syracuse, superbly situated at the head of a beautiful bay, enjoys a very mild climate. It was one of Sicily's if not Magna Graecia's most prestigious cities and at the height of its splendour, rivalled Athens. Syracuse was colonised in the mid-8C BC by Greeks from Corinth who peopled the Island of Ortygia. It soon fell under the yoke of the tyrants, when it developed and prospered. In the 5-4 BC the town had 30 000 inhabitants. Captured by the Romans during the Second Punic War (212 BC), it was occupied successively by the Barbarians, Byzantines (6C), Arabs (9C) and Normans. The river Ciane *(p 237)* was a centre of papyrus production with its papyrus beds. Since the 18C Syracuse has specialised in painting on papyrus, in the Egyptian manner.

Tyrants and intellectuals. – In the Greek world, dictators called tyrants (from the Greek word *turannos*) exercised unlimited power over certain cities, especially Syracuse. Already in 485 BC **Gelon**, the tyrant of Gela, had become master of Syracuse. His brother **Hiero**, an altogether more unpleasant person, nonetheless patronised poets and welcomed to his court both **Pindar** and **Æschylus**, who died in Gela in 456.

Denis the Elder (405-367 BC) was the most famous but even he lived in constant fear. This was symbolised by the sword which he had suspended by a horsehair above the head of Damocles, a jealous courtier. He rarely left the safety of his castle on Ortygia. He wore a shirt of mail under his clothing and changed his room every night. He had Plato sold as a slave when the philosopher came to study the political habits of the people under his dictatorship.

Archimedes, the famous geometrician born at Syracuse in 287 BC, was so absent-minded that he would forget to eat and drink. It was in his bath that he discovered his principle: any body immersed in water loses weight equivalent to that of the water it displaces. Delighted, he jumped out of the bath and ran naked through the streets shouting "Eureka" (I have it!). When defending Syracuse against the Romans, Archimedes set fire to the enemy fleet by focusing the sun's rays with a system of mirrors and lenses. But when the Romans succeeded in entering the town by surprise, Archimedes, deep in his calculations, did not hear them, and a Roman soldier ran him through with his sword.

SIRACUSA

Gelone (Corso)	**AY**	Duomo (Piazza)	**BZ** 9
Matteotti		Federico di Svevia	
(Corso Giacomo)	**BZ** 15	(Piazza)	**BZ** 10
Umberto I (Corso)	**AZ**	Foro Siracusano	**AZ** 12
		Marconi	
Archimede (Piazza)	**BZ** 2	(Piazzale)	**AZ** 14
Capodieci (Via)	**BZ** 3	Necropoli	
Castello		Grotticelli (Via dei)	**AY** 16
Maniace (Via)	**BZ** 4	Pancali (Piazza)	**BZ** 17
Catania (Via)	**AZ** 5	Paradiso (Via)	**AY** 18
Crispi		Regina Margherita	
(Via Francesco)	**AZ** 6	(Viale)	**AZ** 20
Diaz (Viale Armando)	**AZ** 7	S. Giovanni	
Dionisio il		(Viale)	**AY** 21
Grande (Via)	**BY** 8	Teracati (Viale)	**AY** 22
		Testaferrata	
		(Via G.)	**AY** 24
		20 Settembre (Via)	**BZ** 25

★★★ **ARCHAEOLOGICAL AREA** (ZONA ARCHEOLOGICA) (AY)
⊙ *Visit on foot: 2 hours. Access by Via Paradiso* (AY 18)

This area extends over the ancient quarter of Neapolis (the new town) high above and overlooks the Ionian Sea.
From the **Viale Rizzo** (AY) which skirts the area, there is an excellent panorama of the ruins.

Altar of Hiero II (Ara di Ierone II) (AY K). – To the left of the Via Paradiso this 200m – 656ft long altar partly hewn out of the rock, was used for public sacrifices.

★★★ **Greek Theatre** (Teatro Greco) (AY). – The theatre dates from the 5C BC and is one of the largest of the ancient world. The tiers of seats are hewn out of the rock. The first performance of *The Persians* of Æschylus was given in it. A little further on is the **road to the tombs** (AY N), which is hewn out of the rock.

★★★ **Paradise Quarry** (Latomia del Paradiso) (AY L). – This former quarry dates from ancient times. Part of its roof fell in during the 1693 earthquake. An orange grove has been laid out on the excavated material.
The **Ear of Denys**★★★ (B) is an artificial grotto in the form of an earlobe. The grotto was so named in 1608 by the painter Caravaggio as a reminder after the legend recounting how the exceptional echo enabled the tyrant Denys to overhear the talk of the prisoners he confined in a room below.
The **Cordmakers' Cave**★★ (G) takes its name from the cordmakers who used to work there, being able, thanks to the humidity in the air and the fresh atmosphere, to spin and plait their hemp.

★ **Roman Amphitheatre** (Anfiteatro Romano) (AY C). – This 3 or 4C BC amphitheatre measures 140m – 459ft by 119m – 390ft and is hewn out of the rock. There are pines and oleanders.

★★ **OLD TOWN** (CITTÀ VECCHIA) (BZ) *time: 3/4 hour*

On the Island of Ortygia the streets are rich in medieval or Baroque palaces. **Via della Maestranza** (BZ) is particulary rich in the latter. These narrow streets are shaded in summer and are ideal for a stroll.
The **Piazza Duomo** (BZ 9) is particularly attractive lined by palaces adorned by wrought iron balconies and the monumental façade of the **cathedral**★ (Duomo) (BZ D). This was built in the 7C on the foundations of a Doric temple dedicated to Athena. Some of the columns of the latter are to be found reused in the Christian building (north side and interior).
Inside, admire several sculptures (including the Madonna of the Snow) which are attributed to the Gagini, a family of artists who settled in Sicily in the 16C.

★ **Arethusa Fountain** (Fonte Aretusa) (BZ E). – This is the legendary cradle of the city. The nymph Arethusa, pursued by the river-god Alpheus, took refuge on the Island of Ortygia where she was changed into a spring by Artemis. Though near the sea, the fountain, built into a wall, runs with fresh water.
From the nearby platform there is a view of the beautiful Bay of Syracuse.
The **Foro Vittorio Emanuele II** (BZ) a favourite walk for the Syracusans, starts below.

★★ **REGIONAL ARCHAEOLOGICAL MUSEUM P. ORSI**
⊙ **(MUSEO ARCHEOLOGICO REGIONALE)** (AY M¹) *time: 1 hour*

Set in the charming grounds of the **Villa Landolina,** an attractive modern building attributed to Franco Minissi houses the museum built in memory of the archaeologist Paolo Orsi (1859-1935).
It presents the history of Sicily from prehistoric times up to the Greek colonies of Syracuse (7C BC).
After learning about local geology – note the skeletons of the two dwarf elephants-visitors are explained the history of the island, starting from the Upper Palaeolithic, when man made his first appearance in Sicily.
The second part of the visit is devoted to the Greek colonisation (from mid-8C BC onwards), of which many artefacts were salvaged thanks to the excavations carried out at Megara Hyblaea and of course Syracuse: marble kouros, chalk statue of a goddess-mother, ceramics, architectural fragments and small-size replicas of the great sanctuaries of Ortygie, the oldest district in Syracuse...
The third part of the museum is concerned with the various Syracuse colonies. The town became very powerful and in 664 BC it founded Akrai (Palazzolo Acreide).
Then followed Kasmenai (Monte Casale) in 644 BC and Camarina (598 BC): chalk statues, horsemen used in the ornamentation of temples, etc. This part of the building also shows artefacts taken from the Greek colonies inland (large statue of Detemer or Koré) and the excavation sites at Gela and Agrigente, which we owe to the efforts of Paolo Orsi.
The exhibits concerning later history are on display upstairs.

ADDITIONAL SIGHTS

★★ **Catacombs of St John** (Catacombe di San Giovanni) (AY). – After those in Rome these
⊙ are the best Italian example of catacombs. These consist of a main gallery off which branch secondary galleries ending in circular chapels or rotundas, several of the tombs are in the form of arched niches.

★★ **Capuchins' Quarry** (Latomia del Cappuccini) (BY F). – In 413 BC 7 000 Athenian prisoners were interned by Denys of Syracuse in these quarries. The quarries are now overrun by luxuriant vegetation.

★ **Regional Museum: Palazzo Bellomo** (BZ M). – The museum is installed in the beautiful 13C palace which was remodelled in the Catalan style in the 15C. The art gallery has the admirable (despite some damage) **Annunciation** by Antonello da Messina. There is also some goldsmith work, a few charming Sicilian cribs, liturgical objects and furniture.

EXCURSIONS

★ **Ciane Spring** (Fonte Ciane). – *8km – 5 miles to the southwest. It is best to visit by boat.* The **Ciane River**★★ is lined with papyrus beds, which are unique in Italy. It was here that the nymph Cyane was changed into a spring when she opposed the abduction of Proserpine by Pluto.

Castle of Euryalus (Castello Eurialo). – *9km – 6 miles to the northwest of the plan.* This, one of the greatest fortresses of the Greek period, was built by Denys the Elder. Fine panorama.

★★★ TAORMINA   Pop 10 473

Michelin map 988 fold 37 – Town plan in the current Michelin Red Guide Italia

Taormina stands in a wonderful **site** at an altitude of 250m – 820ft and forms a balcony overlooking the sea, facing Etna. It is renowned for its peaceful atmosphere and its beautiful monuments and gardens.

★★ **Greek Theatre** (Teatro Greco). – The theatre dates from the 3C BC but was remodelled by the Romans who used it as an area for their contests.
Performances, of Classical plays, are given in summer. From the upper tiers there is an admirable **view**★★★ between the stage columns, of the coastline and Etna.

★★ **Public Gardens** (Giardino Pubblico). – From this garden of terraces of flowers and exotic plants there are views of the coast and the Sicilian Sea.

★ **Corso Umberto.** – This, the main street of Taormina, has three gateways along its course: Porta Catania, the middle one with the Torre dell' Orologio (Clock Tower) and Porta Messina.
The Piazza del Duomo is overlooked by the Gothic façade of the cathedral and adorned by an attractive baroque fountain. Almost halfway along the **Piazza 9 Aprile** forms a terrace which affords a splendid **panorama**★★ of the gulf. The Piazza Vittorio Emanuele was laid out on the site of the forum and is overlooked by the 15C Corvaia Palace.

★ **Belvedere.** – View of the Aspromonte Massif in Calabria, the Sicilian coast and Etna.

★ **Castle** (Castello). – *4km – 2 miles by the Castelmola road, and then a road to the right. It is also possible to walk up (1 hour Rtn).*
The castle was built in the medieval period on the summit of Monte Tauro (390m – 1 280ft), on the remains of the former acropolis. There are remarkable **views**★ of Taormina.

★ TINDARI

Michelin map 988 fold 37 – 62km – 39 miles to the west of Messina

The ancient Greek Tyndaris, founded in 396 BC, is perched on the summit of the cape of the same name. At the very point stands a **sanctuary** with a Black Virgin which is a place of pilgrimage. The **ruins** are essentially those of the city **ramparts**, the theatre on a site facing the sea and a fine arcaded Roman building (access by the main street, Decumanus) which preceded the forum.

TRAPANI   Pop 73 301

Michelin map 988 fold 35 – Town plan in the current Michelin Red Guide Italia

Trapani has a sheltered port within sight of the Egadi Islands. A pretty coastal road links the town centre with the beach at San Giuliano *(3km – 2 miles to the north).*

Sanctuary of the Annunciation (Annunziata). – Built in the 14C, the church was remodelled and enlarged in the 17C. The campanile is baroque. On the north side the attractive 16C Renaissance **Sailors' Chapel** is crowned with a dome.
Inside the **Chapel of the Madonna**★ contains a Renaissance arch carved in the 16C, a bronze grille dated 1591 and a graceful statue of the Virgin (14C) attributed to Nino Pisano.

★ **Pepoli Museum** (Museo Pepoli). – The museum is located in the former Carmelite convent which adjoins the Annunziata. The works include sculpture (by the Gagini) and paintings (the 15C Trapani polyptych, a *Pietà* by Roberto di Oderisio, a *St Bartholomew* by Ribera and a *St Francis receiving the Stigmata* by Titian). There is also a display of local crafts: coral work and a very delicate crib.

You will find a selection of touring programmes on pp 8-11.

Plan your route with the help of the map of principal sights on pp 4-7.

Practical information

Tourist Information Centres

Consult the **Italian State Tourist Office,** the **E.N.I.T. (Ente Nazionale per il Turismo)** in London at 1 Princes' Street, WI, Tel: (01) 408 1254. Paris, 23 Rue de la Paix, 75002, Tel: 42 66 66 68. New York, 630 Fifth Avenue, New York, NY 10111, Tel: 24 54822. Information may also be obtained from the **Compania Italiana Turismo (C.I.T.),** to be found in many large European towns. The London address is 50 Conduit Street, WI.

In Italy itself, in each regional capital, there is a Regional Tourist Board **(Assessorato Regionale per il Turismo),** in each provincial capital an official tourist information centre called the **A.P.T. (Azienda Promozione Turistica),** and in each resort an **Azienda Autonoma di Soggiorno, Cura e Turismo (A.S.T.),** which is a kind of local tourist information centre. The addresses of these tourist offices and those of the **Italian Automobile Club (A.C.I.)** will be found in the Michelin Red Guide Italia, under the appropriate town.

The symbol ▤ indicates the location of tourist information centres on the town plans found in this guide and in the Red Guide Italia.

REGULATIONS

Exchange. – The Italian unit of currency is the lira : 2 300 = £; 1 300 = $. Money can be changed at the Banca d'Italia, other banks and authorised exchange offices. Banks are usually open Mondays to Fridays from 8.30am to 1.20pm and again for one hour in the afternoon, generally from 3pm to 4pm but this varies according to the different banks. Enquire locally.

The principal credit cards (American Express, Diners Club, Eurocard – Access, Master Charge – and Visa – Barclaycard –) as well as Eurocheques and Travellers Cheques are widely accepted in Italy, with the exception of petrol stations.

Passports. – For a stay not exceeding three months the visitor must have a valid passport or equivalent identity card. Holders of other travel documents should enquire at the nearest Italian Embassy to see if a visa is required and if so for what length of stay.

Vehicle documents and Insurance. – Visitors require a valid driving-licence with an Italian translation or an international driving-licence, the car log-book and the international green insurance card for the vehicle. It is advisable to take out an insurance policy for medical treatment.

MOTORING IN ITALY

Fuel. – Motorists driving in Italy with a foreign registered car may on certain conditions purchase coupons at reduced rates under the Tourist Petrol Concession Scheme. These **coupons** are paid for in foreign currency and are issued (on presentation of car log-book and identification) in the UK by the motoring organisations, C.I.T. and Wasteel Travel, or by the frontier offices of the A.C.I. Apply to the motoring organisations for further information.

On the road. – Speed limits applicable on trunk roads and motorways are as follows (for all vehicles): 50km/h in towns to 90km/h on provincial roads, and 110km/h on motorways (weekends) to 130km/h on motorways (weekdays). Italy has many motorways *(autostrade)* and most of these are toll-roads. The ticket must be kept and given up with payment on leaving the motorway. On some *autostrade* the toll is calculated according to the distance between axles while on others it is according to engine capacity.

Motorway vouchers are available towards payment of the tolls. Apply to the same organisations as for the petrol coupons *(see above)*. A car breakdown service (a tax is levied) is operated by the A.C.I. for foreign motorists carrying the fuel card *(Carta Carburante)*.

The A.C.I. also offers a telephone information service in English (8am to 5pm) for road and weather conditions, as well as for tourist events: Tel: (06) 4212.

Petrol stations generally close for lunch between 12.30pm and 3pm.

Road Maps. – For complete coverage of Italy use the Michelin Map ▦ at a scale of 1: 1 000 000. Other Michelin maps give partial cover: ▦ at 1: 100 000, ▦ and ▦ at 1: 200 000 and ▦ at 1: 400 000. The Touring Club Italiano (T.C.I.), 10 Corso Italia, 20122 Milan, Tel: (02) 852672 publishes among other publications a regional map series at 1: 200 000.

Car ferries. – For the different shipping routes between the peninsula and the various islands consult the Michelin Map ▦. The Michelin Red Guide Italia gives further details. Look under the name of the mainland port or the proper name of the island.

PLACES TO STAY

Hotels and restaurants. – In Italy the choice is wide. To find a hotel or resort use the current Michelin Red Guide Italia which is an annual publication and lists establishments according to grade, comfort, location, amenities and prices. Use the guide to find that overnight stop or that special hotel or unforgettable meal.

Camping. – There are many equipped camping sites in Italy. The local tourist information centres will give particulars on the various sites in the area. Information may also be obtained from the Italian Camping Federation, Federcampeggio, Casella Postale 23, 50041, Calenzano. Tel: (055) 882391. This organisation publishes a map of camping sites and a list of camping grounds offering special rates to holders of the International Camping Card. It also publishes an annual *Campeggi a Villagi Turistici in Italia* in collaboration with the Touring Club Italiano (T.C.I.).

Tourists wishing to spend a ski-ing holiday in Italy can use the SKICALL line to enquire about weather conditions. Dial 0898 12 10 and then 93 (snow reports) or 73 (resort reports).

OPENING TIMES AND PUBLIC HOLIDAYS

Time. – Italian Summer Time (GMT+2 hours) is in force from the last weekend in March to the last weekend in September.

Opening Hours. – **Public buildings** and **national museums** are closed on Mondays (when not a holiday) and certain holidays *(see below)*. Some **museums** may be partially or completely closed for restoration work or because of a shortage of staff. **Churches** are not open to visitors during a service and they often shut between noon or 1pm and 4pm and after 6.30pm. Most **theatrical** and **other entertainments** begin at 9 or 9.30pm. **Shops** in resorts stay open until late in the evening. For banks and petrol stations see under Exchange and On the Road respectively.

Principal Public Holidays. – On the following public holidays offices, shops and schools are closed: 1 and 6 January (Epiphany), Easter Sunday and Monday, 25 April (Anniversary of the 1945 Liberation), 1 May (May Day), 15 August *(Ferragosto:* Assumption), 1 November (All Saints' Day), 25 and 26 December. In addition, each town celebrates the feast of its patron saint. For museums and other sights described in the guide see under Times and Charges.

BOOKS TO READ

We list below only a selection of many books about Italy. Some, which may be out of print, will be available only from libraries.

History and Art

The Grandeur that was Rome by J.C. Stobart *(Sidgwick and Jackson)*
The Italian World by J.J. Norwich *(Thames and Hudson)*
Roman Italy by T.W. Potter *(British Museum Publication Ltd)*
Leonardo da Vinci by Martin Kemp, Jane Roberts and Philip Steadman *(Yale University)*
Michelangelo by Hibbard *(Penguin)*
Venetian Painting: A Concise History by John Steer *(Thames and Hudson)*
Architecture of the Italian Renaissance by Peter Murray *(Thames and Hudson)*
Siena: A City and its History by Judith Hook *(Hamish Hamilton)*
Rise and Fall of the House of Medici by Hibbert *(Penguin)*
Villas of Tuscany by H. Acton *(Thames and Hudson)*
The Art of the Renaissance by Linda and Peter Murray *(Thames and Hudson)*
A History of Italian Renaissance Art by F. Hartt *(Thames and Hudson)*
A Concise Encyclopaedia of the Italian Renaissance by J.R. Hale *(Thames and Hudson)*

Travel

Blue Guides: Northern Italy by A. Macadam; Southern Italy by Paul Blanchard; Sicily by A. Macadam; Florence by A. Macadam; Rome and Environs by A. Macadam; Venice by A. Macadam
Baedeker/AA: Italy (Country Guide); Tuscany (Regional Guide), Florence, Rome and Venice (City Guides)
Mediterranean Island Hopping by Dana Facaros and Michael Pauls *(Gentry Books Ltd)*
D.H. Lawrence and Italy *(Penguin)*
The Path to Rome by Hilaire Belloc *(Penguin)*
Stones of Florence and Venice by McCarthy *(Penguin)*
Venice by John Kent *(Viking)*
Venetian Evenings by James Lees-Milne *(Collins)*
Living in Italy by Y.M. Menzies *(Hale)*
Guide to Tuscany by Bently *(Penguin)*
A Visit to Germany, Italy and Malta by Hans Anderson *(Peter Owen Publishers)*
Room with a View by E.M. Forster *(Penguin)*

Food and Wine

Life beyond Lambrusco (Understanding Italian Fine Wine) by N. Belfrage *(Sidgwick and Jackson)*
Traditional Italian Food by L.B. Birch *(Fontana)*

Literature and Modern Fiction

Italian Short Stories by R. Trevelyan *(Penguin, parallel text)*
The Leopard by Giuseppe Tomasi di Lampedusa *(Flamingo)*
Sicilian Carousel by Lawrence Durrell *(Faber)*
The Slow Train to Milan by Lisa St Aubin de Teran *(Penguin)*

PRINCIPAL FESTIVALS

30 and 31 January

Aosta........................ Fair of St Ours: crafts fair with articles for sale

In February

Viareggio .... Carnival: masked procession, folklore events

Ten days previous to Lent

Venice .... The Carnival. *Further information from the Azienda di Soggiorno, Palazzo Martinengo, San Marco, 4089-30100 Venezia; Tel: (041) 26110*

Last Friday of the carnival

Verona .... Bacchanalian Carnival of the Gnocco: masked processions and competition for the best float; gnocchi made on the spot under a baldachin set up in front of the Church of St Zeno, are distributed to town officials and passers-by

1 April

San Marino .... Investiture of the two Captains Regent *(p 178)*

Holy Week

Taranto .... Processions *(p 185)*

Easter Sunday

Florence .... *Scoppio del Carro:* fireworks display from a decorated float at midday on Piazza del Duomo. The fireworks are set off by a dove which slides along a wire from the high altar in the cathedral to the float

Sulmona .... Feast day of the *Madonna che scappa in Piazza (p 184)*

May

Florence .... May is the month of music: numerous cultural events (concerts, opera, ballet). *Programme from the Azienda di Soggiorno, 15 Via de' Tornabuoni, Florence. Tel: (055) 216544.*

1 May

Cagliari .... Feast of St Efisio, patron saint of Sardinia *(p 217)*

First Sunday in May

Naples .... Feast of the Miracle of St Januarius in the cathedral *(p 125)*

7 to 10 May

Bari .... Feast of St Nicholas: 7 May procession in costumes through the town. 8 May the faithful go in boats to worship a statue of their saint

15 May

Gubbio .... Race of the Ceri *(p 100)*

Second last Sunday in May

Sassari .... *Cavalcata Sarda (p 221)*

Last Sunday in May

Gubbio .... *Palio della Balestra:* archery competition in Piazza della Signoria

1 June to 30 September, even years

Venice .... The Biennale: International Exhibition of Modern Art. *For further information call the Biennale Committee: Tel: (041) 700311*

Beginning of June to end of August

Verona .... Summer Drama Festival

1 to 3 June

Taormina .... Carnival with Sicilian costumes and carts

24 June

Florence .... *Calcio Storico Fiorentino:* ball game on Piazza della Signoria, procession in 16C costumes; fireworks display in Piazzale Michelangiolo

Late June-early July

Spoleto .... *Festival dei Due Mondi:* International Festival of Drama, Music and Dance *(p 183)*

Beginning of July to end of August

Verona .... Musical Season in the setting of the Roman Amphitheatre. *Further information from the Azienda di Soggiorno, 6 Via Dietro Anfiteatro, 37100 Verona. Tel: (045) 592828*

2 July

Siena .... *Palio delle Contrade (p 181)*

16 July
Naples .... Feast of Santa Maria del Carmine (illumination of the campanile) *(p 125)*

Third Saturday in July
Venice .... Feast of the Redeemer on the Island of Giudecca (Saturday night)

First Sunday in August
Ascoli Piceno .... *Festa della Quintana:* procession of representatives from the various districts in 15C costume; horsemen attack a dummy

14 August
Sassari .... *Festa dei Candelieri* (Feast of Candles) *(p 221)*

16 August
Siena .... *Palio delle Contrade (p 181)*

29 August
Nuoro .... Feast of the Redeemer *(p 219)*

End of August to beginning of September
Venice .... International Film Festival on the Lido Island

First Sunday in September
Venice .... Regatta on the Grand Canal

7 September
Florence .... *Festa delle Rificolona* (paper lanterns): musical and folklore events in the different districts

8 September
Loreto .... Feast of the Nativity of the Virgin *(p 109)*
Naples .... Feast of the *Madonna di Piedigrotta*

Second Friday, Saturday and Sunday in September, even years
Marostica .... *Partita a Scacchi:* game of chess with costumed people as the pieces *(p 54)*

Second Sunday in September
Arezzo .... *Giostra del Saracine:* the Saracen's Tournament *(p 48)*
Foligno .... Game of the Quintana *(p 52)*
Sansepolcro .... Cross-box competition, in medieval costumes

13 September
Lucca .... *Luminara di Santa Croce:* night-time procession *(p 110)*

Ten days towards mid-September
Asti .... Wine Festival

Mid-September to mid-October, even years
Florence .... Biennial Antiques Fair in the Palazzo Strozzi

19 September
Naples .... Feast of the Miracle of St Januarius *(p 125)*

Third Sunday in September
Asti .... *Palio* or horse race

1 October
San Marino .... Investiture of the two Captains Regent *(p 178)*

10 December
Loreto .... Feast of the Translation of the Santa Casa *(p 109)*

Christmas to Epiphany
Naples .... Display of cribs in the local churches

Times and charges for admission

Due to the fluctuations in the cost of living and the constant change in the opening times, the information below is given only as a general indication.

The prices quoted below apply to individual adults with no reductions.

Groups should apply in advance in writing or at least telephone ahead; many places have special days for groups; many offer special rates for advance bookings.

For general information on opening times and national holidays see the chapter on Practical Information.

When telephone numbers are given, the local dialling code (prefisso) *is indicated in brackets beforehand.*

Every sight for which there are times and charges listed below is indicated by the symbol ⊙ in the margin of the main part of the guide.

The following opening times have been simplified. Open daily means open all the year round. When there is no mention of mornings or afternoons this means it is open all day without a lunch-time break. Remember in Italy late afternoon can be as late as 7pm.

a

ABRUZZI National Park

Visitor centres. – These are to be found at Civitella Alfedena (near Villetta Barrea), Bisegna (18km – 11 miles north of Pescasseroli), Pescasseroli. Tel: (0863) 91315. Villavallelonga (30km – 19 miles southeast of Avezzano via Trasacco).

ALBA FUCENS

Ruins. – Open daily.

ALBISOLA MARINA

Villa Faraggiana. – Open afternoons April to late September. Closed Tuesdays. 1 500 lire. Tel: (019) 480622.

ALTILIA SAEPINUM

Ruins. – Open daily.

Benevento Gate Museum. – Open daily mornings. Closed Mondays and main public holidays. Tel: (0874) 311147.

Museum near the Theatre. – Same opening times as for Benevento Gate Museum.

ALTOMONTE

Museum. – Open daily mornings and late afternoons. 2 000 lire. Tel: (0981) 948261.

AMALFI

St Andrew's Cathedral: Cloisters of Paradise. – Open daily mornings and afternoons. Closed main religious holidays. 1 000 lire.

ANAGNI

Cathedral Crypt and Treasury. – Open daily mornings and late afternoons. Open afternoons only Sundays and public holidays. Closed 3rd Thursday of each month October to late June. Tel: (0775) 727228.

ANCONA

Church of Santa Maria della Piazza. – Open daily.

National Museum of the Marches. – Open daily mornings Monday to Saturday and Sunday afternoons. Closed official public holidays. 3 000 lire. Tel: (071) 51829.

Podesti Public Gallery. – Open daily. Closed Mondays. 2 000 lire (free on Sundays). Tel: (071) 204262.

ANDALO

Monte Paganella. – Daily access by cable-car. 12 000 lire Rtn in summer, 24 000 lire Rtn in winter (includes ski-ing charges). Access by chairlift from Fai della Paganella. Tel: (0461) 585836.

Times and charges

ANGERA

La Rocca Castle. – Open late March to late October mornings and afternoons. 4 000 lire. Tel: (0331) 931300.

AOSTA

Collegiate Church of St Orso. – Open daily mornings and afternoons. Cloister closed Mondays. Tel: (0165) 362026.

Cathedral. – Open daily mornings and afternoons. Tel: (0165) 40251.

Cathedral treasure in sacristy. – Open April to late September mornings and afternoons. Open afternoons only Sundays and public holidays. The rest of the year open afternoons only Sundays and public holidays. 2 500 lire. Tel: (0165) 40413.

L'AQUILA

Castle: National Museum of the Abruzzi. – Open daily mornings. Closed public holidays. 3 000 lire. Tel: (0862) 27337.

AQUILEIA

Basilica: crypt. – Open daily. Open daily mornings and afternoons. 200 lire. Tel: (0431) 91026.

Basilica: Cripta degli Scavi. – Open daily mornings.

Roman ruins. – Open daily. Tel: (0431) 91016.

Archaeological Museum. – Open daily mornings. 3 000 lire. Tel: (0431) 91016.

Paleo-Christian Museum. – Open daily mornings. Tel: (0431) 91131.

AREZZO

Archaeological Museum. – Open daily mornings. Closed Mondays. 3 000 lire. Tel: (0575) 20882.

Vasari Mansion. – Open daily. Open mornings only Sundays and public holidays. Tel: (0575) 20295.

Museum of Medieval and Modern Art. – Open daily. Closed Sundays afternoons. 3 000 lire. Tel: (0575) 23868.

ARONA

Statue: Colosso di San Carlone. – Open daily mornings and afternoons. Closed Tuesday afternoons and Wednesdays October to late March. Ascent to terrace: 2 000 lire. Ascent to summit: 3 000 lire.

ASCOLI PICENO

Picture Gallery. – Open daily mornings. Open mornings and afternoons in summer. Closed Mondays, 1 January, Easter, 25 April, 1 May, 1 November and 25 December. 2 500 lire.

ASSISI

Lower Basilica: treasury. – Open mornings and afternoons April to late October. Closed Mondays. 3 000 lire. Tel: (075) 812238.

Medieval Castle. – Open daily mornings and afternoons. Closed Mondays and afternoons Sundays and public holidays. 1 500 lire. Tel: (075) 816241.

Pilgrims' Oratory. – Open daily mornings and afternoons. Closed Sundays and public holidays. Tel: (075) 812267.

Carceri Hermitage. – Open daily. Tel: (075) 812301.

Monastery of St Damian. – Open daily mornings and afternoons. Tel: (075) 812273.

St Mary of the Angels Basilica. – Open daily mornings and afternoons. Tel: (075) 8040523.

b

BACOLI

Cento Camerelle. – For permission to visit apply to 161 Via Cento Camarelle.

Piscina Mirabile. – For permission to visit apply to 5 Via Piscina Mirabile.

BAGNAIA

Villa Lante. – Open daily. Closed Mondays and 1 January, 25 April, 1 May, 2 June, 15 August and at Christmas. 2 000 lire. Tel: (0761) 288008.

BAIA

The Baths. – Open daily. 2 000 lire. Tel: (081) 8670797.

BARI

Castle. – Open daily mornings and afternoons. Closed afternoons Sundays and public holidays. 2 000 lire. Tel: (080) 214361.

Picture Gallery. – Open daily mornings and late afternoons. Open mornings only Sundays and public holidays. Closed Mondays and public holidays. Tel: (080) 392421.

Archaeological Museum. – Open daily mornings. Closed Sundays and public holidays. Tel: (080) 5211559.

BARLETTA

Basilica of the Holy Sepulchre. – Open daily mornings and late afternoons. Avoid visiting Sunday mornings.

Municipal Museum. – Open daily mornings. Closed Mondays. Tel: (0883) 31373.

BASSANO DEL GRAPPA

Municipal Museum. – Open daily mornings and afternoons. Closed Mondays and Sunday afternoons. 1 000 lire. Tel: (0424) 22235.

BELLAGIO

Gardens of Villa Serbelloni. – Guided tours (1 1/2 hours) mid-April to mid-October at 11am and 4pm. Closed Mondays. 3 000 lire. Tel: (031) 950204 (Azienda Turistica).

Gardens of Villa Melzi. – Open all day late March to late October. 2 500 lire. Tel: (031) 950318.

BELLUNO

Municipal Museum. – Open mornings and afternoons 2nd Tuesday in April to late October. Closed Mondays, Sunday afternoons, Easter, 1 May and 15 August. The rest of the year open mornings and afternoons Tuesdays to Fridays. Open mornings only Mondays and Saturdays. Closed Sundays. Tel: (0437) 24836.

BENEVENTO

Samnium Museum. – Open daily mornings. Closed Sundays and Mondays. Tel: (0824) 21818.

BERGAMO

Colleoni Chapel. – Open daily mornings and afternoons. Tel: (035) 226311.

Basilica of St Mary Major. – Open daily mornings and afternoons. Open Sunday mornings 11am to 12am.

Bell-Tower of the Palazzo della Ragione. – Open mornings and afternoons early May to late September. The rest of the year open all day Saturdays and Sundays. 1 000 lire (includes use of lift).

Nos 9 and 11 Via Bartolomeo Colleoni. – Open daily Tuesday and Friday mornings. For permission to visit on the other days call Mr. Zerbini. Tel: (035) 248319. Closed towards 15 August.

Carrara Academy. – Open daily mornings and early afternoons. Closed Tuesdays, 1 January, 6 January, Easter Sunday, Easter Monday, 25 April, 1 May, 15 August, 26 August, 1 November, 8, 25 and 26 December. 2 000 lire (free on Sundays). Tel: (035) 399425.

BOLOGNA

Communal Palace. – Open daily mornings and afternoons. Closed Sunday afternoons. October to July, access to the Council Chamber is limited on Mondays, Wednesdays and Fridays, when the Municipal Council holds its sessions. Tel: (051) 290208.

Communal Art Collections. – Open daily mornings. Closed Tuesdays.

Governors' Palace. – Open only during exhibitions. For permission to visit apply to the Information Centre of the City of Bologna. Tel: (051) 290290.

Municipal Archaeological Museum. – Open daily mornings. Closed Mondays and public holidays falling on weekdays. 2 000 lire. Tel: (051) 233849.

Palazzo dell' Archiginnasio: Anatomy Theatre. – Open daily mornings. Closed Sundays and public holidays. For permission to visit apply to the caretaker of the Archiginnasio Library, 1 Piazza Galvani. Tel: (051) 277643.

Torre degli Asinelli. – Open daily. 1 000 lire.

St Stephen's Basilica: Museum. – Open daily mornings and afternoons. Tel: (051) 223256.

National Picture Gallery. – Open daily mornings only. Closed Mondays, 1 January, Easter Sunday to Tuesday, 25 April, 1 May, 15 August, and at Christmas. 3 000 lire. Tel: (051) 243222.

Church of St James Major: St Cecilia's Oratory. – For permission to see the frescoes apply to the sacristan.

Museum of Industrial Art. – Open daily mornings only. Closed Mondays and public holidays.

Davia Bargellini Gallery. – Same admission times as for the Museum of Industrial Art.

BOLSENA

St Christine's. – The Chapel of the Miracle and the Grotto of St Christine are open daily mornings and afternoons. Donations welcome.

BOLZANO

Church and Cloisters of the Dominican Monastery. – Open daily. Closed Sunday afternoons.

Church of the Franciscans. – Open daily mornings and afternoons.

BOMARZO

Park of the Villa Orsini. – Open daily. 5 000 lire. Tel: (0761) 424029.

BOMINACO

Churches. – Open daily mornings and afternoons. For permission to visit apply to the caretaker Mr. Cassiani Berardo. Tel: (0862) 93604. Gratuities welcome.

BORROMEAN ISLANDS

Boats leave from Arona, Stresa, Baveno, Pallanza and Laveno. Pass for the three islands: 6 400 lire.

Isola Bella. – Access: from Arona and Laveno, 8 400 lire Rtn; from Stresa and Baveno, 4 200 lire Rtn; from Pallanza, 5 800 lire Rtn.
Open late March to the 3rd week in October mornings and afternoons. 5 000 lire.

Isola dei Pescatori. – Access: from Arona and Laveno, 8 400 lire Rtn; from Stresa and Baveno, 4 200 lire Rtn; from Pallanza, 5 800 lire Rtn.

Isola Madre. – Access: from Arona, 10 000 lire Rtn; from Laveno, 5 800 lire Rtn; from Stresa, 4 600 lire Rtn; from Baveno 4 200 lire Rtn; from Pallanza, 2 200 lire Rtn.
Open mornings and afternoons late March to 3rd week in October. 5 000 lire.

BRENTA RIVIERA

Boat trips to the villas. – Il Burchiello operates from late March to late October; departure from Venice Tuesdays, Thursdays and Saturdays. Departure from Padua Wednesdays, Fridays and Sundays. Return journey by coach. 98 000 lire (includes admission to the villas, lunch and coach fare). To book apply to C.I.T., Piazza San Marco, Venice, Tel: (041) 5285480; C.I.T., 12 Via Matteotti, Padua, Tel: (049) 663333, or SIAMIC EXPRESS, 42 Via Trieste, Tel: (049) 660944. For the individual opening times of the villas, see under Stra, Mira and Malcontenta.

BRESCIA

Tosio Martinengo Picture Gallery. – Open daily mornings and afternoons. Closed Mondays and public holidays. 2 000 lire. Tel: (030) 59120.

Roman Museum. – Open daily mornings and afternoons. Closed Mondays and official public holidays, 15 February and 8 December. 2 000 lire. Tel: (030) 46321.

Museum of Christian Art. – Closed for restoration work. Part of the collection is on display in the Tosio Martinengo Picture Gallery.

BRESSANONE

Cathedral Treasury. – Open April to late October mornings and afternoons. Closed Sundays and public holidays. 1 200 lire.

Diocesan Museum. – Open all day mid-March to late October. Closed Sundays. 3 000 lire. Open afternoons only mid-December to mid-February. Closed Sundays. 2 000 lire.

BREUIL-CERVINIA

Cable-cars. – Cable-cars for the Rosa Plateau (24 000 lire Rtn) and the Furggen Pass (24 000 lire Rtn) operate daily except from 10 May to 15 June and from 1 to 31 October, when they operate only at weekends. Cable-cars leave every quarter or half hour.

BRINDISI

Archaeological Museum. – Open daily mornings. Closed Sundays and public holidays. Tel: (0831) 23418.

Information in this guide is based on tourist data provided at the time of going to press. Improved facilities and changes in the cost of living make alterations inevitable: we hope our readers will bear with us.

CAMALDOLI

Hermitage. – Guided tours daily mornings and afternoons. Donations welcome.

CAMONICA Valley

National Park of Rock Engravings. – Open daily. Closed 1 January, 25 April, 1 May, 1st Sunday in June, 15 August and 25 December. 2 000 lire. For further information apply to the Centro Camuno di Studi Preistorici, Capo di Ponte. Tel: (0364) 42091.

CAMPO CARLO MAGNO

Grosté Pass. – The cable-car operates from the 1st weekend in July to the 3rd weekend in September mornings and afternoons. Total price for two stages Rtn: 15 000 lire.

CAMPO IMPERATORE

Access. – The cable-car service operates between 8.30am and sunset. 20 000 lire Rtn for skiers. For further information apply to A.P.T., in Aquila. Tel: (0862) 410808. The road is passable from June to late September only.

CANOSA DI PUGLIA

Hypogea. – Open daily mornings only.

CAPRAROLA

Villa Farnese. – Guided tours (villa 1/2 hour, park 1 hour) daily. Park closed Sundays and public holidays. 2 000 lire. Tel: (0761) 646052.

CAPRI, Isle of

Blue Grotto. – Boat trips to the cave are organised daily. Allow 1 hour. 11 550 lire on weekdays, 12 550 Sundays and public holidays. No sailings when the sea is rough.

Tour of the Isle. – Boat trips are organised daily. Allow 2 hours. 12 000 lire (plus 6 450 lire for access to Blue Grotto). No sailings when the sea is rough.

Jupiter's Villa. – Open daily. Open mornings only in winter. Closed Mondays, public holidays and 1st Sunday in June. 2 000 lire. Tel. : (081) 8376218

Carthusian Monastery of St James. – Open daily mornings. Closed Mondays. Tel: (081) 8376218.

Villa San Michele (Anacapri). – Open daily. Open mornings only in winter. 3 000 lire.

Monte Solaro (Anacapri). – The chairlift operates daily except during a short period in winter for maintenance work. 5 000 lire Rtn.

CAPUA

Campania Museum. – Open daily mornings. Closed Mondays. Tel: (0823) 961402.

CARPI

Castello dei Pio. – Open April to late November, late afternoons on weekdays. Open late mornings and late afternoons Sundays. Closed Mondays. Tel: (059) 693153.

CARRARA

Marble Quarries. – Private property. Open daily but check with workers so that you do not hinder the work in progress. Care is required at all times. It is best to visit during the week in the morning, when there is the greatest variety of work in progress. Working hours are generally from 7 to 11am and from 12am to 4pm. There is no quarrying on Saturday afternoons, Sundays, public holidays and around 15 August.

CASAMARI

Abbey. – Open daily mornings and late afternoons. Donations welcome. Tel: (0775) 332371.

CASERTA

La Reggia. – Open daily mornings. 3 000 lire. Tel: (0823) 321127.
Park. – Open daily. 2 000 lire. Tel: (0823) 321127.

CASTEL DEL MONTE

Castle. – Open April to late September mornings and afternoons. Open October to late March mornings only. Closed Sunday afternoons and public holidays. 2 000 lire. Tel: (080) 214361.

CASTELFRANCO VENETO

Giorgione's Birthplace. – Open daily mornings and afternoons Saturdays and Sundays. The rest of the week open afternoons only. Closed Mondays, 1 January, Easter, 24, 25, 26 and 31 December. Tel: (0423) 491240.

CASTELLAMMARE DI STABIA

Antiquarium. – Open daily mornings. Closed Mondays. Tel: (081) 8707228.

Ariadne's Villa. – Open daily. Closed Mondays. The works under way may cause the Villa to be temporarily closed. Tel: (081) 8714541.

San Marco's Villa. – Same visiting times as for Ariadne's Villa.

CASTELLANA

Caves. – Guided tours all year round. Mid-March to late October open all day. In August additional visit at 9pm. The rest of the year mornings only. Visit including the White Cave: 20 000 lire, time: 1 3/4 hours. Visit excluding the White Cave: 10 000 lire, time: 3/4 hour. Tel: (080) 735511.

CERRO

Ceramics Museum. – Open mornings and afternoons Fridays, Saturdays and Sundays. Open afternoons only Tuesdays, Wednesdays and Thursdays. Closed Mondays. 1 000 lire. Tel: (0332) 666530.

CERTALDO

Boccaccio's House. – Open daily early afternoons. For further information apply to the caretaker. Tel: (0571) 667386.

Palazzo Pretorio. – Open daily mornings and afternoons. Open late afternoons in summer. Closed Mondays. 1 000 lire. Tel: (0571) 668270.

CERVETERI

Banditaccia Necropolis. – Open daily mornings. Closed Mondays and Easter Monday. 4 000 lire.

CESENA

Malatestiana Library. – Open daily mornings and afternoons. Closed Monday mornings and Sunday afternoons. September to late June closed Sunday mornings. Also closed public holidays. The manuscripts hall – lit only by daylight – gets dark towards the end of the afternoon. Tel: (0547) 21297.

CHIARAVALLE

Abbey. – Open daily mornings and afternoons. Open afternoons only Sundays and public holidays. Closed Mondays and during church services.

CHIAVENNA

Collegiate Church of St Lawrence: treasure. – Temporarily closed for restoration work.

Botanical and Archaeological Garden. – Open daily afternoons. Closed Mondays, 1 January, Easter, 1 May, 10 August (St Lawrence), 25, 26 and 31 December. 1 000 lire. Tel: (0343) 32821 (library).

CHIETI

Abruzzi Archaeological Museum. – Open daily mornings. Closed 1 January, 25 April, 1 May, 1st Sunday in June, 15 August and 25 December. 3 000 lire. Tel: (0871) 2909

CHIUSI

Etruscan Museum. – Open daily mornings. Closed 1 January, Easter Monday, 1 May, 15 August and 25 December. 2 000 lire. Tel: (0578) 20177.

CIVIDALE DEL FRIULI

Cathedral: museum. – Open daily mornings and afternoons. Sundays and public holidays open 1/2 hour before noon and late afternoons. Tel: (0432) 731398 (tourist bureau).

Archaeological Museum. – Open daily mornings. 2 000 lire. Tel: (0432) 731119.

Tempietto. – Open daily mornings and afternoons. Closed afternoons Sundays and public holidays. Tel: (0432) 731398 (tourist bureau).

CIVITAVECCHIA

National Archaeological Museum. – Open daily mornings. Closed Mondays. Tel: (0766) 23604.

Trajan's Baths. – Open daily mornings. Closed Mondays.

CLITUMNUS, Source of the

Temple of Clitumnus. – Open daily. Closed public holidays. Tel: (0743) 28111 in Spoleto.

COLLODI

Villa Garzoni. – Open daily. December to February open Saturdays and Sundays only. 5 700 lire. Tel: (0572) 428400.

Garzoni Gardens. – Open daily. 7 300 lire.

COMO

Villa Olmo: gardens. – Open daily. Closed Sundays and public holidays. Tel: (031) 262091 (tourist bureau).

COMO, Lake

Boat trips. – These ply from Como to Colico (northeast of lake) and from Como to Lecco: 14 800 lire Rtn. From Como to Tremezzo, Bellagio or Menaggio: 11 600 lire Rtn. From Tremezzo to Dongo, Domaso and Colico: 7 400 to 11 600 lire Rtn. From Bellagio to Lecco: 9 600 lire Rtn.
Hydrofoil service between Como and Tremezzo, Bellagio and Menaggio: 16 000 lire Rtn.
Car ferry service between Bellagio, Varenna, Menaggio and Cadenabbia: 6 500 to 11 000 lire.
With one-day and ten-day tickets visitors are free to travel as they wish: 17 000 lire for the one-day ticket, 53 000 lire for the ten-day ticket.

Night-time trips. – Saturdays in summer. 22 000 lire.

CONEGLIANO

Cathedral. – Open mornings and afternoons. Closed Sunday mornings.

Castle Museums. – Open daily mornings and afternoons. Closed Mondays. 1 200 lire. Tel: (0438) 22871.

CORFINIO

Basilica of San Pelino. – Open all day May to late September. For permission to visit the rest of the year and Sunday afternoons apply to the priest. Tel: (0864) 728121 or 728120. Donations welcome.

CORTINA D'AMPEZZO

Tondi di Faloria. – Cable-car service from Via Marconi to Faloria : 8 900 lire single. From Faloria to Tondi di Faloria: "Tondi" skilift in winter, 1 700 lire and "Girilada" chairlift, 3 000 lire. There is a jeep service during the summer season. 4 000 lire.

Tofana di Mezzo. – "Freccia nel Cielo" cable-car, 24 000 lire Rtn.

Pocol Belvedere. – Bus runs every hour from Piazza Roma. 2 000 lire.

CORTONA

Diocesan Museum. – Open daily mornings and afternoons. Closed Mondays. 3 000 lire. Tel: (0575) 62830.

Museum of the Etruscan Academy. – Open daily mornings and afternoons. April to late September open mornings and late afternoons only. Closed Mondays. 3 000 lire. Tel: (0575) 62767.

CREMONA

Torrazzo. – Visitors may go up to the top 1 April to 15 November every day mornings and afternoons. The rest of the year open Sundays and public holidays only. For the other days of the week apply to the caretaker Mr. Ferdinando Giordano. Tel: (0372) 31524 or 27633. 3 000 lire.

Town Hall. – Guided tours (1 hour) daily mornings and afternoons. Closed Sunday afternoons, Christmas and 1 January. Tel: (0372) 4071.

Municipal Museum. – Open daily mornings and afternoons. Closed Sunday afternoons, Mondays, Christmas and 1 January. 1 000 lire. Tel: (0372) 29349.

CROTONE

Archaeological Museum. – Open daily mornings and afternoons. Open mornings and late afternoons in summer. Closed Sunday and Monday afternoons. Tel: (0962) 23082.

CUMAE

Acropolis. – Open daily. 2 000 lire. Tel: (081) 8543060.

#

DESENZANO DEL GARDA

Villa Romana. – Open daily. Closed Mondays except when they are public holidays. 2 000 lire. Tel: (030) 9143547.

ELBA, Isle of

Napoleonic Museum (Portoferraio). – Open daily. Closed Sunday afternoons, 1 January, 25 April, 1 May, 2 June, 15 August and 25 December. 3 000 lire (includes visit to Napoleon's Villa at San Martino the same day). Tel: (0565) 915846.

Monte Capanne. – Cable-cars operate from May to late September mornings and afternoons. 8 500 lire Rtn.

Marciana: Archaeological Museum. – Open mid-April to mid-October mornings and late afternoons. Closed 15 August and afternoons in April, May and October. 1 500 lire. Tel: (0565) 901015.

Napoleon's Villa (San Martino). – Same times and charges as for the Napoleonic Museum. Tel: (0565) 92688.

EMERALD Cave

Access. – By lift from the road, open daily: 4 000 lire (includes lift and admission to cave). By boat from the port of Amalfi: 5 000 lire or more depending on the type of boat (spring and summer).

ESTE

Atestino National Museum. – Open daily mornings and afternoons. Closed Mondays when they are not public holidays. 2 000 lire. Tel: (0429) 2085.

f

FAENZA

International Ceramics Museum. – Open all day May to late September. The rest of the year open mornings and afternoons. Closed Mondays, Sunday afternoons, 1 January, Easter, 25 April, 1 May, 15 August and 25 December. 4 000 lire. Tel (0546) 21240.

Municipal Picture Gallery. – Open daily mornings. Closed Sundays and public holidays. Tel: (0546) 660799.

FAITO, Monte

Toll-road. – 2 000 lire Rtn per car.

FANO

Municipal Museum. – Open July to late September mornings and late afternoons. The rest of the year open mornings only. Closed Mondays, Sunday afternoons and public holidays. 2 000 lire. Tel: (0721) 876362.

FELTRE

Museum. – Open daily mornings Tuesday to Friday. Open mornings and afternoons Saturdays and Sundays. Closed Mondays. 2 000 lire. Restoration work under way may cause temporary closure. Tel: (0439) 80264.

FENIS

Castle. – Open daily mornings and afternoons. Closed Tuesdays, 25 December and 1 January in the afternoon. 2 000 lire. Tel: (0165) 764263.

FERENTILLO

Abbey of San Pietro in Valle. – Open June to late September mornings and afternoons. The rest of the year open mornings and afternoons Saturdays and Sundays, and afternoons only on weekdays. Donations welcome. Tel: (0744) 780316.

FERENTO

Roman Theatre. – Open all day March to late September. The rest of the year open mornings only. Closed Mondays – or Tuesdays if the Monday is a public holiday not listed below – 1 January, 25 April, 1 May, 1st Sunday in June, 8 and 25 December. Tel: (0761) 225929.

FERRARA

Cathedral Museum. – Open daily mornings and afternoons. Open mornings and late afternoons in summer. Closed Sundays and religious holidays. Donations welcome. For further information apply to Dom Marescotti. Tel: (0532) 901024.

Este Castle. – Open daily mornings and afternoons. Closed Mondays, 25 December and 1 January. In the event of a temporary exhibition the castle remains open on Mondays and there is an admission fee. Tel: (0532) 34301.

Schifanoia Palace. – Open daily. Closed 1 January, Easter Sunday, 1 May, 15 August, 1 November, 25 and 26 December. 2 500 lire. Tel: (0532) 62038.

Palace of Diamonds. – Open daily mornings. Closed Mondays, 1 January, Easter Sunday and Tuesday, 25 April, 1 May, 1st Sunday in June, 15 August and 25 December. 3 000 lire. Tel: (0532) 21831.

Palace of Ludovic the Moor. – The museum is temporarily closed owing to restoration and renovation works. Visitors should be allowed access to the garden and court of honour. Tel: (0532) 66299.

Casa Romei. – Open daily mornings. Closed Mondays, 1 January, Easter Sunday and Tuesday, 25 April, 1 May, 1st Sunday in June, 15 August and 25 December. 2 000 lire. Tel: (0532) 40341.

Palazzina di Marfisa d'Este. – Open daily mornings and afternoons. Closed Sunday afternoons October to late February and 1 January, Easter, 1 May, 15 August, 25 and 26 December. 2 000 lire. Tel: (0532) 36923.

Sant'Antonio in Polesine. – Open daily mornings and afternoons. Closed Sundays and public holidays. Donations welcome. Tel: (0532) 64068.

Ariosto's House. – Open daily mornings and afternoons. Closed Sundays and public holidays. Tel: (0532) 40784.

FIESOLE

Convent of St Francis. – Open mornings and afternoons. Donations welcome. Tel. (055) 59175.

Archaeological Site and Museum. – Open daily. 2 500 lire. Tel: (055) 59477.

Bandini Museum. – Temporarily closed owing to restoration and renovation works. Tel: (055) 59601.

Badia Fiesolina. – For permission to visit apply to the caretaker. Tel: (055) 59155.

FLORENCE

Cathedral:

Inner Gallery and Fresco on the Dome. – Restoration work under way, fresco not visible.

Top of the Dome. – 464 steps. Open daily. Closed Sundays, 1 January, Maundy Thursday to Easter Sunday, 24 June, 15 August, 1 November, 8, 25 and 26 December. 3 000 lire. Tel: (055) 213229.

Crypt of Santa Reparata. – Open daily. Closed Sundays, 1 January, Maundy Thursday, Easter Sunday, 24 June, 15 August, 1 November, 8, 25 and 26 December. 1 500 lire. Tel: (055) 213229.

Campanile. – Open daily. Closed for Easter. 3 000 lire. Tel: (055) 213229.

Baptistry. – Open daily afternoons. Tel: (055) 213229.

Cathedral Museum. – Open daily. Closed Sunday afternoons, 1 January, Easter and 25 December. 3 000 lire (free on Sundays). Tel: (055) 213229.

Palazzo Vecchio. – Open daily. Closed Saturdays and Sunday afternoons, 1 January, Easter, 1 May, 15 August and Christmas. 4 000 lire (free on Sundays). Tel: (055) 2768465.

Uffizi Museum. – Open daily. Closed Mondays, 1 January, 25 April, 1 May, 1st Sunday in June, 15 August and Christmas. 5 000 lire. Tel: (055) 218341.

Corridoio Vasariano. – For permission to visit apply in advance to the Uffizi Secretariat. Guided tours (40min) according to the availability of the guides. Same times and charges as for Uffizi Museum.

Bargello Palace and Museum. – Open daily mornings. Closed Mondays and public holidays. 3 000 lire. Tel: (055) 210801.

Laurenziana Library. – Open daily mornings. Closed Sundays and public holidays, as well as certain days when exhibitions are being prepared. Tel: (055) 210760.

Medici Chapels. – Open daily mornings. Closed Mondays and some public holidays. 4 350 lire. Tel: (055) 213206.

Medici Palace. – Open daily mornings and afternoons. Closed Wednesdays and Sunday afternoons, 1 January, Easter, 1 May, 15 August, 8 and 25 December. Tel: (055) 27601.

Santa Maria Novella: Green Cloisters. – Open daily mornings. Closed Fridays, 1 January, Easter, 1 May, 15 August and Christmas. 3 000 lire (free on Sundays). Tel: (055) 282187.

Pitti Palace:

Palatine Gallery. – Open daily mornings. Closed Mondays, 1 January, 6 January, 7 January, 1 May, 13 August, 14 August and 25 December. 3 000 lire. Tel: (055) 210323.

State Apartments. – Same times and charges as for the Palatine Gallery.

Silver Museum. – Open daily mornings. Closed Mondays. 3 000 lire (includes admission to the Porcelain Museum listed below and the Costume Museum). Tel: (055) 212557.

Modern Art Gallery. – Open daily mornings. Closed Mondays. 4 000 lire. Tel: (055) 287096.

Boboli Garden. – Open daily. Closed 1 January, Easter, 25 April, 1 May, 15 August and Christmas.

Porcelain Museum. – Same times and charges as for Silver Museum.

Convent and Museum of St Mark. – Open daily mornings. Closed Mondays and some public holidays. Tel: (055) 210741.

Academy Gallery. – Open daily mornings. Closed Mondays and some public holidays. 4 000 lire. Tel: (055) 214375.

Foundlings Hospital: Art Gallery. – Open daily mornings. Closed Wednesdays, 1 January, Easter, 1 May, 15 August and 25 December. 3 000 lire (free on Sundays). Tel: (055) 243670.

Times and charges

Santa Croce:

Church. – Open daily mornings and afternoons. Closed during religious services
Tel: (055) 244619.

Santa Croce Museum. – Open daily mornings and afternoons. Closed Wednesdays
1 January, and 25 December. 2 000 lire (includes admission to the Pazzi Chapel)
Tel: (055) 244619.

Pazzi Chapel. – Same times and charges as for the Santa Croce Museum.

Frescoes of Santa Maria del Carmine (in the Brancacci Chapel). – The frescoes are
presently undergoing restoration and the chapel is temporarily closed. For further
information call (055) 2478141.

Last Supper of San Salvi. – Open daily mornings. Closed Mondays, 1 January
6 January, 7 January, 1 May, 13 August, 14 August and 25 December. 2 000 lire
Tel: (055) 677570.

Archaeological Museum. – Open daily mornings. Closed Mondays and public
holidays. 3 000 lire. Tel: (055) 2478641.

Last Supper of Sant'Apollonia. – Open daily mornings. Closed Mondays, 1 January
6 January, 7 January, 1 May, 13 August, 14 August and 25 December. Tel: (055
287074.

Ghirlandaio's Last Supper. – For permission to visit apply to the monastery in the
morning. Closed Sundays. Donations welcome. Tel: (055) 296802.

Florentine House and Museum. – Open daily mornings. Closed Mondays and public
holidays. 2 000 lire. Tel: (055) 216518.

Science Museum. – Open daily mornings. Open afternoons Mondays, Wednesdays
and Fridays. Closed Sundays and public holidays; 5 000 lire. Tel: (055) 293493.

Semi-Precious Stone Workshop. – Open daily mornings. Closed Sundays and public
holidays. 2 000 lire. The stones are not for sale. Tel: (055) 210102.

Buonarroti's House. – Open daily mornings. Closed Tuesdays, 1 January, Easter
25 April, 1 May, 15 August and 25 December. 4 000 lire. Tel: (055) 241752.

Petraia's House. – Guided tours (1/2 hour) daily mornings. The garden is open daily
(no admission fee). Closed Mondays and public holidays. Tel: (055) 451208.

Villa di Castello. – The garden is open daily. Closed Mondays and public holidays
The villa is not open to the public. Tel: (055) 454791.

Villa di Poggio a Caiano. – Open daily mornings only. Guided tours (1 hour) afternoons
Closed Mondays, Sunday afternoons, 1 January, 25 April, 1 May, 2 June, 15 August
and 25 December. Tel: (055) 218741.

Galluzzo Carthusian Monastery. – Guided tours (1/2 hour) daily mornings and
afternoons. Closed Mondays when they are not public holidays. Donations welcome
Tel: (055) 2049226.

FONTANELLATO

Rocca San Vitale. – Open daily mornings and afternoons. Closed Mondays mid-
October to mid-March. 2 000 lire. Tel: (0521) 821118.

FONTE COLOMBO

Monastery. – Open daily. Donations welcome.

La FORESTA

Monastery. – Open daily mornings and afternoons. Donations welcome. Tel: (0746
40085.

FORLÌ

Picture Gallery. – Guided tours (1 hour) daily mornings. Closed Mondays and public
holidays. Tel: (0543) 32771.

FOSSANOVA

Abbey. – Open daily mornings and afternoons. Donations welcome. Tel: (0773) 93061

FRASASSI

Caves. – Open July, August and September: all day every 15min. The rest of the year
open at 9.30am, 11am, 12.30pm, 3pm, 4.30pm and 6pm. 6 000 to 10 000 lire
depending on the season. Tel: (0732) 973001.

FRASCATI

Villa Aldobrandini. – The park only is open daily mornings only. Closed Sundays and
public holidays. For permission to visit apply to Azienda di Soggiorno e Turismo "de
Tuscolo", 1 Piazza Marconi. Tel: (06) 9420331.

Respect the life of the countryside
Go carefully on country roads
Protect wildlife, plants and trees.

g

GAETA

Monte Orlando: Tomb. – For permission to visit apply to Azienda di Turismo, Piazza 19 Maggio, Gaeta. Tel: (0771) 461165 or 462767.

GARDA, Lake

Boat trips. – From Desenzano to Riva del Garda via Sirmione and Salò. 17 000 lire Rtn (boat). 25 200 lire Rtn (hydrofoil).

GARDONE RIVIERA

Vittoriale. – Open daily mornings and afternoons. The villa is closed Mondays. 4 000 lire (park), 10 000 lire (park and villa). Tel: (0365) 20130.

GARGNANO

Villa Feltrinelli. – Not open to the public.

GENOA

Port: boat trips. – These leave from the main harbour Dei Mille. The frequency of these daily trips depends on the number of visitors. Allow 1 hour. 3 500 lire. Tel: (010) 262633.

Cathedral of St Lawrence: Treasury. – Open daily mornings and afternoons. Closed Mondays, Sundays and public holidays. 100 lire. Tel: (010) 296695.

Palazzo Cataldi. – Guided tours (1/4 hour) daily. Closed Saturday afternoons, Sundays and public holidays. Closed all day Saturdays in July and August. Tel: (010) 2094293.

Town Hall. – For permission to visit apply to Direzione Pubbliche Relazioni. Closed Saturdays, Sundays and public holidays.

Palazzo Bianco. – Open daily mornings and afternoons. Closed Mondays, Sunday afternoons and public holidays. 2 000 lire (free on Sunday mornings). Tel: (010) 282641.

Palazzo Rosso. – Same times and charges as for the Palazzo Bianco.

Royal Palace. – Open daily mornings only. 2 000 lire. Tel: (010) 206851.

Palazzo Spinola Gallery. – Open daily. Closed Sundays and Monday afternoons as well as public holidays. 2 000 lire. Tel: (010) 206870.

Villetta Di Negro: Chiossone Museum. – Open mornings and afternoons. Closed Sunday afternoons and Mondays. 2 000 lire. Tel: (010) 542285.

Castelletto. – The lift operates daily. 350 lire.

GRADARA

Rocca. – Open daily mid-May to late September. The rest of the year open mornings only. 3 000 lire. Tel: (0541) 964181.

GRAN PARADISO NATIONAL PARK

Information centres reached from the main Valle d'Aosta road:

Rhêmes-Notre-Dame (information on vultures): Open July and August.

Degioz (by the Val Savarenche road): Open July and August.

Valnontey (turn right in Cogne): Open June to late September. Apply to the Alpino Paradisia Botanical Gardens.

Information centres reached from the Locana road:

Ronco Canavese (turn right in Pont): Open July and August.

Noasca (14km – 9 miles beyond Locana): Open July, August and September. The rest of the year open Sundays and public holidays only.

GRECCIO

Monastery. – Open daily mornings and afternoons.

GROSSETO

Maremma Art and Archaeological Museum. – Open daily mornings and late afternoons. Closed Wednesdays, Sunday afternoons, public holidays in the afternoon, 1 January and 25 December. 3 000 lire (free on Sundays). Tel: (0564) 27290.

Diocesan Museum. – Same times as charges as for the Maremma Museum.

GROTTA GIGANTE

Cave and Museum. – Guided tours (3/4 hour) daily mornings and afternoons: every 30min March to late October, the rest of the year every 60min. Closed Mondays when they are not public holidays and 1 January. 6 000 lire. In summer the admission fee includes the return train journey from Trieste (tourist bureau) and the No 45 bus trip. Tel: (040) 227312 or 327312.

GUBBIO

Consuls' Palace. – Open daily mornings and afternoons. Closed 1 January, 14, 15 and 16 May, and 25 December. 2 000 lire. Tel: (075) 9271989.

Ducal Palace. – Open daily mornings only. Closed 1 January, 25 April, 1 May, 1st Sunday in June, 15 August and 25 December. 2 000 lire. Tel: (075) 9275872.

Cathedral: Episcopal Palace. – The chapel is open only for special festivals. On occasions the sacristan may show visitors round the cathedral. Gratuity.

h – i – j

HERCULANEUM

Ruins. – Open daily. Sometimes closed 1 January and 25 December. The theatre is temporarily closed owing to restoration works. 4 000 lire. Tel: (081) 7390963 or 8611051.

ISEO, Lake

Boat trips. – Boats leave Sarnico or Iseo late morning and return late afternoon. Meals are available on board to visitors who tour the lake. Stops at Lovere and Monte Isola, allow 7 hours. Ticket: 8 900 lire, meal: 12 000 lire. Afternoon excursions from Iseo stop at Monte Isola, allow 2 1/2 hours. 3 700 lire. Apply to I.A.T., 2 Lungolago Marconi, Iseo. Tel: (030) 980209.

ISSOGNE

Castle. – Open daily mornings and afternoons. Closed Mondays, 25 December and 1 January in the afternoon. 2 000 lire. Tel: (0125) 929373.

JESI

Picture Gallery. – Open daily mornings and late afternoons. Closed Mondays, Sunday afternoons, 1 January, Easter, 15 August and 25 December. Tel: (0731) 56859.

l

LAKE DISTRICT

There is a wide choice of boat or hydrofoil (aliscafo) services on the different lakes. Look under the proper name of each lake, where some of these trips will be mentioned. For further information apply to the local tourist information centres.

LAVENO MOMBELLO

Cable-car to Sasso del Ferro. – Operates mornings and afternoons May to late September. The rest of the year operates Saturday and Sunday afternoons. 5 000 lire Rtn. Tel: (0332) 668012.

LECCE

Provincial Museum. – Open daily mornings and afternoons. Closed Saturdays, Sunday afternoons and public holidays. 1 000 lire (free on Sundays). Tel: (0832) 47025.

LORETO

Sanctuary of the Holy House. – Open daily until late afternoon. Tel: (071) 920108.

Picture Gallery. – Open daily mornings and afternoons. Closed Fridays, 1 January, Easter, 1 May, 15 August and Christmas. 2 000 lire. Tel: (071) 92029.

LOVERE

Tadini Museum. – Open May to mid-October afternoons only on weekdays. Open mornings and afternoons Sundays and public holidays. 2 000 lire. Tel: (035) 962780.

LUCCA

Casa Guinigi: Tower. – Ascent of the tower: entrance in Via S. Andrea (behind Via Guinigi). Open daily. Visits are limited to 10min. 2 000 lire. The house itself is not open to the public. Tel: (0583) 41449.

National Museum in the Palazzo Mansi. – Open daily. Closed Monday mornings – except on public holidays –, 1 January, 1 May and 25 December. 3 000 lire. Tel: (0583) 55570.

National Museum in the Villa Guinigi. – Open daily. Closed Sunday and Monday afternoons, all day Monday if it is a public holiday, 1 January, 25 April, 1 May, the Sunday following 2 June, 15 August and 25 December. 2 000 lire. Tel: (0583) 46033.

LUCERA

Museum. – Open daily mornings. Closed Mondays and public holidays. 500 lire. Tel: (0881) 943827.

LUGANO, Lake

Boat trips. – The *Gran Giro del Lago* sails daily late March to mid-October. Departure from Lugano at 2.35pm, return at 5.15pm. 19.60 Swiss francs. For further information on other excursions apply to Società Navigazione del lago di Lugano. Tel: (091) 515223 in Lugano, Switzerland.

MAGGIORE, Lake

Boat trips. – Arona to Locarno: 21 000 lire Rtn. Intra to Laveno: 3 600 lire. Car-ferry: 9 500 to 11 000 lire (single trip with 1 passenger). Intra to Locarno, 17 000 lire Rtn (outward trip by boat, return trip by hydrofoil). One, three and seven day tickets are available, allowing unlimited travel for the given period: 14 300 lire for one day, 28 600 lire for three days and 39 300 lire for seven days.

MALCESINE

Monte Baldo. – Cable-cars operating daily. Departures every 1/2 hour. Time: 15min. Change at San Michele. Closed during the fortnight following Easter, and in November. 12 000 lire Rtn.

MALCONTENTA

Villa Foscari. – Open May to late October Tuesday and Saturday mornings. During this period open 1st Sunday of each month. 5 000 lire. Tel: (041) 969012.

MANTUA

Ducal Palace. – Guided tours (1 hour) daily. Closed Sunday and Monday afternoons; 1 January, 25 April, 1 May, 2 June, 15 August and 25 December. 4 000 lire. Tel: (0376) 320283.

Rotonda di San Lorenzo. – For permission to visit apply to the sacristan of the Basilica of St Andrew.

Palazzo del Te. – Reopening scheduled for 1 September 1989 on the occasion of the exhibition on Jules Romain (visiting times to be fixed at a further date).

Teatro Accademico. – Open daily mornings and afternoons. Closed Sundays and public holidays. 300 lire. Tel: (0376) 327653.

Palazzo d'Arco. – Guided tours (3/4 hour) March to late October Thursday mornings and afternoons, but mornings only Tuesdays, Wednesdays and Fridays. The rest of the year open Thursday mornings, closed the other days. Closed 1 January, 25 April, 1 May, 2 June, 15 August and 25 December. 2 000 lire. Tel: (0376) 322242.

MANSI, Villa

Park. – Open daily mornings and afternoons. Closed over Easter and Christmas. 2 000 lire. Tel: (0583) 929293.

MARLIA

Gardens of the Villa Reale. – Guided tours (1 hour) at 10am, 11am, 4pm, 5pm and 6pm Wednesdays, Thursdays and Sundays in July and August. The rest of the year guided tours every day except Mondays. 3 000 lire July to October, 2 500 lire the rest of the year. Tel: (0583) 30108.

MARMOLADA Massif

Cable-car from Malga Ciapela. – Operates from mid-February to early May and mid-June to late September. 21 000 lire Rtn. Tel: (0437) 722144.

MARMORE Cascade

The waterfalls operate on:

Sundays and public holidays. – November to mid-March from 3pm (1pm on 25, 26 December and 1 January) to 4pm. Mid-March to late April and in September and October, 10am to 12am and 3pm to 9pm. Also on **Saturdays** from 6pm to 9pm. May to late August, 10am to 1pm and 3pm to 11pm. Also on 22 May and 16 August at the same times, and Saturdays 5pm to 10pm.

Weekdays. – Mid-July to late August 5pm to 6.30pm.

Information. – Tel: (0744) 43047. Azienda di Promozione Turistica, Terni.

MASER

Villa. – Open daily afternoons Tuesdays, Saturdays, Sundays and public holidays. Closed on other days, Easter and from 24 December to 6 January. 2 500 lire.

Times and charges

MASSA MARITTIMA

Municipal Museums. – Open daily mornings and afternoons. Closed Mondays and 1 January. 3 500 lire. Tel: (0566) 902289.

Mining Museum. – Open daily mornings and afternoons. Visiting hours are restricted from October to late March. Closed Mondays and 1 January. 2 000 lire. Tel: (0566) 902289.

MATERA

San Pietro Caveoso. – Temporarily closed owing to restoration work.

Ridola National Museum. – Open daily mornings. Closed Mondays, 1 January, Easter, 1 May, 2 June, 15 August and 25 December. 2 000 lire. Tel: (0835) 211239.

MERANO

Princes' Castle. – Open daily April to late October mornings and afternoons. Closed Saturday afternoons, Sundays and public holidays. Admission fee. Tel: (0473) 37834.

MERANO 2000

Cable-car. – Operates daily. 14 500 lire Rtn.

MILAN

Cathedral: Tel: (02) 860358.

Baptistry under the parvis. – Open daily mornings and afternoons. Closed Mondays.

Treasury. – Open daily mornings and afternoons. Closed Mondays. 1 000 lire.

Walk on the roofs. – Open daily. Closed over Christmas and 1 May in the morning. Ascent on foot: 2 000 lire. Ascent by lift: 4 000 lire.

Cathedral Museum. – Open daily mornings and afternoons. Closed Mondays, Easter, 1 May and at Christmas. 4 000 lire.

Scala Museum. – Open daily mornings and afternoons. Closed Sundays November to late April, 1 January, Easter, 1 May, 15 August, 25 and 26 December. 3 000 lire. Tel: (02) 8053418.

Brera Picture Gallery. – Open daily Tuesdays, Wednesdays and Thursdays. On other days open mornings only. Closed all day Monday. 4 000 lire. Tel: (02) 800985 ext. 220.

Castle of the Sforzas. – Open daily mornings and afternoons. Closed Mondays, 1 January, 15 August and Christmas. Tel: (02) 62083943.

Ambrosian Library. – Not open to the public.

Picture Gallery. – Open daily. Closed Saturdays, Easter Sunday and Monday, 1 May, 15 and 16 August, 25 and 26 December. 3 000 lire. Tel: (02) 800146.

Poldi-Pezzoli Museum. – Open daily mornings and afternoons. Also 9pm to 11pm Thursdays (except in August). Closed Mondays (and Sunday afternoons April to late September). Also closed 1 January, Easter, 1 May, 15 and 16 August, 1 November, 25 and 26 December. Also closed some public holidays in the afternoon (including 25 April). 4 000 lire. Tel: (02) 794889.

Modern Art Gallery. – Open daily mornings and afternoons. Closed Tuesdays, 1 January, Easter, 1 May, 15 August and Christmas. Tel: (02) 702819.

Leonardo da Vinci Museum of Science and Technology. – Open daily. Closed Mondays when they are not public holidays, 1 January, Easter, 1 May, 15 August and Christmas. 4 000 lire. Tel: (02) 4817034.

Church of St Mary of Grace: Refectory. – Open daily mornings and afternoons. Open mornings only Mondays, Sundays and public holidays. 4 000 lire. Tel: (02) 4987588.

Archaeological Museum (near the Church of St Maurice). – Open Wednesday mornings and afternoons only.

Church of St Lawrence: Chapel of Sant'Aquilino. – If closed apply to the sacristan, except on Sunday mornings. Tel: (02) 8370991.

MIRA

Villa Widmann-Foscari-Rezzonico. – Open daily mornings and afternoons. Closed Mondays. Tel: (041) 423552.

MIRAMARE

Castle. – Open daily mornings. 3 000 lire. The garden is open all day (no admission fee). From mid-June to mid-September it is also possible to visit the villa in the afternoon. Tel: (040) 224143.

MISURINA, Lake

Toll-road. – 12 000 lire Rtn per car (including the driver). 3 500 lire per passenger.

MODENA

Cathedral Museum. – For permission to visit apply to the sacristan. Tel: (059) 217130, afternoons only. Closed Sundays and public holidays.

Este Library. – Open daily mornings. Closed Sundays and public holidays, as well as Easter week and the 1st fortnight in September. Tel: (059) 222248.

Este Gallery. – Open daily. Open mornings only Tuesdays, Wednesdays and Sundays. Closed Mondays and public holidays. 2 000 lire. Tel: (059) 222145.

MONTE CASSINO

Abbey. – Open daily mornings. Tel: (0776) 26529.

Museum. – Open daily mornings and afternoons. Closed Fridays in summer. Open Sundays and public holidays only in winter. 2 000 lire. Tel: (0776) 26529.

National Archaeological Museum. – Open daily mornings. Closed Mondays and public holidays. Tel: (0776) 301168.

MONTECATINI TERME

Museum of Modern Art. – Open July to late September late afternoons, closed Mondays. Open October to late June afternoons, closed Sundays. Tel: (0572) 78211.

MONTECCHIO MAGGIORE

Villa Cordellina-Lombardi. – Open 13 to 28 April, 4 May to 18 July and 17 August to 15 October: mornings and afternoons Wednesdays, Saturdays and Sundays. The rest of the week open mornings only. Closed Mondays. 2 000 lire. Tel: (0444) 399141.

MONTEFALCO

Communal Tower. – Open daily mornings and afternoons. Apply to Mr. Arnaldo Pietrangeli, 15 Piazza del Commune. 500 lire.

St Francis' Church. – Open daily mornings and afternoons. 2 000 lire. Tel: (0742) 79122.

MONTE ISOLA

Access by boat. – From late March to late September: daily departures from Iseo every 1/2 hour (Sundays and public holidays only late March to mid-June). 3 700 lire Rtn. Daily departures from Sulzano every 1/4 hour. 2 300 lire Rtn. It is also possible to reach the island from other lakeside towns.

MONTE OLIVETO MAGGIORE

Abbey. – Open daily mornings and afternoons.

MONTEPULCIANO

Town Hall. – Open daily mornings. Closed Sundays and public holidays. Tel: (0578) 757442.

Madonna di San Biagio. – Open daily mornings and late afternoons. Closed Mondays and public holidays. Donations welcome. Tel: (0578) 757442.

MONTE SANT'ANGELO

Tomb of Rotharis. – For permission to visit apply to the caretaker. Gratuity.

MONZA

Cathedral: Treasury. – Open daily mornings and afternoons. Closed Mondays. 2 000 lire. Tel: (039) 323404.

Park of the Royal Villa. – Open daily.

MORTOLA INFERIORE

Hanbury Gardens. – Open daily. Closed Wednesdays October to late May. 8 500 lire. Tel: (0184) 39507.

MURANO

Museum of Glass. – Open daily around lunchtime. Also open Sunday mornings. Closed Wednesdays and public holidays. 3 000 lire. Tel: (041) 5225625.

GREEN TOURIST GUIDES

Picturesque scenery, buildings
Attractive routes
Touring programmes
Plans of towns and buildings.

n

NAPLES

St Charles Theatre. – Guided tours (1/2 hour) mornings on request. Closed Mondays. It is advisable to book at least a day in advance by contacting the theatre's Public Relations Office. Tel: (081) 7972111.

Royal Palace. – Open daily mornings. Closed 1 January, 25 April, 1 May, 1st Sunday in June, 15 August and 25 December. 3 000 lire. Tel: (081) 413888.

Egg Castle. – For permission to visit apply to Provveditorato alle Opere Pubbliche (Public Works Department) per la Campania, 21 Via Marchese Campodisola.

St Clare's Church: Cloister. – Open daily mornings and late afternoons. Closed Sunday afternoons and public holidays. Tel: (081) 205561.

Chapel of San Severo. – Open daily mornings. Closed 1 January, Easter, 15 August and Christmas. 2 000 lire.

National Archaeological Museum. – Open daily mornings. 4 000 lire. The following galleries are undergoing renovation work and may be temporarily closed: Galleries VIII to XVI, Coloured Marble Gallery, Greek Portrait and the Emperors' Galleries, Galleries XC to XCV. Tel: (081) 440166.

Carthusian Monastery of St Martin. – Open daily mornings. Closed Mondays. 3 000 lire. Tel: (081) 377005.

Capodimonte Palace and National Gallery. – Open daily mornings. Closed Mondays. 4 000 lire. Tel: (081) 7410801.

Villa Floridiana. – Open daily mornings. Closed Mondays. 2 000 lire. Tel: (081) 377315.

Catacombs of St Januarius. – Guided tours daily mornings Saturdays, Sundays and public holidays. Closed the rest of the week. 3 000 lire.

Cathedral. – Open daily mornings and late afternoons. Closed Easter Sunday and 26 December.

Chapel of St Januarius. – Open daily mornings. Also open late afternoon 1st week in May and 19 to 26 September (Feast of the Miracle). Closed 2nd week in May and last week in September.

Basilica of Santa Restituta. – For permission to visit apply to the sacristan of the cathedral. Closed public holidays, 1st Sunday in May and 19 September. Donations welcome.

Cuomo Palace. – Open daily mornings. Closed Mondays and public holidays. 2 000 lire. Tel: (081) 203175.

Aquarium. – Open daily. Closed Mondays, 15 August, and Sunday afternoons November to late February. 1 000 lire. Tel: (081) 5833111.

NONANTOLA

Abbey. – Open daily.

NOVACELLA

Monastery. – Guided tours (1 hour) daily at 10am, 11am, 2pm, 3pm and 4pm. Closed Sundays and public holidays. 2 000 lire. Tel: (0472) 22189.

o

ORTISEI

Alpe di Suisi. – Cable-car services mornings and afternoons in summer: 9 400 lire Rtn. Cable-car services all day in winter: 8 600 lire Rtn. Closed for 40 days after Easter. Tel: (0471) 76218.

ORVIETO

Palace of the Popes: Cathedral Museum. – Open daily mornings and afternoons. Closed Mondays and a couple of weeks in winter. 3 000 lire. Tel: (0763) 42477.

St Patrick's Well. – Open daily. 3 000 lire. Tel: (0763) 43768.

Faina Archaeological Museum. – Open daily mornings and afternoons. Closed Mondays, 25 December and 1 January. 3 000 lire. Tel: (0763) 41216.

OSTIA

Excavation Site. – Open daily. 4 000 lire. Tel: (06) 738994 in Rome.

Museum. – Same times and charges as for the excavation site, but the museum is closed afternoons, Mondays and public holidays.

OTRANTO

The South Coast: Grotta Zinzulusa. – Near Castro Marina. Open all day March to late October. There is no visiting when the sea is rough. For further information apply to Pro Loco (local tourist bureau) in Castro. Tel: (0836) 97317.

p

Guided tours of the historic centre. – Daily bus tours with commentaries in several languages (except on Mondays). 10 000 lire. For further information and bookings apply to the Tourist Information Centre. Tel: (049) 8750655.

Frescoes by Giotto (Scrovegni Chapel). – Open daily mornings and afternoons. Closed afternoons Sundays, public holidays, as well as 1 January, Easter and Christmas. 2 000 lire.

The Saint's Basilica. – Open daily. No visiting during services Sundays and public holidays. Apply at the sacristy to see the high altar.

St George's Oratory and Scuola di Sant' Antonio. – Open daily mornings. Open mornings and afternoons April to late September. 1 000 lire.

Law Courts. – Open daily mornings and afternoons. Closed Sunday afternoons, Mondays and public holidays. 2 000 lire (1 000 lire on Sundays). Tel: (049) 655200 ext. 423.

Municipal Museum. – Open daily mornings. Closed Mondays, 1 January and Easter. 2 000 lire. Tel: (049) 8750975.

University: Teatro Anatomico. – Open daily mornings and afternoons. Open mornings only in August. Closed Sundays and public holidays. Apply to the caretaker of the University, 2 Via 8 Febbraio. Tel: (049) 651400.

Botanical Gardens. – Open May to mid-September mornings and afternoons. Open mornings only in winter. Closed Mondays, 1 January, Easter, 1 May and 25 December. 1 000 lire. Tel: (049) 656614.

PAESTUM

Museum. – Open daily. 3 000 lire (includes access to ruins). Closed Mondays.

Ruins. – Open daily. 3 000 lire (includes access to the museum).

PALLANZA

Villa Taranto. – Open daily April to late October. 5 000 lire. Tel: (0323) 506667.

PALMI

Municipal Museum. – Open daily mornings. Closed Sundays and public holidays. Tel: (0966) 23530.

PAOLA

Monastery. – Open daily mornings and afternoons. Tel: (0984) 390585.

PARMA

St John the Evangelist's Church: Convent cloisters. – Open daily mornings and afternoons. Closed Sundays.

St John the Evangelist's Church: Pharmacy. – Open daily mornings. Closed Mondays and public holidays. 2 000 lire. Tel: (0521) 33309.

National Museum of Antiquities. – Open daily mornings. Closed Mondays, 1 January and 25 December. 2 000 lire. Tel: (0521) 33718.

National Gallery. – Open daily mornings. Closed Mondays, 1 January, 25 April, 1 May, 15 August and 25 December. 5 000 lire. Tel: (0521) 33317.

Farnese Theatre. – Same times and charges as for the National Gallery above. Tel: (0521) 33309.

Corregio's Room. – Open daily mornings. Closed Mondays, 1 January, 25 April, 1 May, 15 August and 25 December.

Glauco-Lombardi Museum. – Open daily mornings and afternoons. Closed Mondays, Sunday afternoons, 4 April, 1st Sunday in June, 1st Sunday in November and public holidays. Tel: (0521) 33727.

PAVIA

Castle of the Visconti. – Open daily mornings and afternoons. Open mornings only in July, August, December and January. Closed Mondays, 4 April and public holidays. 2 000 lire. Tel: (0382) 33853.

PAVIA, Carthusian Monastery of

Monastery. – Open daily mornings and afternoons. Closed Mondays when they are not public holidays.

PERUGIA

National Gallery of Umbria. – Open daily mornings. Closed 1 January, 25 April, 1st Sunday in June, 15 August and 25 December. 4 000 lire. Tel: (075) 20316.

National Archaeological Museum of Umbria. – Open daily mornings. 2 000 lire. Tel: (075) 27141.

Exchange Building. – Open mornings and afternoons March to late October and 20 December to 6 January. Open mornings only November to late February. Closed Mondays, 1 January, Easter, 1 May, 2 June, 15 August and 25 December. 1 000 lire. Tel: (075) 61379.

Porta Marzia and Via Baglione Sotterranea. – Open mornings and afternoons in summer. Open mornings only in winter.

Hypogeum. – Open daily. Closed afternoons Sundays and public holidays. 2 000 lire. Tel: (075) 393329.

PESARO

Rossini's House. – Temporarily closed owing to restoration works. May be re-opened in summer 1989.

Municipal Museum. – Open mornings and afternoons April to late September. Closed afternoons Sundays and public holidays. The rest of the year open mornings only. Closed Mondays. 3 000 lire (free on Sundays). Tel: (0721) 67815.

Oliveriano Museum. – For permission to visit apply to the caretaker of the Oliveriana Library mornings and afternoons. Closed Saturdays, Sundays and public holidays.

PIACENZA

Farnese Palace: Municipal Museum. – Open daily mornings only Wednesdays, Fridays and Saturdays. Open mornings and afternoons Tuesdays, Thursdays and Sundays (late afternoons June to late September). Closed Mondays and public holidays. 2 000 lire. Tel: (0523) 28270.

Alberoni Gallery. – Tours on request only. Contact the gallery's management the day before. Tel: (0523) 63198.

PIENZA

Cathedral Museum. – Guided tours (1/2 hour) daily mornings and afternoons. Closed Tuesdays. 1 000 lire. Tel: (0578) 748549.

Palazzo Piccolomini. – Guided tours (20min) daily mornings and afternoons. Closed Mondays except Easter Monday. Tel: (0578) 748503.

PIEVE DI CADORE

Museum (Titian's birthplace). – Open mornings and late afternoons mid-June to mid-September. Closed Mondays. 1 000 lire. Tel: (0435) 32262.

PIONA

Abbey. – Open daily mornings and afternoons. Tel: (0341) 940331.

PISA

Leaning Tower. – Open daily. Closed 1 January and 25 December. 4 000 lire. Tel: (050) 560547.

Baptistry. – Open daily mornings and afternoons. Closed 1 January and 25 December. Tel: (050) 561820.

Cemetery. – Open daily. Closed 1 January and 25 December. 2 000 lire. Tel: (050) 561820.

Sinopia Museum. – Open daily mornings and afternoons. Closed 1 January and 25 December. 2 000 lire. Tel: (050) 561820.

National Museum. – Open daily. Closed Mondays, afternoons Sundays and public holidays, 1 January, 25 April, 1 May, 1st Sunday in June, 15 August and 25 December. 3 000 lire. Tel: (050) 23750.

Church of St Mary of the Thorn. – Open daily mornings. Closed Sundays.

PISTOIA

Cathedral: Altar of St James. – For permission to visit call (0573) 25095.

Baptistry. – Open daily mornings and afternoons. Closed afternoons Sundays and public holidays, 1 January, Easter, 1 May and 25 December. Tel: (0573) 25095.

Town Hall. – Open daily mornings and afternoons. Closed Mondays and Sunday afternoons, 1 January, Easter, 1 May and over Christmas. 2 500 lire. Tel: (0573) 3711. The Marino Marini documentation centre will be transferred to the Tau Palazzo located Corso Librano Fedi.

PLOSE

Access. – From the village of Sant'Andrea, southeast of Bressanone, a cable-car takes visitors to Valcroce and a second to Plose (the latter operates only in winter and early spring). For further information apply to the Tourist Information Centre in Bressanone. Tel: (0472) 22401.

POGGIO BUSTONE

Monastery. – Open daily. Donations welcome.

POMPEII

The Dead City. – Open daily. May close on some public holidays such as 1 January, 1 May, 15 August and 25 December. 5 000 lire. The Antiquarium and the following houses are temporarily closed: House of the Vettii, House of the Cryptoportico, House of the Golden Cherubs, House of Ara Massima, House of the Tragic Poet, House of Pansa and Villa di Guilia Felice.

POMPOSA

Abbey. – Open daily mornings and afternoons. Closed Sunday mornings, in December and 1st week in January. Donations welcome.

POPPI

Castle. – Temporarily closed owing to restoration work.

PORTOFINO

Castle. – Open daily. Closed Tuesdays. 1 000 lire. Tel: (0185) 269075.

PORTOFINO VETTA

Access. – Private road with toll: 3 000 lire for car and driver, 500 lire per passenger.

PORTONOVO

Church of Santa Maria. – Temporarily closed owing to restoration work.

POSSAGNO

Temple of Canova. – Open daily mornings and afternoons. Closed Mondays when they are not public holidays. 2 500 lire. Tel: (0423) 544323.

POZZUOLI

Amphitheatre. – Open daily. 2 000 lire.

Solfatara. – Open daily. 3 000 lire. Although it is not compulsory, visitors may hire a guide (fee subject to discussion).

PRATO

Cathedral Museum. – Open daily mornings and afternoons. Closed Sunday afternoons and Tuesdays. 1 000 lire. Tel: (0574) 29339.

r

RAVELLO

Villa Rufolo. – Open daily mornings and afternoons. Closed 25 December, 1 January. Also closed 24 and 31 December in the afternoon. 1 000 lire. Tel: (089) 224322.

Villa Cimbrone. – Open daily. 2 500 lire. Tel: (089) 857138.

Cathedral Museum. – Open June to late September all day to early evening. Open mornings only October to late May. Tel: (089) 857096.

RAVENNA

Tomb of Galla Placidia. – Open daily.

Church of St Vitalis. – Open daily.

National Museum. – Open daily. Closed Mondays and Sunday afternoons. 3 000 lire.

Orthodox Baptistry. – Open daily mornings and afternoons. Closed afternoons Sundays and public holidays, as well as 1 January and 25 December. 100 lire.

Basilica of St Apollinaris in Classe. – Open daily mornings and afternoons.

Basilica of St Apollinaris the New. – Open daily.

Arians' Baptistry. – Open daily mornings and afternoons. Closed Sunday afternoons and public holidays.

Theodoric's Tomb. – Open all day in summer. Open mornings only in winter. 3 000 lire. Tel: (0544) 34424.

Episcopal Palace Museum. – Open daily mornings and afternoons. Closed Tuesdays, Sunday afternoons and public holidays. 500 lire. Tel: (0544) 30323.

Municipal Picture Gallery. – Open daily mornings and afternoons. Closed Mondays, All Saints' Day, Christmas and 1 January. 1 500 lire (2 000 lire during temporary exhibitions). Tel: (0544) 35625.

Times and charges

RECANATI

Palazzo Leopardi. – Guided tours (1/2 hour) daily mornings and afternoons. Closed 1 January, Easter, 15 August and 25 December. 2 000 lire.

Picture Gallery. – Open daily mornings and late afternoons. Closed Sunday afternoons, Mondays, 1 January, Easter, 15 August and 25 December. 1 000 lire. Tel: (071) 982772.

REGGIO DI CALABRIA

National Museum. – Open daily mornings and afternoons. Open mornings only Sundays and Mondays. 4 000 lire. Tel: (0965) 22005.

REGGIO NELL' EMILIA

Parmeggiani Gallery. – Open daily mornings. Open mornings and afternoons Sundays and Wednesdays. Closed public holidays and in August. Tel: (0522) 37775.

RIVA DEL GARDA

Castle: Museum. – Open June to October mornings and afternoons. Some rooms are still undergoing restoration. Closed Mondays. 2 000 lire. Tel: (0464) 554490.

ROME

Palazzo Venezia. – Open daily mornings. Closed 1 January, 1 May and 25 December. 4 000 lire. Tel: (06) 6798865.

Monument to Victor Emmanuel II. – Not open to the public.

Palazzo dei Conservatori. – Open daily mornings. Open mornings and late afternoons Tuesdays. Also open 5pm to 8pm Saturdays October to March and 8pm to 11pm Saturdays April to late September. Closed Mondays, 1 January, Easter, 21 April, 1 May, 2 and 29 June, 15 August and 25 December. 4 000 lire (includes admission to Capitoline Museum).

Capitoline Museum. – Same times and charges as for the Palazzo dei Conservatori.

Palazzo Senatorio. – Not open to the public.

Roman Forum. – Open daily. Closed on main public holidays. 5 000 lire.

House of Livia. – For permission to visit apply to the caretaker.

Coliseum. – Open daily. Closed on main public holidays. 3 000 lire.

Trajan's Markets. – Open daily mornings. Open mornings and afternoons Tuesdays, Thursdays and Saturdays. Closed Mondays, 1 January, Easter Sunday, Easter Monday, 21 and 25 April, 1 May, 15 August, 1 November, 8, 25 and 26 December. 1 500 lire.

Castel Sant'Angelo. – Open daily mornings only. Open some afternoons in summer. Closed Mondays, 1 January, 1 May and 25 December. 3 000 lire. Tel: (06) 6875036.

Vatican City. – It is essential to dress properly. Do not wear shorts, mini-skirts, or have bare shoulders and plunging necklines.

Vatican: Papal Audiences. – These public audiences are held on Wednesdays. To attend, apply at least 48 hours in advance to the Prefettura della Casa Pontificia in the morning. It is advisable but not essential to obtain a letter of recommendation from a parish priest.

Vatican Museums. – Open daily mornings only. Open afternoons (tickets are not sold after 4pm) in July, August, September and during Holy and Easter weeks (mornings only Saturdays). Closed Sundays, except the morning of the last Sunday of each month so long as it is not a public holiday (admission free). Also closed 1 and 6 January, 11 February, 19 March, Easter Sunday and Monday, 1 May, Ascension or Holy Thursday, Corpus Christi, 29 June, 15 August, 1 November, 8, 25 and 26 December. 8 000 lire.

St Peter's Basilica :

Ascent of the Dome. – Open daily except during Papal Audiences. 3 000 lire for the lift. 2 000 lire on foot.

Treasury and Historical Museum. – Open daily. Closed Easter and Christmas. 2 000 lire. Tel: (06) 6983465.

Farnese Palace. – Not open to the public.

Pantheon. – Open daily mornings. Open mornings and afternoons April to late September. Closed Sunday afternoons, 1 January, 1 May and 25 December. Tel: (06) 369831.

San Luigi dei Francesi. – Open daily mornings and afternoons. Closed Thursday afternoons.

Caracalla's Baths. – Open daily. Closed on main public holidays. 3 000 lire.

St Callistus' Catacombs. – Guided tours (1/2 hour) daily mornings and afternoons. Closed Wednesdays, the last week in January, the 1st week in February, 1 January, Easter and Christmas. 3 000 lire. Tel: (06) 735824.

St Sebastian's Catacombs. – Same times and charges as for St Callistus' Catacombs. Closed Thursdays and the last three weeks in November.

Domitilla's Catacombs. – Same times and charges as for St Callistus' Catacombs. Closed Tuesdays and the first three weeks in January.

Tomb of Cecilia Metella. – Open daily mornings. Closed Mondays, 1 January, Easter, 1 May, 15 August and 25 December. 2 000 lire.

St Cecilia in Trastevere. – For permission to visit apply on Sunday morning (11am to 12.30pm) to the Benedictine monastery which stands alongside, at the far end of the courtyard. Tel: (06) 582140.

National Gallery of Modern Art. – Open daily mornings. Also open afternoons during temporary exhibitions. Closed Mondays and public holidays. 4 000 lire. Tel: (06) 802751.

Borghese Gallery. – Open daily. Closed Sunday and Monday afternoons, as well as some public holidays. Tel: (06) 858577.

National Roman Museum. – Open daily mornings. Closed Mondays. 1 000 lire.

Villa Giulia National Museum. – Open daily. Closed Mondays, 1 January, 1 May and 31 December. 4 000 lire. Tel: (06) 3606571.

Quirinal Palace. – Open by appointment only. Apply at least one week in advance in writing to the Ufficio Intendenza del Palazzo Quirinale, Via della Dataria, 00187, Rome. Closed Saturdays, Sundays, public holidays and in August.

Barberini Palace. – Open daily Monday and Tuesday mornings. The rest of the week open all day. Closed some public holidays. 3 000 lire. Tel: (06) 4754430.

Palazzo Braschi: Rome Museum. – Temporarily closed on account of the renovation works. Tel: (06) 6875880.

Palazzo Doria Pamphili. – Open daily mornings. Closed Mondays, Wednesdays, Thursdays and some public holidays. 2 000 lire (plus an additional 2 000 to see the apartments). Tel: (06) 6794365.

Palazzo Spada. – Open daily Monday and Tuesday mornings. The rest of the week open mornings and afternoons. Closed 1 January, Easter Monday, 15 August anc 25 December. 2 000 lire. Tel: (06) 6561158.

Villa Farnesina. – Open daily mornings. Closed Sundays and public holidays. Tel: (06) 650831.

Museum of Roman Civilisation. – Open daily mornings. Also open Thursday afternoons. Closed Mondays and public holidays. 4 500 lire (free on the last Sunday of each month). Tel: (06) 5926135.

ROSELLE

Ruins. – Open daily.

ROSSANO

Diocesan Museum. – Open daily mornings and late afternoons. Closed Sunday afternoons. Gratuity. Tel: (0983) 31282.

RUVO DI PUGLIA

Jatta Archaeological Museum. – Open daily mornings. Closed Mondays, 1 January, Easter, 15 August and 25 December. 3 000 lire. Tel: (080) 811042.

S

SABBIONETA

Guided tours. – The town's main landmarks are included in a guided tour leaving from the Associazione Proloco, 31 Via Gonzaga. Tel: (0375) 52039. There are guided tours mornings and afternoons except on Mondays. 4 000 lire.

SACRA DI SAN MICHELE

Abbey. – Open daily mornings and afternoons. If closed ring the bell. Donations welcome. Tel: (011) 939130.

SAN FRUTTUOSO

Access by boat. – Daily excursions leave from Rapallo or Santa Margherita every 1/2 hour. 12 000 lire Rtn.
Daily excursions leave from Portofino or Camogli every hour. 6 000 lire Rtn.

SAN GIMIGNANO

Collegiate Church: Chapel of Santa Fina. – Guided tours (20min) daily mornings and afternoons. 2 500 lire (includes admission to the People's Palace).

People's Palace. – Ascent of the tower and museum: open daily mornings and afternoons. Closed Mondays November to late March, 1 January, Easter and 25 December. 2 500 lire (includes admission to the Chapel of Santa Fina). Tel: (0577) 940340.

SAN GUILIO Island

Access. – Daily excursions from Orta every 3/4 hour (break for lunch). Time: 5min. 1 500 lire Rtn. Tel: (0322) 844862, in Borgomanero (8.5km ÷ 5 miles south of the lake).

SAN LEO

Museum and Picture Gallery. – Open daily mornings and afternoons. 3 500 lire. Tel: (0541) 916231.

Times and charges

SAN MARINO

Government House. – Open daily mornings and afternoons. Open all day June to late August. 1 500 lire. Tel: (0549) 992102 (tourist bureau).

Arms Museum. – Open daily mornings and afternoons. Open all day June to late August. 2 000 lire.

Museum - Picture Gallery. – Open daily mornings and afternoons. 1 000 lire.

St Francis' Museum. – Open daily mornings and afternoons. 1 000 lire.

Coin and Stamp Museum. – Open daily mornings and afternoons. Open all day June to late August. 1 000 lire.

SANSEPOLCRO

Municipal Museum. – Open daily mornings and afternoons. Closed 1 January, 1 May, 15 August and 25 December. 2 000 lire. Tel: (0575) 76465.

SAN VIGILIO, Punta di

Villa Guarienti. – Not open to the public.

SARZANA

Sarzanello Fortress. – For permission to visit apply at least 24 hours in advance to the Assessorato alla Cultura e Turismo del Comune di Sarzana. Tel: (0187) 626600.

SIBARI

Archaeological Museum. – Open daily mornings and afternoons. Tel: (0981) 79166.

Excavation Site. – Open daily.

SIENA

Town Hall. – Open daily April to late October. Closed Sunday afternoons. Open mornings only in winter. Closed 1 January, Easter, 1 May and 25 December. 5 000 lire. Tel: (0577) 292111.

Town Hall: Tower. – Same visiting times as for the Town Hall. 2 500 lire.

Cathedral:

Paving. – Much of the paving is usually covered by a protective false floor.

Cathedral Museum. – Open daily mid-March to late October. Open mornings only November to mid-March. Closed 1 January and 25 December. 4 000 lire. Tel: (0577) 283048.

Baptistry of St John. – Open daily generally all day. Visiting hours subject to alteration Sundays. Tel: (0577) 283048.

Picture Gallery. – Open daily. Closed Mondays, Sunday afternoons, 1 January, 1 May and 25 December. 3 000 lire. Tel: (0577) 281161.

Birthplace of St Catherine. – Open daily mornings and afternoons. Tel: (0577) 44177.

SIRMIONE

Scaligers' Castle. – Open daily mornings. 3 000 lire. Tel: (030) 916468.

Grottoes of Catullus. – Open daily. Closed Mondays. 3 000 lire. Tel: (030) 916157.

SORRENTO

Correale di Terranova Museum. – Temporarily closed owing to restoration works May reopen for summer 1989. Tel: (081) 8781846.

SPERLONGA

Archaeological Museum. – Open daily. Closed Mondays. 3 000 lire. Tel: (0771) 54028. The cave is not open to the public.

La SPEZIA

Naval Museum. – Open daily mornings and afternoons. Closed Mondays, Fridays Sundays, 1 January, Easter, 15 August and 25 December. 1 000 lire.

STILO

La Cattolica. – Open daily.

STRÀ

Villa Nazionale. – Open daily mornings. Closed Mondays. 3 000 lire. Tel: (049) 502074.

STRESA

Mottarone. – Access by toll-road from Alpino: 4 000 lire Rtn. Access by cable-car 8 000 lire Rtn. Tel: (0323) 30295.

Villa Pallavicino. – Open all day mid-March to late October. 5 500 lire.

STUPINIGI

Palace. – Open daily (closes early afternoons). Also closed Mondays, Fridays and public holidays. 3 000 lire. Tel: (011) 3581220.

SUBIACO

Monastery of Santa Scolastica. – Open daily mornings and afternoons. Closed during religious services. Donations welcome.

Monastery of St Benedict. – Open daily mornings and afternoons. Donations welcome.

SUPERGA

Basilica: Royal Tombs. – Guided tours (20min) daily mornings and afternoons. Closed Fridays, 1 January, Easter, 8 September and 25 December, and the 2nd fortnight in June. Donations welcome. Tel: (011) 890083.

t

TARANTO

National Museum. – Open daily mornings. Closed public holidays. 3 000 lire. Tel: (099) 22112.

TARQUINIA

Etruscan Necropolis. – Guided tours (1 hour) daily mornings. Closed Mondays. 4 000 lire (includes admission to the National Museum). The caretaker shows visitors only a few of the graves. Tel: (0766) 856308.

National Museum. – Open daily mornings. Closed Mondays. 4 000 lire (includes admission to the Etruscan Necropolis). Tel: (0766) 856036.

Church of St Mary. – For permission to visit apply at the house to the left of the church.

TIVOLI

Villa d'Este. – Open daily. Closed 1 January, 25 April, 1 May, 1st Sunday in June, 15 August and 25 December. 5 000 lire. Tel: (0774) 21249 (Azienda di Turismo).

Hadrian's Villa. – Open daily. 4 000 lire.

Villa Gregoriana. – Open daily. 1 500 lire (free on Thursdays). Tel: (0774) 21644.

TODI

Palazzo del Popolo. – The museums are temporarily closed for restoration work. Small groups may be allowed to visit certain sections of the Palazzo in the morning. Apply to D.sa Graziella Rosati or D.r Giorgio Comez, Palazzi Comunali. Tel: (075) 883541.

TOLENTINO

Basilica of St Nicholas. – Open daily mornings and afternoons. Tel: (0733) 973029.

TORGIANO

Wine Museum. – Open daily mornings and afternoons. Open mornings and late afternoons April to late September. 2 000 lire. Tel: (075) 982348.

TORRE ANNUNZIATA

Roman Villa Oplontis. – Open daily. Closed Mondays during the winter season, 1 January, Easter Monday, 1 May and 25 December. Tel: (081) 8621755.

TORRECHIARA

Castle. – Open mid-April to mid-September mornings and afternoons. The rest of the year open mornings only (until 3pm Saturdays and Sundays). Closed Mondays (except Easter Monday), 1 January, 1 May, 15 August and 25 December. 2 000 lire. Tel: (0521) 855255.

TORRE DEL LAGO PUCCINI

Villa Puccini. – Open daily mornings and afternoons. Closed Mondays October to late March. 3 000 lire.

TORRIGIANI

Villa. – Guided tours (allow 1 hour) April to early November mornings and afternoons. 5 000 lire (includes access to the villa and gardens). Tel: (0583) 928008.

TREMEZZO

Villa Carlotta. – Open all day April to late September. The rest of the year open mornings and afternoons. 4 000 lire. Tel: (0344) 40405.

TREMITI Islands

San Nicola: Abbey of Santa Maria al Mare. – For permission to visit apply in advance to the sacristan of St Francis' parish, Mr. Antonio Crisculo in Cagnano Varano on the mainland. Tel: (0884) 8201.

Boat excursions around San Domino. – Apply to Compagnia Navigazione Libera del Golfo in Termoli on the mainland. During the summer season some excursions leave from Rodi Garganico.

TRENTO

Paleo-Christian Basilica. – Same times and charges as for the Diocesan Museum. Also closed on Sunday mornings.

Diocesan Museum. – Open mornings and afternoons. Closed Wednesdays and mid-November to mid-February. 2 000 lire (includes admission to the basilica). Tel: (0461) 34419.

Castle of Good Counsel. – Open daily mornings and afternoons. Closed Mondays and public holidays. 2 000 lire. Tel: (0461) 35112.

TREVISO

Monte di Pietà. – Open daily mornings. Closed Saturdays, Sundays and public holidays. Tel: (0422) 5841.

Monastery (near the Church of St Nicholas). – For permission to visit apply to the caretaker of the Seminario Vescovile in Via San Nicolo. Tel: (0422) 542322.

Bailo Municipal Museum. – Open daily mornings and afternoons. Closed Mondays, Sunday afternoons and public holidays. 1 000 lire. Tel: (0422) 51337.

TRIESTE

Castle. – Open daily mornings. Closed Mondays, 1 January, Easter, 25 April, 1 May, 15 August and 25 December. 1 000 lire. Tel: (040) 725316.

History and Art Museum. – Same visiting hours as for the castle.

Maritime Museum. – Same visiting hours as for the castle. Also closed 6 January, 1 and 3 November, and 8 December. 1 500 lire. Tel: (040) 304987.

TURIN

Egyptian Museum. – Open daily mornings. Closed Mondays. 3 000 lire. Tel: (011) 544091.

Galleria Sabauda. – Open daily mornings. Closed Mondays. 3 000 lire. Tel: (011) 547440.

Palazzo Madama: Museum of Ancient Art. – Temporarily closed owing to restoration work. Tel: (011) 5765 or 3920 during office hours.

National Film Museum. – Temporarily closed owing to restoration work. Tel: (011) 535901 (tourist bureau).

Royal Palace:

Apartments. – Open daily mornings and afternoons. Closed Mondays and official public holidays. 3 000 lire. Tel: (011) 546731.

Royal Armoury. – Open daily mornings. Closed Mondays, Wednesdays and Fridays. Tel: (011) 546889.

Palazzo Carignano: Museum of the Risorgimento. – Open daily. Closed Sunday afternoons and public holidays. 3 000 lire. Tel: (011) 511147.

Mole Antonelliana. – The lift operates all day. Closed Mondays. 3 000 lire Rtn.

Carlo Biscaretti di Ruffia Motor Museum. – Open daily mornings and afternoons. Closed Mondays and over Christmas. 4 000 lire. Tel: (011) 677666.

Borgo Mediœvale. – Open daily (closes mid-afternoons). Closed Mondays and public holidays. 2 000 lire (access to the castle is free on Fridays). There is no admission fee for the park. Tel: (011) 6699372.

TUSCANIA

Church of St Peter: crypt. – For permission to visit apply to the sacristan in the morning or the afternoon.

UDINE

Castle. – Open daily. Owing to the renovation works under way, the visiting hours are subject to alteration. Tel: (0432) 502872.

Cathedral: Oratory of Purity. – For permission to visit apply to the sacristan mornings or late afternoons. Tel: (0432) 203830.

Archbishop's Palace. – Open daily mornings. Closed Saturdays, Sundays and the first three weeks in August.

URBINO

National Gallery of the Marches. – Open daily mornings. Possibility of all-day opening in summer. 4 000 lire. Tel: (0722) 2760.

Raphael's House. – Open daily mornings and afternoons. Open mornings only during the winter season. Closed Mondays. 3 000 lire. Tel: (0722) 320105.

Churches – St John's and St Joseph's Oratories. – Open March to late December mornings and afternoons. The rest of the year open afternoons only. Open Sunday mornings all year round. 1 000 lire. Tel: (0722) 53300.

VARENNA

Villa Monastero. – The park is open May to late September mornings and afternoons. Closed Tuesdays. The villa is not open to the public. 1 500 lire. Tel: (0341) 830129.

VELIA

Excavations and museum. – Open daily. Closed Mondays.

VENICE

St Mark's Basilica:

Chancel (Pala d'Oro and Treasury). – Open daily. Closed Sunday mornings, as well as Wednesday, Thursday and Friday during Holy Week. 500 lire. Tel: (041) 5225205.

Galleries. – Open daily. 500 lire.

Campanile. – Open daily. 1 500 lire. Tel: (041) 5224064.

Doges' Palace. – Open daily. Closed public holidays. 5 000 lire. Tel: (041) 5224951.

Law Courts: Clock Tower. – Temporarily closed owing to restoration work.

Correr Museum. – Open daily around lunchtime. From June to late September also open late afternoons Fridays, Saturdays and Sundays. Closed Tuesdays, public holidays and 21 November. 3 000 lire. Tel: (041) 5222185.

Old Library:

Archaeological Museum. – Open daily mornings. 2 000 lire. Tel: (041) 5225978.

Marciana Library. – Write in advance to the Head Librarian, 7 Piazzetta San Marco, 30134, Venice. Open weekdays only.

Ca' d'Oro: Franchetti Gallery. – Open daily mornings. Closed 1 January, Easter and 25 December. 2 000 lire. Tel: (041) 5238790.

Academy of Fine Arts. – Open daily mornings. Closed 1 January, 25 April, 1 May, 1st Sunday in June, 15 August and 25 December. 4 000 lire. Tel: (041) 5222247.

Church of St Mary of Salvation. – Open daily mornings and afternoons (limited visiting hours on Sunday mornings and winter afternoons). 500 lire. Tel: (041) 5237951.

Church of St George Major: Campanile. – Access by lift daily mornings and afternoons. 1 000 lire.

Church of Santa Maria Gloriosa dei Frari. – Open daily mornings and afternoons. Closed Sunday mornings. 500 lire.

Scuola di San Rocco. – Open April to late October mornings and afternoons. The rest of the year open mornings daily and afternoons Saturdays and Sundays. 5 000 lire. Tel: (041) 5234864.

Scuola di San Giorgio degli Schiavoni. – Open daily mornings and afternoons. Closed Mondays, afternoons Sundays and public holidays, 1 May and 26 December. 3 000 lire. Tel: (041) 5228828.

Scuola dei Carmini. – Open daily mornings and afternoons. Closed Sundays. 3 000 lire (4 000 lire in summer). Tel: (041) 5289420.

Peggy Guggenheim Collection. – Open April to late October afternoons (until 9pm on Saturdays). Closed Tuesdays. During the winter season open for temporary exhibitions. 5 000 lire (free on Saturday evenings). Tel: (041) 5206288.

Museum: Venice in the 18C. – Open 10am to 4pm. Open Sunday mornings. Closed Fridays and public holidays. 3 000 lire. Tel: (041) 5229006.

Palazzo Querini-Stampalia. – The picture gallery is open daily (closes early afternoon from October to late May). Closed Mondays, 1 January, Easter, 25 April, 1 May, 1st Sunday in June, 15 August and 25 December. 5 000 lire. Tel: (041) 5203433.

Museum of Modern Art (Palazzo Pesaro). – Temporarily closed owing to restoration work.

Palazzo Labia. – Open Wednesdays, Thursdays and Fridays. Apply in advance to RAI (Italian Television), 275 Campo San Geremia. Tel: (041) 781111.

Naval Museum. – Open daily mornings. Closed Sundays, 1 January, Easter, Christmas and public holidays. 1 000 lire.

Times and charges

San Michele. – Access daily by means of the vaporetto "Circolare 5".

The Lagoon: Boat trips. – Numerous agencies propose excursions of varying length and price to the islands and towns on the lagoon. Departure point: Riva degli Schiavoni near St Mark's Square, the railway station and the car park on Piazzale Roma. Apply on the spot or to the C.I.T., St Mark's Square.

Brenta Riviera. – See under the heading "Brenta".

VERONA

Juliet's House. – Open daily. Closed Mondays, 1 January, Easter, 1 May, 1 November and 25 December. 3 000 lire. Tel: (045) 38303.

Palazzo del Comune: Lamberti Tower. – Open all day in summer. Open mornings only in winter. Closed Mondays, 1 January, Easter, 1 May, 1 November and Christmas. 2 500 lire (using lift), 1 500 lire (using staircase). Tel: (045) 32726.

Scaliger Tombs. – Temporarily closed owing to restoration work.

Roman Arena. – Open daily. During the musical season in July and August open mornings only. Closed Mondays, 1 January, Easter, 1 May, 1 November and Christmas. 3 000 lire (free on the 1st Sunday of each month). Tel: (045) 8003204.

Old Scaliger Castle: Art Museum. – Open daily. Closed Mondays, 1 and 6 January, Easter, 1 May, 25 and 26 December. 3 000 lire (free on the 1st Sunday of each month). Tel: (045) 592985.

Church of St Anastasia: Giusti Chapel. – Open same times as church, mornings and afternoons. If the chapel is closed, apply to the sacristan.

Roman Theatre. – Open all day April and May. From October to late March and in June, July, August and September, open mornings only on account of the stage performances. Closed Mondays, 1 January, Easter, 1 May, 1 November and Christmas. 3 000 lire (free on the 1st Sunday of each month). Tel: (045) 8000360.

Archaeological Museum. – Same times and charges as for the Roman Theatre.

Castle of St Peter. – Daily access to the terrace and garden all day long. The castle is not open to the public.

Juliet's Tomb. – Open daily. Closed Mondays, 1 January, Easter, 1 May, 1 November and Christmas. 3 000 lire (free on the 1st Sunday of each month). Tel: (045) 8000361.

VESUVIUS

Ascent by the west face. – Paying car-park at the end of the road. Visitors wishing to go to the top to see the crater must be accompanied by a guide. 7 500 lire.

Ascent by the south face. – Visitors wishing to go to the top to see the crater must be accompanied by a guide. 7 500 lire.

VICENZA

Olympic Theatre. – Open daily mornings and afternoons. Closed afternoons Sundays and public holidays, all day 1 January, Easter, 1 May, 15 August, 25 and 26 December. Also closed afternoons 6 January, Easter Monday, 25 April, 8 September, 1 November and 8 December. 3 000 lire (5 000 lire includes admission to the Picture Gallery). Tel: (0444) 234381.

Municipal Museum in the Palazzo Chiericati. – Same times and charges as for the Olympic Theatre. Also closed Mondays. Tel: (0444) 221348.

Villa Valmarana "ai Nani". – Open late March to early November afternoons. Also open Thursday and Saturday mornings. Sundays and public holidays open mornings only. 4 000 lire. Tel: (0444) 221803.

Rotunda. – Open mid-March to mid-October mornings and afternoons. Outside tour only Tuesdays and Thursdays (as well as Fridays, Saturdays and Sundays if the guides are available). 2 000 lire. 5 000 lire for inside tours on Wednesdays. For permission to visit the inside on other days apply to the Amministrazione F.lli Valmarana, Villa Rotonda, Vicenza. 10 000 lire. Tel: (0444) 221793.

VIGO DI FASSA

Catinaccio Massif. – The cable-car operates from Christmas to Easter and from June to late September. 9 000 lire Rtn.

VILLA OPICINA

Access by funicular. – 1 000 lire single ticket.

VINCI

Museum and Library. – Open daily mornings and afternoons. Closed 1 January, Easter, 1 May, 15 August and 25 December. 3 000 lire. Tel: (0571) 56055.

Leonardo da Vinci's Birthplace. – Open daily mornings and afternoons. Closed Wednesdays, 1 January, Easter, 1 May, 15 August and 25 December. Tel: (0571) 56055.

VITERBO

Municipal Museum. – Open March to late September mornings and afternoons. The rest of the year open mornings only. Closed Sunday afternoons, 1 January, Easter, 25 April, 1 May, 25 and 26 December. 1 000 lire. Tel: (0761) 340810.

VITTORIO VENETO

Battle Museum. – Open daily mornings and afternoons. Closed Mondays, the month of February, 1 January, Easter and 25 December. 1 200 lire. Tel: (0438) 57695.

VOLTERRA

Picture Gallery. – Open all day mid-June to mid-September. The rest of the year open mornings only. Closed 1 January and 25 December. 2 500 lire. Tel: (0588) 87580.

Etruscan Museum. – Open mid-March to late October mornings and afternoons. The rest of the year open late mornings only. Closed 1 January and 25 December. 4 000 lire. Tel: (0588) 86347.

SARDINIA

CAGLIARI

Cathedral: Santuario. – Open daily mornings and late afternoons. Tel: (070) 663837.

National Archaeological Museum. – Open daily mornings and afternoons. Closed Mondays. 3 000 lire. Tel: (070) 654237.

Botanical Gardens. – Open daily mornings. Closed Sundays and public holidays.

CALA GONONE

Sea Ox Cave. – For permission to visit apply to the municipality of Dorgali in the morning on weekdays. Tel: (0784) 93113.

MADDALENA Archipelago

Island of Caprera: Museum. – Open daily mornings. Closed Mondays (if the Monday is a public holiday, the closing day is Tuesday). Also closed 1 January, 25 April, 1 May, 1st Sunday in June, 15 August and 25 December. Tel: (0789)727162.

NUORO

Museum of Popular Traditions. – Open daily mornings and afternoons. Closed Sunday afternoons and Mondays. Tel: (0784) 31426.

PORTO CONTE

Neptune's Cave. – Boats leave from Alghero from mid-April to mid-October at 9am and 3pm. In July and August there are additional sailings at 10am and 4pm. 10 000 lire Rtn. Time: 3 hours. Admission to the cave all year round (closed at 3pm in winter): 5 000 lire. Tel: (079) 979054.

SANT' ANTIOCO Island

Remains of Sulcis and Museum. – Open daily mornings and afternoons. Closed 1 January, Easter, 25, 26 and 31 December. 2 000 lire. Catacombs: 1 500 lire. Tel: (0781) 83590.

SASSARI

Sanna National Museum. – Open daily mornings. Also open late afternoons on the 1st Wednesday of each month. 3 000 lire. Tel: (079) 272202.

THARROS

Excavation site and necropolis. – Admission free.

SICILY

AGRIGENTO

Regional Archaeological Museum. – Open daily mornings and afternoons. Closed Saturday and Sunday afternoons. Tel: (0922) 29008.

Phalaris' Oratory. – Open daily. Tel: (0922) 29008 or 29195.

Greco-Roman Quarter. – Open daily.

Pirandello's House. – 115, Strada Porto Empedocle, in Caos. Guided tours daily. Gratuity.

BAGHERIA

Villa Palagonia. – Guided tours (1 hour) daily mornings. 1 000 lire. Tel: (091) 937522.

CATANIA

Ursino Castle and Museum. – Temporarily closed owing to restoration work.

Times and charges

CEFALU

Mandralisca Museum. – Open daily mornings and afternoons. 1 500 lire. Tel: (0921) 21547.

EGADI Islands

Access. – Ferry and hydrofoil trips leaving from Trapani for the islands of Favignana, Levanzo and Marettimo. For further information consult the Michelin Red Guide Italia.

Favignana. – Boat trips. – No regular timetable. Apply to the local fishermen. Approx. price: 25 000 lire for 4 people.

Levanzo: Boat trip to the Grotta del Genovese. – Apply to the fishermen in Cala Dogana. 5 000 lire per person.

Marettimo: Tour of the island. – Apply to the local fishermen. 15 000 lire per person.

ENNA

Castle. – Open daily mornings and afternoons. Closed Sunday afternoons and 2 July. Tel: (0935) 21009.

ERICE

Castle of Venus. – Open early March to late September mornings and afternoons. The rest of the year open mornings only. Closed Sundays, public holidays and in winter. Tel: (0923) 869159.

ETNA, Mount

Ascent of Etna. – Due to the numerous eruptions, the tourist facilities (roads, paths, cable-cars and refuge huts) are subject to change.

South face. – The cable-car will be operational shortly. For the moment the entire trip is made by four-wheel drive vehicles from the Stazione Etna Sud (in front of the Sapienza hut). Time: 3 hours. 28 000 lire Rtn (includes transport and guided tour of volcano). Stazione Etna Sud may be reached by bus from Catania (30km – 19 miles): these leave from the station square at 8am (additional trips at 11.15am in summer). Excursions to Mount Etna may be cancelled on account of bad weather (fog) or the state of the volcano. For further information and details regarding night excursions, apply to the Tourist Information Centre in Catania or to S.I.T.A.S., 45 Piazza Vittorio Emmanuele in Nicolosi. Tel: (095) 911158.

Northeast face. – Four-wheel drive vehicles leave from Piano Provenzana. Time: 3 hours. 28 000 lire Rtn (includes transport and guided tour of volcano). For further information and details regarding night excursions, apply to S.T.A.R. 233 Via Roma in Linguaglossa, tel: (095) 643180, or Piano Provenzana, tel: (095) 643430, or the Tourist Information Centre (Pro Loco) of Linguaglossa, 5 Piazza Annunziata, tel: (095) 643094.

GELA

Greek Fortifications. – Open daily.

Regional Archaeological Museum. – Open daily mornings. Tel: (0933) 912626.

LIPARI Islands

Lipari Museum. – Open daily mornings. Tel: (090) 9811031.

Boat Trips. – Departures from Marina Corta March to early November. The boats take you round both Lipari and Salina. 20 000 lire.

MARSALA

Archaeological Museum. – Open daily mornings. Also open afternoons Wednesdays, Saturdays and Sundays.

MESSINA

Museum. – Open daily mornings. 2 000 lire. Tel: (090) 658605.

MONREALE

Cathedral. – Open daily mornings and afternoons. Visits are not allowed during the services.

Cloisters. – Open all day April to late September (closed Sunday afternoons). The rest of the year open mornings only. 2 000 lire.

Terraces. – Guided tours (20min) mornings and afternoons. Visits are not allowed during the services. 2 000 lire.

MORGANTINA

Ruins. – Open daily. Tel: (0935) 87307.

Museum. – Open daily mornings and afternoons. Tel: (0935) 87307.

PALERMO

La Martorana. – Open mornings and afternoons. Closed afternoons Sundays and public holidays. Tel: (091) 6161692.

Church of St Cataldo. – For permission to visit apply to the caretaker of La Martorana.

Cathedral: Treasure. – Open daily mornings and late afternoons.

Palace of the Normans. – Guided tours (1 hour) daily Monday, Friday and Saturday mornings. Closed other days and when the regional parliament holds an extraordinary session. Tel: (091) 6561111.

Church of St John of the Hermits and Cloisters. – Open mornings and late afternoons in summer (except on Sunday afternoons). During the winter season open mornings only (closed Mondays). Closed public holidays.

Capuchin Catacombs. – Open daily mornings and afternoons. Gratuity. Tel: (091) 212117.

Zisa Palace. – Temporarily closed owing to restoration work.

Regional Gallery of Sicily. – Open daily mornings. Also open Tuesday and Thursday afternoons. 2 000 lire. Tel: (091) 6164317.

Archaeological Museum. – Open daily mornings. Also open Tuesday and Friday afternoons. 2 000 lire. Tel: (091) 587825.

Chiaramonte Palace. – The palace now houses the administrative offices of the university and it is not open to the public.

Botanical Garden. – Open daily mornings (closed early on Saturdays). Closed Sundays and public holidays. Tel: (091) 6162472.

Park of the Favourite: Pitrè Ethnographic Museum. – Open daily mornings. Closed 1 January, Good Friday to Easter Monday and 25 December. 2 000 lire.

PIAZZA ARMERINA

Roman Villa of Casale. – Open daily. 2 000 lire. Tel: (0935) 84322.

RAGUSA

Ibleo Archaeological Museum. – Open daily mornings. Tel: (0932) 22963.

SALINA Island

Boat trips around the island. – See under Lipari.

SEGESTA

Temple. – Open daily, paying car-park.

SELINUS

Archaeological site. – Open daily. 2 000 lire.

SOLUNTUM

Archaeological site. – Open daily. 2 000 lire. Tel: (091) 936557.

STROMBOLI

Ascent to the crater. – Guide compulsory. 15 000 lire per person. Apply to the Tourist Information Centre in Fico Grande.

SYRACUSE

Archaeological area. – Open daily. The last tickets are sold two hours before sunset. Tel: (0931) 66206.

Regional Archaeological Museum P. Orsi. – Open daily mornings. Closed Mondays. 2 000 lire. Tel: (0931) 66222.

St John's Catacombs. – Guided tours (1 hour) daily mornings and afternoons. 1 000 lire. Tel: (0931) 67955.

Capuchins' Quarry. – Temporarily closed owing to restoration work.

Regional Museum: Palazzo Bellomo. – Open daily mornings. 2 000 lire. Tel: (0931) 65343.

Cyane Spring. – By boat, sailings from Porto Grande. Allow 2 to 3 hours. 50 000 lire Rtn for a boat and four passengers. Excursions are on request. Apply to Mr Vella. Tel: (0931) 69076.

Castle of Euryalus. – Open daily. The last tickets (free) are given two hours before sunset. Tel: 711773.

TAORMINA

Greek Theatre. – Open daily. Closed public holidays. 2 000 lire.

Castle. – Open daily. Tel: (090) 393707.

TINDARI

Ruins. – Open daily. Apply to the Tourist Information Centre (Pro Loco) in Patti. Tel: (0941) 21327.

TRAPANI

Pepoli Museum. – Open daily mornings. 2 000 lire. Tel: (0923) 35444.

VULCANO Island

Tour of the island by boat. – March to late October sailings at 9am, return at 1pm. 10 000 lire.

Index

274

VOCABULARY

ON THE ROAD AND IN TOWN

a destra .... to the right
a sinistra .... to the left
aperto .... open
banchina .... pavement
corso .... boulevard
discesa .... descent
dogana .... customs
fiume .... river
ingresso .... entrance
lavori in corso ..... men at work
neve .... snow
passaggio a livello level crossing
passo .... pass
pericolo .... danger
piazza, largo ...... square, place
piazzale .... esplanade
stretto .... narrow
uscita .... exit, way out
viale, corso .... boulevard, avenue
vietato .... prohibited

mercato .... market
mura .... walls
opere .... works
pala .... panel, altarpiece
palazzo .... palace
paliotto .... altar frontal
passeggiata ...... walk, promenade
piano .... floor, storey
pinacoteca .... picture gallery
pulpito .... pulpit
quadro .... picture
rivolgersi a .... to apply to
rocca .... feudal castle
rovine, ruderi ..... ruins
sagrestia .... sacristy
scala .... stairway
scavi .... excavations
seggiovia .... chair-hoist
spiaggia .... beach
tesoro .... treasure
torre, torazzo ..... tower
vista .... view

PLACE AND THINGS TO SEE

abbazia, convento . abbey, monastery
affreschi .... frescoes
arazzi .... tapestries
arca .... monumental tomb
biblioteca .... library
cappella .... chapel
casa .... house
cascata .... waterfall
castello .... castle
Cena .... The Last Supper
chiesa .... church
chiostro .... cloisters
chiuso .... closed
città .... town
cortile .... courtyard
dintorni .... environs
duomo .... cathedral
facciata .... façade
funivia .... cable-car
giardini .... gardens
gole .... gorges
lago .... lake
lungomare .... seashore promenade

COMMON WORDS

yes, no .... **si, no**
Sir .... **Signore**
Madam .... **Signora**
Miss .... **Signorina**
today .... **oggi**
tomorrow morning .. **domani mattina**
morning .... **mattina**
evening .... **sera**
afternoon .... **pomeriggio**
please .... **per favore**
thank you so much .. **grazie tante**
good morning ...... **buon giorno**
goodbye .... **arrivederci**
how much? .... **quanto?**
where? when? ...... **dove? quando?**
where is? .... **dov'è?**
much, little .... **molto, poco**
all .... **tutto, tutti**
large .... **grande**
small .... **piccolo**
dear .... **caro**
the road to...? ...... **la strada per...?**
may one visit? ...... **si può visitare?**

ART AND ARCHITECTURAL TERMS

Ambo: the pulpit of a primitive Christian basilica.

Ambulatory: an aisle curving round the chancel.

Apparatus: the arrangements of stones or bricks in a structure.

Apse: the end of a church behind the choir.

Apsidal Chapel: a chapel springing from the apse.

Archivolt: highest arch above a doorway.

Atrium: forecourt of a Roman house or Byzantine church.

Ciborium: a canopy over an altar.

Corbelling: a projection on a façade (balcony).

Foliage: ornamental foliated scroll or stem.

Gable: a decorative, acute-angled structure over a window or doorway.

Intarsia or tarsia: inlaid wood, marble or metal.

Lintel: the horizontal traverse over an opening.

Machicolations: a corbelled balcony at the top of a wall, supported by consoles or brackets.

Maestà: Madonna and Child in Majesty.

Mascaron: carved medallion in form of human mask.

Matroneum: gallery reserved for women in early Christian churches.

Merlon: the solid part of a parapet between two crenels.

Misericord: the small tilting seat of a church stall.

Modillion: a small console supporting a cornice.

Narthex: the internal vestibule of a church.

Oculus: a round window.

Pietà: Virgin with the dead Christ.

Pilaster: a rectangular column often attached to a wall.

Polyptych: a painted or carved panel divided into several bays (triptych: three bays).

Predella: the base of an altarpiece often decorated with small scenes.

Recessed Orders: concentric receding arches surmounting a doorway.

Sinopia: sketch for a fresco.

Stucco: ornamental moulding made of lime, chalk and marble dust.

Triforium: a small gallery over the aisles of a church.

Tympanum: the part between the lintel and the arch of a doorway.

MANUFACTURE FRANÇAISE DES PNEUMATIQUES MICHELIN

Société en commandite par actions au capital de 875 000 000 de francs

Place des Carmes-Déchaux - 63 Clermont-Ferrand (France)

R.C.S. Clermont-Fd B 855 200 507

© Michelin et Cie, propriétaires-éditeurs, 1989

Dépôt légal 4e trim. 89 - ISBN 2 06 015 342-5 - ISSN 0763-1383

Printed in France - 09.89.70

Photocomposition : LES ATELIERS TYPOGRAPHIQUES, Châtillon-sous-Bagneux – Impression : OUEST-IMPRESSION, Rennes, n° 9690